Data-Driven Business Intelligence Systems for Socio-Technical Organizations

Pantea Keikhosrokiani
University of Oulu, Finland

A volume in the Advances in Business Information Systems and Analytics (ABISA) Book Series

IGI Global
PUBLISHER of TIMELY KNOWLEDGE

Published in the United States of America by
IGI Global
Business Science Reference (an imprint of IGI Global)
701 E. Chocolate Avenue
Hershey PA, USA 17033
Tel: 717-533-8845
Fax: 717-533-8661
E-mail: cust@igi-global.com
Web site: http://www.igi-global.com

Library of Congress Cataloging-in-Publication Data

Names: Keikhosrokiani, Pantea, DATE- editor.
Title: Data-driven business intelligence systems for socio-technical organizations / edited by Pantea Keikhosrokiani.
Description: Hershey, PA : Business Science Reference, [2024] | Includes bibliographical references and index. | Summary: "This book aims to present the strategies, technologies, artificial intelligence and data analytics methods used by enterprises for the data analysis and management of business and healthcare information"-- Provided by publisher.
Identifiers: LCCN 2023046138 (print) | LCCN 2023046139 (ebook) | ISBN 9798369312100 (hardcover) | ISBN 9798369312117 (ebook)
Subjects: LCSH: Business intelligence. | Big data.
Classification: LCC HD38.7 .D374 2024 (print) | LCC HD38.7 (ebook) | DDC 658.4/72--dc23/eng/20240125
LC record available at https://lccn.loc.gov/2023046138
LC ebook record available at https://lccn.loc.gov/2023046139

This book is published in the IGI Global book series Advances in Business Information Systems and Analytics (ABISA) (ISSN: 2327-3275; eISSN: 2327-3283)

British Cataloguing in Publication Data
A Cataloguing in Publication record for this book is available from the British Library.

For electronic access to this publication, please contact: eresources@igi-global.com.

Advances in Business Information Systems and Analytics (ABISA) Book Series

Madjid Tavana
La Salle University, USA

ISSN:2327-3275
EISSN:2327-3283

Mission

The successful development and management of information systems and business analytics is crucial to the success of an organization. New technological developments and methods for data analysis have allowed organizations to not only improve their processes and allow for greater productivity, but have also provided businesses with a venue through which to cut costs, plan for the future, and maintain competitive advantage in the information age.

The **Advances in Business Information Systems and Analytics (ABISA) Book Series** aims to present diverse and timely research in the development, deployment, and management of business information systems and business analytics for continued organizational development and improved business value.

Coverage

- Business Models
- Information Logistics
- Decision Support Systems
- Geo-BIS
- Strategic Information Systems
- Data Strategy
- Business Systems Engineering
- Forecasting
- Management Information Systems
- Statistics

IGI Global is currently accepting manuscripts for publication within this series. To submit a proposal for a volume in this series, please contact our Acquisition Editors at Acquisitions@igi-global.com or visit: http://www.igi-global.com/publish/.

The Advances in Business Information Systems and Analytics (ABISA) Book Series (ISSN 2327-3275) is published by IGI Global, 701 E. Chocolate Avenue, Hershey, PA 17033-1240, USA, www.igi-global.com. This series is composed of titles available for purchase individually; each title is edited to be contextually exclusive from any other title within the series. For pricing and ordering information please visit http://www.igi-global.com/book-series/advances-business-information-systems-analytics/37155. Postmaster: Send all address changes to above address.

Titles in this Series

For a list of additional titles in this series, please visit:
www.igi-global.com/book-series/advances-business-information-systems-analytics/37155

Utilizing AI and Smart Technology to Improve Sustainability in Entrepreneurship
Syed Far Abid Hossain (BRAC University, Bangldesh)
Business Science Reference • © 2024 • 370pp • H/C (ISBN: 9798369318423) • US $290.00

Strengthening Industrial Cybersecurity to Protect Business Intelligence
Saqib Saeed (Department of Computer Information Systems, College of Computer Science and Information Technology, Imam Abdulrahman Bin Faisal University, Saudi Arabia) Neda Azizi (Torrens University, Australia) Shahzaib Tahir (Department of Information Security, College of Signals, Pakistan & National University of Sciences and Technology, Islamabad, Pakistan) Munir Ahmad (School of Computer Science, National College of Business Administration and Economics, Lahore, Pakistan) and Abdullah M. Almuhaideb (Department of Networks and Communications, College of Computer Science and Information Technology, Imam Abdulrahman Bin Faisal University, Saudi Aabia)
Business Science Reference • © 2024 • 373pp • H/C (ISBN: 9798369308394) • US $275.00

AI and Data Analytics Applications in Organizational Management
Tereza Raquel Merlo (University of North Texas, USA & Merlo Management Consulting, USA)
Business Science Reference • © 2024 • 317pp • H/C (ISBN: 9798369310588) • US $300.00

Evolution of Cross-Sector Cyber Intelligent Markets
Eugene J. Lewis (Capitol Technology University, USA)
Business Science Reference • © 2024 • 469pp • H/C (ISBN: 9798369319703) • US $275.00

Leveraging ChatGPT and Artificial Intelligence for Effective Customer Engagement
Rohit Bansal (Department of Management Studies, Vaish College of Engineering, Rohtak, India) Abdul Hafaz Ngah (Faculty of Business Economics and Social DevelopmentUniversiti Malaysia Terenganu, Malaysia) Aziza Chakir (FSJES AC, Hassan II University, Casablanca, Morocco) and Nishita Pruthi (Maharshi Dayanand University, India)
Business Science Reference • © 2024 • 349pp • H/C (ISBN: 9798369308158) • US $265.00

Data Envelopment Analysis (DEA) Methods for Maximizing Efficiency
Adeyemi Abel Ajibesin (American University of Nigeria, Nigeria) and Narasimha Rao Vajjhala (University of New York Tirana, Albania)
Business Science Reference • © 2024 • 389pp • H/C (ISBN: 9798369302552) • US $250.00

IGI Global
PUBLISHER of TIMELY KNOWLEDGE

701 East Chocolate Avenue, Hershey, PA 17033, USA
Tel: 717-533-8845 x100 • Fax: 717-533-8661
E-Mail: cust@igi-global.com • www.igi-global.com

Table of Contents

Section 6
Sustainability Initiatives

Detailed Table of Contents

Section 3
Innovations in Healthcare Intelligence

Technological advancements are revolutionizing the healthcare sector, notably in the treatment and management of attention deficit/hyperactivity disorder (ADHD). This shift from traditional therapeutic and pharmacological interventions towards a more data-driven approach marks a significant change in ADHD care. The integration of big data (BD) and artificial intelligence (AI) has introduced innovative and effective methods for ADHD management. These technologies not only bring analytical accuracy but also an empathetic understanding of patient needs, enhancing the quality of life through improved screening accuracy, early diagnosis, and the facilitation of remote treatments. This chapter explores a novel method that synergizes BD and AI to enhance the screening, diagnosis, treatment, and monitoring of ADHD. It critically analyzes the increased efficiency and effectiveness in identifying and managing ADHD through a comprehensive literature review and an online questionnaire to forty-eight experts from the healthcare industry. The research underscores the indispensability of BD and AI in developing new clinical approaches, particularly in the backdrop of escalating ADHD cases and broader mental health challenges. The findings align strongly with theoretical expectations, demonstrating significant advancements over previous methodologies. By introducing a strategic technological model that optimally utilizes BD and AI in ADHD care, this research not only proposes an advanced support system for patients but also promotes public health and sustainable, equitable ADHD care practices. Furthermore, it highlights the profound implications for future ADHD studies, potentially revolutionizing the realms of ADHD screening, diagnosis, treatment, and monitoring.

The integration of technology in the medical sector, particularly for data acquisition and analysis via the internet of health things (IoHT), offers significant potential for enhancing community health management by monitoring individual lifestyle patterns. A systematic literature review focusing on articles published between 2019 and 2021 explored the behavioral intention toward using IoHT-based healthcare systems. Analyzing 20 selected articles revealed a preference for theories such as the technology acceptance model (TAM), the unified theory of acceptance and use of technology (UTAUT), and the theory of planned behaviour (TPB) to facilitate behavioral change. Key factors influencing behavioral intention toward these systems include performance expectancy, perceived usefulness, effort expectancy, social influence,

The effectiveness of climate-smart approaches is of significant concern because theatres contribute up to 33% of the hospital carbon footprint and 42% of revenue. Despite overwhelming advancements in climate-smart green theatre research, benchmarking remains a challenge. A single index representing their improvements has significant potential to increase control over and to promote their approaches. That is, this study does not stop at an inquiry about climate-smart approaches but also moves a step further and explores a possible outcome measure for the evolution of magnitudes, particularly in favour of the green theatre index (GTI). A function (clinical_theatre_emissions) was created in the R package Carbonr to calculate carbon emission. A time series emission data by theatre were consolidated as GTI using Fisher ideal index. The GTI proves a feasible and accurate consolidated outcome measure for carbon emissions to track and benchmark climate-smart strategies and could be applied in the real-world settings.

Preface

OVERVIEW

In the age of the Fourth Industrial Revolution, the confluence of digital transformation, artificial intelligence (AI), and business intelligence (BI) systems is reshaping the landscape of industries, healthcare, and society at large. *Data-Driven Business Intelligence Systems for Socio-Technical Organizations* is a comprehensive exploration of this transformative era, designed to offer insights, methodologies, and case studies that illustrate the profound impact of data-driven strategies on socio-technical organizations.

The integration of data-driven business intelligence (BI) systems within socio-technical organizations marks a significant milestone in the evolution of modern enterprises. These systems, powered by advancements in artificial intelligence (AI), machine learning (ML), and big data analytics, offer unprecedented opportunities for enhancing decision-making, operational efficiency, and innovation (Figure 1) (Keikhosrokiani, 2022a, 2022b, 2023). Recent advancements in AI and ML have significantly enhanced the capabilities of BI systems, enabling them to process and analyze vast amounts of data with greater speed and accuracy. It is essential to explore how big data analytics capabilities can drive innovation within organizations, emphasizing the crucial role of dynamic capabilities in this process (Mikalef et al., 2019). The effects of big data analytics on firm performance are investigated, highlighting the mediating role of dynamic capabilities and the importance of a conducive environment for leveraging these technologies (Wamba et al., 2017).

As shown in Figure 1, Business Intelligence (BI) operates through an iterative process that transforms raw big data into actionable insights, facilitating informed decision-making in socio-technical organizations. This transformation journey— (1) converting big data into information, (2) information into knowledge, and (3) knowledge into action—is cyclic rather than linear, emphasizing the importance of feedback at each stage.

Big Data to Information: The process begins with the aggregation of big data from diverse sources, including internal systems (like Customer Relationship Management (CRM) and Enterprise Recourse Planning (ERP)) and external sources (social media, market trends, etc.). This raw big data is then cleaned, pre-processes and integrated to ensure accuracy and consistency, making it ready for analysis.

From Information to Knowledge: Using BI tools and technologies, the processed data is analyzed to uncover patterns, trends, and correlations. Statistical methods, predictive analytics, and data mining techniques are often employed at this stage. The insights gained from data analysis are visualized through dashboards, charts, and reports. This step is crucial as it translates complex data sets into an understandable format for decision-makers.

From Knowledge to Action and Decision Making: Stakeholders interpret the visualized data to gain knowledge about business operations, customer behavior, and market trends. Based on the insight from the knowledge gained from data analytics, socio-technical organizations can strategize, make predictions about future trends, and identify areas for improvement or investment. Decisions are made and actions are implemented based on the insights gained. This could involve launching new products, optimizing operations, or tailoring marketing strategies.

After actions are taken, their outcomes are monitored and evaluated against the organization objectives. This stage is crucial for understanding the efficacy of the decisions made and the accuracy of the insights derived. Feedback from the outcomes is fed back into the BI process. This could lead to new questions, the need for additional data analysis, or adjustments in data collection and analysis methodologies.

Figure 1. The business intelligence as iterative process from big data analytics to action

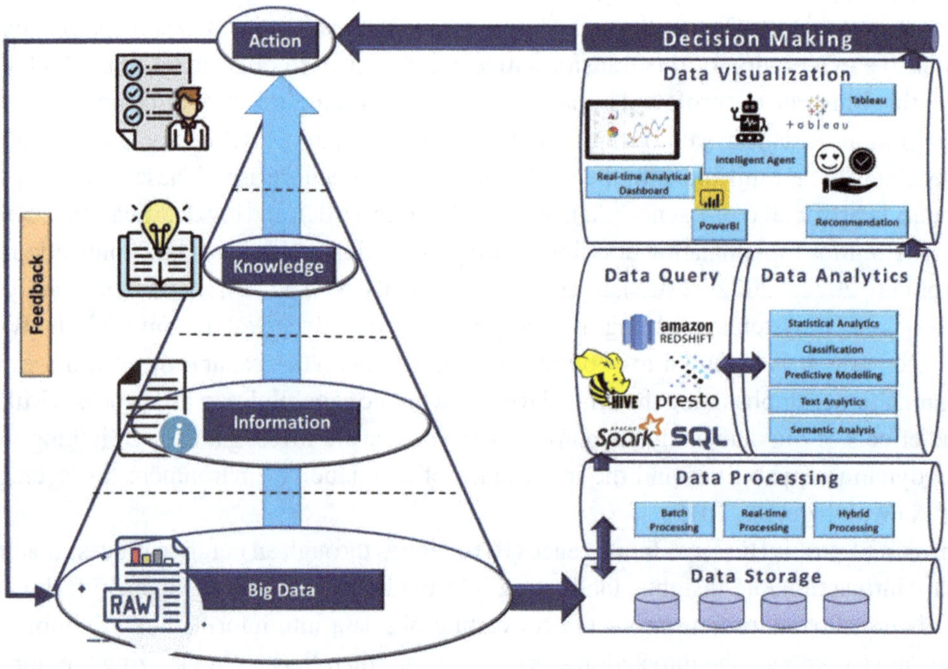

The iterative nature of BI is crucial for continuous improvement and agility in decision-making in socio-technical organizations. As feedback is incorporated, the process begins with refined data collection and analysis that account for the latest business contexts and outcomes. This ongoing cycle ensures that BI systems remain dynamic and aligned with organizational goals, enabling businesses to adapt to changing market conditions and internal dynamics effectively.

In summary, BI is a comprehensive process that transforms data into actionable intelligence, driving informed decision-making through a continuous loop of analysis, action, and feedback. This iterative approach ensures that businesses can remain competitive and responsive in a data-driven world.

While the benefits of data-driven BI systems are considerable, their implementation and integration within socio-technical organizations pose several challenges. Some of considerable challenges and issues are vulnerabilities introduced by ubiquitous IT, including issues related to privacy, security, and ethical considerations. These challenges highlight the need for a balanced approach that considers both the technological and social aspects of BI system deployment.

PURPOSE OF THE BOOK

The purpose of *Data-Driven Business Intelligence Systems for Socio-Technical Organizations* is versatile, aiming to serve as a comprehensive guide for understanding and leveraging the power of business intelligence (BI) and artificial intelligence (AI) in the digital age. This book is crafted to meet the needs of a diverse audience, including researchers, students, university lecturers, business executives, IT professionals, policy makers, system developers, and by providing a deep dive into the strategic application of data-driven technologies across various sectors.

This book aims to clarify the concepts of BI, AI, and digital transformation, explaining how these technologies intersect to create value for socio-technical organizations. The book aims to offer a thorough understanding of the fundamental principles that reinforce these technologies and their practical implications in real-world scenarios.

Through a series of case studies and real-world examples, the book intends to showcase how organizations across different industries have successfully implemented BI and AI systems. This includes detailing the challenges faced, solutions adopted, and the outcomes achieved, providing readers with actionable insights that can be applied to their contexts.

As the adoption of BI and AI technologies accelerates, so do concerns related to privacy, ethics, and social responsibility. The book seeks to engage readers in critical thinking about the socio-technical impacts of data-driven technologies, emphasizing the importance of ethical considerations and the need for organizations to prioritize individual privacy and institutional values in their data practices.

By presenting a wide array of applications and the latest advancements in BI and AI, the book aims to inspire readers to think creatively about how these technologies can be applied within their organizations. It encourages innovation by illustrating the potential for BI and AI to solve complex problems, improve efficiency, and create new opportunities for growth.

Offering guidance on the strategic planning, development, and implementation of BI and AI systems, the book serves as a roadmap for sociotechnical organizations looking to embark on their digital transformation journeys. It includes practical advice on navigating the challenges associated with adopting new technologies, from technical hurdles to organizational change management.

Finally, recognizing the potential of BI and AI to address global challenges, the book highlights the role of technology in driving sustainability initiatives and promoting social good. It aims to encourage organizations to leverage data-driven insights for environmental stewardship and to foster a culture of responsibility towards society and the planet.

In summary, "Data-Driven Business Intelligence Systems for Socio-Technical Organizations" is designed to enable its readers with the knowledge, skills, and ethical framework required to navigate the complexities of the digital era, driving positive change and innovation in their organizations and society at large.

ORGANIZATION OF THE BOOK

The book is organized into six main sections and 16 chapters. A brief description of each of the chapters follows:

SECTION 1: INTRODUCTION TO DIGITAL TRANSFORMATION AND BUSINESS INTELLIGENCE

Chapter 1 explores the evolving landscape of data-driven business intelligence systems within socio-technical organizations, providing an insightful glimpse view at how AI serves as a vital driver for innovation and success. It highlights the advantages of incorporating AI, such as increased operational flexibility and enriched stakeholder engagement. Moreover, it underscores the importance of understanding and integrating data-driven business intelligence systems to maintain a competitive edge in today's business environment.

Chapter 2 evolves from the urgent need to explore innovative strategies for managing the surging data volumes generated by Industry 4.0, Society 5.0, and the Internet of Things (IoT). This chapter aims to highlight the fundamentals of business intelligence, detailing its key components, variations, and application within the digital ecosystem. It introduces the BI theoretical framework and include four case studies across different sectors, followed by empirical research, to illustrate BI's practical relevance and versatility.

SECTION 2: ARTIFICIAL INTELLIGENCE AND MACHINE LEARNING IN BUSINESS

Chapter 3 seeks to examine the role of Business Intelligence (BI) and Data Analytics in enhancing business operations. It focuses on how these technologies equip organizations with the means to derive crucial insights from their data, thereby improving decision-making, operational effectiveness, customer contentment, and gaining a competitive edge. The incorporation of these fields into business practices is essential for fostering growth, innovation, and success within the contemporary, data-centric business environment. The study conducts a systematic literature review from the Scopus database, analyzing 75 scholarly and scientific articles to understand how BI and Data Analytics can significantly benefit businesses.

Chapter 4 reviews the analysis of data from retail businesses and their product manufacturing processes, introducing a scalable business intelligence framework centered around a graph data model and its corresponding management system. To highlight the analytical potential of using a graph database model for business intelligence purposes, the chapter outlines an algorithm designed to uncover insights from the accumulated business data.

Chapter 5 highlights AI-BI's potential and strategic urgency, urging AI investment, data culture, collaboration. Examining AI-infused BI applications, it touts real-world advantages while tackling data alignment challenges. The chapter empowers leaders, managers, technologists to architect AI-BI synergy, redefining success amid evolving industries. Embracing data, it charts course to prosperity, innovation, growth.

Chapter 6 focuses on big data analytics software systems, their testing, and quality assurance-related issues in Hadoop, an open-source framework. It discusses challenges concerning massively parallel data generation from multiple sources, data characterization, software application quality factors, and some software testing mechanism.

Chapter 7 employs Porter's Five Forces model to explore how small and medium-sized enterprises (SMEs) in developing countries can utilize various business intelligence (BI) information systems to outperform their rivals. It finds that factors such as competitive rivalry, the bargaining power of customers and suppliers, along with the threats posed by new entrants and substitute products, significantly affect the competitive edge of enterprises, particularly SMEs in the developing world. The chapter identifies key challenges SMEs face in adopting BI solutions, including limited funds, lack of managerial support, and a shortage of expertise. It advocates for investments and training in BI technologies for SMEs in these regions and calls for further research into the adoption and advancement of such technologies.

SECTION 3: INNOVATIONS IN HEALTHCARE INTELLIGENCE

Chapter 8 explores a novel method that synergizes BD and AI to enhance the screening, diagnosis, treatment, and monitoring of ADHD. It critically analyzes the increased efficiency and effectiveness in identifying and managing ADHD through a comprehensive review of the literature and an online questionnaire to forty-eight experts from the healthcare industry. The research further highlights the indispensability of BD and AI in developing new clinical approaches, particularly in the backdrop of escalating ADHD cases and broader mental health challenges. The findings align strongly with theoretical expectations, demonstrating significant advancements over previous methodologies.

Chapter 9 conducts a systematic literature review focusing on articles published between 2019 and 2021 explored the behavioral intention toward using IoHT-based healthcare systems. Analyzing 20 selected articles revealed a preference for theories such as the Technology Acceptance Model (TAM), the Unified Theory of Acceptance and Use of Technology, and the Theory of Planned Behaviour to facilitate behavioral change. Key factors influencing behavioral intention toward these systems include performance expectancy, perceived usefulness, effort expectancy, social influence, and resistance to change. The findings highlight the importance of user-centric design in developing IoHT-based healthcare systems to effectively meet community health needs, emphasizing that healthcare solutions should be tailored to individual health behaviors and preferences.

Chapter 10 explores the impact of analytics, AI, and big data on patient care, destination selection, and industry dynamics. Personalized patient care is enhanced through data integration, tailoring services to individual needs, improving overall experiences, and treatment outcomes. This focuses on destination selection and industry competitiveness, data-driven decisions on treatment outcomes, cost-effectiveness, quality improvement, and patient satisfaction. The healthcare industry's holistic impact can be examined through Data-driven acumens evolving business models, regulatory frameworks, and strategic alliances. Emphasizing the vital role of global medical tourism sector in delivering more patient-centric, efficient, and competitive medical tourism industry, showcasing its potential for positive global impacts on healthcare accessibility and quality. Valuable insights are offered for policymakers, healthcare providers, and industry stakeholders navigating the evolving landscape.

SECTION 4: AI-AUGMENTED TECHNOLOGICAL APPLICATIONS IN SPECIFIC FIELDS

Chapter 11 proposes a web-based information system designed to assess mental workload by employing a deep learning model. The proposed system aims to utilize a deep learning algorithm for classification and feature extraction from EEG signals to accurately classify mental workload status. The proposed system would become a significant tool for making more effective and precise predictions about employees' mental workload in organizations.

Chapter 12 explores the integration of Inventory Management and Machine Learning, offering a comprehensive guide to harnessing analytical dashboards for improved decision-making. Using classification algorithms, this chapter explores how machine learning techniques can revolutionize inventory control, making predictions more accurate and operations more efficient. It provides a detailed walkthrough of implementing these machine learning models, emphasizing their practical benefits in forecasting and classification tasks within inventory management. Furthermore, it demonstrates how Power BI can be leveraged to visualize inventory data, enabling stakeholders to gain insights into stock trends, performance metrics, and the overall health of the supply chain.

Chapter 13 implements Market Basket Analysis (MBA) and Recommender Systems based on MovieLens Data. In MBA, this chapter identifies movie watching patterns using two types of rule-generating algorithms, namely, the Apriori Algorithm and the FP-Growth Algorithm. Furthermore, it generates three visualization idioms to understand the association rules extracted in the MBA. Secondly, five types of recommender systems, namely memory-based collaborative filtering, model-based collaborative filtering, content filtering, context filtering, and the hybrid method, were implemented to suggest relevant movies to customers. Each recommender system was experimented with three different TopN configurations, and the results were evaluated using information retrieval metrics.

SECTION 5: SOCIAL AND ETHICAL CONSIDERATIONS IN TECHNOLOGY

Chapter 14 designs a comprehensive socio-technical system that facilitates data collecting, processing, and reporting procedures within a university. The system was modeled concurrently, encompassing both the users and stakeholders as well as the software and hardware components. Throughout the development process, a thorough analysis was conducted to understand the requirements and expectations of university personnel regarding the system. This was achieved through the use of qualitative and quantitative data-gathering approaches. Based on the collected findings, prototypes were produced, and input was sought once again. A system that prioritizes user needs, and has a high level of reliability was designed in the last phase. The purpose of the system is to enhance the university's ability to make decisions and plan strategically based on data. Additionally, it is anticipated that the system will boost employee motivation and productivity.

Chapter 15 conducted a sentiment analysis of comments from Meta's new product, "Threads," in competition to Twitter. Authors have tested the system with real-time comments. A dataset of 12,000 comments was extracted from YouTube using the YouTube API containing keywords such as "Threads," "Twitter," and "X." The authors used DistilBERT to weigh the comments and segregate them into positive and negative. Machine learning algorithms were used to analyze the weighted data, and Logistic Regression was found to outperform Random Forest and KNN in providing an accuracy of 85.95%. The study highlights the importance of sentiment analysis in understanding user-generated content and its potential applications in the digital era.

SECTION 6: SUSTAINABILITY INITIATIVES

Chapter 16 goes beyond examining climate-smart tactics by proposing a metric, the "Green Theatre Index (GTI)," to gauge and enhance the adoption of these practices. Utilizing the R package "Carbonr," a function named clinical_theatre_emissions was developed to calculate carbon emissions. GTI, formulated through the Fisher Ideal Index based on time series emissions data from theatres, emerges as a practical and reliable metric for monitoring and benchmarking carbon emissions. This index facilitates the tracking of eco-friendly strategies in healthcare settings, offering a tangible application for real-world implementation.

Finally, I would like to thank the contributors and reviewers for their high-quality intellectual work to publish this book.

Pantea Keikhosrokiani
University of Oulu, Finland

REFERENCES

Keikhosrokiani, P. (2022a). Big Data Analytics for Healthcare: Datasets, Techniques, Life Cycles, Management, and Applications. doi:10.1016/C2021-0-00369-2

Keikhosrokiani, P. (2022b). Handbook of Research on Consumer Behavior Change and Data Analytics in the Socio-Digital Era. doi:10.4018/978-1-6684-4168-8

Keikhosrokiani, P. (2023). *Handbook of Research on Consumer Behavioral Analytics in Metaverse and the Adoption of a Virtual World*. IGI Global. doi:10.4018/978-1-6684-7029-9

Mikalef, P., Boura, M., Lekakos, G., & Krogstie, J. (2019). Big Data Analytics Capabilities and Innovation: The Mediating Role of Dynamic Capabilities and Moderating Effect of the Environment. *British Journal of Management*, *30*(2), 272–298. doi:10.1111/1467-8551.12343

Wamba, S. F., Gunasekaran, A., Akter, S., Ren, S. J., Dubey, R., & Childe, S. J. (2017). Big data analytics and firm performance: Effects of dynamic capabilities. *Journal of Business Research*, *70*, 356–365. doi:10.1016/j.jbusres.2016.08.009

Section 1

Introduction to Digital Transformation and Business Intelligence

Chapter 1
Navigating the Fourth Industrial Revolution:
Empowering Socio-Technical Organizations With Data-Driven Business Intelligence Systems

David Valle-Cruz
https://orcid.org/0000-0002-5204-8095
Unidad Académica Profesional Tianguistenco, Autonomous University of the State of Mexico (UAEMéx), México

J. Patricia Muñoz-Chávez
Technological University of the Metropolitan Zone of the Valley of Mexico, México

Rigoberto García-Contreras
National School of Higher Education, Leon Unit, National Autonomous University of Mexico (UNAM), México

ABSTRACT

Artificial intelligence (AI) has become an integral component in organizational processes, generating several business models that have revolutionized the way companies operate. These advancements have the potential to enable organizations to respond with more agility, achieve greater productivity, and provide superior stakeholders experiences. To provide a more proactive and pragmatic perspective, this chapter explores the current state of data-driven business intelligence systems within the realm of socio-technical organizations. The findings offer an early glimpse into how AI has become a key catalyst for innovation and success in socio-technical organizations, offering benefits ranging from operational agility to improved experience. Furthermore, for the future, understanding and effectively implementing data-driven business intelligence systems is crucial to staying competitive in today's business environment.

DOI: 10.4018/979-8-3693-1210-0.ch001

INTRODUCTION

The sociotechnical perspective emphasizes the dynamic interplay between technology and organizations (Orlikowski, 1992; Pardo & Gil-Garcia, 2005). The rapid emergence of transformative technologies, such as artificial intelligence, Big Data, and the Internet of Things, has created a divergence in the business landscape. Some organizations have flourished, experiencing exponential growth, while others have struggled with organizational adaptation and selection (Valle-Cruz et al., 2021; Valle-Cruz, García-Contreras, et al., 2022; Valle-Cruz, Muñoz-Chávez, et al., 2023).

This dichotomy within the business landscape is a focal point of contemporary research, with different studies shedding light on the various outcomes for organizations navigating the complexities of the sociotechnical environment. The successful implementation of transformative technologies has become a distinguishing factor, enabling certain organizations to thrive and innovate, while others face obstacles in adjusting their structures and operations.

In essence, the sociotechnical perspective provides a framework for comprehending not only the technological changes in organizations but also the resultant organizational dynamics. It prompts to explore how technological advancements shape organizational structures, decision-making processes, and overall functioning.

In response to this evolving phenomena, forward-thinking businesses have shifted their decision-making processes towards data-driven and AI-driven approaches (Valle-Cruz, Fernandez-Cortez, et al., 2022; Valle-Cruz & García-Contreras, 2023). These shifts represent not just subtle adjustments but profound disruptions, marking a sustained journey of innovation (García-Contreras et al., 2021).

Regarding these ideas, this chapter aims to explore the profound and transformative influence of data-driven methodologies within sociotechnical organizations, based on a systematic literature review on Scopus, and it is based in two main research questions:

RQ1: What characteristics and topics does the existing literature in Scopus contain regarding Socio-Technical Organizations with Data-Driven Business Intelligence Systems?

RQ2: Considering the identified topics in the literature, what would be a research agenda for Socio-Technical Organizations with Data-Driven Business Intelligence Systems?"

For this reason, the chapter is divided into six sections. The second section delineates key milestones on the Data-Driven Business Intelligence Systems in terms of cycles of innovation. The third section provides a comprehensive overview of the present state of Data-Driven Business Intelligence Systems within the context of Socio-Technical Organizations in Scopus. The fourth section undertakes both quantitative and qualitative analyses of the documents identified in the state of the art. The fifth section delve into a substantive discussion and propose a forward-looking research agenda. Lastly, the concluding section furnishes final reflections and offer valuable insights.

The chapter seeks to unravel the implications, address inherent challenges, and explore burgeoning opportunities in this ever-evolving landscape. By doing so, the chapter aspires to contribute by enhancing the understanding of how these systems reshape the future of businesses and organizations in the era of the fourth industrial revolution

MILESTONES ON THE DATA-DRIVEN BUSINESS INTELLIGENCE SYSTEMS

A constant in modern organizations is change (Kamel, 2020). Creative destruction and disruptive innovation are amplified by the emerging technologies of the 21st century (Clarke, 2019). In recent decades, the rapid advancement of the socio-digital era and the consequent increase in the application of Artificial Intelligence (AI) as a new operational foundation in various areas of organizations, including those related to products, services, and processes, has transformed the way companies operate and compete. AI is now comprehensively utilized in various aspects of company operations, such as decision-making, process automation, product or service customization, supply chain optimization, customer data analysis, and customer service, among other areas (Iansiti & Lakhani, 2020).

Many companies worldwide have responded swiftly to these transformations, strengthening, and expanding their capabilities in data retrieval and information analysis. This has led to the creation of various business models that have enabled companies to respond with greater agility, achieve higher productivity, and provide an improved customer experience. These models are based on Information and Communication Technologies (ICT), where AI and Big Data play a central role in exploring new frontiers and possibilities. In this context, both business intelligence analysis (BIA) and market information (MI) have become crucial tools in today's business landscape (Chauhan et al., 2022; Lada et al., 2023; Lu et al., 2022).

This transformation, before reaching this point, underwent different stages over several decades, with the following highlights or innovation cycles:

The First Industrial Revolution (1IR) occurred in Britain in the late 18th and early 19th centuries, characterized by economic transformation driven by factors such as the availability of natural resources like coal and iron. It involved the significant introduction of mechanical systems, with the invention and improvement of the steam engine being a pivotal milestone marking the beginning of the modern industrial era. This innovation left a profound impact on key sectors such as the textile industry, mining, railways, maritime transport, and steel production, among others (Lu et al., 2022).

Economic scholars have argued that the technologies introduced during this period were intended to reduce or replace workers' skills, a phenomenon known as "technological crowding out." However, it resulted in the generation and strengthening of new job skills, extending beyond task execution to include the design and maintenance of cutting-edge technologies. The 1IR marked a crucial turning point in human history by introducing unprecedented technological advances and driving economic and social transformations. It laid the foundation for subsequent industrial revolutions, profoundly transforming societies and economies worldwide (García-Contreras et al., 2023).

The Second Industrial Revolution (2IR) took place from the last third of the 19th century to the mid-20th century, with a significant focus on the United States. This period witnessed technological advances, economic transformations, and social changes. It included the mass adoption of electrical energy, enabling mass production and revolutionizing the way goods and services were produced. Key achievements of this revolution included electric power, steel production, automobiles, and airplanes, all of which significantly reshaped the industrial landscape and improved living standards (García-Contreras et al., 2023).

The Third Industrial Revolution (3IR) began in the 1950s and peaked in the late 1990s, marking a turning point in production and manufacturing history. Automation and production processes became fundamental, thanks to advances in information and communication technologies (ICT). A notable example was the introduction of industrial robots that efficiently performed repetitive and hazardous tasks

(García-Contreras et al., 2023). Computer-aided design, manufacturing, and planning systems played essential roles in streamlining processes, enhancing efficiency, and significantly improving productivity.

This gradual transformation, driven by technological innovation, paved the way for the current revolution of the 21st century, known as the Fourth Industrial Revolution (4IR) or Industry 4.0. This stage represents a radical change in the way companies and society operate and develop. Industry 4.0 is characterized by the convergence of advanced technologies such as machine learning, artificial intelligence (AI), the Internet of Things (IoT), Cloud Computing, robotics, data analytics, 3D printing, blockchain, and 5G. These technologies serve as catalysts for technological advancement, revolutionizing daily life, transforming production and the economy through process automation, intelligent decision-making, and interconnected networks (David et al., 2022; Ružarovsk'y et al., 2021; Shahbaz et al., 2020).

At the core of the 4IR is digitalization, which companies have integrated into their operations, enabling them to collect and analyze data in real-time. This has impacted decision-making, streamlined production processes, optimized supply chain activities, shaped organizational culture and procedures, and facilitated mechanisms like product and service customization based on customer needs (David et al., 2022). These transformations are changing the way work is done, allowing companies to increase efficiency and quality. Embracing these digital and technological transformations, which can be considered the "new critical production factor" of the current age, is crucial for organizations to enhance their efficiency and effectiveness, contributing to competitive advantage, profitability, and organizational development. However, as these digital and technological transformations in economic, financial, and labor systems are inevitable and essential for economic, environmental, and social sustainability, there is a growing concern that invites reflection regarding potential economic issues, including potential increases in unemployment and wage reductions (Acemoglu & Restrepo, 2018; Machkour & Abriane, 2020).

DATA-DRIVEN BUSINESS INTELLIGENCE SYSTEMS WITHIN THE CONTEXT OF SOCIO-TECHNICAL ORGANIZATIONS

Sociotechnical theory is an approach to organizational design that considers the interrelationship of social and technical factors in the workplace, with the aim of achieving joint optimization of technical performance and the quality of employees' work life. In this context, it is recognized that organizations are complex systems that cannot be reduced to their individual components (Machkour & Abriane, 2020). By taking into account the interactions and feedback loops between the social and technical subsystems, sociotechnical theory can help design organizations that are more adaptable, resilient, and innovative (García-Contreras et al., 2021).

Sociotechnical theory also emphasizes the importance of human factors in organizational performance. This theory advocates for a participatory and democratic style of management, where employees have autonomy, variety, and meaning in their tasks (Tallarigo, 1999). Furthermore, it promotes collaboration, collegiality, and mutual learning among workers, as well as the alignment of organizational and social goals. These aspects can enhance employee motivation, satisfaction, well-being, as well as their commitment and loyalty to the organization (Parker & Wall, 1998).

In the context of the 4IR, where technology becomes more pervasive, sophisticated, and disruptive, sociotechnical theory helps organizations balance the efficiency and effectiveness of their technical systems with the creativity and flexibility of their human capital (Sony & Naik, 2020). Sociotechnical theory highlights the importance of considering both technical and social factors in the design of technological systems, recognizing that technology is not neutral and that its impact on society is shaped by the social, cultural, and political context in which it is introduced (Orlikowski & Scott, 2008).

Embedded in the sociotechnical view exists a dynamic process between technology, organization, institutional arrangements, and outcomes in the organization due to perception, design, implementation, and use of technology (Fountain, 2004). This approach provides a framework to explain continuous change in organizations because of the implementation and use of technology. The five theoretical constructs in this theory include objective information technologies, organizational forms, enacted technologies, institutional arrangements, and organizational outcomes. Customer engagement and satisfaction, also, affects this organizational dynamics, and it is influenced by different factors, such as political, economic, cultural, customer service, and service quality (Fehrer et al., 2018).

In this regard, the use of emerging technologies creates a dynamic interplay between the organization, technology, and customers. This dynamic interaction implies that results affect customer perception and, in turn, can change organizational outcomes, requiring adjustments in services, products, and internal aspects of organizations, including decision-making process (Figure 1).

Figure 1. Dynamic interaction in sociotechnical organizations
Source: Adapted from Fountain (2014).

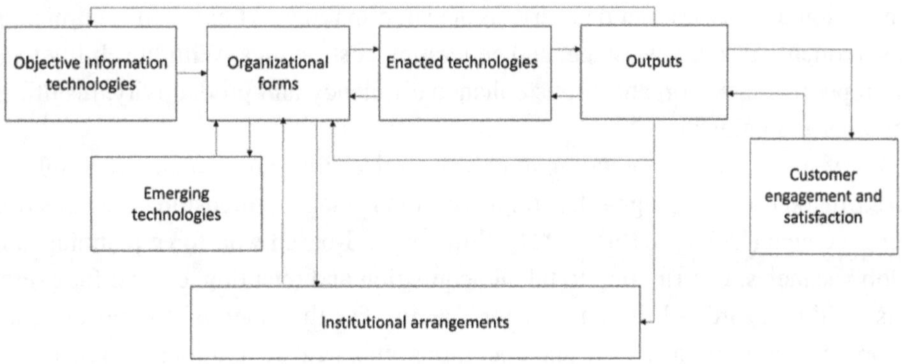

In the field of emerging technologies such as artificial intelligence, Big Data, and the Internet of Things, there is great potential to implement technologies that not only increase profitability but also help improve customer loyalty and satisfaction. However, it is important to recognize that customers can indirectly influence many aspects of an organization, from the design of organizational arrangements to the results achieved.

This influence of customers is cultivated through factors such as perceived success and market acceptance of products and services offered by organizations. Moreover, the implementation of technologies, especially those geared towards process automation, plays a fundamental role in this scenario. The perception and sale of products and services become catalysts for customers to exert their influence, shaping the internal dynamics of organizations indirectly.

Exploring Data-Driven Decision-Making Applications

Although data-driven decision making has its technological basis since data mining systems, in the new century it emerges as a powerful approach boosted by the AI-driven landscape. The combination of advanced analytics and AI algorithms with human expertise enables organizations to make informed, real-time data-driven decisions. This approach carries transformative potential as AI can analyze vast amounts of information, identifying patterns and insights that might elude human decision-makers. Data-driven decision making empowers organizations to move beyond intuition and base their actions on concrete data (Bishop, 2018; Keikhosrokiani, 2022).

Innovation and technology are integral to data-driven decision making. Both technological and process innovation are essential drivers of AI's potential. AI does not just enhance decision-making; it can revolutionize it by offering predictive insights and automating decision processes with unprecedented efficiency and accuracy (Trabucchi & Buganza, 2019). This optimization not only streamlines operations but also confers a competitive advantage in ever-evolving markets.

In this context, planning plays a pivotal role in integrating AI into decision-making. Effective planning and strategic alignment are fundamental for the successful implementation of AI (Duan et al., 2019). Through robust strategies, organizations ensure the seamless integration of AI with their overarching objectives, making it an integral part of the decision-making process. Furthermore, efficiency and process optimization are essential in data-driven decision making. AI excels in optimizing operations and processes, reducing resource wastage, and generating cost savings. With the ability to analyze data and automate repetitive tasks, organizations enhance efficiency and productivity, resulting in positive financial outcomes (Cunningham, 2021).

In the realm of marketing and branding, data-driven decisions are crucial. AI enables the creation of personalized marketing campaigns that improve brand image and customer satisfaction, fostering loyalty and engagement (Huang & Rust, 2021). Similarly, AI-based workforce planning can be applied to optimize job vacancies, contributing to talent acquisition and retention, crucial for overall organizational success. In this regard, AI-driven decision making has the potential to impact positively on all aspects of an organization's performance and operations, enhancing operational efficiency and customer satisfaction (Samarasinghe & Medis, 2020).

Another important topic is related to leadership and organizational culture for the successful adoption of AI in decision-making. Leaders must promote a data-driven mindset, fostering a culture valuing data and AI as facilitators of effective decision-making (Bratasanu, 2018; Latif, 2020). All these aspects have the potential to lead to sustainable competitive advantages for organizations, as AI-powered decision-making allows them to remain competitive in evolving markets. One of the most direct outcomes is value creation as AI tailors products and services to customer needs, enhancing their perceived value in the market.

TRACING THE EVOLUTION OF DATA-DRIVEN BUSINESS INTELLIGENCE SYSTEMS IN SOCIO-TECHNICAL ORGANIZATIONS

This section focuses on analyzing the existing literature in Scopus related to Data-Driven Business Intelligence Systems in Socio-Technical Organizations, both quantitatively and qualitatively. To achieve this, a logical search was conducted (in Scopus) based on the following criteria:

1. Search terms: The search began by specifying the key terms used in the titles, abstracts, and keywords of documents indexed in Scopus. These terms are "data-driven," "business," "intelligence," and "systems." This indicates that the goal was to identify documents related to the intersection of these concepts.
2. Thematic area filters: The search was narrowed down based on the thematic subareas of the documents. It was filtered in two specific thematic areas: "DECI" (Decision Making) and "BUSI" (Business).
3. Document type filter: The search was limited to documents with the document type "ar" (articles). This ensures that only scientific and academic articles are retrieved, rather than other document types such as reviews or conference papers.
4. Scopus search query: As a result of the search criteria, the following query was applied: TITLE-ABS-KEY (data-driven AND business AND intelligence AND systems) AND (LIMIT-TO (SUBJAREA, "DECI") OR LIMIT-TO (SUBJAREA, "BUSI")) AND (LIMIT-TO (DOCTYPE, "ar")).

In total, 55 documents were found, and a content review was conducted in two stages:

1. Screening: In this stage, it was verified whether the documents were related to the topic of Data-Driven Business Intelligence Systems in Socio-Technical Organizations by examining their titles and abstracts. This led to the elimination of 12 documents.
2. Full content review: Finally, a comprehensive review of the remaining 43 documents was conducted to ensure their relevance to the topic. At the end of this stage, 33 documents were deemed to constitute the state of the art on Data-Driven Business Intelligence Systems in Socio-Technical Organizations in Scopus (see Appendices).

A Quantitative View

Quantitative analysis was conducted using Biblioshiny, a bibliometric analysis tool based on the Bibliometrix R package. This powerful tool allows for an in-depth examination of bibliographic data, providing valuable insights into the research landscape. It was fed with the CSV file containing the data sources generated from Scopus, enabling a comprehensive examination of the dataset.

The state-of-the-art landscape in this field began in 2007 but experienced a significant resurgence approximately a decade later, coinciding with what is known as the slope of enlightenment in artificial intelligence applications, eventually leading to a plateau of productivity. This evolution marks a period in which AI applications start to mature and provide tangible and sustainable results. Nowadays, the study in this area is in a developmental phase that attracts the attention of both practitioners and researchers, as its potential to transform different fields and sectors is recognized. This makes it a growing niche in terms of practical opportunities and scientific research, with an increasing focus on exploring the effects and consequences of AI in various aspects of society and the economy (Figure 2).

While there is a wide diversity of researchers from different affiliations in the field of Data-Driven Business Intelligence Systems in Socio-Technical Organizations, the outstanding productivity of the National University of Singapore and the Polytechnic University of Bari stands out. These institutions have led in terms of the quantity of research and contributions in this specific area. However, other prominent universities such as the University of Sussex, Banaras Hindu University, and Copenhagen Business School, along with the Hospital Authority of Hong Kong, have also demonstrated a clear interest in conducting studies related to the potential of Data-Driven Business Intelligence Systems. This underscores the breadth and global scope of research in this field, with various academic institutions and healthcare organizations actively exploring the applications and effects of these systems, as detailed in Table 1.

Despite contributions by universities the United States tops the list with a total of 13 articles, underscoring its significant contribution to this field. India closely follows with 11 articles, demonstrating a growing interest and research activity in this subject. Germany and the United Kingdom share the third position with 8 articles each, reflecting the ongoing commitment of these nations to research in data-driven business intelligence.

Figure 2. Annual scientific production related to data-driven business intelligence systems in socio-technical organizations

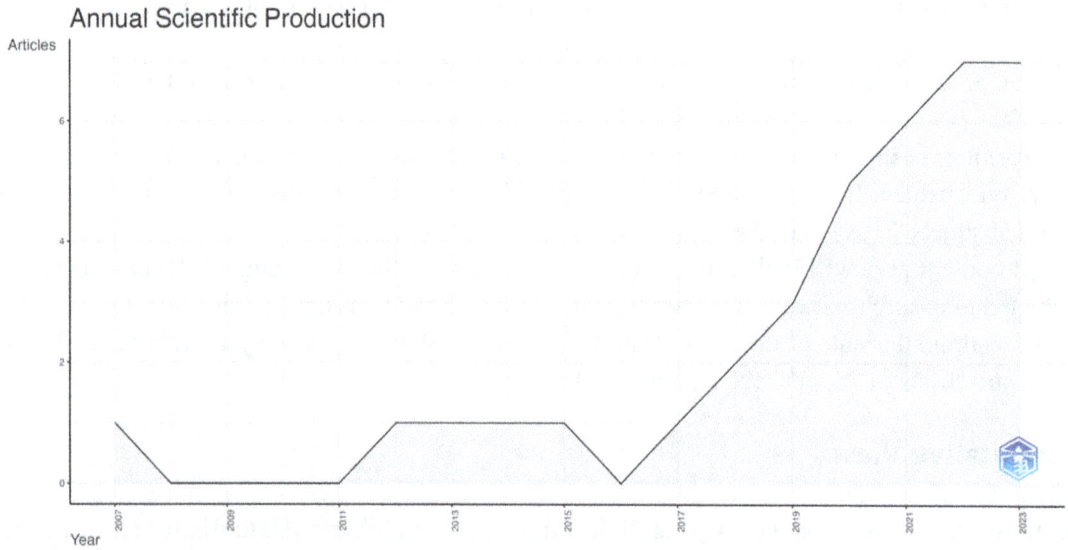

Table 1. Top-ten affiliations studying data-driven business intelligence systems in socio-technical organizations

Affiliation	Articles
National University of Singapore	4
Polytechnic University of Bari	4
Hospital Authority	3
University of Sussex	3
Banaras Hindu University	2
Beijing University of Posts and Telecommunications	2
Catholic University of Eichstaett	2
Chulalongkorn University	2
Copenhagen Business School	2
Indian Institute of Technology Delhi	2

Spain has produced 6 articles, establishing itself as a notable contributor in this domain. Canada, China, Italy, Singapore, and Thailand each have 4 articles, showcasing the geographical diversity of research in this field. These countries are not only actively involved in knowledge generation but are also exploring the applications and effects of data-driven business intelligence systems within the context of socio-technical organizations (Figure 3).

Figure 3. Country scientific production

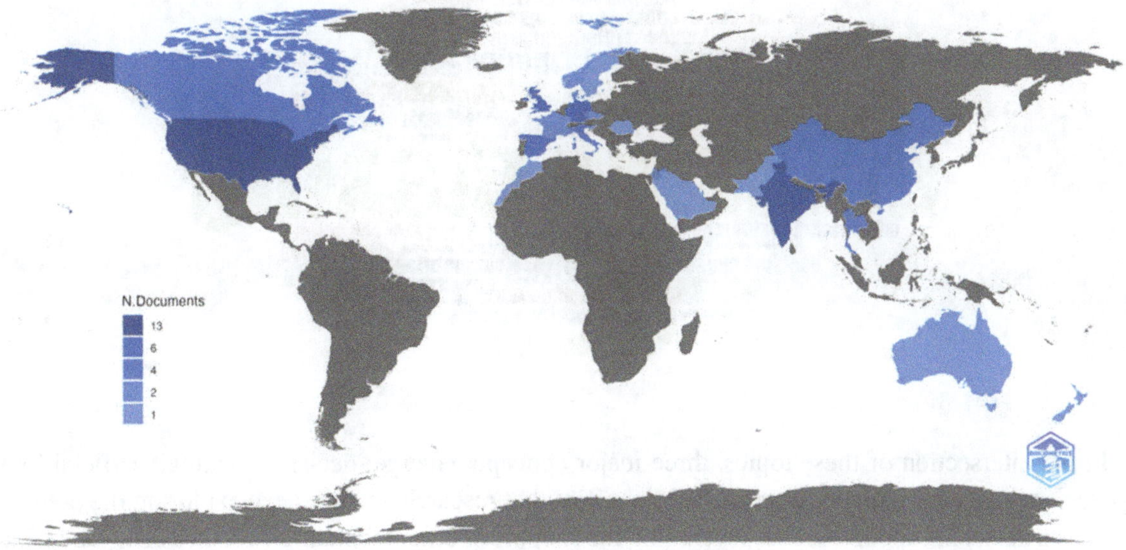

The selection criteria applied in the review of the state of the art have, confirms that the predominant theme is closely related to decision-making. However, it is important to highlight that this interdisciplinary field encompasses a wide range of subtopics and approaches, reflecting the complexity and richness of research in Data-Driven Business Intelligence Systems in Socio-Technical Organizations.

In addition to decision-making, it is evident that other significant topics hold a prominent place in the academic and scientific literature in this field. One of these topics is Big Data, referring to the management and analysis of large volumes of data to extract insights and value. Big Data plays a fundamental role in generating relevant information for informed decision-making.

Moreover, data Analytics is a key component in understanding how data can be translated into valuable information. The ability to effectively analyze data is essential for harnessing the full potential of data-driven business intelligence systems.

Business Intelligence is another central topic, closely related to the collection, analysis, and presentation of business data to support decision-making. In this context, data-driven business intelligence systems play an essential role in generating information that directly impacts decision-making in socio-technical organizations.

The term Data-Driven emphasizes the importance of basing decisions on concrete and reliable data, aligning perfectly with the core focus of this field. Information systems management and business value creation are additional topics that complement and enrich research in Data-Driven Business Intelligence

Systems. Figure 4 provides a visualization of the thematic diversity in the existing literature, emphasizing how these interconnected themes come together to form a comprehensive and multifaceted research landscape. This breadth of topics offers opportunities to explore new research directions and address interdisciplinary challenges in the context of socio-technical organizations.

Figure 4. Word cloud of data-driven business intelligence systems in socio-technical organizations

In the intersection of these topics, three major concepts emerge: decision-making, artificial intelligence, and decision support systems. This signifies that researchers have been exploring the potential of AI as a decision support system, leveraging the support of other technologies such as Big Data, Data Mining, Data Visualization, and Data Storage. The potential of combining these techniques allows for the analysis of information, process optimization, error prevention, and more efficient operations (Figure 5).

AI plays a pivotal role in enhancing decision-making processes by providing valuable insights and predictions derived from vast datasets. Decision support systems, powered by AI, are instrumental in assisting human decision-makers by presenting data-driven recommendations and facilitating informed choices. These systems capitalize on advanced algorithms and machine learning to process and interpret data, making them a valuable asset in the realm of Data-Driven Business Intelligence Systems in Socio-Technical Organizations.

Moreover, the inclusion of Big Data, Data Mining, Data Visualization, and Data Storage technologies amplifies the capabilities of these systems. Big Data tools allow for the management and analysis of large datasets, uncovering hidden patterns and trends that may elude conventional methods. Data Mining techniques aid in the extraction of valuable knowledge from vast data repositories. Data Visualization contributes to the clear presentation of complex information, making it more accessible and understandable to decision-makers. Meanwhile, Data Storage ensures that data is efficiently preserved and readily available for analysis, preventing information silos and enabling timely decision-making.

The symbiotic relationship between these technologies results in an ecosystem where data is transformed into actionable insights, ultimately driving efficiency and effectiveness within socio-technical organizations. This multidisciplinary approach emphasizes the interconnectedness of different technological domains and their collective impact on decision-making processes and the evolution of Data-Driven Business Intelligence Systems. As these technologies continue to advance, their potential for reshaping and optimizing organizational operations is likely to grow, creating a dynamic and ever-evolving research landscape (Figure 5).

However, topics related to decision-making automation based on optimization are losing relevance, making way for emerging research in areas related to the use of AI as decision support or the reinforcement of business intelligence through data-driven processes. This suggests that more creative approaches are being explored to tackle complex problems with the support of AI (Figure 6).

Figure 5. Cooccurrence network for topics related to data-driven business intelligence systems in socio-technical organizations

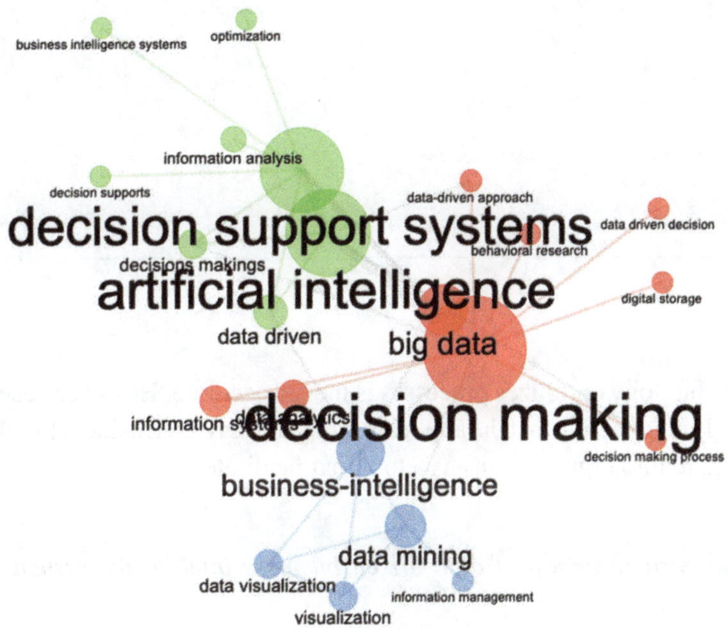

Current research is centered around the synergy between AI and decision-making, where AI could become a strategic partner rather than just an automated tool. The idea is to harness the potential of AI to understand and analyze complex data, enabling organizations to make more informed and strategic decisions. This translates to a greater focus on generating predictive insights and creating more sophisticated decision support systems.

On the other hand, strengthening business intelligence through data analysis refers to the ability to use data to enhance decision-making in all aspects of an organization. Data-driven approaches are applied not only to strategic decision-making but also to process optimization, service personalization, and improving operational efficiency. Research is now aimed at identifying innovative ways to leverage data to drive decision-making at all organizational levels. AI has become a versatile tool for addressing a wide range of challenges in the context of socio-technical organizations. The shift toward a more strategic and sophisticated approach to decision-making, supported by AI, promises to offer creative and effective solutions for current and future problems.

Figure 6. Thematic map of data-driven business intelligence systems in socio-technical organizations

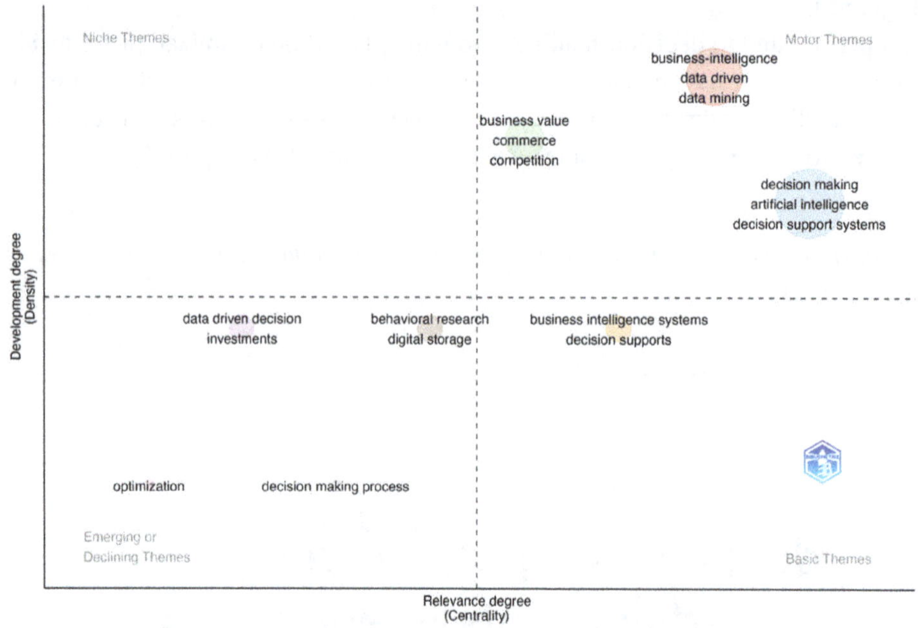

The notion that technology optimizes processes is indeed accurate. However, researchers and professionals are increasingly recognizing that the application of Data-Driven Business Intelligence Systems has the potential to integrate into organizations as a tool that facilitates making better decisions (Figure 7).

Figure 7. Conceptual structure map of data-driven business intelligence systems in socio-technical organizations

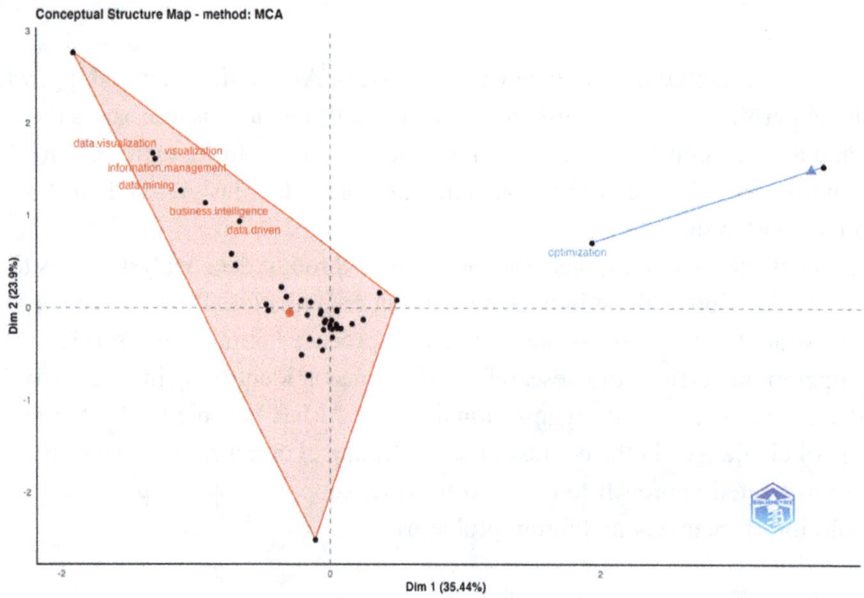

Method: Multiple Correspondence Analysis (MCA) of high frequency keywords

This transition reflects a more profound shift in the role of technology within organizations. While process optimization remains crucial, the focus is expanding beyond mere efficiency gains to harness technology for improving the quality and effectiveness of decision-making. Data-Driven Business Intelligence Systems offer a unique capability to empower organizations with data-driven insights that drive strategic choices and inform actions.

This revolution (the fourth) signifies a fundamental change in how organizations perceive and utilize technology. It's not just about making processes more efficient but about enabling organizations and people to make more informed, strategic, and data-driven decisions. This shift is driving innovation and enhancing the ability of socio-technical organizations to adapt and thrive in an increasingly data-centric and dynamic environment.

A Qualitative View

This subsection delves into the state of the art by comprehensively exploring ten pivotal topics related to various aspects of organizations. These topics provide a multifaceted lens through which it can be assessed the landscape of Data-Driven Business Intelligence Systems in Socio-Technical Organizations, based on ten topics related to key organization' aspects: Data-Driven Decision Making, Innovation and Technology, Planning and Strategy, Efficiency and Optimization, Performance and Operations, Competitive Advantage, Marketing and Branding, Human Resources, Value Creation, and Leadership and Culture.

Data-Driven Decision Making

Data-driven decision making is an indispensable approach in the contemporary AI-driven landscape (Latif, 2020). The fusion of advanced analytics and AI algorithms endows organizations with the capability to make real-time and data-informed decisions (Basile et al., 2023). The potential of this approach is truly transformative. With a continuous stream of data, AI has the capacity to analyze immense volumes of information, uncovering patterns and insights that might elude human decision-makers. Consequently, organizations can transcend reliance on gut feelings and intuition, instead placing their trust in concrete data to steer their actions.

This transition to data-driven decision making is akin to a paradigm shift. In the past, decisions often relied on limited data and experience-based intuition. However, with the advent of AI and data-driven systems, organizations can now harness the power of predictive analytics, machine learning, and big data to inform their strategies (Bohanec et al., 2017). This enables them to make more accurate, agile, and strategic decisions, ultimately leading to better outcomes.

Moreover, data-driven decision making is not limited to a singular department or aspect of an organization and pervades various dimensions, from marketing and branding to workforce planning, impacting overall performance and operations.

Innovation and Technology

Innovation and technology are the cornerstones of successful data-driven decision making (Mishra & Tripathi, 2021). These terms, technological and process innovations are not mere buzzwords; they are pivotal elements in unlocking the full potential of AI. The heart of AI's capabilities is rooted in its capacity to drive innovation, delivering predictive insights, and automating decision-making processes with unprecedented efficiency and accuracy. Through AI-driven innovations, organizations can achieve much more than just operational streamlining; they can secure a significant competitive edge in the face of rapidly changing markets (Nylund et al., 2020).

Innovation is at the heart of AI, and this innovation permeates every facet of an organization's operations. This transformative technology doesn't merely enhance decision-making; it reshapes it. The integration of AI opens up new horizons for creative and data-infused solutions (Valle-Cruz, Fernandez-Cortez, et al., 2022; Valle-Cruz & García-Contreras, 2023). One of the most striking aspects of AI-driven innovation is its potential to disrupt traditional ways of doing business. By utilizing advanced algorithms, machine learning, and data analytics, organizations can uncover novel insights and devise groundbreaking solutions that might have otherwise remained hidden.

The concept of innovation in the context of data-driven decision making extends beyond the mere adoption of AI systems. It encompasses the development of novel processes, policies, and strategies that are tailored to harness the full potential of AI-driven insights. To stay ahead in today's competitive landscape, organizations need to continuously innovate, adapting to the ever-changing technological environment. As such, innovation is not limited to the technology itself but also extends to the way organizations implement and integrate AI-driven insights into their operations (Basile et al., 2023).

The close relationship between innovation and technology in data-driven decision making is essential for organizations looking to outperform their competitors (Nylund et al., 2020). Innovation drives organizations to seek out more efficient and effective ways of leveraging AI technology, allowing them to make informed decisions that are truly data-driven (Lu, 2020). In the quest for data-driven excellence, innovation and technology are key differentiators that enable organizations to navigate the complex and dynamic landscape of the modern business world.

Furthermore, innovation and technology play a vital role in planning the integration of AI into the decision-making process. Effective planning and strategic alignment are crucial for the successful implementation of AI. By developing robust strategies, organizations ensure that AI is seamlessly integrated into their overarching goals, making it an integral part of their decision-making process. This approach not only maximizes the value derived from AI but also positions organizations as industry leaders in the data-driven decision-making landscape (Power, 2015).

Planning and Strategy

Planning is the cornerstone when it comes to integrating AI into the decision-making process. It serves as the foundation on which the successful deployment of AI capabilities is built. Effective planning and strategic alignment are not optional but rather essential prerequisites for harnessing the full potential of AI in organizational decision-making (Mishra & Tripathi, 2021). By meticulously crafting robust strategies, organizations can ensure that AI is not just an add-on, but an intrinsic component seamlessly embedded within their overarching objectives.

The importance of this alignment cannot be overstated. It is not merely a matter of adopting AI technology for its own sake; it is about integrating it thoughtfully and strategically into the very fabric of the organization. This deliberate incorporation transforms AI into a pivotal element of the decision-making process. This is not a superficial integration but a deep and meaningful assimilation that enables AI to inform and enhance decision-making at every level (Williams et al., 2020).

Strategic alignment of AI with organizational goals is more than just a best practice; it is the gateway to optimal outcomes. The strategic roadmap for AI integration should encompass various dimensions, including organizational culture, data management, technology infrastructure, and the specific needs of the organization. By considering these aspects, organizations can ensure that AI aligns seamlessly with their existing workflows, augments their decision-making capabilities, and ultimately drives the achievement of their strategic objectives (Berumen & Cavanaugh, 2021).

One of the core elements in this alignment is understanding that AI is not a standalone solution but rather a transformative force that works in synergy with existing processes. By carefully integrating AI into the existing decision-making framework, organizations can leverage its capabilities without disrupting their operations. This strategic cohesion is pivotal to ensure that AI is not viewed as an isolated tool but as an essential part of the decision-making toolkit.

Efficiency and Optimization

Efficiency and process optimization lie at the very heart of data-driven decision-making. The prowess of AI in this realm cannot be overstated, as it excels in fine-tuning and enhancing operations and processes, yielding substantial reductions in resource wastage and significant cost savings. The application of AI in this context is akin to having a highly adept process manager that can analyze data, pinpoint bottlenecks, and seamlessly automate repetitive tasks (Williams et al., 2020).

Through this dynamic optimization, organizations can achieve a level of operational streamlining that was previously unattainable. By allowing AI to take the reins in analyzing and improving processes, organizations can revamp their operational landscape. The outcome is a significant elevation in efficiency, more effective resource allocation, and a pronounced increase in overall productivity (Mathrani, 2022).

These improvements in operational efficiency have a direct and positive impact on an organization's bottom line. The resource and cost savings, coupled with heightened productivity, contribute to the organization's financial well-being. In essence, AI's capacity to enhance efficiency is not merely an abstract concept but a tangible and impactful advantage for organizations that embrace data-driven decision-making.

By minimizing waste and maximizing productivity, AI-driven process optimization underpins the value of data-driven decisions. This value is not confined to abstract notions but is manifest in the concrete results of reduced costs, improved resource utilization, and, ultimately, a healthier financial outlook for organizations. Hence, the role of AI in bolstering efficiency and process optimization cannot be overstated; it is a requirement in the journey toward harnessing the full potential of data-driven decision-making.

Performance and Operations

Decisions guided by AI have a pervasive and positive impact on every facet of an organization's performance and operations. The influence of data-driven decisions ripples through the organization, transforming not only its overall performance but also the day-to-day operational activities and ultimate business outcomes (Zhou et al., 2021). The profound impact of AI is felt across multiple dimensions.

At the core of AI's transformative potential is its capacity to elevate organizational performance. By enhancing operational efficiency, AI drives an organization to attain higher levels of productivity, effectiveness, and success. It serves as a catalyst for the optimization of internal processes, which, in turn, leads to cost reductions and resource savings. This streamlined approach, enabled by AI, translates into tangible benefits for the organization and its stakeholders (Badakhshan et al., 2022).

The overarching outcome of these enhancements is the emergence of a more agile and competitive organization. In today's fast-paced and dynamic business landscape, adaptability and competitiveness are essential. AI-driven decisions empower organizations to stay ahead of the curve by not only optimizing their internal processes but also by offering superior services to customers. This dynamic positioning gives organizations a competitive edge and enables them to thrive in the face of ever-evolving challenges.

Competitive Advantage

AI-driven decisions empower organizations with the tools to establish and maintain a sustainable competitive advantage. In a business environment characterized by constant change and fierce competition, the utilization of AI's capabilities for data-driven decision-making offers a clear pathway to success (Zhou et al., 2021).

One of the keyways AI contributes to sustainable competitive advantage is through its aptitude for data analysis. AI can handle vast datasets and extract valuable insights from them. This analytical power enables organizations to stay attuned to market trends, customer preferences, and emerging opportunities (Mathrani, 2022). By understanding these critical factors, organizations can proactively adjust their strategies and offerings to align with the evolving landscape.

Moreover, AI-driven decisions allow organizations to be highly responsive to changes in their operating environment. Rapid adaptation is a key driver of success in today's dynamic markets. AI provides organizations with the agility they need to pivot swiftly in response to new challenges or opportunities. By doing so, they can effectively anticipate and respond to customer demands, maintaining a competitive edge (Nylund et al., 2020).

The ability to predict and respond to shifts in market dynamics and consumer behavior positions organizations as industry leaders. They can set the pace and direction of innovation and service quality, outperforming their competitors, and remaining at the forefront of their respective industries.

Furthermore, AI-driven decision-making is not just about maintaining a competitive edge; it is about continuously improving and staying ahead. Organizations that make data-driven decisions are poised to foster a culture of innovation and growth. They are more likely to harness AI's full potential and keep exploring novel ways to enhance their operations and offerings (Zhou et al., 2021).

Marketing and Branding

Within the realm of marketing and branding, data-driven decisions serve as the cornerstone for achieving success. The evaluation of corporate image is increasingly shaped by data-driven marketing strategies. AI plays a pivotal role in this transformation, as it empowers organizations to craft highly personalized marketing campaigns that resonate on an individual level with customers. This personalized approach has a profound impact on the brand image and customer satisfaction, ultimately driving brand loyalty and fostering deeper customer engagement (Diorio et al., 2022).

The power of data-driven marketing strategies lies in their ability to understand and cater to the unique preferences, behaviors, and needs of each customer. AI algorithms can analyze vast datasets, identifying patterns and insights that help create a comprehensive customer profile. Armed with this knowledge, organizations can design marketing campaigns that deliver the right message to the right audience at the right time. This level of personalization makes customers feel understood and valued, significantly enhancing their perception of the brand (Jarek & Mazurek, 2019).

Moreover, data-driven decisions allow organizations to continuously refine their marketing efforts. Through real-time data analysis, they can adapt and optimize campaigns as they unfold, ensuring that their message remains relevant and effective. This adaptability is crucial in a fast-paced and ever-changing market, as it enables organizations to stay ahead of competitors and align their strategies with shifting consumer behaviors (Abrardi et al., 2022).

The result of data-driven marketing is the transformation of marketing into a tailored experience. Customers receive content, products, and offers that are highly relevant to their interests and needs, creating a more meaningful interaction with the brand. Customers are more likely to stick with a brand that consistently understands and caters to their desires.

The personalized approach to marketing also fosters greater customer engagement. When customers feel a strong connection with a brand, they are more inclined to interact with it, whether through social media, reviews, or active participation in brand events. This higher level of engagement not only strengthens the brand-customer relationship but also generates valuable insights and feedback for the organization (Blasco-Arcas et al., 2016).

Human Resources

AI-based workforce planning, particularly in the optimization of job vacancies, is an arena where data-driven decision-making within HR excels. It is well-recognized that the role of HR extends beyond recruitment and payroll; it is a strategic function that profoundly influences an organization's performance and success. Data-driven HR decisions, empowered by AI, play a pivotal role in talent acquisition and retention while optimizing human resource management processes (Aleisa et al., 2023).

When organizations leverage data-driven insights in their HR strategies, they gain a competitive advantage in acquiring and retaining top talent. AI algorithms can process a wide array of data, from resumes and performance metrics to employee satisfaction surveys and market trends. This wealth of information enables HR professionals to make informed decisions about who to hire, when to hire, and how to best retain existing talent. The result is a workforce that is not just skilled but also well-matched to the organization's objectives (Jain, 2018).

Optimizing human resource management processes through data-driven decision making is equally significant. It can encompass workforce scheduling, performance evaluations, training, and development, and much more. By relying on AI and data analysis, organizations can identify areas for improvement and act proactively. This proactive approach enhances efficiency in HR operations, reducing administrative overhead and facilitating strategic HR initiatives that align with broader business goals.

Furthermore, data-driven HR decisions contribute to the development of a highly skilled and motivated workforce. When employees see that their organization invests in data-driven talent management, it sends a clear message that their contributions are valued. Employees are more likely to engage and remain loyal to organizations that prioritize their professional growth and well-being. This engagement, in turn, contributes to higher productivity, greater innovation, and a more collaborative workplace culture (Yu et al., 2023).

An organization's workforce is often considered priceless asset. For this reason, optimizing talent acquisition and retention through data-driven decisions is essential for achieving overall organizational success. A workforce that is strategically aligned with business objectives and actively nurtured through data-driven HR processes can drive innovation, improve performance, and enhance an organization's competitive edge in the market.

Value Creation

The most direct outcome of data-driven decision-making powered by AI is value creation. AI plays a transformative role in tailoring products and services to meet customer needs and align with market trends, all driven by its exceptional data analysis capabilities. This high level of customization has a profound effect on how customers perceive the value of products and services, and in today's competitive landscape, it's pivotal (Lafferty & others, 2019).

The ability to customize offerings to precisely match what customers desire greatly enhances the perceived value of these products and services. When customers receive what they want, they are not only satisfied but also more likely to develop loyalty to a brand. This high degree of customer satisfaction and loyalty is crucial in gaining a competitive edge and sustaining long-term success in the market.

Furthermore, data-driven decisions help organizations make precise predictions about customer preferences and emerging trends. AI can analyze vast datasets to identify patterns and shifts in consumer behavior. Armed with this knowledge, organizations can proactively adapt their products and services to meet evolving market demands, further solidifying their position as innovators and leaders (Diorio et al., 2022).

An additional dimension of value creation is enhanced customer experience. As AI-driven data analytics refines product and service personalization, it also contributes to smoother and more efficient customer interactions. When customers find their needs are intuitively understood and met, their overall experience is enriched. This leads to increased customer satisfaction, word-of-mouth recommendations, and positive brand perception, all of which contribute to higher customer retention and acquisition rates.

Moreover, in the age of social media and online reviews, customer satisfaction and perceived value can have a cascading effect on an organization's reputation. Positive reviews and word-of-mouth recommendations from satisfied customers amplify the organization's presence in the market and attract new customers. Conversely, addressing customer needs with tailored products and services minimizes the chances of negative feedback, strengthening the organization's brand image.

Leadership and Culture

Leadership and organizational culture are instrumental in ensuring the successful integration of AI into decision-making processes. They play pivotal roles in creating an environment where AI-driven data analytics can thrive and bring significant value to the organization. Leadership within an organization is the driving force behind AI's successful adoption in decision-making. Effective leaders recognize the transformative potential of AI and champion its integration into the organization's processes. They are not just supporters but active proponents of data-driven decision making (Bratasanu, 2018).

Leaders should possess the vision to see how AI can enhance decision-making processes and drive the organization toward its goals. This requires not only an understanding of the technology but also the ability to communicate its value to the entire organization. Leaders must be able to inspire and guide their teams through the changes that come with adopting AI. They need to set clear objectives and expectations for AI initiatives, ensuring that every team member understands their role in the data-driven transformation.

Moreover, effective leadership involves allocating resources, both in terms of budget and talent, to support AI initiatives. This includes hiring or upskilling talent with expertise in data analysis, AI, and related fields. It is the leader's responsibility to create an environment where data scientists, analysts, and other experts can thrive and contribute to the success of AI-driven decision-making projects (Titareva, 2021).

However, leadership alone is not sufficient; it must be complemented by a culture that encourages data-driven decision making. This culture shift is crucial because it instills a collective appreciation for the role of data, analytics, and AI in effective decision making.

Organizational culture is the sum of the values, beliefs, and behaviors that characterize an organization derived from the subjective world and the creation of meanings within it. In the context of data-driven decision making, a culture of data emphasizes the importance of collecting, analyzing, and acting upon data to drive outcomes. This culture prioritizes data accuracy, accessibility, and accountability.

To foster such a culture, organizations should promote continuous learning and skill development. This includes training employees in data literacy and providing access to AI tools and resources. When employees at all levels understand the basics of data and AI, they become more open to incorporating data-driven insights into their decision-making processes (Titareva, 2021).

Additionally, organizations should create a safe environment for experimentation and innovation. Encouraging teams to explore new data-driven approaches, even if they may initially lead to failures, is a way to spur innovation. In such a culture, mistakes are seen as learning opportunities that can lead to more effective decision-making processes.

The alignment of leadership and organizational culture with AI initiatives is the key to unlocking the full potential of data-driven decision making. Leaders set the direction, allocate resources, and drive the vision for how AI can benefit the organization. They also lead by example, demonstrating a commitment to data-driven approaches in their decision making. On the other hand, the organizational culture establishes the context in which AI initiatives are carried out. It influences how teams collaborate, share insights, and incorporate data into their workflows. When leadership and culture are aligned with AI, it means that everyone within the organization is on board with the transformation.

TOWARDS A RESEARCH AGENDA FOR DATA-DRIVEN BUSINESS INTELLIGENCE SYSTEMS WITHIN THE CONTEXT OF SOCIO-TECHNICAL ORGANIZATIONS

Regarding the topic of data-driven business intelligence systems in the context of socio-technical organizations, its relevance goes beyond technology management and encompasses the dynamics that unfold between individuals within this environment.

This chapter presents eight interrelated themes that address (1) ethics and governance, (2) human-artificial intelligence collaboration, (3) explainability and transparency, (4) adaptability, (5) data quality and integration (6) transdisciplinary, (7) AI-driven innovation, and (8) workforce replacement.

These topics not only enrich our understanding of technology, but also highlight the importance of ethical considerations, effective collaboration, and comprehensive management of socio-technical impacts in this context. Developing a research agenda for Data-Driven Business Intelligence Systems within the context of Socio-Technical Organizations is of paramount importance as this transdisciplinary field continues to evolve in an AI-driven landscape.

The future direction of research in this domain should encompass a diverse array of topics and priorities that collectively contribute to the responsible and effective use of AI in decision making.

One fundamental area of concern revolves around Ethical AI and Governance (Weber-Lewerenz & Vasiliu-Feltes, 2022). The central role of AI in decision making makes it imperative to address ethical considerations, including data privacy and algorithmic bias. Researchers must work on constructing comprehensive ethical AI frameworks, guidelines, and governance structures to ensure the responsible deployment of AI systems.

Additionally, the dynamics of Human-AI collaboration require in-depth exploration. Research should delve into the development of AI interfaces that facilitate seamless interaction between humans and AI, foster trust-building mechanisms, and devise methods for rendering AI-driven decisions transparent and comprehensible to human users (Wang et al., 2020).

Enhancing AI explainability and transparency stands as a vital component of this agenda. It necessitates the development of interpretable AI models and techniques to demystify how AI reaches specific decisions. This transparency is foundational for building user trust and ensuring compliance with regulatory frameworks (Ehsan et al., 2021).

Bias mitigation and fairness is a core concern, and research should focus on crafting algorithms that are both fair and unbiased, particularly across diverse demographic groups. This endeavor involves the development of techniques for bias detection, correction, and fairness assessment.

AI's adaptability in dynamic environments constitutes a key research priority. Sociotechnical organizations often function in ever-changing contexts, and research must investigate how AI can adapt, make real-time decisions, and effectively respond to unforeseen challenges (Valle-Cruz, García-Contreras, et al., 2023).

Simultaneously, the significance of Data Quality and Integration cannot be overstated. Research should emphasize the prioritization of data quality, the seamless integration of data from diverse sources, and methods that guarantee data consistency, accuracy, and accessibility. These factors underpin the reliability of AI-driven decisions (Janssen et al., 2020). Promoting transdisciplinary collaboration is central to understanding the broader implications of AI in sociotechnical organizations. Researchers should work towards fostering collaboration among experts from diverse fields, including computer science, social sciences, ethics, and business. This transdisciplinary approach offers a holistic perspective on AI's impact.

AI-enabled innovation, as a critical research area, requires an exploration of how AI can drive innovation within organizations. This encompasses investigating AI's role in the value chain. That is, product design and development, production processes, predictive quality management, supply chain optimization, customer experience, human resources optimization, risk management, product life cycle and in service delivery, and business model evolution. The examination of AI ecosystems, including partnerships, AI marketplaces, and industry standards, is vital for a comprehensive understanding of how AI fits into the broader technological landscape. This knowledge is essential for making informed decisions regarding AI implementation.

AI's impact on the workforce is another essential dimension. Research must investigate skill requirements, address job displacement, and develop strategies for upskilling and reskilling to foster a symbiotic relationship between humans and AI in the workplace. Furthermore, long-term organizational strategy development should guide organizations in aligning their core objectives with AI strategies. The creation of roadmaps for AI adoption, identification of key performance indicators, and ROI assessment are integral to this effort.

AI adoption frameworks need to be established, incorporating best practices, readiness assessments, and case studies that showcase successful AI integrations in decision-making processes. Lastly, the research agenda must also consider global and regulatory considerations, especially for organizations operating across multiple regions and markets. This entails a thorough examination of international regulations and standards that influence AI deployment.

CONCLUDING REMARKS

This chapter delved into the current state of data-driven business intelligence systems in the field of socio-technical organizations through an analysis of existing academic literature in Scopus. Examining this situation shows that it could be expected a wave of new technologies, likely driven by cultural changes within organizations. As discussed in the context of this technological wave, adopting data-driven decision making often requires significant cultural changes within organizations. This change requires a shift from traditional intuition-based decision-making methods to a strategic data-centric mindset. One important aspect into this transformation highlights the critical role of cultural change in facilitating the successful integration of data-driven business intelligence systems in socio-technical organizations. This cultural shift can be challenging, particularly in organizations where data has not been a central component of decision processes.

Addressing this challenge involves creating a culture that values data as a strategic asset. Organizations should foster an environment where employees are encouraged to explore data and leverage AI tools. This cultural transformation includes recognizing and rewarding data-driven insights and innovation. Training programs that promote data literacy and analytics skills among employees can facilitate this transition.

To effectively address these challenges, organizations must take a comprehensive approach. A few key strategies could include:

1. Data Governance: Establish robust data governance practices to ensure data security, privacy, and compliance with regulations. Establishing robust data governance practices is critical for organizations seeking to ensure data security, privacy, and regulatory compliance. Alongside, the implementation of comprehensive data quality management strategies is crucial to ensure data accuracy and consistency across systems. Managing the entire data lifecycle, from creation to archiving or deletion, is also paramount to optimizing resources and mitigating risk. Metadata management helps to understand and use data effectively by capturing descriptive information. Also strengthens data security by safeguarding sensitive information, i.e., data integration and interoperability enable a holistic view of information, fostering organizational agility.
2. Change Management: Implement change management strategies that involve employees in the AI adoption process. Start by understanding adoption ensuring the clear communication of benefits, encouraging participation and collaboration, proactively managing resistance to change, and conducting ongoing evaluation.
3. Training and Education: Provide training and educational resources to enhance data literacy and analytical skills among employees. This includes both specific technical skills related to AI and soft skills to adapt to this new and constantly evolving work environment. This strategy must contemplate knowledge management, that is, focus on maximizing the value of an organization's intangible

assets, such as the experience, skills, information, and ideas of its employees that strengthen the use of AI.

4. Leadership Support: Ensure that leadership is committed to AI integration and advocates for a data-driven culture. The leader can achieve this by clearly communicating the importance of AI, encouraging training and development of necessary skills, and creating an environment that fosters collaboration and adaptability in the face of technological evolution. It involves not only strategically guiding, but also cultivating an environment that motivates and empowers individuals in the organization.
5. Pilot Projects: Begin with smaller AI pilot projects to demonstrate the value of AI and build confidence among employees. Embracing AI pilot projects serves as a starting point for organizations looking to integrate artificial intelligence into their operations. Not only do these pilot initiatives demonstrate the tangible value that AI can bring, but they also play a crucial role in instilling confidence among employees who may be apprehensive about the technology. At the same time, investing in comprehensive skills development programs is essential to ensure that the workforce is equipped with the expertise to collaborate seamlessly with AI tools. As successful pilots unfold, organizations must plan strategically by considering factors such as infrastructure requirements, data scalability, and integration with existing systems.
6. Continuous Monitoring: Continuously monitor progress, data security practices and cybersecurity threats, making necessary adjustments. Continuous monitoring is a critical element in the successful implementation and maintenance of any organizational initiative, particularly in the realm of data security and cybersecurity. In the backdrop of integrating advanced technologies such as artificial intelligence, a vigilant approach is essential. Periodic evaluation of the progress of AI applications enables organizations to identify potential inefficiencies or areas for improvement. Equally important is the ongoing assessment of data security practices to ensure that sensitive information remains protected.
7. Feedback Loop: Establish a feedback loop to collect insights from employees and incorporate their input into AI initiatives. The feedback loop is critical to securing AI initiatives within organizations. By creating information channels and sharing experiences with AI technologies, organizations can leverage valuable front-line perspectives. This communication not only fosters a sense of inclusion, but also serves as a practical means to address potential challenges and optimize AI systems. This iterative process ensures that AI systems align more closely with real needs and preferences and contributes to the seamless integration of AI into organizational practices and reinforces overall success.

By effectively addressing these challenges, organizations have the potential to overcome the barriers to AI adoption in decision making. This paves the way for AI to revolutionize decision processes, making them more efficient, data-driven, and ultimately, more successful in achieving organizational goals. In the global sphere characterized by its constant dynamism, the strategic adoption of a data-based business intelligence system in socio-technical organizations is revealed as a crucial element. This implementation is not only intended to enhance customer value creation, but also plays a critical role in fostering organizational development. The ability to effectively leverage information, gleaned from relevant data and harnessing the benefits of AI, positions organizations to anticipate trends, make informed decisions, and adapt nimbly to a constantly evolving business environment. Ultimately, the integration of this business intelligence strengthens the competitive position of organizations and facilitates their ability to effectively meet the changing demands of the global market.

REFERENCES

Abrardi, L., Cambini, C., & Rondi, L. (2022). Artificial intelligence, firms and consumer behavior: A survey. *Journal of Economic Surveys*, *36*(4), 969–991. doi:10.1111/joes.12455

Acemoglu, D., & Restrepo, P. (2018). The race between man and machine: Implications of technology for growth, factor shares, and employment. *The American Economic Review*, *108*(6), 1488–1542. doi:10.1257/aer.20160696

Aleisa, M. A., Beloff, N., & White, M. (2023). Implementing AIRM: A new AI recruiting model for the Saudi Arabia labour market. *Journal of Innovation and Entrepreneurship*, *12*(1), 59. doi:10.1186/s13731-023-00324-w

Alter, S. (2015). Sociotechnical systems through a work system lens: A possible path for reconciling system conceptualizations, business realities, and humanist values in IS development. *1st International Workshop on Socio-Technical Perspective in IS Development*, 1–15.

Badakhshan, P., Wurm, B., Grisold, T., Geyer-Klingeberg, J., Mendling, J., & Vom Brocke, J. (2022). Creating business value with process mining. *The Journal of Strategic Information Systems*, *31*(4), 101745. doi:10.1016/j.jsis.2022.101745

Basile, L. J., Carbonara, N., Pellegrino, R., & Panniello, U. (2023). Business intelligence in the healthcare industry: The utilization of a data-driven approach to support clinical decision making. *Technovation*, *120*, 102482. doi:10.1016/j.technovation.2022.102482

Berumen, A., & Cavanaugh, C. (2021). Developing a KPI-driven data strategy business strategy, data, and management practices. *Graziadio Business Review, 24*(2).

Bishop, S. (2018). *Using data-driven decision-making to enhance performance: A practical guide for organizations*. University of Maryland University College.

Blasco-Arcas, L., Hernandez-Ortega, B. I., & Jimenez-Martinez, J. (2016). Engagement platforms: The role of emotions in fostering customer engagement and brand image in interactive media. *Journal of Service Theory and Practice*, *26*(5), 559–589. doi:10.1108/JSTP-12-2014-0286

Bohanec, M., Robnik-Šikonja, M., & Kljajić Borštnar, M. (2017). Decision-making framework with double-loop learning through interpretable black-box machine learning models. Industrial Management \&. *Data Systems*, *117*(7), 1389–1406.

Bratasanu, V. (2018). Leadership Decision-Making Processes in the Context of Data Driven Tools. *Quality - Access to Success*, 19.

Chauhan, C., Parida, V., & Dhir, A. (2022). Linking circular economy and digitalisation technologies: A systematic literature review of past achievements and future promises. *Technological Forecasting and Social Change*, *177*, 121508. doi:10.1016/j.techfore.2022.121508

Clarke, T. (2019). Creative destruction, technology disruption, and growth. In Oxford Research Encyclopedia of Economics and Finance. doi:10.1093/acrefore/9780190625979.013.393

Cunningham, E. (2021). Artificial intelligence-based decision-making algorithms, sustainable organizational performance, and automated production systems in big data-driven smart urban economy. *Journal of Self-Governance and Management Economics*, *9*(1), 31–41.

David, L. O., Nwulu, N. I., Aigbavboa, C. O., & Adepoju, O. O. (2022). Integrating fourth industrial revolution (4IR) technologies into the water, energy & food nexus for sustainable security: A bibliometric analysis. *Journal of Cleaner Production*, *363*, 132522. doi:10.1016/j.jclepro.2022.132522

Diorio, S., Hummel, C., & Rogers, B. (2022). Revenue operations: A systems approach for turning analytics into growth. *Applied Marketing Analytics*, *7*(4), 306–317.

Duan, Y., Edwards, J. S., & Dwivedi, Y. K. (2019). Artificial intelligence for decision making in the era of Big Data—Evolution, challenges and research agenda. *International Journal of Information Management*, *48*, 63–71. doi:10.1016/j.ijinfomgt.2019.01.021

Ehsan, U., Liao, Q. V., Muller, M., Riedl, M. O., & Weisz, J. D. (2021). Expanding explainability: Towards social transparency in ai systems. *Proceedings of the 2021 CHI Conference on Human Factors in Computing Systems*, 1–19. 10.1145/3411764.3445188

Fehrer, J. A., Woratschek, H., Germelmann, C. C., & Brodie, R. J. (2018). Dynamics and drivers of customer engagement: Within the dyad and beyond. *Journal of Service Management*, *29*(3), 443–467. doi:10.1108/JOSM-08-2016-0236

Fountain, J. E. (2004). *Building the virtual state: Information technology and institutional change*. Rowman & Littlefield.

García-Contreras, R., Muñoz-Chávez, J. P., & Muñoz-Chávez, R. L. (2023). Is the Idea of Human Replacement too Far-Fetched?: Artificial Intelligence as a Partner for the Public Sector. In *Handbook of Research on Applied Artificial Intelligence and Robotics for Government Processes* (pp. 93–113). IGI Global.

García-Contreras, R., Valle-Cruz, D., & Canales-García, R. A. (2021). Organizational selection: SMEs resilience and performance in COVID-19 age. *Estudios Gerenciales*, *37*(158), 73–84.

Huang, M.-H., & Rust, R. T. (2021). A strategic framework for artificial intelligence in marketing. *Journal of the Academy of Marketing Science*, *49*(1), 30–50. doi:10.1007/s11747-020-00749-9

Iansiti, M., & Lakhani, K. R. (2020). *Competing in the age of AI: Strategy and leadership when algorithms and networks run the world*. Harvard Business Press.

Jain, D. S. (2018). Human resource management and artificial intelligence. *International Journal of Management and Social Sciences Research*, *7*(3), 56–59.

Janssen, M., Brous, P., Estevez, E., Barbosa, L. S., & Janowski, T. (2020). Data governance: Organizing data for trustworthy Artificial Intelligence. *Government Information Quarterly*, *37*(3), 101493. doi:10.1016/j.giq.2020.101493

Jarek, K., & Mazurek, G. (2019). Marketing and Artificial Intelligence. *Central European Business Review, 8*(2).

Kamel, S. (2020). The impact of business schools in transforming the society case: AUC School of Business. *Journal of Economic and Administrative Sciences*, *36*(1), 38–63. doi:10.1108/JEAS-10-2018-0110

Keikhosrokiani, P. (2022). Handbook of Research on Consumer Behavior Change and Data Analytics in the Socio-Digital Era. doi:10.4018/978-1-6684-4168-8

Lada, S., Chekima, B., Karim, M. R. A., Fabeil, N. F., Ayub, M. S., Amirul, S. M., Ansar, R., Bouteraa, M., Fook, L. M., & Zaki, H. O. (2023). Determining Factors Related to Artificial Intelligence (AI) Adoption Among Malaysia's Small and Medium-Sized Businesses. *Journal of Open Innovation*, *9*(4), 100144. doi:10.1016/j.joitmc.2023.100144

Lafferty, C., & ... (2019). Sustainable Industry 4.0: Product decision-making information systems, data-driven innovation, and smart industrial value creation. *Journal of Self-Governance and Management Economics*, *7*(2), 19–24.

Latif, S. T. M. (2020). *Study of the effect of choice of organizational culture on artificial intelligence (AI) resources adoption*. NTNU.

Lu, J. (2020). Data analytics research-informed teaching in a digital technologies' curriculum. *Transactions on Education*, *20*(2), 57–72. doi:10.1287/ited.2019.0215

Lu, X., Wijayaratna, K., Huang, Y., & Qiu, A. (2022). AI-enabled opportunities and transformation challenges for SMEs in the post-pandemic era: A review and research agenda. *Frontiers in Public Health*, *10*, 885067. doi:10.3389/fpubh.2022.885067 PMID:35570947

Machkour, B., & Abriane, A. (2020). Industry 4.0 and its Implications for the Financial Sector. *Procedia Computer Science*, *177*, 496–502. doi:10.1016/j.procs.2020.10.068

Mathrani, S. (2022). Enhancing production agility using enterprise systems. *Knowledge Management Research & Practice, 20*(1), 91–103.

Mishra, S., & Tripathi, A. R. (2021). AI business model: An integrative business approach. *Journal of Innovation and Entrepreneurship*, *10*(1), 18. doi:10.1186/s13731-021-00157-5

Nylund, P. A., Ferras-Hernandez, X., & Brem, A. (2020). Automating profitably together: Is there an impact of open innovation and automation on firm turnover? *Review of Managerial Science*, *14*(1), 269–285. doi:10.1007/s11846-018-0294-z

Orlikowski, W. J. (1992). The Duality of Technology: Rethinking the Concept of Technology in Organizations. *Organization Science*, *3*(3), 398–427. doi:10.1287/orsc.3.3.398

Orlikowski, W. J., & Scott, S. V. (2008). Sociomateriality: Challenging the separation of technology, work and organization. *The Academy of Management Annals*, *2*(1), 433–474. doi:10.5465/19416520802211644

Pardo, T. A., & Gil-Garcia, J. R. (2005). *Understanding the Complexity of E-Government: Multi-method Approaches to Social Phenomena*. American Society for Public Administration.

Parker, S., & Wall, T. D. (1998). *Job and work design: Organizing work to promote well-being and effectiveness* (Vol. 4). Sage. doi:10.4135/9781452231518

Power, D. J. (2015). 'Big data' decision making use cases. *Decision Support Systems V—Big Data Analytics for Decision Making: First International Conference, ICDSST 2015, Belgrade, Serbia, May 27-29, 2015 Proceedings, 1*, 1–9.

Ružarovsk'y, R., Holubek, R., Janìček, M., Velìšek, K., & Tirian, G. O. (2021). Analysis of the Industry 4.0 key elements and technologies implementation in the Festo Didactic educational systems MPS 203 I4. 0. *Journal of Physics: Conference Series, 1781*(1), 12030. doi:10.1088/1742-6596/1781/1/012030

Samarasinghe, K. R., & Medis, A. (2020). Artificial intelligence based strategic human resource management (AISHRM) for industry 4.0. *Global Journal of Management and Business Research, 20*(2), 7–13. doi:10.34257/GJMBRGVOl20IS2PG7

Shahbaz, M., Nasir, M. A., Hille, E., & Mahalik, M. K. (2020). UK's net-zero carbon emissions target: Investigating the potential role of economic growth, financial development, and R\&D expenditures based on historical data (1870–2017). *Technological Forecasting and Social Change, 161*, 120255. doi:10.1016/j.techfore.2020.120255 PMID:32904903

Sony, M., & Naik, S. (2020). Industry 4.0 integration with socio-technical systems theory: A systematic review and proposed theoretical model. *Technology in Society, 61*, 101248. doi:10.1016/j.techsoc.2020.101248

Tallarigo, R. (1999). Job and Work Design: Organizing Work to Promote Well-Being and Effectiveness. *Personnel Psychology, 52*(2), 510.

Titareva, T. (2021). *Leadership in an Artificial Intelligence Era*. Academic Press.

Trabucchi, D., & Buganza, T. (2019). Data-driven innovation: Switching the perspective on Big Data. *European Journal of Innovation Management, 22*(1), 23–40. doi:10.1108/EJIM-01-2018-0017

Valle-Cruz, D., Fernandez-Cortez, V., & Gil-Garcia, J. R. (2022). From E-budgeting to smart budgeting: Exploring the potential of artificial intelligence in government decision-making for resource allocation. *Government Information Quarterly, 39*(2), 101644. doi:10.1016/j.giq.2021.101644

Valle-Cruz, D., Fernandez-Cortez, V., López-Chau, A., & Sandoval-Almazán, R. (2021). Does Twitter Affect Stock Market Decisions? Financial Sentiment Analysis During Pandemics: A Comparative Study of the H1N1 and the COVID-19 Periods. *Cognitive Computation*, 1–16. PMID:33520006

Valle-Cruz, D., & García-Contreras, R. (2023). Towards AI-driven transformation and smart data management: Emerging technological change in the public sector value chain. *Public Policy and Administration*. doi:10.1177/09520767231188401

Valle-Cruz, D., García-Contreras, R., & Gil-Garcia, J. R. (2023). Exploring the negative impacts of artificial intelligence in government: The dark side of intelligent algorithms and cognitive machines. *International Review of Administrative Sciences*. doi:10.1177/00208523231187051

Valle-Cruz, D., García-Contreras, R., & Muñoz-Chávez, J. P. (2022). Mind the Gap: Towards an Understanding of Government Decision-Making based on Artificial Intelligence. *DG.O 2022: The 23rd Annual International Conference on Digital Government Research*, 1–9.

Valle-Cruz, D., Muñoz-Chávez, J. P., & García-Contreras, R. (2023). Towards the Understanding of Consumer Behavior in the Metaverse: A Systematic Literature Review Using the PRISMA Methodology. Handbook of Research on Consumer Behavioral Analytics in Metaverse and the Adoption of a Virtual World, 1–21. doi:10.4018/978-1-6684-7029-9.ch001

Wang, D., Churchill, E., Maes, P., Fan, X., Shneiderman, B., Shi, Y., & Wang, Q. (2020). From human-human collaboration to Human-AI collaboration: Designing AI systems that can work together with people. *Extended Abstracts of the 2020 CHI Conference on Human Factors in Computing Systems*, 1–6.

Weber-Lewerenz, B., & Vasiliu-Feltes, I. (2022). Empowering Digital Innovation by Diverse Leadership in ICT—A Roadmap to a Better Value System in Computer Algorithms. *Humanistic Management Journal*, *7*(1), 117–134. doi:10.1007/s41463-022-00123-7

Williams, A., Suler, P., & Vrbka, J. (2020). Business Process Optimization, Cognitive Decision-Making Algorithms, and Artificial Intelligence Data-driven Internet of Things Systems in Sustainable Smart Manufacturing. *Journal of Self-Governance and Management Economics*, *8*(4), 39–48.

Yu, X., Xu, S., & Ashton, M. (2023). Antecedents and outcomes of artificial intelligence adoption and application in the workplace: The socio-technical system theory perspective. *Information Technology & People*, *36*(1), 454–474. doi:10.1108/ITP-04-2021-0254

Zhou, C., Stephen, A., Cao, X., & Wang, S. (2021). A data-driven business intelligence system for large-scale semi-automated logistics facilities. *International Journal of Production Research*, *59*(8), 2250–2268. doi:10.1080/00207543.2020.1727048

Chapter 2
Digital Transformation and Business Intelligence (BI) in the Industry 4.0 (I 4.0) Age

Mune Moğol Sever
https://orcid.org/0000-0003-4706-5859
Anadolu University, Turkey

ABSTRACT

It is crucial to investigate novel methods for handling the rapidly growing volume of data produced by Industry 4.0 (I4.0), Society 5.0 (S5.0), and IoTs (internet of things). Digital solutions are becoming essential for ensuring that the process continues unhindered and for giving prompt responses. To evaluate and conclude the vast amounts of data generated in this intelligent society, newer information technologies are required. Consisting of optimization, modeling, and data mining, BI is a bundle of technology for multi-dimensional analysis to obtain meaningful data and information from big data without the need for business analysts, professionals, or any trained experts. It consists of optimization, modeling, and data mining. This chapter aims to provide an overview of business intelligence, including its components, varieties, and practical uses in the context of the digital ecosystem. Following an explanation of the BI theoretical framework, four case studies from various industries will be covered, followed by empirical research.

INTRODUCTION

New ideas for Industry 4.0 and Society 5.0 emerged due to the need to discover fresh approaches to the exponentially growing amount of data being generated by IoTs (Internet of Things). Digital solutions become essential in order to offer immediate answers that improve analysis and uninterrupted process maintenance.

Through the use of smart technologies, civilization quickly advanced from I 3.0 (Industry 3.0) to I 5.0 (Industry 5.0), becoming an extremely intelligent society. Later on, further technologies were added to Information Technology (IT) and Information Systems (IS) to keep relevant data and aid in decision-

DOI: 10.4018/979-8-3693-1210-0.ch002

making. The center of this ecosystem is BI. It is acknowledged that Business Intelligence (BI) is the use of technology for data analysis (Howson, 2003). IT&IS is now a more dynamic system with BI than it was before, offering more immediate answers. The key here is using smart technology to extract relevant information from huge data to provide a real-time solution. This clever process is known as business intelligence (BI), and it serves as the primary tool for gathering, evaluating, reporting, and disseminating important data for decision support systems.

Although BI is commonly misinterpreted as Business Analytics (BA), it is not. BA is a subset of BI in the broadest sense. As part of this ecosystem, BA employs express analytical tools and procedures, whereas BI is composed of strategies, tools, and technology (Ng & Nagalingham, 2023). Stated differently, business analytics (BA) uses data interpretation methodologies to prepare the firm for action.

BI has a layered architecture including data, logic, and access/interface. In the data layer, data from many sources (external and internal) are collected and sorted for subsequent analysis. All stakeholders want to access data because businesses implement open-source data policies due to their transparent management approach. Besides, digitalization efforts, where objects and people are connected from everywhere via the internet, cause the production of a lot of mass data: big data. To access this mass of data, businesses save it in their databases to prevent data from being lost in the data layer. The second layer of BI is logic. In this part of BI, analytical processes for data such as extracting from the main data warehouse, loading to internal data warehouse or datamarts, transforming to meaningful and useful information, and inferring to achieve knowledge are carried out. The main elements are data warehouses, datamarts, ETL, OLAP tools, etc. for this layer. The last layer, access/interface, stands for a visual representation of the results. In this layer, there exist tools such as reports, dashboards, graphs, and tables that will allow the user to easily read the results.

Web 3.0 technologies create an immersive, 3D, and End-to-end (E2E) environment for businesses and customers. In this connected internet ecosystem, the internet service quality such as speed, and ubiquitousness become important. Real-time data analysis and instant solutions are the main facilitators of this ecosystem. Real-time data and solutions are also the main handicap within the BI context. ETL is a tool that allows you to extract, clean, and analyze data by dividing it into smaller, more meaningful pieces. The ability to perform all these ETL operations instantly and at a speed close to real-time plays an important role in the success of BI. The scholars are mainly focused on real-time solutions for BI.

Artificial Intelligence (AI) is the main facilitator for instantaneous solutions on BI. It is possible to make meaningful inferences from data thanks to deep learning, machine learning, and heuristic algorithms of artificial intelligence that solve problems in a very short time. Due to the ability to learn & and understand from the past, extract meaningful knowledge, and quickly respond AI is the main assistance in the decision-making process within the context of BI.

BI has attracted the attention of researchers due to the need for instant solutions in human-intensive sectors such as tourism and health. Healthcare at Home (HH) Model for preventive medicine in healthcare (Conley et al., 2008), web-based and open-source data sources for home doctors, a diagnostic and therapeutic reporting system, medical images, and pathological examination reporting systems to make decision support for neurological diseases (Tsumoto et al., 2003), global health records spatial distribution of diseases and health concerns (Be´dard et al., 2003; Yi et al., 2008; Lavracˇ et al., 2007), managing processes through metadata to diagnose (Delen et al, 2012), process improvement (Lee et al., 2021), predictions in disease (Methaila et al., 2014), and infection control (Machado et al, 2017) in healthcare, cancer predictions utilizing data mining and BI tools (Subramanian et al., 2016, Lee et al., 2021), heart attack discovering by several data mining algorithms such as decision trees, artificial neural networks

(ANN), and Naïve Bayes (Methaila et al., 2014), destination management in tourism (Bustamante et al., 2020; Höpken et al.2015) event and festival management (Vajirakachorn & Chongwatpol, 2017) utilizing Neural Network (NN) are some of the examples in BI implementation in healthcare and tourism sectors. Even though BI increases data security and data analysis efficiency in the business, shortens the processing time, and has the capacity to respond quickly to technological innovations, there are also some problems with the use of BI in the business and its integration with other existing software and architecture (ERP, CRM, SOA-Services Oriented architectures) that each enterprise have different operations and it means a lot of customization. In addition, communication difficulties between the consultant and the business, slow performance dealing with big data, time-related disruptions during BI installation, poor data quality, and difficulty in training the personnel who will perform data analysis are the pitfalls that may be encountered during the implementation of BI on a business scale. (Nofal & Yusof, 2013; Djerdjouri, 2020; Wong, 2024).

How business intelligence came to be, industrial revolutions and technological developments, and the digital transformation trends are topics examined in the following section. The transformation of the internet environment into a more interactive environment with Web 3.0, the Internet of Things, and the fact that data transmission and production are very fast in an ecosystem where everyone can access the internet from anywhere and where artificial intelligence is active, are also discussed in this section. In this context, considering the vitality of real-time data and instant solutions, what role BI plays in the success of institutions is also among the topics mentioned. BI has a three-layer architecture, and within the scope of this study, three layers defined as data source, logic, and access are explained in detail in the third section. What role artificial intelligence plays in BI to make meaningful inferences from data is also among the topics covered in the chapter. BI is classified in various ways. Within the scope of this study, it has been deemed appropriate to make a classification as follows: traditional BI, Expert systems, Collaborative BI, Self-Service Business Intelligence, and Real-Time. Besides, to show BI live applications and concretize the subject, BI cases from four main sectors, tourism, health, social networks, and energy, were examined. In these case studies, it is discussed which problems businesses found solutions to, what results they achieved, and their gains after implementing BI. The objective of this chapter is mainly to unpack the BI, its elements, types, and applications in real life within the scope of the digital ecosystem.

FROM INDUSTRY 1.0 TO INDUSTRY 5.0: DIGITALIZATION, DIGITAL TRANSFORMATION, AND ENHANCED DECISION-MAKING

In the wake of Industry 1.0 (I 1.0) mechanization, the I 2.0 revolution introduced electricity to society. Industrial automation in I 3.0 and the use of computers marked the beginning of automation. In the I 4.0 era that we are currently living in, cyber-physical systems control and direct ongoing operations. Sensors and embedded technologies allow direct connection between any physical object and any other object. The current physical systems transform into cyber systems in the context of Industry 4.0. After recognizing the cyber-physical duality and cooperation, it's time to allocate certain routine, non-ergonomic jobs for humans to peers: robots and artificial intelligence (AI)—the I 5.0 or Society 5.0.

According to Fitzgerald et al. (2014), digital transformation (DT) is the connecting of people, things, and everything through the use of the internet and digital technologies, which are being reshaped to improve operational procedures and boost performance. With the use of digital technologies, DT is changing the world (Piccinini et al., 2015). Researchers' primary concerns include distributed business structures, the development of social networks and collaborative environments, increased investment in big data solutions and the Internet of Things (IoTs), the importance of service businesses, and sustainability issues, what are the main factors in creating a suitable environment for DT (Bughin, Chui & Manyika, 2010). One of the key elements in the development of such an ecosystem is the distributed or decentralized structure found in many businesses. Because of a vertical hierarchy, decision-making in centralized structures results in delays and time loss. People may communicate more easily and share information more easily under a decentralized and distributed system since the autocratic structure is eliminated. This may cause a more social and sharing corporate network to emerge. In a similar vein, social network integration fosters cooperation between clients, vendors, companies, and other stakeholders.

The fact that the entire system is connected to the internet is unquestionably the most fundamental aspect of digital transformation. Because of this, items need to be linked to the Internet via Internet of Things technologies as well. Big data is produced as a result of a large number of users and quick information transfer in comparison to analog systems. A service-based approach is brought to the agenda by handling such large data, a connected environment, and exchanging data & resources with the other stakeholders (customers, prosumers, suppliers, etc.). In addition to the primary business function, providing quick fixes and handling concerns pertaining to prosumers and consumers in real-time is another business. Businesses and customers can interact in an End-to-End (E2E) environment thanks to the Internet and Web 3.0 technology. The businesses' ability to provide services is largely dependent on the speed of their internet, service, and technology infrastructure in this collaborative ecosystem that is integrated from top to bottom.

Considering the BI paradigm shift, BI, which was initially used as a prediction tool, has now gained a more collaborative, proactive, and agile approach thanks to the interactive internet along with Web 3.0. With personalization, social networks, and institutions making their resources available to everyone, institutions have gone beyond predicting 'what might happen' and become a tool to help investigate 'what we don't know yet' in real-time (Weichbroth et al., 2024). Instantaneous data access is becoming more and more necessary due to sustainability and users' growing environmental consciousness. People may now compare products and firms based on how environmentally conscious they are, thanks to the Internet of Everything (IoE) and the Internet of Everywhere (IoE), as well as transparent operations. People therefore put pressure on businesses to make clean, ecologically friendly products. In an open, cooperative, networked, big data ecosystem, businesses need quick fixes for third parties in order to continue operating. Businesses must swiftly perform business analysis while carrying out their daily activities to obtain information and deliver immediate answers based on big data. At this point, firms will benefit from new-generation real-time business intelligence (BI) systems. In the following section, the theoretical infrastructure and layers of BI will be examined in detail.

BI-THEORETICAL FRAMEWORK

Without the need for business analysts, professionals, or other trained specialists, business intelligence (BI), which combines optimization, modeling, and data mining approaches, is a multi-dimensional analysis to extract useful information and knowledge from huge data (Turban & Aronson, 2001). The ability to retrieve useful information from vast amounts of streaming data while carrying out ongoing operations is essential to the business's performance (Sahay & Ranjan, 2008). This is the goal that BI is pursuing.

The terms DSS and BI are not synonymous. By giving users access to pertinent data and improving data quality, business intelligence (BI) improves decision support systems. In the decision-making process, BI is acknowledged with BA as a subset and primary facilitator of DSS (Phillips-Wren, Daly & Burstein, 2021). BI aids DSS in decision-making processes by providing solution tools and support (Skyrius, Kazakevičienė, & Bujauskas, 2013; Rouhani et al., 2015). Compared to traditional tools, BI is a real-time, data-driven, agile tool that helps find data and gain information to improve the efficiency of the DSS process (Ou & Peng, 2006). To support DSS, there is extensive IT infrastructure in place (Arnott et al., 2019). While DSS is described as IT systems for small-scale, semi-structured, transient, non-routine decisions (Harsh, 1987: p189; Bonczek, Holsapple & Bennett, 1983: p14; Turban & Watkins, 1986: Arnott & Pervan, 2014; Arnott et al., 2019), DSS is now more proactive and real-time data-driven IS systems as a result of the introduction and use of AI in BI. In addition, according to some academics, BI is a catch-all word for large-scale DSS (Arnott, Lizama & Song, 2017). According to Rouhani et al. (2015), BI improves knowledge processing, reduces decision time and cost, and has a beneficial impact on DSS.

In conclusion, business intelligence (BI) is the core element of decision support systems, made up of many digital techniques. BI ensures and makes it easier to extract and evaluate data from a big data environment, readying the system for action in an operational scenario. The main purpose of the DSS is to prepare the system for decision-making after this process. If the DSS is the business's brain, then the business intelligence process (BI) is what the brain does to prepare itself for the DSS's ultimate conclusion.

For business intelligence to be successful, data from all areas of the company must be integrated, and effective analytical tools must be used. For this reason, the theoretical frameworks of business intelligence—which include the system's operation, relationships with databases, data marts, ETL, OLAP tools, BI types, BI tools, Layers, AI, BI, IoT Relations, and Big Data analytics—are crucial. Furthermore, the standard of information content and information accessibility are important factors that contribute to creating a conducive environment for analytical decision-making (Popovič et al., 2012).

Most operational business intelligence is related to business processes. Furthermore, to handle ongoing unstructured issues, workflow, general-purpose software, and service-oriented approaches (SOA) such web-based services call for an operational business intelligence (BI) tool that is more dynamic and case-based (Marjanovic, 2007). Operational BI is the term used to describe BI that feeds real-time data for operational examples. The organization has plenty of unstructured problems that are outside the scope of general-purpose tools and technologies. In these situations, proactive, real-time operational business intelligence is crucial as a short-term solution for companies.

Real-life examples of BI are frequently encountered. Social media platforms are also among those who benefit from BI. For example, Facebook collects data under the headings of engaged users, likes, PTAT (People Talking about This), Twitter collects follower segmentation (interest, location, gender, etc.), comments YouTube collects likes, comments, EMW (Estimated Minutes Watched) as a social media key metrics and to identify users and to analyze their content (HelicalInsight, 2024). When we consider new-generation autonomous vehicles such as Tesla, we see how vital the capacity to produce instant solutions is for these vehicles. In this context, BI tools will inevitably be used in Tesla as well. Tesla ensures safe and efficient driving, especially by using artificial intelligence-supported BI tools and data analytics, to enhance user experience, predictive maintenance, cost advantage, autonomous driving, advanced navigation, emission reduction, and most importantly real-time data analyses employing Power BI (Amira, 2023). Coca-Cola is another leading company that uses BI tools such as Tableau. Based on sales data, Coca-Cola saved costs through BI (Anand, 2021). Uber also uses artificial intelligence-supported BI to separate business and leisure travel. This will make it easier to collectively cost business trips and send invoices to businesses (TechInside, 2024). One of the recently popular platforms is Netflix. Netflix made a turnover of 8.4 billion dollars in the last third quarter of 2023 (Statista, 2024). Considering that it generated approximately 1 billion dollars in 2013 when it started, the answer to how it made this revenue can be explained by data analytics and BI. With BI, Netflix analyzes viewing day, time, location and device, platform searches (key words), whether content was paused, rewound, rewatched, or fast-forwarded, content abandonment times, and scrolling behaviors (Mixson, 2021).

How BI works, its layered architecture, what is in the layers, and the relationships between the layers are among the topics explained in the following section.

The Three BI Layers

By raising the value of company data, business intelligence (BI) is a combination of technologies that improve operational efficiency (Bharadiya, 2023). Commercial Astuteness The umbrella phrase covering data analytics, data warehouse operations, and result visualization is business intelligence (BI). Three steps or layers commonly comprise business intelligence (BI): data, logic, and access/interface (Baars and Kemper, 2008).

In Figure 1, the relationships between every layer are shown. Data is gathered from several data sources for the first layer. Data from various sources were transformed using ETL, sorted, and cleaned before being transferred as a subset of the data warehouse to the internal data warehouse or datamarts. AI, OLAP, etc. based on the company's strategic or managerial choices. This layer handles the logical operations necessary to transform data into meaningful information. Following logical operations, layer 3-interface/access will be used to visualize the findings on tables, graphs, dashboards, etc. The parts that follow will provide more information on three layers: data source, logic, and access.

Data Source

This layer is where the databases are gathered. Data is retrieved and transported to data warehouses from a variety of sources, including databases, application programs, and APIs (Application Programming Interfaces). Sources of data might be either internal or external. Operational, sales, inventory, management, and data from application programs like Management Executive Systems (MES), Customer Relationship Management (CRM), and Enterprise Resource Planning (ERP) are examples of internal data sources. Suppliers, laws, clients, social media, web-based, cloud, and other entities are the sources of external data.

Logic/Rule-Based Operation

Effective analysis methods are used to process data in this layer (Iris & Nagalingham 2023). Within this business intelligence layer, data is transformed into potentially unknown but important knowledge through the application of rules, analytical tools, and other analytical procedures. This layer contains OLAP, AI, ETL, data marts, and warehouses as components of BI.

Figure 1. BI architecture
(Originally prepared by the author)

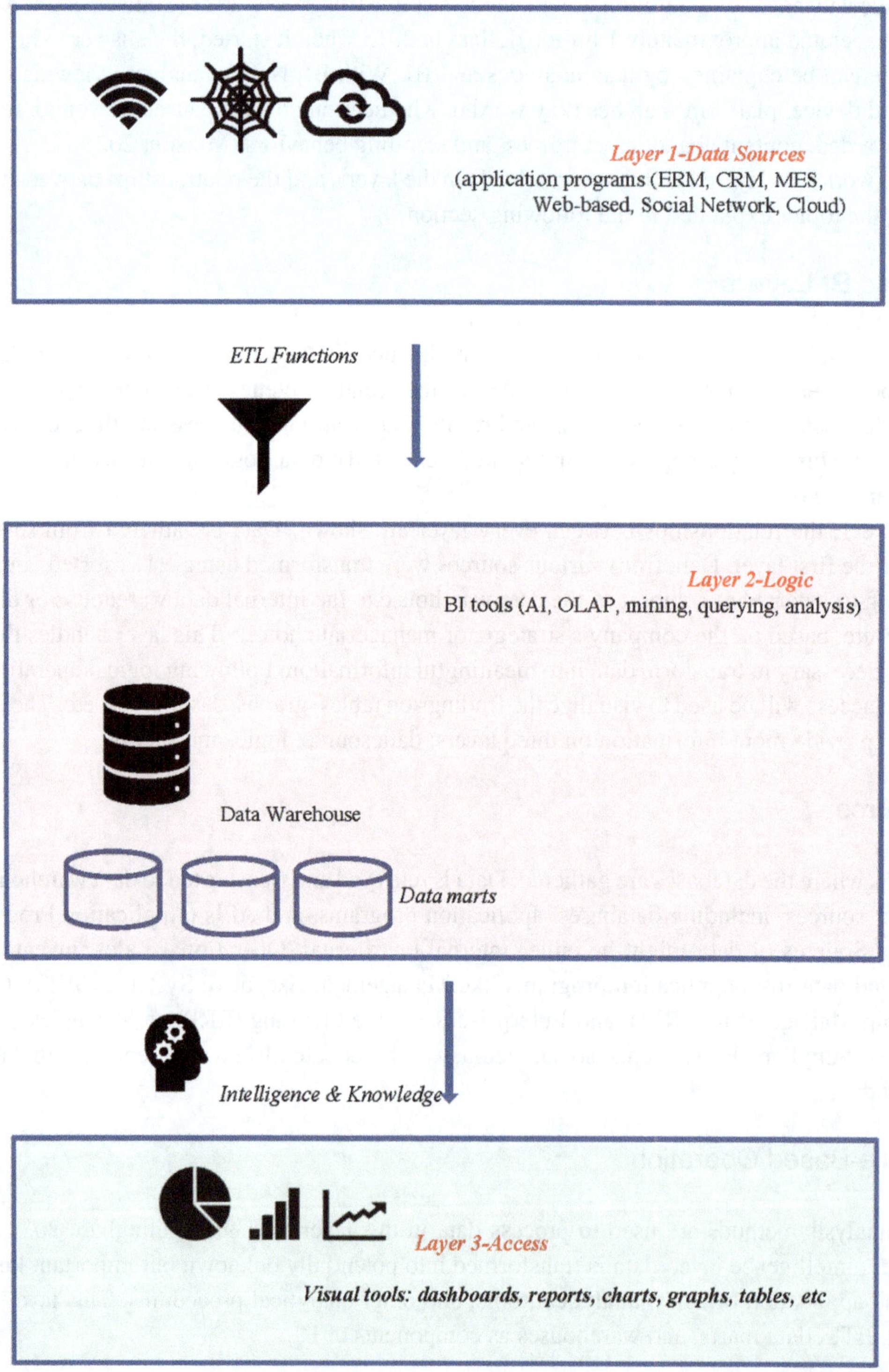

Data warehouse: A data warehouse is a computer system that is used to gather, store, and process operational business data as needed (Hermawan et al., 2018). Due to its capacity to access and aggregate a large amount of disparate data from many data sources, data warehouses are among the most important parts of business intelligence (Vaisman & Zimanyi, 2012). Databases from various, dispersed sources might provide business data. Data can be retrieved from numerous databases even for certain procedures. With the businesses in the digital ecosystem, there are a plethora of data sources to consider, including cyber-physical data generated from inside the facility, which is referred to as inside data, and outside data generated by third parties, such as suppliers, consumers, the government, and other authorities. All parties have their own data storage in this context of blended and fused business models. To generate an immediate answer, data from all sources should be pooled and then segregated for additional analysis.

Data mart: Data Marts called retail outlets of data warehouses (Moody & Kortink, 2000) are the subset or small group of data warehouses. In data marts, data were extracted and collected with specific parameters in small data warehouses. In other words, it is the division of a data warehouse in a selected subject or theme.

ETL (Extract Transform Load): Before using any analytical technique in a big data context, data should be properly chosen. Preparing and integrating operational data with BI tools is the primary purpose of ETL. According to Machado et al. (2019), it is the process of organizing data for querying and/or analysis. ETL uses an iterative, step-by-step technique to provide this. Sorting is the primary purpose of ETL, which is also known as extraction, validation, cleansing, conversion or transformation, loading, or aggregation. A general ETL structure is shown in Figure 2.

Figure 2. The ETL structure

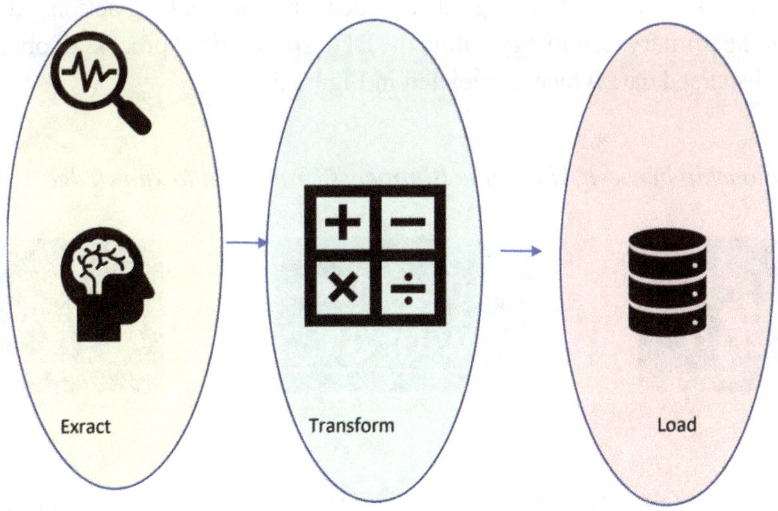

The analyst should ascertain the enterprise's data source in the initial step of extraction, including whether the data is structured or unstructured, and which application programs and database management systems are in use (Jun, et al., 2009). Using predetermined parameters, the system tests and verifies the data in the validation process. Cleaning is the process of removing from the data pool any useless or vague information. The next stage after cleaning is to transform the data into meaningful information using traditional pivot table slicing and dicing operations to obtain a more focused and manageable subset of big data. The process of loading involves obtaining and uploading data into a relevant system—such as a database, application, etc.—so that it can be used for business analysis and knowledge extraction. In conclusion, the primary purpose of ETL in BI is to collect meaningful data using databases and datamarts. From the standpoint of real-time business intelligence, ETL plays a crucial role in preparing the data for immediate solutions. ETL must operate independently, requiring only monitoring from humans, in order to feed data marts (Watson et al., 2009).

OLAP: OLAP is a multidimensional modeling tool designed to help decision-makers by capturing the structure of real-time data for further analysis (Turban & Aronson, 2001: 194). OLAP is a group of methods that primarily make use of cubes as a multidimensional data query tool. A multidimensional array of data for additional analysis can be found at the crossing point of these cubes (Villar Et al., 2018; Zaiane et al., 1998). With the aid of OLAP technology, databases can be edited to extract valuable information from them or data marts.

AI: Organizations now have to deal with real-time data in contrast to old systems because of the development of IoTs and autonomous systems. In a real-time streaming data ecosystem, the system produces hundreds of data, which translates into dozens of queries and preventive measures. By taking into account the 4Vs (volume, velocity, value, and variety) of the big data ecosystem, words from business analytics become big data analytics. As a result, real-time useful data extraction requires artificial intelligence techniques. Algorithms such as AI's Machine Learning (ML) and Deep Learning (DL) can extract meaningful knowledge from a huge data environment in milliseconds. In addition, heuristics like genetic algorithms, memetic algorithms, and Ant colony optimization can be used as AI techniques within the BI logic layer, as can expert systems and fuzzy logic.

While BI works with extracting knowledge from data in a big data environment, AI mimics the way the human brain works in terms of reasoning, making decisions, and taking action. AI takes on the role of the BI's brain, or the primary technology within the BI to speed up the process of obtaining knowledge from massive and dispersed data which is depicted in Figure 3.

Figure 3. The relationship between AI and the BI process (from data to knowledge)

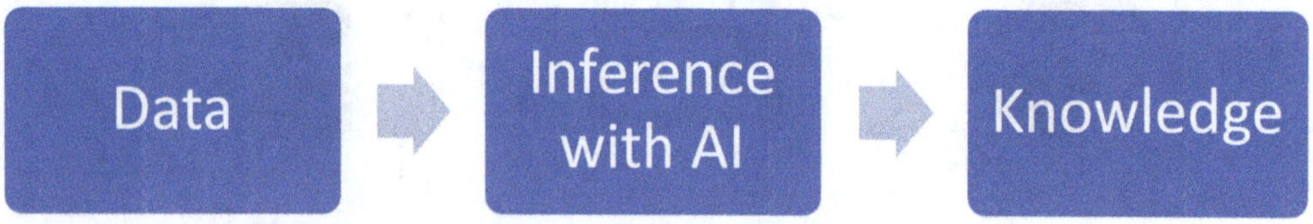

In the context of AI, intelligence can be summed up as follows (Turban & Aronson, 2001: 398):

- Gaining insight and learning from the past
- Deriving significant knowledge from imprecise communications
- Reaction time is short and productivity is high in unfamiliar situations
- Problem-solving strategy is logical and matches the AI directly.

AI can be utilized as a data extractor and improve the data analytics capability of BI because of its rule-based and predictive structure, which includes learning algorithms, deep learning, and machine learning (Bharadiya, 2022). Put differently, AI can provide BI ahead of analytics.

The primary enablers in the BI logic layer for cleaning, mapping, reducing, combining, and inferring are a few software programs. The two primary frameworks for storing, cleaning, reducing, mapping, and analyzing large data are Hadoop Map Reduce and SAP HANA. One massive data processing framework is Hadoop MapReduce (Dittrich & Quian´eRuiz, 2012). The two main steps in MapReduce are mapping and reduction. The initial step involves mapping data. After then, the data is divided into various sections. The final phase of MapReduce is to reduce the data and merge similar subjects (Hadoop, 1.11.2023) One type of In-Memory Cache Database (IMDB) is SAP HANA. For applications needing fast speed for real-time solutions, they store the data in RAM (SAP, 02.11.2023).

Access

Dashboards, reporting systems, visual tools, and other tools are intended for this layer. The user interface layer, sometimes referred to as the "end user layer" (Ong et al., 2011), is what presents the BI tool results as a visual and nontechnical tool. There is so much software to help the end user to interpret results visually. Tableau, Microsoft Power BI, IBM Cognos Analytics, SAS Viya, and SAP Hana are some of them. It is also known that rapid developments in artificial intelligence, artificial intelligence's reasoning ability, contribution to decision-making processes, etc. cause AI to be associated with BI and increase the performance of BI. Besides, AI creates an opportunity for BI due to its automatic data analysis and anomaly detection ability, dynamic pricing and predictive forecasts, agile decision-making ability, and quick response to personalized services and products (Bharadiya, 2023). In this context, innovative solutions involving artificial intelligence in BI processes have also been launched. One of them is Open AI. Open AI launched Dall.e as the first edition of Dall.e series in 2021. Dall.e is an artificial intelligence program developed to create images from texts (Open AI, 2024). Images directly related to texts given in any language are created. This can be considered as a BI tool with an AI add-on that quickly reaches the desired meaningful result based on data. AI is a technology that brings innovative solutions to businesses within the digitalization trend. More easily understandable dashboards, tables, and visuals are created through AI, enabling the end user to use BI tools in a useful way. For these reasons, AI appears as the current technology preferred only in providing solutions to logic operations in BI and visualizing the results.

To summarize, it is necessary to say that BI has a layered architecture. These layers are defined as the input layer, which is expressed as the data source, the rule-based layer, where logical operations are performed, and finally, the access layer, where the results are interpreted after the operations are performed. So, the answers to the questions "Which all BIs are encountered? What kind of a classification is made regarding the types and types of BIs?" are given in the following section.

BI Classification

In its initial iteration, business intelligence (BI) was only a static reporting system that could be used manually or with any spreadsheet program, like Excel. After a few online analytical tools are incorporated, it becomes an OLAP (Online Analytical Processing) that extracts more important information from historical data than ad hoc queries. It eventually begins to look more like a predictive tool than a descriptive one. In the context of a smart society, business intelligence (BI) is now more than just a forecasting tool; it uses real-time data by utilizing digital twins of real-physical systems and cyber-physical systems.

- **Traditional instruments:** ¥Ad-hoc queries, OLAP, and connected databases are basic technologies when it comes to business intelligence. Researchers wishing to analyze data in more dimensions than two can use the Online Analytical Process (OLAP), which provides an online workspace for their research. ETL tools are used to extract data from databases, application programs (ERP, CRM, MES, etc.), and APIs in the OLAP system after the data has been stored in a data warehouse or data mart. The user uses pivot tables to slice and dice crucial parameters to employ OLAP cubes to extract significant information from this enormous historical data pool. Users and analysts employ Multidimensional Expressions (MDX), a multidimensional query language, for ad hoc base query analysis. Traditional BIs are generally used to detect patterns and make predictions from historical data. The information we provide while shopping at a shopping mall creates data for business intelligence to plan our next purchase and for advertising companies and promotions. Companies send us advertisements and informational messages for special campaigns and promotions based on our shopping history. At this point, it is thought that the use of BI in retailing will be more active.
- **Expert System (ES)**: A group of computer programs based on artificial intelligence (AI) designed to aid in decision-making (Zahedi, 1993: 12). Expert systems are computer programs that, typically with a specific goal in mind, solve problems or make decisions based on rules or difficulties. The concept underlying ES is simple. Expert systems incorporate one or more people's expertise and experience (Mach & Abdel-Badeeh, 2010). The process starts whenever the expert converts knowledge to software, enabling customers to call for assistance anytime needed (Turban & Aronson, 2001). Neural networks and machine learning are two AI technologies that ES leverages.
- **Collaborative BI:** Collaborative intelligence, or BI 2.0, mostly functions in a real-time environment (Rizzi, 2012). Because of the emergence of data-sharing technologies and the phenomenon of crowdsourcing, businesses are now willing to share their data, knowledge, and expertise with outside parties. Analytical efficacy and efficiency rise on a platform this open and collaborative. We refer to this type of decision-making environment as collaborative business intelligence.
- **Self-Service Business Intelligence (SSBI):** This type of BI is used by business specialists who are not used to coding methods (Tableau, 22.10.2023). Professionals can use this type of BI service provider more easily than system analysis since they don't need to comprehend system analysis concepts or know how to write code.
- **Open-Source BI**: The foundation and resource for open-source BI is publicly available data from mainstream media, social media, open government, and journals. Data obtained from social media platforms is sometimes referred to as Social Business Intelligence (SBI) (Dinter & Lorenz, 2012; Kaufmann & Chamoni, 2014). In context-rich social media sources, SBI leverages the wisdom of the crowd (Zeng et al., 2010). Following the increasing adoption of shared economy concepts and the emergence of transparent management ideas, Open-Source BI evolved.
- **Real-Time BI (RTBI):** BI is used in tactical, strategic, and operational decision-making processes. The constant evolution of digitalization concepts and technology necessitates the use of BI in continuous, real-time operations. Real-time can be defined as necessary information for ongoing processes with zero latency, information when the process requires it, and immediate achievement of important performance indicators for ongoing operations, even though there is no

universally accepted definition for the term (Azvine et al., 2006). Depending on its operations, strategy, clientele, etc., every business has unique critical performance metrics. Zero latency, for instance, can tolerate a 10-minute wait time for an urgent call response from a hospital, but not for a hotel check-in procedure. To operate successfully and efficiently, businesses should first define their real-time definition and key performance indicators.

With the advent of Industry 4.0 and the Internet of Things (IoTs) into our daily lives, real-time activities have become more and more crucial, and real-time business information (BI) is a key component of decision-making. Real-time BI processes data as soon as it is entered into the system. Sandu (2008) states that the delay should be around milliseconds. This type of BI is used during the operational stages. Unfortunately, most BI applications do not have this feature because of synchronization problems and slow updating of databases (Melchert, Winter & Klesse, 2004). To suppress this latency issue, firms utilize novel ETL technologies to retrieve real-time database data instead of traditional database data extraction procedures. List, Bauer, and Schöpfer (2002). Distributed on Demand-ETL is an attempt to achieve near real-time data solutions for ETL. It combines distributed on-demand data with I-memory caching and effective data partitioning in a parallel architecture that is independent of technology (Machado et al., 2019).

Although there are many BI classifications, this is the most basic classification encountered. When the definitions are examined, they seem to be closer to today's digitalization and self-management principles, where real-time BIs and SSBIs can come to the fore. BI applications will be the subject of the next section, in which sectors and in which operations BI is used.

EMPIRICAL STUDIES

BI is particularly prone to service sectors, even if many innovations and technology were initially used in the manufacturing sector. BI tools are appropriate for service-oriented sectors due to their ability to handle simultaneous production and consumption, direct client interaction, and human insensitivity. Numerous disjointed pieces of software used in management and customer relations, in addition to back-office functions, generate a vast number of data sources. Under these circumstances, the BI turns into a crucial service company partner. In addition, it is known that BI provides solutions and applications to many different issues; Customer relationship management, smart marketing, use of resources, optimizing processes, improvement in quality of data and operations, maintaining security and privacy, brand trust, and creating distinctive image are some of these (Kazemi et al., 2024). Given the volume of face-to-face interactions and transactions, the two most well-known service industries are tourism and health. For this reason, studies from these areas have been mentioned with this intensity.

BI is a good tool for destination management. In order to establish BITOUR, a collaborative data platform, Bustamante et al., 2020 combined four data sources: Twitter, Airbnb, TripAdvisor, and OpenStreetMap. BITOUR enables the analysis of visitor opinions towards specified sites, the length of stay per visitor, and the most popular places for tourists to visit inside specific tourist attractions. Using visual tools, this BI platform assists in analyzing a tourism destination's intensity. In a different study, Höpken et al. (2015) used exploratory data analysis methods including OLAP and data mining to create a destination management information system as a multi-dimensional data model.

Large-scale occasions like festivals and specialized travel agencies can have an impact on a region locally or globally. Because of the significant effects that special events have on the economy and society, many players in the tourism industry are primarily concerned with anticipating and understanding the primary driving force behind tourists during these events. Researchers sought to study visitor purchase patterns, travel experiences, and destination preferences to boost consumer satisfaction, given the influence of large crowds at major events (Vajirakachorn & Chongwatpol, 2017). Regression tools, support vector machines, and a neural network (NN) with six input components are used as BI tools, and Tableau software is used to visualize the results. It is vital to employ diverse BI methodologies within a single research investigation. In addition, the study demonstrates the significance of BI for all tourism stakeholders in tourism management.

Emerging topics in the field of business intelligence (BI) include managing processes through metadata to diagnose (Delen et al., 2012), process improvement (Lee et al., 2021), disease forecasts (Methaila et al., 2014), and infection management (Machado et al., 2017). In healthcare business intelligence, machine learning and learning algorithms are the favored methods. Chronic illnesses, being recurring health issues, produce a large amount of data quickly. BI can be used to diagnose issues related to managing chronic diseases. Researchers who use BI and data mining technologies also address cancer forecasts (Subramanian et al., 2016, Lee et al., 2021). Researchers create big data databases and archives using inputs like body checks, screening records, medical histories, and demographic data in order to employ learning algorithms to extract information about cervical cancer (Lee et al., 2021). Precautions must be made in advance about heart attack instances. Several data mining algorithms, including decision trees, artificial neural networks (ANN), and Naïve Bayes, have been used to uncover the underlying causes of heart attacks (Methaila et al., 2014). The fight against infections is another crucial aspect of health. Healthcare facilities use business intelligence (BI) tools to assist in decision-making (Machato et al., 2017, Ali et al, 2013). Ali et al. (2013) developed a decision and reporting support system to assist with hand hygiene audits, guarantee a corporate data repository, and an infection prevention and control reporting tool for visualization to lower infection rates and promote infection safety plans. Ali et al. (2013) used SQL Server 2008 R2 to create a data mart, SSIS as an ETL solution, and Excel & SSRS for reporting in their project. Another area of medicine that has a wealth of digital data that can be used to apply BI solutions is radiology. Using MySQL 5.0 for database management and Penraho Data Integration 3.0 open-source software for ETL, researchers apply BI solutions in the radiology detection process using open-source data (Prevedello et al., 2008). In 2010, Zhou et al. created a Clinical Data Warehouse (CDW) using OLAP tools and Complex Network Analysis (CAN) to find the clinical association, and a Clinical Information Model (CIM) with an ETL tool to normalize the data. They look for Traditional Chinese Medicine (TCM) information amid the excessive number of clinical settings.

Because streaming data is so easily accessible, web-based and open-source data sources are becoming more and more common in healthcare research. To support decision-making for neurological illnesses, researchers created an expert system for a web-based system for home doctors, a diagnostic and therapeutic reporting system, medical imaging, and pathological examination reporting systems (Tsumoto et al., 2003).

Researchers delved into the spatial distribution of diseases and health concerns as a result of global health records and a knowledge of public health from a global viewpoint (Be´dard et al., 2003; Yi et al., 2008; Lavrac⁼ et al., 2007). In order to enhance the public health decision-making process, researchers combined the Geographic Information Systems (GIS) and OLAP tools to produce a spatial OLAP, or SOLAP (Be´dard et al., 2003). Bedard et al. (2003) identified and ruled out a possible link between environmental factors and health issues in their investigation. In a different study pertaining to public health, researchers attempt to use Google Maps and R software to visualize physically the spatial distribution of cancer incidence and death data (Yi et al., 2008). Data mining is used by Lavrač et al. (2007) for regional public health planning in Slovenia. They try to visualize the results using BI visualizing tools and use a variety of data sources, including the medical status database, the out-patient healthcare statistics database, and the health-care provider's database, to aid in the planning of regional public health institutes (PHIs).

Despite having uses in the service industry, there are certain issues with its implementation. ETL bottlenecks account for the bulk of BI-related issues (Marín-Ortega et al., 2014). Businesses strive to develop an effective ETL system to eliminate data bottlenecks and latency issues to have real-time data and find instantaneous solutions. In the BI process, an ETL pipeline was described. According to Watson and Wixom (2007), the integration of business processes with BI, which is recognized as an ETL process, requires 80% of the time and results in more than 50% of unforeseen project expenses. The pipeline should not be clogged for the system to function.

The primary factors influencing the effectiveness of ETL are data quality, speed, and accuracy (Pan et al., 2018). The ETL is successful in the BI process if the data is obtained instantly and is of sufficient quality for analysis. Increasing data quality will increase the institution's information system quality and data security, thus ensuring user performance and satisfaction (Mudau et al., 2024). But unfortunately, it is challenging to obtain and analyze real-time data due to the absence of standards in health services and the utilization of numerous approaches (Ward et al., 2014). The primary focus of preventative medicine in health care research is real-time or almost real-time data. The Healthcare at Home (HH) Model was created by Conley et al. (2008) by combining various data sources, including clinical hubs, mobile communication devices, and/or home-based network PCs. Scholars aim to produce real-time data using this patient-centered HH model and multi-source data to enhance healthcare interventions and boost decision-making efficiency.

Despite its advantages, this appears to be a disadvantage since it takes time to install BI in the business and integrate it with other software. In addition, problems experienced in the training of data analysts and communication with BI consultants appear as disruptions in the process (Nofal & Yusof, 2013). Resistance of workplace users to use BI and poor data quality are other challenges in implementing BI (Djerdjouri, 2020). Data security and privacy are also challenges in the adoption of BI (Aruldoss et al., 2014). Encryption systems and a multidimensional hierarchical architecture create a suitable environment for data security in BI (Al-Aqrabi et al., 2013). Encryptions, especially with cryptographic systems provided by Blockchain technology, can provide a reliable data environment for BI. Additionally, programming models, social analytics, semantic data, efficient processing of big data, effective machine learning techniques, massive OLAP, efficient distributed storage, and search were mentioned as the challenges in implementing BI in the industry (Ardagna & Damiani, 2014). Although there are many reasons for failure in BI projects, some of them are listed as follows: lack of pre-planning, ignoring fees other than the license fee, data quality, deficiencies in dashboard reliability, and failing to anticipate the change. Besides, customer portfolio, demographics, business practices, and principles should also be determined at the beginning of BI projects. This data is not data to be outsourced or provided by BI consultants (Caroline, 2024).

Enhancing business intelligence (BI) is an essential topic to assist in boosting productivity and performing tasks correctly for practitioners. Examples from service businesses that use BI in practice will be provided so that readers may see how the technology is applied in various industries. Several case studies, especially from the service industries (health, tourism, energy, and social networks) are explained in the next section.

BI SUCCESS MODEL: CASE STUDIES FOR SERVICE INDUSTRIES: BI4S (BI FOR SERVICES)

In this section, a succinct overview of BI software and success stories from particular industries will be covered in detail. This section comprises the case study technique steps like the problem, the accomplishment, and the outcomes as shown in Table 1 to 5. Discussed cases are:

- Transportation: Heathrow Airport Microsoft *Azure & Power BI*
- Health care: INTEGRIS Health *Azure analytics & Power BI &Embedded*
- Tourism: Foxwoods Resort Casino with *SAS Viya*
- Social: LinkedIn sales team performance with *Tableau*
- Energy: Alliant Energy with IBM-*Cognos-AI.*

Heathrow Airport Microsoft *Azure & Power BI*

Nearly every airport has an issue with lines of passengers. Airport management is interested in several concerns, one of which is reducing the waiting line. Heathrow Airport handled 19.4 million passengers in 2021, according to the data (Heathrow, 2023). Airport authorities utilize business intelligence (BI) to manage passenger flow and make managerial choices about staff changes, passenger lines, and security lanes. The management of Heathrow Airport shifted the operational viewpoint from reactive, paper-based models to proactive, digital models that are predictive (Carey, 2018). They bought Power BI, a real-time business intelligence solution that tracks passenger movement and facilitates operational decision-making.

Microsoft Cloud Power BI is a cloud-based, data-driven BI software designed to help professionals work with the latest AI algorithms. It is one of Microsoft's cloud-based BI products. With Power BI's copilot tool, reports may be generated rapidly, comprehend the semantic model, describe a phenomenon, and provide ideas for report topics to the business (Microsoft, 2023; Manis, 2023). Heathrow Airport management was able to instantly manage security lanes, shifts, and breaks utilizing ML algorithms with Power BI after putting it into practice.

Table 1. Heathrow airport Microsoft Azure & Power BI

The problem: a paper-based, reactive model for passenger flow
Accomplishment: a predictive and proactive model for predicting the passenger volume
Outcomes: planning the personnel shifts, security lanes, and breaks utilizing machine learning

By utilizing Microsoft Azure BI tools Heathrow Airport has a more predictive and proactive model for passenger volume measurement, to make personnel planning efficient.

Healthcare: INTEGRIS Health *Azure Analytics & Power BI & Embedded*

The many different technologies and data sources that record electronic health records (EHRs) make them extremely diversified. One of the objectives of large healthcare facilities is to compile all of the recorded data and incorporate it into EHR software using BI technologies. EPIC's HER records are integrated with Power BI by Integris Health, which also integrates the data sources (Mansalis, 2023). With nine facilities and 10,000 employees, Integris Health is the biggest hospital system in Oklahoma. Data is gathered from a variety of sources, including EPIC, Oracle ERP, IoT External, and Claims. Data is initially supplied to Azure Synapse Analysis and Azure Analysis Services during the ETL step to aggregate all the databases from various data sources. Results of the embedded BI tool implementation can be examined on Power BI Wall and Power BI Embedded analytics on EPIC EHR on desktop and mobile devices (Microsoft, 2021).

Table 2. INTEGRIS Health Azure analytics & Power BI & Embedded

Problem: disconnect data
Accomplishment: connection data to discover the data to help healthcare facility workers & employees **Outcomes:** flexibility and adjustment for urgent user needs and ability to get action for the patient

Integris Health solved the disconnected data problem by implementing Azure analytics & Power BI by embedding it into their current Electronic Health Records software (EHR). By connecting all operational data Integris can satisfy the urgent needs of patients and hence help healthcare workers using BI tools.

Tourism: Foxwoods Resort Casino With *SAS Viya*

Another industry with a high transaction volume each day is tourism, which also requires a lot of people and data. One of the main industries that contributes significantly to the economy and driving force of tourism is hospitality. After being forced to close due to COVID-19, Foxwoods Resort Casino, a 9 million-square-foot facility with seven casinos, four hotels, 35 restaurants, and 80 shops, looking for immediate and digital data solutions, converting the problem into an opportunity (SAS Institute 2021).

Table 3. Foxwoods Resort Casino with SAS Viya

Problem: reactive process
Accomplishment: revenue, expense, and demand forecasting by SAS
Outcomes: staff scheduling & planning for each entity in a hotel depending on the SAS BI revenue, expense, and demand forecast.

The management used SAS BI to fulfill their goal of knowing how many employees are assigned to which entity in a hotel based on demand. One of the cloud-based BI programs is SAS Viya. In addition to the drag-and-drop interface, SAS Viya allows teachers and students to write R, Python, and SAS code for discovery and deployment (SAS, 2023).

Social: LinkedIn Sales Team Performance With *Tableau*

Tableau was first used by LinkedIn as part of its sales effectiveness program to generate current reports, respond to inquiries, and determine whether or not the data is actionable. LinkedIn concentrated on four topics by using Tableau (Staniar & Ngo, 2023):

- Product usage: Using LinkedIn

Target search: advance search by target; InMail engagement: using InMail instead of other email accounts; Social Selling Index (SSI): using social media, LinkedIn, developing a professional brand, locating the right people, interacting with insights, and forging lasting relationships.

Table 4. LinkedIn sales team performance with Tableau

Problem: reactive process
Accomplishment: improve the productivity and performance of sales organization
Outcomes: sales effective-sales navigator program

By using Tableau LinkedIn, the company was able to improve revenue by 59%, deal-to-connect decision-maker size by 42%, and build 15% more sales funnels for customer acquisition (Troidl, 2023). In addition, Tableau's implementation will enable 90% of the sales team members at LinkedIn by centralizing petabytes of data from several platforms into a more proactive system with reduced client attrition (Tableau, 2023). Tableau's results are more than twice as good as LinkedIn's, with a 0.57% clicking rate and a 6% discussion rate (LinkedIn, 2023).

Energy: Alliant Energy With IBM COGNOS

An AI BI platform from the IBM family is called Cognos. Cognos AI may test a hypothesis or inquiry by simply articulating it and then extracting pertinent information from the data (IBM, 2023). Alliant Energy employs 3129 people and serves 995,000 retail customers in Iowa and Wisconsin for electricity and 425,000 for natural gas (Alliant Energy, 2023).

Table 5. Alliant Energy with IBM COGNOS

Problem: reactive process
Accomplishment: AI-based BI to help internal customers/employees for ongoing operations to eliminate coal from their portfolio by 2050
Outcomes: enabling data-driven models from each level of the organization in asset management and operation functions.travel budgeting, prioritizing requests of the customer, visual reporting/dashboards, Web-based data acquisition: data modules

Businesses use BI technologies driven by AI to improve reporting and data analysis for internal customers. Furthermore, by 2050, the corporation hopes to remove coal from its energy mix (Cheuvront, 2020). Alliant Energy uses dashboards and Cognos data modules to analyze data more effectively using visualization tools. To reduce electricity use, the company additionally put smart meters in 1000 residences. By using Cognos' cloud-based data analytics, this led to an 11% reduction in electricity consumption (Niccolai, 2011).

In conclusion, this part includes sample applications for the five fundamental service industry sectors: transportation, health, tourism, social networks, and energy. Furthermore, the outputs of BI in the listed sectors are discussed in this section.

CONCLUSION

This chapter provides an explanation of BI terminology and components in the context of digital transformation. Mass data was created as a result of the introduction of IoTs into our lives during the last industrial revolution. New-generation business intelligence (BI) technologies will unavoidably replace older models in business processes and analytics inside this ecosystem, where data is transferred rapidly and immediate resolutions are anticipated.

This section also explains the relationship between DSS and BI, even if their differences and similarities can occasionally lead to conceptual confusion. In its widest sense, BI is a collection of technologies that support DSS. Stated differently, it seemed to be a tool to help DSS make decisions.

Many of the system's devices can connect to the internet and one another thanks to IoT technology in I4.0. When linked things and the internet communicate with one another and with users, instant data is created by means of loTs. Big data is a result of IoT-generated massive data. Mass data generation is also aided by open-source data madness and web-based apps. Therefore, real-time technological solutions are required for the analysis of these instantaneous data as well as for the quick resolution of issues. Instant BI tools now assist organizations in making decisions. Despite this, the BI real-time solution still needs to be developed. By no means are traditional tools (OLAP, etc.) proactive. Artificial intelligence steps in to save the day at this point.

Real-time or nearly real-time solutions to urgent situations become possible with the help of AI and BI. One of the most important technologies for speeding up and enabling useful inferences from large amounts of data is artificial intelligence (AI). In order to move from data to knowledge, sophisticated AI generative algorithms can draw conclusions. Put differently, artificial intelligence (AI) is the most significant BI assistive technology that helps make data intelligible and evaluate it in real-time.

This chapter's case study is restricted to the service industries, particularly the two that require the greatest human resources: healthcare and tourism. These two industries were selected because they make up a sizable portion of the service industry, need a lot of labor, and have urgent procedures. It is essential that the solution must be available right away in one of these industries, healthcare. In the other industry, tourism, there is an urgent need for a solution because decreasing client wait times is critical to boosting customer satisfaction.

Healthcare at Home (HH) Model for preventive medicine in healthcare (Conley et al., 2008), web-based and open-source data sources for home doctors, a diagnostic and therapeutic reporting system, medical images, and pathological examination reporting systems to make decision support for neurological diseases (Tsumoto et al., 2003), global health records spatial distribution of diseases and health concerns

(Be´dard et al., 2003; Yi et al., 2008; Lavracˇ et al., 2007), managing processes through metadata to diagnose (Delen et al, 2012), process improvement (Lee et al., 2021), predictions in disease (Methaila et al., 2014), and infection control (Machado et al, 2017) in healthcare, cancer predictions utilizing data mining and BI tools (Subramanian et al., 2016, Lee et al., 2021), heart attack discovering by several data mining algorithms such as decision trees, artificial neural networks (ANN), and Naïve Bayes (Methaila et al., 2014), destination management in tourism (Bustamante et al., 2020; Höpken et al.2015) event and festival management (Vajirakachorn & Chongwatpol, 2017) utilizing Neural Network (NN) are some of the examples in BI implementation in healthcare and tourism sectors. Applications related to other sectors are included in the case studies and empirical studies section.

DISCUSSION

Although AI is currently described as an expensive and difficult-to-access technology, in the near future it will be used as a tool to help small businesses run their operations at all levels and will be accessible even in a small pizzeria (NG, 2023). Considering the relationship between BI and AI, it is an inevitable fact that AI technology in BI will be the basic core technology in the focus of BI. Or will this BI be mentioned after AI?

It is difficult for people who are not experts in data analysis to use BI tools and interpret the results. Self-service BIs have emerged to solve this handicap. SSBIs are special BIs developed for non-IT users to make automatic reporting (Passlick et al., 2023). For such reasons, it is thought that self-service BIs and SSBIs will become more widespread soon. But what about the privacy issues and ethical considerations of sharing data on those service platforms?

Using institutions' data in shared environments, and platforms, for data analysis and BI reports may raise some privacy and ethical issues. As a result of BI platforms being hacked, data falling into the hands of unwanted third parties may cause losses and grievances for companies. At this point, it should be examined what precautions both cloud platform providers and BI service platforms take regarding data privacy and security. Additionally, the compliance of BI platforms and software with scientific and ethical principles regarding data manipulation, data reliability, and validity is another issue that should be taken into consideration. Despite eliminating all these ethical and security issues, are BI services accessible to everyone at an affordable cost?

Currently, only large companies can invest in BI technologies due to costs and high prices. However, especially utilizing crowdsourcing and shared platforms, the software becoming available to everyone, the decrease in costs, and the rapid developments in artificial intelligence will make it easier for medium and small-sized businesses to obtain these technologies. But how to deal with such mass data has become more important than ever after IoTs.

One of the topics discussed in other chapters is that the digital age is full of management with digital data. Employing the Industry 5.0 and its derivative technologies, objects, machines, and other existing devices have become accessible via the internet. Additionally emerging terms like transhumanism, in an environment where even humans have become digital, this is a natural consequence that after each internet-connected object communicates with each other, the signal and data traffic traveling in the system will intensify and create mass data, big data. The issue of how real-time data analysis and real-time solutions will be achieved has not yet been brought to the agenda. It does not seem possible to classify and sort this data quickly with human intelligence. Therefore, at this point, we encounter AI-supported

BI for processing big data. Although AI may seem like a magic wand, it is beneficial to reconsider BI along with artificial intelligence, like every new technology. As the last word, in an environment where quantum technology and new-generation computers and Chatbots are becoming widespread, it is difficult to predict where BI will evolve.

Funding

This research received no specific grant from any funding agency in the public, commercial, or not-for-profit sectors.

REFERENCES

Al-Aqrabi, H., Liu, L., Hill, R., Ding, Z., & Antonopoulos, N. (2013). Business Intelligence Security on the Clouds: Challenges, Solutions and Future Directions. *2013 IEEE Seventh International Symposium on Service-Oriented System Engineering,* 137-144. 10.1109/SOSE.2013.36

Ali, O. T., Nassif, A. B., & Capretz, L. F. (2013, June). Business intelligence solutions in healthcare a case study: Transforming OLTP system to BI solution. In *2013 Third International Conference on Communications and Information Technology (ICCIT)* (pp. 209-214). IEEE. 10.1109/ICCITechnology.2013.6579551

Alliant Energy. (2023). *Welcome to Alliant Energy.* Retrieved December 19, 2023 from https://www.alliantenergy.com/accountandbilling/customersupport/welcomepage

Amira, V. Y. (2023). *Medium.com. How Tesla is using AI and Big Data Analytics in their Self Driving Cars?* Retrieved January 8, 2024, from https://medium.com/dare-to-be-better/how-tesla-is-using-ai-and-big-data-analytics-in-their-self-driving-cars-7072e410c1b8

Anand, K. (2024). *How Intelligent Businesses Use Business Intelligence.* Retrieved January 7, 2024 from https://www.entrepreneur.com/growing-a-business/how-intelligent-businesses-use-business-intelligence/398669

Ardagna, C. A., & Damiani, E. (2014, September). Business intelligence meets big data: an overview on security and privacy. *NSF Workshop on Big Data Security and Privacy*, 16-17.

Arnott, D., Lizama, F., & Song, Y. (2017). Patterns of business intelligence systems use in organizations. *Decision Support Systems*, *97*, 58–68. doi:10.1016/j.dss.2017.03.005

Arnott, D., & Pervan, G. (2014). A critical analysis of decision support systems research revisited: The rise of design science. *Journal of Information Technology*, *29*(4), 269–293. doi:10.1057/jit.2014.16

Arnott, Gao, Lizama, Meredith, & Song. (2019). Are business intelligence systems different to decision support systems and other business information systems? *ACIS 2019 Proceedings*. 66. https://aisel.aisnet.org/acis2019/66

Aruldoss, M., Lakshmi Travis, M., & Prasanna Venkatesan, V. (2014). A survey on recent research in business intelligence. *Journal of Enterprise Information Management, 27*(6), 831–866. doi:10.1108/JEIM-06-2013-0029

Azvine, B., Cui, Z., Nauck, D. D., & Majeed, B. (2006, June). Real-time business intelligence for the adaptive enterprise. In *The 8th IEEE International Conference on E-Commerce Technology and The 3rd IEEE International Conference on Enterprise Computing, E-Commerce, and E-Services (CEC/EEE'06)* (pp. 29-29). IEEE. 10.1109/CEC-EEE.2006.73

Baars, H., & Kemper, H. G. (2008). Management support with structured and unstructured data—An integrated business intelligence framework. *Information Systems Management, 25*(2), 132–148. doi:10.1080/10580530801941058

Bédard, Y., Gosselin, P., Rivest, S., Proulx, M. J., Nadeau, M., Lebel, G., & Gagnon, M. F. (2003). Integrating GIS components with knowledge discovery technology for environmental health decision support. *International Journal of Medical Informatics, 70*(1), 79–94. doi:10.1016/S1386-5056(02)00126-0 PMID:12706184

Bharadiya, J. P. (2022). Driving Business Growth with Artificial Intelligence and Business Intelligence. *International Journal of Computer Science And Technology, 6*(4), 28–44.

Bharadiya, J. P. (2023). A Comparative Study of Business Intelligence and Artificial Intelligence with Big Data Analytics. *American Journal of Artificial Intelligence, 7*(1), 24. doi:10.11648/j.ajai.20230701.14

Bonczek, R. H., Holsapple, C. W., & Whinston, A. B. (2014). *Foundations of decision support systems*. Academic Press.

Bruckner, R. M., List, B., & Schiefer, J. (2002). Striving towards near real-time data integration for data warehouses. In *Data Warehousing and Knowledge Discovery: 4th International Conference, DaWaK 2002 Aix-en-Provence, France, September 4–6, 2002 Proceedings 4* (pp. 317-326). Springer. 10.1007/3-540-46145-0_31

Bughin, J., Chui, M., & Manyika, J. (2010). Clouds, big data, and smart assets: Ten tech-enabled business trends to watch. *The McKinsey Quarterly, 56*(1), 75–86.

Bustamante, A., Sebastia, L., & Onaindia, E. (2020). Bitour: A business intelligence platform for tourism analysis. *ISPRS International Journal of Geo-Information, 9*(11), 671. doi:10.3390/ijgi9110671

Carey, S. (2018). *Heathrow turns to Power BI to predict passenger volumes ahead of time.* Retrieved from November 22, 2023, from https://www.computerworld.com/article/3427880/heathrow-turns-to-power-bi-to-predict-passenger-volumes-ahead-of-time.html

Caroline, L. (2024). *Top Ten Business Intelligence Failures.* Retrieved January 5, 2024 from https://www.intellectyx.com/blog/top-ten-business-intelligence-failures/

Cheuvront, D. (2020). *Heather Gardner shines a light on analytics and the energy industry.* IBM. Retrieved November, 14, 2023, from https://www.ibm.com/blog/heather-gardner-shines-a-light-on-analytics-and-the-energy-industry/

Conley, E. C., Owens, D. R., Luzio, S. L., Subramanian, M., Ali, A. S., Hardisty, A., & Rana, O. (2008). Simultaneous trend analysis for evaluating outcomes in patient-centred health monitoring services. *Health Care Management Science*, *11*(2), 152–166. doi:10.1007/s10729-008-9061-z PMID:18581822

Dinter, B., & Lorenz, A. (2012). Social business intelligence: a literature review and research agenda. *Thirty Third International Conference on Information Systems*. https://aisel.aisnet.org/icis2012/proceedings/ResearchInProgress/104/

Djerdjouri, M. (2020). Data and Business Intelligence Systems for Competitive Advantage: prospects, challenges, and real-world applications. *Mercados y Negocios*, (41), 5-18. https://www.redalyc.org/articulo.oa?id=571861494009

Fitzgerald, M., Kruschwitz, N., Bonnet, D., & Welch, M. (2014). Embracing digital technology: A new strategic imperative. *MIT Sloan Management Review*, *55*(2), 1.

Hadoop. (n.d.). *Tutorials.* Retrieved November 11, 2023, from https://hadoop.apache.org/docs/r1.2.1/mapred_tutorial.html?source=post_page-----a4bb27bc930--------------------------------#MapReduce+-+User+Interfaces

Harsh, S. (1987). Decision Support Systems Definition and Overview. In *Proceedings of the American Agricultural Economics Association Extension Workshop*. Oklahoma State University.

Heathrow Airport. (2023). *Facts and figures*. Retrieved November 23, 2023, from https://www.heathrow.com/company/about-heathrow/facts-and-figures

Helical Insight. (n.d.). *Significance Of Business Intelligence In Social Media*. Retrieved January 8, 2024, from https://www.helicalinsight.com/significance-bi-social-media-2/

Hermawan, A., Kurnia, Y., Destiandi, N., & Kurnaedi, D. (2018). Modeling data mart using ETL (extract, transform, load) web service concept on the feeder with a dashboard. *IACSIT International Journal of Engineering and Technology*, *6057-6059*. Advance online publication. doi:10.14419/ijet.v7i4.23127

Höpken, W., Fuchs, M., Keil, D., & Lexhagen, M. (2015). Business intelligence for cross-process knowledge extraction at tourism destinations. *Information Technology & Tourism*, *15*(2), 101–130. doi:10.1007/s40558-015-0023-2

Howson, C. (2013). *Successful Business Intelligence, Unlock the Value of BI & Big Data*. McGraw-Hill Education.

IBM. (2023). *IBM Cognos Analytics. Get answers faster with AI. IBM.* Retrieved November 10, 2023, from https://www.ibm.com/products/cognos-analytics

Jun, T., Kai, C., Yu, F., & Gang, T. (2009, May). The research & application of ETL tool in business intelligence project. In *2009 International Forum on Information Technology and Applications* (Vol. 2, pp. 620-623). IEEE. 10.1109/IFITA.2009.48

Kaufmann, J., & Chamoni, P. (2014, January). Structuring collaborative business intelligence: A literature review. In *2014 47th Hawaii International Conference on System Sciences* (pp. 3738-3747). IEEE. 10.1109/HICSS.2014.465

Kazemi, A., Kazemi, Z., Heshmat, H., Nazarian-Jashnabadi, J., & Tomášková, H. (2024). Ranking factors affecting sustainable competitive advantage from the business intelligence perspective: Using content analysis and F-TOPSIS. *Journal of Soft Computing and Decision Analytics*, *2*(1), 39–53. doi:10.31181/jscda21202430

Lavrač, N., Bohanec, M., Pur, A., Cestnik, B., Debeljak, M., & Kobler, A. (2007). Data mining and visualization for decision support and modeling of public healthcare resources. *Journal of Biomedical Informatics*, *40*(4), 438–447. doi:10.1016/j.jbi.2006.10.003 PMID:17157076

Lee, C. K. H., Tse, Y. K., Ho, G. T. S., & Chung, S. H. (2021). Uncovering insights from healthcare archives to improve operations: An association analysis for cervical cancer screening. *Technological Forecasting and Social Change*, *162*, 120375. doi:10.1016/j.techfore.2020.120375

Mach, M. A., & Abdel-Badeeh, M. S. (2010, November). Intelligent techniques for business intelligence in healthcare. In *2010 10th International Conference on Intelligent Systems Design and Applications* (pp. 545-550). IEEE. 10.1109/ISDA.2010.5687209

Machado, G. V., Cunha, Í., Pereira, A. C., & Oliveira, L. B. (2019). DOD-ETL: Distributed on-demand ETL for near real-time business intelligence. *Journal of Internet Services and Applications*, *10*(1), 1–15. doi:10.1186/s13174-019-0121-z

Manis, K. (2023). *Empower Power BI users with Microsoft Fabric and Copilot. Microsoft Power BI Platform.* Retrieved November 22, 2023, from https://powerbi.microsoft.com/en-us/blog/empower-power-bi-users-with-microsoft-fabric-and-copilot/

Mansalis, B. (2023). *Real-world stories with Power BI: INTEGRIS Health, Embeds Power BI reports in Healthcare EMR to Provide Life Saving Data. Microsoft* [Video]. Retrieved October 20, 2023, from https://community.fabric.microsoft.com/t5/2021-MSBizAppsSummit-Gallery/Real-world-stories-with-Power-BI-INTEGRIS-Health-Embeds-Power-BI/td-p/1835298

Marín-Ortega, P. M., Dmitriyev, V., Abilov, M., & Gómez, J. M. (2014). ELTA: New approach in designing business intelligence solutions in era of big data. *Procedia Technology*, *16*, 667–674. doi:10.1016/j.protcy.2014.10.015

Marjanovic, O. (2007, January). The next stage of operational business intelligence: Creating new challenges for business process management. In *2007 40th Annual Hawaii International Conference on System Sciences (HICSS'07)* (pp. 215c-215c). IEEE.

Melchert, F., Winter, R., & Klesse, M. (2004). Aligning process automation and business intelligence to support corporate performance management. *Americas Conference on Information Systems. AMCIS*, 507.

Methaila, A., Kansal, P., Arya, H., & Kumar, P. (2014). Early heart disease prediction using data mining techniques. *Computer Science & Information Technology Journal*, *24*, 53–59. doi:10.5121/csit.2014.4807

Microsoft. (2023). *Create a narrative with Copilot for Power BI.* Retrieved November, 22, 2023 from https://learn.microsoft.com/en-us/power-bi/create-reports/copilot-create-narrative?tabs=powerbi-service

Microsoft Customer Stories. (2021). *Hospital network engages caregivers with Power BI analytics through visual storytelling that saves lives.* Retrieved November 22, 2023 from. https://customers.microsoft.com/en-us/story/1431800255709306489-integris-health-power-bi

Mixson, E. (2021). *Data Science at Netflix: How Advanced Data & Analytics Helps Netflix Generate Billions.* Retrieved January 4, 2024, from https://www.aidataanalytics.network/data-science-ai/articles/data-science-at-netflix-how-advanced-data-analytics-helped-netflix-generate-billions

Moody, D. L., & Kortink, M. A. (2000, June). From enterprise models to dimensional models: a methodology for data warehouse and data mart design. In *International Workshop on Design and Management of Data Warehouses (DMDW'2000) DMDW* (p. 5). Academic Press.

Mudau, T. N., Cohen, J., & Papageorgiou, E. (2024). Determinants and consequences of routine and advanced use of business intelligence (BI) systems by management accountants. *Information & Management, 61*(1), 103888. doi:10.1016/j.im.2023.103888

Ng, A. (2024, January 5). *How AI Could Empower Any Business* [Video]. https://www.youtube.com/watch?v=reUZRyXxUs4

Ng, I., & Nagalingham, S. (2023). Implementation of Business Intelligence Solution for United Airlines. *International Journal of Advanced Computer Science and Applications, 14*(1). Advance online publication. doi:10.14569/IJACSA.2023.0140192

Niccolai, J. (2011). *Residents Cut Energy Bills 11% in Smart Meter Test.* Retrieved November 11, 2023, from https://www.pcworld.com/article/482245/residents_cut_energy_bills_11_in_smart_meter_test.htm

Nofal, M. I., & Yusof, Z. M. (2013). Integration of business intelligence and enterprise resource planning within organizations. *Procedia Technology, 11*, 658–665. doi:10.1016/j.protcy.2013.12.242

Ong, I. L., Siew, P. H., & Wong, S. F. (2011). A five-layered business intelligence architecture. *Communications of the IBIMA, 2011*, 1–11. doi:10.5171/2011.695619

Ou, L., & Peng, H. (2006, June). Knowledge and process based decision support in business intelligence system. In *First International Multi-Symposiums on Computer and Computational Sciences (IMSCCS'06)* (Vol. 2, pp. 780-786). IEEE.

Pan, B., Zhang, G., & Qin, X. (2018, April). Design and realization of an ETL method in business intelligence project. In *2018 IEEE 3rd International Conference on Cloud Computing and Big Data Analysis (ICCCBDA)* (pp. 275-279). IEEE. 10.1109/ICCCBDA.2018.8386526

Passlick, J., Grützner, L., Schulz, M., & Breitner, M. H. (2023). Self-service business intelligence and analytics application scenarios: A taxonomy for differentiation. *Information Systems and e-Business Management, 21*(1), 159–191. doi:10.1007/s10257-022-00574-3

Phillips-Wren, G., Daly, M., & Burstein, F. (2021). Reconciling business intelligence, analytics and decision support systems: More data, deeper insight. *Decision Support Systems, 146*, 113560. doi:10.1016/j.dss.2021.113560

Piccinini, E., Hanelt, A., Gregory, R. W., & Kolbe, L. M. (2015). *Transforming industrial business: the impact of digital transformation on automotive organizations.* Paper Presented at the 2015 International Conference on Information Systems: Exploring the Information Frontier.

Popovič, A., Hackney, R., Coelho, P. S., & Jaklič, J. (2012). Towards business intelligence systems success: Effects of maturity and culture on analytical decision making. *Decision Support Systems*, *54*(1), 729–739. doi:10.1016/j.dss.2012.08.017

Prevedello, L. M., Andriole, K. P., Hanson, R., Kelly, P., & Khorasani, R. (2010). Business intelligence tools for radiology: Creating a prototype model using open-source tools. *Journal of Digital Imaging*, *23*(2), 133–141. doi:10.1007/s10278-008-9167-3 PMID:19011943

Rizzi, S. (2012). Collaborative business intelligence. *Business Intelligence, 1*, 186-205. 10.1007/978-3-642-27358-2_9

Rouhani, S., Ashrafi, A., Zare Ravasan, A., & Afshari, S. (2016). The impact model of business intelligence on decision support and organizational benefits. *Journal of Enterprise Information Management*, *29*(1), 19–50. doi:10.1108/JEIM-12-2014-0126

Sahay, B. S., & Ranjan, J. (2008). Real time business intelligence in supply chain analytics. *Information Management & Computer Security*, *16*(1), 28–48. doi:10.1108/09685220810862733

Sandu, D. I. (2008). Operational and real-time Business Intelligence. *Revista Informatica Economică*, *3*(47), 33-36. https://revistaie.ase.ro/content/47/06Sandu.pdf

SAP. (n.d.). *What is SAP HANA?* Retrieved November 14, 2023, from https://www.sap.com/uk/products/technology-platform/hana/what-is-sap-hana.html

SAS. (2023). *Sas Viya For Learners*. Retrieved November 14, 2023, from https://www.sas.com/tr_tr/software/viya-for-learners.html

SAS Institute. (2023). *Foxwoods Resort Casino relies on SAS® Viya® to determine optimal staffing, enhance the guest experience and maximize profits*. Retrieved November 20, 2023, from https://www.sas.com/tr_tr/customers/foxwoods.html

Skyrius, R., Kazakevičienė, G., & Bujauskas, V. (2013). The relationship between management decision support and business intelligence: developing awareness. In Advances in information systems and technologies (pp. 587-598). Springer. doi:10.1007/978-3-642-36981-0_54

Staniar, B., & Ngo, T. (2023). *How to build a sales effectiveness program for LinkedIn Sales Navigator with Tableau.* Retrieved November 11, 2023, from https://www.tableau.com/blog/how-build-sales-effectiveness-program-linkedin-sales-navigator-tableau

Stoll, J. (2024). *Revenue generated by Netflix from 1st quarter 2013 to 3rd quarter 2023*. Retrieved January 5, 2024, from https://www.statista.com/statistics/273883/netflixs-quarterly-revenue/

Subramanian, P., Palaniappan, S., Vedamanikam, M., Bharat, N. U., & Sinnasamy, S. (2016). Exploring the effectiveness of data mining techniques for lung cancer prediction. Tableau. *Business intelligence: A complete overview*. Retrieved October 22, 2023, from https://www.tableau.com/learn/articles/business-intelligence#bi-analysis

Tableau. (2023). *LinkedIn empowers thousands of salespeople with Tableau, reducing customer churn.* Retrieved November 11, 2023, from https://www.tableau.com/solutions/customer/linkedin-dives-deep-into-petabytes-data-tableau

TechInside. (2019). *Uber'in yapay zekası iş ve eğlence gezilerini ayırt edecek.* Retrieved January 6, 2024 from https://www.techinside.com/uberin-yapay-zekasi-is-ve-eglence-gezilerini-ayirt-edecek/

Troidl, A. (2023). *Boost Social Selling Success With Sales Navigator Analytics.* Tribalimpact.com. Retrieved November 19, 2023, from https://www.tribalimpact.com/blog/boost-social-selling-success-with-sales-navigator-analytics#:~:text=%2B59%25%20total%20revenue%20influenced%20by,Sales%20Navigator%20to%20find%20customers

Tsumoto, S., Hirano, S., & Hanada, E. (2003, November). Internet-based decision support: towards E-hospital. In *Proceedings 27th Annual International Computer Software and Applications Conference. COMPAC 2003* (pp. 595-600). IEEE. 10.1109/CMPSAC.2003.1245401

Turban, E. & Aronson. (2001). *Decision Support Systems and Intelligent systems* (6th ed.). Prentice Hall.

Turban, E., & Watkins, P. R. (1986). Integrating expert systems and decision support systems. *Management Information Systems Quarterly, 10*(2), 121–136. doi:10.2307/249031

Vaisman, A., & Zimányi, E. (2012). Data Warehouses: Next Challenges. In Business Intelligence. eBISS 2011. Lecture Notes in Business Information Processing, vol 96 (pp. 1-26). Springer. doi:10.1007/978-3-642-27358-2_1

Vajirakachorn, T., & Chongwatpol, J. (2017). Application of business intelligence in the tourism industry: A case study of a local food festival in Thailand. *Tourism Management Perspectives, 23*, 75–86. doi:10.1016/j.tmp.2017.05.003

Villar, A., Zarrabeitia, M. T., Fdez-Arroyabe, P., & Santurtún, A. (2018). Integrating and analyzing medical and environmental data using ETL and Business Intelligence tools. *International Journal of Biometeorology, 62*(6), 1085–1095. doi:10.1007/s00484-018-1511-9 PMID:29516156

Ward, M. J., Marsolo, K. A., & Froehle, C. M. (2014). Applications of business analytics in healthcare. *Business Horizons, 57*(5), 571–582. doi:10.1016/j.bushor.2014.06.003 PMID:25429161

Watson, H. J., Wixom, B. H., Hoffer, J. A., Anderson-Lehman, R., & Reynolds, A. M. (2009). Real-time business intelligence: Best practices at Continental Airlines. *EDPACS The EDP Audit, Control, and Security Newsletter, 40*(6), 1–16. doi:10.1080/07366980903484935

Weichbroth, P., Zurada, J., & Olszak, C. (2024). Exploring the Benefits, Challenges, and Opportunities of Collaborative Business Intelligence. *Proceedings of the 57th Hawaii International Conference on System Sciences.* https://hdl.handle.net/10125/106408

Wong, A. (2024). *5 Reasons your business intelligence solution is failing you.* Retrieved January 5, 2024, from https://www.tellius.com/5-reasons-your-business-intelligence-solution-is-failing-you/

Yi, Q., Hoskins, R. E., Hillringhouse, E. A., Sorensen, S. S., Oberle, M. W., Fuller, S. S., & Wallace, J. C. (2008). Integrating open-source technologies to build low-cost information systems for improved access to public health data. *International Journal of Health Geographics*, *7*(1), 29. doi:10.1186/1476-072X-7-29 PMID:18541035

Zahedi, F. (1993). *Intelligent systems for business: expert systems with neural networks*. Wadsworth Pub. Co.

Zaiane, Xin, & Han. (1998). Discovering Web access patterns and trends by applying OLAP and data mining technology on Web logs. *Proceedings IEEE International Forum on Research and Technology Advances in Digital Libraries*, 19-29. . doi:10.1109/ADL.1998.670376

Zeng, D., Chen, H., Lusch, R., & Li, S. H. (2010). Social media analytics and intelligence. *IEEE Intelligent Systems*, *25*(6), 13–16. doi:10.1109/MIS.2010.151

Zhou, X., Chen, S., Liu, B., Zhang, R., Wang, Y., Li, P., Guo, Y., Zhang, H., Gao, Z., & Yan, X. (2010). Development of traditional Chinese medicine clinical data warehouse for medical knowledge discovery and decision support. *Artificial Intelligence in Medicine*, *48*(2-3), 139–152. doi:10.1016/j.artmed.2009.07.012 PMID:20122820

KEY TERMS AND DEFINITIONS

Datamarts: Are the subset or small group of data warehouses.

ERP: The abbreviation of Enterprise Resource Planning. ERP is an integrated software that enables the effective and efficient use of labor, materials, machinery, etc. required for the production of goods and services in businesses and enables joint work between departments.

ES: The abbreviation of Expert System. The software system for solving problems or making decisions based on rules.

ETL: The abbreviation of Extract, Transform, Load. ETL is preparing and integrating the operational data.

I 4.0: The industry 4.0. the fourth industrial revolutions, the collection IoTs that create a cyber physical ecosystem.

IoTs: The Internet of Things (IoTs). The state of physical objects after connecting to the internet through sensors and actuators

OLAP: The abbreviation of Online Analytical Processing. OLAP is a multidimensional modeling tool to captures the structure of the real-time data for further analysis to help decision-makers.

Real-Time Data: The data created instantaneously from the system.

Section 2

Artificial Intelligence and Machine Learning in Business

Chapter 3
How Business Intelligence and Data Analytics Can Leverage Business

Albérico Travassos Rosário
https://orcid.org/0000-0003-4793-4110
GOVCOPP, IADE, Universidade Europeia, Portugal

ABSTRACT

Business intelligence (BI) and data analytics are crucial tools that organizations can leverage to improve their business operations, decision-making processes, and overall performance. These two disciplines involve collecting, analyzing, interpreting, and presenting data to provide valuable insights and inform strategic actions. This study aims to explore how BI and data analytics can leverage business. Provide organizations with the tools to extract valuable insights from their data, leading to better decision-making, operational efficiency, customer satisfaction, and competitive advantage. Integrating these disciplines into business processes can drive growth, innovation, and success in today's data-driven business landscape. Based on the above, it is intended to systematically review the bibliometric literature on how business intelligence and data analytics can leverage business in the Scopus database with the analysis of 75 academic and/or scientific documents.

INTRODUCTION

Companies across the globe are increasingly embracing the data-driven culture. They are leveraging data technologies to improve organizational performance and operations, differentiate customers, provide personalized services, and enhance employees experiences. As a result, businesses are striving to acquire and implement data technologies such as business intelligence (BI) and data analytics. Ram et al. (2016, p.221) defines BI as "the ability of a company to make meaningful use of data it collects in the course of its day-to-day business operations." Data analytics, on the other hand, is the process of collecting, transforming, and organizing data to draw conclusions and predictions. As a result, using BI and data analytics enables companies to identify opportunities and potential threats and improves

DOI: 10.4018/979-8-3693-1210-0.ch003

decision-making by increasing access to knowledge and crucial insights. Hurbean et al. (2023) further explain that analytics technologies provide information and expertise that help eliminate nonproductive tasks and reduce the time needed to make decisions.

With the business intelligence gathered through analytics systems, businesses can identify potential areas of improvement and gaps in performance, thus aiding effective resource allocation. Therefore, BI and data analytics provide tools and opportunities to help business growth and competitiveness.

The internet and computing technologies have increased companies' access to large volumes of heterogeneous data gathered from multiple sources. This data can be either structured or unstructured, simple or complex. For instance, Ram et al. (2016) indicate that approximately 500 million tweets are published daily, Wal-Mart processes about 1 million transactions per hour, and Weibo has 776 million users daily. In addition, there are about 4.88 billion global social media users, accounting for a 59.4% penetration rate (Dixon, 2023).

This significant internet use has led to the concept of 'big data' in which unprecedented large and complex data is generated. Using analytics technologies enables enterprises to analyze big data, which provides crucial insights regarding evolving consumer behaviors and preferences and the current business state. In addition, they can analyze trends, patterns, and anomalies to identify potential opportunities, mitigate risks, and optimize business strategies. However, these data and analytics technologies are associated with multiple challenges, such as data privacy and security, scalability, and the complexity of technologies and tools.

Therefore, this systematic literature review synthesizes data from 75 sources to demonstrate how businesses can leverage BI and data analytics.

METHODOLOGICAL APPROACH

The researcher conducted a bibliometric systematic literature review to identify relevant sources and synthesize findings on how businesses use BI and data analytics. This methodology provides a robust approach to comprehensive and structured analysis of existing research.

Given the rapidly evolving nature of BI and data analytics in today's data-driven business environment, this methodology allows for the systematic identification and analysis of a vast body of literature. It allows the researcher to identify key trends, emerging themes, and the evolution of research in this field, enabling practitioners to gain insights into the current state of knowledge, research gaps, and future directions.

The bibliometric systematic literature review (LRSB) provides a comprehensive overview of the academic landscape by systematically identifying, collecting, and analyzing relevant academic publications, thereby allowing the researcher to identify key trends, emerging research themes, and gaps in the literature.

In contrast to conventional literature reviews, LRSB uses a replicable, scientific, and transparent process that thoroughly searches for both published and unpublished literature on the study topic (Rosário & Dias, 2023a, b, Rosário et al. 2023). Additionally, the researcher offers an audit trail that enables readers to evaluate the research's procedures, conclusions, and the quality of the synthesized studies.

In order to verify the veracity and accuracy of the data presented, the LRSB screens and chooses information sources in a process that consists of three phases and six steps (Rosário, & Dias, 2023a, b; Rosário et al., 2023), (Table 1).

Table 1. Process of systematic LRSB

Fase	Step	Description
Exploration	Step 1	formulating the research problem
	Step 2	searching for appropriate literature
	Step 3	critical appraisal of the selected studies
	Step 4	data synthesis from individual sources
Interpretation	Step 5	reporting findings and recommendations
Communication	Step 6	Presentation of the LRSB report

Source: adapted Rosário and Dias (2023a, b), Rosário, et al. (2023).

The researchers used the Scopus database to find and choose reliable sources that are well-liked by academics and scientists. It is important to note that this study was constrained because it excluded other academic and scientific databases and only looked at the Scopus database until September 2023. The literature search should include peer-reviewed scientific and/ or academic publications.

The literature search process began with identifying the academic database for sourcing the relevant documents, in this case, Scopus. The researcher then conducted the initial search using the keyword "business intelligence," which generated 10,070 documents. Adding the exact keyword "data analytics" reduced the sources to 429.

Since the research focuses on examining how BI and data analytics can leverage business, the researcher limited the search to the subject area of "business, management, and accounting." This filter reduced the sources found to 75 (N=75). The search process is summarized in Figure 2 below.

Table 2. Screening methodology

Database Scopus	Screening	Publications
Meta-search	Keyword: Business intelligence	10,070
First Inclusion Criterion	Keyword: Business intelligence; Data Analytics	429
Screening	Keyword: Business intelligence; Data Analytics Subject area: Business, management and accounting Published until September 2023	75

Source: own elaboration

We used content and thematic analysis methods to identify, examine and present the different documents described by Rosário, & Dias (2023a, b); Rosário, et al., 2023).

The 75 academic and/ or scientific documents that Scopus indexed were then subjected to narrative and bibliometric analysis to enrich the information and possibly uncover any shared themes (Rosário, & Dias, 2023a, b; Rosário, et al., 2023). Of the 75 selected documents, 36 Articles; 26 Conference papers; 7 Reviews; 4 Book chapters; and 2 Books.

PUBLICATION DISTRIBUTION

Peer-reviewed articles on how business intelligence and data analytics can leverage business until September 2023. The year 2020 and 2023 had the highest number of peer-reviewed publications on the subject, with 12 publications. Figure 1 summarizes the peer-reviewed literature published until September 2023.

Figure 1. Documents by year
Source: own elaboration

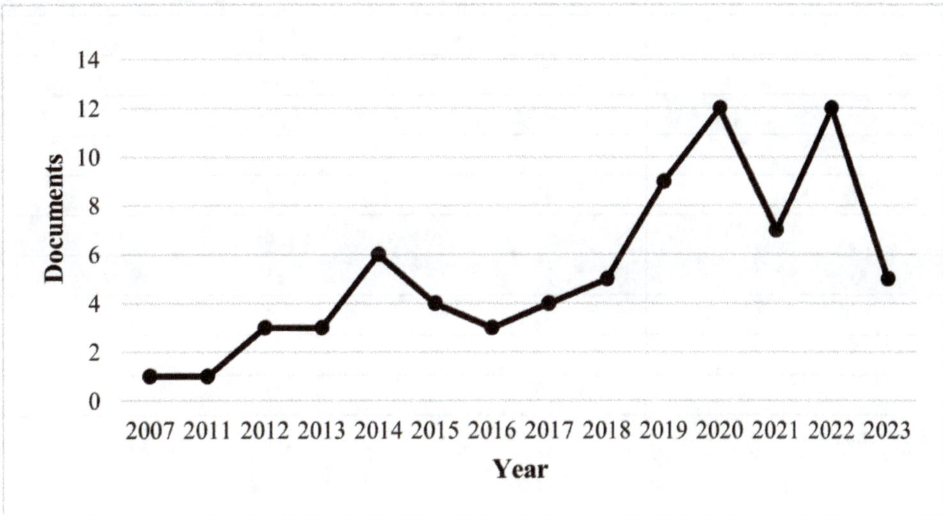

China and USA are highlighted in Figure 2 as having the most publications among the nations with the highest levels of scientific output in related fields.

Figure 2. Scientific production by country

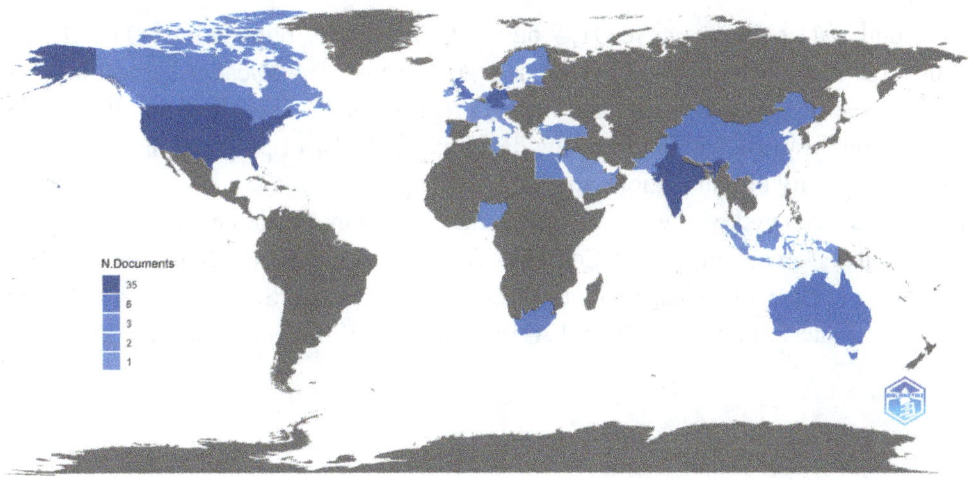

The 10 nations with the highest scientific output for the terms studied are depicted in Table 3 in addition to Figure 2.

This analysis aims to identify which nations are more interested in virtual universe research, focusing on how business intelligence and data analytics can leverage business rather than highlighting countries' productivity.

Table 3. Top 10 countries by number of publications

Country	Number of Publications
India	35
USA	35
Germany	26
UK	14
Autralia	8
Portugal	8
Cnhina	5
Malaysia	5
South Africa	5
Áustria	4

Source: own elaboration

The publications were sorted out as follows: Lecture Notes In Business Information Processing (9); Technological Forecasting And Social Change (4); Industrial Management And Data Systems (3); and with 2 publications (Journal Of Research In Interactive Marketing; Journal Of Management Analytics; Journal Of Education For Business; International Journal On Emerging Technologies; IBM Data Management Magazine; Big Data And Cognitive Computing); and the remaining publications with 1 document.

In Table 4 we analyze the Scimago Journal & Country Rank (SJR), the best quartile, and the H index by MIS Quarterly: Management Information Systems is the most quoted publication with 3,790 (SJR), Q1, and H index 257.

There is a total of 11 publications in Q1, 7 publications in Q2, 7 publications Q3 and 1 publication in Q4. Publications from best quartile Q1 represent 20% of the 75 publications titles; best quartile Q2 represents 13%, best Q3 represents 13% and best Q4 represents 2% of each of the titles of 75 publications. Finally, 30 publications without indexing data represent 54% of publications. As shown in Table 4, the expressive majority of publications are Q1.

The subject areas covered by the 75 scientific and/or academic documents were: Limited to Business, Management and Accounting (75); Computer Science (42); Decision Sciences (32); Engineering (28); Mathematics (12); Economics, Econometrics and Finance (9); Social Sciences (7); Psychology (4); Medicine (3); Materials Science (2); and Agricultural and Biological Sciences (2).

Table 4. Scimago journal & country rank impact factor

Title	SJR	Best Quartile	H index
Journal Of Strategic Information Systems	4,010	Q1	104
MIS Quarterly Management Information Systems	3,790	Q1	257
Journal Of Research In Interactive Marketing	2,830	Q1	50
Information And Management	2,690	Q1	182
Technological Forecasting And Social Change	2,640	Q1	155
Business Research	1,510	Q1	29
Journal Of Management Analytics	1,280	Q1	29
Industrial Management And Data Systems	1,220	Q1	117
International Journal Of Accounting Information Systems	1,160	Q1	60
IEEE Transactions On Engineering Management	1,00	Q1	103
Business Process Management Journal	0,920	Q1	90
Big Data Research	0,710	Q2	33
Big Data And Cognitive Computing	0,680	Q2	23
ACM Transactions On Management Information Systems	0,650	Q2	34
Decision Sciences Journal Of Innovative Education	0,600	Q2	26
Journal Of Education For Business	0,440	Q2	52
Iimb Management Review	0,440	Q2	29
Lecture Notes In Business Information Processing	0,350	Q2	56
Vikalpa	0,350	Q3	30
Informs Transactions On Education	0,350	Q3	4
International Journal Of Enterprise Information Systems	0,340	Q3	26
International Journal Of Systems Assurance Engineering And Management	0,300	Q3	9
Business Systems Research	0,260	Q3	11
Journal Of Business Analytics	0,230	Q3	8
Journal Of Telecommunications And The Digital Economy	0,190	Q3	12
Journal Of Applied Business Research	0,120	Q4	29
International Journal On Emerging Technologies**	0	-*	13
IBM Data Management Magazine	0	-*	3
Tagungsband Multikonferenz Wirtschaftsinformatik 2014 Mkwi 2014	0	-*	7
Proceedings Of The International Conference On Industrial Engineering And Operations Management	0	-*	18
Proceedings Of The European Conference On E Government Eceg	0	-*	15
Proceedings 2017 IEEE 19th Conference On Business Informatics CBI 2017	0	-*	15
Picmet 2018 Portland International Conference On Management Of Engineering And Technology Managing Technological Entrepreneurship The Engine For Economic Growth Proceedings	0	-*	9
Icetech 2015 2015 IEEE International Conference On Engineering And Technology	0	-*	10
IEEE International Conference On Industrial Engineering And Engineering Management	0	-*	24
Atas Da Conferencia Da Associacao Portuguesa De Sistemas De Informação	0	-*	5

Table 4 continued

Title	SJR	Best Quartile	H index
2018 International Conference On Information Technology Systems And Innovation Icitsi 2018 Proceedings	0	-*	8
Understanding The Role Of Business Analytics Some Applications	-*	-*	-*
Towards The Digital World And Industry X 0 Proceedings Of The 29th International Conference Of The International Association For Management Of Technology Iamot 2020	-*	-*	-*
Proceedings Of The 2022 International Conference Quality Management Transport And Information Security Information Technologies IT And Qm And Is 2022	-*	-*	-*
Proceedings Of 2nd IEEE International Conference On Computational Intelligence And Knowledge Economy Iccike 2021	-*	-*	-*
Proceedings 2019 3rd International Conference On Data Science And Business Analytics Icdsba 2019	-*	-*	-*
Journal Of High Technology Management Research	-*	-*	-*
Issues In Information Systems	-*	-*	-*
International Journal Of Recent Technology And Engineering	-*	-*	-*
Human Element Of Big Data Issues Analytics And Performance	-*	-*	-*
Handbook Of Big Data And Analytics In Accounting And Auditing	-*	-*	-*
Ecosystems And Technology Idea Generation And Content Model Processing	-*	-*	-*
Analytics Enabled Decision Making	-*	-*	-*
Advanced Analytics In Power Bi With R And Python Ingesting Transforming Visualizing	-*	-*	-*
2022 International Conference On Interdisciplinary Research In Technology And Management Irtm 2022 Proceedings	-*	-*	-*
2022 International Conference On Data Analytics For Business And Industry Icdabi 2022	-*	-*	-*
2022 IEEE 28th International Conference On Engineering Technology And Innovation ICE Itmc 2022 And 31st International Association For Management Of Technology Iamot 2022 Joint Conference Proceedings	-*	-*	-*
2022 2nd International Conference On Intelligent Technologies Conit 2022	-*	-*	-*
2020 International Conference On Computer Science Engineering And Applications Iccsea 2020	-*	-*	-*
17th International Conference On Wirtschaftsinformatik Wi 2022	-*	-*	-*

Note: *data not available,** discontinued in Scopus as of 2020
Source: own elaboration

The most cited article was "Business intelligence and analytics: From big data to big impact" by Hsinchun et al. (2012), with 378 published citations MIS Quarterly: Management Information Systems 3,790 (SJR), best quartile (Q1) and with H-index (257), this article first provides a framework that identifies the evolution, applications, and emerging research areas of BI&A. BI&A 1.0, BI&A 2.0 and BI&A 3.0 are defined and described in terms of their main characteristics and capabilities.

In Figure 3 we can analyze citation changes for documents published up to September 2023. The period ≤2013-2023 shows a positive net growth in citations with an R2 of 79%, reaching 5017 citations in 2023.

Based on the maximum number of articles included and at least the same number of citations, the h-index is used to evaluate the productivity and impact of a published work 16 of the documents considered for the h-index were cited at least 16 times.

Figure 3. Evolution of Citations Between ≤2013 and 2023
Source: own elaboration

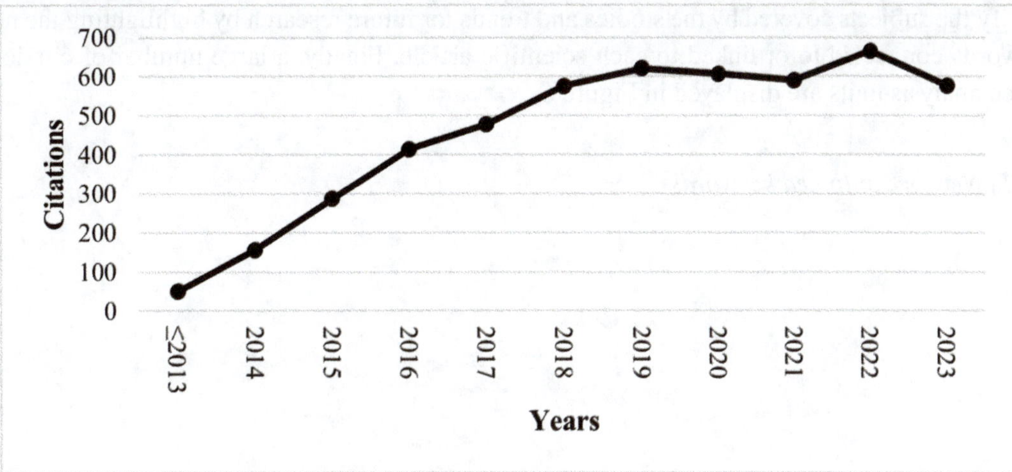

Citations of all scientific and/or academic documents from the period ≤2013 to September 2023, with a total of 5017 citations, of the 75 documents 22 were not cited. The self-citation of documents in the period ≤2013 to September 2023 was self-cited 126 times.

Figure 4. Network of all keywords

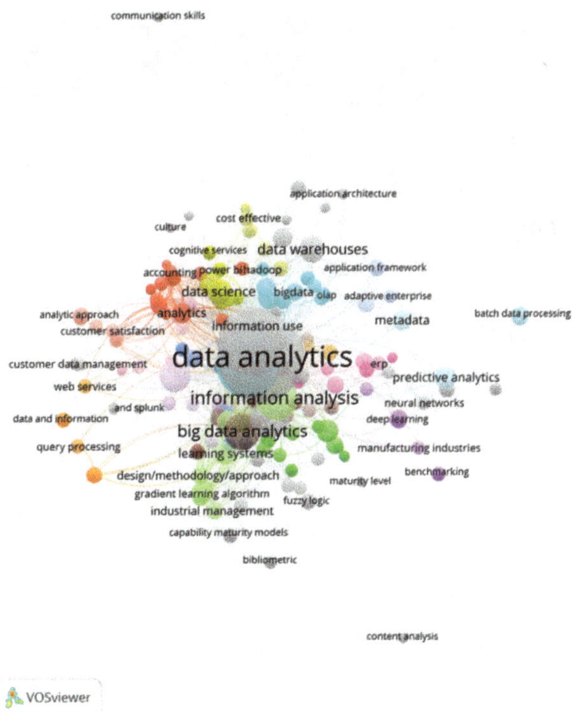

The study examines how business intelligence and data analytics can benefit business and is based on academic and/or scientific documents. We can look at the related keywords in Figure 5. This enables us to identify the subjects covered by the studies and trends for future research by highlighting the network of keywords connected to or linked to each scientific article. Finally, a large number of citations and reference analysis units are displayed in Figure 6.

Figure 5. Network of linked keywords

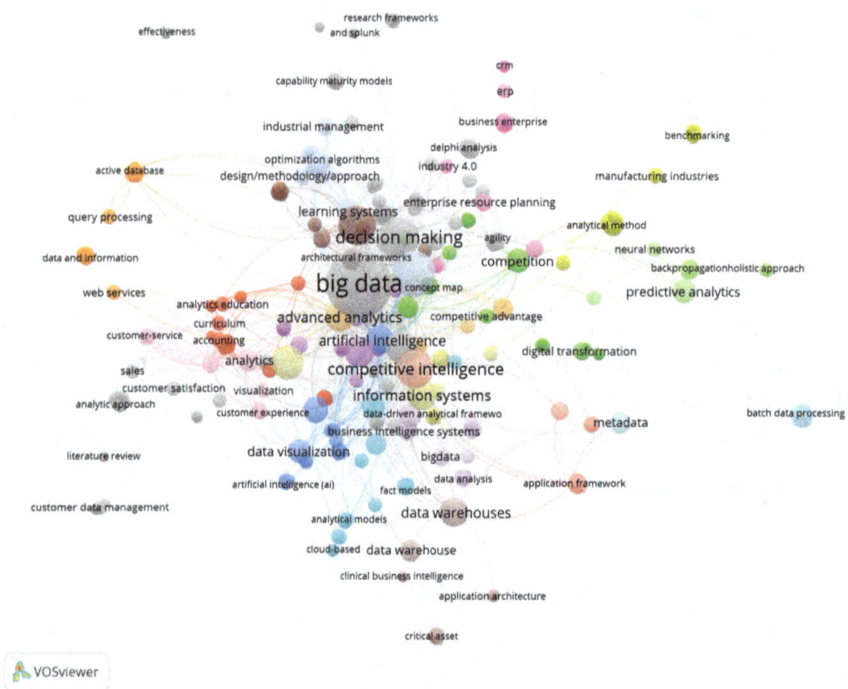

Figure 6. Network of co-citation

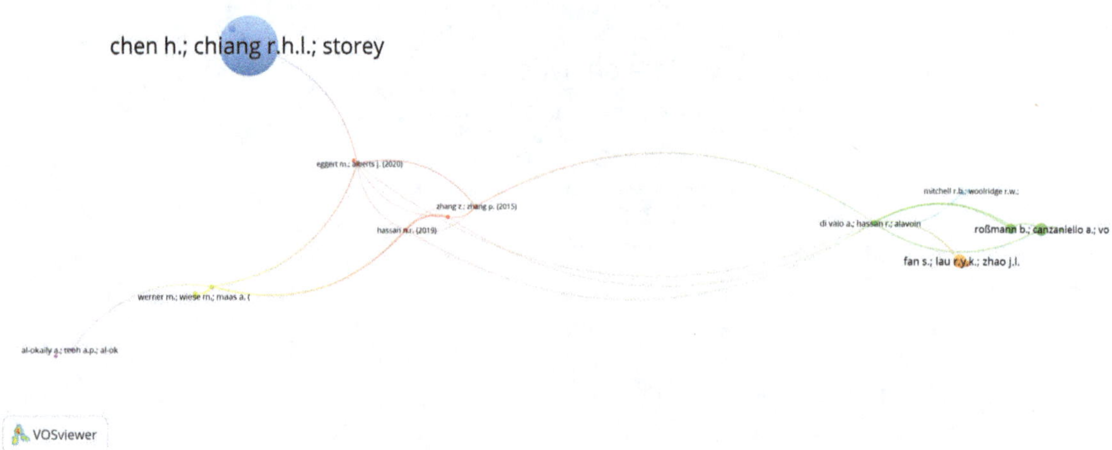

THEORETICAL PERSPECTIVES

Business Intelligence (BI) and data analytics have emerged as major drivers of success in the modern business landscape. This dynamic field represents a strategic intersection of technology, data, and decision-making that can potentially transform businesses across industries. The core premise of BI and data analytics is harnessing structured and unstructured data to derive actionable insights, foster informed decision-making, enhance operational efficiency, and gain a competitive edge (Dedić & Stanier, 2017). In this regard, organizations that employ these advanced tools and techniques optimize their operations and unearth hidden patterns, trends, and opportunities within their data. This literature review synthesizes findings on the pivotal role of BI and data analytics in business.

Business Intelligence

BI is an approach that encompasses the collection, analysis, and transformation of data into actionable insights to support informed decision-making within organizations. Al-Okaily et al. (2023) describe it as the process used to analyze large data sets and present high-quality, accurate reports that empower managers to make business decisions. Similarly, Chen et al. (2012) define BI as a strategy used to generate actionable information that helps executive decision-makers improve business performance. At its core, BI involves utilizing various data sources, such as databases, spreadsheets, and real-time data streams, to gather and consolidate information (Eggert & Alberts, 2020). This data is then subjected to a range of analytics and reporting tools to extract valuable insights, identify patterns, and highlight trends, enabling organizations to make data-driven decisions. In addition, BI systems often employ data visualization techniques, including charts, graphs, and dashboards, to present information in a visually accessible manner, aiding in the interpretation of complex data (Fan et al., 2015; Eom, 2020). Business leaders can leverage BI tools and techniques to generate reports, alerts, and key performance indicators (KPIs) to help stakeholders monitor business performance and respond to emerging opportunities or challenges. As a result, BI serves as an invaluable resource for businesses, helping them streamline operations, optimize processes, and enhance customer experiences.

However, the scope of BI extends beyond just data analysis to involve the integration of historical and real-time data, predictive modeling, and prescriptive analytics. For instance, organizations can use BI to identify historical trends and patterns, understand the present state of their operations, and forecast future outcomes (Ganesan & Gopalsamy, 2019; Graupner et al., 2014). Additionally, BI provides the foundation for strategic planning by delivering insights that help organizations make informed choices about their products, services, resource allocation, and market strategies (Kazeli, 2014; Luen & Hooi, 2016). George and Jeyakumar (2020) explain that the advent of advanced technologies like machine learning and artificial intelligence has led to the evolution of BI, enabling even more sophisticated predictive and prescriptive capabilities further enhancing its capacity to drive business success. Therefore, BI is considered a strategic approach that empowers organizations with the knowledge needed to adapt, innovate, and thrive in the increasingly data-driven business landscape.

Data Analytics

Data analytics is the process of examining, cleaning, transforming, and interpreting large and complex datasets to extract valuable insights, patterns, and meaningful information. Banerjee et al. (2013, p.1) define it as "any fact-based deliberation which leads to insights (diagnostics) and possible implications for planning future action in an organizational setup." Hassan (2019, p.1) identifies data analytics as a subset of BI that involves "extensive use of data, statistical and quantitative analysis, explanatory and predictive models, and fact-based management to drive decisions and actions." Moreover, Kronberga et al. (2017) found that at its core, data analytics involves using a combination of statistical techniques, data mining, machine learning, and computational algorithms to reveal hidden knowledge within data. The primary objective of data analytics is to convert raw data into actionable intelligence, providing organizations with a basis for informed decision-making (Dabab & Weber, 2018). Companies can leverage data analytics to optimize processes, enhance efficiency, identify opportunities, mitigate risks, and gain a competitive edge in various domains, from marketing and finance to healthcare and supply chain management.

Data analytics can be categorized into various types, including descriptive, diagnostic, predictive, and prescriptive analytics, each serving a unique purpose in the data analysis spectrum (Figure 7). For instance, descriptive analytics focuses on understanding past events by summarizing and visualizing data through techniques like data aggregation and data visualization (Banerjee et al., 2013). Diagnostic analytics delves deeper to uncover the reasons behind past outcomes, helping organizations identify patterns and trends that influenced historical data. According to Zhang and Zhang (2015), predictive analytics leverages statistical modeling and machine learning to make informed forecasts about future events and trends based on historical data. Finally, prescriptive analytics takes it a step further by not only forecasting outcomes but also recommending actions to optimize results (Gröger et al., 2014). These diverse applications of data analytics have turned this innovation into an indispensable tool for organizations in today's data-rich world (Diab & Awny, 2020). For instance, data analytics can help improve customer experiences, optimize resource allocation, or guide strategic decisions, thereby enabling businesses to build competitive advantage and informed decision-making.

Figure 7. Classification of business data analytics
Source: Adapted from Banerjee et al. (2013)

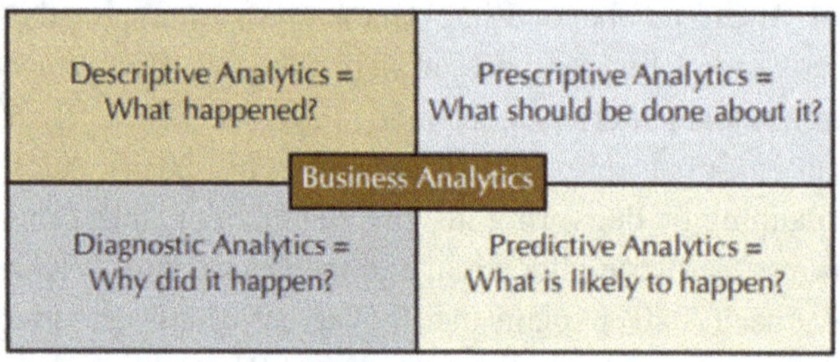

Technologies Supporting BI and Data Analytics

BI and data analytics innovations are supported by various technologies that enable the collection, processing, and analysis of data. These may include big data, artificial intelligence, machine learning, and IoT. The seamless integration of these technologies enables organizations to harness the power of data, gain a competitive edge, and drive informed strategies across various industries and domains.

Big Data

Big data refers to the immense and intricate volume of data generated daily from a multitude of sources, including social media, sensor networks, online transactions, mobile devices, emails, search queries, videos, and audio. This data is characterized by its three key dimensions: volume, velocity, and variety (Figure 8). The volume of big data encompasses the large amount or size of data generated, often classified in terabytes, petabytes, and beyond (Sagiroglu & Sinanc, 2013). The velocity pertains to the rapid generation and flow of data, making it crucial to analyze and act upon in real-time or near real-time. The variety encompasses the diversity of data types, from structured data found in databases to unstructured data like text, images, and video (Rana et al., 2023). Big data technologies such as distributed computing frameworks and NoSQL databases are essential for managing, processing, and extracting insights from this vast and complex data landscape (Zhao et al., 2014; Ziaee et al., 2023). Moreover, big data technologies are foundational for predictive and prescriptive analytics, as they provide the computational power and scalability necessary to analyze data on an unprecedented scale, helping organizations uncover valuable insights, discover patterns, and make data-driven decisions. Therefore, businesses across industries like healthcare, finance, marketing, and logistics are increasingly leveraging big data to gain valuable insights, make predictions, and drive innovation.

Figure 8. The 3 dimensions of big data
Source: Adapted from Sagiroglu & Sinanc (2013)

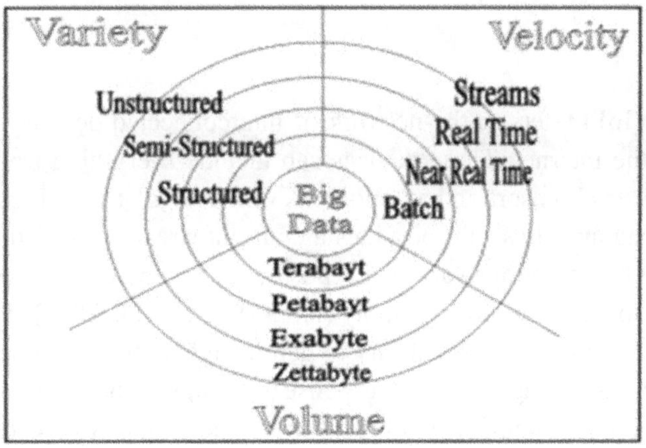

Artificial Intelligence

Artificial Intelligence (AI) encompasses a wide array of technologies and methodologies that enable machines to mimic human cognitive functions. Bharadiya (2023, p.24) defines AI as a "technique for simulating human intellect using a collection of algorithms to create a new computer that can accomplish similar tasks to humans while also performing parallel computing." Therefore, AI involves creating intelligent machines with the capacity to engage in activities previously done by humans with more precision and accuracy (Tcukanova et al., 2022). AI is employed in BI and data analytics to optimize and streamline the data analysis process (Quboa & Mehandjiev, 2017). For instance, AI-driven systems can process natural language queries, making it easier for non-technical users to interact with data and extract information. In addition, AI-powered chatbots and virtual assistants can provide real-time insights and answer queries, enhancing the accessibility and usability of data analytics (Di Vaio et al., 2022; Arora, 2018). AI-based BI and analytics enable companies to identify complex patterns and correlations within data, helping them make more informed decisions and adapt to dynamic business environments. Therefore, leveraging AI technologies can help organizations uncover valuable insights that might remain hidden through traditional analysis methods, thus improving their competitive advantage.

Machine Learning

Machine Learning (ML) is a subset of AI that involves developing algorithms and models that enable systems to learn from data and improve their performance over time. According to Khan et al. (2020b, p.129), ML is used in BI to enhance informed decision-making by facilitating the "process of data gathering, analyses and extracting knowledge." In addition, Bharadiya (2023) explains that ML is used in BI and data analytics to automate data analysis and prediction. ML algorithms can detect patterns and anomalies within datasets, classify data into categories, and make predictions based on historical data. This technology is used to build predictive models, recommendation systems, and sentiment analysis tools (Khan et al., 2020a). As a result, ML can enhance decision-making processes by providing insights that might be challenging to uncover using traditional methods. The automation features also help save time and resources while increasing the accuracy and depth of data analysis.

IoT Technology

The Internet of Things (IoT) refers to the network of interconnected devices and sensors that collect and transmit data over the internet. These devices can include everything from smart appliances and wearable gadgets to industrial sensors and autonomous vehicles. IoT technology is an increasingly vital component of BI and data analytics as it provides a constant stream of real-time data (Trappey et al., 2021). This data can be harnessed for various purposes, such as monitoring equipment performance, tracking customer behavior, and optimizing supply chains (Labde et al., 2022). The continuous data flow from IoT devices offers organizations the ability to gain insights into their operations as they happen, enabling proactive decision-making and quick response to changing conditions (Arora, 2018; Lu, 2020). Integrating IoT data with BI and analytics tools allows organizations to create data-driven strategies, improve operational efficiency, and enhance customer experiences, ultimately leveraging the power of real-time insights to improve organizational competitiveness and growth.

Applications of BI and Data Analytics in Business

With the rapid growth of data-driven culture, BI and data analytics have become popular. Businesses are leveraging these innovations to collect and analyze data for informed decision-making and to improve organizational performance and operational efficiency (Oliveira & Bernardino, 2020). As a result, BI and data analytics are applied in various sectors ranging from marketing to accounting, customer service, and supply chain management. This section synthesizes data on the multiple applications of BI and data analytics in business.

Organizational Performance

Businesses can leverage BI and data analytics to enhance organizational performance. These tools provide companies with valuable insights that aid data-driven decision-making and strategic planning, thus leading to improved efficiency and effectiveness (Awan et al., 2021). For instance, BI and data analytics can be used in performance measurement and benchmarking. In this case, companies can harness historical data and real-time information to track and compare their performance metrics across various departments or teams (Jha et al., 2016; Nourani, 2017). This helps in identifying areas of underperformance, enabling management to take corrective actions promptly. For example, a retail company may analyze sales data to identify low-performing stores and subsequently adjust their marketing strategies or inventory management (Neaga et al., 2015). This strategy helps optimize resource allocation and ensures that the company stays on track to meet its objectives.

Furthermore, BI and data analytics facilitate predictive analytics, enabling organizations to make informed forecasts and predictions about future trends and patterns. As a result, companies can use these tools to analyze customer behavior, market trends, and other relevant data, enabling them to anticipate shifts in demand or changes in customer preferences (Oesterreich et al., 2022; Nambiar & Mundra, 2022). This allows for proactive decision-making, such as adjusting production schedules, launching new products, or modifying marketing campaigns. For instance, a company can use predictive analytics to identify which products are likely to be in high demand during certain seasons, ensuring that they have sufficient stock to meet customer needs (Nascimento et al., 2022). In this way, BI and data analytics boost the current performance of the organization and position it for sustainable growth and adaptability in an ever-evolving marketplace.

Marketing

BI and data analytics have revolutionized the field of marketing by offering data-driven insights and strategies that enhance customer engagement, conversion rates, and overall marketing effectiveness. Fan et al. (2015) explain that these innovations are implemented in marketing intelligence, which enables companies to collect and analyze data for informed marketing decision-making. Zahay et al. (2019) identify customer segmentation and profiling as a major benefit of the modern-day data-driven culture. Analyzing various data sources, such as demographic, behavioral, and transactional data, enables companies to categorize their customer base into distinct segments (Fan et al., 2015). This segmentation enables personalized marketing efforts, allowing organizations to tailor their messages and offers to specific customer groups. This precision in targeting improves the return on marketing investments and enhances the customer experience (Stone & Woodcock, 2014). Other key applications of BI and data analytics in marketing include product ontology and reputation management, establishment of recommender systems, promotional marketing and competitor analysis, pricing strategies, and facilitation of location-based advertising. These applications are summarized in Figure 9 based on Fan et al. (2015) marketing mix framework for big data management.

Moreover, BI and data analytics help in measuring marketing campaign performance. Businesses can use the tools and techniques to track key performance indicators (KPIs) like click-through rates, conversion rates, and return on investment (ROI) in real-time (Zahay et al., 2019). This allows them to make immediate adjustments to underperforming campaigns or scale up successful ones (Verma et al., 2019). For example, a digital marketing agency can analyze the performance of an online ad campaign by tracking user interactions and conversions. If certain ads or platforms are not generating the desired results, the agency can quickly reallocate resources to more effective channels (Olsen & Dupin-Bryant, 2013). This agility in marketing strategy is essential for staying competitive in today's fast-paced digital landscape. It ensures that marketing efforts are well-targeted and continually optimized for maximum impact.

Figure 9. Marketing mix framework for big data management
Source: Adapted from Fan et al. (2015)

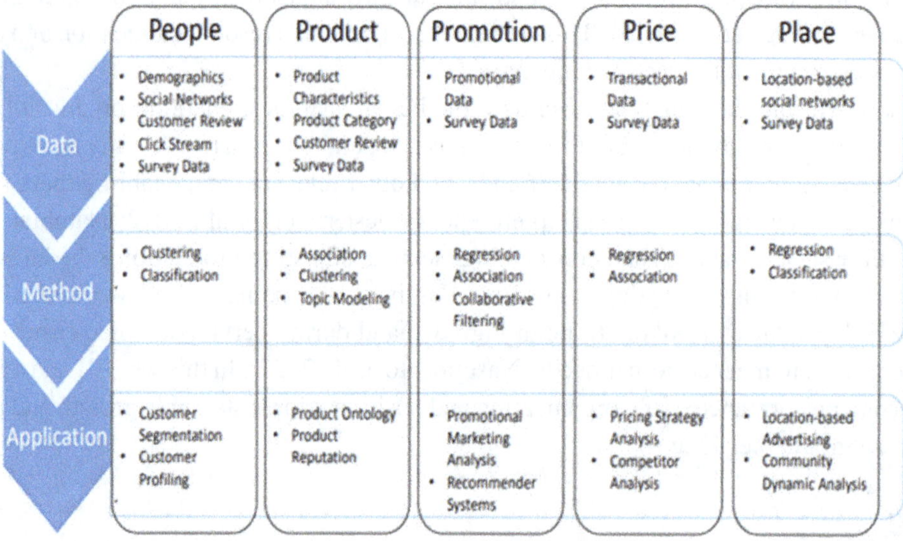

Accounting

Companies can apply BI and data analytics in accounting to gather enhanced insights, provide automation, and improve accuracy in financial reporting and analysis. These tools are particularly instrumental in financial data management and reporting (Werner et al., 2021). They streamline the process of collecting, analyzing, and presenting financial data, making it more efficient and reducing the risk of errors (Rana et al., 2023; Ibrahim et al., 2021). For instance, accounting software equipped with BI capabilities can automatically consolidate financial data from various sources, generating financial reports, balance sheets, and income statements in real time. This automation saves time and ensures that the financial data is accurate and up-to-date, thus aiding decision-making.

Additionally, BI and data analytics can be applied in accounting to detect and prevent fraud. These tools can identify irregular patterns or anomalies in financial transactions, which could indicate fraudulent activities (Ibrahim et al., 2021). For example, a company's BI system can flag unusual expense claims or duplicate invoices, prompting further investigation by the finance team. This proactive approach helps prevent financial losses due to fraud and safeguards the integrity of the company's financial statements (Werner et al., 2021; Ajah & Nweke, 2019). Moreover, these tools enable auditors to perform more thorough and efficient audits by analyzing a large volume of financial data quickly, thereby reducing the risk of financial misstatements (Yaman & Bilgic, 2019). Therefore, BI and data analytics play a fundamental role in making accounting processes more accurate, efficient, and secure, which is crucial for maintaining the financial health and integrity of organizations.

Business Decision-Making

BI and data analytics have become indispensable tools for improving business decision-making across various industries. These technologies provide organizations with a wealth of data-driven insights that empower decision-makers to make informed, strategic choices (Awan et al., 2021). Business decision-makers can use BI and data analytics to visualize data, making it easier to identify trends, patterns, and correlations within the data (Sigman et al., 2016; Anh Hoang et al., 2012). For instance, these tools can transform complex data sets into easily understandable visual representations, such as charts, graphs, and dashboards (Di Vaio et al., 2022). As a result, enterprises can use this data visualization for various applications, such as tracking performing product categories or monitoring customer behaviors. This enables them to make timely decisions about inventory management and marketing strategies.

Furthermore, BI and data analytics offer predictive analytics, allowing businesses to anticipate future scenarios and plan accordingly. Organizations can analyze historical data and apply machine learning algorithms to predict customer behaviors, market trends, and resource requirements (Guru, 2023; Nalchigar & Yu, 2013). This foresight is invaluable for developing proactive strategies. For example, a manufacturing company can use predictive analytics to forecast production demand based on seasonal patterns, ensuring they have the right inventory levels and production capacity in place (Nader, 2022). Additionally, BI and data analytics help decision-makers track the progress of various initiatives and departments, enabling them to adjust and ensure their actions and business practices align with their strategic goals (Mitchell et al., 2021). Therefore, BI and data analytics enable more informed, timely, and proactive decision-making, ultimately leading to better business outcomes and competitiveness in the marketplace.

Customer Service

BI and data analytics have revolutionized the way companies interact with and serve their customers, thus enhancing customer service. For instance, these tools can be leveraged in customer service to create a 360-degree customer view (Padmanabhan et al., 2011). In this case, businesses can aggregate and analyze data from various touchpoints, such as online interactions, social media, and purchase history, to gain a comprehensive understanding of individual customer preferences and behavior (Shongwe et al., 2022; Telukdarie & Sishi, 2018). This knowledge enables customer service representatives to provide personalized assistance, resolve issues more efficiently, and create a more positive customer experience. In addition, they can leverage this information to offer tailored product recommendations, thus enhancing customer satisfaction.

Additionally, companies can utilize BI and data analytics for real-time sentiment analysis. They can monitor customer feedback, reviews, and social media mentions to gauge customer sentiment and identify potential issues or opportunities as they emerge (Arun et al., 2015). This allows for proactive responses to customer concerns, whether it's addressing a service problem promptly or capitalizing on a positive buzz around a product. For example, a company can use sentiment analysis to detect negative feedback on social media, take swift action to resolve customer complaints, and maintain a positive brand image (Sapateiro & Bernardo, 2020). Furthermore, these tools facilitate performance tracking, enabling organizations to monitor the efficiency of their customer service operations. Metrics such as response time, resolution rate, and customer satisfaction scores can be tracked and analyzed to identify areas for improvement (Shongwe et al., 2022). Consequently, BI and data analytics in customer service enhance the customer experience, drive customer loyalty, and enable organizations to stay responsive to customer needs and concerns.

Increasing Company Revenue

BI and data analytics are powerful tools for increasing company revenue by providing insights that drive informed strategies and actions. For instance, these innovations can be applied in sales forecasting. They offer tools and techniques that enable professionals to analyze historical sales data and market trends, allowing organizations to make accurate predictions about future sales (George & Jeyakumar, 2020). Companies can leverage this knowledge to predict future demand and sales patterns, thus optimizing their inventory levels, adjusting production schedules, and planning marketing campaigns more effectively (Miller, 2018). These strategies can ultimately maximize revenue and contribute to organizational growth.

Additionally, businesses can leverage BI and Data analytics to optimize pricing. For instance, these tools can be used to determine the ideal pricing strategy based on factors like competitor prices, market demand, and customer behavior. This enables organizations to set prices that maximize profit while remaining competitive (George & Jeyakumar, 2020). For example, an online retailer can adjust product prices in real time based on market conditions and customer demand, optimizing revenue and profit margins. In addition, BI and data analytics facilitate customer segmentation and targeting (Sapateiro & Bernardo, 2020). They provide mechanisms for analyzing customer data, thus enabling companies to identify high-value customer segments and create tailored marketing and sales strategies to cater to their needs (Kumar, 2020; Jayender & Kundu, 2021). This strategy increases customer loyalty and enhances revenue through upselling and cross-selling opportunities. Thus, BI and data analytics empower organizations to make data-driven decisions that boost revenue by improving sales forecasting, pricing strategies, and customer targeting.

Business Strategy

BI and data analytics have become integral components in the formulation and execution of effective business strategies. Dabab and Weber (2018) explain that successful strategic management requires appropriate tactical and operational management based on the right decision-making and planning. BI and analytics provide tools that empower organizations with critical insights and actionable data to inform strategic decisions and optimize long-term goals (Najdawi & Karan Patkuri, 2021). For example, businesses use BI and data analytics to collect and analyze data on their competitors, such as market share, pricing strategies, and customer feedback. In addition, they use competitive analysis to assess the strengths and weaknesses of competitors' products or services, enabling them to refine their offers and marketing strategies (Minh et al., 2022). Thus, the information gathered through this procedure can help businesses identify opportunities for differentiation and develop strategies to gain a competitive edge.

BI and data analytics technologies support business strategy by empowering businesses to conduct risk assessments. For instance, organizations can use historical data and predictive analytics to evaluate potential risks and uncertainties that may impact their business strategies (Wade, 2020). Understanding these risks can help companies devise contingency plans and risk mitigation strategies. Moreover, these tools facilitate performance monitoring and goal tracking (Vashisht et al., 2020; Santi & Putra, 2018). In this case, businesses can set KPIs and use BI to track their progress in real-time. If the performance falls short of the desired targets, corrective actions can be taken promptly to stay aligned with the strategic objectives. BI and data analytics empower businesses to craft data-driven, adaptable strategies by providing insights into competition, risk, and performance, ultimately enhancing their competitiveness and long-term success.

Supply Chain Management

BI and data analytics have transformed how businesses plan, monitor, and optimize their supply chains, thus impacting supply chain management. For example, the ability to analyze historical sales data, market trends, and external factors empowers companies to accurately predict future demand for their products (Roßmann et al., 2018). This enables them to optimize inventory levels, production schedules, and procurement, ultimately reducing costs and ensuring sufficient product availability (Ziaee et al., 2023; Madugula et al., 2023). For instance, a food distributor can use demand forecasting to ensure they have the right amount of perishable goods in stock, reducing waste and meeting customer demand more efficiently. Therefore, implementing data technologies into the supply chains can help companies achieve high-efficiency levels.

Moreover, BI and data analytics increase supply chain visibility. They provide real-time insights into the entire supply chain, from suppliers to distribution channels (Roßmann et al., 2018). Companies can track the movement of goods, monitor inventory levels, and assess transportation efficiency. For example, a global manufacturer can use these tools to track the location and condition of goods in transit, ensuring that products arrive on time and in optimal condition. Additionally, these BI and data analytics innovations enable performance monitoring and supplier scorecards, allowing organizations to evaluate the performance of suppliers and logistics partners (Jallouli et al., 2022). They can also track KPIs to identify areas for improvement, negotiate better terms, and enhance the overall efficiency of their supply chain operations (Fattah, 2014). These findings indicate that BI and data analytics can strengthen supply chain management by enabling accurate demand forecasting, improving visibility, and facilitating performance monitoring, leading to cost reduction, better service, and enhanced supply chain efficiency.

Business and Customer Value Generation

Companies can leverage BI and data analytics to support operational efficiency by streamlining processes and reducing costs. Organizations can use data analytics to identify bottlenecks, inefficiencies, and areas for improvement within their operations (Mitchell et al., 2021). This efficiency translates to cost savings and improved service quality. Additionally, BI and analytics provide tools that help businesses uncover new opportunities (Badakhshan et al., 2022; Arora, 2018). For example, they can analyze market trends, customer preferences, and emerging technologies to identify unmet needs and gaps in the market. In this case, BI and data analytics create business value by enhancing a company's competitiveness and profitability

BI and data analytics innovations support customer analytics, which allows companies to gain deep insights into customer behavior and preferences. Analyzing data from various touchpoints, including website interactions, purchase history, and feedback, enables organizations to understand their customers better (Oesterreich et al., 2022). This knowledge empowers businesses to tailor their products, services, and marketing efforts to meet customer needs and preferences, thus leading to higher customer satisfaction and increasing sales (Alkhatib et al., 2007). Furthermore, BI and data analytics are paramount in enhancing customer experience and driving customer retention through data-driven decisions. For instance, analyzing customer feedback, behavior, and satisfaction metrics enables businesses to pinpoint pain points and areas for improvement (Catterall, 2012; Choi & Ngo-Ye, 2019). This allows them to develop and offer products and services customized to meet customers' exact needs and demands. This personalized approach enhances customer experience and fosters stronger customer loyalty since satisfied customers are more likely to remain loyal to the brand, increasing customer retention rates.

Challenges Hindering the Adoption of BI and Data Analytics in Business

Despite the opportunities BI and data analytics present for businesses, these technologies are associated with multiple challenges that hinder adoption. These challenges can have severe reputational and financial problems that can undermine a company's ability to exploit the advanced features and tools BI and data analytics offer. These challenges include:

Data Quality and Integration Issues

One of the most fundamental challenges in using BI and data analytics in business is ensuring data quality and consistency. BI and data analytics involves analyzing large amounts of data sourced from multiple sources (Zhao et al., 2014). As a result, the decisions and strategies made rely on the accuracy and consistency of the analyzed data. Therefore, poor data quality can result in inaccurate insights and misleading choices, which can hinder operational efficiency and, consequently, organizational performance and growth (Ram et al., 2016). Moreover, data in organizations is often spread across various systems and departments, which can lead to data silos and inconsistencies. As a result, firms struggle with integrating different data sources and formats, which can be complex and time-consuming. In addition, data cleansing, transformation, and alignment are necessary but can be costly and resource-intensive.

Privacy and Security Concerns

The increasing amount of data being collected and analyzed also raises concerns about data privacy and security. Customers and regulators are becoming more vigilant about how companies handle and protect personal data (Yazici & Nastjuk, 2022). As a result, countries and regions have implemented data privacy regulations that have made it crucial for businesses to maintain compliance. Moreover, organizations understand the severe consequences of data breaches, such as damaging a company's reputation and potential legal repercussions (Ram et al., 2016). Thus, managing data securely while extracting meaningful insights without violating privacy laws is a complex challenge for businesses utilizing BI and Data analytics.

Data Complexity and Scalability

Managing and processing vast amounts of data can be a significant challenge for businesses adopting BI and Data analytics. The complexity of data management and analysis increases as data sources multiply and data volumes grow (Ram et al., 2016). Companies still using traditional data storage and processing infrastructure may struggle to handle the scalability and performance requirements, leading to bottlenecks and inefficiencies. Additionally, the variety of data formats, such as structured, semi-structured, and unstructured data, can complicate analysis efforts (Myla et al., 2019). Organizations must invest in robust data infrastructure and scalability solutions to handle the data stream effectively. Moreover, the complexity of analyzing multi-dimensional data and ensuring that analytics tools are capable of processing large datasets is a crucial consideration in overcoming this challenge.

CONCLUSION

The rapidly growing data culture has led to the significant adoption of BI and data analytics. These innovations provide tools and techniques that enable companies to collect and analyze business data. The analyzed data guide business decision-making, allowing companies to develop products and implement strategies that align with customer needs. At the core of BI and data analytics are other technologies such as big data, AI, machine learning, and IoT technologies. Big data involves the collection of large amounts of structured, semi-structured, and unstructured data. Businesses gather this data from multiple sources, including social media, videos, texts, and images. AI and machine learning innovations are concerned with creating intelligent machines that can mimic human cognitive functions. These machines can conduct tasks done by human employees but with more ease, precision, and accuracy. IoT technology involves building interconnected networks and devices to facilitate information sharing and dissemination over the internet. This innovation ensures a consistent flow of data for analysis, thus aiding data-driven decision-making, planning, and business practices.

BI and data analytics are applied in multiple aspects of business. For instance, companies leverage these tools to improve business performance through proactive decision-making and strategic planning. For example, companies can use BI and data analytics tools to assess performing and underperforming areas for appropriate planning and actions. Other key areas in which BI and data analytics are applied in businesses include marketing, accounting, reporting, customer service, business strategy, revenue growth, and creating business and customer value. BI and data analytics provide tools that companies can use to analyze customer and marketing analytics, monitor key performance indicators, analyze financial data, and create reports. These applications help improve operational efficiency and organizational competitiveness. For example, analyzing customer data helps businesses understand and predict customers' needs, preferences, and behaviors. This knowledge can then be integrated into business practices such as product development and marketing. However, businesses looking to achieve these benefits associated with implementing BI and data analytics must address various dominant challenges such as data security and privacy concerns, complexity, scalability, quality, and integration. Addressing these challenges helps ensure that companies have the appropriate policies, structures, and infrastructure needed to securely and safely implement data technologies, including BI and data analytics.

Business Intelligence and Data Analytics play a crucial role in helping businesses make informed decisions, optimize processes, and gain a competitive edge. BI and Data Analytics promote a culture of data-driven decision-making, where decisions are based on empirical evidence rather than intuition or guesswork. This aligns with the idea that informed decisions tend to yield better outcomes and provide tools and frameworks for measuring and monitoring key performance indicators (KPIs). This supports the theoretical concept of continuous improvement and helps organizations understand where they stand in relation to their goals.

Theoretical implications include the ability to forecast future trends and outcomes. Predictive analytics allows businesses to anticipate market changes, customer preferences, and potential issues, enabling proactive decision-making. BI and Data Analytics help businesses gain a competitive advantage by providing insights into market trends, competitor activities, and customer behavior. This aligns with the theoretical concept of competitive strategy. BI and Data Analytics provide real-time insights into business operations, customer behavior, and market trends. This enables executives and managers to make more informed and timely decisions, reducing the risk of errors. Practical benefits include streamlining operations and optimizing resource allocation. Businesses can identify inefficiencies and areas for improvement, resulting in cost savings and increased productivity. Allow businesses to segment their customer base, understand individual preferences, and personalize marketing efforts. This leads to better customer engagement, retention, and loyalty. By analyzing historical data and using predictive analytics, organizations can identify potential risks and take proactive measures to mitigate them. This helps in reducing financial losses and reputational damage. In industries with strict regulations, BI can help ensure compliance by providing auditing capabilities and tracking data lineage. This ensures that data is used ethically and in accordance with legal requirements. Data Analytics can fuel innovation by uncovering new market trends, customer preferences, and product ideas. Businesses can use these insights to develop new products or services that meet evolving consumer demands.

The theoretical implications of Business Intelligence and Data Analytics revolve around data-driven decision-making and competitive advantage, while the practical implications encompass improved decision-making, operational efficiency, enhanced customer relationships, risk management, revenue growth, compliance, innovation, and employee productivity. When implemented effectively, BI and Data Analytics can significantly boost a business's performance and competitiveness in today's data-driven world.

As the field of Business Intelligence and Data Analytics continues to evolve, several future lines of research are likely to emerge that can further boost business performance: (i) investigate methods and techniques for making AI and machine learning models more interpretable and explainable, especially in sensitive industries like healthcare and finance; (ii) research the ethical implications of AI and Data Analytics, including bias in algorithms, fairness, transparency, and accountability. Develop frameworks and guidelines for ethical AI adoption in business; (iii) explore how augmented analytics, which uses AI and machine learning to automate data preparation and insight discovery, can enhance decision-making processes; (iv) investigate the capabilities and challenges of implementing real-time analytics to enable instant decision-making based on the most up-to-date data; and (v) explore the potential impact of quantum computing on solving complex BI and analytics problems, such as optimization and simulations.

These future lines of research will continue to shape the landscape of Business Intelligence and Data Analytics, providing businesses with new tools and strategies to enhance their decision-making, competitiveness, and overall performance.

ACKNOWLEDGMENT

I would like to express gratitude to the Editor and the Arbitrators. They offered extremely valuable suggestions or improvements. The GOVCOPP Research Center of the University of Aveiro supported the author.

REFERENCES

Ajah, I. A., & Nweke, H. F. (2019). Big data and business analytics: Trends, platforms, success factors and applications. *Big Data and Cognitive Computing, 3*(2 C7 - 32), 1-30. doi:10.3390/bdcc3020032

Al-Okaily, A., Teoh, A. P., & Al-Okaily, M. (2023). Evaluation of data analytics-oriented business intelligence technology effectiveness: An enterprise-level analysis. *Business Process Management Journal, 29*(3), 777–800. doi:10.1108/BPMJ-10-2022-0546

Alkhatib, G., Bataineh, E., Fraihat, H., & Maamar, Z. (2007). An intelligent integrated e-Government framework: The case of Jordan. *Proceedings of the European Conference on e-Government, ECEG.*

Anh Hoang, D. T., Tran, H., Nguyen, B. T., & Tjoa, A. M. (2012). Towards the development of large-scale data warehouse application frameworks. *Lecture Notes in Business Information Processing, 105*, 92–104. doi:10.1007/978-3-642-28827-2_7

Arora, B. (2018). Big data analytics: The underlying technologies used by organizations for value generation. In Understanding the Role of Business Analytics: Some Applications (pp. 9-30). Springer Singapore. doi:10.1007/978-981-13-1334-9_2

Arun, J., Hazaruthin, M. M., & Karthik, M. (2015). Analytics as a service delivery model for the cloud. *Technological Forecasting and Social Change, 168*, C7–C120766. doi:10.1016/j.techfore.2021.120766

Badakhshan, P., Wurm, B., Grisold, T., Geyer-Klingeberg, J., Mendling, J., & vom Brocke, J. (2022). Creating business value with process mining. *Journal of Strategic Information Systems, 31*(4 C7 - 101745). doi:10.1016/j.jsis.2022.101745

Banerjee, A., Bandyopadhyay, T., & Acharya, P. (2013). Data Analytics: Hyped Up Aspirations or True Potential? *Vikalpa, 38*(4), 1–12. doi:10.1177/0256090920130401

Bharadiya, J. P. (2023). A comparative study of business intelligence and artificial intelligence with big data analytics. *American Journal of Artificial Intelligence, 7*(1), 24–30.

Catterall, R. (2012). Hey, what are you calling a "legacy system"? *IBM Data Management Magazine*, (2).

Chen, H., Chiang, R. H. L., & Storey, V. C. (2012). Business intelligence and analytics: From big data to big impact. MIS Quarterly: Management. *Management Information Systems Quarterly, 36*(4), 1165–1188. doi:10.2307/41703503

Choi, J. J., & Ngo-Ye, T. L. (2019). Selecting enterprise applications for curriculum: Insights from a teaching initiative. *Issues in Information Systems, 20*(1), 195–203. doi:10.48009/1_iis_2019_195-203

Dabab, M., & Weber, C. (2018). Business intelligence and data analytics as a driver of dynamic capability strategic approach. *PICMET 2018 - Portland International Conference on Management of Engineering and Technology: Managing Technological Entrepreneurship: The Engine for Economic Growth, Proceedings*. 10.23919/PICMET.2018.8481750

Di Vaio, A., Hassan, R., & Alavoine, C. (2022). Data intelligence and analytics: A bibliometric analysis of human–Artificial intelligence in public sector decision-making effectiveness. *Technological Forecasting and Social Change, 174*, C7–C121201. doi:10.1016/j.techfore.2021.121201

Diab, Z., & Awny, M. M. (2020). Data analytics maturity models: A systematic literature review. Towards the Digital World and Industry X.0. *Proceedings of the 29th International Conference of the International Association for Management of Technology, IAMOT 2020.*

Dixon, S. (2023, Aug 31). *Social media: Statistics & Facts*. Statista. https://www.statista.com/topics/1164/social-networks/#topicOverview

Eggert, M., & Alberts, J. (2020). Frontiers of business intelligence and analytics 3.0: A taxonomy-based literature review and research agenda. *Business Research, 13*(2), 685–739. doi:10.1007/s40685-020-00108-y

Eom, S. (2020). DSS, BI, and data analytics research: current state and emerging trends (2015–2019). *Lecture Notes in Business Information Processing*.

Fan, S., Lau, R. Y. K., & Zhao, J. L. (2015). Demystifying big data analytics for business intelligence through the lens of marketing mix. *Big Data Research, 2*(1), 28–32. doi:10.1016/j.bdr.2015.02.006

Fattah, A. (2014). Cloud analytics: Derive insight without on-premises infrastructure. *IBM Data Management Magazine*, (8).

Ganesan, S., & Gopalsamy, S. (2019). Business intelligence and advanced analytics: Impact and behavior of business decision making process. *International Journal of Recent Technology and Engineering, 8*(3 Special Issue), 375-379. doi:10.35940/ijrte.C1080.1083S19

George, J., & Jeyakumar, M. K. (2020). A dimensional data model for healthcare revenue cycle analytics and business intelligence. *International Journal on Emerging Technologies, 11*(3), 648–653.

Graupner, E., Berner, M., Maedche, A., & Jegadeesan, H. (2014). Business intelligence & analytics for processes: A visibility requirements evaluation. *Tagungsband Multikonferenz Wirtschaftsinformatik 2014, MKWI 2014.*

Gröger, C., Schwarz, H., & Mitschang, B. (2014). Prescriptive analytics for recommendation-based business process optimization. *Lecture Notes in Business Information Processing, 176*, 25–37. doi:10.1007/978-3-319-06695-0_3

Guru, S. K. (2023). Influence of big data analytics on business intelligence. In *Analytics Enabled Decision Making* (pp. 45–58). Springer Nature. doi:10.1007/978-981-19-9658-0_3

Hassan, N. R. (2019). The origins of business analytics and implications for the information systems field. *Journal of Business Analytics, 2*(2), 1–17. doi:10.1080/2573234X.2019.1693912

Hurbean, L., Militaru, F., Muntean, M., & Danaiata, D. (2023). The Impact of business intelligence and analytics adoption on decision making effectiveness and managerial work performance. *Scientific Annals of Economics and Business, 70*(SI), 43-54. doi:10.47743/saeb-2023-0012

Ibrahim, A. E. A., Elamer, A. A., & Ezat, A. N. (2021). The convergence of big data and accounting: Innovative research opportunities. *Technological Forecasting and Social Change, 173*, C7–C121171. doi:10.1016/j.techfore.2021.121171

Jallouli, R., Tobji, M. A. B., Piho, G., & McHeick, H. (2022). Guest Editorial. *Journal of Telecommunications and the Digital Economy, 10*(2), 1–5. doi:10.18080/jtde.v10n2.590

Jayender, P., & Kundu, G. K. (2021). *Intelligent ERP for SCM agility and graph theory technique for adaptation in automotive industry in India.* International Journal of Systems Assurance Engineering and Management. doi:10.1007/s13198-021-01361-y

Jha, M., Jha, S., & O'Brien, L. (2016). Big data and its impact on enterprise architecture. In The Human Element of Big Data: Issues, Analytics, and Performance (pp. 107-124). CRC Press. doi:10.1201/9781315368061

Kazeli, H. (2014). Cloud Business Intelligence. *Lecture Notes in Business Information Processing, 183*, 307–317. doi:10.1007/978-3-319-11460-6_26

Khan, W. A., Chung, S. H., Awan, M. U., & Wen, X. (2020a). Machine learning facilitated business intelligence (Part I): Neural networks learning algorithms and applications. *Industrial Management & Data Systems, 120*(1), 164–195. doi:10.1108/IMDS-07-2019-0361

Khan, W. A., Chung, S. H., Awan, M. U., & Wen, X. (2020b). Machine learning facilitated business intelligence (Part II): Neural networks optimization techniques and applications. *Industrial Management & Data Systems, 120*(1), 128–163. doi:10.1108/IMDS-06-2019-0351

Kronberga, K., Kirikova, M., & Kiopa, D. (2017). Navigating in the land of data analytics. *Lecture Notes in Business Information Processing, 295*, 125–132. doi:10.1007/978-3-319-64930-6_9

Kumar, U. D. (2020). Analytics education. *IIMB Management Review, 32*(1), 108–117. doi:10.1016/j.iimb.2019.10.014

Labde, S., Bhanushali, N., Thaker, R., & Singh, R. (2022). A Project on Statistical Analysis, ETL Automation, and Intelligence Reporting. *2022 2nd International Conference on Intelligent Technologies, CONIT 2022.*

Lu, J. (2020). Data analytics research-informed teaching in a digital technologies curriculum. *Transactions on Education, 20*(2), 57–72. doi:10.1287/ited.2019.0215

Luen, W. K., & Hooi, C. M. (2016). In search of Malaysian companies with successful implementation of business intelligence initiatives. *Proceedings of the International Conference on Industrial Engineering and Operations Management.*

Madugula, S., Pratapagiri, S., Phridviraj, M. S. B., Rao, V. C. S., Polala, N., & Kumaraswamy, P. (2023). Big data for the comprehensive data analysis of IT organizations. *Journal of High Technology Management Research, 34*(2 C7 - 100465). doi:10.1016/j.hitech.2023.100465

Miller, G. J. (2018, September). Quantitative comparison of big data analytics and business intelligence project success factors. In *Conference on Advanced Information Technologies for Management* (pp. 53-72). Cham: Springer International Publishing.

Minh, Q. T., Thai, D. T., Duc, B. T., & Phat, N. H. (2022). Designing a data warehouse framework for business intelligence. *2022 International Conference on Data Analytics for Business and Industry, ICDABI 2022*. 10.1109/ICDABI56818.2022.10041706

Mitchell, R. B., Woolridge, R. W., & Johnson, V. (2021). The role of nontechnical skills in providing value in analytics-based decision culture. *Journal of Education for Business, 96*(1), 1–9. doi:10.1080/08832323.2020.1719961

Myla, S., Marella, S. T., Karthikeya, K., Preetham, B., & Hasane Ahammad, S. K. (2019). The rise of "big data" in the field of cloud analytics. *International Journal on Emerging Technologies, 10*(4), 125–130.

Nader, J. (2022). Lean six sigma and design of experiments: an empirical case study from the dairy industry. *2022 International Conference on Interdisciplinary Research in Technology and Management, IRTM 2022 – Proceedings*.

Najdawi, A., & Karan Patkuri, S. (2021). Modeling business intelligence process: toward smart data-driven strategies. *Proceedings of 2nd IEEE International Conference on Computational Intelligence and Knowledge Economy, ICCIKE 2021 C7 – 9410804*. 10.1109/ICCIKE51210.2021.9410804

Nalchigar, S., & Yu, E. (2013). From business intelligence insights to actions: A methodology for closing the sense-and-respond loop in the adaptive enterprise. *Lecture Notes in Business Information Processing, 165*, 114–128. doi:10.1007/978-3-642-41641-5_9

Nambiar, A., & Mundra, D. (2022). An overview of data warehouse and data lake in modern enterprise data management. *Big Data and Cognitive Computing, 6*(4 C7 - 132). doi:10.3390/bdcc6040132

Nascimento, J., Frazão, N., Teixeira, S., & Ribeiro, A. C. (2022). Dashboard for the management and acceptance of customer orders. *Business Systems Research, 13*(3), 116–129. doi:10.2478/bsrj-2022-0028

Neaga, I., Liu, S., Xu, L., Chen, H., & Hao, Y. (2015). Cloud enabled big data business platform for logistics services: A research and development agenda. *Lecture Notes in Business Information Processing, 216*, 22–33. doi:10.1007/978-3-319-18533-0_3

Nourani, C. F. (2017). Virtual mobile interfaces, business intelligence, and analytics content processing. In Ecosystems and Technology: Idea Generation and Content Model Processing (pp. 189-222). Apple Academic Press. doi:10.1201/9781315365664

Oesterreich, T. D., Anton, E., & Teuteberg, F. (2022). What translates big data into business value? A meta-analysis of the impacts of business analytics on firm performance. *Information and Management, 59*(6 C7 - 103685). doi:10.1016/j.im.2022.103685

Oliveira, A., & Bernardino, J. (2020). *Osspal assessment of self-service BI and analytics software*. Atas da Conferencia da Associacao Portuguesa de Sistemas de Informacao.

Olsen, D. H., & Dupin-Bryant, P. A. (2013). Combining business intelligence and stock market data: A primer for data analytics and business intelligence. *Journal of Applied Business Research, 29*(1), 139–156. doi:10.19030/jabr.v29i1.7562

Padmanabhan, B., Hevner, A., Cuenco, M., & Shi, C. (2011). From information to operations: Service quality and customer retention. *ACM Transactions on Management Information Systems, 2*(4 C7 - 21). doi:10.1145/2070710.2070712

Quboa, Q., & Mehandjiev, N. (2017). Creating intelligent business systems by utilizing big data and semantics. *Proceedings - 2017 IEEE 19th Conference on Business Informatics, CBI 2017.*

Ram, J., Zhang, C., & Koronios, A. (2016). The implications of big data analytics on business intelligence: A qualitative study in China. *Procedia Computer Science, 87*, 221–226. doi:10.1016/j.procs.2016.05.152

Rana, T., Svanberg, J., Öhman, P., & Lowe, A. (2023). *Handbook of Big Data and Analytics in Accounting and Auditing*. Springer Nature. doi:10.1007/978-981-19-4460-4

Rosário, A. T., & Dias, J. C. (2023a). How Industry 4.0 and Sensors Can Leverage Product Design: Opportunities and Challenges. *Sensors (Basel), 23*(3), 1165. doi:10.3390/s23031165 PMID:36772206

Rosário, A. T., & Dias, J. C. (2023b). Marketing Strategies on Social Media Platforms. *International Journal of E-Business Research, 19*(1), 1–25. doi:10.4018/IJEBR.316969

Rosário, A. T., Lopes, P. R., & Rosário, F. S. (2023). Metaverse in Marketing: Challenges and Opportunities. In A. Khang, V. Shah, & S. Rani (Eds.), *Handbook of Research on AI-BasedTechnologies and Applications in the Era of the Metaverse* (pp. 204–227). IGI Global. doi:10.4018/978-1-6684-8851-5.ch010

Roßmann, B., Canzaniello, A., von der Gracht, H., & Hartmann, E. (2018). The future and social impact of big data analytics in supply chain management: Results from a Delphi study. *Technological Forecasting and Social Change, 130*, 135–149. doi:10.1016/j.techfore.2017.10.005

Sagiroglu, S., & Sinanc, D. (2013, May). Big data: A review. In *2013 international conference on collaboration technologies and systems (CTS)* (pp. 42-47). IEEE.

Santi, R. P., & Putra, H. (2018). A systematic literature review of business intelligence technology, contribution and application for higher education. *2018 International Conference on Information Technology Systems and Innovation, ICITSI 2018 - Proceedings C7 – 8696019.*

Sapateiro, C. M., & Bernardo, R. M. (2020). Crossing human factors research and business intelligence. *International Journal of Enterprise Information Systems, 16*(3), 78–92. doi:10.4018/IJEIS.2020070106

Shongwe, T., Malatji, M., & Pretorius, J. H. C. (2022). Telecommunications customer service improvement through big data analytics. *2022 IEEE 28th International Conference on Engineering, Technology and Innovation, ICE/ITMC 2022 and 31st International Association for Management of Technology, IAMOT 2022 Joint Conference – Proceedings.*

Sigman, B. P., Garr, W., Pongsajapan, R., Selvanadin, M., McWilliams, M., & Bolling, K. (2016). Visualization of Twitter data in the classroom. *Decision Sciences Journal of Innovative Education, 14*(4), 362–381. doi:10.1111/dsji.12108

Stone, M. D., & Woodcock, N. D. (2014). Interactive, direct and digital marketing: A future that depends on better use of business intelligence. *Journal of Research in Interactive Marketing*, *8*(1), 4–17. doi:10.1108/JRIM-07-2013-0046

Tcukanova, O. A., Yarskaya, A. A., & Torosyan, A. A. (2022). Artificial intelligence as a new stage in the development of business intelligence systems. *Proceedings of the 2022 International Conference "Quality Management, Transport and Information Security, Information Technologies", IT and QM and IS 2022*. 10.1109/ITQMIS56172.2022.9976832

Telukdarie, A., & Sishi, M. N. (2018). Enterprise definition for industry 4.0. *IEEE International Conference on Industrial Engineering and Engineering Management.*

Trappey, A. J. C., Trappey, C. V., Govindarajan, U. H., & Sun, J. J. H. (2021). Patent value analysis using deep learning models-the case of IoT technology mining for the manufacturing industry. *IEEE Transactions on Engineering Management, 68*(5 C7 - 08941278), 1334-1346. doi:10.1109/TEM.2019.2957842

Vashisht, V., Kamya, S., & Vashisht, M. (2020). Defect prediction framework using neural networks for business intelligence technology-based projects. *2020 International Conference on Computer Science, Engineering and Applications, ICCSEA 2020 C7 – 9132944.*

Verma, A., Yurov, K. M., Lane, P. L., & Yurova, Y. V. (2019). An investigation of skill requirements for business and data analytics positions: A content analysis of job advertisements. *Journal of Education for Business*, *94*(4), 243–250. doi:10.1080/08832323.2018.1520685

Wade, R. (2020). *Advanced Analytics in Power BI with R and Python: Ingesting, Transforming, Visualizing*. Springer International Publishing. doi:10.1007/978-1-4842-5829-3

Werner, M., Wiese, M., & Maas, A. (2021). Embedding process mining into financial statement audits. *International Journal of Accounting Information Systems*, *41*, C7–C100514. doi:10.1016/j.accinf.2021.100514

Yaman, T. T., & Bilgic, E. (2019). Is business analytics education sufficient in business schools? The case in Turkish business schools. *Proceedings - 2019 3rd International Conference on Data Science and Business Analytics, ICDSBA 2019 C7 – 9270212*. 10.1109/ICDSBA48748.2019.00040

Yazici, M. E., & Nastjuk, I. (2022). Security issues in data analytical environments. *17th International Conference on Wirtschaftsinformatik, WI 2022.*

Zahay, D., Sihi, D., Muzellec, L., & Johnson, D. S. (2019). The marketing organization's journey to become data driven. *Journal of Research in Interactive Marketing*, *13*(2), 162–178. doi:10.1108/JRIM-12-2018-0157

Zhang, Z., & Zhang, P. (2015). Seeing around the corner: An analytic approach for predictive maintenance using sensor data. *Journal of Management Analytics*, *2*(4), 333–350. doi:10.1080/23270012.2015.1086704

Zhao, J. L., Fan, S., & Hu, D. (2014). Business challenges and research directions of management analytics in the big data era. *Journal of Management Analytics*, *1*(3), 169–174. doi:10.1080/23270012.2014.968643

Ziaee, M., Shee, H. K., & Sohal, A. (2023). Big data analytics in Australian pharmaceutical supply chain. *Industrial Management & Data Systems, 123*(5), 1310–1335. doi:10.1108/IMDS-05-2022-0309

ADDITIONAL READING

Delgosha, M. S., Hajiheydari, N., & Fahimi, S. M. (2021). Elucidation of big data analytics inbanking: a four-stage Delphi study. *Journal of enterprise information management, 34*(6),1577-1596. doi:10.1108/JEIM-03-2019-0097

Duan, L., & Xiong, Y. (2015). Big data analytics and business analytics. *Journal of managementanalytics, 2*(1), 1-21. doi:10.1080/23270012.2015.1020891

Ghasemaghaei, M., Ebrahimi, S., & Hassanein, K. (2018). Data analytics competency forimproving firm decision making performance. *The Journal of Strategic Information Systems, 27*(1), 101–113. doi:10.1016/j.jsis.2017.10.001

Lee, M., Lee, S., & Koh, Y. (2019). Multisensory experience for enhancing hotel guest experienceEmpirical evidence from big data analytics. *International Journal of Contemporary Hospitality Management, 31*(11), 4313–4337. doi:10.1108/IJCHM-03-2018-0263

Neaga, I., & Liu, S. F. (2014). The Knowledge Management Context of Cloud Based big DataAnalytics. *Proceedings of the 15th european conference on knowledge management (eckm2014), vols 1-3*, 1339-1343.

Pedro, J., Brown, I., & Hart, M. (2019). Capabilities and Readiness for Big Data Analytics.*Centeris2019--international conference on enterprise information systems/projman2019--international conference on project management/hcist2019--international conference onhealth and social care information systems and technologies, 164*, 3-10. doi:10.1016/j.procs.2019.12.147

Talaoui, Y., Kohtamäki, M., Ranta, M., & Paroutis, S. (2023). Recovering the divide: A review ofthe big data analytics-strategy relationship. *Long range planning, 56*(2 C7 - 102290). doi:10.1016/j.lrp.2022.102290

van Rijmenan, M., Erekhinskaya, T., Schweitzer, J., & Williams, M. A. (2019). Avoid being theTurkey: How big data analytics changes the game of strategy in times of ambiguity anduncertainty. *Long range planning, 52*(5 C7 - 101841). doi:10.1016/j.lrp.2018.05.007

Wang, Y. C., Kung, L., Wang, W. Y. C., & Cegielski, C. G. (2018). An integrated big data analytics-enabled transformation model: Application to health care. *Information & Management, 55*(1), 64–79. doi:10.1016/j.im.2017.04.001

KEY TERMS AND DEFINITIONS

Artificial Intelligence: Multidisciplinary field of study that covers several areas of knowledge.

Big Data: Is an area of knowledge that studies how to treat, analyze and obtain information from very large data sets.

Business Intelligence: Refers to capabilities that enable organizations to make better decisions, take informed actions, and implement more-efficient business processes.

Data Analytics: Is a process of inspecting, cleaning, transforming, and modeling data with the goal of discovering useful information, informing lessons, and supporting decision-making.

Data-Driven: A programming paradigm in which program instructions describe the data to be matched and the processing required, rather than defining a sequence of steps to be performed.

Internet of Things: Is a concept that refers to the digital interconnection of everyday objects with the internet, the connection of objects more than people.

Key Performance Indicators: They are management tools for measuring and measuring the resulting level of performance and success of an organization or a certain process, focusing on the "how" and indicating how well the company's processes are doing, allowing its objectives to be achieved.

Machine Learning: Focused on building computer systems that learn from data.

Chapter 4
Scalable Textile Business Intelligence With Operational Data Collection and Analytical Processing

Kamalendu Pal
https://orcid.org/0000-0001-7158-6481
University of London, UK

ABSTRACT

Many textile companies have come to the realization that data is crucial for improving sales and revenue margins. Clothing brands and retailers must develop manufacturing and sales styles that appeal to customers. In recent decades, with advancements in various categories of data analytics and artificial intelligence techniques (e.g., machine learning), the value of data-driven applications has been well acknowledged by textile clothing retailers. They use predictive software outputs for regular operational decision-making. This chapter reviews retail businesses and their products' manufacturing data analytics. It presents a scalable business intelligence framework using a graph data model and its management system. The chapter also highlights that big data technologies and related supporting resources (e.g., the Internet of Things) enable real-time data capture, storage, processing, and sharing. This helps businesses make operational decisions faster and more effectively. This chapter presents an algorithm for extracting knowledge from stored business data to exemplify the analytical value of the graph database model for business intelligence.

INTRODUCTION

The textile and clothing industry is a significant part of the global economy (Pal & Yasar, 2020). In 2000, consumers spent around one trillion US dollars on clothing, with one-third spent in Western Europe, one-third in North America, and one-quarter in Asia. Clothing and textiles account for seventy per cent of total world exports, and developing countries, particularly in Asia, dominate the sector. These global

DOI: 10.4018/979-8-3693-1210-0.ch004

business records and the recent coronavirus pandemic significantly challenge the textile industry. The pandemic has caused disruptions in the industry, including adopting remote work and economic slowdown.

However, the business world started to work better in 2023, and it was arguably the first full post-pandemic year – and with that, the business world observed certain things return to "normal". Travelling increased, many people spent more time at the office, face-to-face commerce no longer took place through protective masks, and people came to retail shops to buy clothes. Here are many channels that either emerged or persisted. Inflation continued to swell, with only recent, partial relief in some parts of the world. Economic uncertainty and a global cost-of-living crisis have been at the forefront of individuals' and business organizations' minds. In particular, the industry needs to understand the changing buying behaviours and preferences.

To make informed decisions in these uncertain times, textile and clothing companies rely on artificial intelligence (AI) techniques for interpreting business operational data. However, more than merely having data and advanced technology is required. Businesses must be able to turn data into insights and insights into action to realize their value. Moreover, AI can aid textile and clothing companies in augmenting data-driven decision-making, improving their capabilities, and maximizing their impact on the business.

Different radio frequency identification (RFID) devices and tags, sensors, actuators, and mobile devices have been integrated into textile manufacturing processes to collect business operations data, as shown in Figure 1. These devices capture massive amounts of data and store it in suitable formats. However, due to the lack of interoperability, data generated by different devices cannot be shared smoothly due to heterogeneity, which has become a severe challenge for the business community. Another issue is finding appropriate storage mechanisms and mining and extracting the hidden information from the data. Graph databases have played an attractive role in storing and processing this massive amount of data in recent decades. Graph data models are crucial in today's data-driven decision-making. They rely on mathematical graph theory-based representations and computations that enable flexible and powerful evaluations of domain objects and their relationships. Thus, graph analytics and graph mining have become popular among academics and practitioners from various business domains.

The main goal of this chapter is to provide an example of how graph data-based business intelligence applications can be used in the clothing industry. However, the real-world operations of the textile and clothing industry are complicated and challenging. The textile and garment manufacturing process involves numerous operational activities, from raw materials to producing finished products. The textile and clothing production process includes various industries and their integrated efforts. For example, the agriculture, chemical, and textile industries work together to produce natural and synthetic fibers, the primary components of fashion and commercial textile products for industrial use. Researchers have described an industrial world that faces challenges in maintaining sustainability, controlling environmental pollution, and ensuring equality in global environmental policies and organizational approaches. Academics and practitioners are introducing new business models that focus on preventing resource waste and improving work practice efficiency.

The textile industry can develop more ecological and sustainable products by carefully selecting materials and constituent ingredients. This includes using materials and components that are recycled, recyclable, and biodegradable, as well as those produced using eco-friendly processes. It also involves minimizing the use of chemicals and energy during production, using water-based solvents and glues, avoiding hazardous and restricted substances, and using renewable materials and innovative manufacturing technologies.

Figure 1. Textile business's dependency on other industrial operations

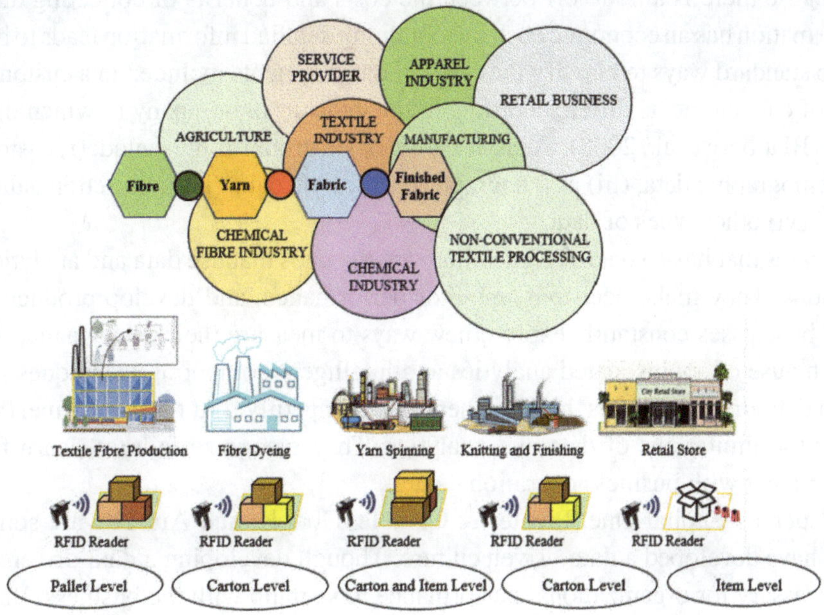

This chapter aims to highlight the importance of systemic approach and data analytics in the textile industry's day-to-day operations. It also emphasizes the value of personalization to enhance customer experience. To identify the various sources of data in the textile industry, the chapter uses Professor Michael Porter's value chain model. The collection and processing of data are crucial in any industry, and this chapter provides a technology-based approach to establish a solid foundation. An example of sales data processing in the textile industry using a graph data model is also provided. Finally, the chapter concludes by discussing future research directions and offering concluding remarks.

BACKGROUND OF CUSTOMER FOCUSED BUSINESS

The textile and clothing industry gathers data from various sources such as manufacturing plants, warehouses, transportation systems specific to the industry, web-based sales, and physical retail outlets. It also includes information from sensors that collect operational data, climate reports, social media posts, digital images, industry operational videos, purchase transaction records, and cell phone GPS signals. All this data is stored in numerical form and processed to obtain insights. In order to put things into perspective, every minute, the world uploads 48 hours of video on YouTube, email users send over 200 million messages, Google receives over two million search queries, Facebook shares more than six hundred thousand pieces of content, and consumers spend almost three hundred thousand dollars on online shopping. These figures highlight the significance of collecting data and processing it effectively.

The customer information file is a crucial component for a customer-focused textile company, and every decision should be based on customer data analysis. Customer information includes everything about customers, such as their names, addresses, phone numbers, transaction histories, and any information from customer contacts. Prioritizing different data elements in the customer information file is a good idea because there is a trade-off between the costs and benefits of collecting data. Storing and processing information has an economic cost, but obtaining detailed information leads to better decisions.

There are no standard ways to classify the types of data elements included in a customer information file. The types of data elements differ according to the industry or company to which they belong. In a research article (Blattberg et al., 2008), a classification of six groups is presented: (i) customer identification data, (ii) demographic data, (iii) psychographic or lifestyle data, (iv) transaction data, (v) marketing action data, and (vi) other types of data.

Retail businesses that have a data-driven culture are the ones that use data and analytics in all aspects of their operations. They make decisions, monitor performance, and develop products based on data insights. These businesses constantly explore new ways to measure their performance and operational environment. The use of sophisticated analytics and intelligent computing techniques is at the core of businesses with data-driven cultures, helping them stay competitive. At the same time, these businesses also understand the limitations of data and analytics. They recognize failures, learn from them, and frequently experiment with business operational data.

Companies such as Capital One, Procter & Gamble, Google, and Amazon are some examples of businesses that have developed a data-driven culture. Though developing a data-driven culture is challenging, it is necessary for organizational performance to keep up with the business. Research specific to different industries shows that businesses need to improve or are getting worse. Losing sight of a data-driven culture can lead to inferior decisions, less innovation, and less talent compared to competitors.

One of the most crucial lessons for retail businesses is to provide an exceptional customer experience by focusing on customer engagement. Retailers can leverage the five digital forces of mobility, big data, cloud service, social media, and analytics to transform the shopper's journey. In this era where physical-to-digital transformation is taking place, easy connectivity, changing consumer behavior, listening to customers, and providing personalized experiences are essential for long-term profitability and customer loyalty. This requires a transformational change in the underlying business model, processes, and tools.

Many organizations across different industries have created successful business models by institutionalizing interactions and enabling continuous conversations with customers across every contact point. However, there are concerns about the usefulness and consistency of these interactions. Inconsistent interactions can lead to consumer mistrust, potentially doing more harm than good.

Understanding customer buying behavior is challenging because customers are social entities. Retail buying behavior can be compared to a football player maneuvering to score a goal. Customers and retailers are increasingly adopting digital channels, making product data, reviews, comparisons, prices, promotions, and stock levels available. This ubiquitous availability of rich data has made digital customer interactions more transactional. While customers demand lower prices, better value, an extensive range, and quicker fulfillment, they consistently seek better deals, which has commoditized retail. Personalized interactions create a serendipitous experience by enriching product discovery and are critical and value-added when they involve personalized interaction.

To foster long-term relationships, retailers must offer meaningful personalization. With various digital forces at play, a one-to-one relationship with customers is no longer a distant dream – it's an opportunity that needs to be seized. The operations, marketing, technology, and corporate teams of textile business will have to work together to design and deliver these personalized interactions, which means that the rules of the retail game need to be redefined.

Advantages of Textile Product Personalization

The textile industry has been changing rapidly in recent decades, and its operations are considered responsible for their day-to-day work that affects society directly or indirectly. With the increase in human population, there is a growing need for approaches that are more adaptable to the sustainability and ecology of the textile industry. Additionally, trends in textile product development are influenced by the globalization of manufacturing networks, digitization of business operations, and multifaceted consumer expectations related to operational sustainability. Industry experts and consumers seek detailed information regarding the environmental impact of textile products' constituent elements, products, and production processes.

Figure 2 represents a diagrammatic representation of textile product sales activities. In these sales activities, customer interactions with the retail textile and clothing business sales items and services are captured using technology-driven data-capturing mechanisms such as RFID tags for data collection, storage, and processing. For example, customers can use touch screen facilities to display product-specific sustainability-related information and provide personal preferences with the help of mobile device touch screen options. This way, textile companies have developed a new mechanism to manage their relationship with customers and try to retain either new or existing customers.

This new way of customer interaction management is commonly called customer relationship management (CRM), which includes personalization options. Reichheld studied the dramatic increase in profits after slight increases in customer retention rates. He showed an example where an increase in retention of five per cent impacted the net present value delivered by customers by as high as ninety-five per cent. The fact exposed by Reichheld is complemented by Winer, who explains that long-term relationships with customers can deliver long-term profits. These facts have changed how marketers see the retail textile and clothing business world.

The approach to customer relationships has shifted from a marketing-focused one to one that centers around the customer. The marketing approach prioritizes maximizing profits in the short term by delivering quality products or services. On the other hand, the customer-centric approach aims to provide value and satisfaction to customers and establish long-term relationships with them.

Companies use various techniques to cater to customer needs and provide personalized experiences to achieve this. Websites, for instance, can personalize their content based on visitor characteristics and captured data. Research shows that customer loyalty programs that offer rewards positively impact customer retention, while mass emails do not. However, extending payment dates enhances the customer experience and strengthens customer relationships.

Textile and clothing businesses can create a strong bond with their customers by gaining a deep understanding of them. These businesses can store vast amounts of customer data that can help them improve customer relationships, advertising, customer service, and experience. Effective promotion and recommendation strategies can be created by knowing the customer group and optimizing the layout of products in retail outlets, placing related products nearby, or making them more accessible to customers.

Customers today are interested in the transparency of product manufacturing information. Textile businesses have changed in recent decades due to process automation and disruptive technologies, which have affected environmental, economic, societal, and supply chain operations. Sustainability has become a significant challenge and a crucial topic of investigation. Including sustainability-related business activities enhances the operational green agenda-related performance of the enterprises and makes them competitive.

Figure 2. Diagrammatic representation of textile product sales activities

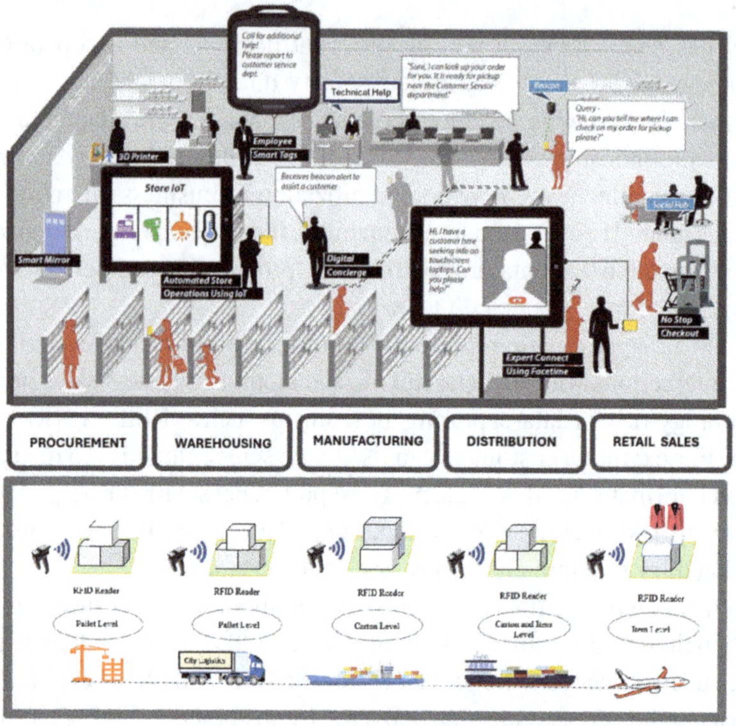

Figure 3. Value chain analysis model

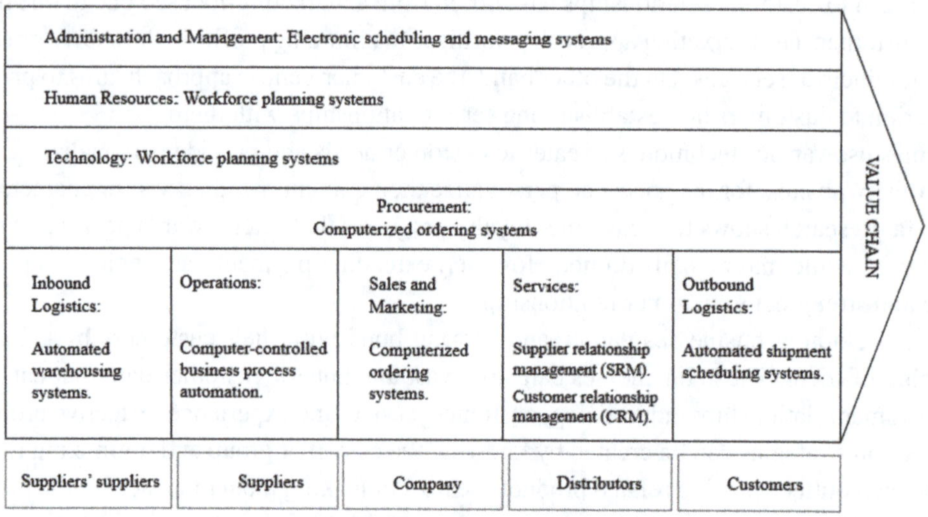

Strategic management techniques such as business performance and value chain analysis are essential to assess the organizational competitive advantage of operations. The value chain analysis model (Porter, 2001) consists of business activities that a textile company can use to analyze and deliver a product or a service. This analysis considers a series of business activities related to raw materials procurement and the sale of finished products. The activities include storing materials in warehouses, logistical production management, storage and transportation costs, product branding and sales-related communication, and sales to consumers and after-sales service plans. The value chain analysis also considers four operational support functionalities: administration and management part of the planning activities, deployment of technological infrastructures, recruitment and training related strategic actions, and manufacturing business infrastructures that look after the financial, legal, and public service-related issues. By breaking down a business's operational activities and assessing how individual activities contribute to its operations, operational supervisors can manage them effectively and improve its competitive advantage.

Sustainability-related issues are the other important factors essential to new industrial value chain operational activities. Sustainability practices provide the safest route to governmental regulations and customer satisfaction (Pal, 2023). Industrial data analytics provide a way to address social issues and create value-added economic revenue (Pal, 2023) while optimizing the operating environment and the effects of the green environment (Pal, 2021). Moreover, the ramifications of massive-collected data analyses on Lean, Agile, Resilient, Green, and Economical (LARGE) issues outcome are providing some guidelines for different categories of supply chain operations (Chun Wu, 2003) (Dora et al., 2016) (Baramichai et al., 2007) (Srivastava, 2007) in present years. Some researchers put forward the panacea of the LARGE ideas of industrial operations as a value-added manifestation. The following section briefly presents a selection of LARGE concepts based on recent research.

RECENT SUPPLY CHAIN DATA ANALYTICS RESEARCH

Industrial manufacturing businesses require to place sustainable work practices to comply with international institution guided regulations. Big data analytics are helping businesses to achieve social dimensions and improve economic values while optimizing the green effects related to corporate sustainability. In addition, the research articles reviews of the researcher-works realised that some western countries (e.g., United Kingdom, United States of America, and Germany) are using vast business operation related data collection and analyses for supply chain management. Developing countries (e.g., India, China) are also under the microscope of industrial manufacturing sustainability related research works. Figure 4 presents a diagrammatic visualization of sustainability related research for few countries.

With the increasing digitization of business activities, fashion companies are also turning towards technology to improve their operations. The widespread availability of mobile devices, the Internet, and social networking services (SNS) has opened up new avenues for data collection, such as website click-through rates, browsing histories, and social media comments (Kauffman et al., 2012). This information can benefit fashion companies by providing insights into customers' interests, demands, and sentiments towards brands and products. These insights can then be utilized for future product design, sales forecasting, trendspotting, product recommendations, personalized service design, and decision-making (Mikalef et al., 2017). To stay competitive and succeed in a data-driven environment, companies must be adept at extracting valuable insights from existing data and using them to inform their business practices (Kauffman et al., 2012) (Mikalef et al., 2017).

Figure 4. Recent research on manufacturing industry and supply chain

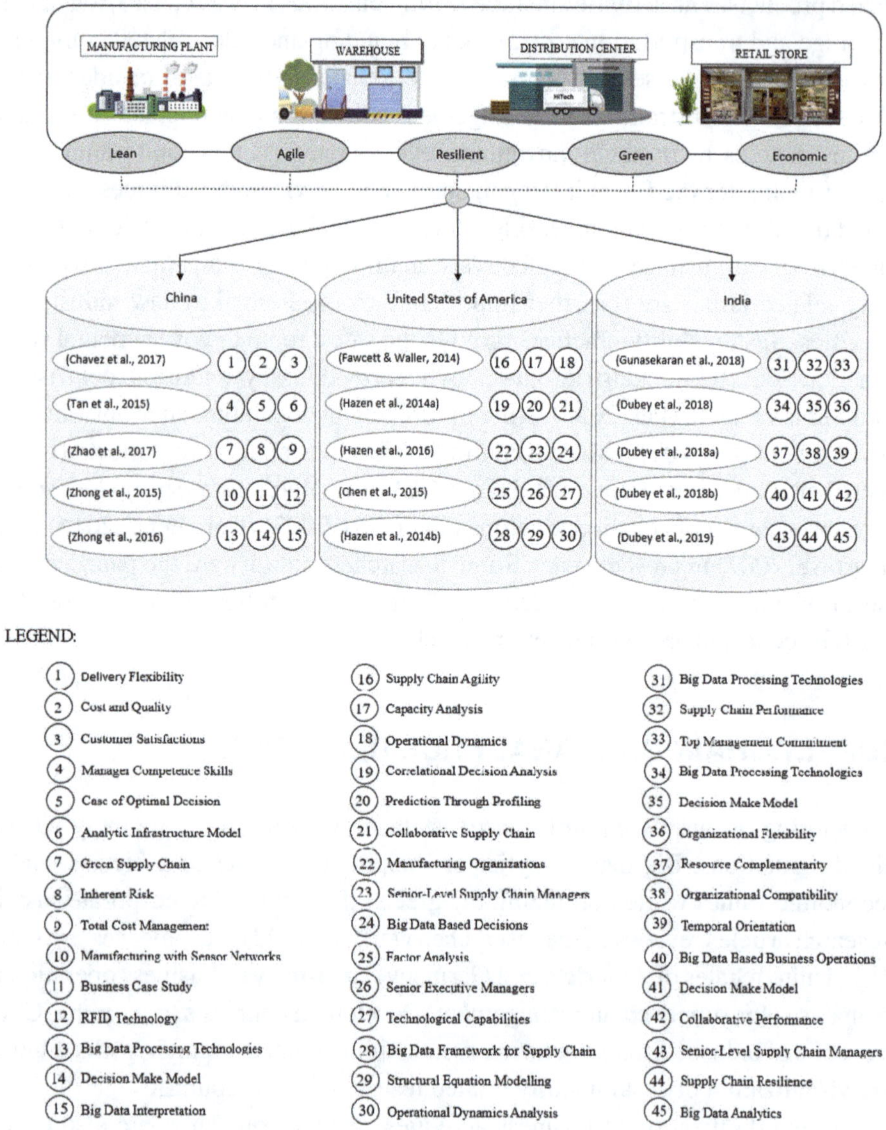

The development of textile products is influenced by various factors such as globalization, digitization, and consumer expectations related to sustainability. As a result, the industry experts require detailed information about the environmental impact of textile products' constituent elements, products, and production processes.

The textile product manufacturing has been fragmented, and the globally dispersed production network acts as a significant stimulus in industry-specific supply chain network deployment, creating value for the entire business operations. The concept of supply chain operations, or value chain networks, is getting more complex due to business processes outsourcing and the need for product traceability monitoring for regulatory purposes and quality assurance management. Supply chain operation managers appreciate the importance of enforcing assessment through achievement by using data-driven decision metrics. The crucial ingredients of traceability management are data gathering, processing, decision-making, and secure information-sharing system architecture. This creates an essential ingredient for attractive industrial operation management using technologies. Business process-generated data drives these decisions and actions. Using available data for analytics design has also gained immense value in handling business operations. However, estimates of the data value are required to accurately understand how data can contribute value to the textile's regular business operations and how to manage the collection and use of various data types.

Figure 5. An organizational overview of the SCOR model

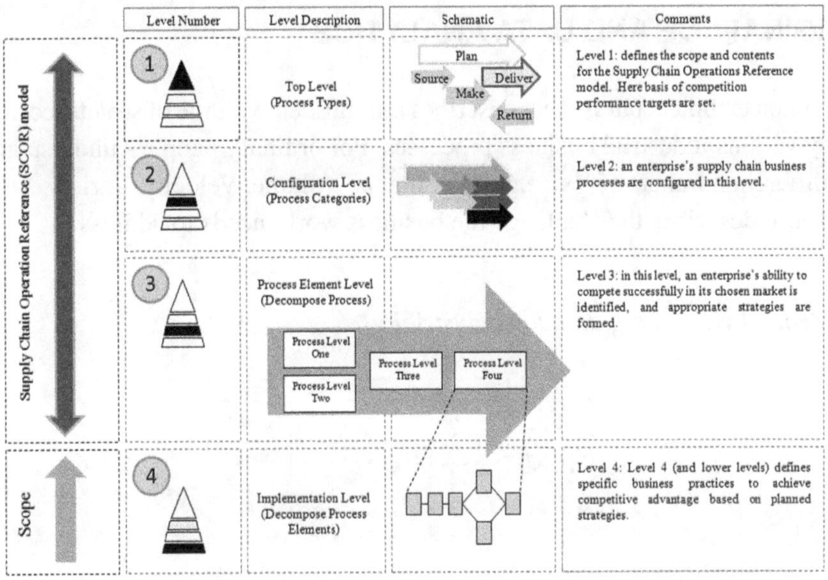

Textile manufacturing and retailing activities have changed in recent decades due to business process automation, and disruptive technologies play an essential role. These activities influence environmental, economic, societal, and supply chain operations. Sustainability has become a significant challenge and crucial topic of investigation. The inclusion of sustainability-related business activities enhances the operational green agenda-related performance of enterprises. It provides them with new advantages that make them competitive by using sustainability agendas around regular operations.

To assess the organizational competitive advantage of operations, strategic management techniques such as business performance evaluation using industry specific SCOR model (as shown in Figure 5) and value chain analysis (Figure 3) play an essential role. The value chain analysis model consists of business activities that a textile company can use to analyze and deliver a product or a service. This analysis considers a series of business activities related to raw materials procurement and the sale of finished products. The activities include storing materials in warehouses, logistical production management, storage and transportation costs, product branding and sales-related communication, and sales to consumers and after-sales service plans.

The value chain analysis also considers four operational support functionalities: administration and management part of the planning activities, deployment of technological infrastructures, recruitment and training related strategic actions, and manufacturing business infrastructures that look after the financial, legal, and public service-related issues, as shown in Figure 3.

In this way, Porter describes breaking down a business operational activity that represents the primary constituent building blocks of competitive advantage. Operational supervisors can then assess how individual activities contribute to the overall business operations and how to manage them effectively. In this way, the SCOR and value chain models are essential for business competitiveness analysis. All these analyses consider business operational data for different business activities, which form the big data source for data analytics design.

BIG DATA SIGINAFACE AND DATA ANALYTICS

Big Data is a common technical phrase that describes a significant volume of structured and unstructured data produced by various industrial business processes. For ordinary people's understanding, it is often presented with different numbers of Vs. (e.g., 4V – that is, Volume, Velocity, Variety, Veracity, and 5Vs or 6Vs), moreover, it describes the challenge the business world needs to address.

Figure 6. A conceptual view of big data for industrial use

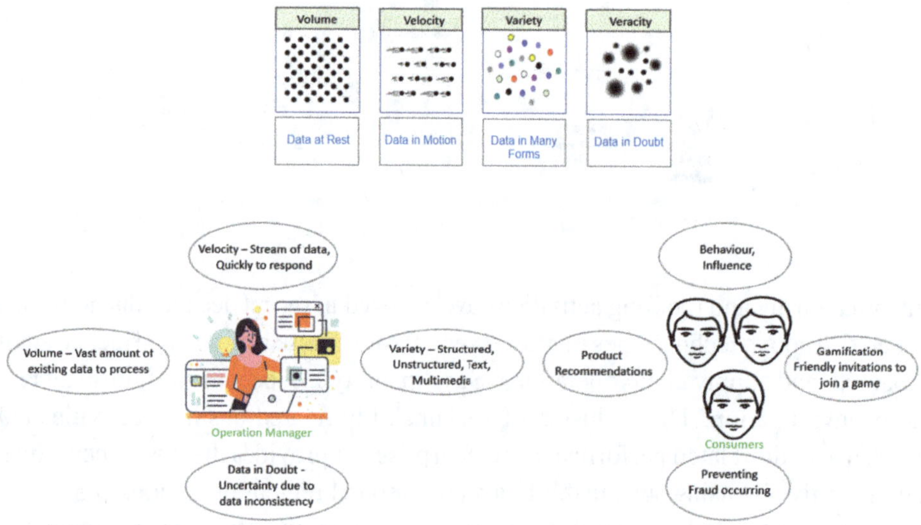

Figure 6 presents a brief overview of big data for industrial use and some relevant socio-technical issues for business application development. For example, consumer behavioural characteristics to design and develop recommendation systems.

Academics and practitioners are assessing bottlenecks in various industrial applications. These bottlenecks have been tackled by various categories of data management models and algorithms. The following section discusses various databases developed to store significant data for analysis.

DATA PROCESSING AND INDUSTRIAL APPLICATIONS

Data processing systems have long been an integral part of regular manufacturing and distribution operations. In the 1970s, third-generation programming applications like COBOL were used to coordinate business operations in manufacturing, including material management, raw material procurement, human resource management, and transportation. In the early 1980s, relational data management systems were introduced for industrial application development.

However, storing data in relational databases has become tedious and inefficient with the increasing volume of semi- or unstructured and interconnected data. This is because relational database systems have constrained data models and deal poorly with relationships. The limitations of traditional database systems, particularly the relational data model, have led to the creation of new-generation database technologies. Among these, Graph Databases have garnered attention in the database community because they are well-suited to processing the graph-like structure of data in modern projects that require a database. Graph database activity has flourished in today's industrial applications.

One of the most crucial elements of a database is its 'database model' or simply 'data model.' In the most general sense, a data model requires conceptual tools to model representations of real-world entities and their relationships. From a database standpoint, a data model comprises three components: a set of data structure types, operators or inference rules, and a set of integrity rules. Graph databases like Neo4j are particularly adept at storing relationship-oriented data naturally and efficiently using nodes and edges.

THE ERA OF BIG DATA ANALYTICS

The main objective of processing Big Data is to generate differentiated, trustworthy value. This is done by applying advanced analytics against the complete data collection, regardless of scale. To understand the critical issues of Big Data, one must understand the data sources of business processes within industrial applications.

Graph database models can be characterized as those where data structures for the schema and instances are modelled as graphs or generalizations of them and data manipulation is expressed by graph-oriented operations and type constructors. The advantages of using a graph data model are that it introduces a level of abstraction that allows more natural modelling of graph data, query languages, operations, and algorithms for storing and querying graphs. A few essential preliminaries of graph databases are described below.

Graph Database Preliminaries

Graph databases store data in the form of *nodes*, *edges*, and *relationships* that provide index-free adjacency. Figure 7. represents a simple product-order database. A graph is a pair G= (V, E) of sets such that $E \subseteq (V \times V)$. The elements of V are vertices or nodes of the graph G, and the element of E are its *edges* or *relationships*. Because academic literature on graph theory typically talks about vertices and edges, which available graph database and its APIs operate on nodes and relationships respectively, these terms are used interchangeably in this chapter.

Order – The order of a graph G, denoted by $|G|$, is the number of vertices of G. Its number of edges is denoted by $||G||$.

Incident Vertex – A vertex *v* is incident with an edge e if $v \in e$; then e is an edge at *v*. An edge $\{x, y\}$ can be written as *xy*.

Vertex Degree – The set of all edges in E at a vertex *v* is denoted E(*v*). The degree of a vertex *v*, denoted as d(*v*), is the number $|E(v)|$ of edges at *v*.

Figure 7. Characteristics of relational and graph database

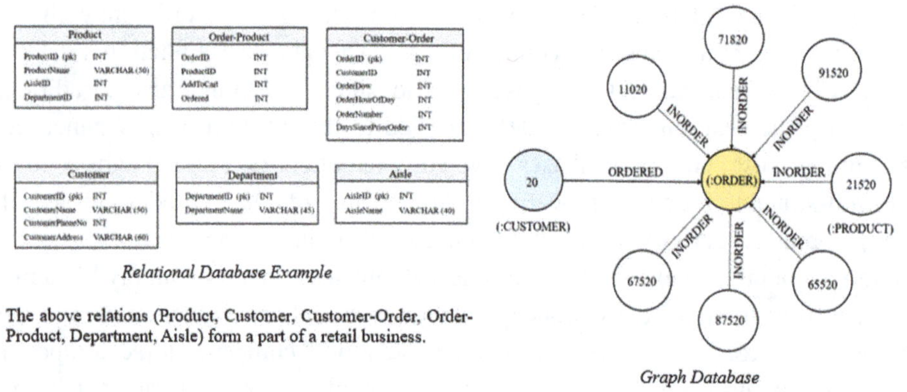

Subgraph – Given two graphs G= (V, E) and G'= (V', E'), G' is a subgraph of G, written as G' ⊆ G and G' contains all the edges $xy \in E$ with x, $y \in V'$, then G' is an induced subgraph of G.

Path – A path is a non-empty graph P = (V, E) of the form V= $\{x_0, x_1, \ldots, x_k\}$, E= $\{x_0x_1, x_1,x_2, \ldots, x_{k-1}x_k\}$. The number of edges in a path is its length.

BIG DATA ANALYTICS

A simple definition is that "BI is a wider group of software applications, technologies, infrastructure, and processes for gathering, storing, accessing, and analyzing data to help business users make operational decisions" (Watson, 2009). The methodology used in this chapter's research is based on the cross-industry standard process for the data mining model conceived initially by IBM research in the mid-1990s. The model consists of six phases for conducting a data mining project. The six phases are (i) understanding business, (ii) data understanding which deals with the initial data collection and analysis, (iii) data preparation, (iv) modelling, (v) evaluation, and (vi) deployment. Figure 10 (b) represents the model.

The research of the current chapter is evaluated by clustering algorithm on a graph shown in Figure 8(a). That graph is known as the connected caveman graph, and it was initially proposed by Duncan J Watts (Watts, 1999). Structurally, it is formed by modifying a set of isolated k-cliques by removing one edge from each clique and connecting it to a neighbouring clique. However, the graph in Figure 10 (a) does not resemble a real network, but the current research project of this chapter chose it as it will help evaluate the implemented algorithm. Such a graph contains communities that can be used to verify the proposed Algorithm 1. The result of the community detection is satisfied by the verification method.

Techniques for Analytics

Most techniques used to analyze big data analytics are based on applied mathematical computation and machine learning paradigms. However, big data analytics techniques are widespread and context specific. These techniques can be classified and discussed according to the data under investigation. Depending on the type of data, four central big data analytics can be defined: (i) text analytics: this technique is used to find out relevant information from textual data, (ii) audio analytics: techniques deployed to extract information from unstructured audio data. Customer service telephone conversations with customers are the primary source of audio analytics. Some of the main techniques used for audio analytics include large vocabulary, continuous speech recognition and phonetics-based systems, (iii) video analytics: methods used to monitor and analyze video streams. Video analytics has been mainly used as a replacement for labor-intensive observation.

Figure 8. Typical types of big data application systems

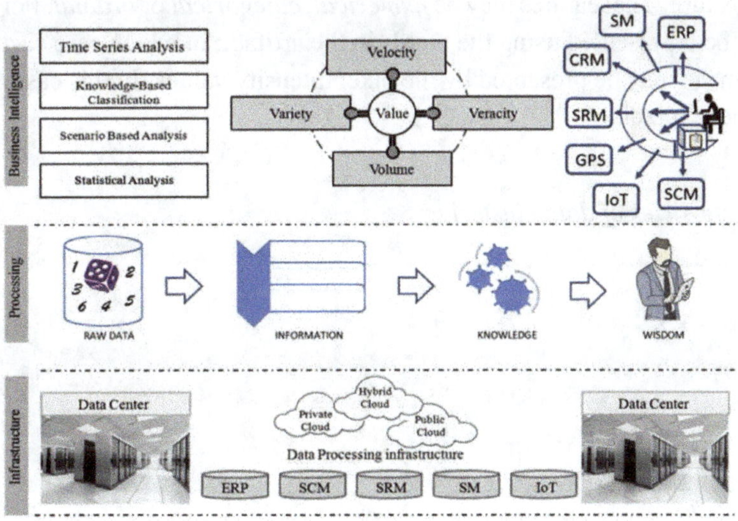

In addition, many business applications of video analytics are being used in manufacturing to collect data on customer demographics and preferences, and (iv) social media analytics: techniques used to analyze structured and non-structured data from social media channels (e.g., Twitter, Facebook). Some exciting techniques used to analyze social media data are community detection, social influence analysis and link prediction. Many successful enterprises have invested large sums of money in business intelligence and data warehousing tools and technologies. These enterprises believe that up-to-date, accurate and integrated information about their supply chain, products and customers is critical for their survival.

In order to solve a problem, the big data-based application uses intelligent reasoning in automated software that helps users apply analytical and scientific methods to business decision-making. The software applications that focus on the industrial decision support systems, providing Big Data-based tools to support a user's global supply chain reasoning process to develop a solution to the problem. Figure 8 represents typical types of big data application systems.

Once the industrial business process data is collected, it needs to be stored for processing purposes. In the data processing phase, the collected data is analyzed for business operational decision making. Data analysis is broadly classified into two different categories: (i) exploratory, and (ii) confirmatory. The main objective of exploratory analysis is to discover patterns and model the data. Exploratory data analysis is usually followed by a phase of confirmatory data analysis which aims at model validation. Many mathematical techniques have been proposed to perform data analysis. Statistical pattern recognition and machine learning is often used with predicative analysis that consists of finding relationships among objects in consideration and predicting future events, based on the knowledge obtained. Pattern recognition comprises of three phases: data representation, learning and inference.

Data Representation

In order to analyze the collected data, the analysis process needs an appropriate representation scheme to represent the data. Again, this representation involves picking a set of properties to identify the objects of interest in the data set. A d-dimensional vector $x = (x_1, x_2, \ldots, x_d)^T$ represents each object, where $x_p, p \in [d]$ denotes a feature. The features may be *numerical*, *categorical* or *ordinal*. For example, a written textual artifact may be represented using the words in the artifact; in which case each x_p denotes a word in the artifact. An image may be presented by the pixel intensity values. In this case, x_p is the numerical intensity value at the pth pixel.

Figure 9. Various categories of data clustering

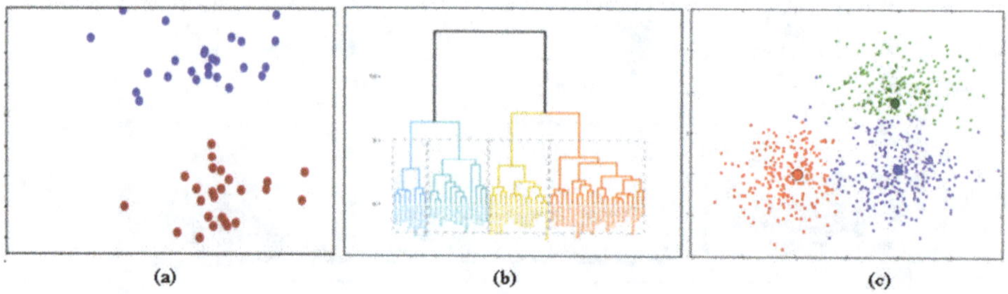

Data Clustering Algorithms

In general, two types of data clustering algorithms (i.e., hierarchical, partitional) have been used in data science historically. As the name suggests, hierarchical clustering algorithms build a hierarchy of clusters where the root of the tree contains all the n points in the data set, and the leaves contain the individual points. Figure 9(a) shows a set of points in two-dimensional space, containing three clusters. Hierarchical clustering generates a dendrogram for the collected data. Figure 9(b) presents a dendrogram generated using the complete-link agglomerative hierarchical clustering algorithm. Partitional clustering algorithms, directly partition the collected data into different clusters, as shown in Figure 9(c). There are different types of clustering algorithms available for data clustering. For example, Figure 9(c) depicts the three clusters, represented by the red, blue and green points, and obtained using the k-means algorithm.

The methodology used in this chapter's research is inspired by the cross-industry standard process for the data mining model conceived initially by IBM research in the mid-1990s. The model consists of six phases for conducting a data mining project. The six phases are (i) understanding business, (ii) data understanding which deals with the initial data collection and analysis, (iii) data preparation, (iv) modelling, (v) evaluation, and (vi) deployment. Figure 10 (b) represents the model.

Figure 10. Connected caveman graph of six cliques

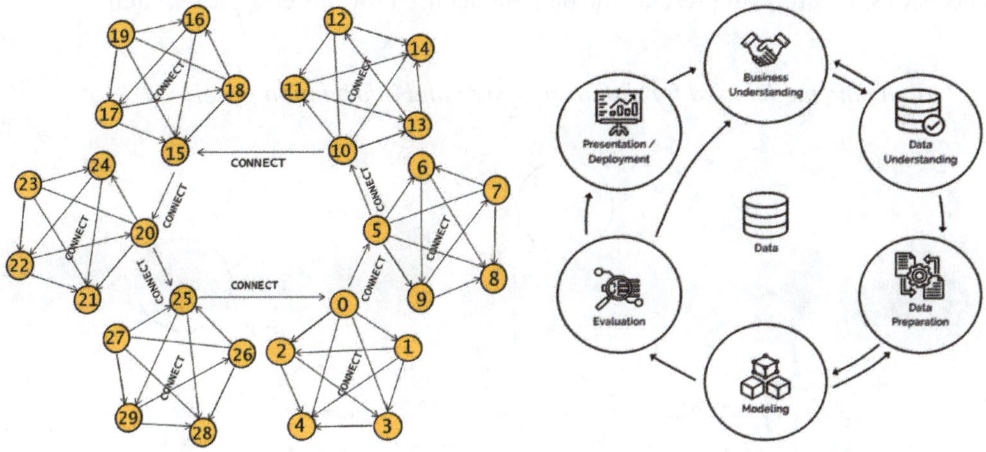

(a) (b)

The research of the current chapter is evaluated by clustering algorithm on a graph shown in Figure 10(a). That graph is known as the connected caveman graph, and it was initially proposed by Duncan J Watts (Watts, 1999). However, the graph in Figure 10(a) does not resemble a real network, but the current research project of this chapter chose it as it will help evaluate the implemented algorithm. Such a graph contains communities that can be used to verify the proposed Algorithm 1. The result of the community detection is satisfied by the verification method.

Algorithm 1: Louvain community detection algorithm

```
G be the initial network;
while Put each node of G in its own community do
  | while some nodes are moved do
  |   | foreach Node in the network do
  |   |   | place n in its neighboring community including its own which maximizes
  |   |   | the modularity gain;
  |   | end
  | end
  | if the new modularity is higher than the previous modularity then
  |   | G = the network between communities of G;
  | else
  |   | Terminate;
  | end
end
```

RETAIL SALES DATA ANLYTIC EXAMPLE

Big data analytics are playing an essential role in today's textile business. It is geared towards storing, processing, and visualizing many real-time business process-related data. In order to do these data-related activities, industrial analytics applications require the appropriate tools and create an operating work area, which helps to get meaningful strategic information from the gathered data. Textile business retail operation is one area that collects vast amounts of business-processes operational data regularly. Retail operation managers must understand their consumer's purchasing patterns and behaviour to make better business decisions. Figure 11 represents the data model used for this chapter research.

Figure 11. Graph data model used for database design and information generated

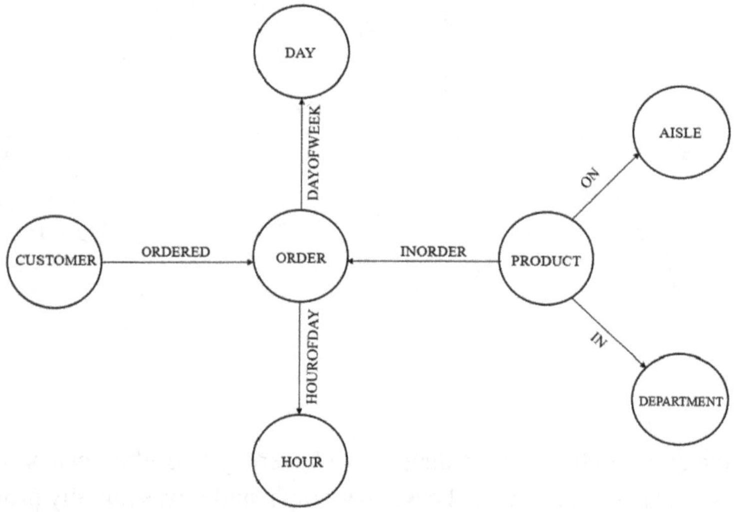

Big data analytics are playing an essential role in today's textile business. It is geared towards storing, processing, and visualizing many real-time business process-related data. In order to do these data-related activities, industrial analytics applications require the appropriate tools and create an operating environment. Retail operation managers must understand their consumer's purchasing patterns (as shown in Figure 12) and behaviour to make better business decisions.

FUTURE RESEARCH DIRECTIONS

As the use of big data-based textile sales analytics becomes more prevalent, various techniques are being implemented to manage regular operations. Researchers are relying on artificial intelligence-based network technologies to address operational issues, with one of the main challenges being algorithmic recommendation systems. This chapter explores the Louvain clustering algorithm that generates non-overlapping product clusters and evaluates the impact of an overlapping community clustering algorithm. In the future, the research will focus on incorporating more detailed information regarding textile retail data, such as order timestamps, customer demographics, and relevant geographic details, to enhance the recommendation system. Additionally, the projects aim to apply service-oriented processing capabilities of analytics and incorporate seasonal variations of products to customers' requirements. It is essential to have the organizational capability to deploy new information and communication technologies such as augmented reality (AR), virtual reality (VR), and the inclusion of new technologies that can capture real-time data streams (i.e., IoT, RFID technology).

Figure 12. Number of orders placed at various hours of a particular day

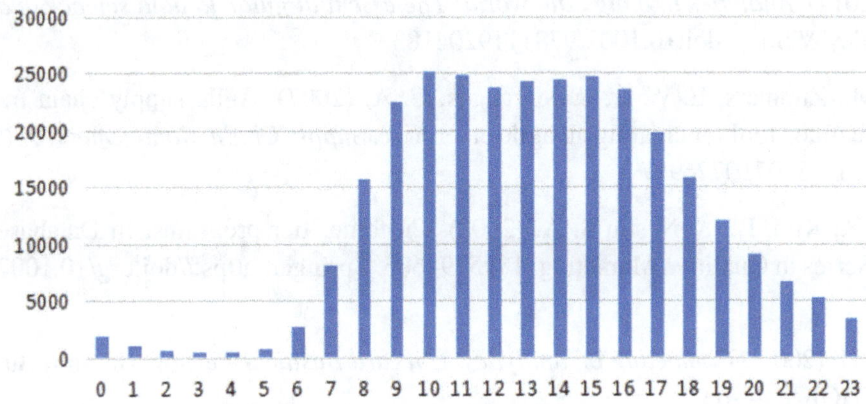

CONCLUSION

This chapter focuses on the importance of making data-driven decisions in business operations for enhanced efficiency. It highlights how business managers can overcome the complexity of decision-making by using techniques like business operational modelling using spreadsheets. However, the reality is that decision-making is more complex than mathematical models can portray.

The chapter emphasizes the role of disruptive technologies, like IoT and real-time data analytics, in making informed decisions for regular business operations. While not all disruptive technologies may be useful for every business model, managers should always be on the lookout for such technologies to assess their potential impact on their resources and capabilities. It also highlights the close relationship between big data and disruptive technologies, where both fuel each other's growth.

To demonstrate innovative ideas, the chapter presents a graph-based framework for data analytics for textile product sales management. The framework uses the Louvain Algorithm to find network communities in retail transactional data and produce a customer recommendation system using the Neo4j graph database. The chapter emphasizes that graph databases are ideal for high-dimensional data in real-world applications and can provide insights into data relationships quickly. The central objective of the chapter is to help managers leverage disruptive technologies and big data for effective decision-making.

REFERENCES

Akter, S., Wamba, S. F., Gunasekaran, A., Dubey, R., & Childe, S. J. (2016). How to improve firm performance using big data analytics capability and business strategy alignment? *International Journal of Production Economics, 182*, 113–131. doi:10.1016/j.ijpe.2016.08.018

Arunachalam, D., Kumar, N., & Kawalek, J. P. (2018). Understanding big data analytics capabilities in supply chain management: Unravelling the issues, challenges and implications for practice. *Transportation Research Part E, Logistics and Transportation Review, 114*, 416–436. doi:10.1016/j.tre.2017.04.001

Baesens, A. (2014). *Analytics in a big data world: The essential guide to data science and its applications.* John Wiley & Sons. doi:10.1002/9781119204183

Baramichai, M., Zimmers, E. W. Jr, & Marangos, C. A. (2007). Agile supply chain transformation matrix: An integrated tool for creating an agile enterprise. *Supply Chain Management, 12*(5), 334–348. doi:10.1108/13598540710776917

Blattberg, R. C., Kim, B., & Neslin S. A. (2008). Customer tier programs. In Database Marketing: International Series in Qualitive Marketing, 18, 579–605. Springer. https://doi.org/10.1007/978-0-387-72579-6_23

Davenport, T. H. (2006). *Competing on analytics, Harvard Business Review*. Harvard Business Press. doi:10.5860/CHOICE.44-6322

Davenport, T. H., & Harris, J. G. (2007). *Competing on analytics – the new science of winning*. Harvard Business School Publishing Corporation. doi:10.5465/amr.2005.17293788

Dora, M., Kumar, M., & Gellynck, X. (2016). Determinants and barriers to lean implementation in food-processing SMEs—A multiple case analysis. *Production Planning and Control, 27*(1), 1–23. doi: 10.1080/09537287.2015.1050477

Dubey, R., Gunasekaran, A., & Childe, S. J. (2018a). Big data analytics capability in supply chain agility: The moderating effect of organizational flexibility. *Management Decision*. Advance online publication. doi:10.1108/MD-01-2018-0119

Dubey, R., Gunasekaran, A., Childe, S. J., Fosso Wamba, S., Roubaud, D., & Foropon, C. (2021). Empirical investigation of data analytics capability and organizational flexibility as complements to supply chain resilience. *International Journal of Production Research, 59*(1), 1–19. doi:10.1080/00207543.2019.1582820

Dubey, R., Gunasekaran, A., Childe, S. J., Luo, Z., Wamba, S. F., Roubaud, D., & Foropon, C. (2018b). Examining the role of big data and predictive analytics on collaborative performance in context to sustainable consumption and production behaviour. *Journal of Cleaner Production, 196*, 1508–1521. doi:10.1016/j.jclepro.2018.06.097

Dubey, R., Gunasekaran, A., Childe, S. J., Roubaud, D., Wamba, S. F., Giannakis, M., & Foropon, C. (2019b). Big data analytics and organizational culture as complements to swift trust and collaborative performance in the humanitarian supply chain. *International Journal of Production Economics, 210*, 120–136. doi:10.1016/j.ijpe.2019.01.023

Dubey, R., Gunasekaran, A., Childe, S. J., Wamba, S. F., & Papadopoulos, T. (2016). The impact of big data on world-class sustainable manufacturing. *International Journal of Advanced Manufacturing Technology, 84*(1–4), 631–645. doi:10.1007/s00170-015-7674-1

Fawcett, S. E., & Waller, M. A. (2014). Supply chain game changers—mega, nano, and virtual trends—and forces that impede supply chain design (ie, building a winning team). *Journal of Business Logistics, 35*(3), 157–164. doi:10.1111/jbl.12058

Fosso Wamba, S., Gunasekaran, A., Papadopoulos, T., & Ngai, E. (2018). Big data analytics in logistics and supply chain management. *International Journal of Logistics Management, 29*(2), 478–484. doi:10.1108/IJLM-02-2018-0026

Giannakis, M., & Louis, M. (2016). A multi-agent based system with big data processing for enhanced supply chain agility. *Journal of Enterprise Information Management, 29*(5), 706–727. doi:10.1108/JEIM-06-2015-0050

Govindan, K., Cheng, T. C. E., Mishra, N., & Shukla, N. (2018). Big data analytics and application for logistics and supply chain management. *Transportation Research Part E, Logistics and Transportation Review, 114*, 343–349. doi:10.1016/j.tre.2018.03.011

Gunasekaran, A., Papadopoulos, T., Dubey, R., Wamba, S. F., Childe, S. J., Hazen, B., & Akter, S. (2017). Big data and predictive analytics for supply chain and organizational performance. *Journal of Business Research, 70*, 308–317. doi:10.1016/j.jbusres.2016.08.004

Hazen, B. T., Boone, C. A., Ezell, J. D., & Jones-Farmer, L. A. (2014). Data quality for data science, predictive analytics, and big data in supply chain management: An introduction to the problem and suggestions for research and applications. *International Journal of Production Economics, 154*, 72–80. doi:10.1016/j.ijpe.2014.04.018

Hazen, B. T., Skipper, J. B., Ezell, J. D., & Boone, C. A. (2016). Big Data and predictive analytics for supply chain sustainability: A theory-driven research agenda. *Computers & Industrial Engineering, 101*, 592–598. doi:10.1016/j.cie.2016.06.030

Kauffman, R. JSrivastava, JVayghan, J. (2012). Business and data analytics: new innovations for the management of E-commerce. Electronic Commerce Research and Applications, 11(2), 85–88. https://doi.org/10.1016/j.elerap.2012.01.001

Keikhosrokiani, P. (2022a). Big Data Analytics for Healthcare: Datasets, Techniques, Life Cycles, Management, and Applications. doi:10.1016/C2021-0-00369-2

Keikhosrokiani, P. (2022b). Handbook of research on consumer behavior change and data analytics in the socio-digital era. doi:10.4018/978-1-6684-4168-8

Keikhosrokiani, P. (2023). *Handbook of Research on Consumer Behavioral Analytics in Metaverse and the Adoption of a Virtual World.* IGI Global., doi:10.4018/978-1-6684-7029-9

Mikalef P, Pappas IO, Krogstie J, & Giannakos M (2017). Big data analytics capabilities: A systematic literature review and research agenda. In Information Systems e-Business Management. https://doi.org/10.1007/s1025 7-017-0362-y

Pal, K. (2017). Supply chain coordination based on web services. In H. K. Chan, N. Subramanian, M. D.-A. Abdulrahman (eds) Supply Chain Management in the Big Data Era, (pp. 137-170). IGI Global. doi:10.4018/978-1-5225-0956-1.ch009

Pal, K. (2020). Information sharing for manufacturing supply chain management based on blockchain technology. In I. Williams (ed) Cross-Industry Use of Blockchain Technology and Opportunities for the Future, (pp. 1-17). IGI Global doi:10.4018/978-1-7998-3632-2.ch001

Pal, K. (2021). Applications of secured blockchain technology in manufacturing industry. In S. K. Pani, B. Patnaik, S. Lun, and X. Liu (ed) Blockchain and AI Technology in the Industrial Internet of Things. IGI Global. doi:10.4018/978-1-7998-6694-7.ch010

Pal, K. (2023). Drivers of sustainable supply chain management using internet of things-based blockchain technology. In A. Taghipour (ed) Government Impact on Sustainable and Responsible Supply Chan. (pp. 171-201). IGI Global. doi:10.4018/978-1-6684-9062-4.ch010

Pal, K., & Yasar, A. (2020). Internet of Things and blockchain technology in textile manufacturing supply chain data management. *Procedia Computer Science*, *170*, 450–457. doi:10.1016/j.procs.2020.03.088

Porter, M. (2001). The value chain and competitive advantage. In *Understanding Business: Processes; Barnes, D. (Edited)* (pp. 50–66). Routledge. doi:10.1201/9781420025569.ch8

Srivastava, S. K. (2007). Green Supply-Chain Management: A State-of-the-Art Literature Review. *International Journal of Management Reviews*, *9*(1), 53–80. doi:10.1111/j.1468-2370.2007.00202.x

Supply Chain Council. (2010). http://supply-chain.org/f/down-load/726710733/SCOR10.pdf

Trkman, P., McCormack, K., de Oliveira, M. P. V., & Ladeira, M. B. (2010). The Impact of Business Analytics on Supply Chain Performance. *Decision Support Systems*, *49*(3), 318–327. doi:10.1016/j.dss.2010.03.007

Watts, D. J. (1999). *Small Worlds. The Dynamics of Networks between Order and Randomness*. Princeton University Press. doi:10.1515/9780691188331

Wu, C. (2003). Lean manufacturing: A perspective of lean suppliers. *International Journal of Operations & Production Management*, *23*(11), 1349–1376. doi:10.1108/01443570310501880

Zhao, R., Liu, Y., Zhang, N., & Huang, T. (2017). An optimization model for green supply chain management by using a big data analytic approach. *Journal of Cleaner Production*, *142*, 1085–1097. doi:10.1016/j.jclepro.2016.03.006

Zhong, R. Y., Huang, G. Q., Lan, S., Dai, Q. Y., Chen, X., & Zhang, T. (2015). A big data approach for logistics trajectory discovery from RFID-enabled production data. *International Journal of Production Economics*, *165*, 260–272. doi:10.1016/j.ijpe.2015.02.014

Zhong, R. Y., Lan, S., Xu, C., Dai, Q., & Huang, G. Q. (2016). Visualization of RFID-enabled shopfloor logistics Big Data in Cloud Manufacturing. *International Journal of Advanced Manufacturing Technology*, *84*(1–4), 5–16. doi:10.1007/s00170-015-7702-1

Chapter 5
Synergizing Success:
Harnessing AI-Infused Business Intelligence to Propel Exponential Business Growth

Princi Gupta
JECRC University, India

ABSTRACT

In business, AI and BI convergence fuels growth and innovation. This chapter probes this union. It delves into intricate AI integration with BI, catalyzing digital-era expansion. Contextualizing this, it addresses shifting decision paradigms. AI's predictive might, coupled with BI's tools, offers a holistic perspective. Strategic blueprints underpin AI-BI integration, detailing systematic approaches from data to deployment. Real-world cases illuminate symbiosis. Amid discourse, strategic considerations align objectives and optimize value. The chapter underscores AI-BI's potential and strategic urgency, urging AI investment, data culture, and collaboration. Examining AI-infused BI applications, it touts real-world advantages while tackling data alignment challenges. The chapter empowers leaders, managers, technologists to architect AI-BI synergy, redefining success amid evolving industries. Embracing data, it charts the course to prosperity, innovation, growth.

INTRODUCTION

Businesses need business intelligence (BI) tools to gather, analyze, and disseminate information in today's competitive, knowledge-based economy so that knowledge workers can make wise decisions. The capacity for managers to obtain "actionable data"—information that can be utilized to present performance measures, comprehend client behavior, and forecast market trends in "real-time"—is essential given how quickly a global economy runs. Applications for business intelligence help with tasks including financial analysis, score carding, data mining, data warehousing, and decision assistance. Producing something helpful to fulfill needs, secure a living, and better the world is what business is

DOI: 10.4018/979-8-3693-1210-0.ch005

all about Documentation of business actions is done electronically or on paper (Mohammad, 2023). As a result, more data about consumer responses and the sector is accessible. Using specialized tools and techniques, this data may be analyzed and mined to find patterns and intelligence that describe how the organization runs. The company may then be encouraged to implement these ideas, which will help it develop and become more adept at satisfying customer requests. The cycle never ends. Business intelligence, which applies to all industries, includes methods and tools for gathering, analyzing, and visualizing data to support executive decision-making. Data mining uses statistical and machine learning techniques to build decision-making models from unstructured data (Nguyen, 2023). The current war against any cyber-attack has increased the need for information security professionals at all levels of any organization. Processing incoming data as sets of information so becomes increasingly important. Additionally, the data will frequently be ambiguous and have both quantitative and qualitative components (Bharadiya, 2022). For these reasons, it is crucial to incorporate subjective judgment, human subjectivity, and imprecision into standard decision-making systems. These authors have adopted an unconventional strategy to improve this decision-making process by implementing a newly emerging technology known as a neural network as part of the infrastructure that will enable artificial intelligence systems to replace humans in order to meet the demand for real-time decision making. By incorporating a newly emerging technology known as a neural network as part of the infrastructure that will allow artificial intelligence systems to replace humans in order to meet the demand for real-time decision making, these authors have adopted an unconventional approach to enhance this decision-making process (Nwanakwaugwu, 2023). Better business decision-making is supported by business intelligence. In essence, Business Intelligence systems are Decision Support Systems (DSS) that are data-driven. Executive information systems, report and query tools, and briefing books are occasionally used interchangeably with business intelligence (Waliszewski, 2020).

Industrial sectors are characterized by vast and diverse data streams emanating from machinery, sensors, supply chains, and operational processes. Big Data Analytics provides the infrastructure, algorithms, and tools necessary to process, analyze, and derive actionable insights from this voluminous and complex data. Within BI frameworks, Big Data Analytics enhances decision-making by facilitating real-time monitoring of production lines, predictive maintenance of equipment, and optimized resource allocation. It enables industries to uncover patterns, trends, and correlations that might be imperceptible through traditional analytics methods. Moreover, by leveraging advanced machine learning and AI techniques, Big Data Analytics empowers organizations to forecast market trends, identify potential risks, and seize emerging opportunities. In essence, the integration of Big Data Analytics into BI frameworks for industrial applications catalyzes operational efficiencies, fosters innovation, and ensures competitiveness in an increasingly data-driven landscape (Pal, 2023).

The chapter aims to delve into the synergistic potential of merging AI with BI, emphasizing its transformative role in amplifying business growth and innovation. By examining practical applications and strategic blueprints, it illuminates how AI-enhanced BI can refine decision-making and streamline operations. Ultimately, the chapter offers invaluable guidance for organizations, empowering them to craft and implement AI-BI strategies that drive exponential growth and secure a competitive edge. Business intelligence components are compiled and discussed in this chapter as shown in Figure 1.

Figure 1. Business intelligence components

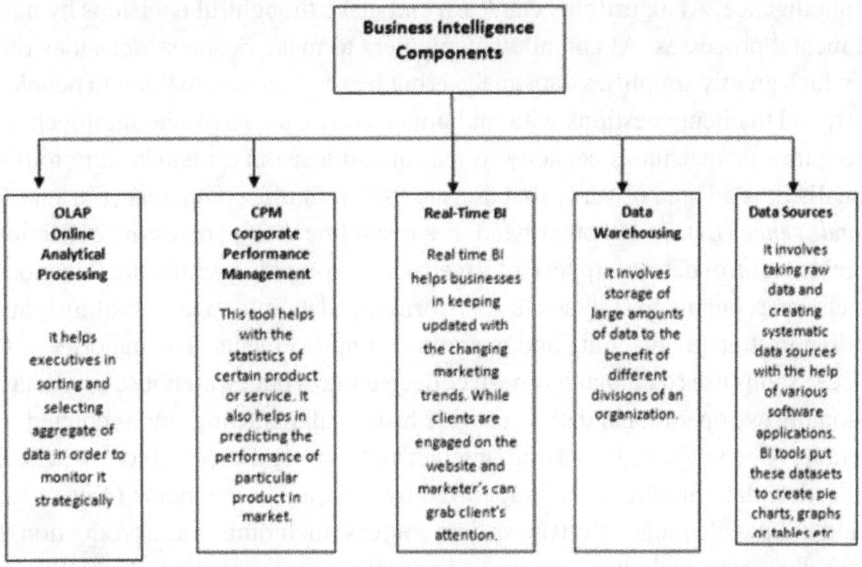

LITERATURE REVIEW

Deciphering the Core Concepts: An In-Depth Look at AI and BI Definitions

Business intelligence (BI) refers to a company's ability to use the data received from regular operations effectively (Kaushik, 2022). The BI may significantly contribute to maximizing organizational effectiveness by identifying new opportunities, highlighting potential hazards, providing more industry insights, and fortifying decision-making frameworks. While business analytics analyses historical data, business intelligence employs both current and past data to execute business operations, drive customer demands, and boost productivity (Bharadiya, 2022). Currently, internal and centralized corporate data are the main sources of data for BI systems. An incomplete understanding of the facts and a partial decision-making process could be caused by a significant amount of useful knowledge contained in unorganized and existent material. In today's rapidly evolving business landscape, data is often considered the new oil. The ability to harness, analyze, and derive actionable insights from vast amounts of data has become a critical factor in achieving success (Rana, 2022).

Artificial Intelligence (AI) is a broad field of computer science that focuses on creating systems and machines capable of performing tasks that typically require human intelligence. These tasks include learning from data, recognizing patterns, making decisions, and even natural language understanding (Fitriana, 2021). AI encompasses various subfields, such as machine learning, deep learning, natural language processing, computer vision, and robotics. Artificial intelligence (AI) takes a different tack from business intelligence (BI), which focuses on streamlining the process of gathering, reporting, and data analysis. Businesses may increase the regularity and quality of their data collection by utilizing BI. As a result, in order to make trusted decisions for our daily routine operations as stakeholders within our enterprise, we need to understand AI, its functionality, and capabilities as well as how it manages data that is dumped on us in an overwhelming sheer volume. We also need better information in order to increase our knowledge (Kaushik, 2022). One of the main objectives of artificial intelligence is to model human intelligence. AI algorithms can learn and make thoughtful decisions by modeling human behaviors and mental processes. AI can allow computers to make business decisions on their own, in contrast to BI, which greatly simplifies data analysis but leaves decision-making to people. For instance, chatbots can respond to client questions without human assistance. Artificial intelligence (AI) refers to a computer program's or machine's capacity to reason and learn in a manner akin to that of a human being. Additionally, it is an area of study that aims to "smarten up" computers (Fitriana, 2021).

Business Intelligence (BI), on the other hand, is a discipline that involves the collection, processing, analysis, and presentation of data to support informed decision-making within organizations (Jain, 2020). BI tools and techniques enable businesses to transform raw data into meaningful insights, reports, and dashboards, aiding in strategic planning and operational improvements. The majority of the time, business intelligence systems uses data that has been collected into a data warehouse or a data mart, but they can also occasionally use operational data to provide historical, real-time, and predicted perspectives of business operations (Chen, 2021). Reporting, interactive "slice-and-dice" pivot-table analytics, visualization, and statistical data mining are all supported by software components (Tavera Romero, 2021). Applications address a wide range of business data sources, including sales, production, financial, and many others, for objectives including corporate performance management. Through a process called benchmarking, information is frequently acquired about other businesses in the same sector that compete with one another in the same market or generate goods that are created there. Organizations are now beginning to recognize that data and content management should not be viewed as two distinct facets of information management, but rather as an integrated organizational approach (Chen, 2021). Business intelligence and enterprise content management are combined in enterprise information management. Operational business intelligence, which is now underserved and unchallenged by suppliers, is where organizations are moving. The top of the pyramid has historically been the only part of the pyramid that business intelligence providers have focused on, but there is currently a paradigm change moving towards taking business intelligence to the bottom of the pyramid with a focus on self-service business intelligence (Bharadiya, 2023).

Deep Dive Into AI-BI Synergy: Technical Evolution and Insights

AI Evolution: AI has its roots in the 1950s, with early developments in symbolic AI and rule-based systems. Over the decades, AI has witnessed breakthroughs in machine learning, neural networks, and deep learning, leading to remarkable advancements in areas like image recognition, natural language processing, and autonomous systems (Tavera Romero, 2021).

BI Evolution: Business Intelligence, although rooted in data processing since the 1960s, saw significant growth in the 1990s with the advent of data warehousing and OLAP (Online Analytical Processing) technologies. As computing power increased and data became more accessible, BI tools evolved to provide more sophisticated analytics and visualizations (Bharadiya, 2023). Both AI and BI have a rich history of evolution:

Table 1 provides a chronological overview of the evolution of AI and BI, delineating their respective developments and their intersection over time. In the early stages (1950s-1980s), AI focused on symbolic reasoning and expert systems, while BI primarily involved basic computerized data processing. The two fields had limited interaction during this period. The subsequent era saw the emergence of knowledge-based AI and early data warehousing in BI, but integration remained rudimentary. During the AI Winter and Data Warehousing era (1990s), AI faced reduced funding, while BI saw the development of data mining. The 2000s witnessed the machine learning renaissance in AI and the rise of advanced analytics in BI, with some data-driven decision-making in the latter. Big Data and Data Science gained prominence, with AI aiding data analysis in BI. The Convergence of AI and BI marked a turning point, leading to AI integration into BI tools and the emergence of AI-powered BI with advanced analytics (Chen, 2021). In the 2020s and beyond, AI-driven BI became common, offering automated insights and real-time data analysis, with AIBI (AI-Powered Business Intelligence) taking a central role (Bharadiya, 2023).

Table 1. Categorical breakdown: Technical evolution of AI-BI synergy

Era	AI Developments	BI Developments	Intersection
Early Stages (1950s-1980s)	Symbolic AI, Expert Systems	Computerized Decision Support Systems (DSS)	Focusing on symbolic reasoning, while BI primarily involved basic computerized data processing with limited analytical capabilities.
Knowledge-Based Systems	Emergence of knowledge-based AI.	Early data warehousing and OLAP systems.	Limited integration, focus on data storage.
AI Winter and Data Warehousing (1990s)	AI experiences reduced funding during the AI Winter.	Development of data mining and multidimensional databases in BI.	AI and BI continue to evolve separately.
Machine Learning Renaissance (2000s)	Machine learning renaissance begins, including deep learning	Rise of advanced analytics and predictive modeling in BI.	Some data-driven decision-making in BI.
Big Data and Data Science	Big data and data science gain prominence	BI adapts to handle massive data. Emergence of data science in BI.	Integration remains limited but AI aids data analysis
Convergence of AI and BI	AI starts to integrate into BI tools.	AI-powered BI tools emerge with enhanced data visualization.	Advanced analytics, AI-driven insights begin to surface.
AI-Powered BI and AI-Driven Insights (2020s and beyond)	AI-driven BI becomes common, offering automated insights and predictive capabilities.	Real-time data analysis, AI-driven decision support systems.	AIBI (AI-Powered Business Intelligence) at the forefront.

Source: Author compilation

Table 1 Categorical Breakdown is as follows: Technical Evolution of AI-BI Synergy provides a comprehensive summary of the technical evolution and insights surrounding the synergy between AI (Artificial Intelligence) and BI (Business Intelligence). It delves into key aspects and developments across different eras, highlighting the gradual convergence of these two fields.

METHODOLOGY

The methodology employed in exploring the transformative intersection of AI and BI within the business landscape in “Synergizing Success: Harnessing AI-Infused Business Intelligence to Propel Exponential Business Growth” is a meticulous journey into the heart of technological integration and its catalytic role in digital-era expansion. The chapter methodically investigates the intricate fusion of AI with BI, navigating through the nuances of shifting decision paradigms. Grounded in a foundation of strategic blueprints, the methodology outlines systematic approaches spanning the entire spectrum from data acquisition to strategic deployment. Real-world cases are intricately woven into the exploration, shedding light on the symbiotic relationship between AI and BI in practical scenarios. Within this discourse, strategic considerations emerge as guiding principles, aligning objectives and optimizing value in the dynamic business landscape. The chapter's methodology emphasizes the potential and strategic urgency of AI-BI integration, urging investments in AI, the cultivation of a data-centric culture, and the fostering of collaborative efforts. By scrutinizing AI-infused BI applications, the methodology highlights tangible real-world advantages while fearlessly addressing the challenges associated with data alignment. Ultimately, the methodology empowers leaders, managers, and technologists, providing a framework to architect the synergy between AI and BI and redefine success within the ever-evolving industries. Through a dedicated embrace of data, this methodology charts a course towards prosperity, innovation, and sustainable growth, envisioning a future where the convergence of AI and BI propels businesses to unprecedented heights of success.

THE SYNERGISTIC CONVERGENCE: AI AND BI AT THE INTERSECTION OF DATA-DRIVEN INSIGHTS

The synergy between AI and BI is where the true potential for transformative business insights emerges (Tamang, 2021). The intersection of these fields involves integrating AI technologies into BI processes. AI can enhance BI by:

Automating Data Analysis and Report Generation

AI-powered algorithms can automate the process of data analysis, allowing for faster and more accurate insights (Rana, 2022). They can identify patterns, correlations, and outliers in large datasets without human intervention. Automated report generation saves time and ensures that reports are consistently generated, reducing the risk of human errors in manual reporting (Ahmad, 2022).

Enabling Predictive Analytics

AI-driven predictive analytics leverages historical data and machine learning models to make forecasts and predictions. This is invaluable for businesses looking to anticipate market trends, customer behavior, and demand patterns. Predictive analytics can aid in proactive decision-making and help businesses stay ahead of the competition (Tamang, 2021).

Uncovering Hidden Patterns and Anomalies

AI can detect hidden patterns and anomalies in data that may not be apparent through traditional BI tools. This is crucial for identifying fraud, unusual operational behavior, or untapped opportunities. Anomaly detection can save businesses from financial losses and improve operational efficiency (Gad-Elrab, 2021).

Enhancing Natural Language Understanding

Natural language processing (NLP) and understanding (NLU) technologies enable users to interact with BI systems in a more conversational and intuitive manner (Keikhosrokiani & Asl, 2022a, 2022b, 2022c; Kng et al., 2022; Suhendra et al., 2022; Zainol et al., 2022). Users can ask questions in plain language, and AI-powered BI systems can understand and provide relevant answers, making data exploration more accessible to non-technical stakeholders.

Personalization and Recommendations

AI can analyze user behavior within BI platforms and offer personalized recommendations and insights. For example, suggesting relevant reports, dashboards, or data sources based on a user's historical interactions. Personalization enhances user engagement and ensures that individuals receive the most relevant information (Tong-On, 2021, Keikhosrokiani, 2022; Keikhosrokiani & Fye, 2023; Xian et al., 2022; Zhao & Keikhosrokiani, 2022).

Real-time Data Processing

AI can process and analyze data in real-time, allowing businesses to react swiftly to changing conditions. Real-time insights are crucial for monitoring key performance indicators (KPIs) and responding to events as they happen (Nwanakwaugwu, 2023).

Continuous Learning and Improvement

AI models used in BI can continuously learn and adapt to changing data patterns. This ensures that insights and predictions remain accurate and relevant over time (Ahmad, 2022). The synergy between AI and BI indeed opens up new possibilities for businesses to gain deeper insights, make data-driven decisions, and stay competitive in a rapidly evolving business landscape. As AI technologies continue to advance, we can expect even more sophisticated integration between AI and BI, leading to further improvements in data analysis and decision-making processes (Tong-On, 2021).

REALIZING COMPETITIVE ADVANTAGE: THE BENEFITS OF AI AND BI INTEGRATION

Table 2 depicts the benefits of combining AI and BI, including enhanced data analysis, predictive analytics, cost savings, and more. The table provides a concise overview of the compelling advantages that arise from integrating AI (Artificial Intelligence) with BI (Business Intelligence) in organizations. This combination enhances data analysis by allowing AI to process complex data swiftly and accurately, offering predictive analytics for informed decision-making, and delivering personalized insights tailored to individual users. Moreover, it automates routine tasks, reduces costs, and ensures data governance and compliance (Gad-Elrab, 2021). AI's ability to facilitate natural language interaction and provide real-time insights gives organizations a competitive edge, while its scalability accommodates growing data volumes. Additionally, data monetization opportunities arise, fostering innovation and adaptation within the organization's operations and strategies (Chen, 2022).

Table 2. Catalysts for success: The benefits of AI and BI integration

Reason for Combining AI and BI	Description
Enhanced Data Analysis	AI can analyze complex data faster and more accurately than traditional methods, uncovering valuable insights.
Predictive Analytics	AI empowers organizations to forecast future trends and make proactive decisions based on data-driven predictions.
Personalized Insights	AI tailors insights to individual users, enhancing the user experience and making data more relevant.
Automation of Routine Tasks	AI automates repetitive tasks such as data preparation and report generation, reducing the workload on human resources.
Improved Natural Language Interaction	AI makes data analysis accessible to non-technical users through natural language queries and responses
Real-time Insights	AI enables real-time data processing and analysis, allowing organizations to respond swiftly to changing circumstances.
Competitive Advantage	AI equips organizations with the ability to adapt rapidly to market shifts and trends, gaining a competitive edge.
Scalability	AI systems can scale seamlessly to handle growing data volumes, accommodating business growth.
Cost Savings	AI leads to significant cost savings by automating tasks, streamlining processes, and reducing manual errors
Data Governance and Compliance	AI ensures data quality and compliance with regulations, reducing the risk of data-related issues.
Data Monetization	AI-driven insights can be leveraged to create new revenue streams by offering data products or services.
Innovation and Adaptation	Combining AI and BI encourages experimentation, fosters innovation, and supports data-driven decision-making.

Source: Author compilation

AI VS. BI: UNVEILING DYNAMICS – DIFFERENCES, DISCOVERIES, SYNERGIES

In a corporate setting, business intelligence and artificial intelligence are becoming more and more important yet frequently misunderstood instruments. Business intelligence and artificial intelligence are currently popular trends with add-on features that give a platform that works (Edge, 2018). Both differ in a variety of qualities and abilities. The study and pattern of human thought serve as the foundation for artificial intelligence, and the algorithm mimics the workings of the human brain. Business intelligence, on the other hand, is actually technology that is utilized to improve business solution decisions (Figalist, 2022). AI (Artificial Intelligence) and BI (Business Intelligence) are two distinct yet interconnected domains that play pivotal roles in the world of data analysis and decision-making. AI focuses on the development of intelligent systems capable of simulating human-like thinking processes, automating tasks, and making complex decisions (Liebowitz, 2020). It relies on both historical and real-time data, harnessing machine learning algorithms to predict outcomes and continuously learn from patterns. In contrast, BI revolves around extracting meaningful insights and patterns from historical data, supporting informed business decisions through reports and visualizations. While AI excels in automation and prediction, BI primarily provides descriptive and diagnostic insights into past events. However, the true power emerges when these two fields synergize. Integrating AI into BI enhances predictive analytics and automation capabilities, making data-driven decision-making more accurate and efficient (Cao, 2020). Furthermore, BI aids in interpreting and communicating the results of AI models to non-technical stakeholders, facilitating a deeper understanding of AI-driven decisions. Together, AI and BI create a formidable data-driven ecosystem, enabling organizations to extract maximum value from their data while making well-informed choices for the future (Figalist, 2022).

Table 3 summarizes the key differences, discoveries, and potential synergies between AI and BI, providing a clear overview of their respective roles and how they can work together to leverage data for informed decision-making.

Table 3. Divergence and convergence: A comparative analysis of AI and BI

Aspect	Artificial Intelligence (AI)	Business Intelligence (BI)	Synergies
Definition and Purpose	Development of intelligent systems to simulate human-like thinking processes and automate tasks.	Use of data analysis tools to extract insights from historical data and facilitate informed decision-making.	Integrating AI to enhance predictive analytics and automation capabilities within BI.
Data Utilization	Relies on both historical and real-time data, using machine learning algorithms for analysis.	Primarily utilizes historical data for reporting and analysis purposes.	AI can improve BI's predictive capabilities by analyzing vast datasets.
Automation and Decision-Making	Excels in automation and complex decision-making through algorithms and learning.	Supports human decision-making by providing insights and information.	AI can automate routine BI tasks and enhance decision support.
Predictive Capabilities	Designed for predictive analytics, forecasting future trends and behaviors based on data patterns.	Primarily descriptive and diagnostic, explaining past events and their causes.	Combining AI's predictive power with BI's historical insights for more accurate forecasting.
User Interaction	Can interact conversationally with users through NLP and chatbots.	Often requires users to have technical expertise and relies on predefined reports.	AI can make BI tools more user-friendly and accessible.
Integration and Synergies	AI can enhance predictive analytics and data preparation within BI.	BI can help interpret and communicate AI results to non-technical stakeholders.	Combining AI and BI creates a powerful data-driven ecosystem.
Use Cases	Applications include NLP, computer vision, healthcare diagnostics, recommendation systems, etc.	Commonly used for financial reporting, sales analysis, marketing evaluation, supply chain optimization, etc.	AI and BI serve different but complementary roles in various industries and domains.

Source: Author compilation

ELEVATE YOUR BI GAME WITH AI ESSENTIALS

AI (Artificial Intelligence) has become increasingly important in the realm of Business Intelligence (BI) as it offers advanced capabilities for data analysis, prediction, and automation (Liebowitz, 2020). Here are some AI fundamentals that are crucial for leveraging AI in the context of Business Intelligence:

Data Quality and Preparation: AI's effectiveness in BI depends heavily on the quality of the data it analyzes. Clean, well-organized data is essential. Data preparation, including cleaning, transformation, and integration, is a fundamental step to ensure AI algorithms can operate effectively (Abusweilem, 2019).

Machine Learning Basics: Understanding the fundamentals of machine learning is vital for implementing AI in BI. This includes knowledge of algorithms such as regression, decision trees, clustering, and neural networks. Knowing when and how to apply these algorithms to different BI tasks is key (Cao, 2020).

Feature Engineering: Feature engineering involves selecting and transforming the right variables (features) in your dataset to make them suitable for AI algorithms. This skill is essential for creating predictive models and extracting meaningful insights from data (Doshi, 2023).

Model Training and Evaluation: AI models need to be trained on historical data and evaluated for their performance. Concepts like over fitting, under fitting, cross-validation, and model evaluation metrics (e.g., accuracy, precision, recall) are fundamental for assessing the quality of AI models (Doshi, 2023).

Data Visualization: Effective data visualization is essential for conveying AI-derived insights to business stakeholders. Understanding how to create informative charts, graphs, and dashboards is crucial for BI professionals working with AI (Chuah, 2022).

Natural Language Processing (NLP): In BI, NLP techniques can be employed to analyze and understand textual data, such as customer reviews, social media comments, or survey responses. NLP skills are valuable for extracting insights from unstructured data sources.

Deep Learning: While not always necessary, understanding deep learning, a subset of machine learning involving neural networks, can be beneficial for tackling complex BI problems like image recognition, voice recognition, and natural language understanding.

AI Tools and Frameworks: Familiarity with AI tools and frameworks like Python, Tens or Flow, PyTorch, scikit-learn, and libraries for data manipulation (e.g. pandas) are essential. These tools facilitate AI model development and deployment within BI environments (Chuah, 2022).

Ethical Considerations: Business intelligence professionals must be aware of ethical considerations when using AI. This includes understanding bias in AI models, data privacy regulations, and responsible AI practices (Abusweilem, 2019).

Continuous Learning: AI is a rapidly evolving field. Staying updated on the latest AI advancements, trends, and best practices is crucial for BI professionals to harness AI effectively for their organization's benefit.

Integration with BI Tools: Understanding how to integrate AI capabilities into existing BI tools and platforms is essential. Many BI tools are incorporating AI features, and knowing how to leverage them is a valuable skill.

Business Context: Finally, AI in BI should always be aligned with the organization's strategic goals and business objectives. Knowing how to identify relevant AI use cases that can drive business value is fundamental (Mehrotra, 2021).

TRANSFORMING INSIGHTS: THE JOURNEY OF AI INTEGRATION IN BUSINESS INTELLIGENCE

In the ever-evolving landscape of business intelligence (BI), organizations are increasingly turning to the transformative power of artificial intelligence (AI) to enhance their decision-making processes. The integration of AI and BI represents a monumental shift in how businesses extract value from their data, offering unprecedented opportunities for deeper insights, predictive analytics, and streamlined operations. This journey of AI integration into BI is not merely an option; it has become a strategic imperative for organizations striving to remain competitive in today's data-driven world (Doshi, 2023). The traditional realm of Business Intelligence primarily focused on collecting, processing, and presenting historical data to inform decision-making. While it undoubtedly served as a vital tool for businesses, it often fell short in providing real-time insights and predictive capabilities. AI, on the other hand, introduces a new dimension by enabling machines to learn from data, adapt to changing circumstances, and make informed predictions. By marrying the capabilities of AI and BI, organizations can bridge the gap between historical data analysis and forward-looking decision support (Mehrotra, 2021). One of the key differentiators between AI and BI is their approach to data analysis. Business Intelligence predominantly relies on predefined queries and structured data to generate reports and dashboards. AI, in contrast, leverages machine learning algorithms and natural language processing to analyze unstructured and complex data sources, including text, images, and voice. This capability opens the door to a wealth of untapped insights hidden within unstructured data, empowering organizations to make data-driven decisions with a more comprehensive view of their business landscape (Phillips-Wren, 2021).

Discoveries through AI integration in BI are not limited to historical patterns; they extend into the realm of predictive analytics. AI algorithms can analyze historical data to identify trends and make predictions about future outcomes. For example, in retail, AI can forecast demand for specific products based on historical sales data, seasonality, and external factors like weather patterns. Such predictive insights enable businesses to optimize inventory management, reduce costs, and meet customer demands more effectively (Ramakrishnan, 2020). The synergy between AI and BI extends further when it comes to personalization. AI algorithms can tailor insights and recommendations to individual users, creating a highly customized experience. Whether it's suggesting products to an online shopper, providing targeted marketing recommendations, or delivering real-time financial insights to a CFO, AI's ability to personalize information enhances user engagement and decision-making. Automation is another area where AI integration in BI yields significant benefits (v, 2021). Traditional BI processes often involve manual data extraction, transformation, and report generation, which can be time-consuming and error-prone. AI automates these routine tasks, allowing organizations to allocate human resources to more value-added activities, such as interpreting results and devising strategies based on AI-generated insights. Real-time insights are a fundamental requirement in today's fast-paced business environment, and AI integration in BI makes this possible. AI algorithms can process and analyze data in real time, enabling organizations to react swiftly to changing market conditions. For example, in financial services, AI-powered trading systems can make split-second decisions based on real-time market data to maximize returns and mitigate risks. Competitive advantage is at the core of AI integration in BI. Organizations that harness the power of AI to drive their BI processes can respond rapidly to market shifts and emerging trends, staying one step ahead of competitors (Nwanakwaugwu, 2023). By making data-driven decisions in real time and predicting future market dynamics, businesses can position themselves for success in an increasingly competitive landscape. The scalability of AI is a crucial asset for organizations experiencing data growth. As data volumes continue to expand, AI systems can seamlessly scale to handle massive datasets, ensuring that organizations can extract insights and value from their data regardless of its size (Ramakrishnan, 2020). While the benefits of AI integration in BI are significant, it's essential to recognize the role it plays in data governance and compliance. AI can help ensure data quality and adherence to regulatory requirements by identifying anomalies, discrepancies, and potential compliance issues within datasets. This not only mitigates risk but also enhances trust in the data used for decision-making. The integration of AI in BI is not merely about optimizing existing processes; it opens the door to new revenue streams and business models. Organizations can monetize AI-driven insights by offering data products or services to external customers, creating additional sources of income and expanding their market reach. Furthermore, the infusion of AI encourages a culture of innovation and adaptation within organizations. It empowers teams to experiment with data, test hypotheses, and uncover new opportunities for growth. This culture of data-driven innovation positions businesses to navigate the complex and ever-changing business landscape successfully. In conclusion, the journey of AI integration in Business Intelligence represents a transformative shift that holds the potential to revolutionize how organizations operate and make decisions (Figalist, 2022). The synergies between AI and BI enable enhanced data analysis, predictive analytics, personalization, automation, and real-time insights, ultimately leading to a competitive advantage in the market. Furthermore, AI-driven data governance, monetization, and innovation opportunities further solidify the case for organizations to embrace this integration as a strategic imperative in the pursuit of success in the data-driven age (Alghamdi, 2022).

CULTIVATING SUCCESS: CASE STUDIES AND INSIGHTS FROM AI IMPLEMENTATIONS IN RETAIL, HEALTHCARE, AND FINANCIAL SERVICES

Table 4 provides a concise overview of the case studies and key lessons learned from each successful AI implementation in the retail, healthcare, and financial services industries. In this table, we delve into illuminating case studies across the retail, healthcare, and financial services sectors, highlighting the objectives, AI implementations, and remarkable outcomes achieved. Case Study 1 in retail saw notable reductions in inventory costs alongside increased online sales, driven by AI-enabled demand forecasting, personalized recommendations, and dynamic pricing. Case Study 2 in healthcare revealed substantial improvements in patient care, including a 30% reduction in diagnostic errors, through AI applications in medical imaging, patient data analysis, and predictive analytics. Case Study 3 in financial services showcased remarkable gains in fraud detection accuracy, expedited customer support, and superior algorithmic trading strategies, all empowered by AI (Al-Okaily, 2022). Furthermore, the 'Lessons Learned' section imparts invaluable insights, emphasizing the significance of clear objectives, data quality, interdisciplinary collaboration, ethical considerations, ongoing learning, pilot projects, and user-centric design in ensuring the triumph of AI implementations across industries (Alghamdi, 2022)."

NAVIGATING THE FUTURE: AI AND BI AS GROWTH CATALYSTS

Driving business growth with the powerful synergy of AI (Artificial Intelligence) and BI (Business Intelligence) is no longer a luxury but a strategic imperative in today's fiercely competitive landscape. These two transformative technologies, when harnessed effectively, enable organizations to make data-driven decisions, optimize operations, and ultimately gain a significant competitive edge (Figalist, 2022).

At the core of this transformative synergy lies the ability to turn vast amounts of data into actionable insights. AI, with its advanced algorithms and machine learning capabilities, can automate data analysis processes, rapidly sift through terabytes of information, and identify patterns, anomalies, and trends that might elude human analysis. This automation not only accelerates decision-making but also ensures that these decisions are grounded in robust data. Moreover, AI facilitates predictive analytics, allowing businesses to forecast future trends, customer behavior, and demand (Al-Okaily, 2022). This is particularly invaluable in dynamic markets where agility and foresight can mean the difference between success and stagnation.

Table 4. AI success stories: Transformative case studies across industries

Case Study	Industry	Objective	AI Implementation	Results
Case Study 1	Retail	Enhance customer experience, optimize inventory, and increase sales	- Demand Forecasting: Improved demand forecasting with AI predictive analytics. – Personalized Recommendations: AI-driven product recommendations. – Dynamic Pricing: Real-time pricing optimization based on AI algorithms.	- 20% reduction in inventory costs. – 15% increase in online sales. – Significant improvement in customer satisfaction scores.
Case Study 2	Healthcare	Enhance patient care, streamline operations, and reduce costs	- Medical Imaging: AI for image analysis and diagnostics. – Patient Data Analysis: NLP for insights from unstructured records. – Predictive Analytics: AI models for disease outbreak predictions.	- 30% reduction in diagnostic errors. – 20% reduction in administrative workload. – Improved patient outcomes and satisfaction.
Case Study 3	Financial Services	Improve fraud detection, customer service, and operational efficiency	- Fraud Detection: Real-time fraud detection with AI algorithms. – Customer Support: Chatbots and virtual assistants. – Algorithmic Trading: AI-driven trading strategies.	- 25% improvement in fraud detection accuracy. – 50% faster customer support response times. – Outperformance in algorithmic trading strategies.
Lessons Learned	N/A	N/A	- Define clear objectives aligned with business goals. – Ensure high-quality data and preprocessing. – Foster cross-functional collaboration. – Address ethical concerns and compliance. – Invest in continuous learning. – Start with pilot projects and scale successful implementations. – Prioritize user experience and user-centric design.	- Successful AI implementations require strategic planning, data quality, collaboration, and ethical consideratio

Source: Author Compilation

AI also adds a layer of intelligence to data interpretation through natural language processing (NLP) and understanding (NLU). By enhancing the natural language interface, AI empowers non-technical users to query BI systems in everyday language, bridging the gap between data experts and decision-makers. Users can ask questions conversationally, enabling a wider array of stakeholders to access and interpret complex data, fostering a more informed and inclusive decision-making culture (Figalist, 2020).

Furthermore, AI can customize BI experiences by tailoring dashboards and reports to individual user preferences and needs. This personalization ensures that users receive the most relevant insights and data visualizations, increasing engagement and the utility of BI systems. Additionally, AI-driven recommendations and insights, based on users' historical interactions with the system, enhance the user experience further (Gad-Elrab, 2021).

In the realm of data visualization, AI contributes by suggesting the most appropriate chart types, color schemes, and even generating interactive visualizations automatically. This feature simplifies the interpretation of complex data, enabling users to grasp insights quickly and act upon them decisively. Real-time data processing is another vital contribution, allowing organizations to monitor key performance indicators (KPIs) and respond rapidly to changing conditions, thus enhancing operational efficiency.

AI's capabilities extend to anomaly detection, a crucial component of risk management and fraud prevention. By constantly monitoring data streams, AI algorithms can identify unusual patterns or outliers that may signify fraudulent activities, operational inefficiencies, or emerging risks. This proactive approach is pivotal in safeguarding an organization's financial stability and reputation. While AI primarily deals with data analysis and automation, BI complements this by providing the infrastructure and tools necessary for data storage, organization, and presentation (Figalist, 2020). Data warehouses centralize data, ensuring a single source of truth for the organization. They often employ data modeling techniques such as star or snowflake schemas, simplifying data retrieval and analysis. BI tools come into play by enabling users to query and analyze this data, generate reports, create dashboards, and perform ad-hoc analysis. These tools not only enhance the accessibility of data but also foster a culture of data-driven decision-making.

Data visualization within BI tools transforms data into meaningful and comprehensible formats, including charts, graphs, heat maps, and more (Tavera Romero, 2021). This visual storytelling aspect is critical in conveying complex information effectively and facilitating quicker and more informed decision-making. Interactive dashboards allow users to explore data, drill down into details, and gain insights in real-time, thus democratizing data analysis within the organization.

Crucially, BI frameworks also address data governance and security concerns, ensuring data accuracy, quality, and compliance with regulatory requirements (Vodithala, 2023). They implement robust security measures such as access controls and encryption to protect sensitive information from unauthorized access and breaches, preserving data integrity and trust.

To fully realize the potential of AI and BI in driving business growth, organizations must not only invest in cutting-edge technologies but also nurture a data-driven culture. This cultural shift requires fostering collaboration between data experts and business decision-makers, promoting data literacy across the organization, and ensuring that data ethics and privacy considerations remain paramount (Gad-Elrab, 2021).

In conclusion, the intersection of AI and BI represents a formidable force for business growth. By combining AI's data analysis, automation, and predictive capabilities with BI's data infrastructure, reporting, and visualization tools, organizations can unlock deeper insights, make data-driven decisions, and navigate the ever-evolving business landscape with confidence. This transformative synergy empowers businesses to not only survive but thrive in today's data-driven era, where strategic decisions and competitive advantages are forged through data intelligence and innovation (Reuille-Dupont, 2023).

DISCUSSION

In unraveling the intricate landscape of AI and BI convergence within the realm of business, "Synergizing Success: Harnessing AI-Infused Business Intelligence to Propel Exponential Business Growth" initiates a profound discussion that explores the transformative synergy between these technological powerhouses. The chapter delves into the nuanced integration of AI with BI, acting as a catalytic force driving expansion in the digital era. Contextualizing this union, the discussion navigates through the shifting paradigms of decision-making, wherein AI's predictive capabilities harmoniously intertwine with BI's analytical tools, presenting a comprehensive and holistic perspective. At the core of this exploration are strategic blueprints that meticulously underpin the integration of AI and BI, outlining systematic approaches from the acquisition of data to its strategic deployment. Real-world cases serve as beacons, illuminating the symbiotic relationship between AI and BI in practical scenarios. Amid this discourse, strategic considerations emerge as guiding principles, aligning objectives and optimizing value in the ever-evolving business landscape. The chapter accentuates not only the potential but also the strategic urgency of AI-BI integration, advocating for imperative investments in AI, the cultivation of a data-centric culture, and fostering collaboration. Through a detailed examination of AI-infused BI applications, the discussion proudly highlights tangible real-world advantages while fearlessly confronting the challenges associated with data alignment. Ultimately, the chapter serves as a catalyst for empowerment, offering a roadmap for leaders, managers, and technologists to architect the synergy between AI and BI. In doing so, it encourages a paradigm shift, redefining success within industries that are continuously evolving. By embracing data as the compass, the discussion charts a course toward prosperity, innovation, and sustainable growth, paving the way for a future where AI and BI work in unison to shape the destiny of businesses.

FUTURE RESEARCH DIRECTIONS

In the realm of advancing business frontiers, the future work for "Synergizing Success: Harnessing AI-Infused Business Intelligence to Propel Exponential Business Growth" envisions a continued exploration of cutting-edge advancements. Further research could delve into refining and optimizing the integration of AI and Business Intelligence, exploring emerging technologies, and adapting strategies to evolving market dynamics. In-depth analyses of industry-specific applications and novel use cases would contribute to a deeper understanding of the symbiotic relationship between AI and BI, paving the way for customized solutions. Additionally, exploring ethical considerations, regulatory frameworks, and the societal impact of AI-infused BI systems will be imperative. Collaborative efforts across interdisciplinary domains and fostering a culture of continuous innovation will undoubtedly be crucial in shaping the future landscape of synergized success in the business realm. Future trends and emerging technologies in harnessing AI-infused Business Intelligence (BI) to propel exponential business growth are exciting and hold immense potential for organizations looking to stay competitive and innovative (Tavera Romero, 2021). Here are some key developments to watch for:

AI-Driven Automation of Business Processes: AI-powered process automation will extend beyond data analysis to streamline entire business operations. Robotic Process Automation (RPA) combined with AI will optimize workflows, reducing manual tasks and boosting efficiency. (Vodithala, 2023).

AI-Powered Data Governance and Compliance: AI will play a central role in maintaining data quality, ensuring compliance with regulations, and managing data privacy. Automated data governance tools will help organizations track and control data access, use, and security (Al Khuwaiter, 2023).

AI-Enhanced Natural Language Understanding: Natural Language Processing (NLP) will continue to advance, making it easier for users to interact with data through conversational interfaces (Reuille-Dupont, 2023). **AI-Powered Predictive Analytics for Customer Retention:**

AI will enable predictive and prescriptive analytics models that can anticipate customer behaviors, such as churn or purchasing trends (Azmat, 2023).

AI-Enhanced Data Visualization and Storytelling: AI-driven data visualization tools will create dynamic and interactive visualizations that adapt to user preferences. Automated data storytelling will help users interpret complex data, enabling faster decision-mking (Salisu, 2021).

Quantum Computing and Advanced Analytics: As quantum computing matures, it will unlock new possibilities for complex data analysis, optimization, and simulations (Mosavi, 2022). Organizations will explore quantum algorithms to solve previously intractable BI problems, such as supply chain optimization or drug discovery.

AI-Enabled Decision Experimentation: AI-driven A/B testing and experimentation will allow organizations to rapidly test and refine decisions, products, and strategies (Arefin, 2021). Continuous experimentation will become a core business practice, driving innovation and growth.

AI for Sustainable Business Practices: AI will play a pivotal role in sustainability efforts, helping organizations optimize resource usage, reduce waste, and lower their environmental footprint. Sustainability-focused AI analytics will inform eco-friendly product design and supply chain management (Mosavi, 2022).

STRATEGIES TO SURMOUNT OBSTACLES AND MAXIMIZE AI-INFUSED BI POTENTIAL

Harnessing the full potential of AI-infused Business Intelligence (BI) to drive exponential business growth is a compelling ambition, but it's not without its share of challenges. Organizations embarking on this transformative journey must strategically navigate these obstacles to maximize the benefits of AI and BI integration (Vodithala, 2023).

One of the foremost challenges is data quality and integration. Often, organizations grapple with data residing in silos, across various departments and systems. To address this, they need to invest in robust data integration solutions that can harmonize data from disparate sources, transforming it into a consistent format. Implementing data governance practices is equally essential to ensure data accuracy and quality, laying a solid foundation for AI-driven analysis (Al-Okaily, 2020).

Another significant hurdle is the availability of talent. Skilled professionals in AI and BI are in high demand, making recruitment a competitive endeavor (Azmat, 2023). To surmount this challenge, organizations should proactively seek out data scientists, data analysts, and AI specialists. Additionally, providing continuous training and up skilling opportunities for existing staff is crucial to bridge the skills gap and ensure that the workforce is well-equipped to harness the full potential of AI-infused BI tools and technologies (Analytics, 2023).

Scalable infrastructure is paramount as data volumes continue to burgeon. Organizations must ensure that their IT infrastructure can seamlessly accommodate increased workloads. Cloud-based solutions often provide the flexibility and scalability needed without significant upfront investments in hardware (Salisu, 2021). A scalable infrastructure ensures that AI-infused BI systems can efficiently process and analyze large datasets, delivering timely insights.

Data privacy and security concerns are another significant challenge. With regulatory requirements like GDPR and CCPA, organizations must ensure strict compliance to avoid legal repercussions (Tumpa, 2020). Establishing a robust security framework that includes encryption, access controls, and comprehensive auditing is essential for safeguarding sensitive data. Additionally, ethical considerations must be central to AI model design to guarantee responsible data usage.

Cultural resistance to AI-infused BI can hamper adoption efforts. Change management strategies are essential to address this challenge. Organizations should foster a culture that embraces data-driven decision-making, with leaders championing the use of AI and BI. Employees must be educated about the benefits and value these technologies bring to their roles, fostering transparency in decision-making processes to build trust in AI recommendations (Rathore, 2022).

Setting clear business objectives is fundamental to AI-infused BI success. Organizations must define specific, measurable goals and Key Performance Indicators (KPIs) aligned with their growth strategies.

AI and BI initiatives should directly contribute to achieving these objectives, whether it's enhancing customer retention, optimizing supply chains, or boosting revenue.

Continuous monitoring and optimization are critical as AI and BI systems are dynamic and require ongoing attention. Regularly assessing the performance of AI models and BI dashboards ensures that insights remain accurate and relevant. Establishing feedback loops helps iterate on models and improve predictive capabilities over time, enhancing the value they deliver.

User-centric design is imperative in ensuring the usability and effectiveness of BI dashboards and AI-powered interfaces (Popescu, 2022). These tools should be intuitive, user-friendly, and tailored to meet the specific needs of different roles within the organization. Providing comprehensive training and support for users ensures that they can effectively leverage these tools to make informed decisions. Data democratization is essential to maximize AI-infused BI potential. By providing access to data and insights to a wide range of employees, not just data specialists, organizations can promote informed decision-making at all levels (Rathore, 2022). Self-service BI tools and natural language interfaces empower non-technical users to explore data independently, democratizing access to information (Al-Okaily, 2023). Last but not least, measuring the Return on Investment (ROI) of AI-infused BI initiatives is vital. Tracking the impact on key metrics, such as revenue growth, cost savings, and customer satisfaction, provides a clear understanding of ROI (Vodithala, 2023). This data-driven evaluation helps justify ongoing investments in AI and BI, demonstrating their tangible contributions to business growth.

In conclusion, the journey to harnessing AI-infused Business Intelligence for exponential business growth is rife with challenges, but with a strategic approach, they can be surmounted. Addressing data quality, talent, infrastructure, security, culture, objectives, monitoring, user experience, data democratization, and ROI measurement is essential. By doing so, organizations can unlock the transformative potential of AI-infused BI, leveraging data-driven insights to fuel innovation, competitiveness, and success in the digital age (Wolniak, 2023).

CONCLUSION

Applications and businesses that leverage human intellect for basic functionality are based on artificial intelligence. The symbol structure and symbolic operations that are typically used in digital computers can be derived from human intelligence. Business intelligence focuses on managing reports and using data mining and data warehousing techniques to analyze data. Business intelligence is used by the firm to acquire actionable insight from the data. The selection of the appropriate module for application development employing business intelligence, artificial intelligence, or both must be made after analyzing the requirements. In conclusion, artificial intelligence allows us to view our data in a way that will be useful to us rather than being overwhelmed by its bulk. AI enables you to truly use your data to your competitive advantage by analyzing all the gathered data and providing real-time recommendations. Utilizing AI will enable you to maximize the value of the data you gather, spot additional trends, develop suggested actions based on those trends, and make sure that these actions and any relevant context are provided to your end customers at the precise time and location they require it. Although AI, like any technology, undoubtedly has some drawbacks, most notably in terms of innate bias or cyber security, the potential advantages are vast. Despite this, a lot of businesses are still catching up when it comes to realizing the potential of AI for business analytics and insight. Businesses that start implementing AI will quickly surpass their rivals in terms of better overall business performance and more revenue. In conclusion, the integration of AI into Business Intelligence represents a potent catalyst for exponential business growth. By synergizing these technologies, organizations unlock the power of data-driven decision-making, predictive insights, and streamlined operations. These case studies vividly illustrate the transformative impact across diverse industries, from retail's inventory optimization and healthcare's patient care enhancement to financial services' fraud detection prowess. The insights gleaned from these implementations underscore the importance of strategic planning, data quality, cross-functional collaboration, ethical considerations, continuous learning, and user-centric design in navigating the AI landscape successfully. As businesses embrace this dynamic fusion of AI and BI, they position themselves to thrive in a rapidly evolving, data-centric world, propelling them toward unparalleled success.

REFERENCES

Abusweilem, M., & Abualoush, S. (2019). The impact of knowledge management process and business intelligence on organizational performance. *Management Science Letters, 9*(12), 2143–2156. doi:10.5267/j.msl.2019.6.020

Ahmad, H., & Mustafa, H. (2022). The impact of artificial intelligence, big data analytics and business intelligence on transforming capability and digital transformation in Jordanian telecommunication firms. *International Journal of Data and Network Science, 6*(3), 727–732. doi:10.5267/j.ijdns.2022.3.009

Al Khuwaiter, M., AlKaabi, N., AlOlama, R., El Khatib, M., & AlAmiri, S. (2023). Managing Outsourcing in IT Software Services-A study of 3 Perspectives and 3 Industries in UAE. *International Journal of Business Analytics and Security, 3*(1), 103–124. doi:10.54489/ijbas.v3i1.206

Al-Okaily, A., Al-Okaily, M., Teoh, A. P., & Al-Debei, M. M. (2023). An empirical study on data warehouse systems effectiveness: The case of Jordanian banks in the business intelligence era. *EuroMed Journal of Business, 18*(4), 489–510. doi:10.1108/EMJB-01-2022-0011

Al-Okaily, A., Teoh, A. P., & Al-Okaily, M. (2023). Evaluation of data analytics-oriented business intelligence technology effectiveness: An enterprise-level analysis. *Business Process Management Journal, 29*(3), 777–800. doi:10.1108/BPMJ-10-2022-0546

Alghamdi, N. A., & Al-Baity, H. H. (2022). Augmented Analytics Driven by AI: A Digital Transformation beyond Business Intelligence. *Sensors (Basel), 22*(20), 8071. doi:10.3390/s22208071 PMID:36298421

Analytics, I. (2023). *India's own Cloud Service Providers*. Academic Press.

Arefin, M. S., Hoque, M. R., & Rasul, T. (2021). Organizational learning culture and business intelligence systems of health-care organizations in an emerging economy. *Journal of Knowledge Management, 25*(3), 573–594. doi:10.1108/JKM-09-2019-0517

Azmat, F., Lim, W. M., Moyeen, A., Voola, R., & Gupta, G. (2023). Convergence of business, innovation, and sustainability at the tipping point of the sustainable development goals. *Journal of Business Research, 167*, 114170. doi:10.1016/j.jbusres.2023.114170

Bharadiya, J. P. (2022). Driving business growth with artificial intelligence and business intelligence. *International Journal of Computer Science and Technology, 6*(4), 28–44.

Bharadiya, J. P. (2023). A comparative study of business intelligence and artificial intelligence with big data analytics. *American Journal of Artificial Intelligence*, *7*(1), 24. doi:10.11648/j.ajai.20230701.14

Cao, L., Zhang, C., & Liu, J. (2020). Ontology-based integration of business intelligence. *Web Intelligence and Agent Systems: An International Journal*, *4*(3), 313–325.

Chen, H., Chiang, R. H., & Storey, V. C. (2022). Business intelligence and analytics: From big data to big impact. *Management Information Systems Quarterly*, 1165–1188.

Chen, Y., & Lin, Z. (2021). Business intelligence capabilities and firm performance: A study in China. *International Journal of Information Management*, *57*, 102232. doi:10.1016/j.ijinfomgt.2020.102232

Chuah, M. H., & Wong, K. L. (2012). Construct an enterprise business intelligence maturity model (EBI2M) using an integration approach: A conceptual framework. *Business Intelligence-Solution for Business Development*, 1-12.

Doshi, R., Hiran, K. K., Mijwil, M. M., & Anand, D. (2023). To That of Artificial Intelligence, Passing Through Business Intelligence. In *Handbook of Research on AI and Knowledge Engineering for Real-Time Business Intelligence* (pp. 1–16). IGI Global. doi:10.4018/978-1-6684-6519-6.ch001

Edge, D., Larson, J., & White, C. (2018, April). Bringing AI to BI: enabling visual analytics of unstructured data in a modern Business Intelligence platform. In Extended abstracts of the 2018 CHI conference on human factors in computing systems (pp. 1-9). doi:10.1145/3170427.3174367

Figalist, I., Elsner, C., Bosch, J., & Olsson, H. H. (2020, August). Breaking the Vicious Circle: Why AI for software analytics and business intelligence does not take off in practice. In *2020 46th Euromicro Conference on Software Engineering and Advanced Applications (SEAA)* (pp. 5-12). IEEE. 10.1109/SEAA51224.2020.00013

Figalist, I., Elsner, C., Bosch, J., & Olsson, H. H. (2022). Breaking the vicious circle: A case study on why AI for software analytics and business intelligence does not take off in practice. *Journal of Systems and Software*, *184*, 111135. doi:10.1016/j.jss.2021.111135

Figalist, I., Elsner, C., Bosch, J., & Olsson, H. H. (2022). Breaking the vicious circle: A case study on why AI for software analytics and business intelligence does not take off in practice. *Journal of Systems and Software*, *184*, 111135. doi:10.1016/j.jss.2021.111135

Fitriana, R., Eriyatno, T. D., & Djatna, T. (2021). Progress in Business Intelligence System research: A literature review. *International Journal of Basic & Applied Sciences IJBAS-IJENS*, *11*(03), 118503–6464.

Gad-Elrab, A. A. (2021). Modern business intelligence: Big data analytics and artificial intelligence for creating the data-driven value. *E-Business-Higher Education and Intelligence Applications, 135.*

Jain, A., Shah, D., & Churi, P. (2020). A Review on Business Intelligence Systems Using Artificial Intelligence. In S. Smys, J. Tavares, V. Balas, & A. Iliyasu (Eds.), *Computational Vision and Bio-Inspired Computing. ICCVBIC 2019. Advances in Intelligent Systems and Computing* (Vol. 1108). Springer. doi:10.1007/978-3-030-37218-7_107

Kaushik, P. (2022). Role and Application of Artificial Intelligence in Business Analytics: A Critical Evaluation. *International Journal for Global Academic & Scientific Research, 1*(3), 1-11. doi:10.55938/ijgasr.v1i3.15

Keikhosrokiani, P. (2022). Handbook of Research on Consumer Behavior Change and Data Analytics in the Socio-Digital Era. doi:10.4018/978-1-6684-4168-8

Keikhosrokiani, P., & Asl, M. P. (2022a). Handbook of Research on Artificial Intelligence Applications in Literary Works and Social Media. doi:10.4018/978-1-6684-6242-3

Keikhosrokiani, P., & Asl, M. P. (2022b). Preface. In Handbook of Research on Artificial Intelligence Applications in Literary Works and Social Media. Academic Press.

Keikhosrokiani, P., & Asl, M. P. (2022c). *Handbook of research on opinion mining and text analytics on literary works and social media*. IGI Global. doi:10.4018/978-1-7998-9594-7

Keikhosrokiani, P., & Fye, G. M. (2023). A hybrid recommender system for health supplement e-commerce based on customer data implicit ratings. *Multimedia Tools and Applications*. Advance online publication. doi:10.1007/s11042-023-17321-6

Kng, C. K., Keikhosrokiani, P., & Asl, M. P. (2022). Artificial intelligence and human rights activism: A case study of Boochani's No Friend But the Mountains and his tweets on justice and equality. Handbook of Research on Artificial Intelligence Applications in Literary Works and Social Media. doi:10.4018/978-1-6684-6242-3.ch006

Liebowitz, J. (2020). *Strategic intelligence: business intelligence, competitive intelligence, and knowledge management*. CRC Press.

Mehrotra, P. (2021). Applications of Artificial Intelligence in the Realm of Business Intelligence. In *Research Anthology on Artificial Intelligence Applications in Security* (pp. 358–386). IGI Global. doi:10.4018/978-1-7998-7705-9.ch018

Mohammad, A. B., Al-Okaily, M., & Al-Majali, M. (2022). Business intelligence and analytics (BIA) usage in the banking industry sector: An application of the TOE framework. *Journal of Open Innovation, 8*(4), 189. doi:10.3390/joitmc8040189

Mosavi, N. S., & Santos, M. F. (2022). Implementation considerations for the applied business intelligence in health care. In *Advances in Decision Science and Management: Proceedings of Third International Conference on Decision Science and Management (ICDSM 2021)* (pp. 183-189). Springer Singapore. 10.1007/978-981-16-2502-2_19

Nguyen, D. K., Sermpinis, G., & Stasinakis, C. (2023). Big data, artificial intelligence and machine learning: A transformative symbiosis in favour of financial technology. *European Financial Management, 29*(2), 517–548. doi:10.1111/eufm.12365

Nwanakwaugwu, A. C., Matthew, U. O., Kazaure, A. A., & Haruna, K. (2023). Data Mining Business Intelligence Applications in Retail Services Using Artificial Neural Networks. In *Handbook of Research on Cybersecurity Risk in Contemporary Business Systems* (pp. 186–210). IGI Global. doi:10.4018/978-1-6684-7207-1.ch010

Pal, K. (2023). A Review of Big Data Analytics for the Internet of Things Applications in Supply Chain Management. *Applied AI and Multimedia Technologies for Smart Manufacturing and CPS Applications*, 221-245. doi:10.4018/978-1-7998-7852-0.ch005

Phillips-Wren, G., Daly, M., & Burstein, F. (2021). Reconciling business intelligence, analytics and decision support systems: More data, deeper insight. *Decision Support Systems*, *146*, 113560. doi:10.1016/j.dss.2021.113560

Popescu, G. H., Valaskova, K., & Horak, J. (2022). Augmented reality shopping experiences, retail business analytics, and machine vision algorithms in the virtual economy of the metaverse. *Journal of Self-Governance and Management Economics*, *10*(2), 67–81.

Ramakrishnan, T., Kathuria, A., & Saldanha, T. J. (2020). Business intelligence and analytics (BI&A) capabilities in healthcare. In Theory and Practice of Business Intelligence in Healthcare (pp. 1-17). IGI Global. DOI: doi:10.4018/978-1-7998-2310-0.ch00

Rana, N. P., Chatterjee, S., Dwivedi, Y. K., & Akter, S. (2022). Understanding dark side of artificial intelligence (AI) integrated business analytics: Assessing firm's operational inefficiency and competitiveness. *European Journal of Information Systems*, *31*(3), 364–387. doi:10.1080/0960085X.2021.1955628

Rathore, P. S., & Sharma, B. K. (2022). Improving healthcare delivery system using business intelligence. *Journal of IoT in Social, Mobile, Analytics, and Cloud*, *4*(1), 11–23. doi:10.36548/jismac.2022.1.002

Reuille-Dupont, J. (2023). *The Power of Algorithms and Big Data: A Marketing Perspective on Consumer Manipulation in Business*. Academic Press.

Salisu, I., Bin Mohd Sappri, M., & Bin Omar, M. F. (2021). The adoption of business intelligence systems in small and medium enterprises in the healthcare sector: A systematic literature review. *Cogent Business & Management*, *8*(1), 1935663. doi:10.1080/23311975.2021.1935663

Sechi, G. M., Migliori, M., Dassi, G., Pagliosa, A., Bonora, R., Oradini-Alacreu, A., ... Team, R. (2020). Business Intelligence applied to Emergency Medical Services in the Lombardy region during SARS-CoV-2 epidemic. *Acta Biomedica*, *91*(2), 39. doi:10.2196/preprints.19062 PMID:32420923

Suhendra, N. H. B., Keikhosrokiani, P., Asl, M. P., & Zhao, X. (2022). Opinion Mining and Text Analytics of Literary Reader Responses: A Case Study of Reader Responses to KL Noir Volumes in Goodreads Using Sentiment Analysis and Topic. In P. Keikhosrokiani & M. Pourya Asl (Eds.), *Handbook of Research on Opinion Mining and Text Analytics on Literary Works and Social Media* (pp. 191–239). IGI Global. doi:10.4018/978-1-7998-9594-7.ch009

Tamang, M. D., Shukla, V. K., Anwar, S., & Punhani, R. (2021, April). Improving business intelligence through machine learning algorithms. In *2021 2nd International Conference on Intelligent Engineering and Management (ICIEM)* (pp. 63-68). IEEE. 10.1109/ICIEM51511.2021.9445344

Tavera Romero, C. A., Ortiz, J. H., Khalaf, O. I., & Ríos Prado, A. (2021). Business intelligence: Business evolution after industry 4.0. *Sustainability (Basel)*, *13*(18), 10026. doi:10.3390/su131810026

Tong-On, P., Siripipatthanakul, S., & Phayaphrom, B. (2021). The implementation of business intelligence using data analytics and its effects towards on performance in the hotel industry in Thailand. *International Journal of Behavioral Analytics*, *1*(2).

Tumpa, Z. N., Saifuzzaman, M., Rabby, S. F., Crearie, L., & Stansfield, M. (2020, December). *Understanding business intelligence in the context of mental healthcare sector of Bangladesh for improving health services. In 2020 IEEE 8th R10 Humanitarian Technology Conference (R10-HTC)*. IEEE.

Vodithala, S., & Bhukya, R. (2023). A Novel Political Optimizer-Based Feature Selection with an Optimal Machine Learning Model for Financial Crisis Prediction. *International Journal of Cooperative Information Systems, 2350020*. Advance online publication. doi:10.1142/S021884302350020X

Waliszewski, K., & Warchlewska, A. (2020). Attitudes towards artificial intelligence in the area of personal financial planning: A case study of selected countries. *Entrepreneurship and Sustainability Issues*, *8*(2), 399–420. doi:10.9770/jesi.2020.8.2(24)

Wolniak, R., & Grebski, W. (2023). Functioning of predictive analytics in business. Silesian University of Technology Scientific Papers. Organization and Management Series, 175, 631-649. doi:10.29119/1641-3466.2023.175.40

Xian, Z., Keikhosrokiani, P. XinYing, C., & Li, Z. (2022). An RFM Model Using K-Means Clustering to Improve Customer Segmentation and Product Recommendation. In P. Keikhosrokiani (Ed.), Handbook of Research on Consumer Behavior Change and Data Analytics in the Socio-Digital Era (pp. 124–145). IGI Global. doi:10.4018/978-1-6684-4168-8.ch006

Zainol, A. F., Keikhosrokiani, P., Asl, M. P., & Anuar, N. A. N. (2022). Artificial intelligence applications in literary works: Emotion extraction and classification of Mohsin Hamid's Moth Smoke. Handbook of Research on Artificial Intelligence Applications in Literary Works and Social Media. doi:10.4018/978-1-6684-6242-3.ch005

Zhao, X., & Keikhosrokiani, P. (2022). Sales prediction and product recommendation model through user behavior analytics. *Computers, Materials & Continua*, *70*(2), 3855–3874. Advance online publication. doi:10.32604/cmc.2022.019750

KEY TERMS AND DEFINITIONS

AI (Artificial Intelligence): AI is the simulation of human intelligence processes by machines, particularly computer systems. It involves tasks such as learning, reasoning, problem-solving, and decision-making. In the context of BI, AI is employed to analyze data, predict outcomes, and generate actionable insights.

Business Intelligence (BI): BI refers to the technologies, processes, and strategies used to collect, analyze, and present business data for informed decision-making. It encompasses tools, software, and practices that transform raw data into meaningful insights.

Data-Driven Decision-Making: Data-driven decision-making is the practice of basing business decisions on empirical evidence and data analysis rather than intuition or gut feeling. It involves using data to inform and validate strategic choices.

Exponential Business Growth: Exponential business growth signifies a rapid and sustained increase in a company's revenue, market share, or profitability over a relatively short period. It often involves significant expansion and scaling of operations.

Predictive Analytics: Predictive analytics is the process of using historical data and statistical algorithms to forecast future trends, behaviors, or outcomes. In the context of BI, it involves AI-driven models for predicting various aspects of business operations.

Synergy: Synergy refers to the combined or cooperative effect of AI and Business Intelligence (BI), where their integration produces results greater than the sum of their individual capabilities. It represents the synergy achieved by leveraging AI's predictive and analytical abilities within the framework of BI for enhanced decision-making.

Chapter 6
Software Engineering Approach for Designing Apparel Business Data Analytics

Kamalendu Pal
https://orcid.org/0000-0001-7158-6481
University of London, UK

ABSTRACT

Apparel products are essential for any society, and its business operations are extensively competitive. The ability to optimize serving business processes while satisfying customer expectations has never been more critical than in today's globalized business world. Therefore, managing and channeling business operational data to work towards customer delight and generate healthy profits is essential to survive prosperously. Practitioners are highlighting the benefits of retail data analytics that are now being applied at every stage of the business process - tracking emerging popular products, forecasting sales, and future demand through predictive intelligence by using intelligent techniques. The chapter focuses on big data analytics software systems, their testing, and quality assurance-related issues in Hadoop, an open-source framework. It discusses challenges concerning massively parallel data generation from multiple sources, data characterization, software application quality factors, and some software testing mechanisms.

INTRODUCTION

James Madison wrote in the Federalist 51 article: "If men were angels, no government would be necessary". Madison was the founding father of the American Constitution. Suppose he had lived in today's industrious world, where every aspect of industrial work practices involves directly or indirectly monitoring, collecting information, and producing decision-making guidance for specific purposes using software applications—commonly known as "Big Data Analytics". Madison might have written in that case: "If software developers of big data analytics were angels, software testing and debugging would be unnecessary". Unfortunately, mistakes are common among most big data analytics developers, and

DOI: 10.4018/979-8-3693-1210-0.ch006

many of them require assistance when designing and writing data analytics software. These errors must be identified and corrected, which is known as software testing and has been around since the inception of computer programs. Complex systems with various domain-specific requirements are continuously being explored by researchers to further advance software design and development (Pal, 2020) (Fitzgerald et al., 2011). The success of a system is dependent on quality results at each stage of development, making superior software development a critical aspect of success (Pal & Karakostas, 2020) (Pal, 2019) (Pal & Williams, 2021). This chapter aims to provide a fundamental comprehension of data analytics software testing in the context of the apparel industry.

Figure 1. Diagrammatic representation of apparel product sales activities

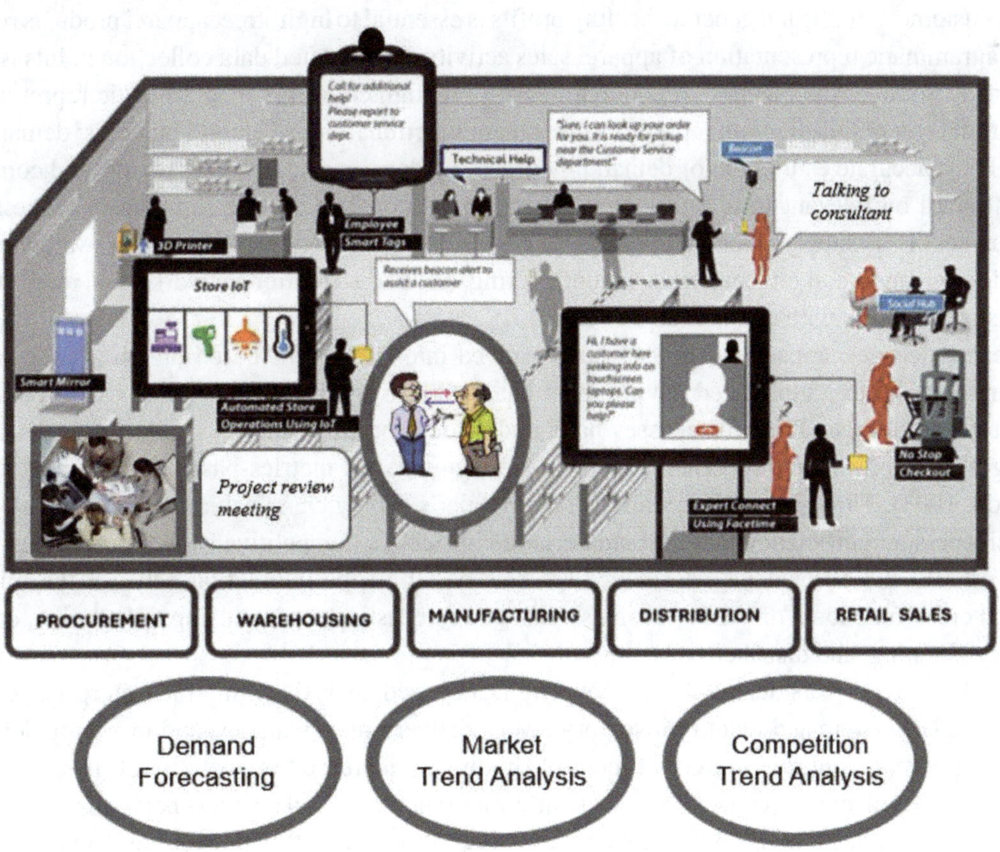

Apparel The demand for ready-to-wear garments has increased tremendously in recent years, leading to a surge in the apparel manufacturing industry. Mass production has reduced the cost of apparel and ensured consistent quality. The apparel industry is a complex combination of textile and garment production, with an extensive range of products to cater to people's diverse requirements.

The industry's success now hinges on cost competitiveness, which has led to the emergence of a post-industrial production system that focuses on mass-customized, low-volume production. In order to achieve supply chain efficiency, advanced technologies like just-in-time delivery, vendor-managed inventory, and third-party logistics are being implemented to improve manufacturing processes and drive cost efficiency.

The apparel industry's technological advancements include computer-aided designing and pattern making, fit analysis software, three-dimensional (3D) scanning technology, automation and robotics, integration of wearable technology, biomimetics, artificial intelligence, and advanced material transport systems. The requirement now is that the industry embrace all these technologies with open arms by being creative enough to design innovative products, introduce new materials and processes, and have flexibility in manufacturing by following proper supply chain practices. However, the apparel manufacturing process engineering (Sinclair, 2011) is beyond the scope of this chapter. The main objective of this chapter is to discuss some of the issues related to apparel manufacturing business automation. In particular, managing, and channelling business processes generated data, as shown in Figure 1, to work towards customer delight and generate healthy profits is essential to high street apparel products retailers.

A diagrammatic representation of apparel sales activities and related data collection points is shown in Figure 1. Some of the business functionalities are highlighted in this diagrammatic representation. The bottom layer of this diagram represents three main functionalities of a retail business: demand forecasting helps accurate estimation of demand by accessing data on sales, market trends, and competitor analysis based on relevant local and global economic factors. The central component of the apparel retail business is its supply chain operations that consist of raw materials procurement, warehousing of finished, semi-finest and raw materials, manufacturing, use of distribution networks, and retail stores to sell finished products with augmented services.

In recent decades, apparel businesses have evolved into new forms based on knowledge and networks in response to a globalized environment characterized by indistinct organizational boundaries and fast-paced change. These businesses have understood the importance of enforcing performance tracking of the goals defined by their corporate strategy through metrics-based management (Kaplan & Norton, 1993). The strategic fit requires that a retailer's supply chain achieves the balance between responsiveness and efficiency that best supports the business's competitive strategy. A supply chain's responsiveness and efficiency performance are best based on the interaction between the following logistical cross-functional drivers of business: demand forecasting, warehousing, scheduling, delivery, inventory planning, and distribution.

These business drivers deal with real-time Big Data-based analysis within the Enterprise Resource Planning (ERP) system and identify inventory levels, delivery miss-matches, and incoming deliveries. Scheduling plays a vital role in SCM. It could help directly increase the visibility of inventory levels, demand, and manufacturing capacity, consequently, more accurate retail business performance. Academics and practitioners are highlighting the benefits of retail operational data, and big data analytics are now being used at every stage of the business process - tracking emerging popular products, forecasting sales and future demand through predictive intelligence, optimizing product production cost and related price offers via customer heat-mapping and many other intelligent techniques.

In addition to this, identifying the customers likely to be interested in particular products and related service types based on their previous purchase behaviours, working out the appropriate way to tackle them through focused targeted marketing methods, and finally working out what to sell them next is what forms the main agenda of retail data analytics. The data analytic systems are designed by individuals who follow well-defined engineering approaches to problem-solving. They include software engineering models, processes, project management, requirements, and tools. Software engineering can be divided into sub-disciplines: software requirements, design, construction, testing, and maintenance (Holcombe,

2008). Today, most big data analytics systems are oriented toward retail and sales industries. Fundamentally, software engineering is concerned with all aspects of software production, including scientific and technological knowledge, methods, design, implementation, testing, and software documentation (Fitzgerald et al., 2011) (Holcombe, 2008) (Lim, 2010).

Big data analytics software development is a research area that provides insights to improve product deliveries and processes. Many studies, data sources, and mining methods have been used. The systematic literature review aims to provide a combined view of the relevant studies on Software Development Analytics in the past decade, emphasizing its application in practical settings. It is worth extracting a set of characteristics (study type, data source, study agenda, development life-cycle activities, stakeholders, mining methods, and analytics scope) and classifying their impact against a taxonomy. The essential data sources, study types, and stakeholders are source code repositories, exploratory case studies, and software developers. Testers also get moderate attention from researchers. Product managers' concerns are being addressed frequently, and project managers are also present but with less prevalence. Mining methods are rapidly evolving, as reflected in their identified long list. Descriptive statistics is the most common method, followed by correlation analysis. Software development is vital in every organization; finding that process mining was present in only one study was unexpected. Time management and cost control were less prevalent. The analysis of security aspects is even more reduced; however, evidence suggests it is an increasing topic of concern. Risk management contributions are also scarce. There is a vast improvement margin for software development analytics in practice. For example, mining and analyzing the activities performed by software developers in their actual case tools (i.e., IDEs). Together with mining developers' behaviours, based on the evidence and trends.

In this way, sharing business operational information enhances customer services and financial performance by offering correct and relevant real-time information. It also improves the supply chain's operational visibility to its collaborative business partners. This also arranges and checks critical performance indicators to focus on variances and sloppiness and tackles the bullwhip effect due to the mismatch of demand information while moving from downstream to upstream. However, a timely and efficient way for an enterprise to formulate an appropriate forward-looking strategy has become crucial in modern retail business. Probing the rich oracles of Business Intelligence (BI) and Business Analytics (BA) application software, retail enterprises can take advantage of Big Data-driven insight to work with optimal lead time and enhance prediction of future to cope with uncertainties. Analytics thus play a vital role in formulating innovative strategies for enhancing the performance of a retail business.

Retail businesses are increasingly seeking to 'win with data'. They rely upon data to gain visibility into expenditure, look for trends in corporate operational cost and related performance, and support process control, inventory monitoring, production optimization, and process improvement efforts. Many retail businesses are awash in data, with many seeking to capture data analysis to gain a competitive advantage (Davenport, 2006). In this way, appropriate data capture, data cleaning, and different data analysis techniques are considered part of an emerging competitive area that will transform how retail supply chains are designed and managed. In addition, due to the massive volume of generated data, the fast velocity of arriving data, and the large variety of heterogeneous data, the Big Data-based applications bring new challenges. It is a hard job to test the correctness of a Big Data-based software system due to its enormous size and timeliness. This is an essential concern for big data-based software system practitioners motivated to develop innovative ways of thinking about how data is produced, organized, and analyzed. Thus, quality assurance for big data-based systems plays a crucial role.

The main objective of this chapter is to provide some perspective on Big Data-based decision-making software and the appropriate software testing mechanisms for these new breeds of applications. The remainder of this chapter is organized as follows. Section 2 discusses the basic concepts of big data and the importance of business analytics, and the advantages of their use are highlighted in the context of supply chain management. Section 3 briefly reviews research in Big Data-based supply chain applications and examines the influence of business analytics on modern supply chain performance. It also includes the conundrum of Big Data quality and dimensions of data quality-related issues. Section 4 provides Big Data-based software application testing approaches to overcome quality challenges. Section 5 examines the scope and process of Big Data-based software applications quality assurance and the general concept of quality factors for Big Data-based applications. Section 6 provides software systems validation methods for Big Data-based applications. Section 7 highlights future research directions of this project. Finally, concluding remarks have been put forward in Section 8.

BACKGROUND OF DATA ANALYTICS

In Big Data and Business Analytics have attracted burgeoning interest among researchers in recent years due to their potential in the business community (Waller & Fawcett, 2013). Notably, research conducted by the IBM Institute for Business Value in collaboration with MIT Sloan Review revealed the importance of Big Data to business managers (LaVallel et al., 2011). The subject has been embraced in notable journals, including Harvard Business Review articles (McAfee & Brynjolfsson, 2013) (Davenport & Patio, 2012), (Barton & Court, 2012) and some articles in MIT Sloan Management Review (LaValle et al., 2011) (Wixom & Ross, 2018). However, despite increasing contributions, Big Data-based software applications in retail business supply chain management (SCM) are still in their infancy.

J R Stock (Stock, 2013) discusses Big Data-driven supply chain management-related issues in one of his recent publications, and he also proposes that Big Data-based analytics for SCM will allow decision-makers to make faster decisions. In an industry survey conducted by Mitsubishi Heavy Industries and consulting company Deloitte (Deloitte & MHI, 2014), supply chain executives were questioned about innovations that drive supply chains. The main objective was to get the views of business executives on emerging technology trends that could dramatically impact future supply chains. The survey also identified areas for analytic-based SCM. The Council for Supply Chain Management Consultants published a report on Big Data in SCM based on interviews with supply chain managers. One of the objectives of this research was to find out the best practices for using Big Data for better SCM performance. Many commercial Big Data applications related to SCM have attracted the attention of academics and practitioners (Watson et al., 2014) (Davenport, 2006) (Davenport & Harris, 2007) (McAfee & Brinjals, 2012) (Deloitte & MHI, 2016). For example, a few research works in corporate marketing management show tremendous opportunities in big data-based business analytics (Viler et al., 2013). The number of publications on supply chain network design using Big Data-based business analytics is also growing ceaselessly (Baseness, 2014) (Dietrich et al., 2014) (Swathi, 2012) (Siegel, 2015) (Watson et al., 2013).

The research literature review shows that SCM's critically critical organizational functions will evolve and adapt to Big Data analytics. An industry report (Deloitte & MHI, 2016) expressed a view about the potential of supply chains to deliver massive economic and environmental rewards for society. However, technological innovation will need to play a crucial role to fulfil this potential. Big Data analytics can improve supply chain visibility, cost savings, and customer service. The key is to generate insightful data analysis and share it between business partners along the retail supply chain so that they can act on it.

In order to solve a problem, Big Data-based applications use intelligent reasoning in an automated software environment that helps users apply analytical and scientific methods to business decision-making. The software applications that focus on the retail supply chain domain are referred to as retail decision support systems, providing Big Data-based tools to support a user in a global supply chain-related reasoning process to solve a problem. This type of reasoning can be considered an intellectual process by which retail managers use diverse artificial intelligence-based inference mechanisms (e.g., rule-based, case-based, model-based, and neutral network-based reasoning) to solve day-to-day operational problems.

Each approach focuses on enriching some aspects of the traditional retail intelligent decision support systems. In addition, these automated software systems regularly use models that are expected to be reasonably accurate reflections of real-world work practices. In the term reasonably accurate, one discovers the need for evaluation. How these models are obtained and deployed across decision-making entities (i.e., human and machine) can introduce inconsistencies, incompleteness, redundancies, and problems in coordination. Consequently, there is a clear need to evaluate big data-based systems that are intended for serious business use.

Moreover, considering both the proliferation of Big Data-based analytics use for global retail business management and the fact that the data upon which these software applications (i.e., analytics) functions rely are often error-prone, there is a critical need to assess the data quality as it pertains to the field of global retail management. As such, poor data quality can directly impact retail supply chain operational decisions, and this will promote several tangible and intangible losses for global businesses. Retail operational managers are seeing the problems and impacts attributed to poor data quality growing in importance.

Many of the issues in Big Data-based retail business-related applications may be familiar. However, there is an evolving positive view of business analytics that is resulting in significant business transformations. Business analytics is now becoming standard for communicating the entire life cycle of enhanced data-driven business decision-making. Big data is the crucial ingredient in estimating many analytical models, and the well-known garbage in, garbage out principle continues to apply. In the Big Data era, the requirement that data must be accurate remains a critical issue. Data quality assurance plays a key role in different problem domains of retail business.

BIG DATA-BASED SOFTWARE APPLICATIONS TESTING APPROACH

Testing Big Data-based applications software is one of the crucial challenges faced by the software development community. This is due to lack of knowledge on what to test; how to test; and how much data to test. In addition, Big Data-based application developers have been facing daunting challenges in creating the best strategies for structured and unstructured data validation; formulating an appropriate software test framework, working with broader use of existing data, integration of new sources of data, and making sure to maintain the standard of in-house quality assurance practices. These challenges are causing inferior quality of data in production, delayed implementation, and an increase in total product cost. Robust Big Data-based applications testing strategy need to be defined for validating structured and unstructured data. Additionally, early identification of defects in Big Data-based software helps to minimize the overall deployment cost and time to market.

Figure 2. A typical big data architecture highlighting the areas of testing

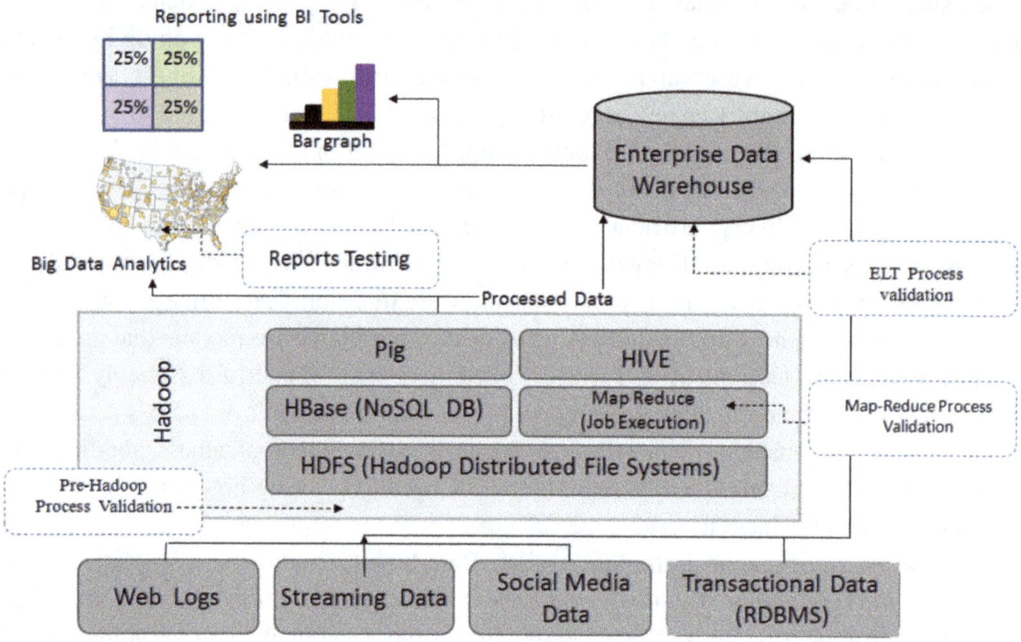

Big Data-based technologies are classified into three distinct types: file systems, computing frameworks, and tools for analytics. File system is responsible for the organization, storage, naming, sharing, and protecting files. Big Data-based application frameworks are often categorized into two: open-source frameworks and commercial frameworks. Known open-source frameworks are - Apache Hadoop (Hadoop, 2017), Spark (Spark, 2017), Storm (Storm, 2017), and S4 (S4, 2017). Google offers Big Query (BigQuery, 2017) to operate on Google Big Table (Chang et al, 2006), Amazon support Big Data through Hadoop cluster, and NoSQL support of columnar database using Amazon DynamoDB (Decandia et al, 2007) are the few examples of commercial frameworks. The brief descriptions of the several Big Data tools can be found in academic literatures (Kune et al, 2016). Technical details of these technologies are beyond the scope of this chapter. Figure 2 represents a typical big data architecture highlighting the areas of testing.

Different software testing mechanisms (e.g. functional, non-functional) are used along with test data and test environment management to make sure that the data from different sources (e.g. retail business in-house data, data from outside sources) is processed error free and is of good quality to perform analysis. Functional testing mechanisms, like validation of map reduce process, structured and unstructured data validation, data storage validation are essential to make sure that the data is correct, in consistent format, and is of quality assured. Except functional validations, other non-functional testing (e.g., failover testing, system performance testing, service level agreement testing) also play a crucial role in Big Data-based applications development.

To discuss different Big Data-based application testing mechanism, this chapter uses an open-source software framework (i.e. Hadoop) for explanation purpose. Hadoop uses its own distributed file system, HDFS (Hadoop Distributed File System), which extends the native file system of the host operating system (e.g., UNIX, Linux, Windows). Hadoop is not actually a single product but is instead a growing collection of components and related projects. Figure 3 shows a typical Big Data architecture diagram and highlights the areas where testing should be focused. A brief description of the relevant technical terms in this architecture is explained in Table-1.

Big Data implementation deals with written complex Pig, Hive programs and running these jobs using Hadoop map educe framework on huge volumes of data across different nodes. Hadoop is a framework that allows for the distribution processing of large data sets across networks of computers. Hadoop uses Map/Reduce, where the application is divided into many small fragments of work, each of which may be executed or re-executed on any node in the cluster. Hadoop utilizes its own distributed file system, HDFS, which makes data available to multiple computing nodes.

A step-by-step process need to follow in testing Big Data systems, using Hadoop ecosystem. First step loading source data into HDFS involves in extracting the data from different source systems and loading into HDFS. Data is extracted using crawl jobs web data and tools like sqoop for transactional data, and then loaded in HDFS by splitting into multiple files. Once this step is completed second step perform map reduce operations involves in processing the input files and applying map and reduce operations to get a desired output. Last setup extracts the output results from HDFS involves in extracting the data output generated out of second step and loading into downstream systems which can be enterprise data warehouse for generating analytical reports or any of the transactional systems for further processing.

BIG DATA ANALYTICS SOFTWARE APPLICATION TESTING

Poor implementation of Big Data-based software applications can lead to poor quality and delays in testing. Performing functional testing can identify data quality issues that originate in errors with coding or distributed node configuration; effective test data and test environment management ensures that data from a variety of sources is of enough quality for accurate analysis and can be processed without error.

Apart from functional testing, non-functional testing (e.g., performance testing, failover testing) plays a key role in ensuring the scalability of the process. Functional testing is performed to identify functional coding issues and requirements issues, while non-functional testing identifies performance bottlenecks and validates the non-functional requirements. The size of Big Data applications often makes it difficult or too costly to replicate the entire system in a test environment; a smaller environment must be created instead, but this introduces the risk that applications that run well in the smaller test environment behave differently in production.

Therefore, it is necessary that the system engineers are careful when building the test environment, as many of these concerns can be mitigated by carefully designing the system architecture. A proper systems architecture can help eliminate performance issues (such as an imbalance in input splits or redundant shuffle and sort), but, of course, this approach alone does not guarantee a system that performs well.

The numerical stability of algorithms also becomes an issue when dealing with statistical or machine learning algorithms. Applications that run well with one dataset may abort unexpectedly or produce poor results when presented with a similar but poorly conditioned set of inputs. Verification of numerical stability is particularly important for customer-facing systems.

Two key areas of the testing problem are (1) establishing efficient test datasets and (2) availability of Hadoop-centric testing tools (e.g. PigUnit, Junit for Pig). Testing should include all four phases shown in Figure 3. Data quality issues can manifest themselves at any of these stages.

Table 1. Technical description in Hadoop framework

Technical Term	Brief Description
Web Logs	Log files from a Web Server and based on the values contained in the Log files, derives indicators about when, how, and by whom a web server is visited.
Streaming Data	Data is delivered either un a streaming format, or as snapshot files of streamed data.
Social Data:	Social interaction data obtained from social networking services.
Transaction Data	Transaction data are data describing an event (the changes because of a transaction).
HDFS	Hadoop uses its own distributed file system, HDFS (Hadoop Distributed File System), which extends the native file system of the host operating system (e.g. UNIX, Linux, Windows).
HBase	Apache HBase is an open source; non-relational database modeled after Google's Bigtable and is written in Java. It runs on top of HDFS (Hadoop Distributed File System). It provides a fault-tolerant way of storing enormous quantities of *sparse data.*
PIG	Apache Pig provides an alternative language to SQL, called Pig Latin, for querying data stored in HDFS. Pig does not require the data to be structured as tables, however, and can be more efficient than SQL if the queries involved require reuse of intermediate results. Pig comes with standard functions for common tasks like averaging data, working with dates, or finding differences between strings.
HIVE	Hive is a tool that structures data in Hadoop into the form of relational-like tables and allows queries using a subset of SQL. Hive is a useful tool for performing queries on large datasets, especially datasets that require full table scans. Hive can be used to support a tester who is interested in doing arbitrary queries to confirm values of calculated statistics or to run reasonableness tests across large swaths of data.
EDW	Enterprise Data Warehouse (EDW) is a retailer's central data repository that is built to support business decisions. EDW contains data related to areas that the retailer wants to analyze. For a retailer, it might be a customer, product or bill of material. EDW is built by extracting data from several operational systems. As the data is fed into EDW it is converted, reformatted and summarized to present a single corporate view. Data is added into the data warehouse over time in the form of snapshots.

Figure 3. Testing phases

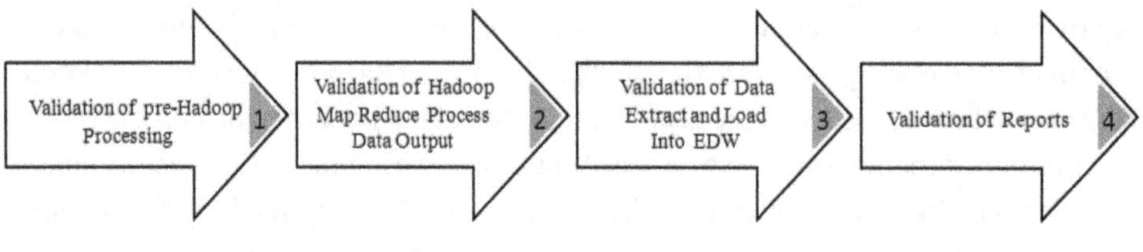

TESTING METHODS FOR VALIDATION OF PRE-HADOOP PROCESSING

Big Data systems typically process a mix of both structured data (e.g. POS transactions, call detail records, general ledger transactions, and call canter transactions). Unstructured data (such as user comments, insurance claims descriptions and web logs) and semi-structured social media data (from sites like Twitter, Facebook, LinkedIn, and Pinterest). Often the data is extracted from its source location and saved in its raw or a processed form in Hadoop or another Big Data database management system. Data is typically extracted from a variety of source systems and in varying file formats (e.g. relational tables, fixed size records, flat CSV files with delimiters, XML files, JSON, and text files). The most important activity during data loading is to compare data to ensure extraction has happened correctly and to confirm that the data loaded into the HDFS (Hadoop Distributed File System) is a complete, accurate copy.

Typical tests include:

- Data type validation: Data type validation is customarily carried out on one or more simple data fields. The simplest kind of data type validation verifies that individual characters provided through user input are consistent with the expected characters of one or more known primitive data types as defined in a programming language or data storage and retrieval mechanism.
- Range and constraint validation: Simple range and constraint validation may examine user input for consistency with a minimum/maximum range or consistency with a test for evaluating a sequence of characters, such as one or more tests against regular expressions.
- Code and cross-reference validation: Code and cross-reference validation includes tests for data type validation, combined with one or more operations to verify that the user-supplied data is consistent with one or more external rules, requirements or validity constraints relevant to an organization, context or set of underlying assumptions. These additional validity constraints may involve cross-referencing supplied data with a known look-up table or directory information service.
- Structured validation: Structured validation allows for the combination of any number of various basic data type validation steps, along with more complex processing. Such complex processing may include the testing of conditional constraints for an entire complex data object or set of process operations with a system.

Testing Methods for Hadoop MapReduce Processes

Hadoop MapReduce: Hadoop MapReduce, as shown in Figure 4, is a software framework for easily written applications that process vast amounts of data (multi-terabyte datasets) in-parallel on large cluster (thousands of nodes) of commodity hardware in a reliable fault-tolerant manner.

Figure 4. Hadoop MapReduce software framework

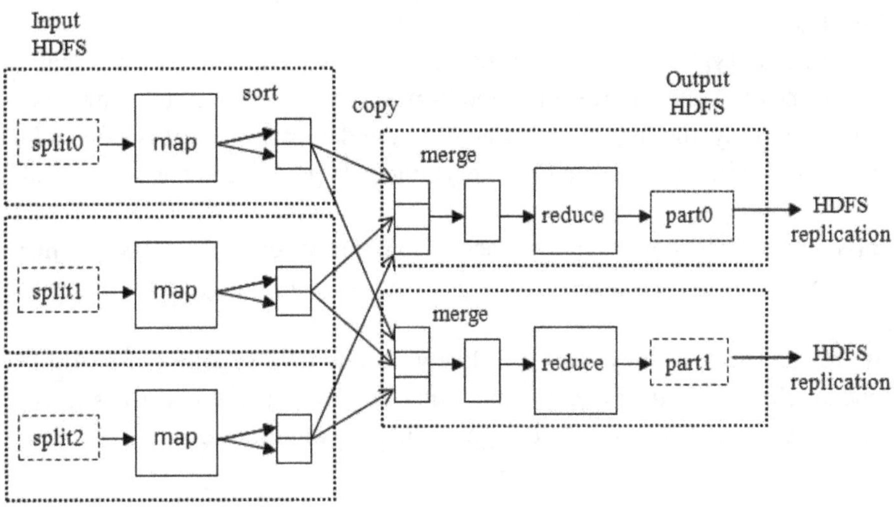

A MapReduce job usually splits the input dataset into independent chunks that are processed by the map tasks in a completely parallel manner. The framework sorts the outputs of the maps, which are then input to the reduced tasks. Typically, both the input and the output of the job are stored in a file system. The framework takes care of scheduling tasks, organizing them, and re-executing the failed tasks.

ETL Process: ETL is a variation of the Extract, Transform, Load (ETL), a data integration process in which transformation takes place on an intermediate server before it is loaded into the target. This capability is most useful for processing the large data set required for BI and BA.

TESTING METHODS FOR DATA EXTRACT AND EDW LOADING

A major part of the data warehouse system is data extraction, transformation, and loading (ETL). The goal is to extract the data, often from a variety of different systems, and transform it so that it is uniform in terms of format and content, and, finally, to load the data into a warehouse where it can serve as the basis for business intelligence needs.

The integrity of the data must be maintained at every step. It must be stored clearly and concisely without loss and should be accessible to all authorized professionals. So, for the data warehouses to deliver value, they require carful ETL testing to ensure that processes work as required.

The different methods for ETL testing depend on the challenges faced in performing this testing. The following are some of the main challenges to overcome.

- No user interface: In data warehouse testing, no user interface is present only data and its relations are there. To test this type of data, the ability to look at data, validate data processing rules, and analyze final data output is required. Consequently, knowledge of database query languages like SQL is essential for testers to do this accurately, where traditional manual testing skills are not enough.
- Huge volume of data: Millions of transactions can be happening every day. It is a challenge to verify the extraction, transformation, and loading of that data in the real-time environment as the code is updated.
- Variety of sources: Typically, a wide variety of systems feed daily transactional data to a data warehouse. Some of the data may even come from systems used in cloud computing or hosted by a third party. Similarly, the format and content of the data will vary. It is often a huge challenge to merge the data while making sure that everything gets processed consistently and in relation to each other.
- Bad or missing data: The information collected from the various source systems may not be complete, may have many special cases requiring exception processing, or may generally be of poor quality.
- Non-static rules: The source systems will likely change over time because of release upgrades with attendant changes in data content and structure. There should be ways to cope with these changes without having to change the design of the data warehouse.

TESTING METHODS FOR REPORTS

Big Data analytics solutions are built to report and analysed data from data warehouses. They can vary in size and complexity depending on the needs of the business, underlying data stores, number of reports, and number of users. The key focus is on validating layout format as per the design mock-up, style sheets, prompts and filter attributes and metrics on the report. Verification of drilling, sorting and export functions of the reports in Web environment is also done. Data generated on the reports should be corrected as per business logic. The test team needs to target the lowest granularity that is present in the data warehouse, understanding each report and the linkages of every field displayed in the report with the schema. Tracing its origin back to the source system is a big challenge and a time-consuming process.

SCOPE AND PROCESS OF BIG DATA APPLICATION QUALITY ASSURANCE

Big Data-based software Quality Assurance (QA) has its roots in assuring the quality of manufactured physical products. In manufacturing product QA is performed by inspecting the product and evaluating its quality near its completion or at various stages of production process. However, software is not as tangible as manufactured engineering products, which are much more physical by nature. But a software product is 'invisible in nature,', and it is characterized by its functionalities. This invisible nature of software product creates extra problems of assessing its quality. In this way, engineering manufactured products are visible, whereas software engineering products are invisible. The majority of the defects in an industrial engineering product can be detected during the manufacturing and fabrication processes. However, defects in software products are invisible that makes its incorrectness identification much harder and as a result software quality assurance is overly complex. Moreover, there are additional problems with assessing software quality, and this is attributed to its recent trend of software product design and development. For example, now-a-days software products are often developed by global teams of professional spanning multiple countries, multiple development platforms, and multiple layers of interfaces between software components.

Different academics and practitioners have different views on the source of the software quality attributes. Juran and his fellow practitioners (Bisgaard, 2008). define software quality as' fitness for use' and 'customer impression' and later' freedom of deficiencies'. A second view is that of Crosby (Crosby, 1979), who defines quality as both the 'conformance to requirements' and 'non-conformance implies defects. A third view is that of Roger Pressman (Pressman, 2000) who states that there are three requirements for software quality, namely 'specific functional requirements', 'adhering to quality standards in the contract' and lastly 'good software engineering practices.

These views on software quality have suggested to approaches of measuring the quality of Big Data-based software applications. The entire process of Big Data-based software development is guided by software engineering techniques, and the assessment of the quality of the software is conducted during the quality assurance process. In software engineering, different techniques are used to design and develop software applications based on business requirements. At the same time, software quality assurance (SQA) mechanisms manage the quality of software during the software development process. SQA defines and measures the inputs and outputs of the development processes and qualifies the quality of the software in terms of defects. To assess the software quality, it is advantageous to identify what aspect of software need to measure.

FACTORS THAT IMPACT SOFTWARE APPLICATION QUALITY

McCall (McCall, 1977) has identified three different categories of factors that software quality can come under. The factors are spread over the lifespan of the application and not only its original development. The first set of factors is associated with the original operation of the software product by a user. The second set of factors is directed towards the revision of the product from an existing product to a new or enhanced product and how the quality of the original design and code allows for this revision. The last set of factors is concerned with the transaction of the product to another target environment, such as a new database or operating system. The factors are outlined in Table 2.

In this chapter, software quality assurance (SQA) is considered as a process for the measurement of deliverables and activities during each stage of Big Data-Based software application development lifecycle. The objective of SQA is to quantify the quality of the products and the activities giving rise to them and to guide a quality improvement effort. For discussion, this chapter considers that Big Data-based software application assurance activities take place at each development stage of the application development lifecycle. The stages are categorized into areas for requirements capture, system design, coding, and testing, and finally release.

Table 2. McCall's Quality factors for new software development

Quality factors for new software developments for		
Product operational	**Product revision**	**Product transaction**
• Correctness • Reliability • Efficiency • Integrity • Usability	• Maintainability • Flexibility • Testability	• Portability • Reusability • Interoperability

In general, big data-based application quality assurance refers to the study and application of various assurance process, methods, standards, criteria, and systems to ensure the quality of Big Data system in terms of a set of quality parameters. Figure 5 shows a sample scope of validation for quality assurance of big data-based supply chain management applications.

Conventional system quality parameters such as performance, robustness, security, etc., can apply to Big Data systems. These are listed below:

System Reliability: Software systems reliability means the ability of an application (e.g., product or service) to perform as expected over time, and this is usually measured in terms of the probability of it performing as expected over time.

System Data Security: Software systems data security could be used to evaluate the security of Big Data applications from different perspectives. Using this criterion, data security could be evaluated at various software system application user hierarchy levels.

System Consistency – The absence of difference when comparing two or more test case outputs in a software testing environment.

Figure 5. The scope of validation for Big Data application system quality

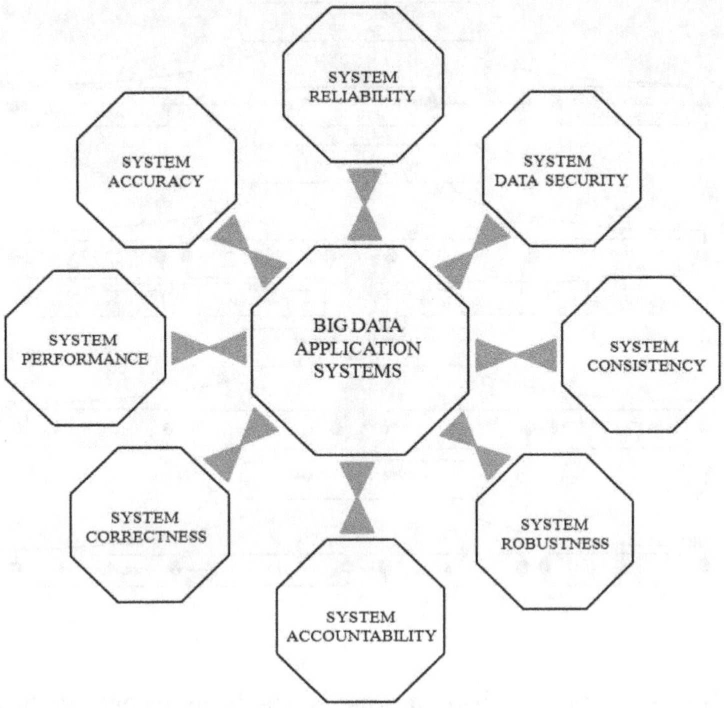

System Robustness: System robustness complements correctness. Correctness addresses the behaviour of a system in a case covered by its specification; robustness characterizes what happens outside of the specification. In this way, robustness is the ability of software systems to react appropriately to abnormal conditions.

Figure 6. represents a quality test process for big data-based application systems. It consists of functional testing, intelligent algorithms testing, and system learning capability testing related issues.

System Accountability: The system accountability quality factor can be divided into three processes. First, one must identify relevant parties for whom they are accountable and to whom they are accountable. Second, if a condition verifies for which a party was previously identified as accountable, a forum of some kind convenes to gather the necessary information and passes a judgment on the accountability of the said party. Third, one must assign positive or negative sanctions to the responsible party.

System Correctness: System correctness is the essential quality criterion for big data analytics applications. It is the quality criteria of software applications to perform their specific tasks, as specified by their specification. If an extensive data-based analytic application does not do what it is meant to, everything else (e.g., excellent graphical user interface and appropriate algorithm for data processing) matters little.

System Performance: This quality criterion indicates the system's performance, such as availability, response time, throughput, and scalability.

System Accuracy: The system accuracy criterion indicates the results of Big Data-based software systems as anticipated.

Figure 6. A quality test process for big data-based application systems

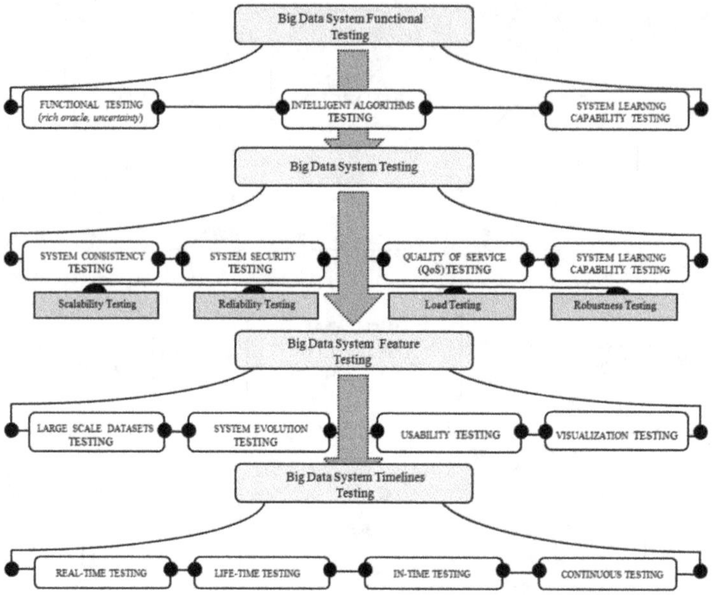

The promise of Big Data-driven decision-making is now being recognized broadly, and there is a growing enthusiasm for business analytics quality assurance-related testing methods. Heterogeneity, scale, timeliness, and privacy problems with supply chain Big Data impede processes at all phases of the pipeline that can create value from this vast data set. The problems start immediately during operational data acquisition, cleaning, and selecting the correct data for decision-making software applications. One of the main problems about what data to keep is what t data to discard, and how to store data makes data dependable for the intended applications. Much supply chain operational data today is not natively structured format; for example, tweets and blogs are weakly structured pieces of text, while images and video are structured formats for storage and display. Therefore, killing the weeds and finding the natural pearl of the data set is a challenging task, and a detailed discussion about the relevant issues is beyond the scope of this chapter.

Nevertheless, this chapter will highlight a simplistic view of Big Data-based software testing that consists of systems functional testing aspects (e.g., rich oracle, uncertainty), intelligent algorithms testing (e.g., scalability, reliability, load, robustness), and system learning capability testing. There are two typical Big Data applications: (a) recommendation systems and (b) prediction systems. Figure 7 summarizes the typical quality factors for prediction and recommendation systems in a fishbone diagram, and a brief description of those factors is presented in the next section.

QUALITY FACTORS FOR PREDICTIVE SYSTEMS

System Correctness: System Correctness is a quality factor used to evaluate the correctness of Big Data applications. Unlike the conventional system, Big Data applications are complex to validate for correctness. For instance, prediction-related software is developed to predict real-world activities. Hence, it is difficult to determine the correct output for those types of software. Correctness is related to the prediction pattern or model. For instance, some models are more likely to predict the point of inflection values, while others do well in predicting continuity. Thus, to verify the correctness of the system effectively, engineers need to evaluate the capability of prediction in the specified conditions and environments.

System Accuracy: System Accuracy is used to evaluate if the system yields true (no systematic errors) and consistent (no random errors) results. Some big data applications are developed to find previously unknown answers; only approximate solutions might be available. This can be called uncontrollable prediction. Some prediction is used to prevent something from happening in the future, and the prediction result will affect actions or behaviours. In turn, those actions can promote the prediction result.

System Stability: System Stability reflects the stability of the system prediction while the environment or data changes. For example, the prediction capability of a system is stable with minor changes when statistical data are acquired from different time limits.

System Consistency: System consistency is a quality that helps evaluate the consistency of the targeted system from different perspectives. Due to the inherent uncertainties in system models, some applications do not produce a single correct output for a given set of inputs. This leads to difficulty in determining the expected behaviours of the software. In such situations, domain-specific experts could provide opinions to support system consistency.

Figure 7. Big Data Application System Quality Factors

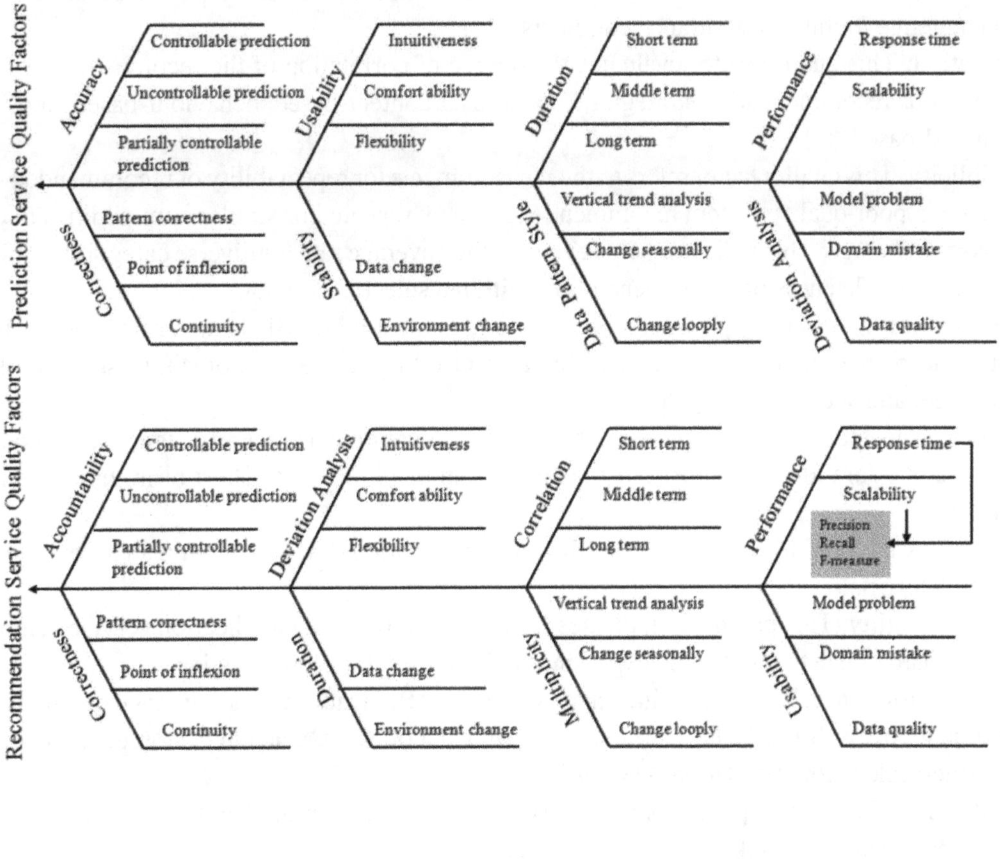

Duration: Duration indicates the expected prediction period. It can measure how up-to-date the data is and whether it is correct despite possible modifications or changes that impact time and date values. For instance, commonly used prediction duration in enterprise management can be divided into short-term, middle-term, and long-term.

Deviation Analysis: Deviation Analysis analyzes the prediction deviation within an accepted range or confidence interval.

System Usability: System usability is a parameter that indicates how well the Big Data application service can be used. It can be subjective due to the diverse experiences of different developers and users. The typical usability factors include intuitiveness, comfortability, and flexibility.

This aspect concerns understandability – the users' effort to recognize the logical concept and its applicability; learnability – the users' effort to learn its application; and operability – the users' effort for operation and operation control.

System Performance: System Performance is a distinct quality factor for Big Data application services. Evaluating how well Big Data is structured, designed, collected, generated, stored, and managed to support large-scale prediction services is helpful.

QUALITY FACTORS FOR RECOMMENDATION SYSTEMS

Correctness: This quality factor reflects whether the recommended service or commodity meets customers' demands. Correctness could be subjective between different persons. Thus, measuring correctness is still a challenge for quality assurance engineers.

Correlation: This quality factor evaluates the degree of correlation of the recommended service. It involves various recommendation strategies, such as user content-based, behaviour-based, and collaboration filtered-based.

Multiplicity: This quality factor refers to the measurements for repeatability of recommended service. For instance, a poor-quality system recommends too many repeated or similar commodities to users.

Category Coverage: This indicator helps evaluate the coverage rate for diverse categories. This factor measures the completeness of recommendations within a selected domain.

Accountability: The quality parameter is critical and mandatory for Big Data service applications and users. It could be measured quantitatively, such as user rating similarity, domain trust value, domain-related degree, and social intimacy degree.

Duration: This factor indicates the expected recommendation period. For instance, commonly used recommendation duration in enterprise management can be divided into short-term, middle-term, and long-term.

Deviation Analysis: This factor analyses the recommendation deviation within an accepted range or confidence interval.

System Usability: This parameter indicates how well the Big Data application service can be used. It can be subjective due to the diverse experiences of different developers and users.

System Performance: This is a distinct quality factor for Big Data application services, and it is helpful to evaluate how well Big Data is structured, designed, collected, generated, stored, and managed to support large-scale recommendation services.

In addition to the typical applications discussed above, there are more Big Data-related applications such as machine learning, ranking, and search systems.

SYSTEM VALIDATION METHODS FOR BIG DATA-BASED APPLICATIONS

The software testing process attempts to verify and validate the capability of a software system to meet its required attributes and functionality. Software testing aims to evaluate an attribute or capability of a software system and determine that it meets its required results. Although crucial to software quality and widely deployed by programmers and testers, the validation of extensive data-based application systems remains an art due to a limited understanding of the principles of software. The difficulty in software testing and validation stems from the complexity of the software. The purpose of validation can be quality assurance, verification, and reliability estimation.

This section presents existing research in software testing methods used to validate several Big Data-based applications, including intelligent, data mining, and learning-based systems.

Program-Based Software Testing

Program-based software testing methods have been used in many Big Data-based applications. This software testing mechanism systematically searches for errors in MapReduce applications and generates corresponding test cases.

Classification-Based Testing

A classification-based testing method for software systems testing usually involves two steps: (a) training a classifier to distinguish failure from successful cases on a select subset of results and (b) applying the trained classifier to identify failures in the primary set of results. A resembling reference model is usually used to train a classifier. More specifically, there are techniques for applying pattern classifications to alleviate the test oracle problems.

Oracle Problem In Software Testing

Testing involves examining the behaviour of a system to discover potential faults. Given an input for a system, distinguishing the corresponding desired, correct behaviour from potentially incorrect behaviour is called the "test oracle problem." Test oracle automation is essential to remove a current bottleneck that inhibits greater overall test automation. Humans should determine whether the observed behaviour is correct without test oracle automation.

Machine Learning-Based Software Testing

Software testing is an investigation process that attempts to validate and verify the alignment of a software system's attributes and functionality with its intended goals. Due to this fact, automated testing approaches are desired to reduce the time and cost. Besides, automation can significantly enhance the testing process performance. Several machine-learning techniques have been used for automated software testing purposes. Artificial neural networks (ANN) and decision tree-based algorithms have been used to predict potential bugs in big data-based applications.

Crowdsourced Software Testing

Software engineering no longer occurs in small, isolated groups of developers. However, it increasingly occurs in organizations and communities (Lim, 2010), which involves delegating various tasks to an unknown workforce – the crowd (Mao, 2011). There is an increasing trend towards globalization, focusing on collaborative methods and infrastructure. Crowdsourcing has gained much attention in practice over the last few years. Many big data-based applications have drawn on this concept to perform tasks and value-creation activities. Nevertheless, despite its popularity, there is still comparatively little well-founded knowledge of crowdsourcing, particularly about crowdsourcing intermediaries.

Model-Based Software Testing

Testing style is abundant in software engineering. Over the last few decades, the industry has used and adopted many of these as solutions to address the increasing demand for assuring software quality. Due to the popularization of object-oriented design and software development, models are used for software implementation. There has been a growth in black box testing techniques collectively dubbed *model-based testing* (MBT). Model-based testing has recently gained attention with the popularization of models (including unified modelling language - UML) in software design and development. Model-based testing or MBT is a general term that signifies an approach that bases standard testing tasks such as test case generation and test result evaluation on a model of the application under test.

FUTURE RESEARCH DIRECTIONS

Challenges always follow opportunities. On the one hand, big data-based supply chain software applications bring many attractive opportunities; on the other hand, big data-based supply chain management application software faces many challenges. These challenges can be broadly categorized as Big Data-based software architectural aspects, hardware performance enhancement-related issues, and parallel software testing capabilities. Big Data-based supply chain application testing is the software life cycle's most expensive and critical phase.

As part of the general Big Data quality assurance research initiative, the current research will continue the concurrency and parallelism issues of Big Data generation and uses in global supply chain business analytics. Big Data is the collection of large and complex data sets. Therefore, dealing with this massive amount of data and executing it on multiple processing nodes is a highly challenging risk of insufficient data and even data quality-related issues at every design and development stage. Some of the future research agendas are: (i) increasing need for integration of large volumes of data available from multiple sources (e.g., text, video, audio); and this integration forces global supply chain operational provision to have constantly clean and reliable data sets; (ii) instant data collection and live deployment are very crucial issues in order to get appropriate business intelligence for a retail organization, which can be overcome only by testing the business intelligence software applications before live deployment; and finally (iii) real-time scalability related issues of large amounts of data generated by devices equipped with sensing components along the global supply chain. In addition, there are emerging needs for research problems and directions on this subject regarding quality control models, automated validation methods, approaches, service platforms, TasS (Testing-as-a-service), and test automation techniques.

CONCLUSION

With the advent of big data management technologies and analytics in supply chain management, academics and practitioners are paying much more attention to building high-quality software services for business applications. However, increasing quality problems result in erroneous data costs in global supply chain industries. Data has always been an integral part of business. Technology transformation has further reinforced this importance. The advent of social media, mobility, and the Internet of Things has not only blurred the lines between online and offline business but also resulted in the availability of a vast amount of unstructured data related to consumer behaviour and interests. With significant insights, Big Data could mean big business for supply chain management. However, industry analysts are echoing growing concerns about data quality. Quality Assurance (QA) can solve the data quality challenge, and a robust and effective QA strategy can deliver significant returns from Big Data.

The design and development of big data-based software applications have proven helpful in a diverse area of application for solving problems in the global supply chain industry – e.g., raw material procurement planning, marketing strategy formulation, and logistics planning. This chapter provides an introductory discussion on Big Data-based business intelligence software systems and their quality assurance-related issues; it includes a discussion on the appropriate software testing mechanisms for the new breeds of Big Data-based applications.

While big data provides solutions to complex business problems like analyzing large volumes of data to derive precise answers, analyzing data in motion poses more significant challenges in testing these scenarios. The data is highly volatile and often unstructured as it is generated from myriad sources–such as weblogs, radio frequency identification (RFID) devices, sensors embedded in different business applications (e.g., in artefact manufacturing machines, global positioning systems, transportation networks), and mostly clustered datasets. The quality data plays a vital role in all supply chain management applications. Data quality is recognized as a relevant performance issue in operating processes, business decision-making activities, and business partners' cooperation requirements.

Moreover, Big Data is changing definitions and benchmarks for breakthrough technologies. The need to stream and collect real-time data from varied data sources and in different formats results in an exponential increase in volume. Further, there is also the need to continuously 'listen' to the stream and sift out irrelevant data. There is no point in responding to a customer tweet after a week or having dirty, noisy data affecting business decisions.

REFERENCES

Arnold, S. E. (1992). Information manufacturing: The road to database quality. *Database*, *15*(5), 32–39. https://dl.acm.org/doi/abs/10.5555/135054.135057

Baesens, A. (2014). *Analytics in a big data world: The essential guide to data science and its applications*. John Wiley & Sons. doi:10.1002/9781119204183

Ballou, D. P., & Pazer, H. L. (1985). Modeling data and process quality in multi-input, multi-output information systems. *Management Science*, *31*(2), 150–162. doi:10.1287/mnsc.31.2.150

Ballou, D. P., Wang, R., & Pacer, H. (1998). Modeling information manufacturing systems to determine information product quality. *Management Science, 44*(4), 462–484. doi:10.1287/mnsc.44.4.462

Battani, C., Cappelli, C., Francians, C., & Maurino, A. (2009). Methodologies for data quality assessment and improvement. *Association for Computing Machinery Computing Surveys, 41*(3), 1-52. https://doi.acm.org/10.1145/1541880.1541883

Bisgaard, S. (2008). Quality Management and Juran's Legacy. *Statistical Quality Control in Healthcare,* 390-401. doi:10.1080/08982110802317398

Blake, R., & Mangiameli, P. (2011). The effects and interactions of data quality and problem complexity on classification. *ACM Journal of Data and Information Quality, 2*(2), 1–28. doi:10.1145/1891879.1891881

Cooke, J. A. (2013). Three trends to watch in 2013, Perspective. *Supply Chain Quarterly, 1*, 11. doi:10.1111/jscm.12034

Crosby, P. (1995). Philip Crosby's Reflections on Quality. McGraw-Hill. , ISBN 13. doi:10.4324/9780203027790-14

Davenport, T. H., Barth, P., & Bean, R. (2012). How Big Data is different. *MIT Sloan Management Review*, (Fall), 22–24. doi:10.7551/mitpress/12588.001.0001

Davenport, T. H., & Harris, J. G. (2007). *Competing on analytics – the new science of wining*. Harvard Business School Publishing Corporation. doi:10.1177/09722629211023024

Davenport, T. H., Harris, J. G., & Morison, R. (2010). *Analytics at work – smart decisions, better results*. Harvard Business Press. doi:10.1108/14754391011050388

Davenport, T. H., & Prusiks, L. (2000). *Working knowledge: how organizations manage what they know*. Harvard Business Press. doi:10.1145/348772.348775

Deloitte & MHI. (2014). *The 2014 MHI Annual Industry Report – Innovation the driven supply chain.* https://www2.deloitte.com/content/dam/Deloitte/dk/Documents/process-and-operations/2015%20MHI%20Industry%20Report.pdf

Deloitte & MHI. (2016). *The 2016 MHI Annual Industry Report – Accelerating change: How innovation is driving digital, always-on Supply Chains.* http://cpbucket.fiu.edu/1168-geb6368x81168_emba-97075%2F2016-industry-report-2016-(1).pdf

Deming, W. E. (2000). *The New Economics for Industry, Government, Education* (2nd ed.). MIT Press. doi:10.7551/mitpress/11458.001.0001

Dietrich, B., Plachy, E. C., & Norton, M. F. (2014). *Analytics across the enterprise: How IBM realize business value from big data and analytics*. IBM Press Books. doi:10.1002/9781118936672

Emery, J.C. (1969). *Organizational planning and control systems: Theory and management.* Macmillan. doi:10.1177/000271627039200187

Fitzgerald, C., Letier, E., & Finkelstein, A. (2011). Early Failure Prediction in Feature Request Management Systems. *IEEE 19th International Requirement Engineering Conference,* 229-238. 10.1109/RE.2011.6051658

Hadoop. (2017). http://hadoop.apache.org

Haug, A., & Arlbjorn, J. S. (2011). Barriers to master data quality. *Journal of Enterprise Information Management, 24*(3), 288-303. doi:10.1108/17410391111122862

Haugh, A., Arlbjorn, J. S., & Pedersen, A. (2009). A classification model of ERP system data quality. *Industrial Management & Data Systems, 109*(8), 1053–1068. doi:10.1108/02635570910991292

HBR. (2012, October). Getting Control of Big Data. *Harvard Business Review*. Advance online publication. doi:10.1002/wcs.1379

Holcombe, M. (2008). *Running an Agile Software Development Project.* Wiley. doi:10.1002/9780470385883

Huh, Y. U., Keller, F. R., Redman, T. C., & Watkins, A. R. (1990). Data quality. *Information and Software Technology, 32*(8), 559–565. doi:10.1016/0950-5849(90)90146-I

Imminent, A., Pacemen, P., & Alaska, E. (2015, October 16). Evaluating the quality of social media data in big data architecture. *IEEE Access : Practical Innovations, Open Solutions, 3*, 2028–2043. doi:10.1109/ACCESS.2015.2490723

Ji, S., Li, Q., Cao, W., Zhang, P. & Muccini, H. (2020). Quality Assurance Technologies of Big Data Applications: A Systematic Literature Review. *Applied Sciences, 10*(8052), 1-31. doi:10.3390/app10228052

Jones-Farmer, L. A., Ezell, J. D., & Hazen, B. T. (2013). Applying control chart methods to enhance data quality. *Technometrics*. Advance online publication. doi:10.1080/00401706.2013.804437

Kahan, B. K., Strong, D. M., & Wang, R. Y. (2002). Information quality benchmarks: Product and service performance. *Communications of the ACM, 45*(4), 184–192. doi:10.1145/505248.506007

Kaplan, R. S., & Norton, D. P. (1993). Putting the Balanced Scorecard to Work. *Harvard Business Review*, (September-October), 4–17. doi:10.1016/B978-0-7506-7009-8.50023-9

Keikhosrokiani, P. (2022a). Big Data Analytics for Healthcare: Datasets, Techniques, Life Cycles, Management, and Applications. doi:10.1016/C2021-0-00369-2

Keikhosrokiani, P. (2022b). Handbook of Research on Consumer Behavior Change and Data Analytics in the Socio-Digital Era. doi:10.4018/978-1-6684-4168-8

Keikhosrokiani, P., Mustaffa, N., & Zakaria, N. (2018). Success factors in developing iHeart as a patient-centric healthcare system: A multi-group analysis. *Telematics and Informatics, 35*(4), 753–775. Advance online publication. doi:10.1016/j.tele.2017.11.006

Keikhosrokiani, P., Mustaffa, N., Zakaria, N., & Abdullah, R. (2020). Assessment of a medical information system: The mediating role of use and user satisfaction on the success of human interaction with the mobile healthcare system (iHeart). *Cognition Technology and Work, 22*(2), 281–305. Advance online publication. doi:10.1007/s10111-019-00565-4

Kune, R., Konugurthi, P. K., Agarwal, A., Chillarige, R. R., & Buyya, R. (2016). The anatomy of big data computing. *Software, Practice & Experience, 46*(1), 79–105. doi:10.1002/spe.2374

Lee, Y. W., Pipino, L., Strong, D. M., & Wang, R. Y. (2004). Process-embedded data integrity. *Journal of Database Management, 15*(1), 87–103. doi:10.4018/jdm.2004010104

Lim, S. L., Quercia, D., & Finkelstein, A. (2010). StakeNet: Using Social Networks to Analyse the Stakeholders of Large-Scale Software Projects. In *Proceedings of the IEEE 32nd International Conference on Software Engineering.* 10.1145/1806799.1806844

Mao, K., Capra, L., Harman, M., & Jia, Y. (2011). A survey of the use of crowdsourcing in software engineering. *Journal of Systems and Software, 126*, 57–84. doi:10.1016/j.jss.2016.09.015

March, S. T., & Hevner, A. R. (2007). Integrated decision support systems: A data warehousing perspective. *Decision Support Systems, 43*(3), 1031–1043. doi:10.1016/j.dss.2005.05.029

McAfee, A., & Brynjolfsson, E. (2013). Big data: The management revolution. *Harvard Business Review, 90*(10), 61–68. doi:10.1111/npqu.11362 PMID:23074865

Pal, K. (2017). A Semantic Web Service Architecture for Supply Chain Management, The 8th International Conference on Ambient Systems, Networks and Technologies (ANT 2017). *Procedia Computer Science, 109C*, 999–1004. doi:10.1016/j.procs.2017.05.442

Pal, K. (2019). Markov Decision Theory Based Crowdsourcing Software Process Model. In Crowdsourcing and Probabilistic Decision-Making in Software Engineering: Emerging Research and Opportunities. DOI: doi:10.4018/978-1-5225-9659-2-ch001

Pal, K. (2020). Framework for Reusable Test Case Generation in Software System Testing. In Software Engineering for Agile Application Development. DOI: doi:10.4018/978-1-7998-2531-9-ch009

Pal, K. & Karakostas, B. (2020). Software Testing Under Agile, Scrum, and DevOps. In *Agile Scrum Implementation and Its Long-Term Impact on Organizations.* doi:10.4018/978-1-7998-4885-1.ch008

Pal, K. & Williams, I. (2021). Software Development Knowledge Management Using Web Portal. In *Digital Technology Advancements in Knowledge Management.* doi:10.4018/978-1-7998-6792-0.ch005

Parssian, A. (2006). Managerial decision support with knowledge of accuracy and completeness of the relational aggregate functions. *Decision Support Systems, 42*(3), 1494–1502. doi:10.1016/j.dss.2005.12.005

Pernici, B. & Scannapieco, M. (2002). *Data quality in Web Information Systems.* doi:10.1007/3-540-45816-6_37

Pipino, L. L., Lee, Y. W., & Wang, R. Y. (2002). Data quality assessment. *Communications of the ACM, 45*(4), 211–218. doi:10.1145/505248.506010

Redman, T. C. (2014). *Statistics in Data and Information Quality*. Wiley. doi:10.1002/9781118445112.stat04018

Ronen, B., & Spiegler, I. (1991). Information as inventory: A new conceptual view. *Information & Management, 21*(4), 239–247. doi:10.1016/0378-7206(91)90069-E

S4. (2017). http://incubator.apache.org/s4.

Sathi, A. (2012). *Big data analytics: Disruptive technologies for changing the game.* doi:10.1002/9781119205005.ch9

Siegel, E. (2015). *Predictive analytics: The power to predict who will click, buy, lie or die.* doi:10.1002/9781119172536

Sinclair, R. (2011). *Textile and Fashion: Materials, Design and Technology.* doi:10.1016/B978-1-84569-646-7.50019-6

Smith, W. B. Jr. (1993). Total Customer Satisfaction as a Business Strategy. *Quality and Reliability Engineering International, 9*(1), 49–53. doi:10.1002/qre.4680090109

Spark. (2017). https://spark.incubator.apache.org

Stock, J. R. (2013). Supply chain management: A look back, a look ahead. *Supply Chain Quarterly, 2*, 22–26. doi:10.4324/9780203124451-17

Storm. (2017). https://storm.incubator.apache.org

Wand, Y., & Wang, R. Y. (1996). Anchoring data quality dimensions in ontological foundations. *Communications of the ACM, 39*(11), 86–95. doi:10.1145/240455.240479

Wang, R. Y. (1998). A product perspective on total data quality management. *Communications of the ACM, 41*(2), 58–65. doi:10.1145/269012.269022

Wang, R. Y., Storey, V. C., & Firth, C. P. (1995). A framework for analysis of data quality research. *IEEE Transactions on Knowledge and Data Engineering, 7*(4), 623–640. doi:10.1109/69.404034

Wang, R. Y., & Strong, D. M. (1996). Beyond Accuracy: What data quality means to data consumers. *Journal of Management Information Systems, 12*(4), 5–33. doi:10.1080/07421222.1996.11518099

Watts, S., Shankaranarayanan, G., & Even, A. (2009). Data quality assessment in context: A cognitive perspective. *Decision Support Systems, 48*(1), 202–211. doi:10.1016/j.dss.2009.07.012

Williamson, O. (1996). The Mechanisms of Governance. doi:10.2307/3117318

Wixom, B. H., & Ross, J. W. (2018). How to Monetize Your Data, MIT Sloan Management Review. *Spring Issue, 58*(3), 10–13. doi:10.7551/mitpress/11633.003.0009

Zeithaml, V. A., Berry, L. L., & Parasuraman, A. (1990). *Delivering quality service: Balancing customer perceptions and expectations.* Free Press. doi:10.5860/CHOICE.28-0390

Chapter 7
The Adoption of Business Intelligence as a Competitive Strategy Among SMEs:
A Developing Country Study

Elisha Mupaikwa
https://orcid.org/0000-0002-0313-7139
National University of Science and Technology, Zimbabwe

ABSTRACT

Business intelligence is central to the competitiveness of small and medium scale enterprises (SMEs) in the developing world. Guided by Porter's five forces model, this chapter discusses how SMEs in the developing world may harness various business intelligence information systems to gain competitive advantages over their competitors. The results of the review show that competitive rivalry among enterprises, influenced by the bargaining power of customers and suppliers, the threats of new entrants, and substitute products, influence the competitiveness of enterprises, and their influence is stronger among SMEs in the developing world. Challenges faced by SMEs in implementing business intelligence solutions include lack of funding, managerial support, and expertise. The chapter recommends investment and training in the development of business intelligence solutions for SMEs in the developing world. It further recommends more research on the acceptance and development of these technologies.

INTRODUCTION

Many SMEs in the developing world have faced challenges that hinder their competitiveness. Many of these challenges are related to stiff competition as a result of the globalisation phenomenon which has eliminated geographical boundaries in the ways enterprises do business. In globalised economies, characterised by competitive rivalry, SMEs in the developing world often suffer shocks that force them to embrace new business models and technologies. While this is meant to enable them to respond to competitive threats and to develop competitive strategies, such actions are mostly reactive, finding

DOI: 10.4018/979-8-3693-1210-0.ch007

organisations unprepared for change, leading to sometimes undesired consequences of the adoption of these new models and technologies. This has been worsened by the digital developments of the internet that have seen the wider usage of e-commerce, exposing SMEs to competition with large multinational enterprises (Keikhosrokiani, 2020, 2022a, 2022b, 2023). In the developing world, the harsh economic environment, particularly on the African continents, and the Asian and South American regions these challenges have been worse because SMEs in these regions face challenges in bargaining for price reductions while competing with large-scale and well-capitalised corporations. Additionally, these SMEs, lack managerial practice to help them to develop their competitiveness, limiting their long-term survival with only a few companies surviving for months to a year (Kamunge, Njeru, and Tirimba, 2014; Bunyasi, Bwisa, and Namusonge, 2014). These SMEs have struggled to establish themselves among leading multinational and national corporations as a result of these challenges and environmental threats against their competitive strategies and efforts. Despite such challenges, SMEs have remained a driving force for nations' economic development employing the majority of citizens and earning foreign currency for nations, particularly those in the developing world. According to Anggadwita and Mustafid (2014) in Indonesia for example SMEs contributed around 60% of the GDP and absorbed more than 97% labour force and this trend seems to be the same across the greater Asian and African communities.

The ability of SMEs to survive in an increasingly competitive global environment is largely predicated upon their capacity to leverage information as a resource (Fourie, 2015; Lateef & Keikhosrokiani, 2022). Currently, organizations that have demonstrated competitive potency are those that have recognized the importance of information and knowledge in the new economy, taking advantage of information technology to achieve high levels of efficiency and effectiveness. Mutula and Van Brakel (2006) agree that information is an important asset that gives SMEs a competitive advantage in the competitive environment because access to information plays a critical role in the informed decision-making process, making it easy for SMEs to make good competitive decisions. However, access to this information is a problem in developing countries, due to lack of ICT infrastructure.

Despite the flurry of research on SMEs' performance, there is no consensus on the factors that drive SMEs' performance and the adoption of ICTs such as BI. Various scholarly articles have investigated the performance of SMEs across different settings, from developed to least-developed countries, and utilized different methodologies (Wang, 2016). However, the research has disproportionately focused more on developed economies and in the context of developing countries (Rosenbusch, Brinckmann, and Bausch 2011). This is revealed by gaps in implementation trends on ICT innovations such as BI, between developing and developed nations (Gono, Handranath, and Ozcan, 2016). Moreover, most studies are focused on one or a few specific variables as potential determinants of SME competitive performance. This points to more scope for empirical analysis in this area, particularly for developing economies because not much is known about the combined effects of internal and external drivers of SMEs' performance (Ipinnaiye et al., 2017). Thus, there is a need to take a more comprehensive look at the drivers of SMEs as the relationship between ICTs and productivity for SMEs in developing countries has not been well established (Cataldo, Pino, and McQueen, 2020).

One of the technological solutions that has enhanced competitiveness across different enterprises including SMEs, creating new and smarter ways to improve performance, grow revenue, develop stronger customer relationships, and increase workforce effectiveness is business intelligence (BI). BI is the only key factor in achieving such results because it supports informed decision-making at every level, enabling managers, executives, and knowledge workers to take the most effective action in a given situation (Chen, Chiang, and Storey, 2012). According to Boateng (2022) therefore, for SMEs in Africa to survive and compete in a globally competitive environment, they must embrace new data analytics technologies. Boateng (2022) however, laments that a few countries in the African sub-region have made conscious efforts to exploit BI and among the countries that had the lowest BI adoption and other IT-driven innovation levels are Chad and Mozambique.

Numerous studies on business intelligence have been conducted, such as that of Mudzana and Maharaj (2015) and Serumaga-Zake (2017), who researched the application of the Delone and McClean model in South Africa to study user satisfaction with BI technologies. Previous research on the theoretical link between business intelligence and SMEs, such as the research of Grabova et al. (2010), Zhi and Guixian (2010), Ponelis and Britz (2011), Guarda et al. (2013), Ponis and Christou (2013) and Tarek and Adel (2016) have also been limited and questions remain as to how SMEs can leverage it and add value to their organizations through improved decision making. In Zimbabwe, the adoption of ICT-based innovations among SMEs was reported by Mveku et al. (2022) to have improved the quality of decisions managers made because it created platforms for collecting, processing, and analysing data from multiple sources. This was beneficial to those managers who were not sufficiently skilled to make decisions and BI provided a reliable alternative to consultancy, resulting in improved competitiveness among these SMEs. However, in an assessment of the relationship between ICT adoption and SME growth in Kenya, Chege and Wang (2020) reported that only 2% of SMEs used ICTs for competitiveness and this was due to inadequate resources and lack of knowledge (Ayoubi and Aljawarneh 2018; Gomwe, Potgiete, and Litheko, 2023).

The chapter therefore argues that the integration of business intelligence and analytics tools in SMEs provides an opportunity for generating innovations that may lead to organizations gaining a competitive advantage in their value chains. This is done using the Five-Forces model which enables organizations to analyze the current situation of their industry in a structured way. The model comprises the following: barriers to entry, threat of substitutes, bargaining power of suppliers, bargaining power of buyers, and rivalry among competitors. The purpose of this chapter is to discuss the application of business intelligence among small and medium-scale enterprises in the developing worlds and indicate how organizations may realize their full potential by integrating business intelligence tools and, methods in their operations.

Overview of the Porter's Five Forces Model

Despite its criticisms, Porter's five forces model has remained arguably, the most widely used model for understanding the competitiveness of business organizations. This model provides a general view of the firm, its competitors, and the firm's environment as shown in Figure 1. The model is commonly used as it serves as a starting point for a more robust assessment of a firm's performance (Nguza-Mduba, 2020).

Central to Porter's model is the competitive rivalry that exists between the firm and its competitors. These organizations always strive to outperform one another and to achieve this; they develop competitive strategies to counter threats to their continued viability and survival. These threats according to Laudon and Laudon (2024) are the bargaining power of customers, the bargaining power of suppliers, threats of new entrants, and threats of substitute products. When rivalry intensifies and there are many players in the markets, profits may begin to tumble. The intensity of these factors determines the level of profitability and competitiveness of enterprises through their understanding of their environment and their assessment of competitiveness (Mugo, 2020). Among some researchers that have used Porter's five forces model to study the competitiveness of SMEs in the developing world context is Omsa, Abdullah, and Jamali (2017) among furniture manufacturers in Indonesia's Eat Java where, the power of buyers significantly affected the differentiation strategy, the power of supplies significantly affected the cost leadership strategy and focus strategy but did not significantly affect the differentiation strategy, and the threat of rivalries affected the differentiation strategy and focus strategy.

Figure 1. Porter's five forces model (Laudon and Laudon, 2014)

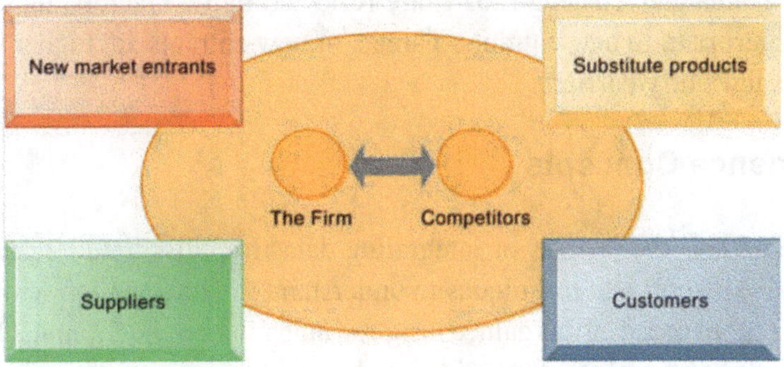

Bargaining Power of Buyers

The bargaining power of buyers increases when buyers can bargain for price reductions and demand better quality and services. Buyers become powerful if they are few but need to buy many products if they need standard products or they have alternative markets and if they can easily form alliances (Laudon and Laudon, 2014; Yunna and Yisheng 2014). For example, Nguza-Mduba (2020) reported that large players in the South African tourism industry always wanted to pay low prices irrespective of the product or service offered. When doing so, they tend to have bargaining power over small tourism businesses.

Bargaining Power of Suppliers

The power of suppliers refers to the ability of suppliers to control the power of resources and with it their bargaining power. Often this occurs when other suppliers have a stable market position or products and services that are unique to those suppliers making it difficult for customers to change their suppliers. The strong bargaining power of suppliers allows suppliers to sell low-quality materials to their buyers and their bargaining power increases when there are few suppliers but many buyers, when suppliers are large and threaten to forward-integrate, few substitute products, and these suppliers hold scarce resources and the costs of switching from the suppliers are high (Laudonon and Laudon, 2014; Mugo, 2020).

The Threat of Substitute Products

Threats of substitute products and services are influenced by customer price sensitivity, economic efficiency of alternatives, number of available alternatives, and forwarding costs. The threat of substitute products becomes real when buyers can easily find substitute products with attractive prices or better quality and when buyers can switch from one product or service with little cost (Nashruddin, 2019). Laudon and Laudon (2014) cite four major strategies for countering these competitive forces to prevent substitute products. These strategies are; becoming a low-cost leadership, product differentiation, focusing on the market niche, and strengthening customer and supplier intimacy.

Threats of New Entrants

Threats of new entrants into business influence the strategic competitiveness of organisations. These threats according to Yunna and Yisheng (2014) are reflected by two factors, that is, barriers to entry and the reaction of enterprises to new entrants. Threats of new entrants are higher when the industry is profitable and there a few entry barriers.

Business Intelligence Concepts

Business intelligence (BI) is the process of integrating data from disparate internal and external data sources, applying analysis tools and techniques to understand the information within the data, making decisions, and taking actions based on this gained insight (Gangadharan and Swami, 2004). This transforms raw data into meaningful and useful information used to enable more effective strategic, tactical, and operational insights and decision-making to drive business performance (Evelson and Nicolson, 2008).

Business intelligence is important for analysing competition strategies, determining their strengths and weaknesses, and examining technological dynamics (Nenzhelele and Pellissier, 2013). This is achieved by analyzing a wide range of data and responding promptly to customers or other parties. The results help enterprises in several ways: identifying major competitors, new markets, concepts, products, or opportunities; supporting, relaunching, or repositioning the existing brand; generating ideas for new products, tracking market trends and formulating strategic plans. According to Ragazou et al.,(2023), therefore BI might be a difference between a company with ordinary performance and a company with great performance. This is because firms frequently experience lower operating expenses and can create differentiation strategies when BI is integrated into the enterprise's value chain. This is motivated by built-in business intelligence (BI) capabilities to gather information about the company's clientele, including demographic and psychographic details about their tastes, spending patterns, and consumption patterns. If the company uses this information to its advantage, it can produce unique products that are challenging for rival businesses to imitate. Ahmed, Ahmad, Khoso, Arif, and Palwishah (2014) examined the competitive intelligence and marketing effectiveness of organizations in Pakistan, diffusing BI into sub-variables that included market opportunities, competitor risks, competitor threats, technological intelligence, technical intelligence, and strategic intelligence. The results of the research show that all the sub-variables are significantly used by the organisations in Pakistan to make their marketing effective and that BI is important to make marketing effective for a business. Egberi and Okpako-Uyeh (2011) assessed the BI and marketing effectiveness of corporate organizations in Nigeria and reported that there was a significant positive relationship between competitive intelligence and organizational profitability.

Business Intelligence Information Systems

The information technology revolution has created many opportunities and challenges for many organizations. Technology has levelled the competitive environment, where a world without computers, mobile phones, and the Internet is inconceivable, as information technology has brought buyers and sellers together (Chung and Wang, 2004). Figure 2, depicts some of the information systems that are used by BI.

Figure 2. BI information systems

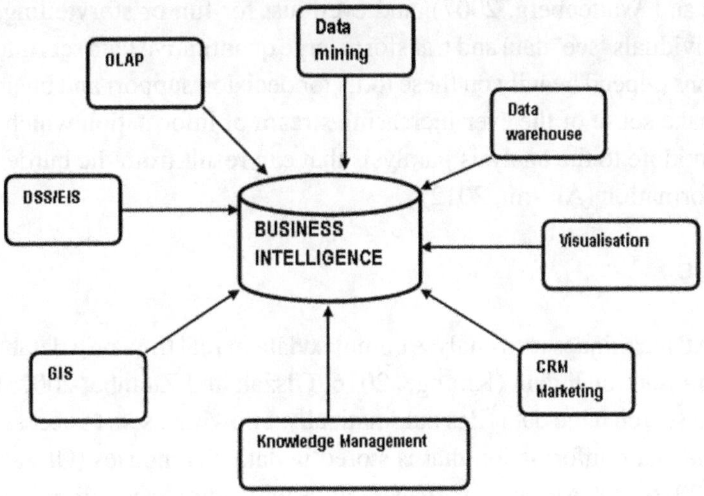

where: OLAP = On-Line Analytical Data Processing, CRM = Customer Relationship Management, DSS = Decision Support Systems, GIS = Geographic Information Systems.

Data Warehouses

Data warehouses refer to collections of business data that are organised and validated in readiness for analysis to aid decision-making (Kirange, 2016; Olszak and Ziemba, 2003; Shollo and Galliers, 2016). A data warehouse is considered the core component of a BI system (Negash, 2004) because it stores aggregated information as well as data that has been analyzed through ETL tools for ease of use by those in the various stages of decision-making (Kirange, 2016; Olszak and Ziemba, 2003; Shollo and Galliers, 2016). The major role data warehouses have played is to assert the role of knowledge as a source of competitive advantage among SMEs that operate under extreme competitive pressures, derived from scanning the environment to identify threats to competitiveness.

In the South African tourism industry context, data collected for storage in the data warehouse included data about products tourists purchase, services they experience, destination choices they evaluate, and the kind of accommodations they select so that tourism firms can fully understand the behaviour of tourists to increase their satisfaction and boost business revenues and profits (Vajirakachorn and Chongwatpol, 2017). Such data then becomes a backbone for research and development (R&D) to facilitate innovations and developments of new products and services. A data warehouse cannot be complete without the deployment of ETL tools which ensure that all data collected and compiled is appropriately loaded into the warehouse.

Data Visualization

Data visualization is the visual and interactive exploration and graphic representation of data of any size, type (structured and unstructured), or origin. The purposes of visualizing data are multi-fold, ranging from general comprehension and understanding of ideas, supporting information behaviours (analysis and decision support, information seeking, browsing, navigation), to artistic (beauty) expression and appreciation (Viégas and Wattenberg, 2007), and even just for fun or storytelling. Data Visualization technologies help individuals 'see' data and transform large quantitative data sets into useful information. Countless organisations depend heavily on these tools for decision support and business intelligence and to help individuals make sense of the ever-increasing stream of information which bombards them and provides a creative antidote to the analysis paralysis that can result from the burden of processing such a large volume of information (Alazmi, 2012).

OLAP Techniques

The main aim of OLAP techniques is to analyse complex data in real time on a database that is constantly being updated with transactional data (Kirange, 2016; Olszak and Ziemba, 2007; Shollo and Galliers, 2016). The OLAP can search huge data files automatically, allowing users to access, analyse, and model business problems and share information that is stored in data warehouses (Olszak and Ziemba, 2007; Shollo and Galliers, 2016). OLAP helps managers with multi-dimensional tools to analyze data from multiple perspectives to discover hidden information and act as may be necessary. According to Hart and Porter (2004), OLAP is a powerful, highly interactive BI tool that enables users to, amongst other things:

a) Perform fast and dynamic analysis of aggregate data;
b) View information from multiple perspectives or dimensions;
c) Carry out trend analysis over sequential periods;
d) 'Drill-down' through various levels of data to retrieve the underlying details.

One area in which OLAP has been applied is the customer-focus studies. Customer focus involves addressing the needs and anticipations of current and potential customers by developing a wide-ranging insight into customer needs and then conveying recognized value to customers (Islamgaleyev et al., 2020). Business organisations such as SMEs can implement customer focus as a strategic orientation that identifies their capability to develop and convey improved customer value through the processing of market insight (Aziz et al., 2021). The anticipated results of a customer-focus strategy consist of the creation of value for the customer which brings about customer loyalty and business organization performance (Madhani, 2020). Literature shows that customer-focused strategy inspires customer interaction actions which lead to uniqueness and value in customer experience. The actual manifestation of customer-focus strategy is contingent on the entrenchment of customer-focus as a culture throughout the business organization (Lee and Lee, 2020). Customer-focus culture and practices ensure the enhancement of the business organization's overall performance and the development of competitive advantage. Customer focus is recognized as an internal resource of any business organization that can improve business performance and several studies have been carried out to validate this assertion. Among these studies in the developing world context is Abrokwah-Larbi (2023) who used the Resource-based View model in studying the impact of customer focus on the performance of West African economies. The results show that customer focus has a positive and significant relationship with financial performance, customer performance, internal business process performance, and learning and growth performance, thus supporting the literature on the positive impact of customer focus on SME performance. Among the tools that were used were AI-based innovations and OLAP tools for customer relationship management.

Customer Relationship Management (CRM)

The concept of CRM involves creating knowledge and relationships and shaping customer perceptions and perceptions about the firm and its products, and all this is done through modern digital technologies. According to Josiah and Ekpo (2019), the implementation of CRM results in improved market performance of sales and profitability across different forms of organisations, SMEs included. This is because CRM adopts advances in database technologies and the recent innovations of BI.

In the Cross River State of Nigeria, Josiah and Ekpo (2019), found out that CRM had a significant relationship with the performance of SMEs and this was true across the various components of CRM, namely, inquiry management, customer management, customer relationship upgrading, technology and customer services. Similarly, in Saudi Arabia, a study by Alenazi and Alanzi (2023) confirmed a positive relationship between CRM and the competitiveness of SMEs and further encouraged SMEs to invest in CRM systems. Additionally, in Nigeria, Nwankwo and Kanyangale (2023), reported that CRM contributed to the survival of SMEs through improved strategies for complaints handling and also further recommended SMEs to adopt CRM technologies that are customer-oriented. However, literature on the adoption of CRM among South African SMEs shows gaps in factors that influence the adoption of these technologies despite the low usage of these technologies in getting customer feedback (Fourie, 2015).

Decision Support Systems

Decision support systems (DSS) describe a set of technologies that aid users, particularly those in senior management positions in their decision-making routines. A successful DSS integrates data from multiple sources and applies analytics to provide insights to decision-makers. The implementation of DSS is considered crucial to the sustenance of the competitive advantages of enterprise because the business environment is dynamic and the impact of competitive pressure is dominant among SMEs. According to Kitsios and Kamaritou (2018), research on DSS adoption and use has previously focused on larger enterprises with few researchers having paid attention to the application of DSS among SMEs, particularly in the developing world context. Among some DSS services that have been proposed is the web-based DSS by Ponis and Christou (2013) which computes market trends and predicts supplier/customer-related trends.

Data Mining

Extracting knowledge from the huge amount of data available to a company has been recognised as one of the most valuable ways to obtain a competitive advantage. In this sense, the recognition of the importance of data mining allowed this research area to be among the fields of computer science that have produced the biggest amount of research and development in recent years. Data mining refers to some techniques that are designed to identify relationships between data within a data warehouse to aid enterprises no matter their seizes and complexity, in making appropriate decisions based on available knowledge. The data mining process involves discovering various patterns, generalizations, regularities, and rules in data resources (Kirange, 2016; Olszak and Ziemba, 2007; Shollo and Galliers, 2016). Knowledge acquired from data mining may be used to predict the outcome of a decision (Shollo and Galliers, 2016). Techniques for data mining include classification, estimation, prediction, time series analysis, and market basket analysis (Zeng et al., 2006). These techniques are usually aligned with the needs of an organization to help decision-making by discovering various patterns, generalizations, regularities, and rules in data resources.

Data explosion as a result of the rapid digital transformation is critical for SMEs because, during the DM process, organizations can radically learn more about their business and translate the new knowledge into better decision-making and performance, transforming traditional SMEs into organizations with a competitive advantage. For example, suppose an SME aims to mine its customer data, the potential benefit would entail creating cross-selling avenues at a higher margin, improving its customer retention and satisfaction rates, identifying the most profitable customer group, enhancing the SME's marketing and sales strategy (Tan, Yeoh, Boo and Liew, 2013). In the mining of inventory data, on the other hand, SMEs can gain an advantage by forecasting the inventory that will help reduce the total value of stock held. This would create a positive implication in allowing timely inventory purchases from the supplier, creating a supplier lock-in, and leading the SME to a better trading agreement (Waller & Fawcett, 2013). It is therefore evident that DM can create business opportunities to enable SMEs to stay ahead of their competition and leverage the possibilities.

In Nigeria, data mining was used to predict customer behaviour by Afolabi et al.,(2019) and the major data mining models used were Statistical models, clustering, classification, Psychological prediction Modeling, Particle Swarm Optimization, Neuro-Fuzzy, and Graph Mining. The use of data mining in CRM among SMEs in the Kenyan banking sector was investigated by Miller and Nyauncho (2015). On an individual customer basis, the main benefits of this work were well-prepared customer marketing calls and better anticipation of customer needs, rather than just reacting to customer requests. Other possibilities according to Miller and Nyauncho (2015) included:

a) Finding customers whose relationships can be revived and expanded.
b) Increasing knowledge of which financial institutions are competitors.
c) Prioritizing customers, and establishing segments for service.
d) Understanding whom the SME customers do business with, including whom they pay and who pays them.

Among several DM innovations is cloud mining which has been used to collect and analyse cloud-based data using advanced analytics. Cloud mining is a process of applying data mining techniques to large repositories of data in the cloud. Cloud mining has been used for grouping users with common browsing behaviour, grouping web pages with similar content extracting user profiles from the clusters designed, and clustering that will form the basis of personalisation. Some of the clustering known methods are fuzzy clustering, partitioning, model-based, and hierarchical.

With an increase of companies that offer cloud services in Zimbabwe such as Yo Africa, Utande, and Realtime BYTES, organizations have all the room to install their services in the cloud due to its advantage. This means more structured and unstructured data streams will continue to grow which when exploited can give rich business knowledge and insights (Kavu et al., 2014). Another area that has benefited from the application of data mining among Nigerian SMEs is targeted marketing (Afolabi, Worlu and Uwadia, 2016). As one of the competitive strategies for competitiveness based on Porter's forces model, targeted marketing enables suppliers to focus on the market niche. According to (Ogechukwu et al., (2013), the main problems of marketing encountered by SMEs in Nigeria have to do with the fact that they do not understand, and do not know how to apply marketing concepts. These businesses do not have the knowledge and skills required for basic marketing. Important marketing ingredients which include marketing research, market segmentation, and marketing planning and control are often overlooked as not important, leading to poor quality products, unawareness of competition, poor promotion, poor distribution, and poor pricing methods. It is therefore important for SMEs to focus on target marketing to grow their business. Data mining techniques, therefore, become necessary for uncovering hidden patterns and predicting future trends and behaviours in the financial markets. Additionally, Rajagopal (2011) was able to identify high-profit, high-value, and low-risk customers by using a data mining technique called customer- clustering, while Rossi et al., (1996) used the purchase history data for targeted marketing using a random effects choice model to measure household preferences and sensitivities using the Bayesian method of inference.

Decision Support Systems (DSS)

Decision support systems are handy when managers' decision-making skills are deficient and managers believe that their use of DSSs would improve their performance. Duan and Xu, (2014). Also reported that the usage of DSS by SMEs in developed countries had remained low although there was evidence from the literature that reported that among SMEs, managers who used DSS positively viewed these technologies. According to Duan and Xu (2014), research on the application of DSS for facilitating competitive intelligence among SMEs is under-explored and there is evidence of the low adoption of these technologies particularly in the developing world. Among DSS services that have been proposed in the web-based DSS by Ponis and Christou (2013) which computed market trends and predicted supplier/customer-related trends.

Knowledge Management

Over decades, knowledge management (KM) has played a pivotal role in supporting the competitiveness of organizations and the benefits of using these technologies have also been extended to SMEs in the developing world. The concept of knowledge management (KM) involves leveraging what is already known to work to achieve the greatest impact and improve performance. According to Nuryanti and Andreas (2017), there is a strong relationship between KM and corporate performance which in turn has a direct positive relationship with the competitiveness of an enterprise. Enterprises, therefore, have come to realize KM as a foundation for competitive advantage, with knowledge presenting what has happened; what is happening, and what could happen (Stodder, 2013). This process involves both individualistic and collective knowledge resources (Azam, Khilji, and Khan, 2016). In both circumstances, the transformation of intangible tacit knowledge into explicit knowledge takes place, actively capturing and organizing explicit knowledge that organisations generate to maximize effectiveness and efficiency. The process of KM comprises people, processes, and technology. Among some of the advantages of using KM as reported by Choochote and Nurse (2012) are improved research, rapidity, and flexibility in decision-making and internal communication. However, some SMEs in the developing world still lack an understanding of the requirements for building, using, and managing KM systems (Choochote and Nurse, 2012). Thus, BI has become evident as a logical enabler of information management that is a key necessity of decision-making.

The implementation of KM in developing countries has been limited particularly among SMEs. In comparing the importance of KM between African SMEs, to European and American SMEs, Gavurova et al., (2020) reported that many SMEs in Africa faced challenges in KM for competitiveness and suggested that policy interventions be developed to support technological innovations to aid organizational performances. However, Azam et al., (2020) cite several organizations in the developed world that have implemented KM, and among them are Siemens, BP Group, Coca-cola, The World Bank, Ericson software, and Atkins. Across these organizations, KM has transformed organizations into knowledge-driven enterprises, enabling them to utilize their knowledge resources to exploit new opportunities and enhance their competitive strategies. Among some competitive advantages reported among SMEs that used KM practices in Indonesian by Azam et al., (2020) are, superiority in prices, superiority in quality and design, superiority in customer responsiveness, and superiority in innovations. Among some tools that have been used recently in KM are social media tools that have been used to support business intelligence through AI and data analytics. These technologies have facilitated collaboration and the co-creation of knowledge among inadequately resourced SMEs.

Geographical Information Systems Mapping

The use of Geographical Information Systems (GIS) and their adoption by SMEs in the developing world has not been researched adequately. In many developing countries, technologies such as GIS have been used by governments and private organizations in managing interrelationships between retail and service providers, wholesale goods, and service providers (Mennecke and West, 2001; Mei et al., 2021). Among some writers who have investigated the use of GIS in developing countries in Amande, Painho, and Oliveira (2018) in Mozambique where these technologies were used to counter competitive pressures in both public and private sector organisations. The use of GIS and GPS permits SMEs to utilize satellite imagery, street maps, real-time traffic analysis, and route planning and public transportation (Arsad et al., 2018). According to Erdin and Ozkaya (2020), GIS can be used for resource management, land review, and business planning. For this technology to achieve this, it utilizes its computing strengths for data management, data integration, advanced query processing, analysis, and visualization of spatial data. However, generally, there is a consensus in the literature that there is a difference in adoption patterns of these technologies between developed and developing nations as evidenced by lower adoption levels amongst developing nations.

Business Intelligence Technologies

BI technologies have continued to gain popularity among both small-scale enterprises and large-scale enterprises. They have also gained the interest of researchers and system developers, resulting in several innovations in BI technologies. These innovations have evolved in their level of sophistication and functionality over time, with newer versions coming up to accommodate the dynamic requirements of the business environment and the need to embrace big data across a wide spectrum of enterprises. Tutunea and Rus (2015) reviewed some of these BI solutions which have been in the form of both open-source and commercial software from vendors such as Actuate, Jaspersoft, Pentaho, and SpagoBI. Among the vendors who have developed commercial solutions are Information Builder, Microstrategy, Panorama Software, QlikTech, Actauate, Microsoft, Oracle, IBM, SAP and SAS Institute (Tutenea and Rus, 2015). Table 1 shows the different BI solutions that have been used.

Table 1. BI technologies

Vendor	Product
IBM	IBM Cognos Express
SAP	Business Objects Edge
SAS	SAS BI
Microsoft	Performance Pint Server 2007
Microstrategy	Microstrategy Reporting Suite
Oracle	Oracle BI Suite Standard Edition
QlikView	QlikView
Information Builders	Web Focus 7
Actuate	Actuate BI
Vai	S2K Analytics

(Source: Tutunea and Rus, 2015)

Other technologies that have been developed in recent years include among others, Scoro, Dundas BI, Microsoft Power BI, Zoho Analytics, SeekTable, Data Pine and Tableau. Fernandez et al., (2016) also report on several BI projects that have been implemented although the data is not segregated according to organisational size. Among these cases were Cognos BI offered to Bayer in Germany, to consolidate processes carried out by the organisation in several countries that it operates. This enables the company to improve its decision-making through the use of standardised reports and dashboards. The uses of such technologies reduce operational and consultation costs, In addition to this Fernandez et al., (2016) also cited Sbaro Inc. which operated restaurants in the Italian-American cuisine restaurants in the USA where the BI solution Aloha Enterprises, integrated data from several of its restaurants and applied business analytics. This reduced labour costs and improved the management of employees. From a study by Magona, Khumalo and du Plessis (2021) in South Africa, one of the dominant BI solutions was IBM Cognos which improved decision-making among SMEs by incorporating functionalities from several applications such as Oracle, SAP, Microsoft and Teradata. This solution provided statistical analysis and reporting tools which provided intuitive content, data protection, contextualised smart search and automatic visualisation.

Key functionalities among the generic BI solutions are:

i) Customisable dashboards that allow faster real-time decision-making;
ii) Localisation and business data visualisation in geographic or spatial data;
iii) Interactive reports;
iv) What-if analysis; and
v) Sharing and distribution of information to users.

However, regardless of the choice of BI solutions, generally, these technologies must have the following characteristics:

i) Data collection, analysis and visualisation
ii) Reporting and customisable dashboards

iii) Predictive analysis
iv) Integration with other systems, and
v) User security.

Application of the Different Business Intelligence Tools in SMEs

In the contemporary environment, intense competitive forces have exerted pressure on firms to innovate ways of enhancing their performance and competitive advantage. Therefore, every firm competing in an industry has a competitive strategy, whether it is explicitly developed through a planning process or may have evolved implicitly through the various activities of the various functional departments (Porter, 1980). Developing a competitive strategy is developing a broad formula for how a business is going to compete, what its goals should be, and what policies will be needed to carry out those goals. Strategy implies the exploitation of unique advantages of the organization in facing the challenges of the environment. In addition, competitive strategies are designed to give firms an understanding of the changes in the environment a view of the opportunities available to the firm, and a quick response to any barriers arising. Firms pursue pace-keeping by making better use of their resources to achieve sustainability and create a competitive advantage, making them superior to competing firms (Alnidawi and Omran, 2016). The strategy involves an organization deciding where it wants the business to go and how to get there. Strategy is a set of decision-making rules for the guidance of organizational behaviour (Walumweya and Phiri, 2022). A good strategy could be considered simple, consistent, and has a long-term objective.

BI has proliferated due to its effective application for disseminating, assimilating, and processing information businesses use to sense issues related to decision-making. This technology has also contributed to business performance, data integration from disparate sources, data warehousing, planning, forecasting, budgeting, and the decision-making that guides business operations toward desired performance. For substantiality of the decision-making, BI as an IS-led application provides the appropriate level of data accuracy and confidentiality of information which produces relevant knowledge (Brinkhues et al., 2014). BI's growing contribution to the business's growing performance has been recognized particularly for SMEs (Guarda et al., 2013) through improving decision support, in everchaning environments (Guarda et al., 2013; Isık et al., 2013). Korte et al. (2013) further suggest that BI can act as a driver to maintain a sustained competitive advantage over competitors and help a business preserve existing customers while at the same time making the business more attractive to new customers. BI also assists businesses in appreciating their capabilities in terms of strengths and weaknesses relative to those of competitors. This would then inform the business on which areas to make amends and which ones to concentrate on to attain a competitive edge over competitors or to sustain the competitive advantage if already attained. Further, management would then be in a position to make fact-based decisions on what next steps they ought to take to make their businesses a success. As a result, businesses that have adopted a BI system and can utilize it fully are inevitably destined for success because BI makes it easy for management to have immediate access to information about the status or any activities taking place in the various departments.

Geopolitical Dynamics

Although research generally acknowledges that BI plays a vital role in the attainment of organisational competitiveness, there has been uneven adoption of BI technologies between developed and developing economies. For example, Mudzana (2016) reported that BI adoptions have been dominant in North America, followed by Latin America and Western Europe, while Africa, the Middle East, Japan and Eastern Europe had fewer adopters of BI. Among SMEs in Bosnia and Herzegovina, according to Kasim et al., (2018), the most used systems among SMEs were Enterprise Resource Planning Systems (ERPs) and Customer Relationship Management (CRM) while only 17.8% used BI. Additionally in Burkina Faso, Ouédraogo, Compaoré and Nassè (2022) reported that only 7 out of the 60 SMEs investigated used BI and among these 60 SMEs, only 4 used systems for linking data from various sources and examples of BI tools that were used included ApacheSuperset, an open source software. This low adoption of BI in developing countries has hindered SMEs' efforts to internalise their businesses (Nahan-Suomela and Lautamäki, 2013). According to Zahor et al., (2023), many African SMEs face resource constraints which inhibit their efforts to internationalise their businesses and to compete in global markets. In addition to this, domestic market instability has sometimes forced African SMEs to explore international markets while at the same time, they lack technologies that enhance their responsiveness to environmental threats. Unequal patterns in the adoption of BI across the globe while providing unlimited opportunities for SMEs in the developed world, these technologies have created competitive pressures among SMEs in the developing world. This has mainly been a result of the development of big data and the Internet of Things (IoT). These technologies present large volumes of dynamic data to SMEs pressuring them to invest in newer digital infrastructures while their counterparts in the developed world would invest in R&D for product and service development for improved competitiveness. According to Miocevic and Crnjak-Karanovic (2011), such cognitive and information-based capabilities have a significant impact on the export performance of enterprises and their agility.

Factors Influencing the Adoption of BI

Several researchers have investigated factors that influence the adoption of BI in developing countries. Amon some theoretical approaches that have been used are TOE (Hmoud et al, 2023; Ghanem, 2021; Rahayu and Day, 2015), DoI, UTAUT, TAM, and TPB (Salisu et al, 2021). From these studies, in most developing countries, the adoption of BI is determined by technological (relative advantage, complexity, compatibility, observability, trialability), organisational characteristics(absorptive capacity, organisational resource availability, top management support, organisational size, top management support, presence of a champion) and environmental characteristics(competitive pressure, vendor support, government support), manager's characteristics(manager's innovativeness, manager's IT knowledge, manager's attitude towards IT). In South Africa, the adoption of BI technologies was found to be influenced by both organisational and environmental factors. Organisational readiness according to Akin-Adetero and Kabanda (2020) includes awareness, management support, business resources, human resources, employees' pressure, formal governance and technological readiness. Environmental readiness included market forces, support from industry, government readiness and sociocultural factors.

Challenges

There is agreement among studies that the main challenge for any business is gaining access to the systems needed to store and analyze such vast amounts of data. While, scale, timeliness, complexity, and privacy are considered the challenges of big data Mining, Raj (2016), and Ayoubi and Aljawarneh (2018 list various factors that affect SMEs' planning to adopt BI solutions and these are:

a) BI solutions are often expensive;
b) While off-the-shelf BI tools are available, the learning curve of such tools for non-technical business users is often steep;
c) Hosting a BI solution requires the support of a non-trivial, and often costly, hardware infrastructure;
d) While there is a wide range of BI solutions available, SMEs often lack in-depth knowledge of BI to select the most appropriate solution for addressing the business's needs;
e) Generating BI is often a non-trivial task that requires good knowledge and understanding of database modelling and data warehousing. Such technical know-how is often not readily available within most SMEs;
f) Limited IT resources;
g) Lack of top management commitment to the BI projects;
h) Low-level awareness;
i) Unfavourable perceptions towards BI, and security concerns.

This is supported by Gomwe, Potgiete, and Litheko (2023) who reported that in South Africa's North-West province, SMEs struggled to implement business intelligence as a strategy due to a lack of top management support, funding, staff motivation, education, and training, and internal environment commitment. In addition to these challenges, many SMEs in the developing world are owned by sole proprietors who often influence decision-making, sometimes interfering against the professional judgment of managers. This has often resulted in professional advice on innovations such as BI Investments being ignored. These reports were found to be true in South Africa and Zimbabwe by Gono et al., (2016) and Mveku et al., (2022), where SME owners disapproved of investments in new ICT-based innovation due to a lack of awareness of the potential benefits of using these technologies. Such challenges were also reported by Francis (2020) among SMEs in Nigeria where top management seemed not to support BI innovations and lacked clear vision and knowledge about BI services. In the context of SMEs in South Africa, Kikawa, Kalema and Carol (2019), reported that in Tshwane, technological, organisational, and environmental characteristics constraints influenced the adoption of BI among SMEs. Furthermore, in South Africa, Schoeman and Seymour (2022) reported fear-based perceptions related to BI among managers who feared losing control of AI-enabled processes. While these factors are legitimate barriers for SMEs to adopt a BI solution, they should not prove detrimental in promoting the implementation of BI solutions in SMEs.

Conclusion

There is a low usage of BI for supporting competitiveness among SMEs in the developing world. However, the use of these technologies provides opportunities for improved competitive strategies in the operational environment characterized by competitive rivalry, threats of new entrants, threats of substitute products, bargaining power of buyers, and bargaining power of suppliers. The use of different technologies of BI enables SMEs to develop innovations that may reduce the influence of these environmental factors through adopting strategies for low-cost production and low-cost leadership, customer segmentation, and product differentiation. However, several challenges confront SMEs in the developing world to adopt these BI innovations.

Recommendations

In the developing world context, SMEs are diverse, and recommending universal standards for the adoption of business intelligence is at present, impractical. The study therefore recommends research into universally accepted standards for BI adoption particularly in the developing world. The study acknowledges the one–size–fits principle is not feasible and this may be due to the diverse nature of these SMEs in the developing world, ranging from manufacturing, services, and tertiary. In addition to this, research institutions, business associations and the government must drive technological diffusion into SMEs by educating SME owners and managers on the benefits organisations realise from the implementation of business intelligence solutions.

REFERENCES

Abrokwah-Larbi, K. (2023). The impact of customer focus on the performance of business organisations: Evidence from SMEs in an emerging West African economy. *African Journal of Economic and Management Studies*.

Afolabi, I. T., Worlu, R. E., Adebayo, O. P., & Jonathan, O. (2019). Predicting Customer Behavior with Combination of Structured and Unstructured Data. 3rd International Conference on Science and Sustainable Development (ICSSD 2019). IOP Conf. Series. *Journal of Physics: Conference Series, 1299*, 012041. doi:10.1088/1742-6596/1299/1/012041

Afolabi, I.T., Worlu, R. E. & Uwadia, C. O. (2016). Data Mining Approach for Target Marketing SMEs in Nigeria. *Covenant Journal of Informatics & Communication Technology, 4*(2).

Akin-Adetoro, A & Salah Kabanda,S. (2020). Factors affecting the adoption of BYOD in South African small and medium enterprises. *Electron J Inf Syst Dev Ctries*.

Alazmi, A. R. R., & Alazmi, A. A. R. (2012). Data mining and visualization of large databases. *International Journal of Computer Science and Security*, *6*(5), 295–314.

Alenazi, S. A. & Alanazi, T.M. (2023).The Mediating Role of Sustainable Dynamic Capabilities in the Effect of Social Customer Relationship Management on Sustainable Competitive Advantage: A Study on SMEs in Saudi Arabia. *Sustainability. 15*(1952). doi:10.3390/su15031952

Alnidawi, A. B., & Omran, M. F. (2016). Human resource management activities adopted in the value chain model and their impact on the organizational sustainability - An empirical study of Jordanian pharmaceutical companies. *International Business Research*, *9*(9), 106–117. doi:10.5539/ibr.v9n8p106

Amande, N., Painho, M., & Oliveira, T. (2018). Geographic information technology usage in developing countries. A case study in Mozambique. *Geo-Spatial Information Science*, *21*(4), 331–345. doi:10.1080/10095020.2018.1523995

Anggadwita, G. & Mustafid, Q.Y. (2014). Identification of factors influencing the performance of small medium enterprises (SMEs). *Procedia-Social and Behavioral Sciences, 115,* 415-523.

Ayoubi, E., & Aljawarneh, S. (2018). Challenges and Opportunities of Adopting Business Intelligence in SMEs: Collaborative Model. *DATA '18, October 1–2, 2018, Madrid, Spain*. Association for Computing Machinery.

Azam, M., Khilji, A. B., & Khan, W. (2020). Knowledge management as a strategy & competitive advantage: A strong influence on success (A survey of knowledge management case studies of different organizations). *Public Policy and Administration Research*, *6*(10).

Aziz, N. A., Ismail, R., Omar, R., & Rahmana, I. (2021). Customer orientation and marketing innovation: A study of SMEs performance in East Coast Malaysia. *International Journal of Academic Research in Business & Social Sciences*, *11*(18), 202–219. doi:10.6007/IJARBSS/v11-i18/11628

Boateng, R. (2022). *Data-driven enterprises in Africa- An evaluation of winners and losers*. Centre for the Study for the Economics of Africa.

Brinkhues, R., Maçada, A. C., & Casalinho, G. (2014). Information Management Capabilities: Antecedents and Consequences. *Twentieth Americas Conference on Information Systems, Savannah, AISel.*

Bunyasi, G. N. W., Bwisa, H., & Namusonge, G. (2014). Effect of Access to Business Information on the Growth of Small and Medium Enterprises in Kenya. *International Journal of Business and Social Science*, *5*(10), 121–128.

Cataldo, A., Pino, G., & McQueen, R. J. (2020). Size matters: The impact of combinations of ICT assets on the performance of Chilean micro, small, and medium enterprises. *Information Technology for Development*, *26*(2), 292–315. doi:10.1080/02681102.2019.1684870

Chege, S. M., & Wang, D. (2020). Information technology innovation and its impact on job creation by SMEs in developing countries: An analysis of the literature review. *Technology Analysis and Strategic Management*, *32*(3), 256–271. doi:10.1080/09537325.2019.1651263

Chen, H., Chiang, R. H., & Storey, V. C. (2012). Business intelligence and analytics: From big data to big impact. *Management Information Systems Quarterly*, *36*(4), 1165–1188. doi:10.2307/41703503

Chung, Y., & Wang, W. (2004). The Levels of Information Technology Adoption, Business Network and a Strategic Position Model for Evaluating the Supply Chain. *Journal of Electronic Commerce Research*, *2*(5), 55–98.

(2015). Country: Evidence from Indonesia. *Procedia: Social and Behavioral Sciences*, *195*, 142–150.

Egberi, A. K., & Okpako-Uyeh, B. (2011). Competitive intelligence and marketing effectiveness of corporate business organizations in Nigeria. *International Journal of Economic Development Research and Investment*, (2), 3.

Erdin, C., & Ozkaya, G. (2020). Contribution of small and medium enterprises to economic development and quality of life in Turkey. *Heliyon*, *6*(2), 2. doi:10.1016/j.heliyon.2020.e03215 PMID:32055722

Evelson, B., & Nicolson, N. (2008). *Topic Overview: Business Intelligence-An Information Workplace Report*. Forrester.

Fernandez, J. L., Guiterrez, J. E., Castro, L. A., & Rodriguez, L. (2016). Integrating business analytics into SMEs in Mexico: Challenges and applications. *Avances en Interacción Humano-Computadora, 1*(1), 41–45. doi:10.47756/aihc.y1i1.13

Fourie, L .E. (2015). Categorizing South African SMEs according to Customer Relationship Building practices. *Corporate Ownership & Control, 13*(1).

Francis, O. O. (2020). Evaluation of the implementation of business intelligence systems on SME results in Lagos State, Nigeria. *International Journal of Novel Research in Computer Science and Software Engineering*, *7*(3), 1–12.

Gangadharan, G., & Swami, S. N. (2004). Business intelligence systems: design and implementation strategies. Information Technology Interfaces. *26th International Conference on, 2004*, 139-144.

Gavurova, B., Cepel, M., Belas, J., & Dvorsky, J. (2020). Strategic management in SMEs and its significance for enhancing the competitiveness in the V4 countries: A comparative analysis. *Management & Marketing. Challenges for the Knowledge Society*, *15*(4), 557–569. doi:10.2478/mmcks-2020-0032

Ghanem, S. K. R., & Hamid, N. A. A. (2021). Factors Influencing SME Performance: The Mediating and Moderating Role of Social Media Adoption and Organizational Culture. *Proceedings of the Second Asia Pacific International Conference on Industrial Engineering and Operations Management Surakarta*.

Gomwe, G., Potgiete, M., & Litheko, A. (2020). Business intelligence as a competitive advantage for SMMEs in the North West Province of South Africa. *Journal of Contemporary Management, 20*(1).

Gono, S., Harindranath, G., & Özcan, G. B. (2016). The adoption and impact of ICT in South African SMEs. *Strategic Change*, *25*(6), 717–734. doi:10.1002/jsc.2103

Grabova, O., Darmont, J., Chauchat, J. H., & Zolotaryova, I. (2010). Business intelligence for small and middle-sized enterprises. *SIGMOD Record*, *39*(2), 39–50. doi:10.1145/1893173.1893180

Guarda, T., Santos, M., Pinto, F., Augusto, M. & Silva, C. (2013). Business intelligence as a competitive advantage for SMEs. *International Journal of Trade, Economics & Finance, 4*(187).

Hart, M. L., & Porter, G. (2004). The impact of cognitive and other factors on the perceived usefulness of OLAP. *Journal of Computer Information Systems*, *45*(2), 47–56.

Hmoud, H., Al-Adwan, A. S., Horani, O., Yaseen, H., & Al Zoubi, J. Z. A. (2023). Factors influencing business intelligence adoption by higher education institutions. *Journal of Open Innovation*, *9*(3), 9. doi:10.1016/j.joitmc.2023.100111

Ipinnaiye, O., Dineen, D., & Lenihan, H. (2017). Drivers of SME performance: A holistic and multivariate approach. *Small Business Economics*, *48*(4), 883–911. doi:10.1007/s11187-016-9819-5

Isık, Ö., Jones, M. C., & Sidorova, A. (2013). Business intelligence success: The roles of BI capabilities and decision environments. *Information & Management*, *50*(1), 13–23. doi:10.1016/j.im.2012.12.001

Josiah, J. U., & Ekpo, N. S. (2019). Effect of Customer Relationship Management (CRM) on the Performance of SMEs on Hospitality Industry in Cross River State. *International Journal of Marketing and Communication Studies*, *4*(2).

Kamunge, M. S., Njeru, A., & Tirimba, O. I. (2014). Factors Affecting the Performance of Small and Micro Enterprises in Limuru Town Market of Kiambu County. Kenya. International Journal of Scientific and Research Publications, 4(12).

Kasim, T., Zijad, D., Mahir, H., & Merima, H. (2018). The use of business intelligence (BI) in small and medium-sized enterprises (SMEs) in Bosnia and Herzegovina, Economic Review. *Journal of Economics and Business, University of Tuzla. Faculty of Economics*, *16*(2), 23–37.

Kavu, T. D., Mastara, P., Phiri, L., & Jari, B. (2014). A Cloud Mining Model for SMEs in E-commerce in Zimbabwe. *International Journal of Scientific and Engineering Research*, *5*(4).

Keikhosrokiani, P. (2020). The Role of m-Commerce Literacy on the Attitude towards Using e-Torch in Penang, Malaysia. In *E-Business in the 21st Century* (Vol. 7, pp. 309–333). World Scientific. doi:10.1142/9789811231841_0013

Keikhosrokiani, P. (2022a). Big Data Analytics for Healthcare: Datasets, Techniques, Life Cycles, Management, and Applications. doi:10.1016/C2021-0-00369-2

Keikhosrokiani, P. (2022b). Handbook of Research on Consumer Behavior Change and Data Analytics in the Socio-Digital Era. doi:10.4018/978-1-6684-4168-8

Keikhosrokiani, P. (2023). *Handbook of Research on Consumer Behavioral Analytics in Metaverse and the Adoption of a Virtual World*. IGI Global. doi:10.4018/978-1-6684-7029-9

Kikawa, C. R., Kalema, B. M., & Carol, M. N. (2019). A statistical analysis of business intelligence acceptance by SMEs in the city of Tshwane, Republic of South Africa. *Academy of Entrepreneurship Journal*, *25*(2).

Kirange, S. (2016). Role of business intelligence in decision-making for SMEs. KHOJ. *Journal of Indian Management Research and Practices*, (Special Issue), 41–47.

Kitsios, F., & Kamariotou, M. (2018). Decision support systems and strategic planning: Information technology and SMEs' performance. *Int. J. Decision Support Systems*, *3*(1/2), 53. doi:10.1504/IJDSS.2018.094260

Korte, D., Ariyachandra, T., & Frolick, M. (2013). Business intelligence in the hospitality industry. *International Journal of Innovation, Management and Technology*, *4*(4), 429–434.

Lateef, M., & Keikhosrokiani, P. (2022). Predicting Critical Success Factors of Business Intelligence Implementation for Improving SMEs' Performances: A Case Study of Lagos State, Nigeria. *Journal of the Knowledge Economy*. Advance online publication. doi:10.1007/s13132-022-00961-8

Laudon, K. C., & Laudon, J. P. (2014). *Management Information Systems, Managing the Digital Firm* (13th ed.). Pearson Education Limited.

Lee, S. M., & Lee, D. (2020). Untact: A new customer service strategy in the digital age. *Service Business*, *14*(1), 1–22. doi:10.1007/s11628-019-00408-2

Madhani, P. M. (2020). Building a customer-focused strategy: Conceptual frameworks and research Propositions. *SSRN*, *17*(3), 5–25. doi:10.2139/ssrn.3717410

Magona,T ., Khumalo, S & du Plessis, T. (2021). Affordability of business intelligence tools suitable for SMEs decision making. *South African Journal of Information Management.*

Mei, A. W. S., Hong, P. L., Keikhosrokiani, P., Xin, C. H., Ying, T. X., & Samat, N. (2021). A GIS-based Mobile Application to Improve Tourism Experience: A Case Study of Terengganu, Malaysia. *2021 International Congress of Advanced Technology and Engineering*, 1–10. 10.1109/ICOTEN52080.2021.9493443

Miller, M., & Nyauncho, E. (2015). *Effective data mining and analysis for SME banking. Project technical note*. FSD Kenya.

Miocevic, D., & Crnjak-Karanovic, B. (2011). Cognitive and Information-Based Capabilities in the Internationalization of Small and Medium-Sized Enterprises: The Case of Croatian Exporters. *Journal of Small Business Management*, *49*(4), 537–557. doi:10.1111/j.1540-627X.2011.00335.x

Mudzana, T. (2016). *Business intelligence information systems success: A South African study* [Doctor of Philosophy Thesis]. University of Kwazulu-Natal, South Africa.

Mudzana, T., & Maharaj, M. (2015). Measuring the success of business-intelligence systems in South Africa: An empirical investigation applying the DeLone and McLean Model. *South African Journal of Information Management*, *17*(1), 1–7. doi:10.4102/sajim.v17i1.646

Mugo, P. (2020). Porter's five forces influence competitive advantage in the telecommunication industry in Kenya. *European Journal of Business and Strategic Management*, *5*(2), 30–49. doi:10.47604/ejbsm.1140

Mutula, S., & Van Brakel, P. (2007). ICT skills readiness for the emerging global digital economy among small businesses in developing countries: A case study of Botswana. *Library Hi Tech*, *25*(2), 231–245. doi:10.1108/07378830710754992

Mveku, B., Muzvidziwa, E., Mutero, T., & Matapo, S. (2022). The impact of ICT adoption decision-making: Case of Zimbabwean SME owner-managers. *International Journal of Research and Innovation in Applied Science*, *VII*(VI).

Nahan-Suomela, R., & Lautamäki, S. (2013). The role of market orientation in the internationalization of SMEs. In *Cultural and Technological Influences on Global Business* (pp. 242–257). IGI Global. doi:10.4018/978-1-4666-3966-9.ch013

Negash, S. (2004). Business Intelligence. *Communications of the Association for Information Systems*, *13*, 177–195. doi:10.17705/1CAIS.01315

Nenzhelele, T. E., & Pellissier, R. (2013). Towards a universal definition of competitive intelligence. *South African Journal of Information Management*, *15*(2), 1–7.

Nguza-Mduba, B. (2020). *Intuitive competitive intelligence: the entrepreneurial path to success for small and medium-sized enterprises (SMEs) in the tourism sector in the Eastern Cape Province* [Doctor of Business Administration thesis]. University of Kwazulu-Natal.

Nuryanti, H., & Andreas, S. P. (2017). The influence of knowledge management on business performance and competitive advantage in Riau food products on small and medium enterprises in Pekan Baru. *International Journal of Scientific & Technology Research*, *6*(10).

Nwankwo, C. A., & Kanyangale, M. I. (2023). Customer Relationship Management and Survival of Manufacturing Small and Medium Enterprises in Nigeria. Journal of Economic and Social Development (JESD) – Resilient Society, 10(2).

Olszak, C. M., & Ziemba, E. (2003), Business intelligence as a key to management of an enterprise. *Proceedings of Informing Science and IT Education Conference*. 10.28945/2672

Olszak, C. M., & Ziemba, E. (2007). Approach to building and implementing business intelligence systems. *Interdisciplinary Journal of Information, Knowledge, and Management*, *2*(1), 135–148. doi:10.28945/105

Omsa, S., Abdullah, I. H., & Jamali, H. (2017). Five Competitive Forces Model and the Implementation of Porter's Generic Strategies to Gain Firm Performances. *Science Journal of Business and Management*, *5*(1), 9–16. doi:10.11648/j.sjbm.20170501.12

Ouédraogo, D., Compaoré, I., & Nassè, T. B. (2022). Practice of business intelligence by SMEs in Burkina Faso. *International Journal of Management & Entrepreneurship Research*, *4*(1), 48–58. doi:10.51594/ijmer.v4i1.262

Ponelis, S. & Britz, J. (2011). The role of business intelligence in information-intensive small businesses: initial results from an interpretive study. *MWAIS 2011 Proceedings, 9*(23), 345-361.

Ponis, S. T., & Christou, I. T. (2013). Competitive intelligence for SMEs: A web-based decision support system. *International Journal of Business Information Systems, 12*(3), 243–258. doi:10.1504/IJBIS.2013.052449

Porter, M. E. (1980). *Competitive Strategy: Techniques for Analyzing Industries and Competitors*. Free Press.

Ragazou, K., Passas, I., Garefalakis, A., & Zopounidis, C. (2023). Business intelligence model empowering SMEs to make better decisions and enhance their competitive advantage. *Discover Analytics*.

Raj, R., Wong, H. S., & Beaumont, A. J. (2016). Business Intelligence Solution for an SME. *CASE (Philadelphia, Pa.)*.

Rajagopal, S. (2011). Customer Data Clustering Using Data Mining Technique. International Journal of Database Management Systems, 3(4).

Rosenbusch, N., Brinckmann, J., & Bausch, A. (2011). Is innovation always beneficial? A meta-analysis of the relationship between innovation and performance in SMEs. *Journal of Business Venturing, 26*(4), 26. doi:10.1016/j.jbusvent.2009.12.002

Salisu, I., Sappri, M. B. M. & Omar, M. F. B. (2021) The adoption of business intelligence systems in small and medium enterprises in the healthcare sector: A systematic literature review. *Cogent Business & Management, 8*(1).

Scheps, S. (2008). *Business Intelligence For Dummies*. Wiley Publishing.

Schink, H. (2009). Current state and future challenges of real-time ETL. *Proceedings 2nd student conference on software engineering and database systems*.

Schoeman, F., & Seymour, L. F. (2020). Understanding the Low Adoption of AI in South African Medium Sized Organisations. *Proceedings of 43rd Conference of the South African Institute of Computer Scientists and Information Technologists.*

Serumaga-Zake, P. A. (2017). The role of user satisfaction in implementing a Business Intelligence System. *South African Journal of Information Management, 19*(1), 1–8. doi:10.4102/sajim.v19i1.736

Shollo, A., & Galliers, R. D. (2016). Towards an understanding of the role of business intelligence systems in organizational knowing. *Information Systems Journal, 26*(4), 339–367. doi:10.1111/isj.12071

Stodder, D. (2013). *Achieving greater agility with business intelligence: Improving speed and flexibility for BI, analytics, and data warehousing*. TDWI Research.

Tarek, B. H., & Adel, G. (2016). Business intelligence versus entrepreneurial competitive intelligence and international competitiveness of North African SMEs. *Journal of International Entrepreneurship, 14*(4), 539–561. doi:10.1007/s10843-016-0194-8

Tutunea, M. & Rus, V. (2015). Business intelligence solutions for SMEs. *Procedia Economics and Finance, 3,* 865-870.

Uwagaba, J., Omotosho, T. D., & George, G. O. (2023). *Exploring the Barriers to Artificial Intelligence Adoption in Sub-Saharan Africa's Small and Medium Enterprises and the Potential for Increased Productivity*. World Wide Journal of Multidisciplinary Research and Development.

Vajirakachorn, T., & Chongwatpol, J. (2017). Application of business intelligence in tourism industry: A case study of a local food festival in Thailand. *Tourism Management Perspectives, 23*, 75–86. doi:10.1016/j.tmp.2017.05.003

Viégas, F. B., & Wattenberg, M. (2007). Artistic data visualization: Beyond visual analytics. *Proceedings of the 2nd International Conference on Online Communities and Social Computing*. 10.1007/978-3-540-73257-0_21

Waller, M. A., & Fawcett, S. E. (2013). Data science, predictive analytics, and big data: A revolution that will transform supply chain design and management. *Journal of Business Logistics*, *4*(3), 77–84. doi:10.1111/jbl.12010

Walumweya, M., & Phiri, J. (2022). Adopt effective competitive strategies in response to environmental challenges for the national public broadcasting corporation in developing countries: A participatory approach. *Open Journal of Business and Management*, *10*(1), 175–191. doi:10.4236/ojbm.2022.101011

Wang, Y. (2016). What are the biggest obstacles to the growth of SMEs in developing countries? An empirical evidence from an enterprise survey. *Borsa Istanbul Review, 16*(3).

Yunna, W., & Yisheng, Y. (2014). The competition situation analysis of the Shale gas industry in China: Applying Porter's five forces and scenario model. *Renewable & Sustainable Energy Reviews*, *40*, 798–805. doi:10.1016/j.rser.2014.08.015

Zahor, N., Khan, Z., Meyer, M., & Laker, B. (2023). Internal entrepreneurial behaviour of internationalising African SMEs-Towards a new research agenda. *Journal of Business Research*, 154.

Zeng, L., Xu, L., Shi, Z., Wang, M., & Wu, W. (2006). *Techniques, processes, and enterprise solutions of business intelligence.* Paper presented at the 2006 IEEE International Conference on Systems, Man, and Cybernetics, Taipei. 10.1109/ICSMC.2006.385050

Zhi, Z., & Guixian, Z. (2010). Notice of retraction: developing a framework for business intelligence systems in Southwest, China. *2010 3rd International Conference on Computer Science and Information Technology,* (7), 182-184.

KEY TERMS AND DEFINITIONS

Business Intelligence: The technology-driven process of collecting, processing, and analysing information to enhance the competitiveness of an enterprise.

Competitive Intelligence: The ability of an enterprise to apply knowledge solutions to gain a competitive advantage.

Competitive Strategy: Policies and procedures that a business uses to gain a competitive advantage.

Competitiveness: The capacity of an enterprise to outperform its competitors.

Data Mining: The process of extracting hidden meanings, trends, and patterns from large datasets.

Data Warehouse: A storage facility for large datasets in a big data environment.

Porter's Forces: A model used to study the competitive environment of a business.

SME: Enterprises that employ a limited number of employees.

Section 3
Innovations in Healthcare Intelligence

Chapter 8
ADHD Healthcare Intelligence: A Synergistic Approach with Big Data and AI for Better Screening, Diagnosis, Treatment, and Monitoring

Antonio Pesqueira
https://orcid.org/0000-0003-1530-6451
ISCTE, University Institute of Lisbon, Portugal

Maria José Sousa José Sousa
https://orcid.org/0000-0001-8633-4199
ISCTE, University Institute of Lisbon, Portugal

Andreia de Bem Machado Bem Machado
https://orcid.org/0000-0002-4404-0341
Federal University of Santa Catarina, Brazil

Sama Bolog
University of Basel, Switzerland

Luiz Vieira
Takeda Pharmaceuticals, USA

Ioana Bolog
Alnylam, Switzerland

ABSTRACT

Technological advancements are revolutionizing the healthcare sector, notably in the treatment and management of attention deficit/hyperactivity disorder (ADHD). This shift from traditional therapeutic and pharmacological interventions towards a more data-driven approach marks a significant change in ADHD care. The integration of big data (BD) and artificial intelligence (AI) has introduced innovative and effective methods for ADHD management. These technologies not only bring analytical accuracy but also an empathetic understanding of patient needs, enhancing the quality of life through improved screening accuracy, early diagnosis, and the facilitation of remote treatments. This chapter explores a novel method that synergizes BD and AI to enhance the screening, diagnosis, treatment, and monitoring of ADHD. It critically analyzes the increased efficiency and effectiveness in identifying and managing ADHD through a comprehensive literature review and an online questionnaire to forty-eight experts from the healthcare industry. The research underscores the indispensability of BD and AI in developing new clinical approaches, particularly in the backdrop of escalating ADHD cases and broader mental

DOI: 10.4018/979-8-3693-1210-0.ch008

health challenges. The findings align strongly with theoretical expectations, demonstrating significant advancements over previous methodologies. By introducing a strategic technological model that optimally utilizes BD and AI in ADHD care, this research not only proposes an advanced support system for patients but also promotes public health and sustainable, equitable ADHD care practices. Furthermore, it highlights the profound implications for future ADHD studies, potentially revolutionizing the realms of ADHD screening, diagnosis, treatment, and monitoring.

1. INTRODUCTION

Attention-Deficit/Hyperactivity Disorder (ADHD) is a prevalent neurological disorder, affecting 8-10% of school-age children globally. Characterized by symptoms of impulsivity, hyperactivity, and inattention, ADHD significantly impacts cognitive, intellectual, behavioral, emotional, and social functioning. Despite its widespread occurrence, precise etiology remains elusive, although genetic imbalances in catecholamine metabolism in the cerebral cortex are recognized as a major contributing factor. ADHD's implications extend beyond the individual, affecting family dynamics, educational achievements, and societal participation. Effective screening, diagnosis, treatment, and monitoring are paramount. Current research links increased ADHD symptoms with heightened engagement in digital platforms, such as social media and smartphone use, suggesting a potential intersection between technology and ADHD management. This nexus is particularly critical in the context of rising ADHD diagnoses and the urgent need for innovative approaches to manage this growing challenge (Black, Grant, 2014; Breaux, et al., 2023).

Technological advancements, notably the integration of Big Data (BD) and Artificial Intelligence (AI), are already revolutionizing ADHD care. Traditionally managed with therapy and medication, ADHD treatment is undergoing a paradigm shift due to these technological innovations. The promise of BD and AI lies in their potential to enhance screening accuracy, enable early diagnosis, and facilitate streamlined treatment, including remote care options. These technologies, however, require careful integration into existing healthcare workflows, underscoring the need for collaboration across educational, medical, and psychological sectors (Washington, et al., 2020; Tsai, Ong, Chen, 2023).

This chapter explores the intersection of BD and AI in ADHD management, focusing on their role in monitoring and screening. The research investigates how technological integration can improve ADHD care and examines the disruptive influence of these technologies on patient care and community medical practices. It also evaluates BD and AI frameworks and applications that best facilitate ADHD management, acknowledging the potential risks such as privacy infringements, accessibility challenges, and the possibility of bias in diagnosis and treatment. In doing so, this study builds upon existing literature and incorporates insights from healthcare professionals, advocating for a strategic technological model that enhances BD and AI utility in ADHD care. This research model aims to optimize the use of these technologies in ADHD management, providing advanced support to patients while ensuring public health and sustainable, equitable care practices.

The primary aim of this study is to investigate the application of BD and AI in enhancing ADHD screening, diagnosis, treatment, and monitoring. Specifically, it seeks to:

1. Establish the role of BD and AI in ADHD management, particularly in improving diagnostic accuracy and treatment effectiveness.

2. Identify gaps in current ADHD care methodologies and how BD and AI can address these.
3. Propose a comprehensive model for integrating BD and AI into ADHD care, considering patient involvement and public health implications.

Therefore, this research adopts a multi-faceted approach, comprising a thorough literature review, analysis of data correlations, and expert consultations. It examines the current landscape of ADHD care, the emerging role of BD and AI, and the potential of these technologies to transform patient outcomes. The study also considers the challenges and risks associated with integrating BD and AI into ADHD care, proposing strategies to mitigate these. This research is significant for several reasons. First, it addresses a critical and growing healthcare challenge: the effective management of ADHD. Second, it explores the potential of cutting-edge technologies in transforming healthcare practices, particularly in ADHD care. Third, by proposing a model for integrating BD and AI into ADHD management, this study contributes to the development of more effective, efficient, and equitable healthcare solutions. Finally, the research has broader implications for public health, education, and societal well-being, underscoring the importance of innovative approaches in addressing complex health disorders like ADHD.

2. THEORETICAL FRAMEWORK

2.1. Attention-Deficit/Hyperactivity Disorder (ADHD)

As mentioned above (p. 2), it is believed that ADHD develops due to a genetic imbalance in catecholamine metabolism in the cerebral cortex, although it is not fully understood. The brain operates two main attentional systems: the default mode network, active during rest, and the task-positive network, active during focused tasks. Typically, these systems are balanced; however, in ADHD, abnormal synchronization disrupts this balance, leading to attention difficulties (Black, Grant, 2014).

There has been a notable increase in adult ADHD cases, prompting debates on whether this trend is due to previously undiagnosed childhood cases or the impact of modern lifestyles, such as the widespread use of smartphones and the constant stream of information. Recent research links ADHD symptoms with increased digital engagement, including social media, smartphones, and internet dependency. This rise in ADHD diagnoses has heightened concerns about effective screening, diagnosis, treatment, and monitoring, underlining the need for innovative solutions due to its extensive impact on families, schools, and society (Breaux, Dvorsky, Becker, 2021).

According to Jain et al. (2017), the diagnosis of ADHD is complex due to symptoms overlapping with other conditions that may be coexisting with ADHD. In addition to screening guidelines, clinical interviews and longitudinal family histories can be used to identify patients who require further evaluation to differentiate ADHD from psychiatric comorbidities. Nevertheless, most psychiatrists, neurologists, pediatricians, and family practitioners rely on subjective assessments of perceived behavior in their diagnostic procedures (Gualtieri, Johnson, 2005).

ADHD patients often display remarkable hyperfocus on activities that are highly stimulating or enjoyable, suggesting that their central challenge is regulating attention, particularly for tasks perceived as monotonous. The 'low dopamine hypothesis' posits that insufficient dopamine levels lead to inconsistent neuron activity within attention networks, affecting focus and time perception. Individuals with ADHD might resort to behaviors that increase dopamine, such as consuming caffeine, nicotine, or using stimulant medication. Early treatment with stimulants can utilize the brain's neuroplasticity, improving attention and concentration. Dopamine levels also influence time perception, with high levels leading to overestimation and low levels to underestimation, often resulting in poor time management and disorganization in those with ADHD. Training in visual focus, complemented by physical exercises, can enhance concentration and focus (Hansen, et al., 2021).

As previously mentioned, the frequent use of smartphones, characterized by rapid context shifts, has been linked to attention deficits in both children and adults. The current literature on ADHD covers clinical characteristics, diagnostic frameworks, comorbidities, and a range of treatment approaches, including medication, behavioral therapy, and psychosocial interventions. The DSM-5 identifies three types of ADHD: Inattentive Type, Hyperactive-Impulsive ADHD, and Combined Type ADHD (Black, Grant, 2014).

Treatment typically involves a combination of behavioral and pharmacological approaches, tailored to individual patient needs (Hoseini, et al.,2014; Black, Grant, 2014).

Despite the comprehensive understanding of ADHD in terms of clinical aspects and traditional treatment approaches, there is a noticeable gap in research focused on technological interventions in ADHD treatment, which warrants further investigation. The prevailing treatment model is evolving to integrate behavioral and pharmacological methods, customized to the patient's age and specific needs. However, the role of technology and the full potential of technology-enhanced interventions in this integration remains underexplored (Breaux, et al., 2023; Husain, 2020; Leffa, et al., 2022).

This gap presents an opportunity for new research avenues, particularly given the increasing use of digital tools. With ADHD diagnoses rising, harnessing technological advancements to refine patient management strategies is increasingly important. ADHD, a complex and multi-faceted disorder, requires comprehensive evaluation for accurate diagnosis and offers various treatments, including medication, behavioral therapy, and psychosocial interventions (Breaux, et al., 2023; Husain, 2020; Leffa, et al.,2022).

While prior research has extensively covered ADHD's clinical aspects and traditional treatment methods, few studies explore how new technologies can revolutionize ADHD care. This includes examining how these technologies can improve diagnostic precision, treatment effectiveness, and patient monitoring—also moving beyond the conventional scope of clinical and pharmacological treatments to explore how technologies like AI can be effectively incorporated into ADHD management strategies. Hence there is considerable research on ADHD concerning its symptoms, diagnosis, and traditional treatments, yet there is an imperative need to pivot towards incorporating technology-driven interventions. Exploring how digital tools can supplement and enhance standard treatments is becoming a crucial area of focus (Raichle, 2015; Keller, et al., 2021).

2.2. ADHD, Big Data, Artificial Intelligence

The current landscape of ADHD diagnosis and treatment, while improved by technological advances, still has notable gaps and limitations that could be addressed by integrating BD and AI. In the context of advancing ADHD management, the integration of BD and AI presents a transformative prospect. The main challenge in ADHD treatment is the subjectivity and variability of diagnostic criteria (see also above p. 3). Traditional diagnostic methods rely heavily on clinical interviews and subjective assessments, which can lead to inconsistencies and a lack of standardization across healthcare providers. This lack of objectivity can lead to both overdiagnosis and underdiagnosis of ADHD, particularly in populations where symptoms may manifest differently, such as adults or females (Yang, et al., 2022; Rahman, 2023).

In addition, current treatment protocols for ADHD, which consist primarily of pharmacological interventions and behavioral therapies, often take a "one-size-fits-all" approach. This may be ineffective for some patients due to the heterogeneous nature of ADHD. The variability in response to medication, the presence of comorbid conditions, and the differences in individual patient profiles require a more personalized approach to treatment. Furthermore, the ongoing monitoring and management of ADHD is often challenging. Traditional methods may not effectively track long-term progress and adherence, particularly in remote or underserved areas. This lack of continuous and comprehensive monitoring can lead to suboptimal treatment outcomes and increased healthcare costs (Yang, et al., 2022; Rahman, 2023).

BD and AI offer promising solutions to these challenges, their incorporation introducing a new paradigm of objectivity and precision. The application of BD to ADHD care can lead to the development of more standardized and objective diagnostic tools. Sophisticated AI algorithms can leverage large datasets from diverse sources like electronic health records and genomic records, enhancing our understanding of ADHD. (Megahed, et al., 2023; Nikolic, et al., 2023; Hong, 2023; Wada, et al., 2022). They thus facilitate more objective diagnostic criteria and monitoring methods, and overcome the limitations of traditional approaches (Breaux, et al., 2023; Husain, 2020; Leffa, et al., 2022).

The role of BD and AI in the early screening and detection of ADHD is noteworthy. Innovations in AI enable the parsing of behavioral data from digital platforms, identifying children at elevated ADHD risk. This early detection facilitates timely interventions, enhancing long-term prognoses. Furthermore, by analyzing diverse populations, AI algorithms can identify patterns and correlations that may not be apparent in smaller samples. This can help develop diagnostic criteria that are more nuanced and tailored to different demographic groups. In the realm of personalized medicine, AI can analyze patient data to predict individual responses to different treatment modalities. By considering a wide range of variables, including genetic information, lifestyle factors, and comorbidity profiles, AI can help clinicians design personalized treatment plans that are more likely to be effective for each patient. This shift towards personalized medicine is pivotal in the evolution of ADHD treatment. AI's role in crafting cognitive training programs tailored to individual needs augments the success of non-pharmacological interventions (Spiel, et al.,2022; Lyu, et al.,2023; Nikolic, et al., 2023; Alawida, et al., 2023; Peters, et al.,2023;).

In addition, the integration of BD and AI in treatment monitoring can revolutionize ADHD management. Wearable technology and mobile applications, combined with AI algorithms, can provide real-time monitoring of symptoms and treatment adherence. The data processed through AI algorithms reveal behavioral patterns and shifts, aiding in evaluating treatment efficacy and necessitating therapeutic adjustments (Yang, Li, Wei, 2023; Vajawat, Varshney, Banerjee, 2021). This can facilitate more timely interventions, reduce the need for frequent in-person consultations, and improve overall treatment outcomes. The use of natural language processing (NLP) algorithms to assess speech patterns and linguistic nuances offers another layer of diagnostic precision. In diagnosis and treatment, the use of AI has not been fully explored. Most studies on this topic have used small sample sizes and have not examined a significant amount of unstructured clinical notes, as well as open-source social media data (e.g., Reddit and PubMed). As a result, large language models derived from deep learning and unstructured electronic health records have not yet been explored as a means of understanding ADHD, although this methodology has been used in other clinical settings (Yang, et al. 2022).

AI could serve as a viable alternative to the use of traditional statistical methods in analyzing disease models in complex, multifactorial disease states, thereby aiding treatment selection based on existing therapies and providing the basis for domain-based therapeutic discovery (Tai, et. Al 2019). AI techniques such as machine learning and deep learning are instrumental in interpreting complex datasets.

To determine the most effective means of improving the quality of life for a person with ADHD, it is important to understand the symptoms and diagnostic process. A qualified healthcare professional, such as a physician, psychologist, psychiatrist, or neuropediatrician, should be able to diagnose ADHD after a comprehensive clinical evaluation that may include interviews, questionnaires, observations, and a review of the patient's medical history. The use of AI, in conjunction with machine learning resources and big data analytics, may lead to the development of this diagnosis. As AI is applied to neuroscience, it will be possible to identify neural patterns associated with ADHD, which will aid in the diagnosis of the condition. For example, AI algorithms trained on brain imaging scans can differentiate between individuals with and without ADHD. Furthermore, using the Social Responsiveness Scale (SRS), a set of parent-administered questionnaires used to assess severity, machine learning algorithms have been trained to differentiate ADHD from autism spectrum disorders. Correspondingly, while current ADHD diagnosis and treatment methods have their merits, the integration of BD and AI offers significant potential to address existing gaps. By increasing the objectivity of diagnostic tools, personalizing treatment approaches, and improving ongoing monitoring, these technologies can revolutionize ADHD care, leading to better patient outcomes and more efficient healthcare systems (Yang, et al., 2022; Rahman, 2023).

However, this technological integration is not without its challenges. AI and BD methods are susceptible to biases and inconsistencies, leading to potential overdiagnosis or underdiagnosis, particularly in specific demographics. Data quality is paramount, as incomplete, or skewed data can lead to algorithms perpetuating diagnostic and treatment inequities. Ethical considerations are also significant, with concerns around data privacy, informed consent, and the potential misuse of sensitive health information. The opacity of AI decision-making processes necessitates transparency to foster trust among healthcare providers, patients, and the broader community. Addressing these challenges requires a multidisciplinary approach, involving collaborations among computer scientists, medical professionals, legal professionals, and patients. Standardized protocols for data acquisition and algorithm training are essential to mitigate inherent biases. Ensuring data integrity, representativeness, and security is crucial (Jalil, et al., 2023; Liu, et al.,2023; Huang, et al., 2023; Hong, 2023; Lee, 2023).

Despite the potential of BD and AI to enhance ADHD management, reliance on these technologies must be balanced with a commitment to ethical principles and equitable healthcare. The future of ADHD management will likely witness a composite approach, where AI and BD supplement the expertise of clinicians. The convergence of BD and AI in ADHD management marks a significant shift towards more objective, precise, and personalized methodologies. While these technologies offer promising pathways for enhancing diagnosis and monitoring, the challenges and ethical implications associated with their use must be addressed. As the field progresses, the balanced integration of AI and BD alongside traditional clinical discernment is anticipated to substantially improve outcomes for individuals with ADHD. This review underscores the profound impact and future potential of BD and AI in revolutionizing ADHD management, setting a course for a more informed and effective approach to this complex disorder (Chen, et al.,2022; Falcetta, et al., 2023).

Table 1 provides an overview of the ADHD research areas and the applications of BD and AI. This table encapsulates the wide range of research avenues within the ADHD domain and exemplifies the multifaceted applications of BD and AI in advancing our understanding and management of ADHD.

Table 1. Integration of BD and AI in ADHD monitoring and screening

ADHD Domain Area	Examples of BD and AI Implementation	References
Behavioral inhibition and executive functions	Theoretical model construction linking inhibition to executive functions in ADHD	(Breaux, et al.,2023; Husain, 2020; Leffa, et al.,2022)
Adult ADHD prevalence and correlates	National surveys and comorbidity studies	(Black, Grant, 2014; Breaux, et al.,2023)
ADHD self-report scales	Development and validation of screening scales	(Breaux, et al.,2023; Husain, 2020; Leffa, et al.,2022)
ADHD diagnosis and treatment in children	Parent-reported surveys and treatment guidelines	(Breaux, et al.,2023; Husain, 2020; Leffa, et al.,2022)
Multimodal treatment strategies	Clinical trials comparing treatment strategies	(Wada, et al.,2022; Vajawat, Varshney, Banerjee, 2021)
Brain imaging in ADHD	Large-scale clinical and population-based studies	(Black, Grant, 2014; Breaux, et al.,2023)
ADHD and Autism Spectrum Disorders	Overlapping phenomenology and diagnostic considerations	(Vajawat, Varshney, Banerjee, 2021; Wada, et al.,2022)
Behavioral disorder tests using AI	Development of AI-based screening tools for ADHD	(Black, Grant, 2014; Breaux, Dvorsky, Becker, 2021; Breaux, et al.,2023)
Comorbidity analysis in brain disorders	Machine learning techniques for early detection	(Hansen, et al.,2021; Breaux, Dvorsky, Becker, 2021)
BD and AI in education	Studies on the application of AI and BD in educational contexts	(Black, Grant, 2014; Breaux, Dvorsky, Becker, 2021; Breaux, et al.,2023)
Knowledge representation frameworks	Research on AI frameworks for intelligent functions	(Wada, et al.,2022; Vajawat, Varshney, Banerjee, 2021)
BD and AI in e-commerce	Reviews on the role of AI and BD in various sectors	(Keller, et al.,2021; Leffa, et al.,2022; Raichle, 2015)
Screening for ADHD in specific settings	Studies on ADHD screening in epilepsy monitoring units	(Black, Grant, 2014; Breaux, Dvorsky, Becker, 2021; Breaux, et al.,2023)
Monitoring ADHD treatment	Research on measures to monitor ADHD treatment effects	(Black, Grant, 2014; Breaux, et al.,2023)
ADHD and substance use disorder	Studies on the comorbidity and treatment of ADHD and SUD	(Keller, et al.,2021; Leffa, et al.,2022; Raichle, 2015)
Objective ADHD-screening systems	Development of activity monitoring systems for ADHD screening	(Breaux, et al.,2023; Husain, 2020; Leffa, et al.,2022)
Task completion in adult ADHD	Commentary on task completion as a measure of ADHD treatment response	(Wada, et al.,2022; Vajawat, Varshney, Banerjee, 2021)
ADHD and learning disabilities	Research on the comorbidity of ADHD and learning disabilities	(Wada, et al.,2022; Vajawat, Varshney, Banerjee, 2021)

Source: Literature review based on presented references.

2.3. Multimodal Large Language Models (M-LLMs), Use Cases

The literature review explores the interplay between ADHD and Multimodal Large Language Models (M-LLMs), focusing particularly on their potential to enhance ADHD screening, diagnosis, treatment, and monitoring. The review integrates recent advancements in AI, BD, and their applications in healthcare, while identifying challenges and proposing new avenues for research (Liu, et al., 2023; Huang, et al., 2023; Hong, 2023).

The introduction of Generative Pretrained Transformer 4 (GPT-4) marks a significant milestone in the evolution of Large Language Models (LLMs), introducing capabilities for multimodal processing. These advancements, particularly in medicine, offer a comprehensive approach to interpreting complex medical data. M-LLMs can process diverse data types such as images, videos, sounds, and documents, presenting new opportunities in medical diagnostics and treatment. Their integration within clinical settings could facilitate improved communication and in-depth analyses across multiple data formats, potentially revolutionizing healthcare delivery (Breaux, et al., 2023; Husain, 2020; Leffa, et al., 2022).

The potential impacts of M-LLMs on ADHD diagnosis and treatment are substantial. They can analyze varied inputs like text, visual evidence, and audio recordings, enabling holistic assessments and streamlined diagnostic processes. This integration heralds a new era for 5G-enabled telehealth and virtual reality solutions, offering nuanced approaches to ADHD patient care. M-LLMs can enhance communication across language barriers, maintaining the nuances of medical terminology, crucial for patient-centered care. Their ability to decipher complex scientific data and analyze sentiment and context is pivotal for monitoring mental health, particularly in ADHD cases (Liu, et al., 2023; Huang, et al., 2023; Hong, 2023).

However, there are challenges in the current literature and technological integration. Despite several approved AI-based unimodal medical technologies, integrating these into clinical practice is challenging due to specificity and cost. M-LLMs, offering versatile and integrated solutions, could redefine this landscape. Yet, the lack of interoperability in healthcare systems remains a significant hurdle. M-LLMs could potentially integrate disparate medical software systems, improving clinical decisions and patient outcomes. Additionally, regulatory challenges, data privacy concerns, and the "black box" nature of AI decision-making are significant issues that need addressing (Wada, et al.,2022; Vajawat, Varshney, Banerjee, 2021; Sexton, et al., 2012; Peters, et al., 2023).

The future of M-LLMs in healthcare, especially in ADHD treatment, necessitates a multidisciplinary approach. This includes integrating prompt engineering into medical education, fostering AI literacy among patients, and ensuring healthcare providers are proficient in AI and data analysis. Regulatory agencies must establish stringent standards and guidelines for the safe and ethical deployment of LLMs in healthcare. This encompasses setting benchmarks for AI application accuracy and safeguarding patient data privacy. Moreover, promoting interdisciplinary collaboration is crucial in research, education, and technology innovation (Kasneci, et al., 2023; Short, Short, 2023).

Another perspective is the role of evidence-based medicine. For the widespread adoption of AI technologies like LLMs in healthcare, adherence to evidence-based medicine is crucial. Clinical validation through rigorous, prospective clinical trials is necessary to ensure that AI applications meet or exceed existing care standards. This is essential in supporting the adoption of AI technologies in healthcare, particularly in the context of ADHD, where precision and accuracy in diagnosis and treatment are critical (Liu, et al.,2023; Rospigliosi, 2023).

The literature review highlights the transformative potential of M-LLMs in ADHD treatment while acknowledging the challenges and complexities involved. The integration of AI into healthcare, particularly for ADHD, necessitates a comprehensive understanding of these technologies, interdisciplinary collaboration, and stringent regulatory frameworks to ensure safe, effective, and ethical applications (Teubner, et al., 2023; Tsai, Ong, Chen, 2023).

3. EMPIRICAL METHODOLOGICAL APPROACH

The methodology of the research study focuses on enhancing ADHD screening, diagnosis, treatment, and monitoring through the integration of BD and AI. The study primarily utilized an online questionnaire, targeting 48 expert participants. These individuals were selected for their proximity to the research team, their deep knowledge of relevant topics, and their influential positions within the industry. This selection was strategic, aiming to ensure informed, reliable responses that are essential for research involving expert participants, as their insights are invaluable in enhancing the value and involvement in group activities. This approach also helps to mitigate selection biases typical in web-based surveys, such as the "volunteer effect". The online questionnaire format was chosen due to its cost-effectiveness, rapid data collection, and higher participation rates compared to traditional paper-based methods. To ensure quality responses, the study employed a multimodal approach, including personalized messages and follow-ups, which is crucial in expert-based surveys. This methodology not only boosts participation rates but also ensures that the responses are from genuinely engaged and knowledgeable participants (Masih, 2022; Jacob, Bourke, Heuss, 2022).

The research aimed to explore how BD and AI are being incorporated into ADHD monitoring and screening. It delved into analyzing key data correlations and recommended strategies for technology adoption, emphasizing patient involvement. The study was guided by three primary research questions: the establishment of technological integration between BD and AI for ADHD monitoring and screening; understanding the concept of ADHD; and the impact of BD and AI on ADHD patient care and community medical practices. The paper also discussed which BD and AI frameworks and applications are best suited for ADHD management.

The questionnaire covered diverse topics like "LLM Use Cases in ADHD," "Applications and Trends of AI in ADHD," "Applications and Trends of BD in ADHD," "Medical Pedagogy for AI and BD in ADHD," and "AI/BD Advantages and Support to ADHD". It included demographic inquiries and a set of 57 assertions, aiming to gather comprehensive data. Responses were captured using a 5-tiered Likert scale, ranging from "strongly disagree" to "strongly agree," to quantify feedback categorically. The survey was disseminated digitally, targeting professionals in the healthcare sector and authorities in ADHD research.

Data analysis was conducted using SPSS, version 27.0. It began with a descriptive review of respondent demographics, followed by an assessment of the questionnaire's reliability through alpha coefficients. Advanced techniques like Factor Analysis were used to identify complex correlations among variables. A scree plot helped in determining significant factors for further examination. Additionally, an Inter-Item Correlation Matrix was formulated to understand the dynamics between survey elements. This analysis was crucial in refining the questionnaire and ensuring its validity. The combination of Cronbach's alpha, Factor Analysis, and the Inter-Item Correlation Matrix reinforced the reliability of the survey tool, making it an accurate instrument for evaluating AI and BD's role in ADHD treatment and management. The methodology employed in this study was meticulous and carefully structured to ensure the collection of high-quality data from knowledgeable participants. The use of advanced statistical techniques ensured the reliability and validity of the findings, thereby contributing significantly to the research on the integration of BD and AI in ADHD care.

3.1. Results

3.1.1 Profile of the Experts

Table 2 offers a detailed breakdown of the organizational affiliations of the respondents. Out of a total of 48 participants, the majority hail from pharmaceutical or biotech companies, representing 27% of the cohort. Private practice and hospitals are equally represented, each accounting for 19% of the respondents. Interestingly, 17% of participants are classified as retired. Clinics constitute 10% of the total sample and medical device companies constitute 8%. The varied distribution underscores the diverse backgrounds and sectors from which the participants originate, providing a comprehensive perspective for the study.

Table 2. Descriptive statistics: Type of organizations

Type of Organizations	N	%
Pharmaceutical/biotech	13	27%
Private Practice	9	19%
Hospital	9	19%
Retired	8	17%
Clinic	5	10%
Medical device company	4	8%
Grand Total	**48**	**100%**

Table 3 delineates the distribution of experts across various academic and professional positions. A total of 48 experts were consulted in the study, the largest proportion of whom were Executive Directors, accounting for 25% (N=12). Medical Doctors formed the second largest group, constituting 22.9% (N=11) of the respondents. Psychologists followed closely at 18.8% (N=9), while Nurses comprised 16.7% (N=8). Psychiatrists represented 12.5% (N=6) of the experts. The smallest groups were Vice Presidents or Senior Vice Presidents (VP/SVP) and Executives, each representing 2.1% (N=1 for both) of the total. This distribution underscores the diverse range of professionals involved in the conversation surrounding the relevance of AI and BD to ADHD treatment and screening. The input from an array of specialists augments the study's credibility, ensuring a comprehensive understanding of the subject matter from various vantage points.

Table 4 delineates the distribution of 48 experts across various therapeutic disciplines. The largest contingent, comprising 31% of the cohort, specializes in the Central Nervous System, succeeded by Psychology, representing 19%. Notably, Mental Health and Mental Health Disorders collectively account for 23% of the specialists. Endocrinology experts contribute 10%, whereas Immunology and Dermatology experts consist of 8%. Lesser represented fields, each at 2%, encompass Rare Diseases, Diabetes, Alzheimer's, and Neuroscience.

Table 3. Academic/professional position of the experts

Academic/Professional Position	N	%
Executive Director	12	25%
Medical Doctor	11	22.9%
Psychologist	9	18.8%
Nurse	8	16.7%
Psychiatrist	6	12.5%
VP/SVP	1	2.1%
Executive	1	2.1%
Grand Total	**48**	**100%**

Table 4. Therapeutic area of the experts

Therapeutic Area	N	%
Central Nervous System	15	31%
Psychology	9	19%
Mental Health	6	13%
Mental health disorders	5	10%
Endocrinology	5	10%
Immunology and Dermatology	4	8%
Rare Diseases	1	2%
Diabetes	1	2%
Alzheimer's	1	2%
Neuroscience	1	2%
Grand Total	**48**	**100%**

About the academic discourse on the significance of AI and BD in ADHD diagnosis and treatment, table 4 accentuates the vast array of expertise drawn upon. The pronounced representation from the Central Nervous System and Psychology domains underscores the importance of neuro-cognitive perspectives in this research. By including experts from a broad spectrum of therapeutic fields, the study adopts a holistic and interdisciplinary stance, highlighting the intricate nature of ADHD and the expansive potential of AI and BD in its holistic understanding and management.

Table 5 provides a geographical breakdown of the 48 experts' national affiliations. A notable 40% hail from Spain, making it the most represented nation. Switzerland follows with 19%, and both Germany and Italy each contribute 17% to the total. Portugal, with a representation of 8%, completes the list.

In the broader context of the study on the role of AI and BD in ADHD intervention and screening, table 5 underscores the European-centric nature of the expertise engaged. Spain's predominant representation may indicate the country's heightened interest or advancements in this particular research area. The balanced input from Germany and Italy, both significant players in the European research landscape, further enhances the study's continental scope. Switzerland's representation is also commendable, suggesting a potential hub of expertise. Portugal's contribution, while modest, ensures a more diversified European perspective. Collectively, the table illustrates the study's commitment to harnessing a broad array of European insights, crucial for a nuanced understanding of AI and BD's impact on ADHD treatment modalities.

Table 5. Country of the experts

Row Labels	N	%
Spain	19	40%
Switzerland	9	19%
Germany	8	17%
Italy	8	17%
Portugal	4	8%
Grand Total	**48**	**100%**

3.1.2 Statistical Analysis (Reliability, Correlation Matrix, Exploratory Factor Analysis)

A Cronbach's alpha coefficient analysis was conducted to estimate the internal consistency and reliability of the questionnaire items. This assessment is essential for affirming the study's validity. The initial phase involved calculating Cronbach's alpha for the entire dataset and subsets of items categorized by the initial digit in their labels. The computation utilized the following formula:

$$\alpha = (N / (N-1)) * (1 - (\Sigma(\sigma^2 Yi) / \sigma^2 X)),$$

where N is the number of items, $\sigma^2 Yi$ is the variance of each item, and $\sigma^2 X$ is the variance of the total scores across items.

After the analysis, the Cronbach's alpha for the entire dataset was determined to be approximately 0.638, signifying moderate reliability. However, the subgroup alpha values fluctuated between 0.342 and 0.578. These figures fall short of the accepted benchmark of 0.7 for robust internal consistency, yet they denote an enhancement from the preliminary metrics.

Furthermore, Table 6 outlines the mean factor scores alongside the reliability coefficients (Cronbach's alpha) for the scales associated with the three domains. The overarching Cronbach's Alpha reached 0.91.

Table 6. Reliability coefficients

Dimensions	**Cronbach Alpha**
LLM Use Cases	0.578
Applications and Trends of AI	0.414
Applications and Trends of BD	0.359
Medical Pedagogy	0.342
AI/BD advantages and support to ADHD screening and treatment	0.414

The internal consistency levels, while moderate, suggest that the reliability of the scale could benefit from further enhancement, particularly by integrating theoretical frameworks and content validity assessments. Subsequent analytical procedures were employed to elucidate the interrelations between three numerical ratings: the influence of AI and BD on ADHD treatment and screening, and the impact of LLM. The derived correlation analysis provided these insights:

- A slight negative correlation (r = -0.355) between the influences of AI and BD on ADHD was observed, implying that an upswing in AI's perceived impact might coincide with a minor decline in BD's perceived impact, and vice versa.
- A moderate negative correlation (r = -0.633) between BD's influence on ADHD and the impact of LLM was noted, reflecting a significant inverse relationship, where an increase in BD's perceived influence corresponds with a reduction in LLM's perceived impact, and vice versa.
- A weak positive correlation (r = 0.351) was found between the influences of AI on ADHD and the impact of LLM, suggesting a slight concurrent increase in their perceived influences.

Understanding correlations is essential in analyzing the impact of technologies on ADHD. Strong correlations (close to 1 or -1) suggest significant relationships, while correlations near 0 imply little or no linear connection. These do not signify causation but potential impacts. Advanced techniques like Principal Component Analysis (PCA) and Exploratory Factor Analysis (EFA) are critical for revealing hidden relationships within research on ADHD.

PCA serves to uncover dataset structures, key factors, and the effects of BD and AI on ADHD treatment and clinical practices. The explained variance ratio in PCA indicates how much variance each principal component accounts for. Identifying where the explained variance levels off—usually between 70-80% for descriptive research and around 90% for more precise investigations—helps discern natural data clusters. The creation of a scree plot, which shows a flattening curve (Figure 1), helps determine the number of components to include by indicating where additional factors do not significantly increase explained variance. By examining factor loadings, we identify which variables strongly correlate with each component, aiding the interpretation of data groupings. The first five principal components are particularly scrutinized for their loadings, revealing the strength of the relationship with survey items. High loadings on a component suggest the items are closely related, measuring similar underlying constructs. This nuanced analysis is vital for a comprehensive understanding of factors influencing ADHD in the context of AI and BD (as illustrated in Figure 1).

By analyzing the items with the highest factor loadings for each component, hypotheses regarding the components' nature can be formulated. For example, if PC1 exhibits high loadings for 'Treatment Effectiveness' items, it might be indicative of that particular aspect (as shown in Figure 1).

The scree plot is a crucial tool for visually evaluating a dataset's dimensionality, here applied to survey data concerning ADHD treatment and management. It graphically displays each principal component's explained variance alongside the aggregate explained variance, aiding in discerning the significant contributors to the data structure.

The initial steep decline of the plot, indicated by a dark blue line with circles, shows that the first few components explain most of the variance, underscoring their significance. As the cumulative variance, shown by a pink line with squares, steadily increases, it becomes apparent that subsequent components add diminishing insight, with the 'elbow' in the plot suggesting the ideal number of factors to keep.

Figure 1. Scree plot of principal components

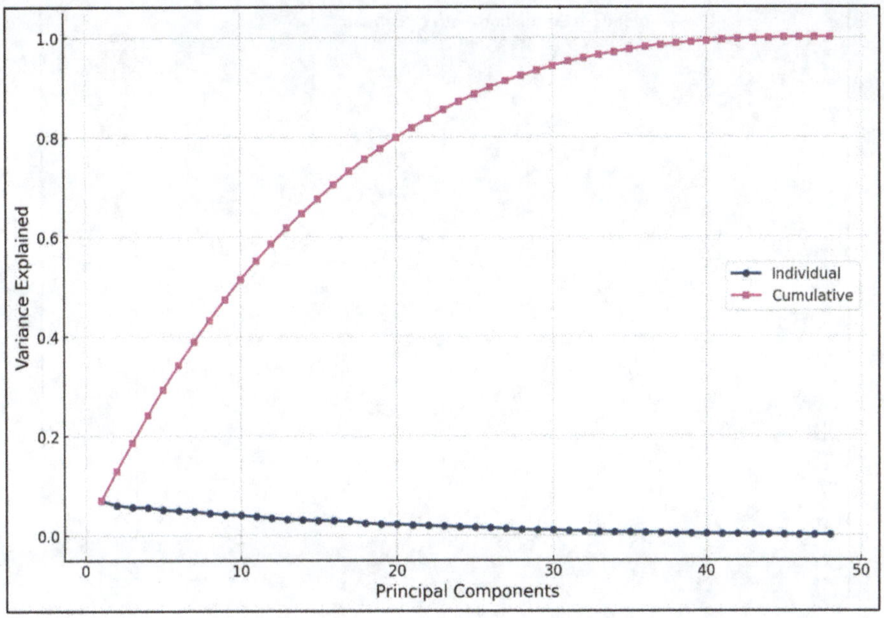

This dataset's complexity, evident from the levelling off of variance, reveals multiple factors that influence survey responses, affirming the survey's construction and the validity of the data interpretation. The scree plot not only aids in analysis but also confirms the methodological rigor, highlighting the nuanced nature of the constructs studied and providing a basis for further refinement of the survey for greater reliability and validity.

The analysis offers essential item-level insights, enabling scale refinement by identifying items with weak correlations, thus enhancing the scale's internal consistency and the study's overall reliability and validity. A thorough item examination through the inter-item correlation matrix signifies a commitment to the scale's psychometric robustness, with each item ideally reflecting the intended construct (Boeldt, McMahon, McConnochie, 2020).

The inter-item correlation matrix (Figure 2) is fundamental in survey research, facilitating more sophisticated analyses and improving data interpretability. The heatmap visually represents the matrix, with each cell showing the Pearson correlation between items, crucial for swiftly identifying correlations and supporting the research process.

The heatmap delineates (Figure 2) the inter-item correlation matrix, with variables numerically denoted as "Q1" to "Q54" for clarity. Its color spectrum, extending from cool blues to warm reds, intuitively signals negative to positive correlations respectively, with neutral tones indicating negligible associations. Figure 2 reveals a minimum correlation of approximately -0.46, hinting at moderate inverse relationships between certain items, potentially reflective of oppositely phrased items or different construct dimensions.

The maximum correlation, predictably, is 1.0 along the diagonal where items correlate with themselves. High off-diagonal correlations may flag potential redundancies or closely related items. An average correlation around 0.014 suggests a general lack of association among items, indicating a wide construct scope but also posing questions about the scale's coherence.

Figure 2. Inter-item correlation matrix heatmap

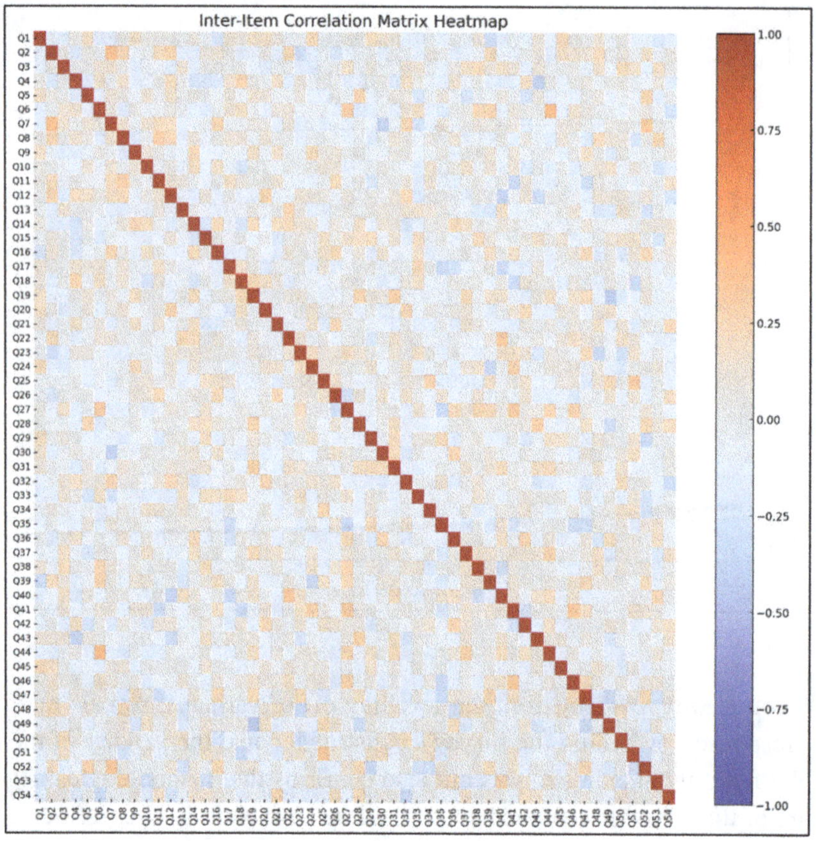

This heatmap acts as a diagnostic tool, shedding light on the relationships among survey items. The array of correlations portrays the construct's complexity and suggests the scale captures multiple dimensions. A low average correlation implies diversity in items, useful for a multidimensional construct but potentially problematic for scale consistency. Individual item analysis, anchored in the study's theoretical framework, is crucial for evaluating each item's relevance to the construct. High positive correlations among items are expected and desirable, whereas items with strong negative correlations may require re-evaluation for conceptual alignment. This matrix, as part of a broader psychometric assessment, informs scale refinement aimed at improving measurement accuracy.

3.1.3 Data Analysis

In addressing the research questions concerning the impact of BD and AI on ADHD patient care and the effectiveness of various BD and AI frameworks in managing ADHD, the analysis of the collected data is pivotal.

Figure 3 box plots provide a visual summary of the surveyed perceptions on the impact of AI, BD, and Language Learning Models (LLMs) on ADHD.

Figure 3. Impact of AI, BD, and language learning models (LLMs) on ADHD

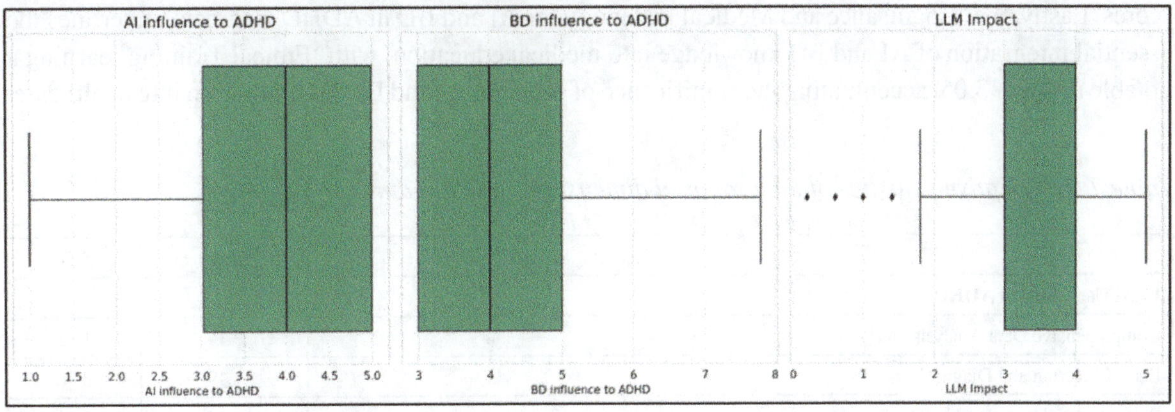

Figure 3 presents three boxplots illustrating the ratings for 'AI influence on ADHD', 'BD influence on ADHD', and 'LLM Impact'. The AI-related plot indicates a compact range of ratings, mostly above the scale's midpoint. The BD-related plot also displays a median of 4 but includes an outlier above 7, hinting at a data entry error or anomaly. The LLM-related plot shows a tighter range with outliers significantly below the main cluster.

The influence of AI is reflected in a symmetrical distribution with a median value of 4, signalling a generally positive reception—indicating most respondents view AI's role in ADHD in a favorable light. The interquartile range, extending from slightly over 3 to 5, denotes a majority consensus with minimal extreme responses or outliers, suggesting a widely held belief in AI's benefits for ADHD management (as image 3).

Similarly, the distribution of responses regarding the impact of BD on ADHD mirrors the pattern observed for AI, with comparable median and interquartile ranges, indicating analogous opinions among participants about their effects on ADHD care. However, the existence of a data point beyond the scale's limit of 1-5 points to a potential anomaly, which could require a review of data collection procedures or data cleansing to ensure the validity of the findings. The 'LLM's Impact' boxplot reveals a tight IQR and a consistent median of 4, as with the other two categories, yet the range of responses is less varied. This might indicate a more uniform opinion that LLMs have a positive impact on ADHD, but with less intense positive sentiment compared to AI and BD. The outlier near 0 is notably discordant with the rest of the data and might represent a data entry error, a misinterpretation of the scale, or a respondent with a significantly different opinion from the cohort. The presence of anomalies in the responses to BD and LLMs may prompt further investigation or consideration in the analysis, ensuring that conclusions drawn are based on accurate and reliable data.

Table 7 offers an exhaustive synopsis of LLM, AI, and BD employment in ADHD. It is divided into segments that illuminate different aspects of AI and BD in the management and diagnosis of ADHD. 'LLM Use Cases in ADHD' details possible LLM applications, with 'Early Detection and Diagnosis' and 'Personalised Treatment Plans' showing promise, as reflected by mean values of 4.19 and 4.10, respectively. 'Speedy Clinical Diagnosis' however, draws caution with a lower mean of 2.77. 'Prospective Applications and Progressions of AI in ADHD' highlights the transformative potential of AI in ADHD management, especially in 'Genomic Analysis' and 'Treatment Monitoring', with means of 4.50 and 4.71, respectively. The 'Emerging Trends and BD Applications in ADHD' section pinpoints 'Educational

Gaming' and 'Digital Therapeutics' as key future interventions in ADHD, indicated by their high mean scores. Lastly, the 'Cognisance and Medical Pedagogy for AI and BD in ADHD' segment underlines the essential integration of AI and BD knowledge into medical education, with 'Ethical Training' earning a notable mean of 3.05, accentuating the significance of ethics in AI and BD incorporation into healthcare.

Table 7. Descriptive statistics of the proposed dimensions and sub-dimensions

	Mean	S.D.
LLM Use Cases in ADHD		
Comprehensive Data Analysis	3.17	1.43
Early Detection and Diagnosis	4.19	0.76
Personalized Treatment Plans	4.10	0.86
Continuous Monitoring and Adjustment	3.96	0.82
Educational Support	2.90	1.32
Enhanced Patient Engagement	3.06	1.37
Support for Healthcare Professionals	3.23	1.42
Research Advancements	2.94	1.52
Cost Efficiency	3.08	1.56
Community Support	2.90	1.46
Ethical and Responsible AI Practices	3.96	0.77
Global Health Impact	3.06	1.42
Prospective Applications and Progressions of AI in ADHD		
Effective Treatment Design	3.81	0.82
Speedy Clinical Diagnosis	2.77	1.49
Hybrid AI Algorithms	2.75	1.41
Genomic Analysis	4.50	0.51
Continuous Data Collection	3.02	1.41
Personalized Treatment Plans	4.13	0.84
Objective Testing	2.98	1.52
Early Detection	3.25	1.41
Treatment Monitoring	4.71	0.46
Educational Tools	2.52	1.37
Emerging Trends and BD Applications in ADHD		
Objective Testing	3.35	1.38
Aggregated Data Analysis	2.85	1.38
Real-time Data Analysis	2.44	1.34
Wearable Devices	3.08	1.37
Database Development	3.00	1.52
Genetic Databases	2.92	1.29
Digital Therapeutics	4.44	0.50

Table 7 continued

	Mean	S.D.
Educational Gaming	4.54	0.50
Treatment Outcome Analysis	3.83	0.83
Cognizance, and Medical Pedagogy for AI and BD in ADHD		
Understanding BD and AI	2.92	1.25
AI Training in Medical Education	2.56	1.30
BD in Medical Curricula	2.79	1.41
Continuous Medical Education (CME)	3.10	1.26
Practical Training	2.71	1.35
Interdisciplinary Collaboration	3.85	0.85
Ethical Training	3.08	1.30
Research and Development	2.92	1.43
Policy and Regulation Education	2.92	1.35
Public and Patient Education	3.08	1.30
Advantages and Support AI and BD Offer to ADHD Management		
Diagnosis	4.56	0.50
Medication Management	2.94	1.37
Comorbid Conditions	2.79	1.29
Behavioral Interventions	3.13	1.39
Educational Support	3.19	1.35
Social Skills	3.06	1.28
Self-esteem	4.08	0.79
Lifestyle and Diet	3.06	1.42
Transitioning Ages	3.15	1.40
Legal and Ethical Concerns	4.48	0.50
Workplace Accommodations	2.94	1.39
Parental and Family Support	2.96	1.32
Adherence to Treatment	4.63	0.49

The analysis from Table 7, highlights the critical and diverse applications of LLMs, AI, and BD in ADHD management, reflecting a clear academic consensus, particularly in domains such as 'Genomic Analysis' and 'Personalized Treatment Plans'. These areas are recognized as key drivers for future research. Moreover, the integration of patient care, ethical considerations, and education is essential for a comprehensive adoption of AI and BD in the ADHD field.

Themes such as 'Objective Testing' and 'Early Detection' are prominent in the discourse, each with significant mentions. 'Personalized Treatment Plans' and 'Genomic Analysis' also draw considerable attention. On the other hand, themes like 'Continuous Data Collection', 'Treatment Monitoring', and 'Effective Treatment Design' show moderate engagement. However, 'Speedy Clinical Diagnosis', 'Hybrid AI Algorithms', and 'Educational Tools' indicate emergent areas that have not yet achieved widespread attention. This distribution reflects a focused interest in leveraging AI for objective testing and early detection to improve ADHD management.

The emphasis on wearable devices and real-time analytics in the context of ADHD underscores BD's role in providing continuous and insightful monitoring, thus improving diagnostic and treatment efficacy. The discussion also touches on the potential of databases, including genetic databases, in fostering personalized treatments through a deeper genetic understanding of ADHD. The data suggests AI and BD are poised to revolutionarily enhance ADHD care. The above table reveals a prioritization of 'AI Training in Medical Education' and 'BD incorporation into Medical Curricula', each with a notable frequency. 'Interdisciplinary Collaboration' and 'Continuous Medical Education (CME)' follow closely, while 'Ethical Training' and 'Practical Training' receive moderate emphasis. In contrast, areas such as 'Understanding BD and AI', 'Research and Development', 'Policy and Regulation Education', and 'Public and Patient Education' has not yet gained substantial attention, suggesting these are less discussed in the current academic landscape.

4. DISCUSSION

The data presented in the previous figures provides a comprehensive analysis of the perceived impact of AI, BD, and Lifelong Learning Models (LLMs) on the management of ADHD. The key findings indicate a positive reception of AI in ADHD care, as shown by a balanced distribution of ratings without outliers, reflecting general optimism about AI's role in ADHD management. However, the impact of BD shows a notable outlier, suggesting a potential anomaly or an extreme value. The influence of Lifelong Learning Models (LLMs) also demonstrates consensus, albeit with some variability, indicated by an outlier at the lower end.

The compact range of scores for AI impact, with most scores above the midpoint of the scale, indicates a consensus about the beneficial role of AI in ADHD treatment. The lack of significant outliers in this category suggests a uniformity of opinion, demonstrating that the majority of respondents view the potential of AI in a positive light. This consistency is critical to understanding the collective optimism about AI's role in advancing ADHD care, particularly in facilitating more accurate and early diagnosis and in developing more effective treatment monitoring systems.

For BD, although there is a notable outlier, the median rating and interquartile range remain consistent with AI ratings, indicating a general optimism about BD's impact on ADHD. The outlier in BD's impact may represent an exceptional viewpoint or a data entry error, but it does not diminish the overall positive sentiment toward BD in ADHD treatment. The innovative applications of BD, such as educational gaming and digital therapeutics, are recognized as promising avenues for ADHD intervention, suggesting a recognition of BD's potential beyond traditional data analysis.

Significant potential is also identified in areas such as 'Early Detection and Diagnosis' and 'Personalized Treatment Plans' for ADHD, highlighting optimism in the academic community about AI's ability to revolutionize ADHD management. This is particularly noticeable in the strong belief in AI's role in genomic analysis and treatment monitoring. The study emphasizes the importance of ethical training in integrating AI and BD into healthcare. The broader thematic distribution across literature points to 'Objective Testing' and 'Early Detection' as primary areas of interest, underscoring their crucial role in ADHD treatment and screenings. Wearable devices and real-time data analytics, crucial in BD applications, are poised to transform ADHD care through enhanced monitoring and diagnostic precision. The focus on understanding ADHD's genetic makeup through databases is expected to lead to more personalized treatment strategies.

The discussion of LLMs, while showing a narrower range of responses, also indicates a positive perception, albeit with a notable outlier well below the main cluster. This outlier could represent an individual perspective that differs from the consensus or a misunderstanding of the rating scale. However, the overall positive median for the impact of LLMs confirms the perceived usefulness of these models in the treatment of ADHD.

The study's emphasis on ethical training in the integration of AI and BD into healthcare is a critical observation. It underscores the need for responsible use of these technologies to ensure that their integration into ADHD treatment is both ethically sound and beneficial to patient care.

The key findings of this study show a positive perception of the impact of AI on ADHD management, with a balanced distribution of ratings and no significant outliers. Optimism for AI, particularly in the areas of genomic analysis and treatment monitoring, is evident. While the impact of BD shows some outliers, the overall sentiment remains positive, especially in its innovative applications. The importance of ethical training in the use of AI and BD in healthcare is a key takeaway, emphasizing the need for responsible and effective integration of these technologies in ADHD care.

The study also addresses knowledge transfer and development, emphasizing 'AI Training in Medical Education' and 'BD Integration into Medical Curricula'. However, it suggests a need for a more balanced approach that includes 'Ethical Training' and 'Practical Training' in future research. Additionally, the research underscores the transformative role of BD and AI in ADHD patient care. Accurate diagnosis is crucial for differentiating ADHD from similar conditions, with AI and BD showing promise in improving this accuracy. The management of ADHD medication, especially stimulants, becomes critical due to potential side effects and misuse. The study highlights the need for integrated care plans, given ADHD's high comorbidity with other disorders.

To provide more context, it was relevant to present some notions of comparative analysis with traditional approaches to ADHD diagnosis and treatment versus future diagnosis and treatment with artificial intelligence, LLM, and Generative AI. The following table (see Table 8) provides an overview of the traditional approaches to diagnosing and treating ADHD, which have focused primarily on clinical assessment, patient history, and standardized testing. Treatment modalities typically include pharmacological interventions, behavioral therapies, and educational support. However, this conventional approach faces challenges such as subjective diagnosis, one-size-fits-all treatment plans, and limited long-term monitoring.

In contrast, the integration of AI, LLM, and generative AI represents a transformative approach to ADHD treatment. AI and LLM offer improved diagnostic accuracy, personalized treatment plans, and continuous monitoring. Specifically, generative AI promises to generate novel treatment strategies and patient education materials (see Table 8).

Traditional methods of diagnosing and treating ADHD have provided a fundamental understanding of the disorder and have shaped current clinical practice. While sometimes limited by subjectivity and generalization, these methods provide critical insight into the individual experience of ADHD, emphasizing the human element in health care.

Traditional diagnostic approaches to ADHD rely primarily on clinical assessments, including detailed patient histories, behavioral observations, and standardized rating scales. These methods focus on the subjective experiences of patients and their observable behaviors, which are critical to understanding the multifaceted nature of ADHD. This personal interaction between clinicians and patients allows for a nuanced appreciation of individual differences in ADHD presentation that may be missed by purely data-driven methods.

Table 8. Comparative analysis table traditional vs. future approaches in ADHD diagnosis and treatment

Aspect	Traditional Approach	Future Approach (AI, LLM, Generative AI)
Diagnosis	Based on clinical assessments and patient history.	AI and LLM-enhanced diagnostics incorporate data analysis for more accurate and objective identification of ADHD.
Treatment Personalization	Generally standardized treatment plans.	Personalized treatment plans developed through AI analysis, considering individual patient profiles and comorbidities.
Treatment Modalities	Pharmacological treatments, behavioral therapy.	Integrates traditional methods with innovative solutions like digital therapeutics and educational gaming, identified by AI and BD analysis.
Monitoring and Management	Periodic follow-ups and self-reported symptoms.	Continuous real-time monitoring using wearable devices and AI algorithms, facilitates timely interventions.
Educational and Support Tools	Standard educational materials and support programs.	Customized educational materials and support programs generated by Generative AI, tailored to individual learning styles and needs.
Research and Development	Limited by slower, traditional research methods.	Expedited by AI and BD, enabling rapid analysis of large datasets for new insights into ADHD.
Ethical and Practical Training	Not a primary focus.	Emphasizes the need for ethical and practical training in AI and BD use in medical education.
Comorbidity Management	Managed separately or in conjunction with ADHD treatment.	AI-driven analysis offers integrated management plans, addressing ADHD and comorbid conditions holistically.

Conventional treatment modalities for ADHD include pharmacotherapy, behavioral interventions, and psychoeducation. Medications, such as stimulants and non-stimulants, have been extensively studied and remain a cornerstone in the management of ADHD symptoms. Behavioral therapies, such as cognitive behavioral therapy (CBT), provide patients with strategies to manage their symptoms and improve functional outcomes. These treatments are supported by a wealth of empirical evidence and clinical experience and offer proven efficacy for many individuals with ADHD.

Traditional methods often take a holistic approach, considering the patient's environment, family dynamics, and educational or vocational challenges. This approach is essential for a disorder such as ADHD, where external factors have a significant impact on symptom expression and management. It also allows for the integration of support systems, such as family therapy and educational accommodations, which are critical to comprehensive care.

Traditional treatment plans for ADHD are often flexible, allowing for adjustments based on individual responses to therapy. This adaptability is critical given the heterogeneity of ADHD, where patients may respond differently to the same treatment.

While traditional methods have their strengths, they also have limitations, such as potential biases in diagnosis and a one-size-fits-all approach to treatment. The integration of AI and BD into ADHD care, as discussed in previous responses, can address these limitations by providing more objective diagnostic tools, personalized treatment plans, and continuous monitoring. However, this integration should not replace traditional methods but rather complement them to create a more robust, comprehensive approach to ADHD care.

Overall, traditional methods of ADHD diagnosis and treatment provide a human-centered perspective that is critical to understanding the complexity of the disorder. While the integration of AI and BD promises to enhance these methods, a balanced approach that combines the strengths of both traditional and modern techniques is essential for a comprehensive understanding and effective treatment of ADHD.

Advice on lifestyle changes is essential for individuals with ADHD, and treatment modalities need to adapt to different life stages. The study also addresses legal and ethical treatment issues, including medication regulation and ethical considerations. In the workplace, specific accommodations may be necessary for adults with ADHD, and employers should be informed about these requirements. Family support is emphasized as crucial, especially for children with ADHD. The study also highlights the challenges in ensuring long-term treatment adherence due to ADHD symptoms. This calls for a comprehensive and personalized approach to managing ADHD, involving collaboration among healthcare professionals, mental health specialists, educators, and families.

The study categorizes the interplay of AI and BD in ADHD treatment and screening into six aspects: data sources, tools, applications, education and training, technology integration, research and development, and community and global impact. These categories showcase the transformative potential of AI and BD in ADHD screening and treatment.

Emerging technologies like LLM and a future version of ChatGPT (hypothetically ChatGPT 5) promise further advancements in ADHD care. These technologies could aid in comprehensive data analysis, early detection, diagnosis, personalized treatment plans, continuous monitoring, and patient engagement. They may also support healthcare professionals with current ADHD treatment information and contribute to cost efficiency in healthcare delivery.

The research validates the integration of BD and AI in ADHD monitoring and screening, the concept of ADHD, and the disruptive influence of these technologies on ADHD patient care and community medical practices.

The study advocates for a strategic technological model to enhance the utility of BD and AI in ADHD care, aiming to optimize their use in ADHD management. This approach is expected to provide advanced, reassuring support to patients while ensuring public health and sustainable, equitable ADHD care practices. The overarching narrative is one of cautious optimism, pointing towards a more technologically integrated approach to managing ADHD.

The following overview (Table 9) encapsulates the core aspects, their descriptions or exemplars, and the significance of each aspect of the research questions posed.

Table 9 delineates the multifaceted interplay of AI and BD in advancing ADHD treatment and screening. It categorizes the involvement into six distinct aspects:

- Data Sources: It underscores the diverse data reservoirs, ranging from Electronic Health Records (EHRs) to innovative tools like Multimodal Lifelong Learning Models. Such expansive data sources facilitate informed decision-making and real-time monitoring.
- AI and BD Tools: The table postulates potential advancements, such as the hypothetical ChatGPT 5, highlighting the progression in AI and the potential for enhanced patient engagement.
- Applications: AI's potential in early detection, personalized treatment plans, and continuous monitoring is emphasized, promising improved patient outcomes and adaptability.
- Education and Training: The table accentuates the importance of integrating AI in continuous medical education, ensuring up-to-date knowledge, and fostering a responsible ethical use of technology.

Table 9. Core Aspects, descriptions, significance of each aspect of the research questions

Aspect	Description / Example	Benefits / Importance
Data Sources	- Electronic Health Records (EHRs)	- Comprehensive analysis for accurate diagnosis and treatment
	- Genomic Databases	- Informed decision-making
	- Wearable Devices and Mobile Apps	- Real-time monitoring and personalized treatment
AI and BD Tools	- Multimodal Lifelong Learning Models (LLM)	- Processing diverse data types
	- ChatGPT 5 (hypothetical)	- Enhanced patient engagement and educational support
	- BD Analytics	- Research advancements and cost efficiency
Applications	- Early Detection and Diagnosis	- Timely intervention
	- Personalized Treatment Plans	- Improved treatment outcomes
	- Continuous Monitoring and Adjustment	- Adaptability to patient's progress
Education and Training	- AI Training in Medical Education	- Skillful medicine-machine interaction
	- Continuous Medical Education (CME)	- Up-to-date knowledge and best practices
	- Ethical Training	- Responsible and ethical use of AI and BD
Technology Integration	- Digital Therapeutics	- Innovative ADHD management solutions
	- Objective Testing	- Unbiased diagnosis and treatment monitoring
	- Mobile Applications and Digital CBT Platforms	- Accessible and interactive ADHD management
Research and Development	- Clinical Trials and Research Studies	- New diagnostic tools and treatment methods
	- Publicly Available Databases	- Facilitated research and development
Community and Global Impact	- Online Forums and social media	- Community support and experience sharing
	- Scalable AI solutions	- Global health impact and accessible ADHD care

- Technology Integration: With a mention of digital therapeutics and mobile applications, it stresses innovative solutions for ADHD management, ensuring unbiased and interactive care approaches.
- Research and Development: Highlighting the role of AI in facilitating research through publicly available databases and innovative diagnostic tools.
- Community and Global Impact: Emphasizes the global scale of AI solutions and the communal benefits, from support forums to scalable ADHD care.

The table robustly encapsulates the transformative potential of AI and BD in ADHD screening and treatment, demonstrating their indispensable role in modern medical research.

BD holds significant potential for advancing the treatment and screening of ADHD. Key data sources that can be harnessed include Electronic Health Records (EHRs), genomic databases, pharmacy and insurance records, school reports, wearable device metrics, psychometric assessments, neuroimaging data, social media discussions, digital therapeutic usage, and research data from clinical trials. The analysis of these disparate data points using BD analytics and AI algorithms can enhance understanding of ADHD etiology, optimize treatment modalities, and monitor patient progress, which may lead to the development of novel diagnostic tools and therapies.

Emerging technologies like LLM and a future version of ChatGPT, hypothetically called ChatGPT 5, promise further advancements. These could be instrumental in comprehensive data analysis, early detection, and diagnosis of ADHD. They may also facilitate personalized treatment plans, offer continuous monitoring and adjustment of treatments, provide tailored educational support, and improve patient engagement.

Moreover, these models could assist healthcare professionals by supplying current information on ADHD treatment, support research by analyzing extensive datasets, and contribute to cost efficiency in healthcare delivery. Additionally, they could strengthen community support for individuals and families affected by ADHD. Future iterations, such as ChatGPT 5, are expected to ensure ethical AI practices, focusing on privacy and consent, and could be instrumental in augmenting global health efforts by making ADHD management solutions more universally accessible and scalable.

5. CONCLUSION

5.1. Theoretical Implications of the Study Findings

The study's findings indicate that the integration of Large Language Models (LLMs), AI, and BD can greatly improve ADHD treatment. This enhancement comes through enabling early detection, personalized care plans, and precise genomic analysis. These technologies hold the potential to refine diagnostic accuracy and tailor interventions. Consequently, it's crucial to explore their ethical implications further and incorporate them into medical education. The growing emphasis on AI and BD in ADHD treatment represents a significant shift towards a data-driven, patient-specific approach in healthcare. This shift necessitates a reevaluation of current practices and the development of new frameworks to guide their ethical and effective integration into clinical settings.

5.2. Policy Implications

Future ADHD treatment guidelines should focus on personalized approaches, informed by AI and BD analytics, with particular emphasis on genetic and behavioral data to customize treatments. These protocols should integrate Large Language Models (LLMs) for comprehensive screening and monitoring, ensuring they continuously adapt to patient responses. Policies must mandate stringent ethical standards, as well as data privacy and security measures. Additionally, systematic education in AI and BD for healthcare providers is essential. Interdisciplinary collaboration will be crucial, with continuous support for research and development necessary to refine and validate these technologically advanced interventions within ADHD care frameworks.

5.3. Future Recommendations

The recommendations for future research in the field of integrating BD and AI in ADHD treatment and management cover a wide array of areas, highlighting the complexity and ongoing development of this field. A primary focus should be the further validation of AI and BD tools in diagnosing and treating ADHD. This requires conducting extensive studies across varied populations to verify the effectiveness and applicability of these technologies. Concurrently, addressing the ethical and privacy concerns associated with AI and BD in healthcare, particularly in sensitive areas like ADHD, is imperative. This includes investigating the long-term efficacy and safety of AI and BD-driven ADHD treatment plans through longitudinal studies to understand the sustainability of these interventions.

Another crucial area is integrating AI and BD into medical education. Future research should aim to prepare healthcare professionals for technological advancements in ADHD treatment, ensuring they have the necessary skills and knowledge. Additionally, exploring patient-centric models in ADHD care is essential, particularly focusing on including patient feedback in developing and refining AI and BD applications. Given the frequent co-occurrence of ADHD with other conditions, research should also examine the use of AI and BD in diagnosing and treating these comorbid conditions. The potential applications of technological advancements in BD and AI, including emerging models like a hypothetical ChatGPT 5, in ADHD diagnosis and treatment warrant investigation.

Global and cross-cultural studies are vital to understanding how AI and BD applications in ADHD care can be adapted to various cultural and healthcare contexts. This research should also assess the broader impact of AI and BD integration on healthcare systems, focusing on cost-effectiveness, healthcare delivery models, and patient access to advanced care.

Interdisciplinary research involving AI experts, healthcare professionals, ethicists, and patients is essential for developing comprehensive ADHD care models that effectively utilize AI and BD. Such collaboration can foster the development of real-time monitoring and adaptive interventions, providing responsive and timely ADHD care. Strategies for public and patient education are crucial to enhance understanding and acceptance of AI and BD in ADHD treatment. Alongside this, investigating the legal and regulatory implications of using these technologies in healthcare, with a focus on ADHD, is necessary to ensure legal compliance and protect patient rights.

Finally, enhancing data security and confidentiality in AI and BD applications is paramount. Research should focus on robust data protection measures to safeguard patient information against breaches and misuse. Future research in this field needs to be comprehensive, multifaceted, and responsive to the dynamic changes in technology, healthcare needs, and ethical considerations. Addressing these diverse areas can significantly advance ADHD treatment and monitoring, ensuring the integration of AI and BD in healthcare is both effective and responsible.

5.4. Conclusions

Given the provided study context, the nature, and implications of outliers in research on the integration of BD and AI into ADHD treatment and monitoring can be more specifically contextualized. The study reflects a positive perception of the impact of AI on ADHD treatment, with a balanced distribution of ratings and no significant outliers. This uniformity suggests a consensus on the promising role of AI, particularly in genomic analysis and treatment monitoring.

The lack of significant outliers in the AI ratings is consistent with the broader medical research community's growing confidence in AI's capabilities and resonates with the themes of "objective testing" and "early detection". This consensus suggests that the potential of AI in ADHD treatment is widely recognized and accepted, making it a fundamental aspect of future ADHD treatment strategies. In contrast, the impact of BD shows some outliers, where these outliers, although few, are critical as they may represent innovative perspectives or unique applications of BD in ADHD treatment, such as educational games and digital therapeutics. The presence of these outliers suggests that while there is optimism about the role of BD, there are divergent opinions or experiences that may not yet be fully explored or understood within the ADHD treatment paradigm. This highlights potential areas for future research, particularly in exploring the capabilities and limitations of BD in specific innovative applications.

The study's focus on ADHD management, including medications, treatment methods, and integrated care plans, suggests that insights from outliers in BD and AI research could significantly improve personalized treatment strategies. This is particularly relevant given the high comorbidity of ADHD with other disorders and the need for lifestyle modifications across the lifespan. Outliers may offer innovative approaches or highlight underexplored areas in these aspects. The mention of emerging technologies such as Large Language Models (LLM) and potential future iterations underscores the evolving nature of ADHD treatment and monitoring. Outliers in current AI and BD research may pave the way for the integration of these newer technologies into ADHD care, enhancing comprehensive data analysis, early detection, diagnosis, personalized treatment plans, continuous monitoring, and patient engagement.

The highlighted areas may require further investigation and are indicative of the evolving nature of ADHD care in the context of rapidly advancing technologies. These outliers serve as indicators of both the potential and the challenges of integrating AI and BD into ADHD treatment, signaling the importance of a strategic, ethically informed approach to their application in healthcare.

Overall key findings reveal a positive perception of AI's impact on ADHD management. This includes a balanced distribution of ratings with no significant outliers, indicating growing confidence in AI's ability to enhance ADHD care, particularly in areas like genomic analysis and treatment monitoring. While BD's impact shows some outliers, there remains a sense of optimism, especially in innovative applications such as educational gaming and digital therapeutics. The study stresses the importance of ethical training in integrating these technologies into healthcare, highlighting the necessity of responsible AI and BD usage.

Also, this research aligns with broader thematic trends in literature, particularly in 'Objective Testing' and 'Early Detection', which are deemed essential in improving ADHD treatment. The use of BD, especially through wearable devices and real-time data analytics, is poised to transform ADHD care by offering more precise monitoring and diagnostics. The focus on analyzing ADHD's genetic components through databases is also expected to pave the way for more individualized treatment strategies.

The study also delves into knowledge transfer and development, underscoring the importance of incorporating AI and BD into medical education. However, it notes that areas like 'Ethical Training' and 'Practical Training' require more attention, indicating a gap for future research to explore. AI and BD's potential to enhance diagnostic accuracy, crucial in differentiating ADHD from similar conditions, is another promising area.

The management of ADHD, especially concerning medication and treatment methods, is highlighted as a critical area. Integrated care plans are essential due to ADHD's high comorbidity with other disorders. The study also focuses on the necessity for lifestyle modification advice and the adaptation of treatment methods as individuals with ADHD navigate different life stages. It emphasizes legal and ethical issues in treatment, along with the need for specific workplace accommodation for adults with ADHD. Family support, particularly for children with ADHD, is emphasized as crucial for effective management.

The study categorizes the interaction between AI and BD in ADHD treatment and screening into various aspects, including data sources, applications, and their integration into educational and training programs. This categorization reflects the transformative potential of AI and BD in ADHD care, signaling a new era marked by improved screening, diagnosis, treatment, and monitoring.

Emerging technologies, like Large Language Models (LLM) and hypothetical future iterations such as ChatGPT 5, hold promise for further advancements in ADHD care. These technologies could play a key role in comprehensive data analysis, early detection, diagnosis, personalized treatment plans, continuous monitoring, and enhancing patient engagement.

The overarching narrative is one of cautious optimism, pointing towards a more technologically integrated approach to managing ADHD. The integration of AI and BD in ADHD management marks a significant advancement, offering improved treatment methods, enhanced diagnostic accuracy, and sophisticated data analysis. This shift towards data-centric methods indicates a departure from traditional ADHD care practices, emphasizing the need for a cohesive strategy for integrating and governing these advanced technologies in healthcare.

Contribution of Individual Authors

The research presented in this paper represents a collective effort where each author has contributed equally and significantly. The development and execution of the study were carried out through a collaborative process, ensuring a harmonious blend of expertise and insights from all team members. Each author was involved in the conceptualization of the research theme and objectives, ensuring that the study's focus on integrating Big Data and Artificial Intelligence for enhancing ADHD screening, diagnosis, treatment, and monitoring was robust and comprehensive. The methodology was developed jointly, with each author contributing their unique perspective and skills to design a rigorous and effective approach. Data collection and analysis were carried out as a team, with each member actively participating in the process, ensuring the integrity and accuracy of the data. The interpretation of results was a collective endeavor, with all authors engaging in critical discussions to derive meaningful conclusions from the findings.

Sources of Funding for Research Presented

The research detailed in this paper was conducted without any funding. Importantly, it did not receive financial contributions from private corporate entities associated with the authors' affiliations. The perspectives, findings, and conclusions articulated in this study are exclusively those of the authors. They do not represent or mirror the views, research agendas, or stances of any business corporations linked to the authors' affiliations. Moreover, this study did not benefit from any external financial support. The role of the universities involved was strictly confined to a research capacity. Their contributions were channeled through the support extended to the authors, in line with their respective academic affiliations.

Conflict of Interest

By the highest standards of academic integrity, the authors declare that there are no conflicts of interest associated with this research. The investigation and the findings presented in this paper were conducted with complete impartiality. The authors have no financial, personal, or professional affiliations that could have inappropriately influenced their work. The absence of funding from private corporate companies, as previously stated, further reinforces the lack of any potential conflict. All research activities, from conception to conclusion, were carried out independently of any external business interests. This independence ensures the integrity and objectivity of this research. Moreover, the universities affiliated with the authors have only contributed to a research capacity, without exerting any influence over the study's outcomes. The authors have adhered strictly to ethical research practices, maintaining transparency and objectivity throughout the process.

REFERENCES

Alawida, M., Mejri, S., Mehmood, A., Chikhaoui, B., & Isaac Abiodun, O. (2023). A Comprehensive Study of ChatGPT: Advancements, Limitations, and Ethical Considerations in Natural Language Processing and Cybersecurity. *Information (Basel), 14*(8), 462. doi:10.3390/info14080462

Black, D. W., & Grant, J. E. (2014). *DSM-5® guidebook: The essential companion to the diagnostic and statistical manual of mental disorders*. American Psychiatric Pub.

Breaux, R., Dvorsky, M. R., & Becker, S. P. (2021). ADHD in COVID-19: Risk, resilience, and the rapid transition to telehealth. *The ADHD Report, 29*(2), 1–9. doi:10.1521/adhd.2021.29.2.1

Breaux, R., Shroff, D. M., Cash, A. R., Swanson, C. S., Carlton, C., Bertollo, J. R., & Dahiya, A. V. (2023). Telehealth delivery of the RELAX intervention for families of adolescents diagnosed with ADHD: Preliminary treatment outcomes and evidence of acceptability and feasibility. *Evidence-Based Practice in Child and Adolescent Mental Health, 8*(1), 24–38. doi:10.1080/23794925.2021.1970053

Chen, Z. S., Galatzer-Levy, I. R., Bigio, B., Nasca, C., & Zhang, Y. (2022). Modern views of machine learning for precision psychiatry. *Patterns (New York, N.Y.), 3*(11), 100602. doi:10.1016/j.patter.2022.100602 PMID:36419447

Falcetta, F. S., de Almeida, F. K., Lemos, J. C. S., Goldim, J. R., & da Costa, C. A. (2023). Automatic documentation of professional health interactions: A systematic review. *Artificial Intelligence in Medicine, 137*, 102487. doi:10.1016/j.artmed.2023.102487 PMID:36868684

Gualtieri, C. T., & Johnson, L. G. (2005). ADHD: Is objective diagnosis possible? *Psychiatry (Edgmont, Pa.), 2*(11), 44. PMID:21120096

Hansen, A. S., Telléus, G. K., Mohr-Jensen, C., & Lauritsen, M. B. (2021). Parent-perceived barriers to accessing services for their child's mental health problems. *Child and Adolescent Psychiatry and Mental Health, 15*(1), 1–11. doi:10.1186/s13034-021-00357-7 PMID:33514400

Hong, W. C. H. (2023). The impact of ChatGPT on foreign language teaching and learning: Opportunities in education and research. *Journal of Educational Technology and Innovation, 5*(1).

Hoseini, B. L., Ajilian, M., Taghizade, M. H., Khademi, G., & Saeidi, M. (2014). *Attention deficit hyperactivity disorder (ADHD) in children: A short review and literature*. Academic Press.

Huang, H., Zheng, O., Wang, D., Yin, J., Wang, Z., Ding, S., Yin, H., Xu, C., Yang, R., Zheng, Q., & Shi, B. (2023). ChatGPT for shaping the future of dentistry: The potential of multi-modal large language model. *International Journal of Oral Science, 15*(1), 29. doi:10.1038/s41368-023-00239-y PMID:37507396

Husain, F. (2020). Investigating current state-of-the-art applications of supportive technologies for individuals with ADHD. *arXiv preprint arXiv:2005.09993.*

Jacob, C., Bourke, S., & Heuss, S. (2022). From Testers to Cocreators—the Value of and Approaches to Successful Patient Engagement in the Development of eHealth Solutions: Qualitative Expert Interview Study. *JMIR Human Factors, 9*(4), e41481. doi:10.2196/41481 PMID:36102548

Jain, R., Jain, S., & Montano, C. B. (2017). Addressing diagnosis and treatment gaps in adults with attention-deficit/hyperactivity disorder. *The Primary Care Companion for CNS Disorders*, *19*(5), 24623. doi:10.4088/PCC.17nr02153 PMID:28906602

Jalil, S., Rafi, S., LaToza, T. D., Moran, K., & Lam, W. (2023, April). Chatgpt and software testing education: Promises & perils. In *2023 IEEE International Conference on Software Testing, Verification and Validation Workshops (ICSTW)* (pp. 4130-4137). IEEE. 10.1109/ICSTW58534.2023.00078

Kasneci, E., Seßler, K., Küchemann, S., Bannert, M., Dementieva, D., Fischer, F., Gasser, U., Groh, G., Günnemann, S., Hüllermeier, E., Krusche, S., Kutyniok, G., Michaeli, T., Nerdel, C., Pfeffer, J., Poquet, O., Sailer, M., Schmidt, A., Seidel, T., ... Kasneci, G. (2023). ChatGPT for good? On opportunities and challenges of large language models for education. *Learning and Individual Differences*, *103*, 102274. doi:10.1016/j.lindif.2023.102274

Keller, A., Rimestad, M. L., Friis Rohde, J., Holm Petersen, B., Bruun Korfitsen, C., Tarp, S., Briciet Lauritsen, M., & Händel, M. N. (2021). The effect of a combined gluten-and casein-free diet on children and adolescents with autism spectrum disorders: A systematic review and meta-analysis. *Nutrients*, *13*(2), 470. doi:10.3390/nu13020470 PMID:33573238

Lee, H. (2023). The rise of ChatGPT: Exploring its potential in medical education. *Anatomical Sciences Education*, ase.2270. doi:10.1002/ase.2270 PMID:36916887

Leffa, D. T., Grevet, E. H., Bau, C. H. D., Schneider, M., Ferrazza, C. P., da Silva, R. F., Miranda, M. S., Picon, F., Teche, S. P., Sanches, P., Pereira, D., Rubia, K., Brunoni, A. R., Camprodon, J. A., Caumo, W., & Rohde, L. A. (2022). Transcranial direct current stimulation vs sham for the treatment of inattention in adults with attention-deficit/hyperactivity disorder: The TUNED randomized clinical trial. *JAMA Psychiatry*, *79*(9), 847–856. doi:10.1001/jamapsychiatry.2022.2055 PMID:35921102

Liu, Y., Han, T., Ma, S., Zhang, J., Yang, Y., Tian, J., ... Ge, B. (2023). Summary of ChatGPT-related research and perspective towards the future of large language models. *Meta-Radiology*, 100017.

Lyu, Q., Tan, J., Zapadka, M. E., Ponnatapura, J., Niu, C., Myers, K. J., Wang, G., & Whitlow, C. T. (2023). Translating radiology reports into plain language using ChatGPT and GPT-4 with prompt learning: Results, limitations, and potential. *Visual Computing for Industry, Biomedicine, and Art*, *6*(1), 9. doi:10.1186/s42492-023-00136-5 PMID:37198498

Masih, E. A. (2022). Feasibility of using QR code for registration & evaluation of training and its ability to increase response rate–The learners' perception. *Nurse Education Today*, *111*, 105305. doi:10.1016/j.nedt.2022.105305 PMID:35220149

Megahed, F. M., Chen, Y. J., Ferris, J. A., Knoth, S., & Jones-Farmer, L. A. (2023). How generative ai models such as chatgpt can be (mis) used in spc practice, education, and research? an exploratory study. *Quality Engineering*, 1–29.

Nikolic, S., Daniel, S., Haque, R., Belkina, M., Hassan, G. M., Grundy, S., ... Sandison, C. (2023). ChatGPT versus engineering education assessment: A multidisciplinary and multi-institutional benchmarking and analysis of this generative artificial intelligence tool to investigate assessment integrity. *European Journal of Engineering Education*, 1–56. doi:10.1080/03043797.2023.2248042

Peters, M. A., Jackson, L., Papastephanou, M., Jandrić, P., Lazaroiu, G., Evers, C. W., Cope, B., Kalantzis, M., Araya, D., Tesar, M., Mika, C., Chen, L., Wang, C., Sturm, S., Rider, S., & Fuller, S. (2023). AI and the future of humanity: ChatGPT-4, philosophy and education–Critical responses. *Educational Philosophy and Theory*, 1–35. doi:10.1080/00131857.2023.2213437

Rahman, M. M. (2023). AI for ADHD: Opportunities and Challenges. *Journal of Attention Disorders*, *27*(8), 797–799. doi:10.1177/10870547231167608 PMID:37039127

Raichle, M. E. (2015). The brain's default mode network. *Annual Review of Neuroscience*, *38*(1), 433–447. doi:10.1146/annurev-neuro-071013-014030 PMID:25938726

Rospigliosi, P. A. (2023). Artificial intelligence in teaching and learning: What questions should we ask of ChatGPT? *Interactive Learning Environments*, *31*(1), 1–3. doi:10.1080/10494820.2023.2180191

Sexton, C. C., Gelhorn, H. L., Bell, J. A., & Classi, P. M. (2012). The co-occurrence of reading disorder and ADHD: Epidemiology, treatment, psychosocial impact, and economic burden. *Journal of Learning Disabilities*, *45*(6), 538–564. doi:10.1177/0022219411407772 PMID:21757683

Short, C. E., & Short, J. C. (2023). The artificially intelligent entrepreneur: ChatGPT, prompt engineering, and entrepreneurial rhetoric creation. *Journal of Business Venturing Insights*, *19*, e00388. doi:10.1016/j.jbvi.2023.e00388

Spiel, K., Hornecker, E., Williams, R. M., & Good, J. (2022). ADHD and technology research–investigated by neurodivergent readers. In *Proceedings of the 2022 CHI Conference on Human Factors in Computing Systems* (pp. 1-21). 10.1145/3491102.3517592

Tai, A. M., Albuquerque, A., Carmona, N. E., Subramanieapillai, M., Cha, D. S., Sheko, M., Lee, Y., Mansur, R., & McIntyre, R. S. (2019). Machine learning and big data: Implications for disease modeling and therapeutic discovery in psychiatry. *Artificial Intelligence in Medicine*, *99*, 101704. doi:10.1016/j.artmed.2019.101704 PMID:31606109

Teubner, T., Flath, C. M., Weinhardt, C., van der Aalst, W., & Hinz, O. (2023). Welcome to the Era of ChatGPT et al. *Business & Information Systems Engineering*, *65*(2), 95–101. doi:10.1007/s12599-023-00795-x

Tsai, M. L., Ong, C. W., & Chen, C. L. (2023). Exploring the use of large language models (LLMs) in chemical engineering education: Building core course problem models with Chat-GPT. *Education for Chemical Engineers*, *44*, 71–95. doi:10.1016/j.ece.2023.05.001

Vajawat, B., Varshney, P., & Banerjee, D. (2021). Digital gaming interventions in psychiatry: Evidence, applications and challenges. *Psychiatry Research*, *295*, 113585. doi:10.1016/j.psychres.2020.113585 PMID:33303223

Wada, M., Noda, Y., Iwata, Y., Tsugawa, S., Yoshida, K., Tani, H., Hirano, Y., Koike, S., Sasabayashi, D., Katayama, H., Plitman, E., Ohi, K., Ueno, F., Caravaggio, F., Koizumi, T., Gerretsen, P., Suzuki, T., Uchida, H., Müller, D. J., ... Nakajima, S. (2022). Dopaminergic dysfunction and excitatory/inhibitory imbalance in treatment-resistant schizophrenia and novel neuromodulatory treatment. *Molecular Psychiatry*, *27*(7), 2950–2967. doi:10.1038/s41380-022-01572-0 PMID:35444257

Washington, P., Park, N., Srivastava, P., Voss, C., Kline, A., Varma, M., Tariq, Q., Kalantarian, H., Schwartz, J., Patnaik, R., Chrisman, B., Stockham, N., Paskov, K., Haber, N., & Wall, D. P. (2020). Data-driven diagnostics and the potential of mobile artificial intelligence for digital therapeutic phenotyping in computational psychiatry. *Biological Psychiatry: Cognitive Neuroscience and Neuroimaging*, *5*(8), 759–769. doi:10.1016/j.bpsc.2019.11.015 PMID:32085921

Yang, J., Li, H. B., & Wei, D. (2023). The Impact of ChatGPT and LLMs on Medical Imaging Stakeholders: Perspectives and Use Cases. *Meta-Radiology*, 100007.

Yang, X., Chen, A., PourNejatian, N., Shin, H. C., Smith, K. E., Parisien, C., Compas, C., Martin, C., Costa, A. B., Flores, M. G., Zhang, Y., Magoc, T., Harle, C. A., Lipori, G., Mitchell, D. A., Hogan, W. R., Shenkman, E. A., Bian, J., & Wu, Y. (2022). A large language model for electronic health records. *NPJ Digital Medicine*, *5*(1), 1–9. doi:10.1038/s41746-022-00742-2 PMID:36572766

Chapter 9
Intersecting Minds and Machines:
A Review of Behavioral Intentions Towards Health Intelligence Systems

Cheryll Anne Augustine
Universiti Sains Malaysia, Malaysia

Pantea Keikhosrokiani
https://orcid.org/0000-0003-4705-2732
Universiti Sains Malaysia, Malaysia & University of Oulu, Finland

Nasuha Lee Abdullah
https://orcid.org/0000-0002-5951-5207
Universiti Sains Malaysia, Malaysia

ABSTRACT

The integration of technology in the medical sector, particularly for data acquisition and analysis via the internet of health things (IoHT), offers significant potential for enhancing community health management by monitoring individual lifestyle patterns. A systematic literature review focusing on articles published between 2019 and 2021 explored the behavioral intention toward using IoHT-based healthcare systems. Analyzing 20 selected articles revealed a preference for theories such as the technology acceptance model (TAM), the unified theory of acceptance and use of technology (UTAUT), and the theory of planned behaviour (TPB) to facilitate behavioral change. Key factors influencing behavioral intention toward these systems include performance expectancy, perceived usefulness, effort expectancy, social influence, and resistance to change. The findings highlight the importance of user-centric design in developing IoHT-based healthcare systems to effectively meet community health needs, emphasizing that healthcare solutions should be tailored to individual health behaviors and preferences.

DOI: 10.4018/979-8-3693-1210-0.ch009

1. INTRODUCTION

In alignment with the United Nations Sustainable Development Goal No. 3 (SDG 3), which aims to ensure healthy lives and promote well-being for all at all ages, it is imperative to address the challenges of sustainable development through enhancing health outcomes. Alarmingly, it has been observed that every two seconds, an individual between the ages of 30 and 70 succumbs prematurely to noncommunicable diseases, including cardiovascular disease, chronic respiratory conditions, diabetes, or cancer (Organization, 2020). Two primary objectives of their agenda are to diminish premature mortality from non-communicable diseases by one third through prevention and treatment, and to enhance mental health and well-being. Additionally, there is a focus on augmenting the capability of all nations, especially those in the developing world, to implement early warning systems, mitigate risks, and manage both national and global health threats. Achieving these goals necessitates efficient and ongoing healthcare monitoring. The escalation of lifestyle-related diseases, sedentary habits, demanding work environments, advancements in healthcare monitoring technologies, and the growing utilization of remote devices are identified as key factors necessitating the development of a systematic and analytical approach to healthcare. While healthcare monitoring devices are anticipated to be technologically sophisticated, offering both advanced and basic features across various price points, the process of data collection and analysis has yet to reach its full potential. (Keikhosrokiani, 2020b; Keikhosrokiani, Mustaffa, & Zakaria, 2018; Keikhosrokiani, Mustaffa, Zakaria, & Sarwar, 2012; Keikhosrokiani et al., 2015). This shortfall may stem from the overwhelming volume of data sent to hospitals, where it is not effectively segregated or analysed. Moreover, there is a noticeable deficiency in the availability of valuable input and real-time data from patients.

The integration of the Internet of Things (IoT) into contemporary healthcare, known as the Internet of Health Things (IoHT), represents a significant advancement in the application of IoT technologies within the realm of e-health (Rahman, Hossain, Islam, Alrajeh, & Muhammad, 2020). This innovation offers a cost-effective and technologically efficient means for medical providers to engage and communicate with patients. IoHT supports a wide array of healthcare services, including pediatric care, elderly supervision, patient monitoring (M. S. Hossain, 2017), chronic disease diagnosis, and the enhancement of overall societal health and fitness. IoHT solutions not only facilitate improved patient care in a more timely manner but also ensure patient safety. As sustainable cities witness burgeoning populations, healthcare challenges escalate correspondingly. Enormous volumes of healthcare-related raw data are continuously collected from diverse sources in real time. This includes a vast range of patient data acquired routinely. However, the task of disease diagnosis is significantly hindered by a lack of skilled labour, delays in procedural functions, and outdated manual methods. In such scenarios, the accurate identification of medical conditions becomes paramount. The early diagnosis of chronic diseases is considerably facilitated when medical professionals have insight into the physiological and genetic factors influencing the patient's health.

This raises a red flag as mortality rates continue to climb, primarily attributed to heart and chronic diseases, according to a survey conducted by the World Health Organization (Organization, 2020) and analysis from the Peterson-KFF Health System Tracker, a comprehensive resource dedicated to monitoring and evaluating the performance of the U.S. healthcare system. Despite a sudden surge in Covid-19 deaths in January 2022, heart disease remains the persistent leading cause of death in the U.S. from March 2020 to February 2022, as illustrated in Figure 1. This prevalent cardiovascular ailment, which poses a significant threat to communities, is heavily influenced by individual habits. Given the diversity of habits among individuals, the adoption of IoHT-based healthcare systems by medical professionals to monitor and promote healthier behaviours becomes essential in fostering a generation with improved health outcomes. Patients grappling with cardiovascular or other chronic diseases often grapple with the consequences of unhealthy habits such as sedentary lifestyles, poor dietary choices, inadequate sleep, and smoking, among others. Recent studies underscore the significance of early disease detection and diagnosis facilitated by healthcare systems leveraging Big Data (Jagadeeswari, Subramaniyaswamy, Logesh, & Vijayakumar, 2018). Hence, the objective of this studyis to scrutinize existing research concerning the behavioural inclination towards utilizing IoHT-based healthcare systems, with a focus on elucidating relevant theories and effective determinants.

Figure 1. Average daily deaths in the United States by cause

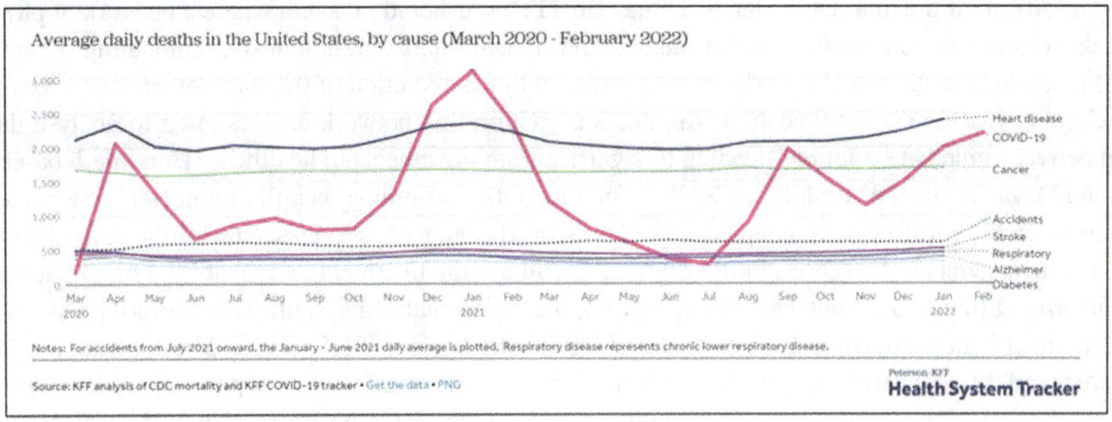

This Systematic Literature Review (SLR) is conducted following the methodologies and guidelines outlined by (Kitchenham & Charters, 2007). An SLR systematically plans, assesses, and reports on existing research relevant to a defined research area, question, topic, or field of interest. Consequently, this SLR aims firstly to explore the existing studies on behavioural intentions regarding the use of Internet of Health Things (IoHT)-based healthcare systems. The second objective is to identify various theories employed to predict behavioural intentions towards IoHT-based healthcare systems utilization. The third goal is to discover different influential factors that predict such behavioural intentions. This SLR distinguishes itself by pinpointing the most prevalent theories and factors that significantly impact the intention to employ IoHT-based systems within the healthcare sector. It includes an analysis of articles from 2019 to 2021 that delve into the behavioural intentions surrounding the adoption of IoHT-based systems in healthcare.

The structure of this chapter is as follows: Section 1 introduces the research, including the problem statement and the study's objectives. Section 2 provides background information on the Internet of Health Things (IoHT) and the current state of healthcare systems. Section 3 outlines the methodology employed in conducting the SLR. Section 4 presents a summary of the findings, results, and discussions. Finally, Section 5 concludes this systematic literature review.

2. BACKGROUND

The Internet of Things (IoT) encompasses the extensive network of physical devices globally interconnected via the internet, collectively gathering and sharing data. When applied to the realm of e-health and digital healthcare systems, this concept evolves into the Internet of Health Things (IoHT). By integrating sensors into a wide array of devices, these otherwise inert objects gain a form of digital consciousness, enabling them to transmit real-time information autonomously, without human intervention. The IoT is thus merging digital and physical realities, fostering a smarter, more reactive environment around us (Ranger, 2020). Within the context of sustainable cities, the healthcare sector is progressively embracing IoHT technologies. The monitoring capabilities of IoHT assets offer considerable advantages to healthcare providers, including doctors, nurses, and support staff, who frequently require precise information regarding the whereabouts of patients and medical assets (Oracle, 2022).

The advent of the Internet of Health Things (IoHT) has ushered in an era where a network of physical devices can communicate, interact, detect, and transmit data autonomously, eliminating the need for human intervention. IoHT represents a new phase in the evolution of the Internet, characterized by machine-to-machine communication. Applications within this network are designed to analyse data and deliver immediate solutions, leading to significant improvements in healthcare (Jemima Jebaseeli, Anand Deva Durai, & Dinesh Peter, 2020). The integration of remote health monitoring systems and smart wearable IoHT devices, coupled with cloud-based healthcare services, enables the early diagnosis and management of diseases. Furthermore, it facilitates the treatment and rehabilitation of patients, transforming traditional healthcare into a smarter, more personalized system. This evolution has given rise to what is now known as the Personalized Healthcare System (PHS) (Papa, Mital, Pisano, & Del Giudice, 2020). IoHT technologies have enhanced the healthcare industry by supporting patient remote monitoring, tracking patient location, granting access to electronic health records and medical data, transmitting medical data/biomedical signals, and providing rapid emergency services. These advancements aid in decision-making and the overall treatment process.

Contemporary healthcare systems in hospitals fall short in their capacity to monitor patients' detrimental habits, a critical oversight given that many community-affecting diseases stem from individual behaviours. Given the variability of habits from one individual to another, actively monitoring and fostering change in these unhealthy practices is essential for cultivating a healthier generation. Particularly, patients battling cardiovascular or other chronic conditions often suffer further due to unhealthy habits, including insufficient exercise, poor dietary patterns, inadequate sleep, smoking, among others. Recent research underscores the significance of early detection and diagnosis of diseases through healthcare systems that leverage Big Data, highlighting an avenue for improving patient outcomes by addressing the root behavioural causes (Jagadeeswari et al., 2018 & Vijayakumar, 2018).

The expansion of the Internet and digital technologies has significantly broadened the horizons of healthcare and health communication beyond its traditional confines (Palfrey and Gasser, 2011; Schiavo, 2013), highlighting the need for a shift in habits towards healthier behaviours to preempt future health issues. In this context, the integration of the Internet of Health Things (IoHT) and big data heralds a transformative era in healthcare. This integration enhances the efficiency of healthcare processes and procedures, allowing for the prediction, autonomous analysis, and prescription of health-care trends and patterns through big data analytics. Consequently, a novel, intelligent paradigm has emerged, wherein IoT and big data analytics serve as synergistic technologies poised to revolutionize the healthcare sector (Saheb & Izadi, 2019). The effective implementation and adoption of Big Data in healthcare unlock immense potential across various domains, notably in enhancing the quality of care and patient support. This potential is encapsulated in the five main characteristics of Big Data, known as the 5Vs: volume, velocity, variety, veracity, and value (Mehta & Pandit, 2018).

Big Data analytics plays a crucial role in this study, serving as the foundation upon which medical professionals depend to offer patients accurate medication, advice, and treatment plans. The insights gleaned from this research could significantly enhance the hospital's patient management system, enabling the provision of early care and preventive measures through societal outreach. Consequently, this study aims to empirically examine behavioural intentions towards the implementation of a healthcare system in hospitals, with a particular focus on the significant role of habit modification.

Existing Healthcare Systems

The research conducted reveals that several hospital management systems are currently operational in select Malaysian hospitals, yet they fall short of incorporating the core functionality proposed in this study, specifically the analysis of Big Data related to patient habits.

The Hospital Information System (HIS) utilized by Public Health Ministry hospitals is grounded in the Sistem Pengurusan Pesakit (SPP) framework (Figure 2). The SPP, a domestically developed hospital management information system, boasts Intellectual Property Rights (IPR) exclusively held by the Ministry of Health Malaysia. There has been a concerted effort to continually enhance the SPP through version upgrades, reflecting modifications based on user feedback. In the latest iteration, SPPV3.0, eight distinct modules have been introduced. The operational cycle of the Sistem Pengurusan Pesakit (SPP) initiates with patient registration at the service counter, advancing to patient admission procedures, management of orders to various departments including Pathology, Radiology, Pharmacy, Dietetics, and Catering, and culminating in the Bill and Payment Management Module (Figure 3). Additionally, the Patient Management System facilitates appointment scheduling. Moreover, the Staff Management feature within the system enables efficient administration of staff-related information, encompassing rosters, shift schedules, and annual leave tracking.

E-Soft Hospital Information System

In 1990, Everise introduced SMI Malaysia's Ultimate Business Software, marking a significant advancement with the launch of their Manufacturing Resource Planning (MRP) software system tailored for the manufacturing sector. Two decades later, in 2010, Everise achieved another milestone with the completion of the E-Soft Hospital Information System. This network-based, client-server software is meticulously crafted for the healthcare industry, promoting scalability, central governance of business protocols, and reductions in maintenance and operational expenses. E-Soft HIS stands out as a cost-efficient, healthcare Enterprise Resource Planning (ERP) software solution, characterized by its simplicity in management, readiness for deployment, scalability, and affordability. Specifically designed to cater to the needs of small, medium, and large hospitals and clinics in Malaysia, E-Soft HIS integrates a comprehensive suite of 9 modules. These modules encompass Patient Registration with MyKad, Outpatient Management, Inpatient & Ward Management, Doctor's Consultation Desktop, Pharmacy for Dispensary and Labelling, Stock Control System, Laboratory, Procedure and Surgery, Patient Billing and Insurance, and the User Management module, thereby offering a holistic approach to healthcare management (E-Soft, 2022).

Figure 2. The cycle of Sistem Pengurusan Pesakit (SPP)

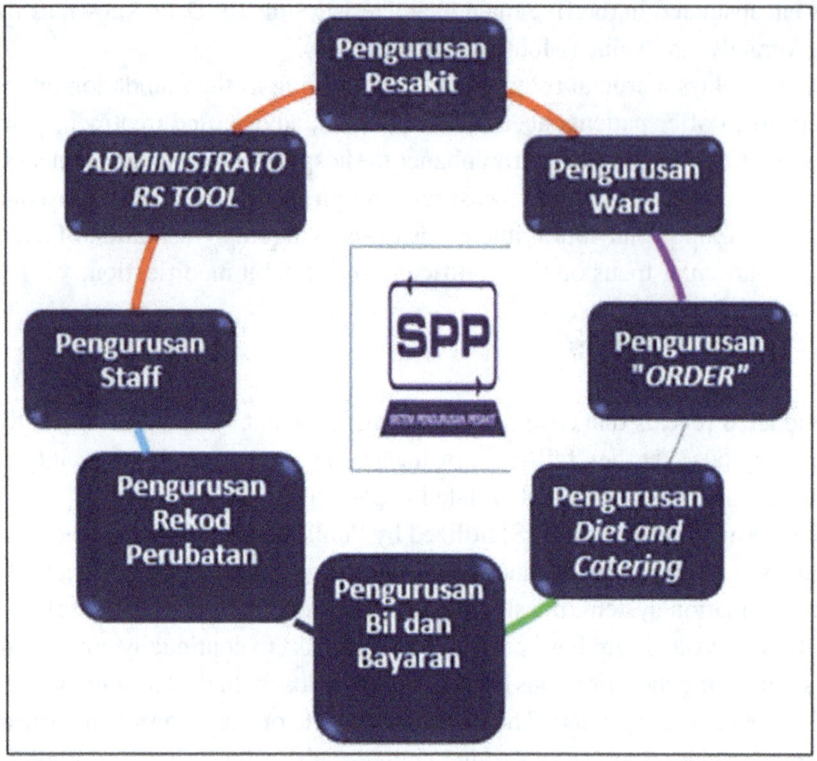

Figure 3. Sub-module of SPP

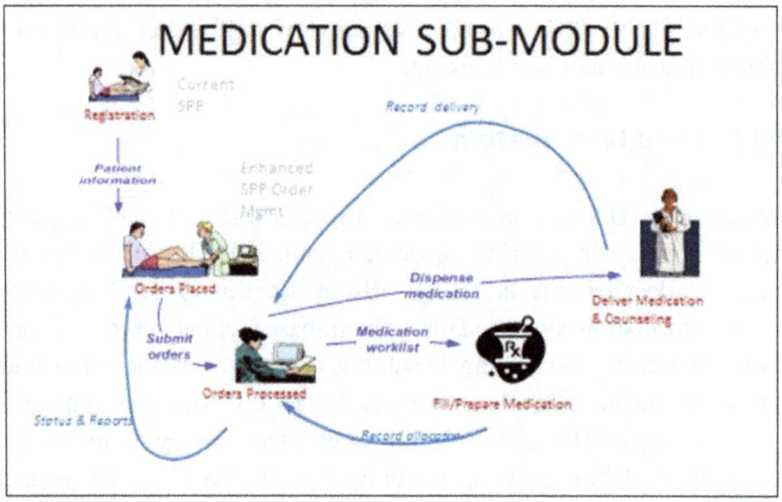

Doctor Assist Software

Doctor Assist™ by Mywam Sdn. Bhd (MyWam, 2022) was developed with the ambitious goal of revolutionizing the healthcare industry by enabling doctors to operate digitally and smartly, while also enhancing patient awareness regarding treatment options tailored to their specific needs and conditions. This comprehensive information system is thoughtfully designed and supported locally, catering to a wide range of operational levels, from private clinics to major hospitals. Doctor Assist™ is renowned for its ability to diminish paperwork, boost productivity, and concurrently reduce superfluous expenses. Moreover, it supports wireless data access over a secure network and acts as an effective local data storage and management system. Doctor Assist™ is founded upon three core principles:

1) A user-friendly customer/patient registration platform equipped with SMS and care line services
2) A digital handwriting recognition system to facilitate seamless communication among healthcare professionals
3) A dispensary and settlement system that accommodates both itemized and non-itemized billing.

In short, while these Hospital Information Systems (HIS), including Doctor Assist™, excel in streamlining hospital and clinic management and administrative workflows, they have yet to fully embrace the potential of Big Data. The significance of Big Data and its capacity for analysing and enhancing patient health—both in terms of general well-being and in identifying and preventing potential illnesses or diseases—is undervalued. There is a pressing need for these systems to leverage Big Data analytics to foster a healthier lifestyle among patients by gaining insights into their daily habits, with the ultimate aim of encouraging positive habit transformation.

A Habit-Change Support Web-Based System With Big Data Analytical Features for Hospitals (Doctive)

The system architecture of the healthcare system called "Doctive" (Augustine & Keikhosrokiani, 2021) is described in detail in the *Figure 4*. There are two interconnected components: Doctive itself and the Behabit mobile application, which is linked to an IoT-enabled smartwatch (Ravichandran & Keikhosrokiani, 2021). The Behabit app is instrumental in gathering and monitoring the user's demographic information, alongside a variety of health metrics such as heart rate, step count, calories burned, mood, exercise intensity, and habits. It aims to positively influence users' habits through emotional and persuasive techniques. This collected data is then transmitted to the Hadoop cloud platform via the internet, making it accessible to the Doctive system. The primary function of Doctive is to aggregate, organize, and analyze this data, empowering users to lead healthier lifestyles and mitigate the risk of chronic diseases. Leveraging cloud technology, Doctive retrieves data and employs machine learning algorithms and tools to facilitate doctors in tracking and understanding changes in users' or patients' habits (Augustine & Keikhosrokiani, 2021). Additionally, it utilizes data visualization tools, such as Tableau, to aid doctors in their analysis, providing a comprehensive and insightful overview of patients' health trajectories.

Figure 4. Doctive system architecture

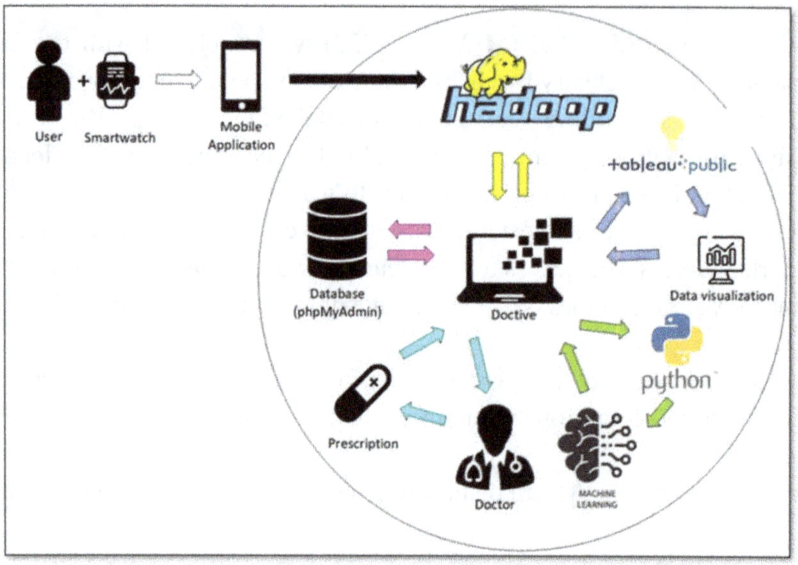

Since the 1980s, the study of individual behaviour and behavioural intentions in the context of information technology has emerged as a focal area within the information systems discipline, leading to the development of several models aimed at understanding technology acceptance (Davis, 1989, 1993; Venkatesh, Morris, Davis, & Davis, 2003). Originating from the Theory of Reasoned Action in 1980 and evolving into the Theory of Planned Behaviour, Behavioural Intention (BI) is defined as the motivational factors that influence an individual's decision to engage in a particular action. The principle posits that the stronger an individual's intention to perform a behaviour, the more likely the behaviour is to be executed.

3. METHODOLOGY

This study encompasses a systematic review executed in four stages, as depicted in Figure 5. The initial phase involved screening the literature for the keyword "behavioural intention towards healthcare system" across three distinct databases. Initially, PubMed was considered; however, it was unable to yield the necessary papers for this investigation. Consequently, ScienceDirect and Springer, renowned for their extensive coverage of big data and healthcare systems, were selected as the electronic databases for this research. The screening process in ScienceDirect revealed a vast collection of 6,381 papers, while Springer provided a significantly lower count of 2,882 papers. To refine these results, duplicate publications were meticulously removed. Subsequent filtration, focusing on journal articles published from 2019 to 2021, left 2,509 papers from ScienceDirect and 1,240 from Springer. These papers underwent further scrutiny to discard those irrelevant based on several criteria: review of articles, title and abstract screening, full paper evaluation, absence of theoretical frameworks, lack of mention of behaviour change, absence of a proposed theoretical model, and lack of system or device involvement. Consequently, this rigorous process concluded with the inclusion of eight papers from ScienceDirect and twelve from Springer, totalling twenty articles. The analysis proceeded with a qualitative approach, utilizing word clouds and node-network visualization to illustrate connections between the selected papers. Methodology for this SLR is adopted from (Pantea Keikhosrokiani, 2021b) (Pantea, Norlia, Nasriah, & Ahmad Suhaimi, 2019).

Figure 5. Four steps of the systematic review

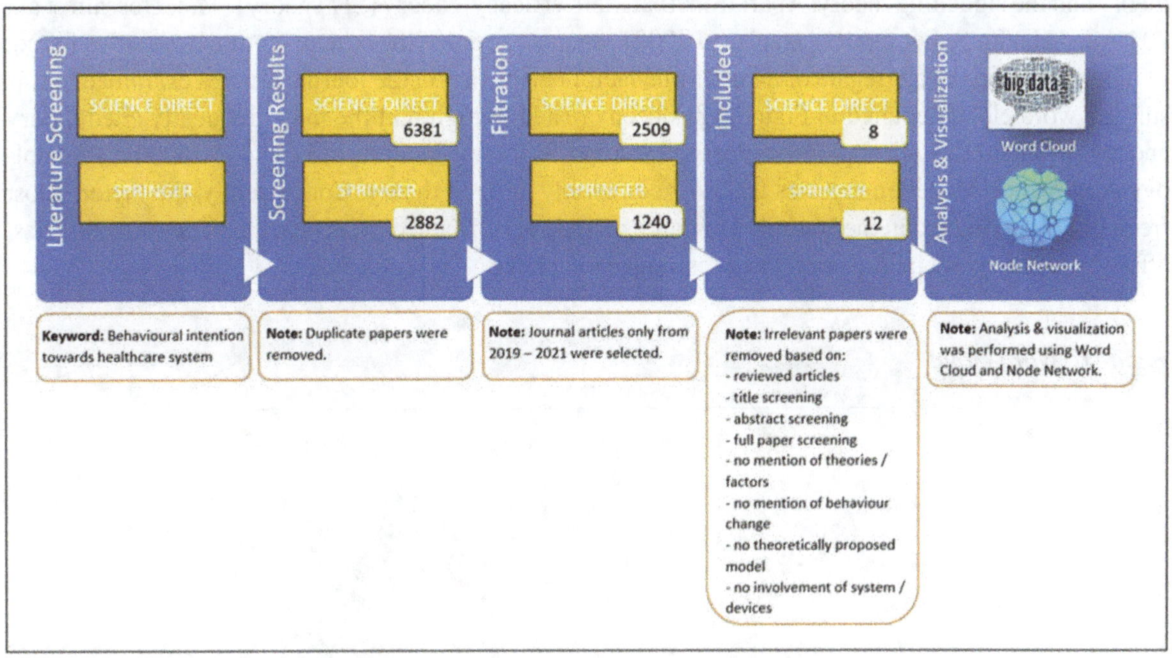

4. RESULTS AND DISCUSSION

As outlined in the methodology, this study undertook a systematic literature review (SLR), resulting in the inclusion of 20 journal articles, with 8 sourced from ScienceDirect and 12 from the Springer electronic database. These databases were specifically selected for their comprehensive coverage of big data, healthcare systems, and behavioural intentions. The studies included in this review encompass a variety of theories and their associated factors related to behavioural change intentions, which were notably absent in numerous articles during the filtration phase. Among these, the Technology Acceptance Model is one of the many theories frequently employed to facilitate behavioural change (Al-Jumaili et al., 2021; Dhagarra, Goswami, & Kumar, 2020; M. I. Hossain, Yusof, Hussin, lahad, & Sadiq, 2021; Papa et al., 2020; Shahbaz, Gao, Zhai, Shahzad, & Hu, 2019) Theory of Acceptance and Use of Technology (UTAUT) (Barchielli, Marullo, Bonciani, & Vainieri, 2021; A. Hossain, Quaresma, & Rahman, 2019; Macdonald, Perrin, Hyett, & Kingsley, 2019; H. Wang, Tao, Yu, & Qu, 2020), UTAUT2 (Idoga, Toycan, Nadiri, & Çelebi, 2019; Lee & Lee, 2020; Talukder, Sorwar, Bao, Ahmed, & Palash, 2020), Theory of Planned Behaviour (TPB) (Anderson & Ozakinci, 2019; Ataei, Gholamrezai, Movahedi, & Aliabadi, 2021; M. I. Hossain et al., 2021; Mustapa, Amin, & Frewer, 2020; Mwaliko et al., 2021; Papa et al., 2020), Task-Technology Fit (TTF) (Shahbaz et al., 2019; H. Wang et al., 2020) and Theory of Reasoned Action (TRA) (M. I. Hossain et al., 2021; Papa et al., 2020). There are also studies that postulate the credentials of the TAM together with TTF contribute substantially to the enhancement of behavioural intentions to use the big data analytics system in healthcare, which ultimately lead towards actual use of the system (Shahbaz et al., 2019).

There are also a few other uncommon theories found in this study, which are Theory of Diffusion of Innovation (DOI) (Al-Dhaen, Hou, Rana, & Weerakkody, 2021), Signal-mechanism-consequence (SMC) (W. Wang, Chen, Xiong, & Wang, 2021) theory that is divided into the diffusion of innovation theory and the signalling theory. Apart from that, Self-efficacy Theory (SE Theory) (M. I. Hossain et al., 2021) and Health Belief model (Ataei et al., 2021) are also some of the other uncommon theories found.

Drawing upon the aggregate of theories and factors identified in the journal articles examined in this study, a word cloud depicted in Figure 6 has been created to highlight the most frequently cited theory and the prevalent factors employed across the studies. From this analysis, it is evident that the Technology Acceptance Model emerges as the most commonly utilized theory. Concurrently, the factors most frequently encountered in the compiled research include performance expectancy, perceived usefulness, effort expectancy, social influence, and resistance to change.

Figure 6. Word cloud

4.1 Theories

Theories are designed to elucidate, forecast, and comprehend phenomena, and often serve to contest and expand upon the prevailing body of knowledge within the confines of critical boundary assumptions (California, 2022). The theories applied across the 20 scholarly articles reviewed in this study have been summarized below, accompanied by a brief explanation and their associated factors.

4.1.1 Diffusion of Innovation (DOI)

The Diffusion of Innovation (DOI) Theory, formulated by E.M. Rogers in 1962, stands as one of the foundational theories in social science (LaMorte, 2019a). Originally conceptualized within the field of communication, it describes the process by which an idea or product gains traction and spreads throughout a particular demographic or social structure over time (LaMorte, 2019a). This process leads individuals within a social system to adopt new ideas, behaviours, or products. Adoption signifies a change in behaviour, such as the purchase or utilization of a new product, or the engagement in a novel behaviour. A crucial aspect of adoption is the individual's perception of the innovation as new or innovative, facilitating the diffusion process (LaMorte, 2019a).

The journey to adopting an innovation, and thus achieving diffusion, encompasses several stages: recognizing the need for the innovation, deciding whether to adopt or reject it, initially trying the innovation to evaluate it, and ultimately continuing its use. There are five primary factors that influence the adoption of an innovation: relative advantage, compatibility, complexity, triability, and observability. These factors vary in their impact across the five categories of adopters.

4.1.2 Technology Acceptance Model

he Technology Acceptance Model (TAM) serves as a framework within information technology to understand the adoption and usage of new technologies, particularly in workplace environments, and its applicability has been demonstrated in older populations as well (Allen, 2020). This theory suggests that an individual's decision to accept and use technology is influenced by their perceptions of the technology's usefulness (the benefits derived from using the technology) and ease of use. The TAM further indicates that individual differences, system characteristics, social influences, and facilitating conditions collectively impact the user's perceived usefulness and ease of use of the technology.

According to the TAM, the adoption of technology triggers a cognitive assessment process where perceived ease of use and perceived usefulness play pivotal roles. These perceptions then drive the user's behavioural intention, leading to actual use behaviour (Davis, 1989, 1993). This model underscores the importance of user perceptions in determining the acceptance and effective utilization of technology (Davis, 1989, 1993)

4.1.3 Theory of Acceptance and Use of Technology (UTAUT)

The Unified Theory of Acceptance and Use of Technology (UTAUT) asserts that four key factors—performance expectancy, effort expectancy, social influence, and facilitating conditions—play a crucial role in technology acceptance (Williams, Rana, & Dwivedi, 2015(Chao, 2019 #103)). Empirical evidence has consistently demonstrated UTAUT's robust capability to elucidate a significant portion of the variance observed in technology usage and acceptance behaviours across diverse contexts, including communication technologies, online education, and health informatics.

4.1.4 Theory of Planned Behaviour (TPB)

The Theory of Planned Behaviour (TPB) (Ajzen, 1991) originally introduced as the Theory of Reasoned Action in 1980, aims to predict an individual's intention to engage in a behaviour within a specific context of time and place. This framework is designed to encapsulate behaviours over which individuals have the ability to exert self-control. Central to this theory is the notion of behavioural intent, which is considered a key determinant of action.

TPB has been effectively applied to predict and elucidate a broad spectrum of health-related behaviours and intentions, ranging from smoking and drinking to the utilization of healthcare services, breastfeeding, and substance abuse. Under the TPB framework, both motivation (intention) and capability play critical roles in the realization of a behaviour. It distinguishes three categories of beliefs—behavioural, normative, and control—which influence behaviour. The theory encompasses six constructs—attitude, behavioural intention, subjective norms, social norms, perceived power, and perceived behavioural control—that together account for an individual's perceived efficacy in managing the behaviour in question.

4.1.5 Task-Technology Fit (TTF)

The Task-Technology Fit (TTF) Model, proposed by (Goodhue & Thompson, 1995) offers an analytical framework to understand technology adoption by assessing how well a technology aligns with users' tasks or requirements. Distinct from preceding research that predominantly concentrated on the precursors to technology use and intentions, TTF was pioneering in its focus on the post-adoption phase of technology utilization (Goodhue & Thompson, 1995).

This model is built around five core constructs: task characteristics, technology characteristics, task-technology fit, technology utilization, and performance impact. Together, these elements provide a comprehensive view of how the suitability of technology for a given task influences its adoption and the subsequent performance outcomes.

4.1.6 Theory of Reasoned Action (TRA)

The Theory of Reasoned Action (TRA), conceived by Martin Fishbein and Icek Ajzen in 1975 represented a significant advancement over the preceding information integration theory (Fishbein & Ajzen, 1975). This development emerged from Fishbein and Ajzen's efforts to discern the distinctions between attitudes and behaviours. A novel aspect introduced by TRA was the concept of behavioural intention, positioning it as a mediator that bridges the gap between mere attitudinal predictions and the actual prediction of behaviour (Fishbein & Ajzen, 1975). This distinction underscores the theory's recognition that various factors may moderate the direct influence of attitudes on behaviour.

TRA introduced two pivotal components to enhance its predictive capability: personal attitude towards the behaviour and subjective norms, or the perceived expectations of others. These elements collectively contribute to the prediction of an individual's behavioural intention. Hence, while personal attitudes might incline an individual towards a certain behaviour, the perceived social pressures or expectations can influence them to consider alternative actions.

4.1.7 Self-Efficacy Theory

The concept of "self-efficacy" was introduced by Albert Bandura, a Canadian-American psychologist and Stanford University professor, in 1977 (Lopez-Garrido, 2020). Bandura's theory posited that self-efficacy encompasses an individual's belief in their ability to successfully execute a course of action in future scenarios. Simply put, it reflects a person's confidence in their capability to achieve success in specific situations (Lopez-Garrido, 2020).

The theory of self-efficacy underscores the significance of the individual's self-perception regarding their own abilities as crucial determinants of achieving successful outcomes (Gallagher, 2012).

4.1.8 Health Belief Model

The Health Belief Model (HBM) (LaMorte, 2019b) was developed in the early 1950s by social scientists at the U.S. Public Health Service, sought to comprehend why people were not engaging in disease prevention behaviours or undergoing early detection screenings. Initially aimed at understanding public reluctance, the HBM evolved to assess patient responses to symptoms and adherence to treatments. At its core, the HBM posits that an individual's likelihood to undertake a health-related action hinges on their perceived risk of acquiring an illness and their belief in the effectiveness of the recommended health behaviour or intervention.

Rooted in psychological and behavioural theories, the HBM (LaMorte, 2019b) operates on the principle that health-related actions are motivated by the desire to avoid illness or to recover if already sick, and the belief that specific health actions can prevent or cure diseases. Ultimately, an individual's decision to engage in healthy behaviours is often shaped by their assessment of the advantages and potential obstacles. The HBM consists of six constructs, with the initial four - perceived susceptibility, perceived severity, perceived benefits, and perceived barriers - laying the foundation. The latter two constructs, cue to action and self-efficacy, were integrated as the model expanded with ongoing research (LaMorte, 2019b).

Table 1 outlines the theories applied in each study, accompanied by the factors influencing behavioural change intention. These factors are categorized according to different domains, including health wearable devices, healthcare innovation, and the utilization of big data analytics in healthcare.

Table 1. Extraction of theory and factors from each study

Study	Theories	Factors	System/Area
(Al-Dhaen et al., 2021)	Diffusion of Innovation (DOI)	-Relative advantage -Compatibility -Complexity -Observability -Trialability -Novelty seeking -Age -AI awareness -Motivation -Training	Internet of Medical Things (IoMT)
(Al-Jumaili et al., 2021)	Technology Acceptance Model (Tam, Tyquin, Mehta, & Larkin); TAM has five main domains	Perceived usefulness (Publishing), perceived ease of use (PEU), attitude toward using (ATU), facilitating conditions (FC) and behavioural intention to use (BIU)	Informational Technology
(Anderson & Ozakinci, 2019)	Theory of Planned Behaviour for Supported Self-Management	Behavioural (Instrumental, Experiential) Subjective Norm (Norms, Pressure) Perceived Behavioural Control (Self-Efficacy, Controllability)	Supported Self-Management for Long-Term Conditions
(Tam et al., 2021)	Theory of Planned Behaviour (TPB)	Trust, Perceived Value, Problem Recognition, Constraint Recognition, Involvement Recognition, Past Experience, Attitude	Private Health Insurance

Table 1 continued

Study	Theories	Factors	System/Area
(Idoga et al., 2019)	Unified Theory of Acceptance and use of Technology Extended (UTAUT2)	UTAUT (Performance Expectancy, Effort Expectancy, Social Influence, Facilitating Conditions), UTAUT2 (Hedonic Motivation, Price Value, Habit)	hospitals in Benue state, northcentral Nigeria
(Lee & Lee, 2020)	Internal factors: KAPB External factors: UTAUT2	KAPB (knowledge, attitude, belief), UTAUT2 (Technological factors, social factors)	Health wearable device
(Macdonald et al., 2019)	Theory of Acceptance and Use of Technology (UTAUT); Multiple Regression method	Self-Efficacy, Attitude, Effort Expectancy, Performance Expectancy	Smart Insoles
(Mustapa et al., 2020)	theory of planned behaviour (TPB) has overlapping concepts with the risk perception attitude (RPA) framework, where perceived risk was reported as a predictor for behavioural intention.	Engagement, Trust in Key Players, Religiosity, Perceived Benefits, Perceived Risk	Intention to adopt Nutrigenomics
(Mwaliko et al., 2021)	theory of planned behaviour (TPB); Bivariate analysis was conducted to investigate the relationship between the external variables and intention.	External variables, Attitudes, Subjective Norms, Perceived behavioural control, behavioural intentions	Healthcare: Early detection of cervical cancer
(Barchielli et al., 2021)	UTAUT model: to analyse the acceptance of innovations, Multidimensional Item Response Theory: to identify the main dimensions characterizing the UTAUT model	Performance expectancy, effort expectancy, social influence, facilitating conditions	Healthcare & innovations
(Shahbaz et al., 2019)	TAM and TTF models to explain BDA adoption in the healthcare sector from both viewpoints (the user's perception of technology and the task-technology fitness); RTC as a moderator	Perceived trust, Perceived security, Task-Technology Fit (TTF), Technology Acceptance Model (Tam et al.); Perceived Ease to Use, Perceived Usefulness	to use the big data analytics system in healthcare
(W. Wang et al., 2021)	signal-mechanism-consequence (SMC) theory; 1)The diffusion of innovation theory 2) signalling theory	Responsible AI signals (Autonomy, Beneficence, explainability, justice, non-maleficence) Mechanism (employee engagement), consequences (attitude tow. AI, Satisfaction tow. AI, usage intention tow. AI)	AI Adoption
(Talukder et al., 2020)	include three context-specific predictors/factors namely self-actualization, resistance to change, and technology anxiety to the UTAUT2 model	-Technology Anxiety -Resistance to change -Performance Expectancy -Effort Expectancy -Social Influence -Facilitating Conditions -Hedonic Motivation -Functional Congruence -Self-Actualization	Wearable Health Technology (WHT)
(Papa et al., 2020)	The Theory of Reasoned Action (TRA), The Theory of Planned Behaviour (TPB) and The Technology Acceptance Model (Tam et al.)	1.Intention to use 2.Attitude towards adoption 3.Perceived usefulness 4.Perceived ease of use 5.Intrusiveness 6.Comfort	Smart Healthcare Devices
(M. I. Hossain et al., 2021)	TAM; Theory of Reasoned Action (TRA); Theory of Planned Behaviour (TPB); Self-efficacy Theory (SE Theory)	1.Interpersonal Influence 2.Personal Innovativeness 3.Trustworthiness 4.Attitude towards a Wearable Device 5.Self-Efficacy 6.Health Interest 7.Perceived Value 8.Intention to Use	Continuous Glucose Monitoring Systems (CGMs) device

Table 1 continued

Study	Theories	Factors	System/Area
(Ataei et al., 2021)	Theory of planned behaviour (TPB) and the health belief model (HBM)	TPB – Self-identity, Moral norm, attitude, subjective norm, perceived behavioural control HBM – cues to action, perceived susceptibility, health motivation, perceived severity, perceived benefits, perceived barriers, perceived self-efficacy	Intention to use green pesticides, agriculture
(Sinha, Singh, Gupta, & Singh, 2020)	-	Anthropomorphism, Technophobia and behavioural intention to accept robotics at workplace	Robotics
(A. Hossain et al., 2019)	Unified Theory of Acceptance and Use of Technology (UTAUT)	-Performance Expectancy -Effort Expectancy -Social Influence -Facilitating Conditions -Personal Innovativeness in IT -Resistance to change -Use behaviour	Electronic Health Record
(Dhagarra et al., 2020)	technology acceptance model (Tam et al.) **extend TAM from patient centric perspective by incorporating variables such as patients' cognitive belief, trust and privacy concerns in addition to TAM variables.	-Perceived usefulness -Trust -Privacy concern -Perceived ease of use	Technology Acceptance in Healthcare
(H. Wang et al., 2020)	Unified Theory of Acceptance and Usage of Technology (UTAUT) and Task-Technology Fit (TTF) models	-social influence -facilitating conditions -effort expectancy -Performance expectancy -technology characteristics -task characteristics -task-technology fit	Health Wearable devices (HWDs)

The table below has summarised 20 studies involved in this systematic review which mainly aims in studying the behavioural intention towards using an IoHT-based healthcare system. Therefore, in *Table 2*, the aim, method used along with tools and the respondents involved have been summarised.

Table 2. Summary of findings of each study

Aim	Method	Tool	Respondents
The continuous intention by healthcare professionals to use the Internet of Medical Things (IoMT) in combination with responsible artificial intelligence (AI)	Quantitative approach	A self-administered Questionnaire, online survey; Only closed and multiple-choice questions were included	276 healthcare professionals; who have experiences of using IoMT
To assess the extent to which healthcare students use five informational technologies for daily academic purposes; to examine the changes in student perceptions toward these technologies over five years.	cross-sectional descriptive study	Electronic surveys and administered using Qualtrics Survey Software;	administered to convenience samples of students at the colleges of pharmacy, medicine, and dentistry in participating universities; Total of 3,113 valid surveys collected in 2015, 2018, and 2020

Table 2 continued

Aim	Method	Tool	Respondents
To explore healthcare professionals' beliefs towards Supported Self-Management for Long-Term Conditions using the Theory of Planned Behaviour.	Mixed methods (Qualitative & Quantitative)	Online questionnaire; Phase 1 TPB-based beliefs, comprising 51- items across 4 overarching variables: Demographics, Intention, Beliefs and Optional Feedback. This was published online using SurveyMonkey Gold©,	HSV staff with direct (patient contact) and/or indirect (Service level) involvement in an existing regional SSM for LTCs project were eligible. No exclusions were placed upon age, gender, race, organization, profession, type of patient contact, project involvement, time in current role, time working with LTCs, or experience of SSM.
examined the motivational factors that affected young adults' attitude and behavioural intentions towards PHI.	Quantitative approach	An online questionnaire	594 Australian young adults aged between 18 and 30 years. Within this age group, the survey sought an equal split of participants who were members and non-members of PHI schemes.
To examine, identify and evaluate the factors affecting healthcare professionals' intention to accept the cloud-based health centre (CBHC) in developing countries.	Quantitative research approach	close-ended questionnaire: 7point Likert-scale measurement	300 (final outcome used) healthcare professionals selected from medical health institutions in Benue State Nigeria.
examined the effects of internal and external factors on actual use behaviour, health improvement expectancy, and continuous use intention of healthcare wearable devices	Quantitative method	Measurement items in the questionnaire taken from previous studies; double translation protocol. Pilot study	Data collected from *medical personnel and general public* through a survey questionnaire. 288 useable questionnaires healthcare wearable devices/apps users.
to use an established theoretical framework to determine a model of psychosocial factors that best predicts participant intention to use smart insoles.	Mixed method study	Participants were invited to complete the questionnaire twice, one week apart, to determine test-retest reliability.	Requirements: to have diabetes, be English language speakers, be ambulant and able to attend the main campus in a regional city. Fifty-three adults with diabetes from regional Australia completed the questionnaire.
to analyse Malaysian stakeholders' intentions to adopt nutrigenomics, and determines the factors that influence their intentions	Quantitative method	face-to-face surveys held with 421 adult respondents in major public hospitals.	421 adults (aged 18 years and older) and comprising two stakeholder groups: *healthcare providers (n = 221) and patients (n = 200)*
to predict primary health care providers' behaviour in examining women who present with abnormal discharge or bleeding	quantitative, cross-sectional, questionnaire-based study	59-item questionnaire	primary health care practitioners in western Kenya
An in-depth analysis of the paths towards the acceptance and use of technology	two stage *regression models* and validated using a *SEM covariance analysis.*	standardized web questionnaire made of twelve questions that operationalize the main constructs of the UTAUT model.	Italian nurses operating in 6 healthcare departments located in the Tuscany Region. Total 62 nurses. 54 valid responses
To explore the adoption mechanism of big data analytics in healthcare organizations to inspect elements correlated to behavioural intention using the technology acceptance model and task-technology fit paradigm.	Quantitative approach	7-point Likert scale in which the agreement of the participants to a given statement	A total of 400 questionnaires were distributed remaining 224 responses were selected for the analysis
investigates how signals of AI responsibility impact healthcare practitioners' attitudes toward AI, satisfaction with AI, AI usage intentions, including the underlying mechanisms.	Quantitative method	seven-item Likert-type scale ranging from 'strongly disagree' to 'strongly agree'.	healthcare practitioners working in the West China Hospital and other Grade A tertiary hospitals in China

Table 2 continued

Aim	Method	Tool	Respondents
to develop a theoretical model on the basis of extended Unified Theory of Acceptance and Use of Technology (UTAUT2) with additional constructs- resistance to change, technology anxiety, and self-actualization, to investigate the key predictors of WHT adoption by elderly.	Quantitative method	Questionnaire with 2 sections: Section (A) portrays demographic statistics as multiple-choice quires such as profession, gender, age, and WHT usage experience. Section(B) questions that symbolize the constructs of the planned UTAUT2 model with an additional three constructs. five-point Likert-scale with doable response points	Targeted: individuals who had knowledge/experience of using WHT. data were collected through a cross-sectional survey on older citizens of age >=60 years in Wuhan, China at various public places of the city such as parks, playgrounds, and community centres. Out of 300 hard copies and 98 online (e-mail based) surveys, 344 were received completed (Response rate of 86%).
To evaluate the contribution of smart innovation in an industry which the engagement and the respectfulness of the patients being represent not only an economic matter but also enabling the emergence of new solutions by developing technologies that support ethics issues as well	Quantitative methodology	-	data was collected from 273 respondents. The age group of the respondents was between 25 and 40 years
To explore the factors that influence users' intention to adopt CGMs device on the Internet of Things (IoT) based healthcare.	Quantitative approach	A survey questionnaire was delivered to the respondents through online via the link of Google form. Designed into two sections, named as 1) Demographic, and 2) Assessment (five-point Likert-scale) questions.	data needs to be collected from the users who are using the device at present and also the people who have experience of using CGMs devices before. this study collected data from Germany and Sweden. 97 data were accepted from 114 of total data collected.
To examine farmers' intention to use green pesticides using two models – the theory of planned behaviour (TPB) and the health belief model (HBM)	Mixed method	research instrument was a questionnaire. Structural equation modelling was used for data analysis. Interview conducted at the farmers' home and farm and each interview lasted 30–40 min.	500 farmers were invited to participate in the survey
To explores the antecedents of employees' intention to accept robotics at workplace using two-step analyses: Twitter Analysis and Survey-based analysis	Mixed approach	A survey questionnaire: (a) demographic profile of the respondents and (b) main questions.	864 responses from an online survey conducted in India among the employees working in IT sector in the Delhi NCR region of India (technological & urban hub)
to identify the critical factors affecting the physicians' adoption of EHR in healthcare system of Bangladesh by extending the Unified Theory of Acceptance and Use of Technology (UTAUT) to include Personal Innovativeness in Information Technology and Resistance to Change.	Qualitative method	cross-sectional survey questionnaire method	Respondents; physicians having various types of specializations from 30 hospitals private and public hospitals in Dhaka, Bangladesh. The study distributed 300 questionnaires, of which 249 (83% response rate) were returned and found to be valid for further analyses.
to understand relationships that predict patients' acceptance of technology in healthcare services.	Quantitative approach	survey-based strategy consisting of structured self-administered questionnaire.	responses obtained from survey of 416 patients availing healthcare service at various primary health centres in New Delhi, India.

Table 2 continued

Aim	Method	Tool	Respondents
to develop and empirically test a model by integrating the Unified Theory of Acceptance and Usage of Technology (UTAUT) and Task-Technology Fit (TTF) models to understand how consumers accept health wearable devices (HWDs).	Quantitative method	Web-based questionnaire survey	inclusion criteria included: 1) adults who owned a smartphone, as HWDs often need to be matched with smartphone platforms; and 2) those who were potential users of HWDs; as the HWDs acceptance in the present study was explored for both users and non-users of HWDs. Of 608 questionnaires, we obtained 406 valid samples

The word cloud depicted in Figure 7 was created using the abstracts of the 20 academic papers included in this study. The University of Melbourne (2022) defines an abstract as a concise summary of a research paper or thesis, not merely a shortened version, but an original, standalone piece (Melbourne, 2022). An effective abstract should be self-explanatory, without requiring external references or the full paper for understanding. Thus, aggregating all abstracts yields a simplified yet comprehensive word cloud that highlights the key components of the research, centring on themes such as healthcare, user intention, technology, and health, as well as behaviour, factors, models, acceptance, and devices.

Figure 7. General word cloud of collected studies

To identify closely related papers, the study "Predicting Smartphone Users' Behaviour Towards a Location-Aware IoMT-Based Information System" (Pantea Keikhosrokiani, 2021b) served as the foundational paper for generating a network of related publications spanning from 2006 to 2021, as depicted in Figure 8. In this figure, each node represents an academic paper linked to the foundational study, organized by similarity. The size of each node corresponds to its citation count, while its colour indicates the year of publication. Papers with stronger connections are represented by thicker lines and are grouped closer together in the network.

This visualization notably features several works by author Keikhosrokiani, with a significant concentration of publications between 2019 and 2021 that are closely interconnected. Among these, key papers include "Success factors in developing iHeart as a patient-centric healthcare system: A multi-group analysis" (Pantea Keikhosrokiani et al., 2018) which boasts the highest citation count among Keikhosrokiani's works; "User Behavioural Intention Toward Using Mobile Healthcare System" (Pantea et al., 2019), identified as the most similar to the foundational study; "Assessment of a medical information system: the mediating role of use and user satisfaction on the success of human interaction with the mobile healthcare system (iHeart)" (Pantea Keikhosrokiani, Mustaffa, Zakaria, & Abdullah, 2020), noted for having the greatest number of references; and "Behavioural intention to use of Mobile Medical Information System (mMIS)" (Pantea Keikhosrokiani, 2020a). These papers, particularly influential and constructive for this study, spotlight and propose advancements in medical information systems, especially concerning heart diseases.

Figure 8. Network of connected papers

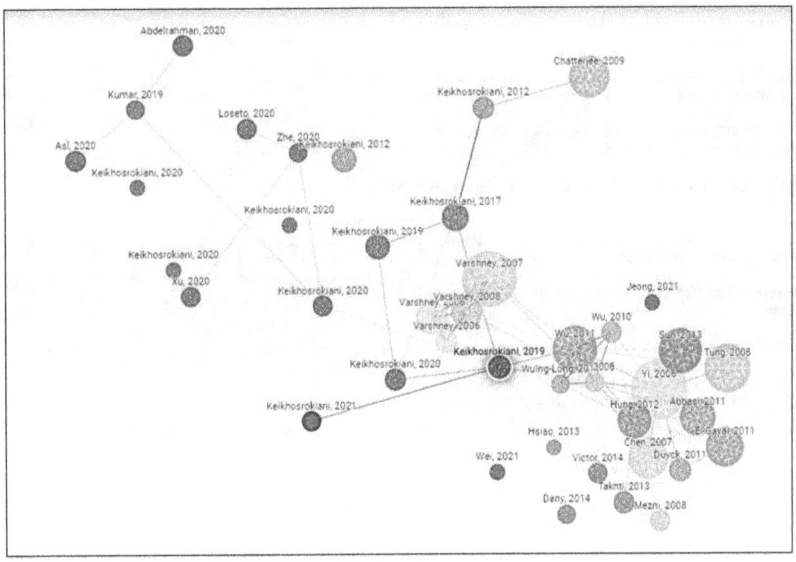

Derivative Works

The study also presents a table of derivative works based on the foundational paper previously discussed. In essence, derivative works are creations that are based on, or derived from, one or more pre-existing works, as defined by the Office (Office, 2020). These works often incorporate significant copyrightable elements from the original source. Despite the highest cited paper in this table, "Factors affecting E-marketing adoption and implementation in tourism firms: An empirical investigation of Egyptian small tourism organizations" (El-Gohary, 2012) accumulating 264 citations at the time of retrieval, it is not directly related to the foundational study. Nonetheless, it might have integrated findings from the foundational paper.

With 41 citations, the article "A Literature Review on Attitudes of Health Professionals towards Health Information Systems: From e-Health to m-Health" (Sezgin & Yıldırım, 2014) closely aligns with both the foundational study and the current research.

he table, depicted as Figure 9, also references graphs based on Figure 8. The most relevant graph reference to this study is "IoT for Enhanced Decision-Making in Medical Information Systems: A Systematic Review" (Pantea Keikhosrokiani, 2021a) by the same author, Pantea Keikhosrokiani. Thus, the compilation of derivative works not only illustrates the influence of the foundational study but also aids in identifying pertinent academic articles that significantly contribute to the current research.

Figure 9. Derivative works

Title⇕	Last author⇕	Year▴	Citations⇕	Graph references⇕
Predicating Smartphone Users' Behaviour Towards a Location-Aware IoMT-Based Information System: An Empirical Study	Pantea, Keikhosrokiani	2021	0	5
Do Consumers Care About Aesthetics and Compatibility? The Intention to Use Wearable Devices in Health Care	Taewoo, Roh	2021	0	5
IoT for Enhanced Decision-Making in Medical Information Systems: A Systematic Review	Pantea, Keikhosrokiani	2021	0	9
Assessment of a medical information system: the mediating role of use and user satisfaction on the success of human interaction with the mobile...	Rosni, Abdullah	2019	13	5
A cross-sectional investigation of acceptance of health information technology: A nationwide survey of community pharmacists in Turkey.	Sevgi, Özkan-Yildirim	2016	18	5
Trends of Factors and Theories in Health Information Systems Acceptance: 2002 – 2014 Review	Sevgi Özkan, Yildirim	2016	3	5
A Literature Review on Attitudes of Health Professionals towards Health Information Systems: From e-Health to m-Health	Sevgi Özkan, Yildirim	2014	41	4
The adoption of PDA for future healthcare system: an emerging market perspective	A., Chong	2014	27	4
Factors Determining Nurses Hospital Information System Usage	S., Abedini	2013	5	5
Factors affecting E-Marketing adoption and implementation in tourism firms: An empirical investigation of Egyptian small tourism organisations	H., El-Gohary	2012	264	4

Prior Works

In addition to derivative works, a comprehensive summary of prior works spanning from 1977 to 2006 has been organized into a table, depicted in Figure 10. "Prior Works" encompasses a wide range of creations, including but not limited to authorship pieces, inventions, intellectual property, materials, documents, or other work products such as research, reports, software, databases, systems, applications, presentations, textual works, content, or audio-visual materials. These are contributions made, invented, designed, developed, or improved by a participant, either individually or collaboratively, before their engagement with the company. Such works are especially relevant if they pertain to or are implicated by the participant's role within the company.

The journal article accruing the highest number of citations, "The Theory of Planned Behaviour" published in 1991 (Ajzen, 1991) boasts 56,487 citations and 18 graph citations. This theory is renowned for its applicability in predicting and elucidating a broad spectrum of health behaviours and intentions, marking it as a pivotal piece of scholarly work in the field.

Following closely, the second most cited article, titled "Perceived Usefulness, Perceived Ease of Use, and User Acceptance of Information Technology" from 1989 (Davis, 1989) delineates critical factors within the Technology Acceptance Model. This model serves as a key framework for comprehending the adoption and utilization of emerging technologies, predominantly within workplace settings such as healthcare centres or hospitals.

The book *Belief, Attitude, Intention, and Behaviour: An Introduction to Theory and Research* (Fishbein & Ajzen, 1975) authored by Fishbein, M., & Ajzen, I., ranks as the third highest cited work according to the table below. It discusses the concepts of belief and attitude, which are pivotal factors associated with the Theory of Planned Behaviour, a framework extensively referenced in numerous studies included in this analysis.

Figure 10. Prior works related to origin paper

Title	Last author	Year	Citations	Graph citations
Understanding information technology acceptance by individual professionals: Toward an integrative view	J., Probst	2006	987	13
Implementation of a WAP-based telemedicine system for patient monitoring	Yuan-ting, Zhang	2003	327	12
User Acceptance of Information Technology: Toward a Unified View	Fred D., Davis	2003	25105	19
Investigating healthcare professionals' decisions to accept telemedicine technology: an empirical test of competing theories	P. H., Hu	2002	1028	13
A Theoretical Extension of the Technology Acceptance Model: Four Longitudinal Field Studies.: Four Longitudinal Field Studies.	Fred D., Davis	2000	15241	16
Understanding Information Technology Usage: A Test of Competing Models	Peter A., Todd	1995	7774	14
The theory of planned behavior	I., Ajzen	1991	56487	18
Perceived Usefulness, Perceived Ease of Use, and User Acceptance of Information Technology	Fred D., Davis	1989	41171	15
User Acceptance of Computer Technology: A Comparison of Two Theoretical Models	P. R., Warshaw	1989	20471	19
Belief, Attitude, Intention, and Behavior: An Introduction to Theory and Research	I., Ajzen	1977	34899	16

5. CONCLUSION

The rapid progression of smart Internet of Health Things (IoHT) devices, sensors, cloud computing, data analytics, and smartphones has significantly transformed community lifestyles. This evolution, particularly evident within the healthcare ecosystem, represents a hallmark of the Big Data era, facilitating a novel approach to living that enhances decision-making efficiency. The advent and pervasive reach of wireless communication technology have made remote healthcare management a tangible reality. Nonetheless, healthcare systems dedicated to patient-centric prediction, prevention, analysis, diagnosis, and treatment are still in their nascent stages of development. Wearable technology, such as smartwatches, smartphones, smart clothing, bracelets, clips, headbands, and shirts, is capable of monitoring vital health metrics including heart rate, body temperature, blood pressure, and daily activities. These devices have become commonplace, continuously generating vast datasets that, when properly monitored and analysed, hold the potential to pre-empt noncommunicable diseases within the community. This systematic review delves into existing research on behavioural intentions regarding the use of IoHT-based healthcare systems, identifying relevant theories and determining effective factors across different healthcare domains. This exploration aims to discern the behavioural intentions toward adopting IoHT-based healthcare systems, highlighting the importance of features such as patient management, administration, tracking, monitoring, and analysis for the benefit of medical professionals and the broader community alike, paving the way for a healthier future. Despite the comprehensive advantages presented, this study acknowledges its limitations. While research on behavioural intentions dates back to as early as 1975 (Fishbein & Ajzen, 1975), the articles meeting the search criteria predominantly span the last three years. Consequently, several studies that could offer valuable insights into behavioural intentions toward healthcare systems, by integrating various theories and factors, may have been overlooked due to the selection criteria.

Conversely, it is evident that there has been a surge in the number of articles addressing behavioural intention and IoHT-based healthcare systems in recent years. This study specifically reviews articles published in English, leading to the exclusion of relevant research published in other languages during the article selection process. Despite this limitation, the aim of this study is to guide IoHT developers and healthcare professionals in creating futuristic healthcare systems. These systems are designed to lower mortality rates through early diagnosis, habit analysis, disease monitoring, and prevention, all while ensuring user-friendly design and systematic development to facilitate technology adoption. Ultimately, this approach fosters positive user behaviour towards IoHT-based healthcare systems, characterized by reliable performance, minimal effort, substantial usefulness, and a positive impact on adherence.

REFERENCES

Ajzen, I. (1991). The theory of planned behavior. *Organizational Behavior and Human Decision Processes*, *50*(2), 179–211. doi:10.1016/0749-5978(91)90020-T

Al-Dhaen, F., Hou, J., Rana, N. P., & Weerakkody, V. (2021). Advancing the Understanding of the Role of Responsible AI in the Continued Use of IoMT in Healthcare. *Information Systems Frontiers*. Advance online publication. doi:10.1007/s10796-021-10193-x PMID:34493926

Al-Jumaili, A. A., Ahmed, K. K., Al-Jalehawi, A. K., Al-Fatlawi, B. G., Al-Rekabi, M. D., Al-Sawad, O. S., Shari, F. H., & Sorofman, B. (2021). Evaluating the use of informational technologies by students of healthcare colleges for academic purposes over a five-year period. *Education and Information Technologies*, *26*(5), 5269–5289. doi:10.1007/s10639-021-10533-z PMID:33867808

Allen, R. (2020). *Digital Marketing Models: The Technology Acceptance Model*. Retrieved from https://www.smartinsights.com/manage-digital-transformation/digital-transformation-strategy/digital-marketing-models-technology-acceptance-model/

Anderson, N., & Ozakinci, G. (2019). "It all needs to be a full jigsaw, not just bits": Exploration of healthcare professionals' beliefs towards supported self-management for long-term conditions. *BMC Psychology*, *7*(1), 38. doi:10.1186/s40359-019-0319-7 PMID:31234924

Ataei, P., Gholamrezai, S., Movahedi, R., & Aliabadi, V. (2021). An analysis of farmers' intention to use green pesticides: The application of the extended theory of planned behavior and health belief model. *Journal of Rural Studies*, *81*, 374–384. doi:10.1016/j.jrurstud.2020.11.003

Augustine, C. A., & Keikhosrokiani, P. (2021). *A Habit-Change Support Web-Based System with Big Data Analytical Features for Hospitals*. Doctive. doi:10.1007/978-3-030-70713-2_10

Barchielli, C., Marullo, C., Bonciani, M., & Vainieri, M. (2021). Nurses and the acceptance of innovations in technology-intensive contexts: The need for tailored management strategies. *BMC Health Services Research*, *21*(1), 639. doi:10.1186/s12913-021-06628-5 PMID:34215228

California, U. S. (2022). *Research Guide on Theoritical Framework*. Retrieved from https://libguides.usc.edu/writingguide

Davis, F. D. (1989). Perceived Usefulness, Perceived Ease of Use, and User Acceptance of Information Technology. *Management Information Systems Quarterly*, *13*(3), 319–340. doi:10.2307/249008

Davis, F. D. (1993). User acceptance of information technology: System characteristics, user perceptions and behavioral impacts. *International Journal of Man-Machine Studies*, *38*(3), 475–487. doi:10.1006/imms.1993.1022

Dhagarra, D., Goswami, M., & Kumar, G. (2020). Impact of Trust and Privacy Concerns on Technology Acceptance in Healthcare: An Indian Perspective. *International Journal of Medical Informatics*, *141*, 104164. doi:10.1016/j.ijmedinf.2020.104164 PMID:32593847

E-Soft. (2022). *Hospital Information System (HIS)*. Retrieved from https://www.e-soft.com.my/hospital.html

El-Gohary, H. (2012). Factors affecting E-Marketing adoption and implementation in tourism firms: An empirical investigation of Egyptian small tourism organisations. *Tourism Management*, *33*(5), 1256–1269. doi:10.1016/j.tourman.2011.10.013

Fishbein, M., & Ajzen, I. (1975). *Belief, attitude, intention and behaviour: An introduction to theory and research* (Vol. 27). Academic Press.

Gallagher, M. W. (2012). Self-Efficacy. In V. S. Ramachandran (Ed.), *Encyclopedia of Human Behavior* (2nd ed., pp. 314–320). Academic Press. doi:10.1016/B978-0-12-375000-6.00312-8

Goodhue, D. L., & Thompson, R. L. (1995). Task-Technology Fit and Individual Performance. *Management Information Systems Quarterly*, *19*(2), 213–236. doi:10.2307/249689

Hossain, A., Quaresma, R., & Rahman, H. (2019). Investigating factors influencing the physicians' adoption of electronic health record (EHR) in healthcare system of Bangladesh: An empirical study. *International Journal of Information Management*, *44*, 76–87. doi:10.1016/j.ijinfomgt.2018.09.016

Hossain, M. I., Yusof, A. F., Hussin, A. R. C., lahad, N. A., & Sadiq, A. S. (2021). Factors influencing adoption model of continuous glucose monitoring devices for internet of things healthcare. *Internet of Things : Engineering Cyber Physical Human Systems*, *15*, 100353. doi:10.1016/j.iot.2020.100353

Hossain, M. S. (2017). Cloud-Supported Cyber–Physical Localization Framework for Patients Monitoring. *IEEE Systems Journal*, *11*(1), 118–127. doi:10.1109/JSYST.2015.2470644

Idoga, P. E., Toycan, M., Nadiri, H., & Çelebi, E. (2019). Assessing factors militating against the acceptance and successful implementation of a cloud based health center from the healthcare professionals' perspective: A survey of hospitals in Benue state, northcentral Nigeria. *BMC Medical Informatics and Decision Making*, *19*(1), 34. doi:10.1186/s12911-019-0751-x PMID:30782166

Jagadeeswari, V., Subramaniyaswamy, V., Logesh, R., & Vijayakumar, V. (2018). A study on medical Internet of Things and Big Data in personalized healthcare system. *Health Information Science and Systems*, *6*(1), 14. doi:10.1007/s13755-018-0049-x PMID:30279984

Jemima Jebaseeli, T., Anand Deva Durai, C., & Dinesh Peter, J. (2020). IOT based sustainable diabetic retinopathy diagnosis system. *Sustainable Computing : Informatics and Systems*, *28*, 100272. doi:10.1016/j.suscom.2018.08.004

Keikhosrokiani, P. (2020a). Behavioral intention to use of Mobile Medical Information System (mMIS). In P. Keikhosrokiani (Ed.), *Perspectives in the Development of Mobile Medical Information Systems* (pp. 57–73). Academic Press. doi:10.1016/B978-0-12-817657-3.00004-3

Keikhosrokiani, P. (2020b). Emotional-persuasive and habit-change assessment of mobile medical information Systems (mMIS). In P. Keikhosrokiani (Ed.), *Perspectives in the Development of Mobile Medical Information Systems* (pp. 101–109). Academic Press. doi:10.1016/B978-0-12-817657-3.00006-7

Keikhosrokiani, P. (2021a). IoT for Enhanced Decision-Making in Medical Information Systems: A Systematic Review. In G. Marques, A. Kumar Bhoi, I. de la Torre Díez, & B. Garcia-Zapirain (Eds.), *Enhanced Telemedicine and e-Health: Advanced IoT Enabled Soft Computing Framework* (pp. 119–140). Springer International Publishing. doi:10.1007/978-3-030-70111-6_6

Keikhosrokiani, P. (2021b). Predicating Smartphone Users' Behaviour Towards a Location-Aware IoMT-Based Information System: An Empirical Study. *International Journal of E-Adoption*, *13*(2), 52–77. doi:10.4018/IJEA.2021070104

Keikhosrokiani, P., Mustaffa, N., & Zakaria, N. (2018). Success factors in developing iHeart as a patient-centric healthcare system: A multi-group analysis. *Telematics and Informatics*, *35*(4), 753–775. doi:10.1016/j.tele.2017.11.006

Keikhosrokiani, P., Mustaffa, N., Zakaria, N., & Abdullah, R. (2020). Assessment of a medical information system: The mediating role of use and user satisfaction on the success of human interaction with the mobile healthcare system (iHeart). *Cognition Technology and Work*, *22*(2), 281–305. doi:10.1007/s10111-019-00565-4

Keikhosrokiani, P., Mustaffa, N., Zakaria, N., & Sarwar, M. I. (2012). A proposal to design a Location-based Mobile Cardiac Emergency System (LMCES). *Studies in Health Technology and Informatics*, *182*, 83–92. PMID:23138083

Keikhosrokiani, P., Zakaria, N., Mustaffa, N., Wan, T.-C., Sarwar, M. I., & Azimi, K. (2015). *Wireless Networks in Mobile Healthcare*. doi:10.1007/978-3-319-12817-7_30

Kitchenham, B., & Charters, S. (2007). *Guidelines for performing Systematic Literature Reviews in Software Engineering*. Academic Press.

LaMorte, W. W. (2019a). *Diffusion of Innovation*. Retrieved from https://sphweb.bumc.bu.edu/otlt/mph-modules/sb/behavioralchangetheories/behavioralchangetheories4.html

LaMorte, W. W. (2019b). *The Health Belief Model*. Retrieved from https://sphweb.bumc.bu.edu/otlt/mph-modules/sb/behavioralchangetheories/behavioralchangetheories2.html

Lee, S. M., & Lee, D. (2020). Healthcare wearable devices: An analysis of key factors for continuous use intention. *Service Business*, *14*(4), 503–531. doi:10.1007/s11628-020-00428-3

Lopez-Garrido, G. (2020). *Self-Efficacy Theory*. Academic Press.

Macdonald, E. M., Perrin, B. M., Hyett, N., & Kingsley, M. I. C. (2019). Factors influencing behavioural intention to use a smart shoe insole in regionally based adults with diabetes: A mixed methods study. *Journal of Foot and Ankle Research*, *12*(1), 29. doi:10.1186/s13047-019-0340-3 PMID:31139261

Melbourne, U. o. (2022). *Writing an Abstract*. Retrieved from https://services.unimelb.edu.au/__data/assets/pdf_file/0007/471274/Writing_an_Abstract_Update_051112.pdf

Mustapa, M. A. C., Amin, L., & Frewer, L. J. (2020). Predictors of stakeholders' intention to adopt nutrigenomics. *Genes & Nutrition*, *15*(1), 16. doi:10.1186/s12263-020-00676-y PMID:32962632

Mwaliko, E., Van Hal, G., Bastiaens, H., Van Dongen, S., Gichangi, P., Otsyula, B., Naanyu, V., & Temmerman, M. (2021). Early detection of cervical cancer in western Kenya: Determinants of healthcare providers performing a gynaecological examination for abnormal vaginal discharge or bleeding. *BMC Family Practice*, *22*(1), 52. doi:10.1186/s12875-021-01395-y PMID:33706721

MyWam. (2022). *Doctor Assist: Hospital Management System*. Retrieved from https://wammap.com/hospital-information-system

Office, U. S. C. (2020). *Copyright in Derivative Works and Compilations*. Retrieved from https://www.copyright.gov/circs/circ14.pdf

Oracle. (2022). *What is IoT?* Retrieved from https://www.oracle.com/internet-of-things/what-is-iot/

Organization, W. H. (2020). *The top 10 causes of death*. Retrieved from https://www.who.int/news-room/fact-sheets/detail/the-top-10-causes-of-death

Pantea, K., Norlia, M., Nasriah, Z., & Ahmad Suhaimi, B. (2019). User Behavioral Intention Toward Using Mobile Healthcare System. In A. Information Resources Management (Ed.), Consumer-Driven Technologies in Healthcare: Breakthroughs in Research and Practice (pp. 429-444). IGI Global.

Papa, A., Mital, M., Pisano, P., & Del Giudice, M. (2020). E-health and wellbeing monitoring using smart healthcare devices: An empirical investigation. *Technological Forecasting and Social Change*, *153*, 119226. doi:10.1016/j.techfore.2018.02.018

Publishing, H. H. (2020). *Mind & Mood*. Retrieved from https://www.health.harvard.edu/topics/mind-and-mood

Rahman, M. A., Hossain, M. S., Islam, M. S., Alrajeh, N. A., & Muhammad, G. (2020). Secure and Provenance Enhanced Internet of Health Things Framework: A Blockchain Managed Federated Learning Approach. *IEEE Access : Practical Innovations, Open Solutions*, *8*, 205071–205087. doi:10.1109/ACCESS.2020.3037474 PMID:34192116

Ranger, S. (2020). *What is the IoT? Everything you need to know about the Internet of Things right now.* Retrieved from https://www.zdnet.com/article/what-is-the-internet-of-things-everything-you-need-to-know-about-the-iot-right-now/

Ravichandran, B. D., & Keikhosrokiani, P. (2021). *An Emotional-Persuasive Habit-Change Support Mobile Application for Heart Disease Patients.* BeHabit. doi:10.1007/978-3-030-70713-2_25

Saheb, T., & Izadi, L. (2019). Paradigm of IoT big data analytics in the healthcare industry: A review of scientific literature and mapping of research trends. *Telematics and Informatics*, *41*, 70–85. doi:10.1016/j.tele.2019.03.005

Sezgin, E., & Yıldırım, S. Ö. (2014). A Literature Review on Attitudes of Health Professionals towards Health Information Systems: From e-Health to m-Health. *Procedia Technology*, *16*, 1317–1326. doi:10.1016/j.protcy.2014.10.148

Shahbaz, M., Gao, C., Zhai, L., Shahzad, F., & Hu, Y. (2019). Investigating the adoption of big data analytics in healthcare: The moderating role of resistance to change. *Journal of Big Data*, *6*(1), 6. doi:10.1186/s40537-019-0170-y

Sinha, N., Singh, P., Gupta, M., & Singh, P. (2020). Robotics at workplace: An integrated Twitter analytics – SEM based approach for behavioral intention to accept. *International Journal of Information Management*, *55*, 102210. doi:10.1016/j.ijinfomgt.2020.102210

Talukder, M. S., Sorwar, G., Bao, Y., Ahmed, J. U., & Palash, M. A. S. (2020). Predicting antecedents of wearable healthcare technology acceptance by elderly: A combined SEM-Neural Network approach. *Technological Forecasting and Social Change*, *150*, 119793. doi:10.1016/j.techfore.2019.119793

Tam, L., Tyquin, E., Mehta, A., & Larkin, I. (2021). Determinants of attitude and intention towards private health insurance: A comparison of insured and uninsured young adults in Australia. *BMC Health Services Research*, *21*(1), 246. doi:10.1186/s12913-021-06249-y PMID:33740968

Venkatesh, V., Morris, M. G., Davis, G. B., & Davis, F. D. (2003). User Acceptance of Information Technology: Toward a Unified View. *Management Information Systems Quarterly*, *27*(3), 425–478. doi:10.2307/30036540

Wang, H., Tao, D., Yu, N., & Qu, X. (2020). Understanding consumer acceptance of healthcare wearable devices: An integrated model of UTAUT and TTF. *International Journal of Medical Informatics*, *139*, 104156. doi:10.1016/j.ijmedinf.2020.104156 PMID:32387819

Wang, W., Chen, L., Xiong, M., & Wang, Y. (2021). Accelerating AI Adoption with Responsible AI Signals and Employee Engagement Mechanisms in Health Care. *Information Systems Frontiers*. Advance online publication. doi:10.1007/s10796-021-10154-4

Williams, M. D., Rana, N. P., & Dwivedi, Y. K. (2015). The unified theory of acceptance and use of technology (UTAUT): A literature review. *Journal of Enterprise Information Management*, *28*(3), 443–488. doi:10.1108/JEIM-09-2014-0088

Chapter 10
Transforming Medical Tourism Through an Integrated Business Intelligence Platform:
Data-Driven Insights and Healthcare Industry Impact

Md. Ashrafuzzaman
https://orcid.org/0000-0002-3366-9144
Military Institute of Science and Technology, Bangladesh

Rabita Rahman Era
Military Institute of Science and Technology, Bangladesh

Saira Binte Awal
Military Institute of Science and Technology, Bangladesh

Israt Sultana
Military Institute of Science and Technology, Bangladesh

Arjun Thimmaiah
Kalam Institute of Health Technology, India

Amit Kumar Sharma
Kalam Institute of Health Technology, India

Jitendra Sharma
Kalam Institute of Health Technology, India

ABSTRACT

Medical tourism has evolved significantly, leveraging data-driven insights in its core operations. This chapter explores the impact of analytics, AI, and big data on patient care, destination selection, and industry dynamics. Personalized patient care is enhanced through data integration, tailoring services to individual needs, improving overall experiences, and treatment outcomes. This focuses on destination selection and industry competitiveness, data-driven decisions on treatment outcomes, cost-effectiveness, quality improvement, and patient satisfaction. The healthcare industry's holistic impact can be examined through data-driven acumens evolving business models, regulatory frameworks, and strategic alliances. Emphasizing the pivotal role of global medical tourism sector in delivering more patient-centric, efficient, and competitive medical tourism industry, showcasing its potential for positive global impacts on healthcare accessibility and quality. Valuable insights are offered for policymakers, healthcare providers, and industry stakeholders navigating the evolving landscape.

DOI: 10.4018/979-8-3693-1210-0.ch010

1. INTRODUCTION

Medical tourism, a rapidly expanding industry intertwining healthcare with travel and hospitality, encompasses a diverse array of medical procedures falling into three main categories. Firstly, curative treatments address specific health issues, ranging from cardiac surgeries to organ transplants, hip and knee replacements, and innovative therapies like stem cell treatments and newly approved drugs available in certain countries. Secondly, rejuvenation and aesthetic offerings cater to those seeking cosmetic surgery, stress relief programs, spa treatments, and procedures aimed at enhancing physical appearance and overall well-being. Lastly, traditional systems of medicine, including Ayurveda, Yoga & Naturopathy, Unani, Siddha, Homeopathy (AYUSH), Traditional Chinese Medicine (TCM), and Tibetan Medicine, appeal to medical tourists seeking alternative or complimentary healing methods, particularly in destinations rooted in these holistic approaches.

Despite the growing popularity of medical tourism, prospective patients face significant challenges in making informed decisions about healthcare providers, treatments, and associated costs (Snyder et al., 2013). Existing platforms often lack comprehensive and transparent information, leading to uncertainty and hesitation among patients seeking medical treatment abroad (Skountridaki, 2017). Additionally, issues such as language barriers, legal complexities, and concerns about quality assurance further compound the challenges faced by medical tourists.

In this context, there is a pressing need for a comprehensive and user-friendly platform that addresses these challenges and empowers patients to make informed decisions about medical tourism. Such a platform would provide transparent and detailed information about healthcare providers, treatment options, success rates, and costs, facilitating a seamless and confident experience for patients seeking medical treatment abroad. Moreover, by offering multilingual support, legal guidance, and access to verified reviews and testimonials, the platform would help alleviate common concerns and barriers associated with medical tourism, ultimately enhancing the accessibility, transparency, and quality of care for international patients.

1.1 Medical and Wellness Tourism

1.1.1 Exploring the Broader Economic Impact

Medical tourism and wellness tourism are distinct yet interconnected aspects of the travel industry, each contributing to the broader economic landscape of healthcare-related travel. While medical tourism primarily focuses on seeking specific medical treatments, wellness tourism adopts a holistic approach to personal well-being, encompassing physical, mental, spiritual, and environmental wellness.

Within the realm of wellness tourism, tourists can be categorized into two groups based on their motivations. Firstly, there are those primarily motivated by wellness, selecting destinations or trips based on their wellness-related goals. Their travel experiences revolve around activities that promote overall well-being. Secondly, there are those who seek wellness while traveling, incorporating wellness experiences into leisure or business trips. These travelers aim to maintain their well-being while on the road, integrating wellness practices into their travel routines.

It's important to recognize that while there may be some overlap between medical tourism and wellness tourism, they largely operate in separate domains, catering to different consumer needs. While medical tourism addresses specific healthcare needs, wellness tourism offers opportunities for holistic wellness enhancement and relaxation. Together, they contribute to the diverse landscape of healthcare-related travel, offering travelers a range of options to meet their individual preferences and goals.

1.1.2 Wellness Tourism Categories

Wellness tourism targets individuals actively seeking ways to maintain and improve their health and well-being, encompassing physical, mental, spiritual, or environmental wellness. It aligns closely with the leisure, recreation, and hospitality industries, emphasizing holistic well-being and offering activities that contribute to a comprehensive sense of wellness. Motivations for wellness tourism stem from a desire to engage in activities that promote overall wellness and relaxation. Beyond healthcare, wellness tourism contributes to the growth of the global wellness industry, encompassing various sectors such as spa services, wellness retreats, fitness programs, and eco-tourism. Collectively, these factors highlight the significance of wellness tourism in promoting holistic well-being and its broader economic contribution to the wellness industry.

1.1.3 Distinguishing Features of Medical Tourism

Medical tourism consists of various distinguishing features as follows:

a) **Target Audience:** Primarily serves individuals with health-related concerns seeking specific medical treatments or enhancements.
b) **Common Procedures:** Involves medical procedures such as cosmetic surgery, orthopedic surgery, cardiac surgery, and dental treatments.
c) **Motivations:** Patients are drawn to medical tourism destinations due to factors like the availability, quality, and affordability of healthcare services.
d) **Success Factors:** Success in medical tourism is influenced by factors including the healthcare sector's status, government regulations, patient safeguards, training standards, insurance frameworks, and travel logistics.

1.1.4 Medical Tourism Industry

The details of medical tourism industry are as follows:

a) **Target Audience:** Targets individuals actively seeking ways to maintain and improve their health and well-being.
b) **Scope:** Aligns closely with leisure, recreation, and hospitality industries, emphasizing holistic well-being.
c) **Motivations:** Wellness tourism involves activities focused on physical, mental, spiritual, or environmental wellness, contributing to a comprehensive sense of well-being.
d) **Economic Contribution:** Contributes to the growth of the global wellness industry, encompassing various sectors beyond healthcare.

1.1.5 Medical Value Travel (MVT)

Medical Value Travel (MVT) has emerged as a fusion product of the healthcare and tourism industries, witnessing significant global growth. Countries like Thailand, Mexico, the United States, Singapore, India, Brazil, Turkey, and Taiwan attract a substantial number of patients, contributing to the estimated USD 60-80 billion global MVT market. India, in particular, stands out as a key player in MVT, offering high-quality healthcare services, including complex surgical procedures, at a fraction of the cost compared to other nations. Additionally, India emphasizes wellness through traditional therapies, making it a favored destination for holistic well-being. This complementary approach, which integrates traditional practices with modern allopathic methods, underscores India's prominence in the MVT landscape. As healthcare and tourism continue to grow globally, the fusion of these industries showcases the potential for economic growth and international collaboration. With millions engaging in medical tourism and wellness tourism gaining momentum, the economic impact extends beyond healthcare, influencing sectors like hospitality, recreation, and local economies. Countries adept at navigating the intersection of healthcare and tourism stand to benefit significantly, contributing to the evolution of the global medical and wellness tourism landscape.

1.2 Origins and Evolution of Medical Tourism

The concept of medical tourism has ancient roots, dating back to civilizations where individuals sought healing in distant lands with therapeutic climates and natural springs. Modern medical tourism is closely linked with globalization, advances in medical technology, and shifts in healthcare dynamics.

Early instances involved patients from developing countries seeking treatments in more developed nations due to limited access to specialized care. Over time, patients from developed countries explored overseas options for medical treatments, driven by factors such as lower costs and reduced waiting times (Rao, 2013).

1.3 Impetus of Medical Tourism

Medical tourism's growth is driven by various factors, including economic incentives. Rising healthcare costs in Western countries, leading to substantial medical bills, have prompted patients to seek more affordable alternatives. Countries like India, Thailand, and Mexico offer high-quality healthcare services at a fraction of the cost, particularly for elective procedures like cosmetic surgery, dental work, and fertility treatments.

Reducing waiting times for medical procedures is another significant driver. Publicly funded healthcare systems often have extended waiting lists, and medical tourism provides a solution by offering timely care, crucial for individuals requiring urgent or specialized treatments.

1.4 Benefits of Medical Tourism

Medical tourism offers advantages for patients, healthcare providers, and host countries. Increased access to cutting-edge medical technologies and procedures is a significant benefit, with destinations investing in state-of-the-art facilities. Patients and their families also benefit from combining medical care with leisure travel, contributing to the tourism industry and the host nation's economy.

1.5 Challenges and Ethical Considerations

While medical tourism presents numerous benefits, challenges and ethical considerations exist. Variability in healthcare quality and standards across different countries is a primary concern. Patients must navigate a complex landscape of healthcare providers, emphasizing the need for thorough research and selection of reputable institutions.

Post-operative care and follow-up present challenges for patients traveling overseas for medical procedures, highlighting the importance of clear communication and coordination between healthcare providers in different countries.

1.6 Impact on Healthcare Systems

Medical tourism's impact extends beyond individual patients and host countries to strain the healthcare infrastructure of popular destinations, potentially leading to longer wait times for local patients. The resources dedicated to serving international patients may divert attention and resources from domestic healthcare needs.

1.7 Purpose of Employing Data Mining Techniques

Data mining techniques are employed in the context of medical tourism to enhance decision-making processes. This involves extracting valuable insights and patterns from large datasets for several purposes:

a) **Improved Targeting:** Identifying patterns and trends in patient preferences and behavior helps tailor marketing and promotional efforts effectively, optimizing resource allocation and budgets.
b) **Personalized Services:** Understanding patient data enables the offering of personalized services, such as tailoring treatment packages, providing language-specific services, and customizing post-procedural care to enhance patient satisfaction and loyalty.
c) **Resource Optimization:** Analyzing demand patterns and treatment trends assists in optimizing resource allocation within the medical tourism ecosystem, aiding in capacity planning, staffing, and logistics management.
d) **Quality Assurance:** Monitoring and assessing the quality of healthcare services through data analysis, including patient outcomes and satisfaction scores, enables identifying areas for improvement and maintaining high standards of care.
e) **Risk Management:** Identifying potential risks early on by analyzing historical data helps implement risk mitigation strategies, ensuring a smoother experience for medical tourists.
f) **Competitive Advantage:** Understanding market dynamics through data mining provides a competitive advantage by analyzing competitors' offerings, pricing strategies, and customer reviews to refine services and remain competitive in the medical tourism landscape (Gupta et al., n.d.).

2. BACKGROUND

2.1 Evolution of Medical Tourism

Medical tourism, also known as health tourism or medical travel, has undergone a remarkable evolution, transforming from a niche industry into a thriving global phenomenon. This evolution can be traced through key stages:

Stage 1: Historical Beginnings

The roots of medical tourism reach back to ancient times when individuals embarked on journeys in search of better health and healing. Ancient Greeks visited the sanctuary of Asklepios in Epidauria for therapeutic purposes, and Roman and European citizens sought health remedies at mineral springs and bathhouses. These early forms of medical tourism were often intertwined with religious or cultural beliefs (Connell, 2013a).

Stage 2: Emergence of Specialization

The modern era of medical tourism began in the late 20th century with the increasing specialization and advancement of healthcare services. Patients from countries with limited healthcare infrastructure sought specialized treatments and advanced medical procedures available in more developed nations. The rise of international travel and globalization facilitated this shift toward seeking healthcare abroad (Lunt et al., 2014).

Stage 3: Economic Considerations

Economic factors played a significant role in the evolution of medical tourism. As healthcare costs in developed countries soared, patients explored more cost-effective alternatives abroad. This trend was particularly notable in elective procedures such as cosmetic surgery, dental treatments, and fertility treatments. Patients realized they could receive high-quality care at a fraction of the cost in destinations like India, Thailand, and Malaysia (Lamarque et al., 2020; Sheppard et al., 2014).

Stage 4: Quality and Accreditation

As medical tourism gained momentum, concerns arose about the quality and safety of healthcare services in destination countries. This led to the development of accreditation standards and international healthcare certifications. Organizations like the Joint Commission International (JCI) began accrediting hospitals and clinics worldwide, ensuring they met international healthcare standards. Accreditation played a crucial role in building trust among medical tourists (Angela et al., 2020).

Stage 5: Diversification of Services

Medical tourism expanded beyond traditional healthcare procedures to include a wide range of medical and wellness services. Patients began seeking not only curative treatments but also wellness experiences, such as spa treatments, stress relief programs, and holistic therapies. This diversification broadened the appeal of medical tourism (Carrera & Bridges, 2006).

Stage 6: Government Support and Promotion

Recognizing the economic potential of medical tourism, many countries actively promoted it as part of their national healthcare strategies. Governments offered incentives, streamlined visa processes, and invested in healthcare infrastructure to attract international patients. This governmental support further accelerated the growth of medical tourism (Banerjee et al., 2015).

2.2 Factors Driving Medical Tourism

Medical tourism, the practice of traveling abroad for healthcare services, has gained popularity due to several key factors:

a) Cost Considerations

One of the primary drivers of medical tourism is cost savings. Many individuals from high-cost healthcare countries seek medical treatments abroad because they can often receive the same quality of care at a significantly lower cost. This cost advantage is particularly evident in elective procedures, such as cosmetic surgery, dental work, and fertility treatments. Patients realize that they can access these treatments without breaking the bank by choosing destinations like India, Thailand, or Mexico (Angela et al., 2020; Connell, 2006).

b) Treatment Quality and Specialization

While cost savings are a significant factor, individuals seeking healthcare services abroad are also driven by the desire for high-quality medical treatment. Many renowned hospitals and clinics worldwide offer specialized medical services and advanced procedures that may not be available or affordable in their home countries. Patients prioritize their health and well-being, and the availability of world-class healthcare facilities in medical tourism destinations encourages them to travel for treatment (Lamarque et al., 2020; Sheppard et al., 2014).

c) Access to Advanced Procedures

Another key factor driving individuals to seek healthcare services abroad is access to advanced medical procedures and treatments. Some countries are at the forefront of medical innovation and offer cutting-edge treatments, including organ transplants, cardiac surgeries, and stem cell therapies. Patients who require these specialized procedures may opt to travel abroad to receive the latest medical advancements.

d) Reduced Waiting Times

Long waiting times for medical procedures can be a frustrating experience for patients in some countries. Medical tourism destinations often offer shorter wait times, allowing individuals to receive treatment more promptly. This reduction in waiting times can be especially appealing for patients with urgent medical needs (Lunt et al., 2014).

e) Privacy and Confidentiality

Privacy concerns can also drive individuals to seek healthcare services abroad. Some patients may prefer to keep their medical procedures and conditions confidential, away from their local communities or social circles. Medical tourism allows them to receive treatment discreetly and maintain their privacy (Carrera & Bridges, 2006).

Thus, the evolution of medical tourism reflects a dynamic interplay of historical practices, economic considerations, quality assurance measures, diversification of services, and active government support. The factors driving medical tourism underscore the importance of cost-effectiveness, high-quality treatment, access to advanced procedures, reduced waiting times, and the preservation of patient privacy.

f) Complementary Therapy

Medical tourism destinations allow complementary therapy where the modern scientific treatment can be supported with Ayurvedic Therapy, Homeopathic Treatment, Massage therapies and other traditional therapies which increases the feel-good wellness factor and enhances healing.

3. DATA COLLECTION AND PREPROCESSING IN MEDICAL TOURISM

3.1 Source of Medical Data

3.1.1 Patient Records From Recognized Hospitals

According to Smith et al. (2018), the cornerstone of medical data in the realm of medical tourism is patient records from established and recognized hospitals. These records offer a comprehensive overview of a patient's medical history, past treatments, medications, and other critical health metrics. Such records serve as a vital foundation for any medical procedure or consultation. As Siddiqua, Omanin., and Ashrafuzzaman., (2022) described in their chapter for the big medical data analytics for diagnosis, vast medical data can be collected and analyzed to be used for carefully access data of each patient and classify them to avail the preferable hospital for their treatments.

3.1.2 Electronic Health Records (EHRs)

Jones and Brown (2019) highlighted the pivotal role of Electronic Health Records (EHRs) in modern healthcare. EHRs streamline the exchange of medical data across borders, ensuring that healthcare professionals in different countries have immediate access to a patient's medical history and can make informed decisions without delay.

3.1.3 Quality Checks and Accreditation

Lee and Wang (2020) pointed out the challenges associated with the accuracy of medical data obtained from unaccredited institutions. The study emphasized the importance of stringent quality checks to validate the authenticity and reliability of medical records, particularly when sourced from less-regulated environments.

3.1.4 Telemedicine Platforms

Garcia and Martinez (2021) explored the emerging role of telemedicine platforms in collecting real-time medical data. These platforms facilitate remote consultations with specialists from around the world, enabling patients to access expert opinions and treatments without the need for physical travel.

3.1.5 Specialized Medical Data

Research by Clark and White (2017), Davis et al. (2019), and Harris (2022) focused on specific types of medical data, such as laboratory results and diagnostic imaging. These studies underscored the importance of standardizing formats and protocols to ensure the accuracy, reliability, and interoperability of specialized medical data. Ashrafuzzaman et al., (2022) pronounced in big data analytics techniques for healthcare, the use of medical dataset and techniques for the effective management of data and life cycle of individuals by the secured applications of massive medical data.

3.1.6 Data Security and Blockchain Technology

Patel and Johnson (2018) highlighted the complexities of cross-border data transmission and potential risks from data breaches. However, Kim and Lee (2021) presented a promising perspective, suggesting that advancements in blockchain technology could enhance the security, transparency, and accuracy of medical data in the context of medical tourism.

3.2 Data Preprocessing Steps

3.2.1 Data Cleaning

As emphasized by Smith et al. (2017), data cleaning is a fundamental step that involves identifying and rectifying errors, inconsistencies, missing values, outliers, and duplicates in the dataset. This ensures the integrity and reliability of the data being analyzed.

3.2.2 Data Integration

Data integration combines information from various sources, such as surveys, patient records, hospitals, and clinics, into a cohesive dataset. This comprehensive view enhances the depth and richness of the data, providing a holistic perspective on the medical tourism landscape.

3.2.3 Data Transformation

Normalization and standardization techniques, including z-score normalization and min-max scaling, are employed to bring the data to a uniform scale. This facilitates fair comparisons and analyses across different variables and datasets.

3.2.4 Feature Selection

Brown and Jones (2020) discussed the importance of feature selection techniques in narrowing down the focus to the most relevant variables. By reducing dimensionality and eliminating redundant or less influential features, this step enhances the effectiveness and efficiency of subsequent analyses.

3.2.5 Handling Categorical Data

Categorical variables are converted into numerical values using techniques such as one-hot encoding or label encoding. This conversion ensures compatibility with machine learning algorithms and maintains the integrity of the data structure.

3.2.6 Data Reduction

Methods like Principal Component Analysis (PCA) may be employed to reduce the dimensionality of the dataset while retaining essential information. This not only enhances computing efficiency but also mitigates the risk of overfitting in predictive models.

3.2.7 Handling Imbalanced Data

To address potential biases in the analysis, strategies like oversampling, under sampling, or generating synthetic samples may be employed to balance class distributions within the dataset.

3.2.8 Temporal Data Processing

If the dataset contains time-series data, appropriate techniques must be applied to account for trends, seasonality, and periodic patterns. This ensures that the temporal aspects of the data are accurately captured and analyzed.

3.2.9 Validation and Splitting

At the end, the preprocessed dataset is divided into training and testing subsets for model development and validation. Techniques like cross-validation are employed to assess the robustness, reliability, and generalizability of the analytical models derived from the data.

In summary, data collection and preprocessing are critical stages in the analysis of medical tourism data. These stages ensure the accuracy, reliability, and usability of the data, thereby laying a solid foundation for informed decision-making, research, and policy development in the field of medical tourism.

4. DATA MINING TECHNIQUES IN MEDICAL TOURISM

4.1 Overview of Techniques

In the dynamic field of medical tourism, data mining techniques play a crucial role in extracting valuable patterns and insights from the vast amount of data generated. Researchers have employed various algorithms and tools to enhance decision-making processes, improve patient experiences, and optimize service quality.

a) Clustering Algorithms

Clustering algorithms, are employed to group medical tourists based on their preferences and demographics. This strategy aids in understanding diverse patient demands, enabling healthcare professionals to tailor treatments to individual needs. The clustering approach helps in classifying nations based on factors like healthcare quality and cost-effectiveness, assisting patients in making informed decisions about where to seek medical treatment (Dryglas & Salamaga, 2018).

b) Association Rule Mining

Association rule mining, highlighted by Johnson and Lee (2017), has been utilized to identify trends in consumers' preferences for travel and healthcare facilities. This technique assists in developing targeted marketing campaigns to attract medical tourists by understanding their preferences and expectations (Ediansyah et al., 2022).

c) Predictive Modeling

Wang and Li (2018) demonstrated how predictive modeling, utilizing machine learning algorithms, can estimate patient influx. This enables hospitals and tourist organizations to allocate resources efficiently, ensuring optimal service delivery and resource utilization.

d) Sentiment Analysis

Sentiment analysis, involves analyzing internet reviews and comments to gauge patient satisfaction and identify areas for improvement. Understanding patient sentiments is crucial for healthcare professionals to enhance services and attract more medical tourists (Ruhanen, 2019)

e) Natural Language Processing (NLP)

Zhao et al., (2023) explored the use of natural language processing (NLP) techniques to extract relevant data from unstructured sources such as patient evaluations and social media platforms. This approach provides insightful knowledge about patient preferences and experiences, contributing to data-driven decision-making support system.

In continuity, clustering, association rule mining, predictive modeling, sentiment analysis, and natural language processing collectively contribute to the data mining approaches in medical tourism.

These techniques empower stakeholders in the medical tourism sector to enhance patient experiences, streamline operations, and make well-informed decisions.

4.2 Clustering and Classification Algorithms in Decision Support

Patients engaging in medical tourism often face the challenge of choosing countries, doctors, and hospitals for their medical procedures. Clustering and classification algorithms have been employed in several studies to assist patients in making well-informed decisions. These algorithms categorize nations, physicians, and hospitals based on various factors, providing tailored information to meet individual preferences and medical requirements.

4.3 Clustering Algorithm for Country Classification

Clustering algorithm was used in many studies to classify nations based on their healthcare infrastructure and cost-effectiveness. This classification aided individuals in deciding where to receive medical treatment by considering factors such as quality and affordability (Torkzadeh et al., 2021).

4.4 Clarification Algorithm for Doctor Information

Debata et al., (2015) utilized a clarification algorithm to offer patients precise information about doctors' specializations and expertise. This approach ensures that patients can make decisions based on detailed and relevant information about the medical professionals they are considering (Debata et al., 2015).

4.5 Hospital Recommendations With Clustering

Hasanzadeh et al., (2021) focused on improving hospital recommendations by employing clustering approaches that considered quality indicators and patient satisfaction. These algorithms refine the recommendations, taking into account the unique needs and preferences of patients (Hasanzadeh et al., 2021).

4.6 Personalized Decision-Making With Clustering and Clarification

Halkiopoulos et al., (2021) introduced a cutting-edge strategy that combined clustering and clarification algorithms to suggest nations, medical professionals, and hospitals. This approach ensures that patients have access to comprehensive and personalized decision-making, incorporating individual preferences and medical history (Halkiopoulos et al., 2021). Yang (2020) expanded on this strategy, providing even more personalized recommendations based on patient-specific data (Yang et al., 2020). Ashrafuzzaman Md., et al., (2023) stated the ways to get the benefits of AI and meta-verse in their study on the application of meta-verse in the healthcare sector to improve quality of life which will pave the ways to integrate this knowledge in medical tourism sector.

4.7 Classification for Access to Advanced Medical Technology

Habibi et al., (2022) utilized sophisticated clustering algorithms to classify nations based on their access to cutting-edge medical technology. This enables patients to choose locations with advanced treatment alternatives, aligning with their medical needs and preferences (Habibi et al., 2022).

4.8 Improving Doctor Credentials and Communication

In a study by Dhakate & Joshi (2023) clustering algorithms were employed to enhance the credentials and communication abilities of doctors. Clarification algorithms played a crucial role in improving the patient-doctor contact experience, contributing to overall patient satisfaction (Dhakate & Joshi, 2023).

4.9 Hospital Organization and Information With Clustering

Ebrahim & Ganguli (2019) utilized clustering algorithms to organize hospitals based on the specialized procedures and treatments they provided. This facilitates easier decision-making for patients, helping them select facilities that align with their unique medical requirements (Ebrahim & Ganguli, 2019). Cavmak & Cavmak, et al., (2020) employed a clarification algorithm to provide detailed information on hospital facilities, assisting patients in selecting facilities that match their preferences (Cavmak & Cavmak, 2020).

4.10 Cultural and Linguistic Compatibility

Martin (2022) used clustering algorithms to group nations based on cultural and linguistic compatibility. This ensures that patients from other countries feel comfortable in their chosen medical tourism destination, contributing to a positive overall experience (Martin et al., 2022).

4.11 Comprehensive Medical Tourism Packages

Panteli (2021) integrated clustering and clarification algorithms to suggest medical tourism packages. These packages included travel, lodging, and post-treatment care, offering a comprehensive solution to patients' travel requirements (Panteli et al., 2021). In fact, the combined use of clustering and clarification algorithms empowers patients with detailed and individualized information, enhancing their decision-making processes in medical tourism. These advanced techniques contribute to a more personalized, efficient, and satisfying experience for medical tourists. The specific pattern of the impact of social media and digital marketing on consumer behavior are potted in the handbook of research on consumer behavior change and data analytics in the socio-digital era which can be studied to compresence the medical data and visualize the authentic medical tourism packages during the selection of destination including the physicians and treatment facilities (Ashrafuzzaman et. al., 2022).

5. PROPOSED ALGORITHM FOR THE INTEGRATED MEDICAL TOURISM PLATFORM

Figure 1. Flow chart for the algorithm

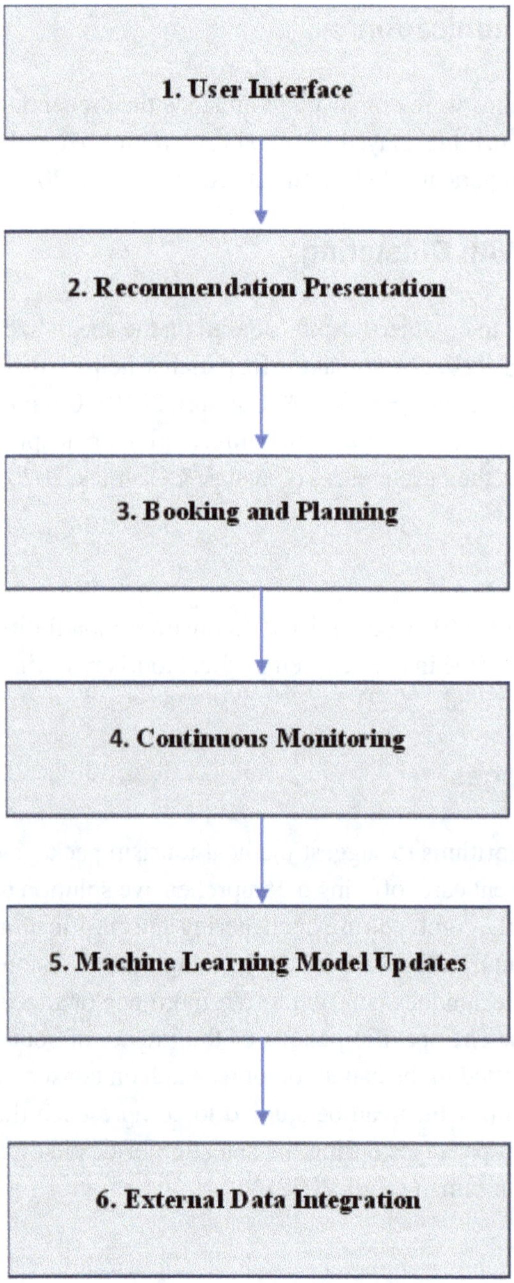

Figure 2. Flow chart for the user interface

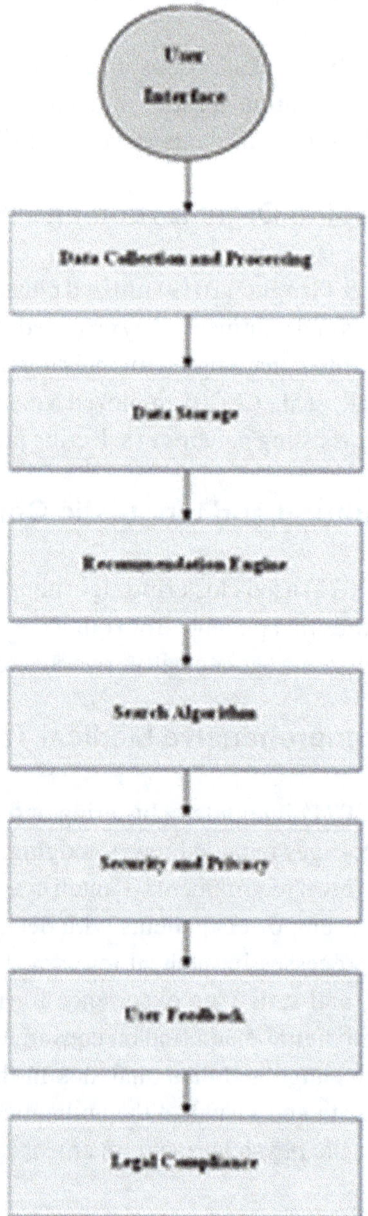

5.1 User Interface and AI Integration in Medical Tourism Platform

5.1.1 User Interface

The user interface and AI integration in medical tourism platform involves some steps: (a) data collection and preprocessing, (b) data storage, (c) recommendation engine, (d) search algorithms, (e) security and privacy, (f) user feedback, and (g) legal compliance.

a) Data Collection and Preprocessing

i. Data Sources

Data is gathered from diverse channels, including medical facilities, healthcare quality assessment organizations, public health databases, and patient reviews. These sources provide comprehensive information on medical facilities, doctors, specialties, quality metrics, and geographical details.

ii. Data Preprocessing

Raw data undergoes preprocessing steps involving cleaning, transforming, and structuring to ensure data quality and consistency.

b) Data Storage

i. Patient Profiles

Individual patient details, medical history, and preferences are stored for personalized recommendations.

ii. Medical Facility Details

Information on facilities' specialties, provider qualifications, location, and equipment is recorded for tailored suggestions.

iii. Quality Metrics

Objective quality measures, such as certifications and patient satisfaction scores, are stored to ensure recommendations are based on quality healthcare options.

c) Recommendation Engine

i. User Input

The recommendation engine receives input from users, including their medical requirements, preferences, and criteria.

ii. Data Analysis

Utilizing data mining and machine learning techniques, the engine analyzes user input and the extensive dataset to generate personalized suggestions.

iii. Personalized Recommendations

Based on the analysis, the recommendation engine provides personalized suggestions for medical facilities, doctors, and regions aligned with the user's criteria.

d) Search Algorithms

i. Proximity

Algorithms analyze a user's location to recommend nearby medical facilities, reducing travel time.

ii. Quality Rating

Facilities and doctors with higher quality ratings are prioritized, emphasizing excellence and reliability.

iii. Cost

Cost-related data helps users find healthcare options within their budget, promoting cost-effective choices.

iv. Patient Reviews

Insights from patient feedback enhance user trust in recommended options.

e) Security and Privacy

i. Data Encryption

Patient data is encrypted during transmission and at rest to protect sensitive information.

ii. Access Controls

Access to patient data is restricted to authorized personnel, ensuring data security and privacy compliance.

f) User Feedback

Users can provide feedback, reviews, and ratings for healthcare providers, contributing to the quality assessment process.

g) Legal Compliance

The platform adheres to regional and international data protection laws and healthcare regulations, ensuring compliance with GDPR and HIPAA.

5.2 Recommendation Presentation

The medical tourism platform offers a range of personalized recommendations to assist users in making informed decisions about their healthcare journey. Users receive details on suggested medical facilities, including specialties, quality ratings, and costs, enabling them to evaluate options and select the most suitable facility for their needs. Additionally, recommendations for healthcare providers include information on qualifications, experience, and patient reviews, empowering users to choose trusted professionals for their medical care. Furthermore, users can explore healthcare destinations based on their medical needs and preferences, with suggestions tailored to match their requirements. These personalized recommendations enhance the user experience, providing valuable guidance and support throughout the medical tourism process.

5.3 Booking and Planning

The medical tourism platform offers a comprehensive suite of services to streamline the user experience and ensure a seamless journey for users. Appointment booking functionality enables users to schedule medical appointments directly, facilitating efficient communication with medical facilities and eliminating logistical hurdles. Additionally, the platform assists users with travel arrangements, including flight bookings, visa requirements, and local transportation, simplifying the process of planning and organizing travel for medical purposes. Furthermore, users can conveniently secure accommodations through the platform, with options filtered based on preferences such as location, amenities, and budget constraints. These integrated services enhance convenience, accessibility, and peace of mind for users seeking medical treatment abroad, contributing to a positive and hassle-free experience.

5.4 Continuous Monitoring

Data quality is paramount in ensuring the effectiveness of a medical tourism platform. Continuous checks and validation mechanisms are implemented to uphold data accuracy, preventing errors or inconsistencies that could compromise user experience and decision-making. Additionally, monitoring user interactions offers valuable insights to enhance the user experience and recommendation quality, enabling iterative improvements based on user feedback and behavior. Regular evaluation of the recommendation engine's performance is conducted to ensure the accuracy and relevance of suggestions, optimizing the platform's ability to provide personalized and valuable recommendations to users. These measures collectively contribute to the reliability, efficacy, and user satisfaction of the medical tourism platform.

5.5 AI for User Interface Decision Making

Artificial intelligence (AI) revolutionizes the medical tourism landscape by offering a plethora of indispensable features. Through the analysis of user data, AI provides personalized recommendations for medical treatments, hospitals, and destinations, tailoring suggestions to individual preferences and needs. Additionally, AI calculates estimated costs for medical treatments, aiding users in effective budgeting. It offers a comprehensive range of treatment options based on medical conditions, empowering users with information to make educated choices. Moreover, AI facilitates doctor matching by pairing users with specialized healthcare professionals, ensuring optimal care. It provides real-time updates on the availability of healthcare options, keeping users informed throughout their journey. Quality assurance is another area where AI shines, as it assesses the quality and safety of medical facilities and providers, upholding high standards of care. Additionally, AI helps bridge language and cultural barriers for international users, ensuring seamless communication and understanding. Through the analysis of user feedback, AI evaluates the reputation and satisfaction levels of healthcare providers, aiding users in decision-making. Furthermore, AI assists users with travel planning, streamlining the process and ensuring a smooth journey. It also monitors user health post-treatment, offering support and alerts if necessary, and utilizes predictive analytics to forecast potential health risks, contributing to proactive healthcare management. Overall, AI serves as a powerful tool in optimizing the medical tourism experience, offering personalized assistance, enhancing accessibility, and ensuring the highest standards of care and user satisfaction.

5.6 External Data Integration

In this step, external data, such as travel information, is integrated for a comprehensive medical tourism experience. Finally, the user interface seamlessly integrates data collection, preprocessing, recommendation engines, search algorithms, security measures, and AI capabilities to offer a comprehensive and personalized medical tourism platform. Continuous monitoring, user feedback analysis, and legal compliance ensure a reliable and user-friendly experience for patients seeking medical recommendations and travel planning.

6. USER EXPERIENCE AND USER INTERFACE DESIGN IN MEDICAL TOURISM

In the realm of medical tourism, designing an effective User Experience (UX) and a user-friendly User Interface (UI) for online platforms is pivotal. These platforms serve as crucial tools in assisting individuals in making informed decisions about their medical preferences when seeking healthcare services abroad. A well-crafted UX/UI not only enhances usability but also instills trust and confidence in users.

6.1 User Experience Design for Medical Preference Platforms

Effective UX design for a medical tourism platform necessitates a comprehensive understanding of user needs, behaviors, and preferences. Prioritizing the user's journey from initial research to final decision-making is paramount, ensuring that the platform meets the diverse requirements of potential medical tourists. User-friendly navigation is integral to the UX design, enabling easy access to relevant information about medical procedures, destinations, and facilities. The platform should offer intuitive exploration pathways, enhancing the user experience and facilitating informed decision-making. Moreover, personalized recommendations tailored to individual medical needs (Keikhosrokiani, 2022a, 2023; Keikhosrokiani & Fye, 2023; Xian et al., 2022; Zhao & Keikhosrokiani, 2022), budget constraints, and preferences enhance user engagement and satisfaction. Incorporating user research and feedback into the design process ensures that the platform aligns with user expectations, ultimately enhancing its effectiveness in serving the needs of medical tourists.

6.2 User Interface Design for Clarity and Accessibility

In designing the user interface (UI) for medical preference platforms, several key considerations are paramount. Firstly, a clean, intuitive, and accessible design is essential, allowing users to easily find information, navigate the platform effortlessly, and perform tasks with minimal friction. Secondly, clear and concise communication is crucial, involving the use of straightforward language, visual hierarchy, and effective utilization of colors and typography to ensure that information is presented in an easily understandable manner. Lastly, accessibility features must be integrated to accommodate users with disabilities, ensuring inclusivity and user-friendliness for a diverse audience. These features may include screen reader compatibility and adjustable font sizes, among others, to enhance accessibility and usability for all users.

7. CONSIDERATIONS FOR A USER-FRIENDLY MEDICAL PREFERENCE PLATFORM

In order to propose a user-friendly medical preference platform, important characteristics need to be considered. For instance, the information provided by the platform must be accurate and transparent; the platform needs to have multilingual support; data handling must be secured; multiple communication channels need to be offered to provide ease of contact; reviews and testimonials have to be performed, user must be able to access the platform using mobile devices, and finally, related educational contents need to be provided.

a) Information Accuracy and Transparency

Ensuring the accuracy and transparency of information regarding medical procedures, costs, and destination facilities is paramount. Users must be able to trust the platform's data, leading to well-informed decisions.

b) Multilingual Support

Since medical tourists come from diverse linguistic backgrounds, offering multilingual support ensures accessibility for a global audience. Translation services or content localization can enhance the user experience and broaden the platform's reach.

c) Secure Data Handling

Given the sensitive nature of health information, robust security measures must be in place to protect user data and privacy. Compliance with data protection regulations is not only necessary but builds trust among users.

d) Ease of Contact

Offering multiple communication channels, such as live chat, email, or phone support, enhances user satisfaction. Providing avenues for users to reach out for inquiries or assistance contributes to a positive user experience.

e) Reviews and Testimonials

Including authentic reviews and testimonials from previous medical tourists can build trust and credibility. Users often rely on the experiences of others when making decisions, and positive feedback can influence their choices positively.

f) Mobile Responsiveness

Many users access platforms via mobile devices. Ensuring that the platform is responsive and mobile-friendly is critical for a seamless user experience on various screen sizes. Responsive design contributes to accessibility and convenience.

g) Educational Content

Providing educational resources about medical procedures, travel tips, and destination information empowers users to make well-informed choices. Educational content enhances the overall user experience and supports users in their decision-making process.

In practical, a thoughtfully designed UX/UI for medical preference platforms involves a deep understanding of user needs, user-friendly navigation, personalized recommendations, clarity in communication, accessibility features, information accuracy, multilingual support, secure data handling, ease of contact, reviews and testimonials, mobile responsiveness, and educational content. These considerations collectively contribute to a user-friendly, trustworthy, and effective platform for individuals exploring medical tourism options. Figure 3 shows fishbone diagram of the algorithms for integrated medical tourism platform.

8. IMPACT ANALYSIS OF DATA-DRIVEN MEDICAL TOURISM

Data-driven medical tourism platforms have brought about transformative changes in various sectors, leaving a significant impact on the healthcare industry, tourism sector, technology industry, research and academia, patient and general public, insurance and finance industry, as well as government and policymakers.

Figure 3. Fishbone diagram of the algorithms for integrated medical tourism platform

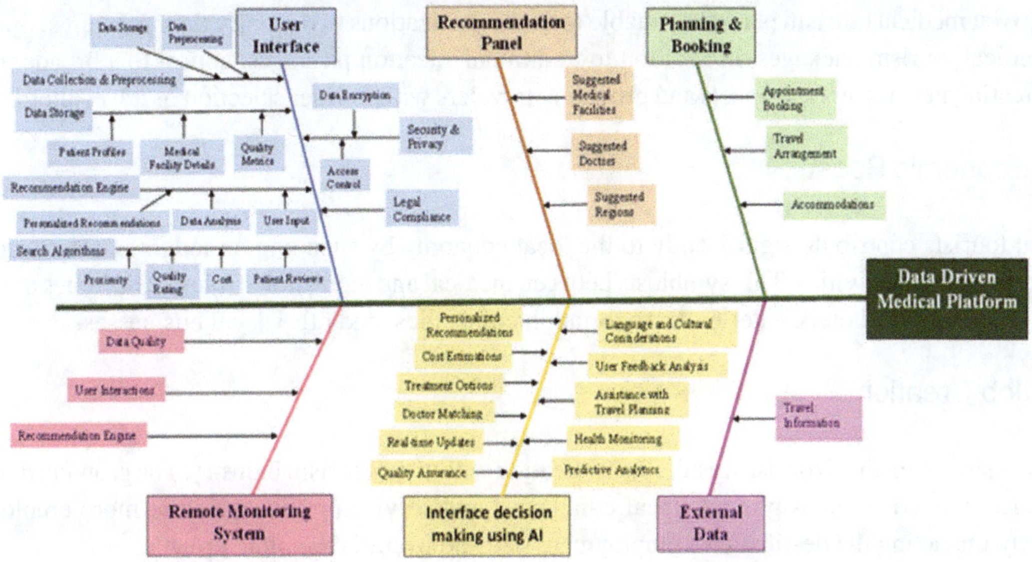

8.1 Healthcare Industry and Medical Tourism Amalgamation

8.1.1 Enhanced Reputation and Increased Revenue

Data-driven medical tourism platforms contribute to the improved reputation of hospitals and healthcare organizations. Endorsements on these platforms, based on data-driven suggestions related to cost, quality, and specialization, attract foreign patients, ultimately increasing revenue. Financial growth allows for investments in infrastructure and personnel training, leading to an overall enhancement of services.

8.1.2 Global Reach and Quality Improvement

The platforms broaden healthcare providers' global reach, fostering cooperation, knowledge exchange, and cultural understanding. The competition among international patients motivates healthcare organizations to improve quality standards by enhancing services and implementing cutting-edge technologies. Overall, data-driven medical tourism platforms elevate the global healthcare landscape.

8.1.3 Increased Tourism

Countries recognized as medical tourism destinations experience a surge in tourism. The influx of medical tourists and their companions results in increased tourism-related activities, benefiting hotels, restaurants, and local businesses.

8.1.4 Diversification

Data-driven medical tourism platforms enable tourist organizations to diversify their offerings. Specialized medical tourism packages, in addition to traditional vacation packages, appeal to a broader client base, creating new income prospects and providing travelers with a wider selection of travel alternatives.

8.1.5 Economic Boost

Medical tourists contribute significantly to the local economy by spending on lodging, transportation, and various tourist activities. This symbiosis between medical and recreational tourism becomes a crucial source of income for hotels, eateries, transportation companies, and other local businesses.

8.1.6 Job Creation

The expansion of medical tourism results in job creation within the tourism industry. The growing demand for tourism-related services prompts local companies and service providers to hire more employees, positively impacting the destination's employment rate and overall economic growth.

8.2 Healthcare Technology Industry

8.2.1 Software Development Opportunities

Data-driven medical tourism platforms drive opportunities in the technology industry, necessitating the expertise of software engineers, data scientists, and IT specialists. This leads to employment creation and business expansion in the technology sector, fostering innovation and technical breakthroughs.

8.2.2 Innovation and Knowledge Transfer

Innovations produced by these platforms extend beyond immediate use. Technologies such as data analysis, user interfaces, and real-time data integration have broader implications. Best practices and lessons learned from these platforms spark innovation in the technology sector, facilitating knowledge transfer.

8.3 Research and Academia

8.3.1 Research Opportunities

Data-driven medical tourism platforms provide valuable data sets for research institutions. Patient preferences, healthcare outcomes, and travel patterns become significant resources for academics to analyze, contributing to a better understanding of patient behavior, healthcare trends, and the impact of medical tourism on healthcare systems.

8.3.2 Educational Value

The platforms offer real-world case studies that can be integrated into academic curricula. Universities and colleges leverage these platforms to teach students about data science, business analytics, healthcare management, and tourist studies, providing hands-on experience and preparing students for careers in related fields.

8.3.3 Interdisciplinary Collaboration

The multidimensional nature of data-driven medical tourism platforms encourages collaboration among academic departments. Researchers from various domains, including healthcare, data science, economics, and tourism, collaborate to investigate different aspects of medical tourism, promoting knowledge sharing and interdisciplinary creativity.

8.4 Patient and General Public

8.4.1 Informed Decision-Making

Data-driven medical tourism platforms empower patients by providing extensive data about healthcare solutions worldwide. This transparency enhances patients' ability to make informed decisions based on cost, quality, specialization, and location.

8.4.2 Accessibility to Specialized Treatments

Access to specialized medical treatments becomes more feasible for patients through these platforms. Medical tourists can research global healthcare options and find suitable solutions for unusual medical issues or advanced operations, thereby improving health outcomes and quality of life.

8.4.3 Cost Savings

Patients can discover cost-effective treatment solutions by comparing rates and services across different healthcare providers and countries. This financial advantage makes high-quality healthcare more accessible and affordable, particularly for individuals without complete insurance coverage.

8.4.4 Global Healthcare Awareness

Data-driven medical tourism platforms contribute to global healthcare awareness by providing information about foreign healthcare providers, medical breakthroughs, and treatment options. This awareness promotes a global perspective on healthcare and encourages information exchange among patients and communities.

8.5 Insurance and Finance Industry

8.5.1 Specialized Insurance Plans

The development of medical tourism opens avenues for insurance firms to offer specialized coverage for medical tourists. These insurance plans cover overseas treatments, travel-related fees, and unforeseen medical issues during medical tourism trips, providing peace of mind and financial security.

8.5.2 Financial Services for Medical Tourists

Recognizing the specific financial needs of medical tourists, financial institutions offer specialized services such as currency conversion, foreign payment solutions, and medical expenditure management. These services aim to streamline financial transactions for medical tourists, facilitating effective navigation of overseas healthcare systems.

8.5.3 Risk Assessment and Management

Data-driven medical tourism platforms provide valuable data for insurance firms to assess and manage risks. Analyzing previous medical tourism data helps insurers understand the risks associated with procedures, countries, and healthcare providers, allowing them to provide affordable premiums while ensuring comprehensive coverage.

8.5.4 Market Growth and Investment Opportunities

The expansion of medical tourism creates investment opportunities in insurance and finance. Companies can invest in insurance products, financial services, and technological solutions tailored to medical tourists, building a robust ecosystem that supports the financial aspects of medical tourism.

8.6 Government and Policymakers

8.6.1 Economic Growth

Governments benefit from the economic growth associated with medical tourism. Income generated from increased medical tourism can be invested in local infrastructure and public services, contributing to overall economic growth.

8.6.2 Regulation and Quality Assurance

With the rise of medical tourism, policymakers play a crucial role in developing and enforcing regulations to ensure patient safety and service quality. These regulations help maintain standards, build trust, and protect the interests of both patients and healthcare professionals.

8.6.3 Healthcare Planning and Resource Allocation

Data-driven medical tourism platforms offer insights into healthcare utilization patterns and patient preferences, aiding policymakers in healthcare planning and budget allocation. Informed decisions about infrastructure development and workforce training can be made to meet the increasing demands of both local and foreign patients.

8.6.4 Global Collaboration and Diplomacy

The growth of medical tourism fosters international cooperation and diplomacy. Governments can form alliances, enter agreements, and streamline visa processes to promote medical tourism and facilitate the safe movement of patients across borders. This collaboration enhances diplomatic connections and encourages international healthcare cooperation.

Data-driven medical tourism platforms play a pivotal role in shaping diverse sectors, impacting economic growth, regulation, technology innovation, research, patient empowerment, financial services, and global collaboration. Their multifaceted significance positions them as catalysts for positive change and development in the global healthcare and tourism landscape

9. MARKETING INDUSTRY

Data-driven medical tourism platforms serve as powerful tools in marketing hospitals, doctors, and specific regions as desirable medical tourism destinations. This not only facilitates targeted promotion but also enables data-driven marketing, provides a competitive advantage, and offers cost-efficient advertising, benefiting both patients and healthcare providers.

9.1 Targeted Promotion

Leveraging the platform as a smart marketing tool allows hospitals and physicians to advertise their services to a global audience actively seeking specific medical treatments. The platform highlights the distinct strengths and specializations of healthcare practitioners, attracting patients who require their expertise. This targeted promotion ensures that marketing efforts reach the right audience, increasing the likelihood of successful patient acquisition.

9.2 Data-Driven Marketing

The data analytics capabilities of the platform provide crucial insights into patient preferences, treatment trends, and healthcare outcomes. Healthcare providers can use this information to personalize their marketing initiatives effectively. Understanding the needs and preferences of potential patients enables providers to develop tailored marketing strategies that resonate with their target demographic, resulting in more successful patient acquisitions.

9.3 Competitive Advantage

Hospitals and clinicians featured on the platform gain a competitive advantage by showcasing their expertise, success rates, and patient testimonials. This transparent display of their capabilities fosters trust and confidence in potential patients, enhancing the likelihood of these providers being chosen for medical requirements. The platform acts as a valuable tool for healthcare organizations to distinguish themselves in a competitive market.

9.4 Cost-Efficient Advertising

Marketing through the platform can be a cost-effective alternative to traditional advertising strategies. Hospitals and physicians can save on marketing expenses while accessing a global audience actively seeking medical services. This cost efficiency translates to a higher return on investment (ROI) for healthcare providers, making marketing through the platform an attractive and economically viable option.

This platform emerges as an effective marketing tool for both patients and healthcare providers. It enables customized advertising, data-driven marketing, a competitive edge, and cost-effective promotional strategies. By supporting improved marketing, the platform contributes to the growth of the medical tourism sector, empowering consumers to make informed decisions and assisting healthcare providers in reaching their target audience more effectively.

10. ETHICAL AND LEGAL CONSIDERATIONS

Addressing ethical and legal considerations is imperative in the development and operation of data-driven medical tourism platforms. Protecting patient data, upholding privacy rights, and ensuring compliance with relevant laws and regulations are essential for maintaining trust and ethical responsibility. Here's a detailed overview of how the platform addresses these concerns:

10.1 Data Privacy and Security Measures

The platform will implement robust data privacy and security measures to safeguard sensitive patient information. It will adhere to international data protection standards, such as GDPR in Europe and HIPAA in the United States, based on the jurisdiction of operation. These measures include encryption, access controls, and regular security audits.

10.2 Informed Consent

Patients using the platform will receive clear and transparent information about data collection, storage, and usage. Informed consent will be obtained from patients, ensuring they understand how their data will be utilized and giving them the choice to opt in or out. This ensures that patient participation is based on a clear understanding of data handling practices.

10.3 Data Encryption

Patient data will be encrypted during transmission and storage to prevent unauthorized access. Strong encryption protocols will be employed to secure sensitive information, including medical records, personal details, and payment data. This encryption ensures the confidentiality and integrity of patient data.

10.4 Access Controls

Access to patient data will be restricted to authorized personnel only. User authentication and role-based access controls will be implemented to ensure that data can only be accessed by individuals with the appropriate permissions. This prevents unauthorized access and protects patient confidentiality.

10.5 Regular Auditing and Monitoring

Continuous auditing and monitoring of data access and usage will be conducted to identify and address potential security breaches or unauthorized activities promptly. Proactive monitoring helps maintain data integrity, privacy, and compliance with security protocols.

10.6 Compliance with Regional Laws

The platform will adhere to legal requirements and regulations specific to each region of operation. This includes compliance with data protection laws, healthcare regulations, and any other relevant legislation. Adhering to regional laws ensures that the platform operates ethically and legally within the boundaries of each jurisdiction.

10.7 Ethical Guidelines

Ethical guidelines will be established within the platform to govern the responsible use of patient data. These guidelines will promote transparency, fairness, and accountability in data handling and decision-making. Ethical considerations will guide the platform's practices, ensuring the ethical treatment of patient information and maintaining public trust.

By addressing these ethical and legal considerations, the data-driven medical tourism platform ensures the responsible and secure handling of patient data, fostering trust among users and stakeholders. This commitment to ethical and legal standards is crucial for the platform's long-term success and positive impact on the healthcare and tourism sectors.

11. TESTING AND USER FEEDBACK

Patients engaging in medical tourism, the practice of seeking healthcare services abroad, highlight the importance of thorough testing and user feedback to ensure the safety and quality of medical treatments. Several research studies have shed light on various aspects of testing and feedback systems in the context of medical tourism.

11.1 Pre-Travel Health Exams and Post-treatment Evaluations

One study emphasized the value of pre-travel health exams and post-treatment evaluations (Mamun & Andaleeb, 2013). It suggested that comprehensive testing before travel and systematic patient feedback after a surgery significantly enhance the overall medical tourism experience and outcomes. This approach emphasizes the importance of evaluations in ensuring the safety and efficacy of medical care for international patients.

11.2 Influence of Customer Feedback on Services

Another research work explored how customer feedback influences the services offered by medical tourism companies (Dang et al., 2020). The study found that ongoing feedback loops involving patients and healthcare professionals are crucial for streamlining the medical tourism process. Feedback systems contribute to the iterative development of services, enhancing patient satisfaction and safety standards.

11.3 Technology Features in Testing and Feedback

The technological aspects of testing and user feedback in medical tourism were examined by another research group (Ayuningtyas & Ariwibowo, 2020). Their focus was on how telemedicine systems and mobile applications can be utilized to track patients' health in real time and obtain immediate feedback. This research argued that these technological advancements not only enable early interventions but also provide valuable information for improving medical practices and treatment plans.

11.4 Cultural Sensitivity in Patient Feedback

An investigation delved into the cultural nuances of patient feedback in medical tourism, especially among individuals from different origins (Viken et al., 2021). This study underscored the significance of culturally sensitive feedback systems that allow patients from diverse cultural backgrounds to express their experiences and concerns freely. Healthcare practitioners must be aware of cultural variations in feedback expression to effectively interpret and respond to the feedback.

11.5 Impact of User Feedback on Reputation

A longitudinal research effort aimed to examine how user feedback over time affects the credibility and reputation of medical tourism locations (Ahani et al., 2021). According to this study, locations that actively incorporate patient input into their healthcare procedures experience an improvement in their reputation with potential medical tourists. Positive reviews not only attract more patients but also build trust in the quality of treatments offered, contributing to the growth of medical tourism destinations.

12. FUTURE PERSPECTIVES OF MEDICAL TOURISM

As medical tourism continues to grow globally, future trends and perspectives are shaping the landscape of this industry.

12.1 Technological Advancements

The future of medical tourism heavily relies on technological advancements. Innovative medical procedures, telemedicine, and remote diagnostics will enable patients to access cutting-edge treatments worldwide (de la Hoz-Correa et al., 2018) explores this trend in depth.

12.2 Personalized Healthcare

With the advent of precision medicine, medical tourism is expected to become more personalized. Patients can anticipate tailored treatment plans based on their unique genetic profiles. (Bishop and James A Litch, 2000) offer insights into the integration of personalized healthcare into medical tourism.

12.3 Emerging Destinations

While traditional medical tourism hubs like Thailand and India continue to thrive, emerging destinations in Eastern Europe, Latin America, and Africa are gaining prominence. These trends in destination diversification are discussed in (de la Hoz-Correa et al., 2018).

12.4 Regulatory Framework

The future of medical tourism will be influenced by regulatory frameworks that ensure patient safety and the quality of care. Robust regulations and accreditation processes are necessary for the industry's growth (Mishra & Sharma, 2021).

12.5 Sustainable Practices

Sustainability is becoming a critical consideration in the healthcare sector. Future medical tourism is likely to see an increased focus on sustainable practices, including eco-friendly healthcare facilities and responsible medical tourism practices (Darwazeh et al., 2021).

12.6 Global Collaboration

International collaboration among healthcare providers, insurers, and governments will play a pivotal role. Cross-border partnerships can enhance the accessibility and affordability of medical treatments.

12.7 Changing Demographics

The aging population in many Western countries will continue to drive medical tourism. Elderly patients seeking cost-effective healthcare options abroad will be a significant demographic.

12.8 Post Pandemic Resilience

The COVID-19 pandemic has disrupted global healthcare systems and medical tourism. However, as the world recovers, the industry is expected to rebound with new measures for pandemic resilience.

The evolving landscape of medical tourism presents a dynamic future with technological advancements, personalized healthcare, emerging destinations, regulatory frameworks, sustainable practices, global collaboration, changing demographics, and post-pandemic resilience shaping the industry.

DISCUSSION

Data-driven medical tourism underscores the transformative impact of integrated platforms on healthcare and tourism globally. The emphasis on user experience and interface design highlights the significance of user-friendly platforms for informed decision-making in medical tourism. This is crucial in a landscape where technology plays a pivotal role in shaping the industry. The impact analysis provides valuable insights into the far-reaching changes across various sectors, including healthcare, technology, research, patient empowerment, insurance, finance, and government. These data-driven platforms serve as catalysts for positive development, contributing to economic growth, job creation, innovation, and international collaboration. Ethical and legal considerations are meticulously addressed, emphasizing the importance of data privacy, security measures, informed consent, encryption, access controls, and compliance with regional laws. This commitment ensures the responsible handling of patient data, fostering trust and ethical responsibility in an era where data protection is paramount. Testing and user feedback are highlighted as essential components in ensuring the safety and quality of medical treatments within the context of medical tourism. The emphasis on pre-travel health exams, post-treatment evaluations, customer feedback loops, technological features, and cultural sensitivity underscores the commitment to enhancing the overall medical tourism experience. The future perspectives of medical tourism outlined key trends, including technological advancements, personalized healthcare, emerging destinations, regulatory frameworks, sustainable practices, global collaboration, changing demographics, and post-pandemic resilience. These trends showcase the dynamic nature of the industry, presenting both opportunities and challenges that will shape its evolving landscape. The integration of data-driven insights into medical tourism represents a transformative era with the envisioned creation of an Integrated Medical Tourism Platform. This platform, characterized by seamless connectivity, informed decision-making, and enhanced patient experiences, stands to revolutionize the industry. The commitment to ethical standards, user-centric design, and continuous improvement positions this platform as a positive force in the evolving landscape of medical tourism.

CONCLUSION

In overall, the integration of data-driven insights into medical tourism has paved the way for a transformative era, laying the foundation for the creation of a new platform that can revolutionize integrated medical tourism on a global scale. The amalgamation of healthcare analytics, artificial intelligence, and big data techniques has not only enhanced patient care and personalized treatment but has also redefined the dynamics of destination selection and industry competitiveness. As the industry continues to evolve, the vision for a new platform emerges "The Integrated Medical Tourism Platform" that is characterized by seamless connectivity, informed decision-making, and enhanced patient experiences. This platform will leverage data to not only cater to individual healthcare needs but also serve as a comprehensive resource for prospective medical tourists. The competition among destinations will be fueled by transparent data on treatment outcomes, cost-effectiveness, and patient satisfaction, fostering a continuous cycle of quality improvement and innovation. The impact on the industry as a whole is substantial, influencing the development of new business models, shaping regulatory frameworks, and fostering strategic alliances. The creation of this integrated platform will empower stakeholders to navigate the evolving landscape of medical tourism with greater precision, capitalizing on emerging trends and meeting the dynamic demands of the global healthcare market.

Lastly, the culmination of data-driven insights in medical tourism propels the industry towards a future where a unified platform serves as a catalyst for positive change. This platform will not only prioritize patient-centric care but also contribute to the efficiency and competitiveness of the global medical tourism sector. As the synergy between healthcare and data analytics continues to unfold, the creation of this integrated platform stands as a testament to the industry's commitment to providing accessible, high-quality healthcare services on a global scale.

REFERENCES

Ahani, A., Nilashi, M., Zogaan, W. A., Samad, S., Aljehane, N. O., Alhargan, A., Mohd, S., Ahmadi, H., & Sanzogni, L. (2021). Evaluating medical travelers' satisfaction through online review analysis. *Journal of Hospitality and Tourism Management*, *48*, 519–537. doi:10.1016/j.jhtm.2021.08.005

Angela, J., Suryono, I., & Wijaya, S. (2020). Profiling Indonesian Medical Tourists: A Motivation-Based Segmentation Study. *Journal of Economics, Business, &. Accountancy Ventura*, *23*(2), 205–217. Advance online publication. doi:10.14414/jebav.v23i2.2290

Ashrafuzzaman, Md., Milu, M., A, Anika., K, Farzana., A, & Rahman, M. (2022). Big Data Analytics Techniques for Healthcare. Big Data Analytics for Healthcare Datasets, Techniques, Life Cycles, Management and Applications, 49-62. doi:10.1016/B978-0-323-91907-4.00015-7

Ashrafuzzaman, Md., ASM, H, R, Adib., Sharif, H, M., & Tareq, A, M. (2022). The Impact of Social Media and Digital Marketing on Consumer Behavior. Handbook of Research on Consumer Behavior Change and Data Analytics in the Socio-Digital Era, 275-294. doi:10.4018/978-1-6684-4168-8.ch012

Ashrafuzzaman, Md., H, R., Rayesa, T., Nawrin, T., & Tasnuba, M. (2023). Application of Metaverse in the Healthcare Sector to Improve Quality of Life. Handbook of Research on Consumer Behavioral Analytics in Metaverse and the Adoption of a Virtual World, 292-320. doi:10.4018/978-1-6684-7029-9.ch014

Ayuningtyas, D., & Ariwibowo, D. A. (2020). The strategic role of information communication technology in succeeding medical tourism. *Enfermeria Clinica*, *30*, 170–173. doi:10.1016/j.enfcli.2020.06.039

Banerjee, S., Nath, S. S., Dey, N., & Eto, H. (2015). Global Medical Tourism: A Review. In New Business Opportunities in the Growing E-Tourism Industry (pp. 114–131). IGI Global. doi:10.4018/978-1-4666-8577-2.ch007

Bishop & Litch. (2000). Medical tourism can do harm. *BMJ (Clinical Research Ed.)*, *320*(7240), 1017. doi:10.1136/bmj.320.7240.1017 PMID:10753174

Carrera, P. M., & Bridges, J. F. (2006). Globalization and healthcare: Understanding health and medical tourism. *Expert Review of Pharmacoeconomics & Outcomes Research*, *6*(4), 447–454. doi:10.1586/14737167.6.4.447 PMID:20528514

CavmakD.CavmakS. (2020). Using AHP to Prioritize Barriers in Developing Medical Tourism: Case of Turkey. https://papers.ssrn.com/abstract=3766688

Connell, J. (2013a). Contemporary medical tourism: Conceptualisation, culture and commodification. *Tourism Management*, *34*, 1–13. doi:10.1016/j.tourman.2012.05.009

Dang, H.-S., Nguyen, T.-M.-T., Wang, C.-N., Day, J.-D., & Dang, T. M. H. (2020). Grey System Theory in the Study of Medical Tourism Industry and Its Economic Impact. *International Journal of Environmental Research and Public Health*, *17*(3), 961. doi:10.3390/ijerph17030961 PMID:32033177

Darwazeh, D., Clarke, A., & Wilson, J. (2021). Framework for Establishing a Sustainable Medical Facility: A Case Study of Medical Tourism in Jordan. *WORLD (Oakland, Calif.)*, *2*(3), 351–375. doi:10.3390/world2030022

de la Hoz-Correa, A., Muñoz-Leiva, F., & Bakucz, M. (2018). Past themes and future trends in medical tourism research: A co-word analysis. *Tourism Management*, *65*, 200–211. doi:10.1016/j.tourman.2017.10.001

Debata, B. R., Patnaik, B., Mahapatra, S. S., & Sree, K. (2015). Interrelations of service quality and service loyalty dimensions in medical tourism: A structural equation modelling approach. *Benchmarking*, *22*(1), 18–55. doi:10.1108/BIJ-04-2013-0036

Dhakate, N., & Joshi, R. (2023). Classification of reviews of e-healthcare services to improve patient satisfaction: Insights from an emerging economy. *Journal of Business Research*, *164*, 114015. doi:10.1016/j.jbusres.2023.114015 PMID:37192884

Dryglas, D., & Salamaga, M. (2018). Segmentation by push motives in health tourism destinations: A case study of Polish spa resorts. *Journal of Destination Marketing & Management*, *9*, 234–246. doi:10.1016/j.jdmm.2018.01.008

Ebrahim, A. H., & Ganguli, S. (2019). A comparative analysis of medical tourism competitiveness of India, Thailand and Singapore. *Tourism: An International Interdisciplinary Journal*, *67*(2), 102–115.

Ediansyah, A., Arief, M., Hamsal, M., & Abdinagoro, S. B. (2022). A decade of medical tourism research: Looking back to moving forward. *Journal of Hospitality and Tourism Insights*, *6*(5), 2158–2172. doi:10.1108/JHTI-06-2022-0250

Gupta, P., Pandey, B., Hussain, S., Kumar, A., Sharma, R., Yadav, M. K., Bhati, S., Khandelwal, A., Shyamal, S., Khan, A., Mohata, V., Khan, F., Sharma, K., Arora, K., Gandhi, T., Kumar, P., & Kundu, P. (n.d.). *Challenges and Strengths of Medical Tourism in Delhi NCR*. Academic Press.

Habibi, A., Mousavi, M., Jamali, S. M., & Ale Ebrahim, N. (2022). A bibliometric study of medical tourism. *Anatolia*, *33*(3), 415–425. doi:10.1080/13032917.2021.1954042

Halkiopoulos, C., Dimou, E., Kompothrekas, A., Telonis, G., & Boutsinas, B. (2021). The E-Tour Facilitator Platform Supporting an Innovative Health Tourism Marketing Strategy. In V. Katsoni & C. van Zyl (Eds.), *Culture and Tourism in a Smart, Globalized, and Sustainable World* (pp. 609–623). Springer International Publishing. doi:10.1007/978-3-030-72469-6_39

Hasanzadeh, M., Delafrooz, N., Gholipoor Soleimani, A., & Shahroodi, K. (2021). Explaining the Model of Customer Value Co-Creation Behavior in the Development of Medical Tourism Industry of Guilan Province. *Urban Tourism*, *8*(2), 141–159. doi:10.22059/jut.2021.327185.927

Keikhosrokiani, P. (2022a). Big Data Analytics for Healthcare: Datasets, Techniques, Life Cycles, Management, and Applications. In Big Data Analytics for Healthcare: Datasets, Techniques, Life Cycles, Management, and Applications. doi:10.1016/C2021-0-00369-2

Keikhosrokiani, P. (2022b). Handbook of research on consumer behavior change and data analytics in the socio-digital era. In Handbook of Research on Consumer Behavior Change and Data Analytics in the Socio-Digital Era. doi:10.4018/978-1-6684-4168-8

Keikhosrokiani, P., & Fye, G. M. (2023). A hybrid recommender system for health supplement e-commerce based on customer data implicit ratings. *Multimedia Tools and Applications*. Advance online publication. doi:10.1007/s11042-023-17321-6

Lamarque, M., Moro Gutiérrez, L., Lamarque, M., & Moro Gutiérrez, L. (2020). Therapeutic Itineraries and Processes of Illness Care in Latin American Migrants: Conflicts, Negotiations, and Adaptations. *Migraciones Internacionales*, *11*. Advance online publication. doi:10.33679/rmi.v1i1.1796

Lunt, N., Smith, R. D., Mannion, R., Green, S. T., Exworthy, M., Hanefeld, J., Horsfall, D., Machin, L., & King, H. (2014). *Implications for the NHS of inward and outward medical tourism: A policy and economic analysis using literature review and mixed-methods approaches*. NIHR Journals Library. https://www.ncbi.nlm.nih.gov/books/NBK263160/

Mamun, M., & Andaleeb, S. (2013). Prospects and Problems of Medical Tourism in Bangladesh. *International Journal of Health Services : Planning, Administration, Evaluation*, *43*(1), 123–141. doi:10.2190/HS.43.1.i PMID:23527458

Martin, J. C., Bustamante-Sánchez, N. S., & Indelicato, A. (2022). Analyzing the Main Determinants for Being an Immigrant in Cuenca (Ecuador) Based on a Fuzzy Clustering Approach. *Axioms*, *11*(2), 2. Advance online publication. doi:10.3390/axioms11020074

Mishra, V., & Sharma, M. G. (2021). Framework for Promotion of Medical Tourism: A Case of India. *International Journal of Global Business and Competitiveness*, *16*(S1, Suppl 1), 103–111. doi:10.1007/s42943-021-00027-7

Omanin Siddiqua, P., Omanin, A., Faiza, S., Jafrin, & Ashrafuzzaman, M. (2022). Big medical data analytics for diagnosis. Big Data Analytics for Healthcare Datasets, techniques, Life Cycles, management and Applications, 111-124. doi:10.1016/B978-0-323-91907-4.00013-3

Panteli, A., Kompothrekas, A., Halkiopoulos, C., & Boutsinas, B. (2021). An Innovative Recommender System for Health Tourism. In V. Katsoni & C. van Zyl (Eds.), *Culture and Tourism in a Smart, Globalized, and Sustainable World* (pp. 649–658). Springer International Publishing., doi:10.1007/978-3-030-72469-6_42

Rao, G. (2013). *Medical Tourism: Global Perspective* [dataset].

Ruhanen, L. (2019). The prominence of eco in ecotourism experiences: An analysis of post-purchase online reviews. *Journal of Hospitality and Tourism Management, 39*, 110–116. doi:10.1016/j.jhtm.2019.03.006

Sheppard, C. E., Lester, E. L. W., Chuck, A. W., Kim, D. H., Karmali, S., de Gara, C. J., & Birch, D. W. (2014). Medical tourism and bariatric surgery: Who pays? *Surgical Endoscopy, 28*(12), 3329–3336. doi:10.1007/s00464-014-3613-8 PMID:24969849

Skountridaki, L. (2017). Barriers to business relations between medical tourism facilitators and medical professionals. *Tourism Management, 59*, 254–266. doi:10.1016/j.tourman.2016.07.008

Snyder, J., Crooks, V. A., Johnston, R., & Dharamsi, S. (2013). "Do your homework…and then hope for the best": The challenges that medical tourism poses to Canadian family physicians' support of patients' informed decision-making. *BMC Medical Ethics, 14*(1), 37. doi:10.1186/1472-6939-14-37 PMID:24053385

Torkzadeh, L., Jalilian, H., Zolfagharian, M., Torkzadeh, H., Bakhshi, M., & Khodayari-Zarnaq, R. (2021). Market segmentation in the health tourism industry: A systematic review of approach and criteria. *Journal of Policy Research in Tourism, Leisure & Events, 0*(0), 1–20. doi:10.1080/19407963.2021.1988622

Viken, A., Höckert, E., & Grimwood, B. S. R. (2021). Cultural sensitivity: Engaging difference in tourism. *Annals of Tourism Research, 89*, 103223. doi:10.1016/j.annals.2021.103223

Xian, Z., Keikhosrokiani, P., XinYing, C., & Li, Z. (2022). An RFM Model Using K-Means Clustering to Improve Customer Segmentation and Product Recommendation. In P. Keikhosrokiani (Ed.), Handbook of Research on Consumer Behavior Change and Data Analytics in the Socio-Digital Era (pp. 124–145). IGI Global. doi:10.4018/978-1-6684-4168-8.ch006

Yang, Y., Hu, J., Liu, Y., & Chen, X. (2020). Doctor Recommendation Based on an Intuitionistic Normal Cloud Model Considering Patient Preferences. *Cognitive Computation, 12*(2), 460–478. doi:10.1007/s12559-018-9616-3

Yee, L. S., & Keikhosrokiani, P. (2022). Hospital data analytics system for tracking and predicting obese patients' lifestyle habits. In *Big Data Analytics for Healthcare*. Datasets, Techniques, Life Cycles, Management, and Applications. doi:10.1016/B978-0-323-91907-4.00004-2

Zhao, X., & Keikhosrokiani, P. (2022). Sales prediction and product recommendation model through user behavior analytics. *Computers, Materials & Continua, 70*(2), 3855–3874. Advance online publication. doi:10.32604/cmc.2022.019750

Zhao, Y., Zhang, L., Zeng, C., Lu, W., Chen, Y., & Fan, T. (2023). Construction of an aspect-level sentiment analysis model for online medical reviews. *Information Processing & Management, 60*(6), 103513. doi:10.1016/j.ipm.2023.103513

Section 4
AI-Augmented Technological Applications in Specific Fields

Chapter 11
Deep-Mental Workload Intelligent System:
An AI-Augmented System to Predict Employee Mental Workload Based on EEG Data Using Deep Learning

Guo Foong Ng
Universiti Sains Malaysia, Malaysia

Pantea Keikhosrokiani
https://orcid.org/0000-0003-4705-2732
University of Oulu, Finland

Minna Isomursu
University of Oulu, Finland

ABSTRACT

Recently, the measurement of mental workload has emerged as a crucial aspect of well-being process in socio-technical organizations. Excessive mental workload reduces work productivity, whereas insufficient mental workload leads to the underutilization of human resources. Significant research utilizing machine learning algorithms, such as SVM and KNN, based on electroencephalogram (EEG) signals, has been used for stress classification in the past few years. However, issues with mental workload and classification accuracy persist across these studies. Therefore, this chapter proposes an AI-augmented web-based information system to assess mental workload by employing a deep learning model. The proposed deep learning algorithm is used for the classification and feature extraction from EEG signals to accurately classify mental workload status. The proposed AI-augmented system would become a significant tool for making more effective and precise predictions about employees' mental workload in organizations.

DOI: 10.4018/979-8-3693-1210-0.ch011

INTRODUCTION

Mental workload, which is also known as psychological load, can be defined as the quantity of brain activity per unit of time, the rate at which brain resources are used or the psychological pressure a person is under (Qu et al., 2020). Recently, machine learning, is widely used in the study of mental workload to make a prediction based on a large scale of historical dataset. Understanding of the mental workload is crucial to the employer to increase the employees' performance in consideration of the fact that excessive mental workload can result in frustrated emotions, errors in decision-making and analysis whereas inadequate mental workload can cause waste of human resources and affect job performance (Alifah et al., 2019; Aoki, 2017; Chen et al., 2022a; Keikhosrokiani et al., 2012; Keikhosrokiani & Kamaruddin, 2022; Qu et al., 2020; Teoh Yi Zhe & Keikhosrokiani, 2021).

In this fast-paced world and data-driven organizations, most businesses are forced to make an effort in order to keep up with the demands from their consumers (Keikhosrokiani, 2021, 2022b). In fact, this scenario leads to an increased workload for employees to prioritize productivity and efficiency. This can result in fatigue in physical, psychological as well as emotional to the employee who is exposed to excess demands. Eventually, their working performance will become less efficient, and their productivity will be lowered. Workload prediction as well as workload management are important for employers to take care of the mental health of their employees. Consequently, this study aims to develop a web application, which is an intelligent web-based information system to predict employee mental workload using deep learning. The system applies deep learning techniques to classify the employee's mental workload based on an electroencephalogram (EEG) data set. Firstly, a deep learning algorithm is proposed to predict the employee mental workload using EEG dataset. Then a web-based information system is developed for monitoring employee mental workload and providing proper advice based on the level of mental workload. Finally, an analytical dashboard is created to keep track of employees' mental workload status.

This chapter reviewed the concept of mental workload, mental workload classification using EEG dataset, and different artificial intelligence algorithms used for the classification of mental workload. Then, the details of the proposed web-based system, as a tool to track employee mental workload in data driven organizations, are presented. Afterwards, the performance comparison of deep learning algorithms, system implementation, testing, and user interfaces are shown. Finally, the chapter is wrapped up with conclusion and future work.

BACKGROUND

Mental Workload

The term "mental workload" refers to the amount of cognitive effort or mental demand required to perform a task or activity. It can be influenced by a variety of factors, including the complexity of the task, the amount of information being processed, the level of skill or expertise required, and the time pressure or other constraints under which the task is being performed (Keikhosrokiani, 2019, 2022a, 2022b; Keikhosrokiani et al., 2018, 2020; Keikhosrokiani & Asl, 2022). Mental workload can have important implications for productivity, performance, and overall well-being. High levels of mental workload can lead to fatigue, stress, and decreased performance, while low levels of mental workload can lead to boredom and reduce motivation. It is therefore important to be able to accurately measure and manage mental workload to optimize performance and well-being.

There are several different ways to measure mental workload, including self-port measures, physiological measures, and performance measures. Self-port measure is a method that asks employees to report on their own cognitive effort or mental demand which is typically based on subjective ratings or questionnaires. It is important to consider the limitations despite the method is useful for assessing mental workload. The limitations are that self-report measures rely on the accuracy and honesty of the individual's responses, which may be influenced by factors such as fatigue, stress, or motivation. Besides, the measures may be influenced by individual differences in perception and interpretation. As a results, self-report measures may not always provide a reliable or objective assessment of mental workload (Jaiswal et al., 2023; Reid & Nygren, 1988; Rubio Valdehita et al., 2017).

Physiological measures refer to measuring changes in employees' physiological responses (Appel et al., 2019; Cho, 2021; Reimer et al., 2009; Wang et al., 2023). This measure can include a wide range of physiological parameters, such as heart rate, blood pressure, pupil dilation, and skin conductance. However, all the physiological parameters may be influenced by factors other than mental workload such as stress anxiety, or physical activity, which affect the accuracy of the measurement. Furthermore, performance measures examine the changes in employees' performance on a task or activity. These measures can include a wide range of performance-based metrics, such as response time, accuracy, number of errors, or speed of completion. The limitation of this method is that the measure might be influenced by factors such as skill level, experiences, or motivation.

On the other hand, electroencephalogram (EEG), is another tool that can be used to measure mental workload, as it allows researchers to examine brain activity and identify specific patterns or changes that are associated with different levels of mental workload (Couceiro et al., 2019; Qu et al., 2020). Generally, there are many techniques used to measure mental workload and it is important to do so. By measuring the mental workload, it is possible to identify situations where an individual may be experiencing high levels of mental workload and take steps to reduce it. This can help to improve performance and reduce the risk of errors or accidents.

Electroencephalogram (EEG) Signal

Electroencephalography (EEG) is a technique for measuring the electrical activity of the brain using sensors (electrodes) placed on the scalp. The brain produces a variety of electrical signals, which are known as brain waves, that are generated by the coordinated activity of millions of neurons in the brain. There are several types of pf brain waves that can be detected by using EEG, including alpha waves, beta waves, gamma waves, and theta waves (Bellamy, 2021). These electrical signals can be recorded using Electroencephalography (EEG), and the resulting EEG records are known as Electroencephalogram. The electroencephalogram reflects the patterns of brain activity at the time the measurement was taken.

EEG signals are typically measured in terms of frequency (measured in hertz, or Hz) and amplitude (measured in microvolts). The frequency of a brain wave reflects the number of cycles per second that the brain wave oscillates, while the amplitude reflects the size or intensity of the brain wave. EEG is a non-invasive technique that is widely used in research and clinical practice to study brain function and to diagnose and monitor neurological and psychiatric disorders. Recently, EEG signals played an important role to classify mental workload as the mental issues arise and become a concern to the community.

Existing Classification Algorithms and Models

The development of mental workload classifiers using EEG signals and machine learning techniques has become more prevalent in recent years as machine learning has progressed to become more advanced (Bellamy, 2021; Parveen & Bhavsar, 2023; Qu et al., 2020; Zhu et al., 2023). Many researchers have successfully implemented various algorithms and models to classify mental workload based on EEG signals. These algorithms and models often utilize machine learning techniques, such as support vector machines (SVM) and decision trees, to analyze the EEG data and predict levels of mental workload. Some of these algorithms and models have been shown to be effective at accurately classifying mental workload, while others have not been as successful. In this session, an overview of some of the existing algorithms and models used in each of the related works will be discussed.

A study proposed a mental states classifier with machine learning algorithms using alpha activity decline based on EEG signals (Qu et al., 2020). The study used alpha activity decline as a measure of mental workload and employed several machine learning algorithms to classify mental states based on this measure. Alpha activity baseline refers to a decrease in the amplitude of alpha brain waves, which are a type of EEG signal that are associated with relaxation and lack of mental effort. They perform data preprocessing such as independent component analysis and band pass filtering to remove noise and artifacts and to extract features relevant to mental workload classification. This included selecting specific frequency bands of the alpha brain waves and calculating the alpha activity decline. The feature extraction is done by Autoregressive Coefficient. The machine learning algorithms for the classification used in this study include linear discriminant analysis (LDA), quadratic discriminant analysis (QDA), and support vector machines (SVM). These algorithms are used to build models that can predict the class of a given input based on a set of labeled training data. They evaluated the performance of the different algorithms on a dataset of EEG signals recorded from participants during different mental workload tasks. They found that the SVM algorithm was the most effective at classifying mental states based on alpha activity decline, achieving the highest classification accuracy.

Another study by (Walter et al., 2011) proposed a mental workload classifier using Support Vector Machines (SVM) and Convolutional Neural Network (CNN) based on EEG signals. In this study, EEG signals were recorded from participants during different Mental Workload Task (MWL) and the recorded EEG signals were used to train and test the SVM and CNN models. The SVM model was trained using different feature extraction techniques, including power spectral density (PSD) and wavelet transform (WT), to extract features from the EEG signals. The CNN model was trained using raw EEG signals as input was able to learn features directly from the data. They evaluated the performance of the SVM and CNN models on dataset of EEG signals and found that the CNN model outperformed the SVM model in terms of classification accuracy. They also found that the CNN model was able to achieve good generalization performance, meaning that it was able to generalize well to new data not seen during training. Overall, this study suggests that CNNs are a promising approach for the classification of MWL using EEG signals, and they can outperform SVM models for this task.

In another study, (Asgher et al., 2020) worked on identifying patterns in brain activity that are associated with mental stress. The mental stress recognition is proposed by using k-nearest neighbor (kNN) classifier on EEG signals. This study used EEG to collect brain activity data from individuals while they performed tasks that were designed to induce mental stress. The raw EEG data was likely preprocessed to remove noise and artifacts, and to ensure that it was in a suitable format for analysis. This may have included steps such as filtering, down sampling, and epoching the data. Various techniques are used to extract features from the preprocessed EEG data that were relevant for identifying mental stress. The techniques included power spectral analysis and time-frequency analysis. They then used a machine learning algorithm called a k-nearest neighbor (kNN) classifier to classify the extracted features as either indicative of mental stress or not indicative of mental stress. The kNN classifier works by finding the k data points in the training set that are most similar to given data point and using the majority class among these k points to classify the given data point. The results of the study showed that the kNN classifier was able to accurately identify mental stress with an accuracy of 89%.

The use of electroencephalography (EEG) data and machine learning techniques to estimate mental workload was investigate by (Rahman et al., 2015). The study utilizes a deep neural network architecture consisting of a bidirectional long short-term memory (BLSTM) layer and a long short-term memory (LSTM) layer to process the EEG data. The BLSTM layer is responsible for capturing the temporal dependencies in the data by processing the input sequence in both forward and backward directions, while the LSTM layer is responsible for learning long-term dependencies in the data. In addition to the deep neural network, the study also employs an evolutionary algorithm to optimize the network's parameter. Evolutionary algorithms are a class of optimization algorithms that mimic the process of natural selection to find the optimal solution to a problem. In this study, the evolutionary algorithm is used to find the optimal set of parameters for the deep neural network that maximizes the accuracy of the mental workload estimation. The study used a dataset collected from 32 participants while they performed a cognitive task. The EEG data was preprocessed to extract features relevant to mental workload estimation, such as power spectral density and event-related spectral perturbation. These features were then used as input to the deep neural network, which was trained to predict the mental workload of the participants. The accuracy of the mental workload estimation was evaluated using various metrics, including mean absolute error and root mean squared error. For the results, the evaluation is done based on two tasks that are No task and SIMKAP-based multitasking activity. The proposed model achieves 86.33% and 82.57% accuracy for the two tasks.

Furthermore, cognitive analysis of working memory load from EEG by a deep recurrent neural network was done in another study by (Das Chakladar et al., 2020). The study utilizes a hybrid combination of convolutional neural network (ConvNet) and deep recurrent neural network (RNN) architecture to process the EEG data. ConvNet was used to handle the variations in space and frequency domains because of its ability to learn 2D data representations. The extracted ConvNet feature vectors (FV) were fed into recurrent LSTM layers to learn the temporal variations. The dataset in this study is collected from the EEG cognitive database of the Psychological Departments, NIMHANS. The data were collected using 64 scalp electrodes and analyzed on a computer workstation. The brain activity during the task was recorded and the data were split into four different classes corresponding to the different levels of cognitive load. The EEG data from each trial were processed and used to create nine frames for training. The 22-fold dataset was split using a leave-subject-out cross validation technique. The ConvNet network used in the study consisted of nine convolutional layers and one fully connected layer. The ConvNet outputs were reshaped as sequences of frames and later used to investigate the temporal sequence in map. Two models included Bidirectional LSTM (BiLSTM) and long short-term memory (LSTM) were evaluated to extract the temporal information. In the results, the proposed hybrid network demonstrated significant improvements in finding better classification accuracy which up to 92.5% over various existing LSTM models.

The comparisons of the discussed EEG classification techniques are listed in table 1 below. The type of classifiers used, and the accuracy achieved covered in the table will be useful in determining which classifiers to be used in this project.

Table 1. Comparison of related EEG classification techniques

Proposed Work	Main Focus	Proposed Classification Method	Accuracy	Notes
(Qu et al., 2020)	Mental state classification using alpha activity decline	Support Vector Machine (SVM)	74.55%	-
(Walter et al., 2011)	Mental workload classification	Support Vector Machine (SVM)	70.64%	-
		Convolutional Neural Networks (CNN)	83.42%	
(Asgher et al., 2020)	Mental stress recognition	K-Nearest Neighbor (kNN)	91.26% when k=1,2	The feature used to train the classifier was the mean power of beta band of EEG signal
		Fuzzy K-Nearest Neighbor (FKNN)	81.98% when k=5	
(Rahman et al., 2015)	Mental workload classification based on EEG data	Deep neural network architecture consists of a BLSTM and LSTM layer, Evolutionary algorithm	86.33% for No Task	The accuracy of the mental workload estimation was evaluated using various metrics, including mean absolute error and root mean squared error.
			82.57% for SIMKAP based multitasking activity	
S. Kuanar et al [11]	Cognitive analysis of working memory load from EEG	Hybrid model of CNN + RNN Convolutional Neural Network (CNN) + Bidirectional long short-term memory (BLSTM)	92.5%	-

PROPOSED METHOD

System Module and Architecture

The proposed solution for this study (Figure 1) is a web-based information system that enables the users to undergo mental workload prediction. The system is used to analyze the electroencephalogram (EEG) for mental workload classification. Deep learning is being used in this project to perform classification on the electroencephalogram (EEG) and decision making. Machine learning techniques, especially deep learning can capture variance characteristics in the EEG signals and classify mental workload levels accurately. The main target users for the system are employers, employees, and admin.

As illustrated in Figure 2, the proposed system consists of three modules including account management module, data classification module, as well as analytical dashboard module. The account management module is a module that includes the login and user registration features for the system. Users may also update their personal details in their profile page.

The second critical module is the Data Classification Module. This complex component comprises several sub-modules, each performing a specific function to ensure reliable and accurate mental workload predictions. The initial phase in this module is data preprocessing. In this stage, the uploaded EEG data is refined and denoised, purging any unwanted signals. This purification ensures the EEG data more accurately represents neural activity, setting the stage for effective classification. After that, the data progresses to the Feature Abstraction sub-module where distinctive attributes are extracted from the EEG, serving as crucial factors for subsequent classification. Then, the Classification sub-module steps into action. The preprocessed and feature-extracted EEG data is scrutinized and segregated into various mental workload categories. The classification is based on separate ratings files that function as labels, facilitating an efficient and systematized process. The Model Evaluation sub-module then evaluates the classification for performance metrics, such as accuracy, precision, and recall. This assessment ensures that the system's predictions meet the desired standard of quality and reliability. The final sub-module, Prediction, is integral for operationalizing the system. It applies the developed model in a practical context, enabling the prediction of mental workload status for new EEG data uploaded to the web application.

Finally, the analytical dashboard module is implemented to display the results of the prediction. The module should visualize and present all the analytics results to the user. The system should allow employers to view the employee list with their EEG prediction results.

Figure 1. Overall architecture diagram for employee mental workload information system

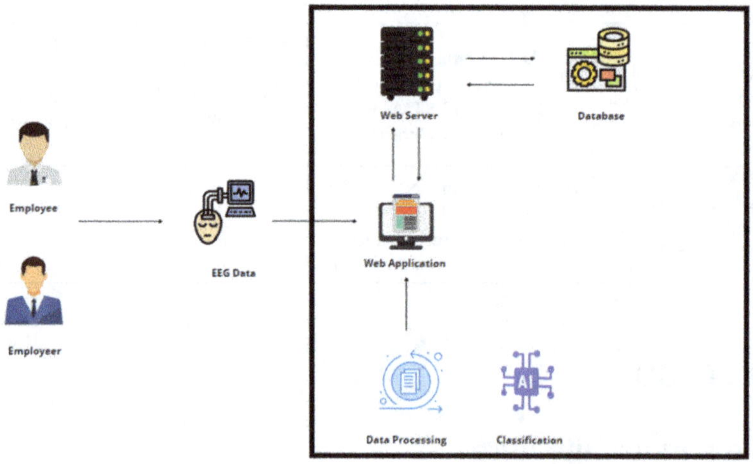

Figure 2. Overall module diagram for employee mental workload information system

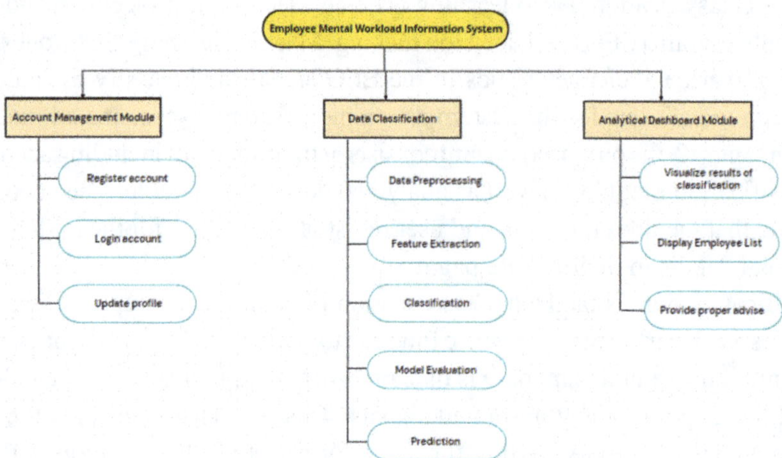

Development Methodology

Agile development methodology is being chosen to be implemented in this study. Agile development is well-suited for web-based information systems like the proposed system as it allows for rapid prototyping and iteration. With agile development, the system can be developed in small increments, with each iteration building on the previous one. This allows for flexibility and the ability to quickly respond to changing requirements or feedback from stakeholders. Generally, agile development is a flexible, iterative approach to software development that emphasizes faster prototyping, continuous delivery, and collaboration with stakeholders. It is based on the Agile Manifesto, a set of values and principles that prioritize customer satisfaction, working software, and teamwork over other aspects of software development, such as processes and tools. Overall, agile development has several advantages including faster delivery, greater flexibility, improved collaboration, higher quality, greater control, and greater visibility.

System Requirements

Functional Requirements

Functional requirements refer to specific actions or behaviors that a system or component must be able to perform to meet the needs of the users or stakeholders. They describe what the system should do, rather than how it should be implemented. Table 2 shows the list of functional requirements identified for this project.

Table 2. Functional requirements for the proposed system

Modules	Functional Requirements
Account Management	• The system shall allow employers to create an employer account by entering their personal information (e.g., Name, Email, Password). • The system shall allow employees to create employee accounts by entering their personal information. • The system shall allow users to view and update their personal information. • System shall allow users able to log in to their account using their email address and password
Data Classification	• System should use deep learning algorithms to classify collected EEG data into different mental workload level (very low, low, balanced, high, very high).
Analytical Dashboard	• The system should provide an interactive dashboard for users to view and analyze their EEG data and prediction results. • The system should be able to provide visualization of the data (e.g., chart, graph) to help users understand and interpret the results. • System should be able to provide proper advice based on the predicted results. • System should allow employer to view on his/her employee list with their EEG prediction result visualization.

Non-Functional Requirements

Non-functional requirements defined as the system capabilities and the desired level of service. Non-functional requirements are those that specify how a system should behave or perform, rather than what it should do. They describe the quality attributes of the system, such as its reliability, usability, performance, security, and maintainability. Table 3 lists out the non-functional requirements in this project system.

Table 3. Non-functional requirements for the proposed system

Non-Functional Requirement	Description
Reliability	• System should be always available to provide reliable service unless there is no Internet connection or a poor Internet connection.
Usability	• The system should be user-friendly, easy to use and understand for the user. • System should provide interactivity between users and components (e.g., buttons should give response whenever clicked by user).
Performance	• System should perform well and respond quickly to user request.
Security	• System should protect the collected EEG data and personal information of users from unauthorized access.
Maintainability	• The system should be easy to maintain and update over time. • System should display an error message to handle undesired events.

Intelligent Component Framework

Figure 3 illustrates the overall framework of the intelligent component that is implemented in this study. The framework includes data collection, data preprocessing, feature extraction, model training, model evaluation and classification.

Figure 3. Intelligent component framework

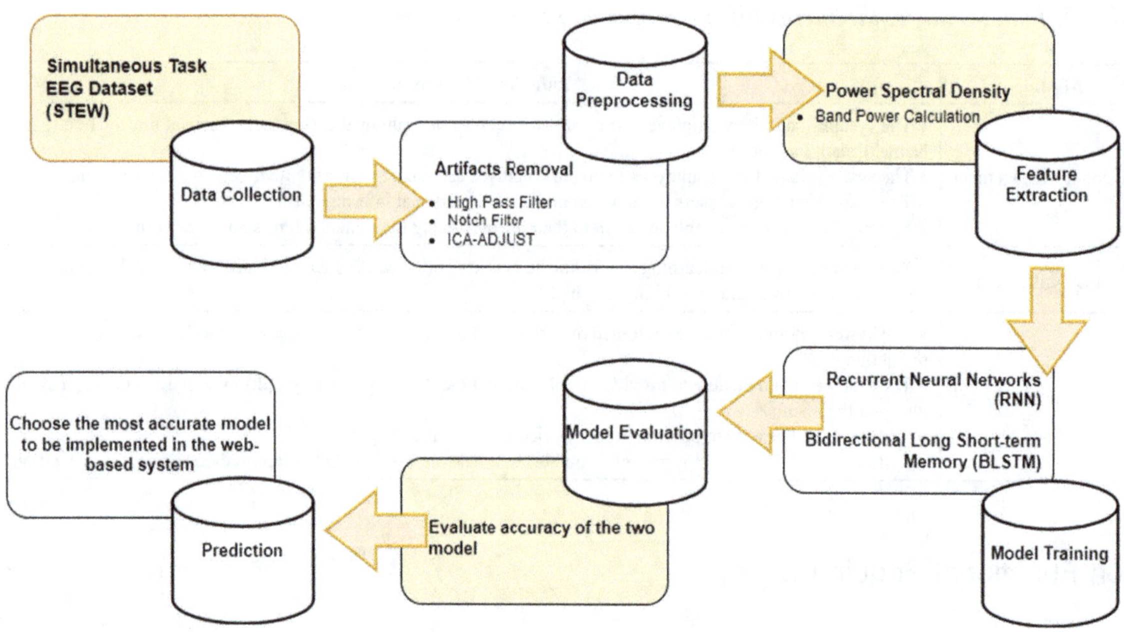

Data Collection

In data collection, the system is using an available dataset named Simultaneous Task EEG dataset (STEW) (Eraslan et al., 2016; Lim et al., 2018). The EEG signals were collected from 48 subjects (all males) via 14 electrodes, sampled at 128 Hz. The data was collected using Emotiv EPOC device. The participants were asked to perform the Simultaneous Capacity (SIMKAP) multitasking activity. The signals have been recorded in the resting state and the working state. After each segment of the experiment, the subjects were asked to self-report their workload levels on a scale of 1 to 9, which was then divided into three categories: low (1-3), balanced (4-6), and high (7-9).

Data Preprocessing

During the Data Preprocessing phase, since the raw EEG data can be easily contaminated, the raw EEG data is pre-processed to remove artifacts caused by muscle movement and different noises such as power line interference (Eraslan et al., 2016). Automatic detection algorithm is used to identify artifacts in the EEG data. The raw EEG data is processed by applying a high-pass filter to remove slow drift and a low-pass filter to remove high-frequency noise (Lim et al., 2018). The data is then re-referenced to average and converted to epochs (time windows).

Feature Extraction

Feature extraction is important before model training. Feature extraction helps to extract the relevant information from the preprocessed EEG data and create a new set of features or variables that can be more easily analyzed and understood. In this study, frequency domain method is used for extracting features from the EEG data as the frequency domain method can provide insight into the underlying neural mechanisms and brain processes that are reflected in the EEG signa. In the feature domain method, the signal power is calculated for each channel at five well-known Power Spectral Density bands, at which the brain wave signals are divided into the categories Delta (0.5-4Hz), Theta (4-8Hz), Alpha (8-12Hz), Beta (12-30Hz), and Gamma (30-100Hz) (Mognon et al., 2011).

Model Training

After the feature extraction, the dataset is then gone through the model training. K-fold cross validation is recommended to be used to train the deep learning model. In K-fold cross validation, the data is partitioned into k-folds, and the training and test sets are created by rotating which fold is used as the test sets. This approach can be useful for maximizing the amount of data used for training and for getting a more robust estimate of model performance (Mognon et al., 2011). After splitting the dataset into train set and test set, the train dataset is used to train the Recurrent Neural Network (RNN) model, Bidirectional Long Short-Term Memory (BLSTM) model, Combination of RNN and BLSTM.

Model Evaluation and Prediction

After training the models, the next phase is to evaluate the models' performance on the test set. This typically involves using the model to make predictions on the test set and then comparing the predictions to the true values to compute evaluation metrics such as accuracy, precision, and recall. The models with the higher accuracy in performance will be selected to implement in the web-based system.

System Implementation

For this study, the web application leverages the Django web framework due to its well-recognized versatility and capacity to integrate machine learning models, such as the RNN model used for mental workload prediction from EEG data. The Django framework adheres to the Model View Template (MVT) design pattern, facilitating clean separation of concerns in the codebase. In line with this design philosophy, each module in the application is structured as an independent "app" within the broader Django project. Each "app" possesses its model.py and view.py files, the former being instrumental in creating database models, and the latter managing the execution of business logic.

As for data persistence, the application opts for PostgreSQL, an advanced open-source relational database. PostgreSQL is chosen for its robustness, scalability, and adherence to the SQL standards. It also supports a range of advanced data types, full-text search, and provides extensibility which can be beneficial in the future as the system evolves.

This architecture allows for a smooth interaction between the front-end and back-end components of the system, and the clear separation of components makes the system more maintainable and easier to update or modify in the future.

FINDINGS

Model Evaluation

Table 4 presents a performance comparison of three different deep learning models used for EEG-based mental workload prediction: a Recurrent Neural Network (RNN), a Bidirectional Long Short-Term Memory (BLSTM) network, and a combined RNN+BLSTM model. The models are evaluated on five different classes of mental workload, ranging from 'Very Low' to 'Very High'.

The highest accuracy achieved is 48% by the BLSTM model. Despite the relatively low accuracy, this model is chosen for integration into a web application for mental workload prediction. The reason for this choice could be due to the model's superior performance in predicting the 'Very Low' and 'High' mental workload classes, as indicated by the F1-Scores of 0.67 and 0.50 respectively. However, it's important to note that the accuracy of these models is lower than expected. There could be several reasons for this:

Small Dataset: Deep learning models typically require large amounts of data to learn effectively. In this case, the dataset consists of only 96 data files from 48 subjects, which might not be sufficient for the models to learn the complex patterns in the EEG signals.

Complexity of the Task: Mental workload prediction from EEG signals is a challenging task due to the high dimensionality and non-stationarity of EEG signals, as well as the subjectivity and variability of mental workload.

Compared to traditional machine learning models, deep learning models have the advantage of being able to learn complex non-linear relationships and automatically extract features from raw data. However, they also require more data and computational resources, and can be more difficult to interpret. In short, while the performance of the models is lower than expected, they still provide a valuable tool for mental workload prediction from EEG data. Future work could focus on collecting more data, exploring different features, addressing class imbalance, and experimenting with different model architectures and hyperparameters to improve performance.

Table 4. Performance comparison of EEG assessment models

Algorithm	Class	Precision	Recall	F1-Score	Accuracy
RNN	Very Low	0.26	0.83	0.39	25%
	Low	0.00	0.00	0.00	
	Balanced	0.00	0.00	0.00	
	High	0.45	0.22	0.25	
	Very High	0.25	1.00	0.20	
BLSTM	Very Low	0.50	1.00	0.67	48%
	Low	0.00	0.00	0.00	
	Balanced	0.00	0.00	0.00	
	High	0.38	0.75	0.50	
	Very High	0.00	0.00	0.00	
RNN+BLSTM	Very Low	0.36	1.00	0.53	39%
	Low	0.00	0.00	0.00	
	Balanced	0.00	0.00	0.00	
	High	0.50	0.50	0.50	
	Very High	0.00	0.00	0.00	

User Interface Design

The user interface diagram for the proposed employee mental workload prediction Information system provides a comprehensive view of the system's hierarchical structure. The diagram begins with the Login and Register page, which serves as the entry point for all users.

Under the Login page, there are three distinct user types: Employee, Employer, and Admin. Each user type has a unique set of pages that they can access, reflecting their different roles and responsibilities within the system.

Employer: Once logged in, the Employer is directed to a Dashboard Page, which serves as a central hub for all their activities. From here, they can navigate to their Profile Page to view or update their personal information. The EEG Assessment Page allows the Employer to perform EEG Assessment. Lastly, the Employee List Page provides a comprehensive list of all the employees under their purview.

Employee: The Employee user type has a similar structure to the Employer, with access to the Dashboard Page, Profile Page, and EEG Assessment Page. However, they do not have access to the Employee List Page, reflecting their individual role within the system.

Admin: The admin user type has a distinct panel separate from the other users. This panel provides a broader view of the system, with access to the Employee List, Employer List, and Company List. This allows the admin to manage all aspects of the system, including users and companies. However, this admin is not a use case and for the target employers or employees.

Figure 4 provides a clear and concise representation of the system's user interface design, highlighting the different user types and their respective access levels. Screenshots of the web-based system are provided in the appendix for further reference. Some sample user interfaces are shown in the Appendix.

Figure 4. User interface design

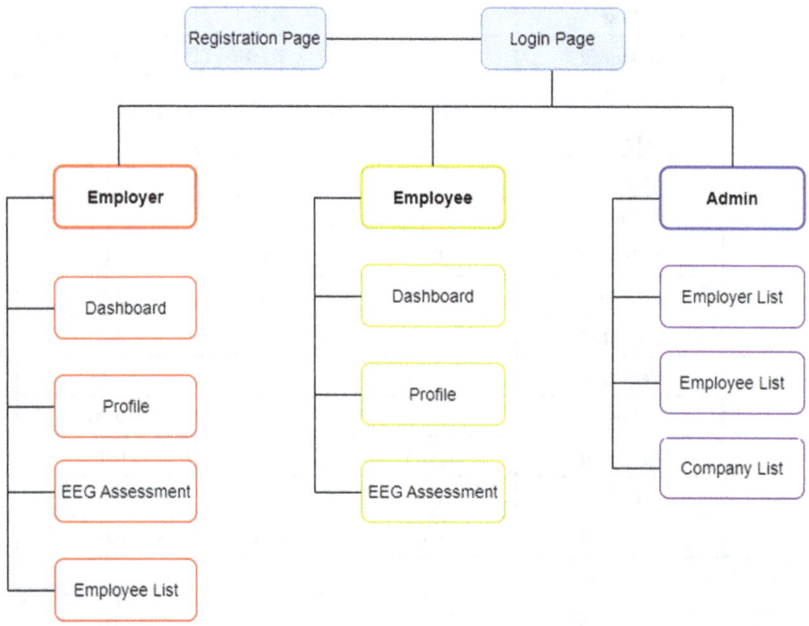

System Testing and Evaluation

Testing Strategy

The testing strategy for this study is comprehensive and robust, designed to ensure that the system is operational and meets both system requirements and user expectations. The strategy comprises four key stages: Unit Testing, Integration Testing, System Testing, and Acceptance Testing. Each stage plays a crucial role in the overall testing process, focusing on different aspects of the system to ensure its functionality, reliability, and usability.

1. Unit Testing

Unit Testing forms the first stage of our testing strategy. This process involves testing the smallest testable parts of the system, such as individual pieces of code or standalone functions, to ensure they function as expected. For instance, a function responsible for user registration is tested with various inputs to verify field validation and form submission. The advantage of Unit Testing lies in its ability to identify and rectify errors early in the development process, saving time and resources in the long run.

2. Integration Testing

Following Unit Testing, we proceed to Integration Testing. This stage involves testing the interaction between different modules or components of the system once they have been combined. The aim is to ensure that data exchange between these modules' functions correctly. For example, the Analytical Dashboard module might be tested in conjunction with the Data Classification Module to ensure that the data generated is displayed correctly. Integration Testing is crucial as it helps detect errors that only become apparent when parameters are passed between modules.

3. System Testing

The third stage of our testing strategy is System Testing. At this point, all modules have been integrated, and the system is tested to verify if it meets the desired functional and non-functional requirements. This involves testing the entire system in a full test cycle, mimicking the actual user flow. Testers interact with the system via its Graphical User Interface (GUI), using both correct and incorrect inputs to assess how the system responds.

4. Acceptance Testing

The final stage of our testing strategy is Acceptance Testing. This stage is performed to verify whether the final system meets the criteria for delivery to end users. It involves a user acceptance survey, which provides valuable feedback on the system's functionality, user experience, and navigation.

Test Cases

The test cases presented in this section are designed to evaluate the functionality and performance of the Web-Based Employee Mental Workload Information System that utilizes EEG data and deep learning algorithms. The test cases cover the three modules of the system, including Account Management Module, Data Classification Module, and Analytical Dashboard Module, it is aimed at ensuring that the system meets the stated functional and non- functional requirements. The below tables show the list of test cases in each module.

Summary of Test Results

The summary of the test results is shown in Table 5. In addition to the testing strategies, the User acceptance survey was conducted as part of the evidence for test results in the evaluation of the Employee Mental Workload Information System. The survey was conducted online and a total of fifteen responses were collected. The survey aimed to gather feedback from users regarding their acceptance and satisfaction with the system. The survey includes the age range, education level, familiarity with deep learning, opinions on AI determining the mental workload status, opinions on the system towards mental workload management, and the system feedback from the respondents.

Based on the survey results, it can be concluded that most of the respondents are not familiar with deep learning but most of them believed that AI technologies can help to analyze EEG data to determine mental workload status. Furthermore, most of the respondents think that this system can effectively help to manage the mental workload of employees.

Around 60% of the respondents agree that the system's features meet their expectations and requirements. Other than that, most of the respondents agree with the scope, and good in features of the overall system.

Table 5. Summary of test results

Module	Test Case ID	Description	Test Case Result
Account Management	TC 01	Employer and Employee login to the system with correct email address and password.	Pass
	TC 02	Employer and Employee will fail to login with incorrect email address and password.	Pass
	TC 03	Employer and Employee log out of the system.	Pass
	TC 04	Employer register account	Pass
	TC 05	Employee register account.	Pass
	TC 06	Employee and Employer can view and update personal information.	Pass
	TC 07	Admin manages user account.	Pass
Data Classification	TC 08	Employer and Employee perform EEG assessment.	Pass
	TC 09	Employer and Employee will fail to perform EEG assessment with unacceptable file format	Pass
	TC 10	System predicts the mental workload by using uploaded EEG data	Pass
Analytical Dashboard	TC 11	System displays the dashboard with EEG prediction result	Pass
	TC 12	Employer view the list of his/her employees	Pass
	TC 13	Employer can view the employee's EEG Chart	Pass
	TC 14	System provides proper advice based on EEG results	Pass

CONCLUSION AND FUTURE WORK

The developed Employee Mental Workload Information System using EEG data offers several advantages over similar existing systems. Its unique incorporation of EEG assessment provides a more accurate and data-driven approach to measuring mental workload. By leveraging EEG analysis, organizations can gain valuable insights into employees' cognitive states, enabling better workforce management.

The system's Account Management Module enhances user experience by allowing efficient registration, login, and personal information updates for both employees and employers. This streamlined functionality ensures appropriate access rights and adds convenience to the system.

The Analytical Dashboard Module offers visual representations of EEG prediction results, empowering employers to make informed decisions and allocate resources effectively. It provides a summarized overview of employees' mental workload, facilitating comprehensive workload management within organizations.

However, the system does have limitations. It currently lacks flexibility in data visualization options, restricting users to default chart types. Additionally, the system only accepts text file formats for EEG data upload, potentially inconveniencing users with data in alternative formats. Compared to existing stress management solutions, the system's combination of EEG assessment and deep learning surpasses subjective self-assessment methods. It offers more accurate workload predictions. However, the requirement for specialized equipment for EEG data acquisition may limit its practicality in certain settings.

In conclusion, the Employee Mental Workload Information System excels in leveraging EEG assessment, efficient Account Management, and informative Analytical Dashboard functionalities. Improvements can be made to enhance data visualization options and broaden file format compatibility. Overall, the system presents an innovative approach to managing employee mental workload, requiring careful consideration for successful implementation and adoption.

The proposed web-based application leverages deep learning algorithms and publicly accessible EEG datasets to monitor and manage employee mental workload. It provides an invaluable tool for employers, offering real-time monitoring of mental workload status, and a user-friendly analytical dashboard for tracking mental workload status.

The objectives of proposing a deep learning model for predicting mental workload, developing a comprehensive information system, and providing an informative dashboard have been achieved in an integrated manner, enhancing the system's effectiveness. All these elements work in synergy, with the deep learning model powering the predictions, the web-based information system facilitating real-time monitoring, and the dashboard allowing easy tracking and comprehension of mental workload data.

The system was developed using Django and React technologies, demonstrating the potential for high-level Python web frameworks in the creation of sophisticated data analysis tools. Django, a Python-based web framework, provided the backbone for the application, while React, a JavaScript library, contributed to building a user interface that is both interactive and user-friendly. These technologies were critical in achieving the design goals of the system.

As we look towards the future, the system has immense potential for refinement and expansion. Enhanced precision in mental workload predictions can be pursued through the utilization of more extensive and diverse EEG datasets. Adding flexibility in data visualization on the dashboard and increasing the range of acceptable EEG data file formats are also worth considering for improved user experience. The integration of different machine learning or deep learning models may be explored for potential advancements in performance and accuracy of predictions. Finally, considering the practical constraints of EEG data collection, the incorporation of more readily available mental workload measurement methods could be considered.

In short, the Employee Mental Workload Information System marks a substantial stride in the field of employee workload management. It is a testament to the power of blending deep learning, EEG analysis, and advanced web technologies for the development of practical and efficient solutions. While there are opportunities for further enhancement, the system serves as a robust base for the future evolution of mental workload prediction tools.

REFERENCES

Alifah, S. K., Widyantara, P. B., & Puspasari, M. A. (2019). The Effect of Mental Workload towards Mental Fatigue on Customer Care Agent Using Electroencephalogram. *Proceedings of the 5th International Conference on Industrial and Business Engineering*, 173–177. 10.1145/3364335.3364367

Aoki, K. (2017). Mental Fatigue Measurement Using Visual Synchronization Tasks. *Proceedings of the 6th International Conference on Bioinformatics and Biomedical Science*, 37–43. 10.1145/3121138.3121164

Appel, T., Sevcenko, N., Wortha, F., Tsarava, K., Moeller, K., Ninaus, M., Kasneci, E., & Gerjets, P. (2019). Predicting Cognitive Load in an Emergency Simulation Based on Behavioral and Physiological Measures. *2019 International Conference on Multimodal Interaction*, 154–163. 10.1145/3340555.3353735

Asgher, U., Khalil, K., Ayaz, Y., Ahmad, R., & Khan, M. J. (2020). Classification of Mental Workload (MWL) using Support Vector Machines (SVM) and Convolutional Neural Networks (CNN). *2020 3rd International Conference on Computing, Mathematics and Engineering Technologies (ICoMET)*, 1–6. 10.1109/iCoMET48670.2020.9073799

Bellamy, S. (2021). *Can mental workload in EEG tasks be classified using machine learning algorithms?* Northeastern University. doi:10.17760/D20399921

Chen, B., Wang, L., Li, B., & Liu, W. (2022). Work stress, mental health, and employee performance. *Frontiers in Psychology*, *13*, 1006580. doi:10.3389/fpsyg.2022.1006580 PMID:36425815

Cho, Y. (2021). Rethinking Eye-Blink: Assessing Task Difficulty through Physiological Representation of Spontaneous Blinking. *Proceedings of the 2021 CHI Conference on Human Factors in Computing Systems*. 10.1145/3411764.3445577

Couceiro, R., Duarte, G., Durães, J., Castelhano, J., Duarte, C., Teixeira, C., Branco, M. C., de Carvalho, P., & Madeira, H. (2019). Biofeedback Augmented Software Engineering: Monitoring of Programmers' Mental Effort. *Proceedings of the 41st International Conference on Software Engineering: New Ideas and Emerging Results*, 37–40. 10.1109/ICSE-NIER.2019.00018

Das Chakladar, D., Dey, S., Roy, P. P., & Dogra, D. P. (2020). EEG-based mental workload estimation using deep BLSTM-LSTM network and evolutionary algorithm. *Biomedical Signal Processing and Control*, *60*, 101989. doi:10.1016/j.bspc.2020.101989

Eraslan, E., Can, G., & Atalay, K. (2016). Mental workload assessment using a fuzzy multi-criteria method [Procjena mentalnog opterećenja primjenom neizrazite metode s više kriterija]. *Tehnicki Vjesnik (Strojarski Fakultet)*, *23*(3).

Jaiswal, D., Chatterjee, D., Sarkar, A. S. M., Ramakrishnan, R. K., Pal, A., & Ghosh, R. (2023). Assessment of Mental Workloads Using Differential Dermal Potentials Recorded from in and around Ear. *Proceedings of the 8th Workshop on Body-Centric Computing Systems*, 1–6. 10.1145/3597061.3597257

Keikhosrokiani, P. (2019). Perspectives in the development of mobile medical information systems: Life cycle, management, methodological approach and application. In *Perspectives in the Development of Mobile Medical Information Systems*. Life Cycle, Management, Methodological Approach and Application. doi:10.1016/C2018-0-02485-8

Keikhosrokiani, P. (2021). The role of m-commerce literacy on the attitude towards using e-torch in Penang, Malaysia. In *E-business In The 21st Century* (2nd ed.). Essential Topics And Studies. doi:10.1142/9789811231841_0013

Keikhosrokiani, P. (2022a). Big Data Analytics for Healthcare: Datasets, Techniques, Life Cycles, Management, and Applications. doi:10.1016/C2021-0-00369-2

Keikhosrokiani, P. (2022b). Handbook of Research on Consumer Behavior Change and Data Analytics in the Socio-Digital Era. doi:10.4018/978-1-6684-4168-8

Keikhosrokiani, P., & Asl, M. P. (2022). Handbook of Research on Artificial Intelligence Applications in Literary Works and Social Media. doi:10.4018/978-1-6684-6242-3

Keikhosrokiani, P., & Kamaruddin, N. S. A. B. (2022). IoT-Based In-Hospital-In-Home Heart Disease Remote Monitoring System with Machine Learning Features for Decision Making. In Studies in Computational Intelligence (Vol. 1021). doi:10.1007/978-3-030-97929-4_16

Keikhosrokiani, P., Mustaffa, N., & Zakaria, N. (2018). Success factors in developing iHeart as a patient-centric healthcare system: A multi-group analysis. *Telematics and Informatics*, *35*(4), 753–775. Advance online publication. doi:10.1016/j.tele.2017.11.006

Keikhosrokiani, P., Mustaffa, N., Zakaria, N., & Abdullah, R. (2020). Assessment of a medical information system: The mediating role of use and user satisfaction on the success of human interaction with the mobile healthcare system (iHeart). *Cognition Technology and Work*, *22*(2), 281–305. Advance online publication. doi:10.1007/s10111-019-00565-4

Keikhosrokiani, P., Mustaffa, N., Zakaria, N., & Sarwar, M. I. (2012). A proposal to design a location-based mobile cardiac emergency system (lmces). In *Global Telehealth 2012* (pp. 83–92). IOS Press. doi:10.3233/978-1-61499-152-6-83

Lim, W. L., Sourina, O., & Wang, L. P. (2018). STEW: Simultaneous Task EEG Workload Data Set. *IEEE Transactions on Neural Systems and Rehabilitation Engineering*, *26*(11), 2106–2114. doi:10.1109/TNSRE.2018.2872924 PMID:30281467

Mognon, A., Jovicich, J., Bruzzone, L., & Buiatti, M. (2011). ADJUST: An automatic EEG artifact detector based on the joint use of spatial and temporal features. *Psychophysiology*, *48*(2), 229–240. doi:10.1111/j.1469-8986.2010.01061.x PMID:20636297

Parveen, F., & Bhavsar, A. (2023). Attention Based 1D-CNN for Mental Workload Classification Using EEG. *Proceedings of the 16th International Conference on PErvasive Technologies Related to Assistive Environments*, 739–745. 10.1145/3594806.3596582

Qu, H., Shan, Y., Liu, Y., Pang, L., Fan, Z., Zhang, J., & Wanyan, X. (2020). Mental Workload Classification Method Based on EEG Independent Component Features. *Applied Sciences (Basel, Switzerland)*, *10*(9), 3036. Advance online publication. doi:10.3390/app10093036

Rahman, T., Ghosh, A. K., Shuvo, M. H., & Rahman, M. (2015). Mental stress recognition using K-nearest neighbor (KNN) classifier on EEG signals. *Int. Conf. Materials, Electronics & Information Engineering (ICMEIE)*, 1–4.

Reid, G. B., & Nygren, T. E. (1988). The Subjective Workload Assessment Technique: A Scaling Procedure for Measuring Mental Workload. In P. A. Hancock & N. Meshkati (Eds.), *Advances in Psychology* (Vol. 52, pp. 185–218). North-Holland. https://doi.org/https://doi.org/10.1016/S0166-4115(08)62387-0

Reimer, B., Mehler, B., Coughlin, J. F., Godfrey, K. M., & Tan, C. (2009). An On-Road Assessment of the Impact of Cognitive Workload on Physiological Arousal in Young Adult Drivers. *Proceedings of the 1st International Conference on Automotive User Interfaces and Interactive Vehicular Applications*, 115–118. 10.1145/1620509.1620531

Rubio Valdehita, S., López Núñez, M. I., López-Higes Sánchez, R., & Díaz Ramiro, E. M. (2017). Development of the CarMen-Q Questionnaire for mental workload assessment. *Psicothema*. Advance online publication. doi:10.7334/psicothema2017.151 PMID:29048320

Teoh Yi Zhe, I., & Keikhosrokiani, P. (2021). Knowledge workers mental workload prediction using optimised ELANFIS. *Applied Intelligence*, *51*(4), 2406–2430. Advance online publication. doi:10.1007/s10489-020-01928-5

Walter, C., Cierniak, G., Gerjets, P., Rosenstiel, W., & Bogdan, M. (2011). *Classifying mental states with machine learning algorithms using alpha activity decline*. ESANN.

Wang, X., Tian, Q., Zhu, M., Wang, Y., Wang, B., Jing, X., Yokoi, H., Li, L., Liu, Z., Huang, W., Chen, S., Liu, Z., & Li, G. (2023). Towards Optimizing the Quality of Long-Term Physiological Signals Monitoring by Using Anhydrous Carbon Paste Electrode. *IEEE Transactions on Biomedical Engineering*, *70*(2), 423–435. doi:10.1109/TBME.2022.3193115 PMID:35867372

Zhu, W., Zhang, C., Liu, C., Yuan, J., Li, X., Wang, Y., & Jiang, C. (2023). Recognition of Pilot Mental Workload in the Simulation Operation of Carrier-Based Aircraft Using the Portable EEG. *Proceedings of the 2023 3rd International Conference on Human Machine Interaction*, 43–49. 10.1145/3604383.3604391

APPENDIX

User Interface Design

Figure 5. Login page

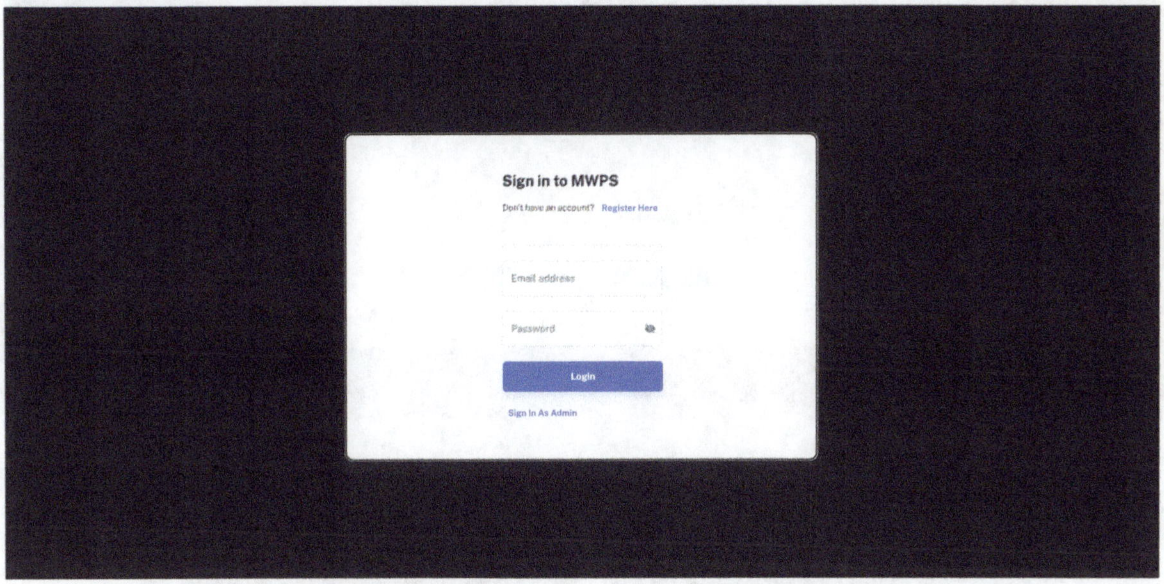

Figure 6. Employer registration page

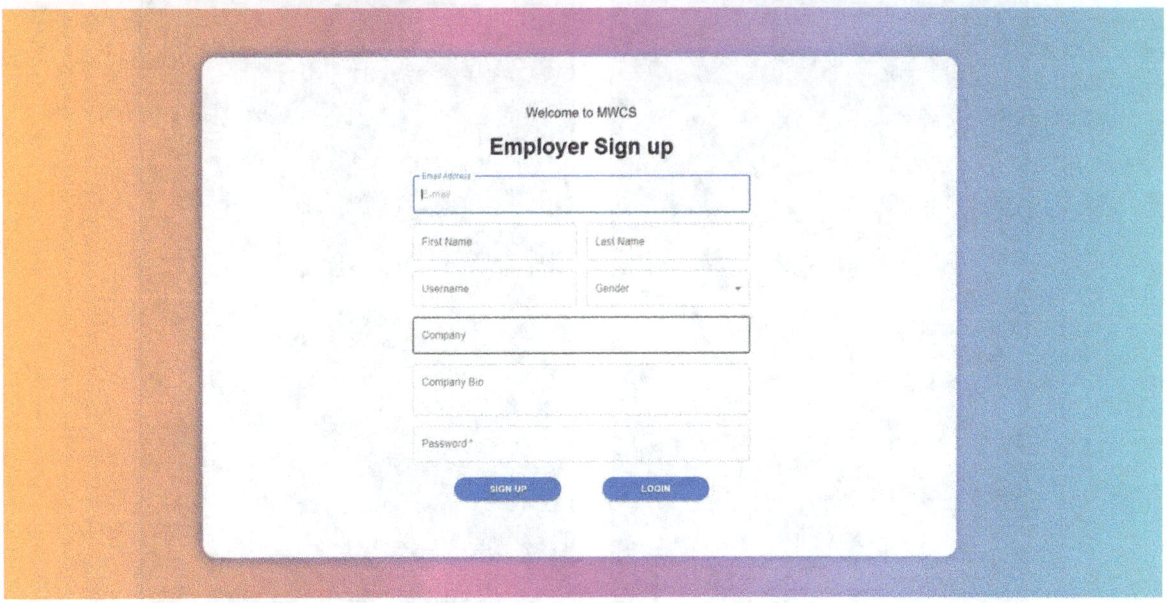

Figure 7. Employee registration page

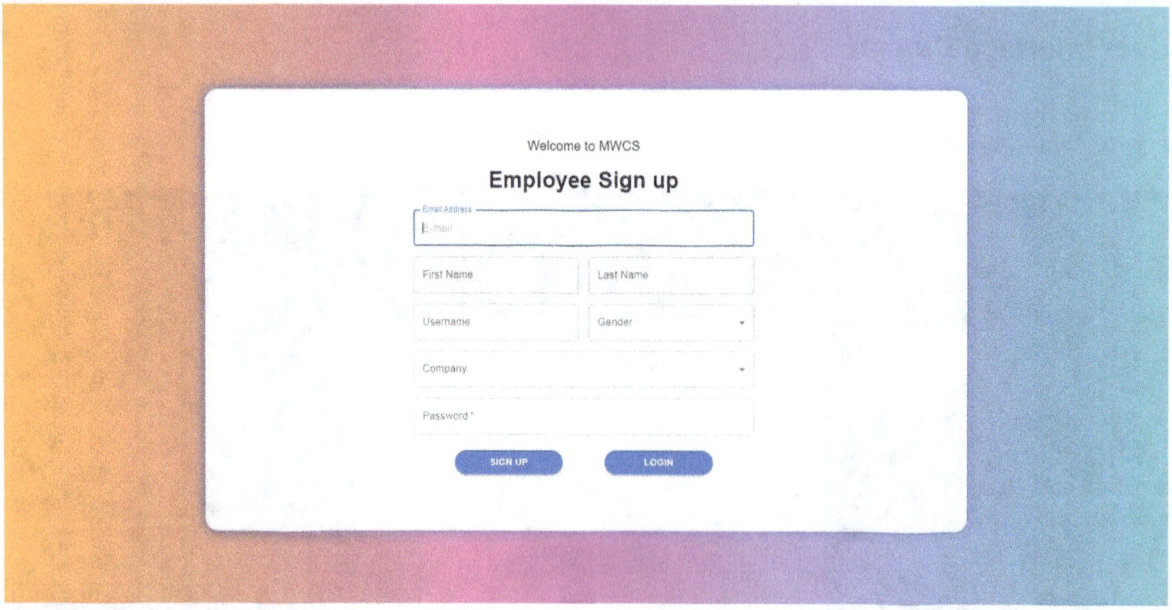

Figure 8. Employee nav bar

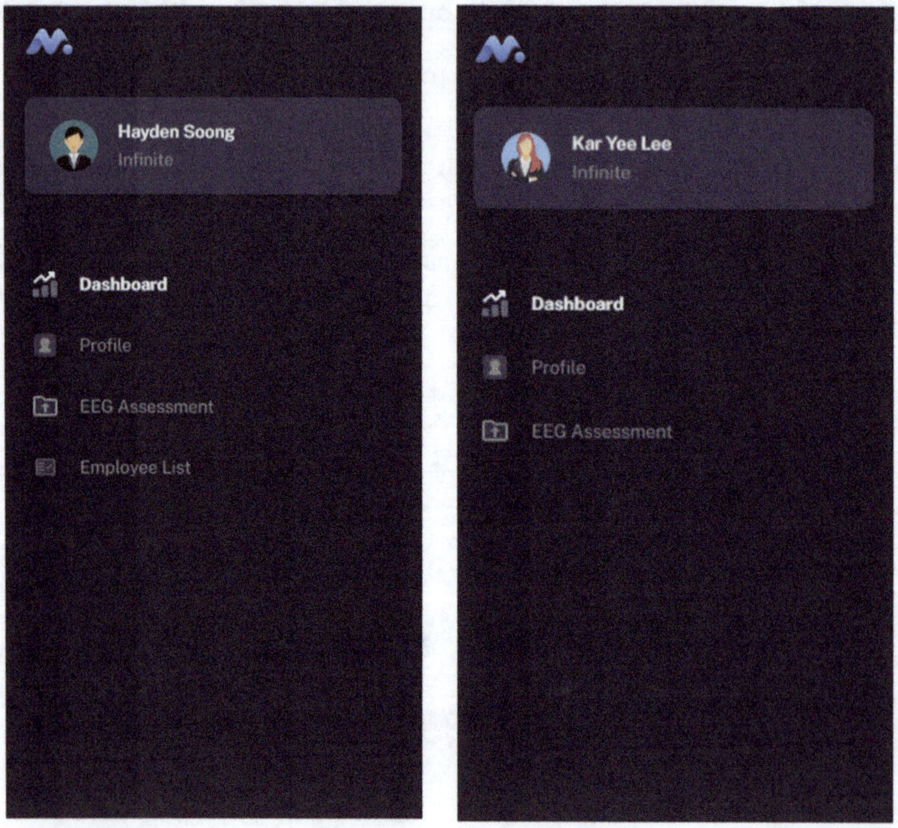

Figure 9. Dashboard

Figure 10. Visualization of weekly and monthly mental workload status distribution

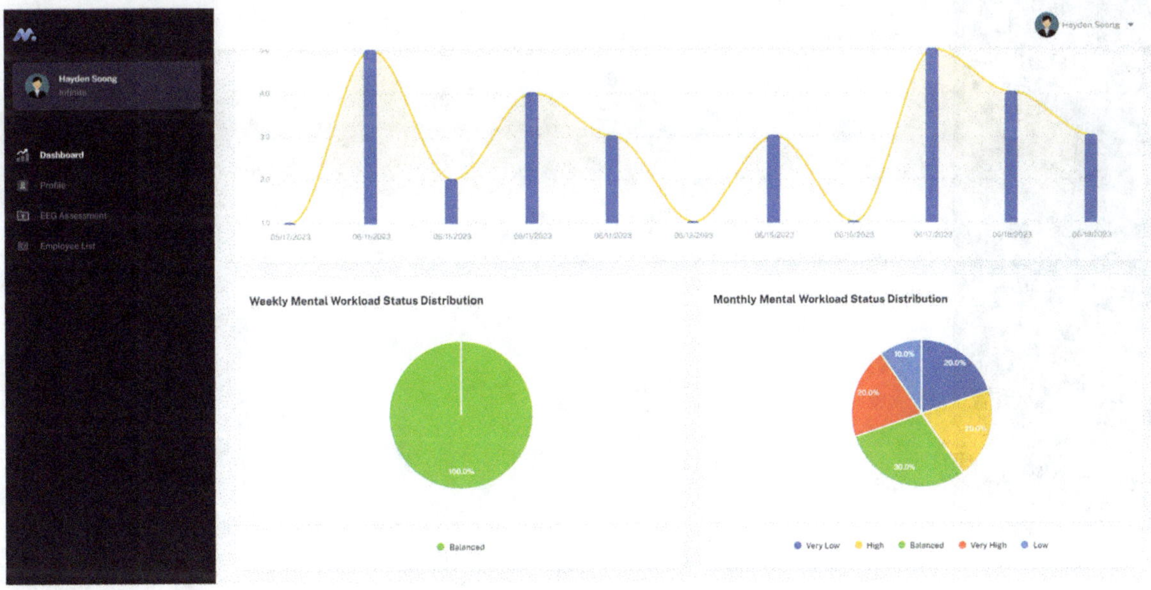

Figure 11. Advice based on EEG results

Figure 12. Tooltip showing mental workload status

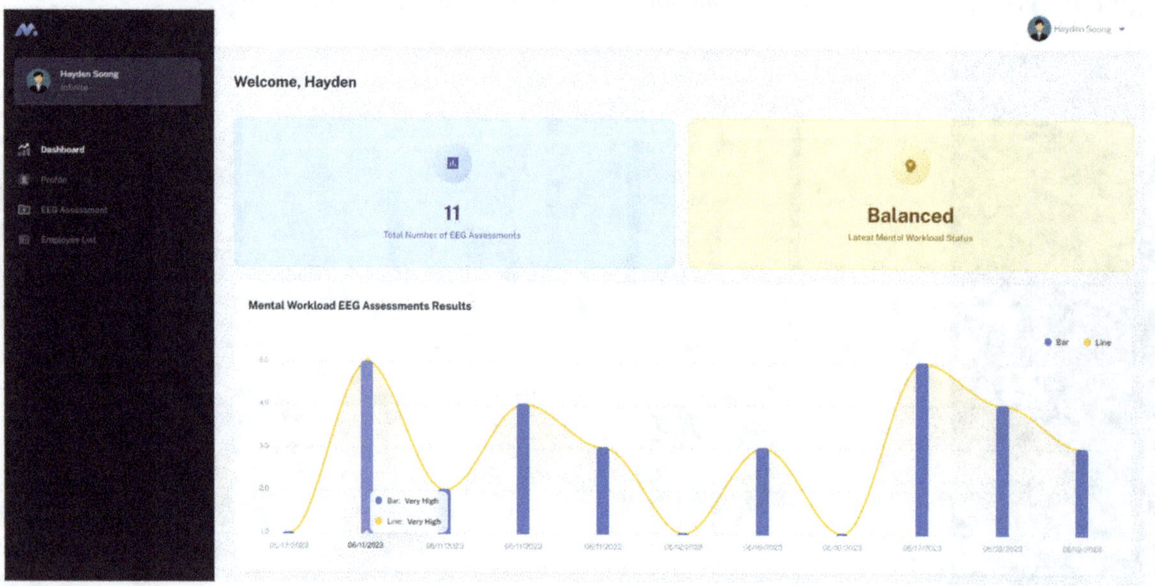

Figure 13. Account popover

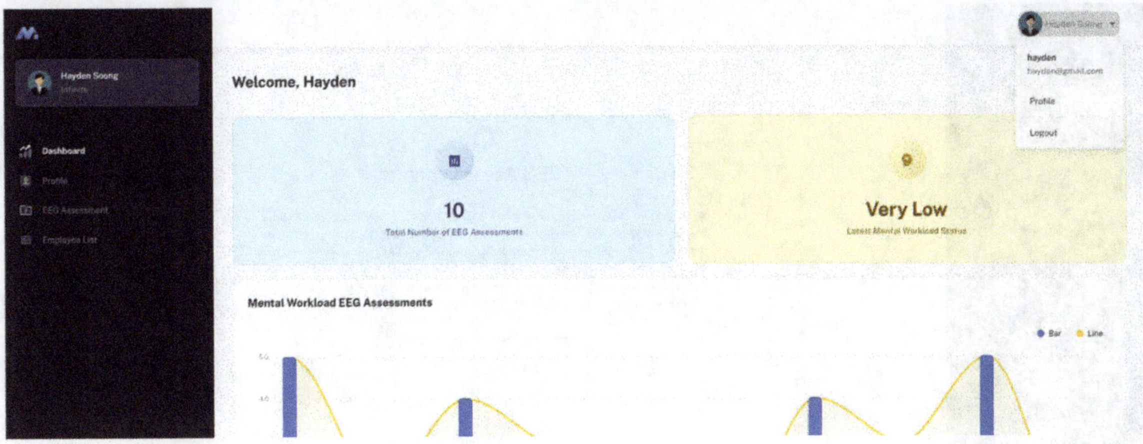

Figure 14. Profile page with update details form

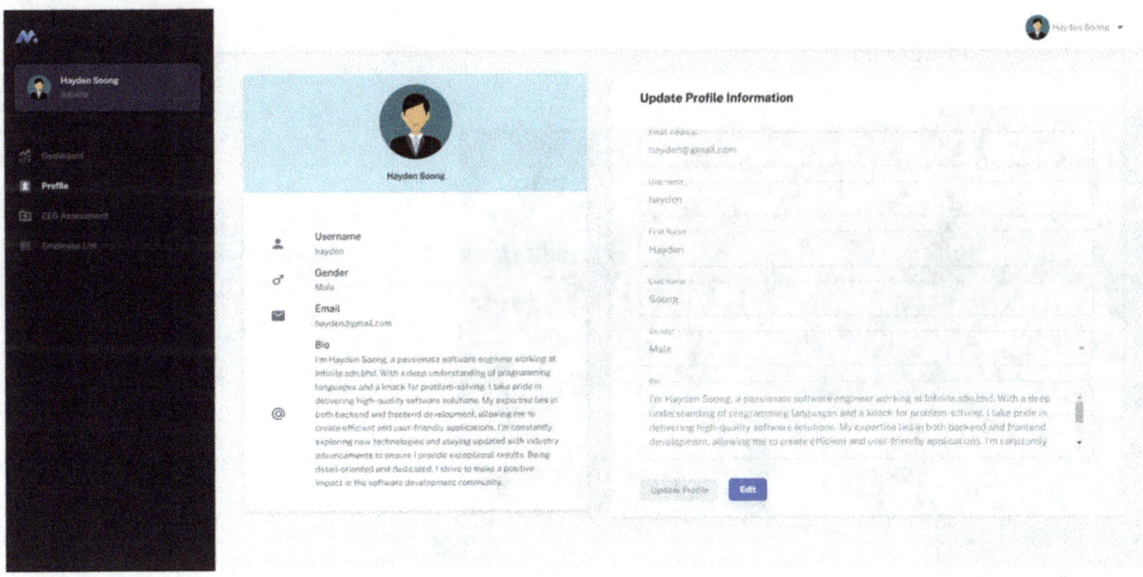

Figure 15. EEG assessment page

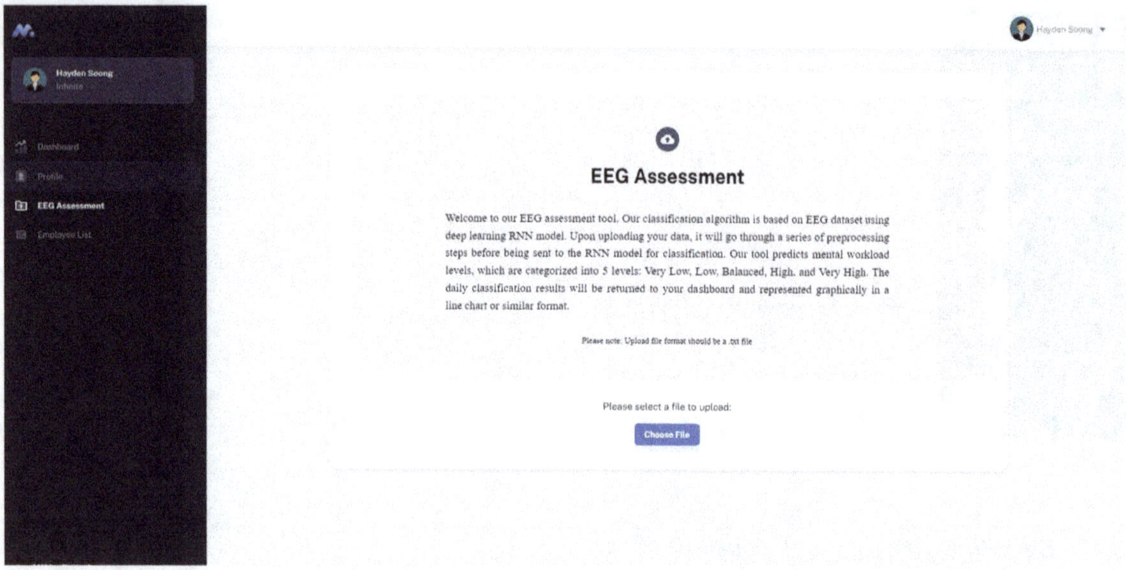

Figure 16. Upload EEG data

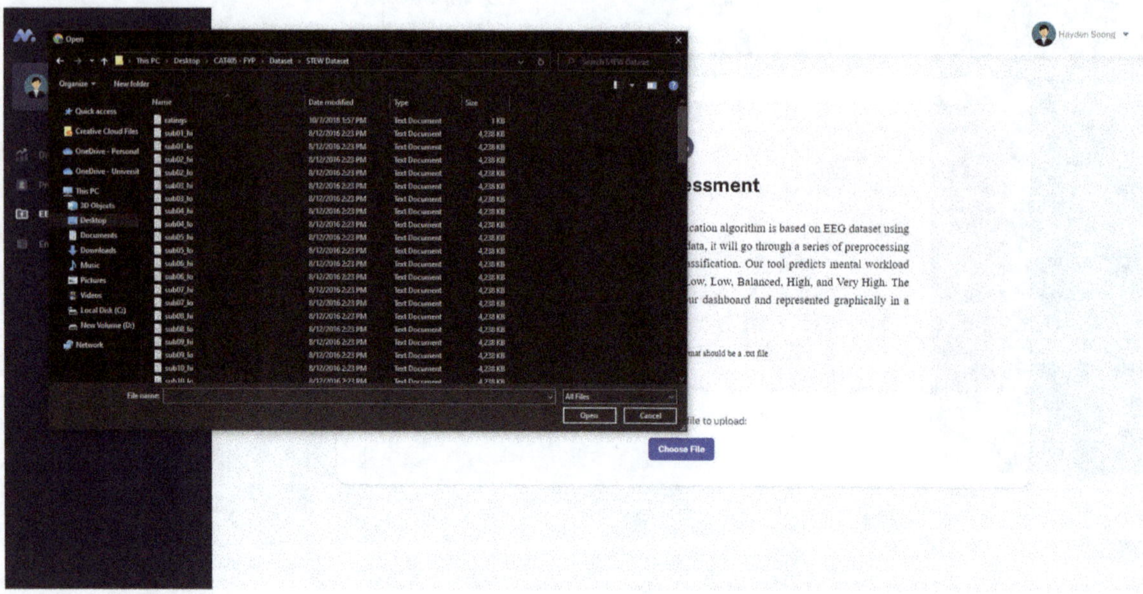

Figure 17. Uploaded EEG data

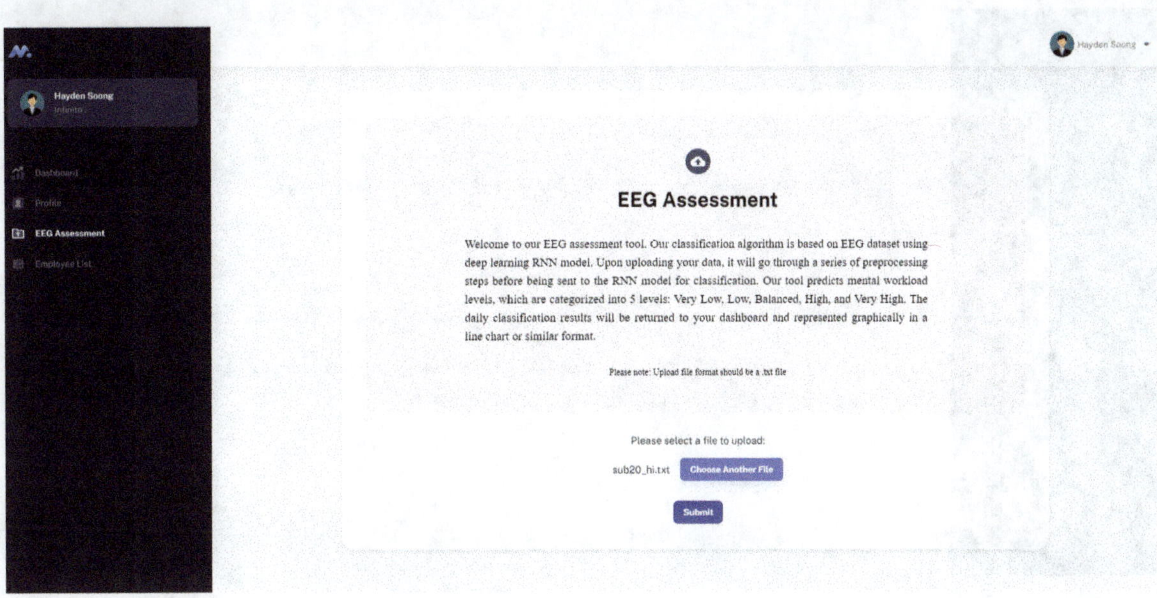

Figure 18. Upload successfully message

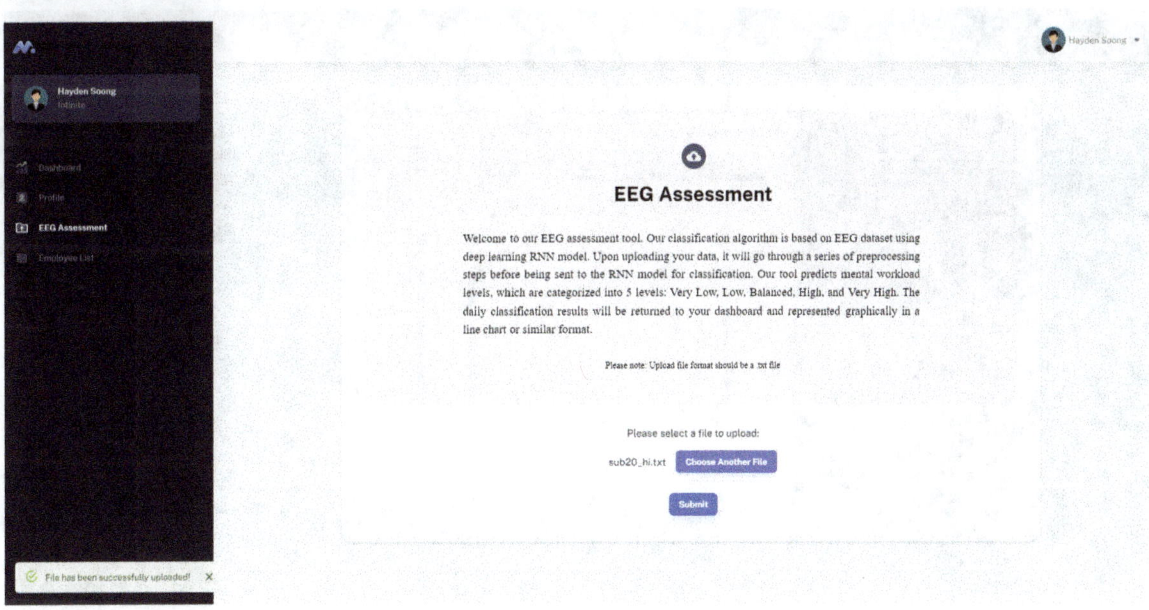

Figure 19. Employee list page

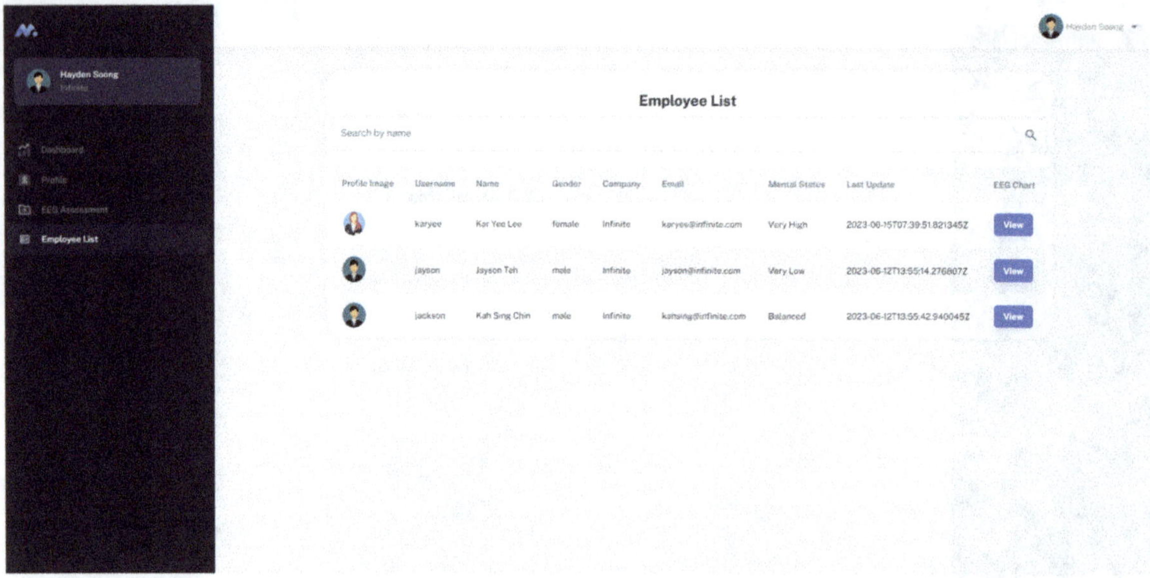

Figure 20. View employee EEG chart

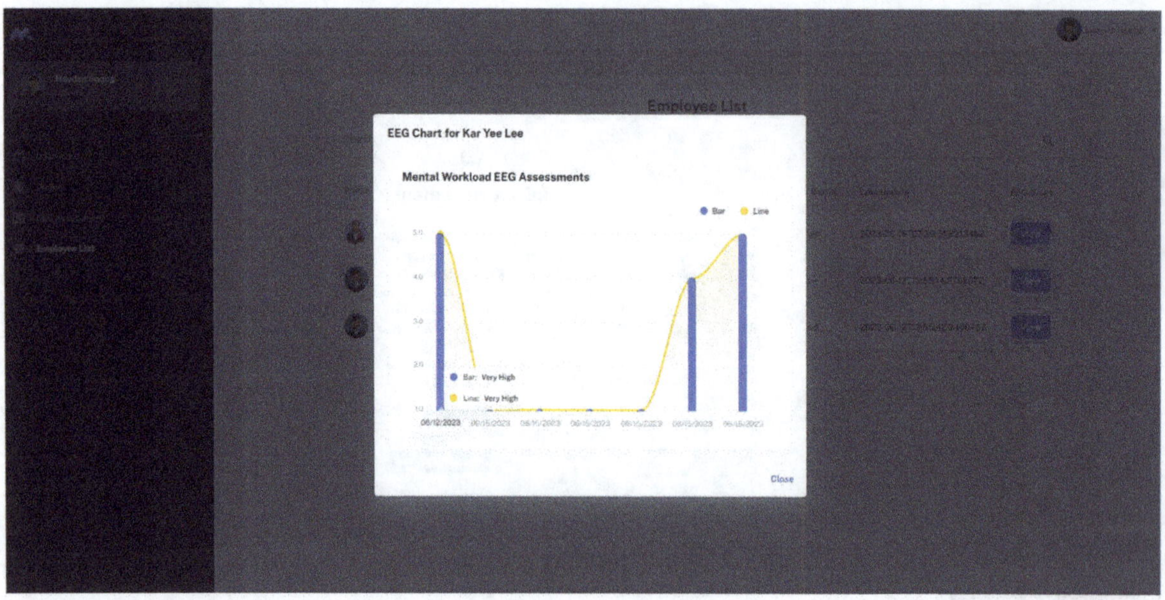

Figure 21. Search bar for specific employee

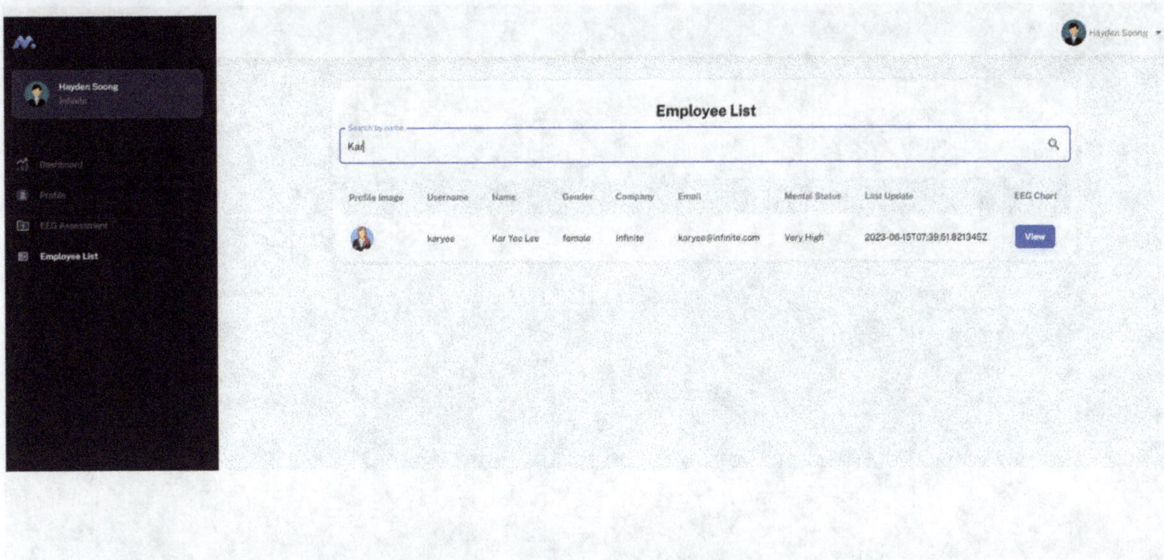

Figure 22. 404 not found page

Figure 23. Admin login panel

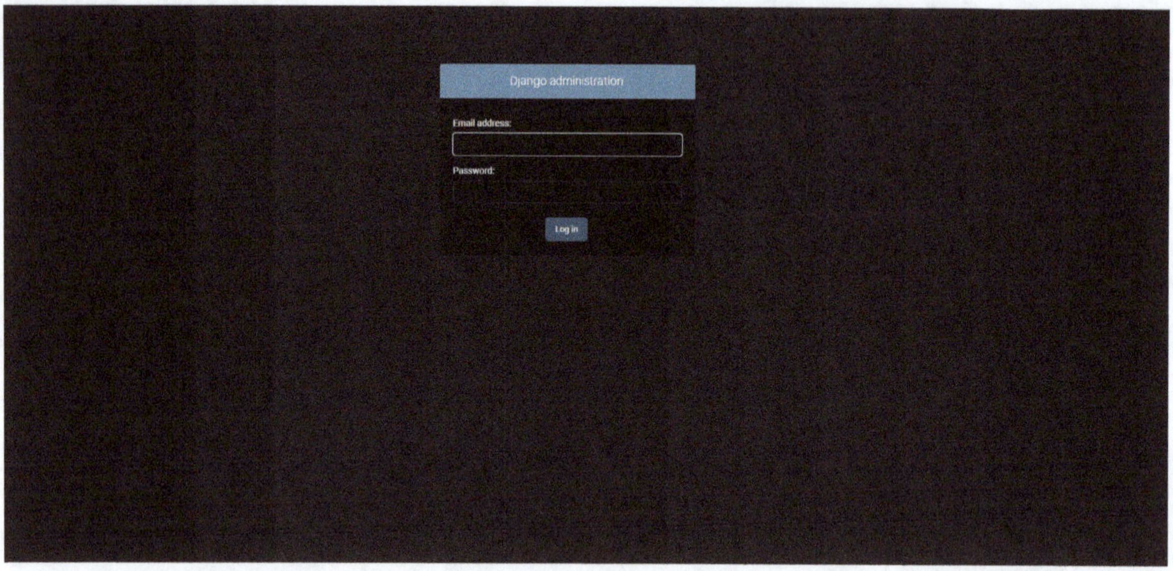

Figure 24. Admin platform

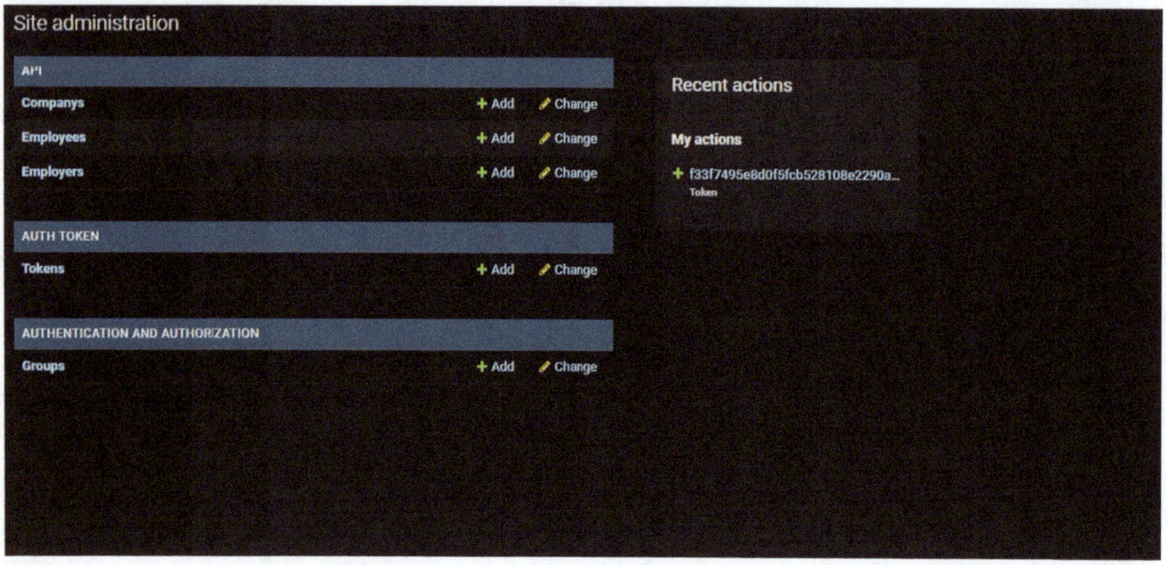

Figure 25. Create user

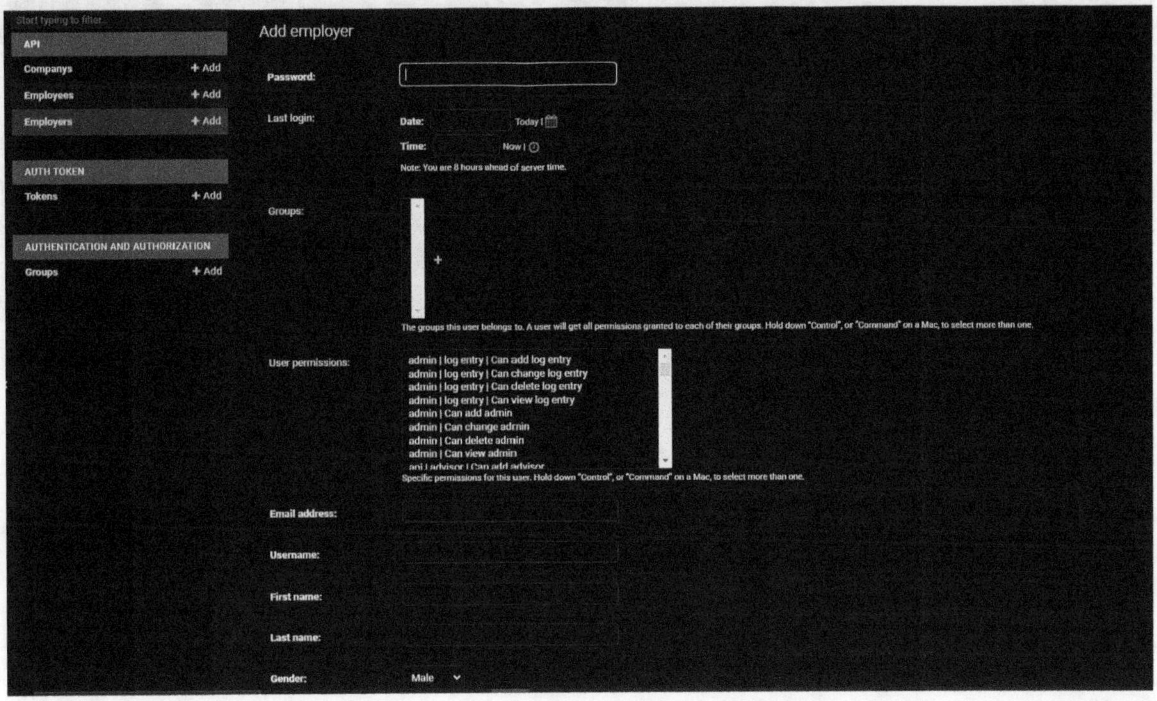

Figure 26. Update personal details

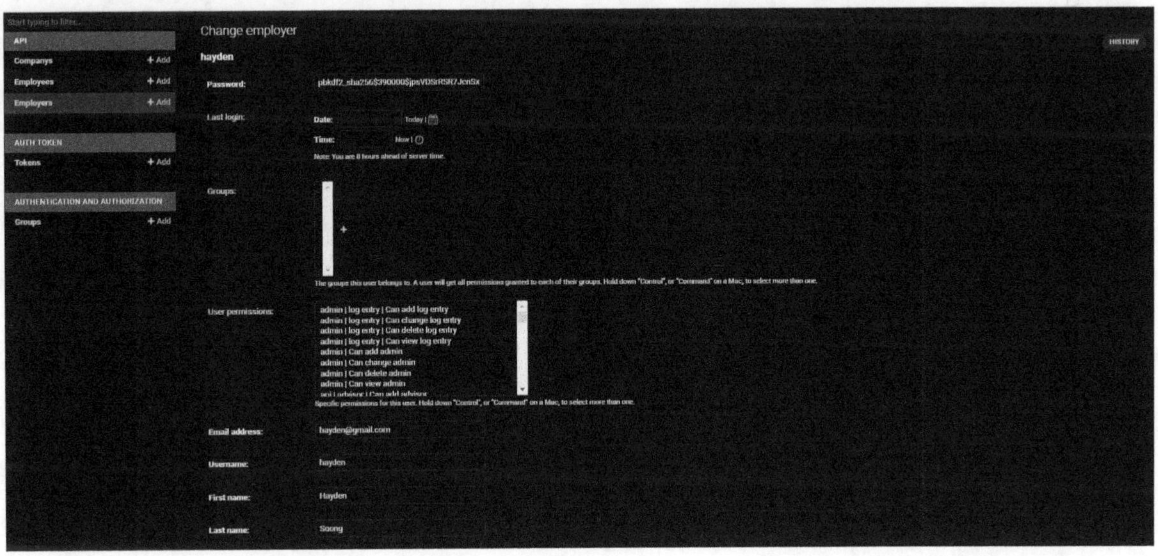

Figure 27. Delete user account

Chapter 12
Inventory Classification and Management System Using Machine Learning and Analytical Dashboard:
A Case Study of a Manufacturing Industry

Renouthani A. P. Jayendran
Universiti Sains Malaysia, Malaysia

Pantea Keikhosrokiani
https://orcid.org/0000-0003-4705-2732
University of Oulu, Finland

Sian Ling Chui
Ideal Vision Integration Sdn. Bhd., Malaysia

ABSTRACT

This chapter explores the integration of inventory management and machine learning, offering a comprehensive guide to harnessing analytical dashboards for improved decision-making. At the core of modern inventory management lies the challenge of balancing stock levels to meet demand without incurring excess or shortfall. Using classification algorithms, this chapter explores how machine learning techniques can revolutionize inventory control, making predictions more accurate and operations more efficient. It provides a detailed walkthrough of implementing these machine learning models, emphasizing their practical benefits in forecasting and classification tasks within inventory management. Furthermore, it demonstrates how Power BI can be leveraged to visualize inventory data, enabling stakeholders to gain insights into stock trends, performance metrics, and the overall health of the supply chain. By integrating machine learning outputs into Power BI dashboards, businesses can achieve a holistic view of their inventory dynamics, facilitating informed decision-making processes.

DOI: 10.4018/979-8-3693-1210-0.ch012

INTRODUCTION

An improvised business processes are anticipated to yield greater returns and good competitive benefits (Heck, Berg, Davarynejad, Duin, & Roskott, 2010). In this view, business processes are seldom termed as 'intangible' (Heck, Berg, Davarynejad, Duin, & Roskott, 2010). There are five crucial steps that need to be considered as key processes in Inventory Management (IM) as follows: forecasting, purchase, goods receipt, storage, and goods issue.

Analysis is executed to determine activities that comprise chances to improvise performance (Heck, Berg, Davarynejad, Duin, & Roskott, 2010). Such activities are improvise material requirements planning, good registration of supplier-contracts, restrict approved suppliers by automatic means, up-to-date budget control, improvise '3-way-match' between packing note, purchase note as well as invoice, good supplier reliability observation, improvise visibility of inventory turnover, enhance visibility of dead stock, decrease waste via good expiration dates information, good rush orders handling and fewer faults via single master data registration (Heck, Berg, Davarynejad, Duin, & Roskott, 2010). To measure reliability and sufficient performance is significant to accomplish the goals set by the top management (Heck, Berg, Davarynejad, Duin, & Roskott, 2010. When organizations experience stock-out on critical inventory items, production halts would happen (Sheakh, 2018). The highly developed inventory management is meant to meet all rising challenges of most corporate entities and this in response to the fact that inventory becomes an asset of distinct feature (Sheakh, 2018). The ROI of inventory management can be seen in aspect of revenue and profits increase, positive atmosphere among employee and increase of overall customer satisfaction (Sheakh, 2018).

The selected manufacturing industry conducts an annual review meeting of all projects, machines, and systems. Therefore, every team leader and system admin present their reports on their projects, systems, or machines to the management team. Throughout the review meeting, management will discuss solutions and improvements for existing projects, systems, or machines with the respective team leads. As a result, all team leaders need to be well-prepared, as they aim to develop a roadmap for the upcoming year after these discussions. However, the system department's admin faces difficulties presenting the performance of the internal system. This internal system comprises of eight subsystems: IMS (Inventory Management), HR (Human Resources Management), CRS (Change Request System), PM (Preventive Maintenance), TNM (Task Notification Management), SF (Service Form), Procurement Management, and SE (Sample Evaluation). Among these subsystems, the admin faces significant challenges with the Inventory Management System (IMS). Therefore, this study focuses on the IMS to address the admin's two main challenges.

The first challenge in the selected manufacturing industry is the *Lack of Visibility in performance*. The IMS lacks visibility regarding its performance when management intends to review annual reporting. The IMS is a system that records all stock-ins and stock-outs. During the stock-out period, specific items are assigned to specific projects; therefore, the details of the projects, along with the date and quantities of items, are recorded to facilitate traceability. However, there is no visibility showing IMS performance beyond mere recording purposes. There is no crucial information on whether the stock meets the project's demand or whether the company is spending hundreds to thousands on purchasing values that are unnecessary for the project or overstocking beyond the actual demand. So far, the IMS admin needs to manually track the records and manage the updates on the IMS weekly. Moreover, the admin has no summarized information about on-loan items that have been returned on time and their condition. The admin must go to the store and check the items for their condition and go through the entries to identify any item that missed its actual return date.

The second problem noticed in the selected manufacturing industry is *the Imprecise Annual Report*. The company's second problem is come up with annual precise report to present during annual meeting. Currently, the admin must manually compile the data and interpret the data using Excel. The report is not informative nor straight-forward, as it consists of data with few words that concludes whole interpretation. Thus, presenting the report is confusing and some important information might be misinterpreted. The current report is complex to understand and difficult to wrap up proper decisions due to the limited visualization tool.

Therefore, this study aims to find the relationship between supply and demand by plotting line graph through classification method, to identify over-stock and under-stock in IMS and to know about the next demand item using different classification algorithms, and finally develop an analytical dashboard required for IMS annual reporting, tracking, and decision making.

LITERATURE REVIEW

ABC Analysis

ABC Analysis and Just in Time are most common and effective inventory management techniques. According to Liu & Wu, (2014), ABC analysis uses mathematical statistics method and involve wide factors corresponding to the property weight that classified into A, B and C. These 3-classification features are classified by priority level (Bialas et al., 2020; Kučera & Suk, 2019; Liu & Wu, 2014). These categories allow managers to concentrate on crucial A items and spend the least time on insignificant many C items. The traditional ABC analysis is performed based on only 1 criterion, the annual dollar usage of SKU (stock-keeping units). The rule is based on either 80-20 or 90-10 rule (Chen et al., 2008). This rule recommends that number of SKUs in 'A' item list is lower than the total number of SKUs. ABC analysis can be conducted by selecting acceptable criterion to classify SKU. Then, gather the necessity information then calculate criterion I. of each SKU and organize SKUs in descending order of criterion I. Afterwards, cumulative percentage of SKUs and its equivalent cumulative percentage of criterion I is calculated.

The ABC analysis is criticized because the classification merely is based single criterion (Chen et al., 2008). In most of the situations, other criteria are crucially playing a role in deciding of which group an SKU must be classified in. Other criteria can be considered is datedness, fixability, urgency and time lead. Business processes of the enterprise inventory management categorisation is affected highly in inventory problems and not merely on the information result sharing. ABC analysis in inventory stock management implementation achieves efficiency, improvise profit margins, and increase efficiency of the management. It creates an appropriate level of control over each inventory category. However, there are concerns that the inventory classification based on the single criterion of ABC analysis might not meet all of an organization's inventory control system need (Saeed et al., 2023). Therefore, organizations are required to implement proper control policies by determining the most effective criteria for their inventory classification. Moreover, a two-fold improvement is required. This involves using inventory management with the aim of reducing the organization's inventory levels and holding costs by avoiding overstock and applying an agent system to automate inventory management processes. This system should also timely respond to demand deviations from forecasted demand by making corrections in replenishment policies. This is because a timely reaction to changes in the environment can lead to better results, which can be achieved either by human decision-making or a decision-support system. This involves comparing forecasted demand with actual demand and then making the appropriate corrections.

Just in Time

The Just in Time (JIT) technique, known as a Japanese philosophy, is rational in its approach to assembly, aiming to have the right items in the right quality and quantity, and at the opportune time (Atnafu & Balda, 2018). With the use of JIT, there are increases in quality and profits, improved effectiveness, enhanced communication, reduced costs, and a decrease in waste. The characteristic of JIT is a process designed to prepare for an immediate response to demand without the need for overstocking, either by the desire of the approach application or as a concern for wastefulness. This approach further emphasizes that the main objective of the JIT technique is to achieve zero inventory. The less a firm spends on storing and handling inventory, the less it needs to discount for outdated quality. Empirical results show that JIT, which includes the layout of equipment, supplier quality, reduction in setup time, and pull production, has a positive impact on operational excellence in Jordanian industrial companies (Haraisa, 2017). To enhance and achieve operational excellence and a competitive advantage, the industrial firms need to significantly focus on their JIT systems, which consist of these four variables (Al Haraisa, 2017). This technique can also be applied to this study, as it covers the second objective of the study.

Inventory Business Process

Improvised business processes are expected to yield greater returns and significant competitive advantages (van Heck et al., 2010). From this perspective, business processes are sometimes referred to as 'intangible'. Five crucial steps must be considered key processes in Inventory Management (IM), as shown and briefly illustrated in Figure 1 (van Heck et al., 2010). The initial step is forecasting and establishing inputs for scheduling and planning. This process is essential to predict future demand to ensure continuous production. Purchasing is viewed as placing orders for value. A good receipt involves checking when goods arrive. The purchase order is compared with the price and quantity of the arrived goods for the purpose of verification. If the inspection of new goods is cleared, they are then added to stock. Goods are issued according to the client's order requirements, which are conducted in the warehouse.

An analysis is conducted to identify activities that offer opportunities to improve performance. These activities include improving material requirements planning, efficiently registering supplier contracts, limiting approved suppliers through automated means, maintaining up-to-date budget control, enhancing the '3-way-match' process between the packing note, purchase note, and invoice, monitoring supplier reliability effectively, increasing inventory turnover visibility, enhancing visibility of dead stock, reducing waste through accurate expiration date information, handling rush orders effectively, and reducing errors through a single master data registration (Singh et al., 2020; van Heck et al., 2010). Measuring reliability and performance adequately is crucial to achieving the goals set by top management. When an organization experiences a stock-out of a critical inventory item, production halts can occur (Sohail & Sheikh, 2018). Advanced inventory management is designed to meet the rising challenges faced by most corporate entities, in response to the recognition of inventory as an asset with distinct characteristics. The ROI of inventory management is evident in terms of increased revenue and profits, a positive atmosphere among employees, and enhanced overall customer satisfaction. Six crucial techniques were identified including: (1) balanced score card, (2) return on investment, (3) net present value, (4) critical success factors, (5) supply chain operations reference model. From the listed techniques, KPI was chosen as the most suitable and relevant performance metric for IM.

Figure 1. Crucial inventory business process steps (van Heck et al., 2010).

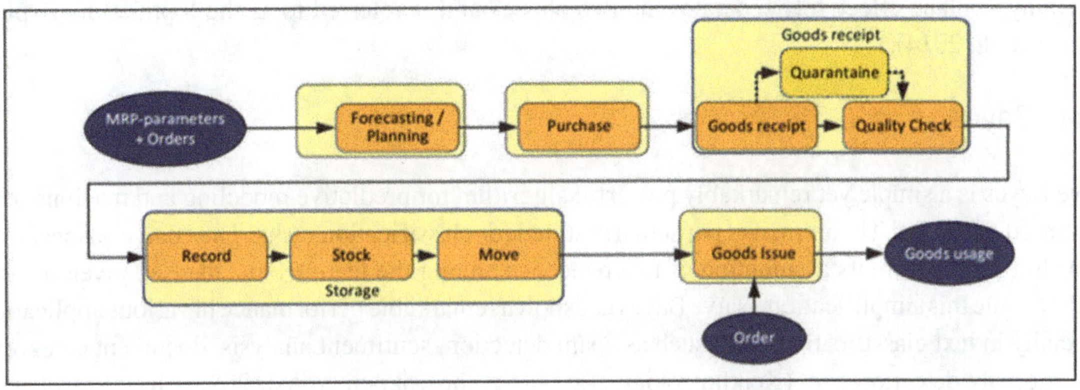

Using Classification Approaches

Random Forest

Random forest is known as most accurate classifier as well as works efficiently especially on large dataset (Abdelrahman & Keikhosrokiani, 2020; Ajesh et al., 2016; Keikhosrokiani, 2022; Keikhosrokiani & Asl, 2022a, 2022b; Zhao & Keikhosrokiani, 2022). Random forest consists of decision trees of combined individual learners. Each of the decision trees is constructed on a different bootstrap sample, which was drawn randomly from the training data. At splitting of each node during the decision tree construction, a random subset of m variables is chosen from its original variable set and best split is based on this m variables are used. Prediction on unknown case constructed are aggregated (major voting for classification). When there is missing data in large set as well as no pre-processing, then random forest can effectively be used for prediction.

K-Nearest Neighbor (KNN)

The K-nearest neighbours (KNN) algorithm is a simple, yet powerful machine learning technique used for both classification and regression problems. Its principle is straightforward: it classifies a new data point based on the majority vote or average of its 'K' nearest neighbours in the feature space (Wang, 2019). KNN calculates the distance between the query example and every training data point to identify the nearest neighbours. It selects the 'K' closest training examples, where 'K' is a user-defined constant. In classification tasks, KNN assigns the label most common among the K nearest neighbours to the query example. For regression tasks, it usually takes the average of the values of its nearest neighbours.

SVM

The support vector machine (SVM) exhibits optimal classification performance with limited training data, and its diagnostic precision is less dependent on the kernel function and parameters, making it suitable for engineering applications (Pisner & Schnyer, 2020). It considers an infinite number of hyperplanes, among which SVM selects the hyperplane that maximizes the margin. The margin refers to the distance between the classifier and the nearest training point (support vector). The chosen maximum margin hyperplane effectively separates the two classes and is referred to as the 'optimal hyperplane' (Bahari et al., 2014).

Naïve Bayes

Naïve Bayes is a simple yet remarkably powerful algorithm for predictive modeling and machine learning. Based on Bayes' Theorem, it is particularly suited for classification tasks. The "naïve" aspect of the algorithm comes from its assumption of independence among the features in a dataset, given the class label. Despite this simplification, Naïve Bayes has shown remarkable performance in various applications, especially in text classification tasks such as spam detection, sentiment analysis, document categorization, anomaly detection, etc. (Keikhosrokiani, 2022; Keikhosrokiani & Asl, 2022a; Keikhosrokiani & Fye, 2023; Keikhosrokiani & Pourya Asl, 2022; Romano et al., 2023; Vishwakarma & Kesswani, 2023; Xian et al., 2022). Naïve Bayes classifier uses probabilistic approach (Redjeki et al., 2015). It estimates opportunities df of conditional class that assumes the attributes are conditionally independent and given the class labeled Y.

However, due to the better performance, random forest classifier is selected for this study to recommend next demand item for admin of IMS. This enables admin to see breakdown from least demand to high demand items (least to most votes). Admin can justify the items of high demand by viewing its class whether those items are in class 'overstock', 'understock' or 'good'. Based on the item class, admin can define stock availability and avoid zero over-stock or under-stock.

Data Visualization

Dashboard design assists industries in displaying crucial data for each performance indicator, recommends ways to collect this data, and illustrates data visualization approaches for better decision- making (Gürdür Broo et al., 2022; Gürdür, Raizer, et al., 2018; Gürdür, Vulgarakis Feljan, et al., 2018). The subjective knowledge of experts plays a significant role in identifying the related KPIs and stakeholders, thus affecting the data visualization design and the dashboard. The analytical dashboard to either hover or click on the visualization feature element to investigate detail about a specific KPI as per shown in supply chain level. While in Warehouse Level, user is able to hover onto bar chart to study the accurate package numbers picked and placed by a specific automated storage and retrieval systems. Finally, in the intelligent agent level, viewer is able to observe well-detailed information by click onto any of the agent and allowing the centre panel of information active for that specific agent.

METHODOLOGY

Data Science Lifecycle

Figure 2 shows the data science lifecycle, which consists of six main steps. The lifecycle starts with business understanding, aligned with the current problem in the selected manufacturing industry. The main issues raised in the selected company was the risk of wrong decision, cash-flow interruption, and customer dissatisfaction to disrupt organization profits. Therefore, this study aims to study the relationship between supply and demand using classification, to identify over-stock and under-stock in IMS using random forest algorithm, to determine the sources and techniques required to extract data from IMS, and to develop analytical dashboard for IMS annual reporting and weekly tracking.

Figure 2. The proposed data science lifecycle adopted from CRISP-DM

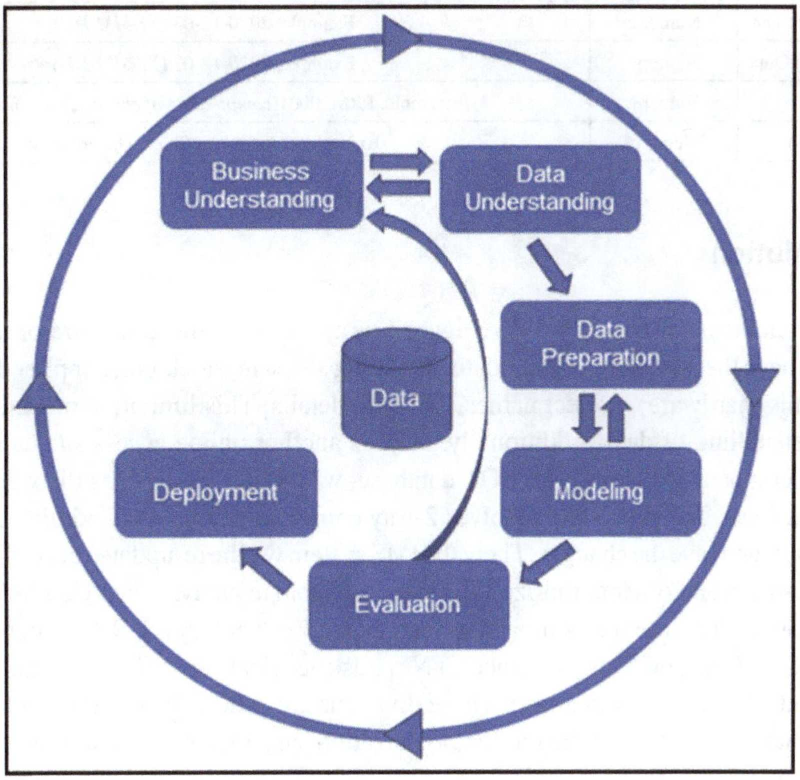

The second step of the development lifecycle focused on data understanding to ensure that data represented on IMS system is tally and accurate as per recorded on the MySQL database. Table 1shows list of attributes, category, and attributes example in the selected manufacturing industry database.

The next step of the proposed lifecycle centred on data cleaning for the collected data thoroughly and constructing new attributes, which may be helpful for future work. Integrating and formatting data as required in this step to store all data values in proper manner. Afterwards, in the modelling step,

Random Forest Model was developed based on the understock and overstock auto generated data. This model helps to output next demand item that admin need to consider on its stock availability. Then, the analytical dashboard was developed using PowerBI. In the next step, the performance of the classifier is evaluated, and the analytical dashboard usability is tested by the admin and other users in the selected industry. Finally, the proposed classification model and analytical dashboard are modified according to the users' comments and deployed onto the industry system. A full guidance is given to the admin to have hands-on the Dashboard.

Table 1. List of attributes, category and attributes example

Attributes	Category	Attributes Examples
Category	Categorical	Example: camera, lens, light source, controller, dongle, cables, monitor, PC, etc.
Part Number & Serial Number	Numeric	Example: SN124679. Both part number and serial number may have same format (*consists of both char + integer*).
Date Stock In & Stock Out	Numeric	Example: 2020-12-03 (*YY-MM-DD*)
Date Loan In & Loan Out	Numeric	Example: 2020-12-03 (*YY-MM-DD*)
Project Name	Numeric	Example: PRM20001(*combination of character and integer*).
Class (*New attributes*)	Categorical	Example: Good, Over-Stock, Under-Stock

Proposed Solution

In the selected manufacturing industry, IMS (Figure 3) is a system where administrators and other authorized employees have the authority to enter data, including stock-in, stock-out, supplier details, customer details, part details (hardware), project names, and loan details. This limitation on personnel in charge is to prevent mishandling of data. Additionally, there is another online access site called Ipage. Ipage is a web hosting company that uses a MySQL database, with PhpMyAdmin as the web application for managing the database. The procedure involves 2-way communication where admin can directly make changes on MySQL and save the changes. Then, the IMS system will be re-updated accordingly. In MySQL data warehouse, admin and other authorized engineers are able to analyze data via PhpMyAdmin itself.

In the warehouse, there are a few divisions such as IMS (inventory), HR (HR management), CRS (change request), PM (preventive maintenance), TNM (task notification), SF (service form), Procurement Management, and SE (sample evaluation). These divisions are called Data Marts. Figure 4 shows each division that is managed and controlled in the organization system website in the selected manufacturing industry.

As shown in Figure 3, admin can extract the information from IMS (export as Excel file) and import it into PowerBI Desktop. The engineers responsible for hardware inspection or stock management will log in to the IMS system. They will then enter the details of the goods into the system. These details will automatically register in the PhpMyAdmin web application, which has been built within the Ipage web hosting service. All the details of the goods are stored in a MySQL database within the PhpMyAdmin application. This application carries out the ETL (extract, transform, and load) process, where the admin is authorized to access and modify the details displayed in columns and rows. The admin is also able to export the SQL file as a backup and re-upload it to Ipage in the event of damage. Additionally, the admin can use Jupyter Notebook as a reference by importing stock details and running the code to output the result for the next demanded item. This process helps in checking stock availability, thereby avoiding overstocking and understocking.

Figure 3. Process flow of the proposed solution

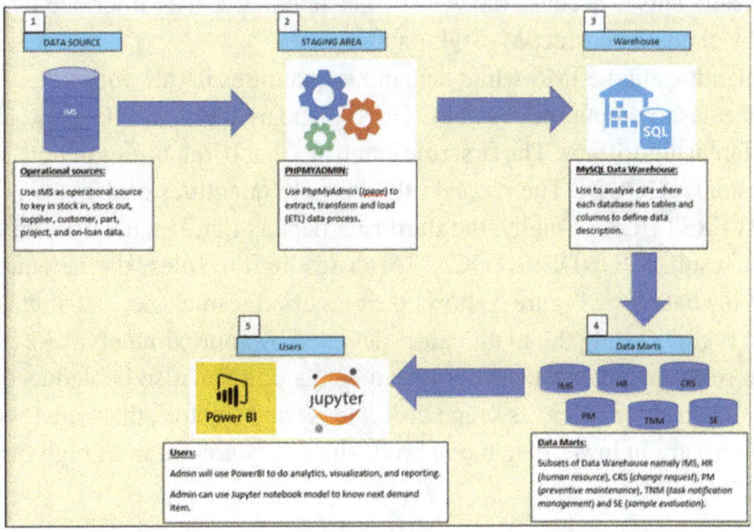

Figure 4. Organization system website task divisions

RESULT AND DISCUSSION

Sources And Techniques to Extract Data From IMS

MySQL database in the selected manufacturing industry is main source that holds actual data of IMS. With the help of phpMyAdmin, data is exported in PDF file. The technique used here highly dependent on phpMyAdmin itself. This is because the website has interactive user interface whereby allow admin to export the data by choosing correct MySQL database.

The supply is quantities in the IMS while demand is quantities in the workorder. Both quantities undergo three defined rules to output the result of 'Good', Under-stock' and 'Over-stock'. These rules are classified using different algorithms. The first rule identifies that IF quantities of both supply and demand are equal THEN result is 'GOOD'. The second rule shows IF quantities of demand is LESS than supply THEN result is 'OVERSTOCK'. Finally, the third rule depicts that IF quantities of demand is MORE than supply THEN result is 'UNDERSTOCK'. After testing the rules, the new attributes (classified result) are saved in the database. Figure 5 shows the classified results (new attributes) in the database.

As illustrated in Figure 6, only the item 'cable' deviated by approximately 0.35%, while all other 17 items show a linear relationship between supply and demand. It can also be deduced that starting from the items 'battery', 'scanner', 'reader', 'storage disk', 'lens', and 'motor', there are less steady quantities. This means these items are in lower demand as well, since they are not in as high quantities as the first three items.

Figure 5. Classified result based on supply and demand

Column1	Project Name	Category	Part Number	Quantity in IMS	Quantity in workorder	Class	Date Stock Out
0	ALT21001	Controller	USB-0808-02	1	1	good	22/2/2021
1	ALT21001	Controller	LIC-4256N	1	1	good	22/2/2021
2	CRE20001	mouse	mouse	0	1	under-stock	17/6/2020
3	CRE20001	keyboard	keyboard	0	1	under-stock	17/6/2020
4	CRE20001	Dongle	HALCON DONGLE	1	1	good	17/6/2020

Figure 6. Supply vs. demand (line graph)

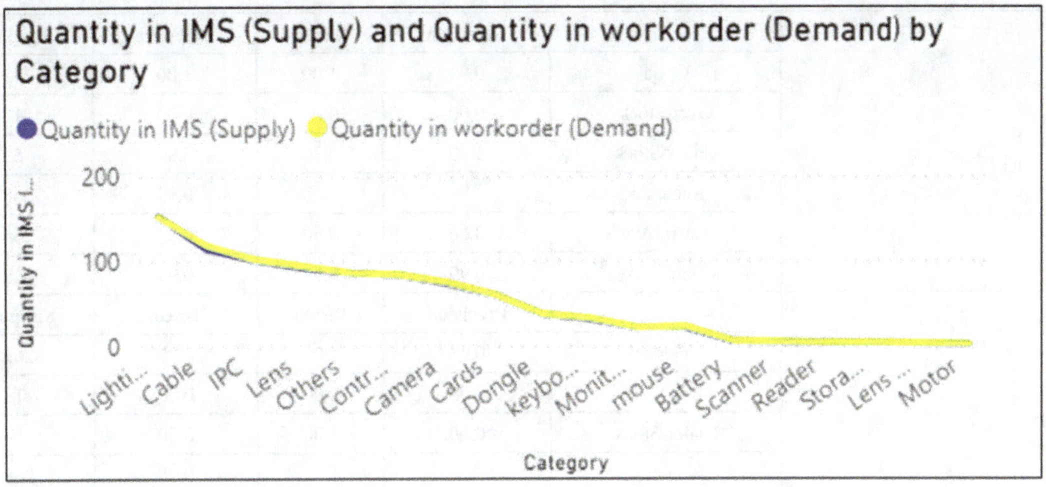

Results to Identify Over-Stock and Under-Stock

Four supervised classification algorithms are selected for this study as shown in Table 2. For SVM, four kernels have been tested to determine which kernel performs best. Overall, only the 'linear' kernel demonstrated the best performance, achieving an accuracy of 1.00, followed by the polynomial kernel with an accuracy of 0.99. The radial basis function and sigmoid kernels also were tested. Hence, the linear kernel is chosen due to its accuracy. However, tuning the hyper-parameters can be challenging, and the final model is complex to interpret. To obtain a good model, a larger dataset is required, but this study is limited by the size of the dataset.

Table 2. SVM performance evaluation based on kernels

		Precision	Recall	F1-Score	Support
Kernel: Linear	Good	1.00	1.00	1.00	262
	Over-Stock	0.00	0.00	0.00	1
	Under-Stock	1.00	1.00	1.00	5
	Accuracy			1.00	268
	Macro Avg	0.67	0.67	0.67	268
	Weighted Avg	0.99	1.00	0.99	268
		Precision	**Recall**	**F1-Score**	**Support**
Kernel: Radial Basis Function	Good	0.98	1.00	0.99	262
	Over-Stock	0.00	0.00	0.00	1
	Under-Stock	0.00	0.00	0.00	5
	Accuracy			0.98	268
	Macro Avg	0.33	0.33	0.33	268
	Weighted Avg	0.96	0.98	0.97	268

Table 2 continued

		Precision	Recall	F1-Score	Support
Kernel: Polynomial	Good	0.99	1.00	1.00	262
	Over-Stock	0.00	0.00	0.00	1
	Under-Stock	1.00	0.80	0.89	5
	Accuracy			0.99	268
	Macro Avg	0.66	0.60	0.63	268
	Weighted Avg	0.99	0.99	0.99	268
Kernel: Sigmoid		**Precision**	**Recall**	**F1-Score**	**Support**
	Good	0.98	1.00	0.99	262
	Over-Stock	0.00	0.00	0.00	1
	Under-Stock	0.00	0.00	0.00	5
	Accuracy			0.98	268
	Macro Avg	0.33	0.33	0.33	268
	Weighted Avg	0.96	0.98	0.97	268

As shown in Table 3, KNN exhibits lower accuracy compared to other algorithms, and its classification is entirely based on the nearest neighbour principle. Moreover, choosing the right K-value is challenging, as it requires testing all K-values until constant stability (equilibrium) is achieved.

Table 3. KNN performance evaluation

		Precision	Recall	F1-Score	Support
KNN	Good	0.97	1.00	0.99	261
	Over-Stock	0.00	0.00	0.00	1
	Under-Stock	0.00	0.00	0.00	6
	Accuracy			0.97	268
	Macro Avg	0.32	0.33	0.33	268
	Weighted Avg	0.95	0.97	0.96	268

As shown in Table 4, for Naïve Bayes, the attributes are assumed to be mutually independent. However, all the attributes in this study are highly dependent on the project. Items are purchased based on the project, and supply and demand quantities depend on each other. Supply quantities are determined based on project demand quantities to avoid understocking and overstocking. Thus, Naïve Bayes is rejected for deployment into the organization system for this study.

As shown in Table 5, Random Forest outperformed the other algorithms and, therefore, has been selected for deployment into the system for this study. This selection is due to its ability to illustrate the breakdown from the least demanded/least voted tree node to more specific, high demand/majority votes. Administrators can clearly observe this breakdown without the need for additional technical testing or adhering to conditional rules, such as with KNN (which requires testing all K-values), Naïve Bayes (which assumes conditional independence), and SVM (which is limited by dataset size and has a complex final model interface). Notably, its accuracy is only 1% shy of achieving the full accuracy target, similar to SVM with a linear kernel. Thus, achieving high accuracy is indeed feasible.

Table 4. Naïve bayes result

		Precision	Recall	F1-Score	Support
Naïve Bayes	Good	0.99	1.00	0.99	265
	Over-Stock	0.00	0.00	0.00	1
	Under-Stock	0.00	0.00	0.00	2
	Accuracy			0.99	268
	Macro Avg	0.33	0.33	0.33	268
	Weighted Avg	0.98	0.99	0.98	268

Table 5. Random forest result

		Precision	Recall	F1-Score	Support
Random Forest	Good	0.98	1.00	0.99	262
	Over-Stock	0.00	0.00	0.00	1
	Under-Stock	1.00	0.40	0.57	5
	Accuracy			0.99	268
	Macro Avg	0.66	0.47	0.52	268
	Weighted Avg	0.98	0.99	0.98	268

From the results of all four classifiers, Naïve Bayes, SVM, and Random Forest demonstrate accuracy. SVM with a linear kernel exhibits the highest accuracy, with a value of 1.00, while KNN shows the lowest accuracy, with a value of 0.97. There are no scores for precision, recall, F1-score, and support for the class 'over-stock' since only one item is classified in this category (the least represented class). In contrast, for the class 'good', Naïve Bayes, SVM, and Random Forest show high precision values. SVM with a linear kernel scored the highest precision, 1.00, and KNN scored the lowest precision, 0.97, in the class 'good'. The majority of items are classified under the class 'good' as compared to both 'over-stock' and 'under-stock' classes.

Next Demand Item Using Random Forest

The admin must load the IMS dataset, which uses numerical values ONLY, into Jupyter Notebook. Then, the notebook will automatically output the result, providing insight to the admin about the next items to stock. Based on the current result shown in Figure 7, the admin needs to stock items ranging from Category 1 to Category 11, such as Battery (Category 1), Cable (Category 2), Camera (Category 3), Cards (Category 4), Controller (Category 5), Dongle (Category 6), IPC (Category 7), Keyboard (Category 8),

Lens (Category 9), Lens Mount (Category 10), and Lighting (Category 11). Although it may seem like a lot of stocking due to the wide range of categories, these are the common and demanded items required for every customer project. Thus, it is advisable to stock up on these items.

Figure 7. Random forest classification result

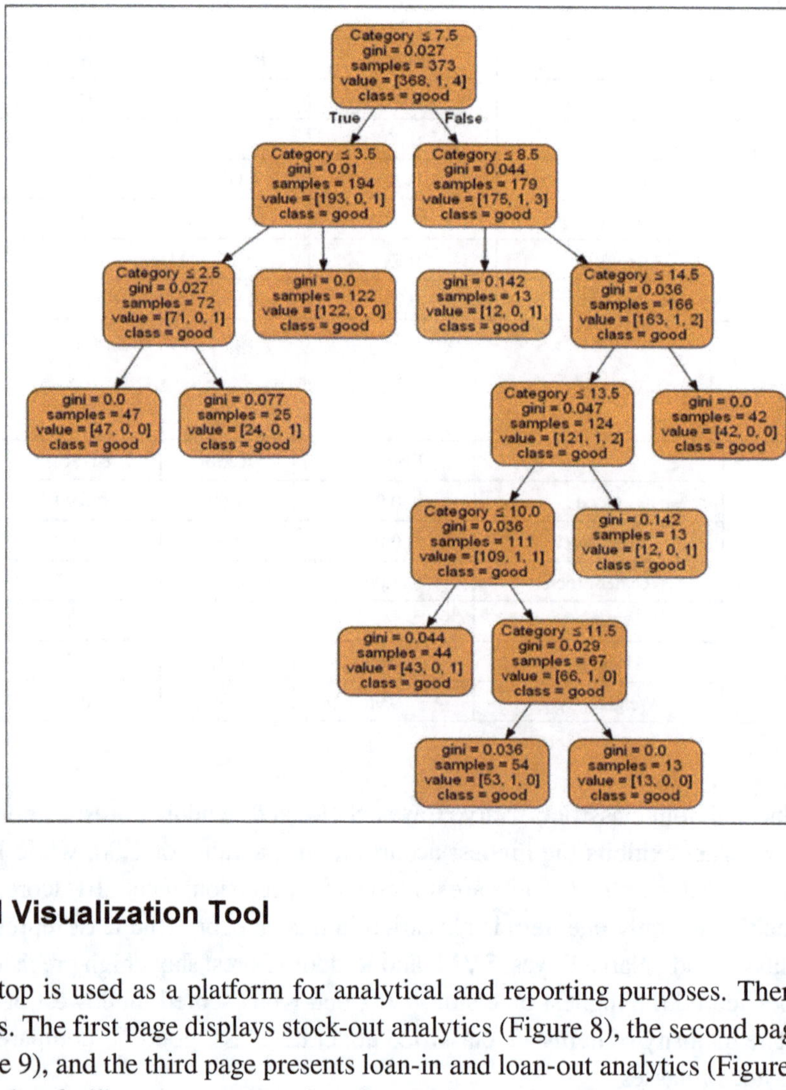

Analytic and Visualization Tool

Power BI Desktop is used as a platform for analytical and reporting purposes. There are three main dashboard pages. The first page displays stock-out analytics (Figure 8), the second page shows stock-in analytics (Figure 9), and the third page presents loan-in and loan-out analytics (Figure 10). These three pages are created to facilitate an easy user interface and to avoid compressing everything into a single dashboard, which may limit visual details. The visualization features created in the dashboard include the Decomposition Tree, Slicer, Line Graph, Tree Map, Stacked Area Chart, and Clustered Column Chart.

Stock Out Dashboard

As shown in Figure 8, six features were created. The first feature is a date slicer, which allows the admin to adjust the date according to their task to analyze quantities in the IMS system. When the admin adjusts the date, all other six features will adjust accordingly per date. The second feature is a decomposition tree, which allows the admin to view item part numbers specifically based on category. This category is adjusted to correspond with the project name, breaking down the tree from the project name to the categories existing in a particular project, and then further breaking down specifically to part numbers. The third feature is a tree map, which shows items from most to least quantity in IMS. For example, light blue (lighting) shows the most quantity (QTY: 152) in IMS, while light pink (motor) shows the least quantity (QTY: 1). The fourth feature is a line graph, where only the item 'cable' deviated about 0.35%, while all other 17 items show a linear relationship between supply and demand. The fifth (stacked area chart) and sixth feature (slicer) work together, allowing the admin two options: either observe the quantity in IMS by filtering the project name in the slicer feature or observe a wide range in the stacked area chart.

Figure 8. 1st dashboard page (stock out)

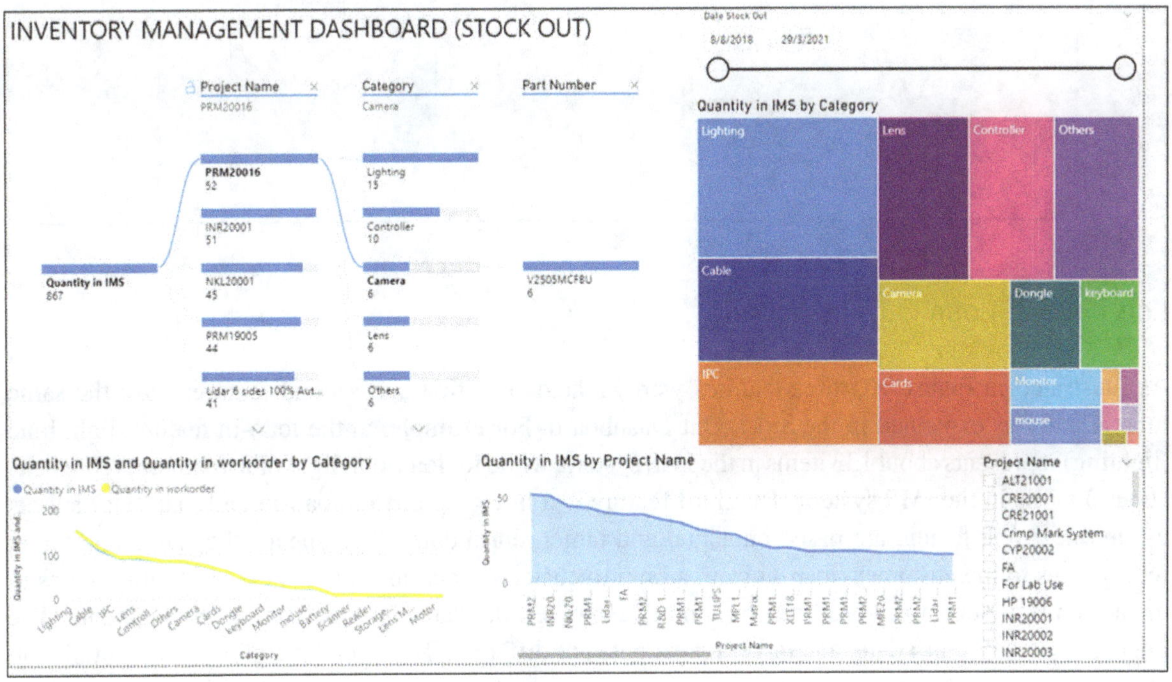

Stock In Dashboard

As depicted in Figure 9, three features were created. The first, second, and third features have the same functionality as explained in the Stock Out Dashboard. For example, in the tree map, light blue (Others) shows the highest quantity (QTY: 35) in IMS, while light pink and purple (battery & scanner, respectively) show the least quantity (QTY: 1) in IMS. The fourth feature is a clustered column chart, where most items are categorized by project name. However, approximately 117 item quantities have not been finalized with a project name; therefore, these items are labeled as 'blank'.

Figure 9. 2nd dashboard page (stock in)

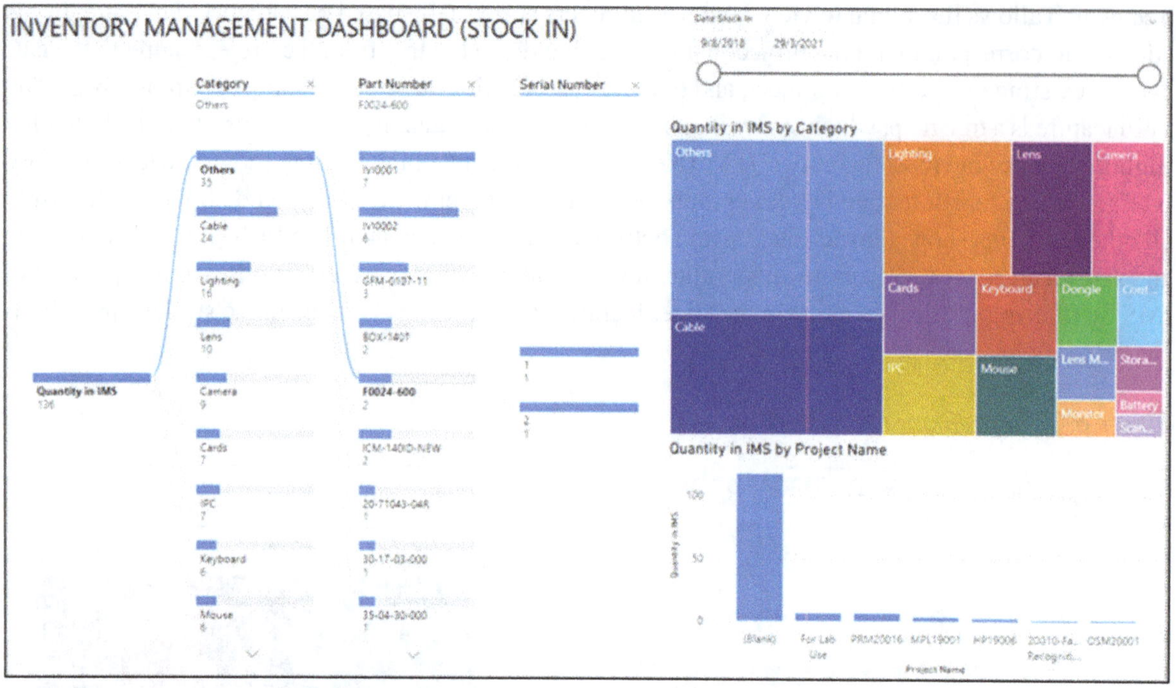

Loan In and Loan Out Dashboard

As illustrated in Figure 10, three features were created. The first and second features have the same functionality as explained in the Stock Out Dashboard. For example, in the loan-in feature, light blue (lighting) represents about 133 items in the IMS system, while for loan-out, light blue (camera) represents about 3 items in the IMS system. The third feature is a line graph. Both loan-in and loan-out datasets in the line graph feature are based on actual and target return dates. This means the actual and target return dates to the customer (loan-in from admin to customer) and the actual and target return dates to the admin (loan-out: from customer to admin). However, the date slicer is fixed to the loan date. The loan date, actual return date, and target return date are different. The loan date refers to the initial plan to loan the items, the actual return date is the actual date the item was returned to the owner, and the target return date is the pre-defined date to return the item to the owner earlier than the actual date. In loan-in, the quantities increase steadily from the year 2019 to 2020, with a high peak of about 115 items. Then, it decreases to 48 items in the IMS system. In loan-out, there is a steady decrease from the year 2020 to 2021. The quantities for loan-in increase steadily with a high peak of 115 and then decrease to 48. Meanwhile, for loan-out, the quantities decrease steadily from 12 items in 2020 to 1 item in 2021.

Figure 10. 3rd dashboard page (loan in and loan out)

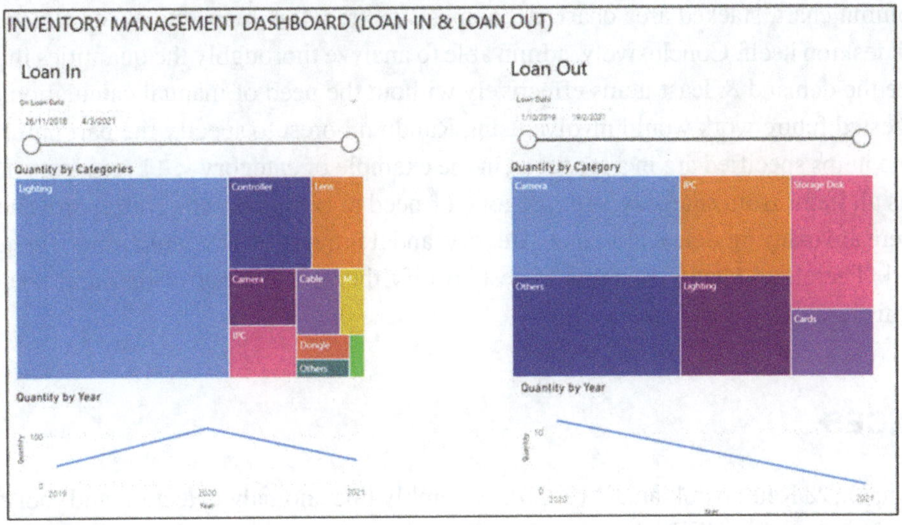

CONCLUSION

The proposed business intelligence system was successfully deployed in the selected manufacturing industry. From the results, it can be deduced that there are currently few overstocked and understocked items. Thus, supply and demand have a significant linear relationship. This indicates that all items have successfully met the project requirements accordingly. Consequently, there is minimal or no cash flow interruption. All objectives have been successfully achieved.

There is a linear relationship between supply and demand, even though only the item 'cable' deviated by about 0.35%. Consequently, the items purchased successfully fulfill the project requirements. By meeting the project's requirements, the admin can confidently stock out items to the customer side without worrying about customer dissatisfaction.

Approximately, 1.72% of the inventory is understocked, and 0.19% is overstocked. Consequently, both overstock and understock are below 2%, which will not severely affect the business's cash flow. This is because the overstocked items can be used for laboratory feasibility studies or for the next upcoming project. The understocked items can be explained with solid reasons, such as delays in item delivery to the admin side due to the pandemic or any other convincing reason for the customer.

The Random Forest Classification method is used to recommend the next demand item in the business intelligence system developed for the selected manufacturing industry. After thoroughly analysing other machine learning classification algorithms, Random Forest emerges as the best choice. Even though the SVM classifier shows high accuracy, the algorithm requires a technical background. Since the Admin is on the Business side, it would not be easy and effective for a person with a business background to explain in detail how the margins work to management. At least with Random Forest, there is a tree node breakdown, which would be easier for them to understand how and why it is necessary to purchase a specific item. This is because the breakdown shows a progression from more general to specific items.

PowerBi desktop is the analytic tool used for annual reporting and visualization required are line graph, clustered column chart, stacked area chart, decomposition tree, tree map, and slicer which available in the PowerBi desktop itself. Conclusively, admin able to analyze thoroughly the quantities in IMS system and visualize the demand & least items effectively without the need of manual calculation as in excel.

The suggested future work would involve using Random Forest to specify the part number of items. Currently, the items specified are in a range, as in the example of category < 11 (category 11: lighting), which means all items from category 1 to category 11 need to be purchased. This approach is not effective since there are many models within one category, and it is questionable which specific model should be purchased. Therefore, having Random Forest specify the part number of the item could provide a solution to this issue.

REFERENCES

Abdelrahman, O., & Keikhosrokiani, P. (2020). Assembly line anomaly detection and root cause analysis using machine learning. *IEEE Access : Practical Innovations, Open Solutions, 8*, 189661–189672. Advance online publication. doi:10.1109/ACCESS.2020.3029826

Ajesh, A., Nair, J., & Jijin, P. S. (2016). A random forest approach for rating-based recommender system. *2016 International Conference on Advances in Computing, Communications and Informatics (ICACCI)*, 1293–1297. 10.1109/ICACCI.2016.7732225

Al Haraisa, Y. E. (2017). Just-In-Time System and Its Impact on Operational Excellence: An Empirical Study on Jordanian Industrial Companies. *International Journal of Biometrics, 12*, 158. https://api.semanticscholar.org/CorpusID:55492018

Atnafu, D., & Balda, A. (2018). The impact of inventory management practice on firms' competitiveness and organizational performance: Empirical evidence from micro and small enterprises in Ethiopia. *Cogent Business & Management, 5*(1), 1503219. doi:10.1080/23311975.2018.1503219

Bahari, N. I. S., Ahmad, A., & Aboobaider, B. M. (2014). Application of support vector machine for classification of multispectral data. *IOP Conference Series. Earth and Environmental Science, 20*(1), 012038. doi:10.1088/1755-1315/20/1/012038

Bialas, C., Revanoglou, A., & Manthou, V. (2020). Improving hospital pharmacy inventory management using data segmentation. *American Journal of Health-System Pharmacy, 77*(5), 371–377. doi:10.1093/ajhp/zxz264 PMID:31754716

Chen, Y., Li, K. W., & Liu, S. (2008). A comparative study on multicriteria ABC analysis in inventory management. *2008 IEEE International Conference on Systems, Man and Cybernetics*, 3280–3285. 10.1109/ICSMC.2008.4811802

Gürdür, D., Raizer, K., & El-Khoury, J. (2018). Data visualization support for complex logistics operations and cyber-physical systems. *14th International Joint Conference on Computer Vision, Imaging and Computer Graphics Theory and Applications*. 10.5220/0006569402000211

Gürdür, D., Vulgarakis Feljan, A., El-khoury, J., Kumar Mohalik, S., Badrinath, R., Pradeep Mujumdar, A., & Fersman, E. (2018). Knowledge Representation of Cyber-physical Systems for Monitoring Purpose. *Procedia CIRP*, *72*, 468–473. doi:10.1016/j.procir.2018.03.018

Gürdür Broo, D., Bravo-Haro, M., & Schooling, J. (2022). Design and implementation of a smart infrastructure digital twin. *Automation in Construction*, *136*, 104171. doi:10.1016/j.autcon.2022.104171

Keikhosrokiani, P. (2022). Handbook of Research on Consumer Behavior Change and Data Analytics in the Socio-Digital Era. doi:10.4018/978-1-6684-4168-8

Keikhosrokiani, P., & Asl, M. P. (2022a). Handbook of Research on Artificial Intelligence Applications in Literary Works and Social Media. doi:10.4018/978-1-6684-6242-3

Keikhosrokiani, P., & Asl, M. P. (2022b). Introduction to artificial intelligence for the analytics of literary works and social media: A review. In Handbook of Research on Artificial Intelligence Applications in Literary Works and Social Media. doi:10.4018/978-1-6684-6242-3.ch001

Keikhosrokiani, P., & Fye, G. M. (2023). A hybrid recommender system for health supplement e-commerce based on customer data implicit ratings. *Multimedia Tools and Applications*. Advance online publication. doi:10.1007/s11042-023-17321-6

Keikhosrokiani, P., & Pourya Asl, M. (2022). *Handbook of research on opinion mining and text analytics on literary works and social media*. IGI Global. doi:10.4018/978-1-7998-9594-7

Kučera, T., & Suk, A. (2019). The application of ABC analysis in the logistic warehousing processes. *Transport Means: Proceedings of the International Scientific Conference*.

Liu, J. C., & Wu, Y. (2014). Application of ABC Analysis in Inventory Management. *Advanced Materials Research*, *1030–1032*, 2515–2518. . doi:10.4028/www.scientific.net/AMR.1030-1032.2515 PMID:31267820

Pisner, D. A., & Schnyer, D. M. (2020). Support vector machine. In A. Mechelli & S. Vieira (Eds.), *Machine Learning* (pp. 101–121). Academic Press. doi:10.1016/B978-0-12-815739-8.00006-7

Redjeki, S., Guntara, M., & Anggoro, P. (2015). Naive bayes classifier algorithm approach for mapping poor families potential. *Int. J. Adv. Res. Artif. Intell*, *4*(12), 29–33. doi:10.14569/IJARAI.2015.041205

Romano, M., Contu, G., Mola, F., & Conversano, C. (2023). Threshold-based Naïve Bayes classifier. *Advances in Data Analysis and Classification*. Advance online publication. doi:10.1007/s11634-023-00536-8

Saeed, A. M. M., Widyaningsih, A., & Khaled, A. S. D. (2023). Activity-based costing (ABC) in the manufacturing industry: A literature review. *Journal of Development Economics*, *8*(2).

Singh, P., Ghosh, S., Saraf, M., & Nayak, R. (2020). A Survey Paper on Identifying Key Performance Indicators for Optimizing Inventory Management System and Exploring Different Visualization Tools. *2020 4th International Conference on Intelligent Computing and Control Systems (ICICCS)*, 627–632. 10.1109/ICICCS48265.2020.9121036

Sohail, N., & Sheikh, T. H. (2018). A study of inventory management system case study. *Journal of Dynamical and Control Systems*, *10*(10), 1176–1190.

van Heck, G., van den Berg, J., Davarynejad, M., van Duin, R., & Roskott, B. (2010). Improving Inventory Management Performance Using a Process-Oriented Measurement Framework. In J. E. Quintela Varajão, M. M. Cruz-Cunha, G. D. Putnik, & A. Trigo (Eds.), *ENTERprise Information Systems* (pp. 279–288). Springer Berlin Heidelberg. doi:10.1007/978-3-642-16402-6_30

Vishwakarma, M., & Kesswani, N. (2023). A new two-phase intrusion detection system with Naïve Bayes machine learning for data classification and elliptic envelop method for anomaly detection. *Decision Analytics Journal, 7*, 100233. https://doi.org/https://doi.org/10.1016/j.dajour.2023.100233

Wang, L. (2019). Research and Implementation of Machine Learning Classifier Based on KNN. *IOP Conference Series. Materials Science and Engineering*, *677*(5), 052038. doi:10.1088/1757-899X/677/5/052038

Xian, Z., Keikhosrokiani, P., XinYing, C., & Li, Z. (2022). An RFM Model Using K-Means Clustering to Improve Customer Segmentation and Product Recommendation. In P. Keikhosrokiani (Ed.), Handbook of Research on Consumer Behavior Change and Data Analytics in the Socio-Digital Era (pp. 124–145). IGI Global. doi:10.4018/978-1-6684-4168-8.ch006

Zhao, X., & Keikhosrokiani, P. (2022). Sales prediction and product recommendation model through user behavior analytics. *Computers, Materials & Continua*, *70*(2), 3855–3874. Advance online publication. doi:10.32604/cmc.2022.019750

Chapter 13
Narrative Threads and Cinematic Connections Using Intelligent Systems to Enhance Movie Recommendations with Market Basket Analysis and Advanced Algorithms

Kah Win Lee
Universiti Sains Malaysia, Malaysia

Jia Hui Wong
Universiti Sains Malaysia, Malaysia

Pantea Keikhosrokiani
https://orcid.org/0000-0003-4705-2732
University of Oulu, Finland

Moussa Pourya Asl
https://orcid.org/0000-0002-8426-426X
University of Oulu, Finland

ABSTRACT

Movie streaming services are businesses driven by data and strategies to predict future viewing patterns based on historical data. Without unsupervised learning techniques, industries like movie streaming services might face laborious tasks and issues in anticipating customer preferences and forecasting changes in customer behavior. In this chapter, market basket analysis (MBA) and recommender systems were implemented on MovieLens Data. In MBA, movie watching patterns were identified using two types of rule-generating algorithms, namely the apriori algorithm and the FP-growth algorithm. Three visualization idioms were generated to understand the association rules extracted in the MBA. Secondly, five types of recommender systems, namely memory-based collaborative filtering, model-based collaborative filtering, content filtering, context filtering, and the hybrid method, were implemented to suggest relevant movies to customers. Each recommender system was experimented with three different TopN configurations, and the results were evaluated using information retrieval metrics.

DOI: 10.4018/979-8-3693-1210-0.ch013

1. INTRODUCTION

In an age where storytelling transcends traditional mediums, the intersection of narrative theory and digital innovation opens up new avenues for understanding and enhancing viewer engagement in the cinematic landscape. In the competitive landscape of movie streaming services, providers are striving to enhance the viewing experience and cater to the varied preferences of their audience to maintain user engagement within their platforms. This endeavor requires service providers to deliver an exceptional user experience, suggest content that aligns with user interests, and, ideally, anticipate the movies users might choose to watch next. Providers unable to meet these expectations risk facing increased customer churn, diminished service ratings, or a decline in customer lifetime value (CLV). A crucial strategy for enriching the user experience involves analyzing individual users' past ratings patterns. This analysis allows providers to recommend movies similar to those a user has previously enjoyed.

Moreover, recognizing that some viewers prefer binge-watching, accurately predicting subsequent movie choices becomes essential. Providers must delve into users' viewing histories to uncover potential patterns of association between watched titles. For instance, discovering that viewers of "Avengers: Age of Ultron" are likely to watch "Avengers: Infinity War" next enables providers to make precise recommendations. Such targeted suggestions not only enhance content relevance but also significantly boost overall user satisfaction.

Therefore, this research will address two problems. First, it aims to predict the "rating" a user would assign to a movie or its attribute based on users' rating histories, thereby suggesting relevant items. To achieve this objective, the study will construct and evaluate three types of recommender systems: Collaborative Filtering System, Content-based System, and Hybrid (Keikhosrokiani, 2022; Keikhosrokiani & Fye, 2023; Low et al., 2024; Xian et al., 2022; Zhao & Keikhosrokiani, 2022). Second, the research intends to use users' rating histories to identify association rules among movies to determine which movies users are likely to watch next. The difference between recommender systems and Market Basket Analysis (MBA) lies in their scope; MBA represents the buying patterns of the entire population, whereas recommender systems focus on specific users or items. Recommender systems answer the question "What are the movies that users with interests similar to yours like?" On the other hand, association rules tackle the question, "What are the movies that frequently watched together (Timur, 2020)?".

By implementing the two algorithms described, this chapter aims to develop a reliable movie recommendation system that enhances the user experience. As a result, movie service providers are likely to gain popularity by accurately recommending movies, leading to an increase in both user retention rates and service ratings.

2. BACKGROUND

2.1 Domain Background

Originating as a product of 19th-century scientific exploration, cinematography has transformed into the leading form of entertainment media, now commanding a multi-billion-pound industry. The evolution of the movie industry over more than a century encompasses a journey from the early days of black and white silent films to the advent of sound in the 1920s, the introduction of color in the 1930s, and the rise of mainstream 3D movies in recent times. According to Grand View Research, (*Movies And*

Entertainment Market Size Report, 2030, n.d.), the global movies and entertainment market, valued at $90.92 billion in 2021, is projected to grow to $169.6 billion by 2030, with a compound annual growth rate (CAGR) of 7.2% from 2022 to 2030. The movie sector claimed the largest market share, accounting for 55.4% of revenue in 2021 (*Movies And Entertainment Market Size Report, 2030*, n.d.). With a strategic focus on expanding into untapped markets such as India, the Asia Pacific region is anticipated to experience the highest CAGR of 8.2% from 2022 to 2030 (*Movies And Entertainment Market Worth $169.6 Billion by 2030*, n.d.). In response to this growth, leading subscription streaming services like Netflix, Prime Video, Disney+, and HBO — which rank among the top ten in popularity (*Top 10 Most Popular Subscription Streaming Services - All Top Everything*, n.d.), are leveraging big data analytics and technology to discover associations between movies. This approach enables them to proactively recommend films to customers based on their viewing behaviors, preferences, and movie details.

The "Movies Dataset," accessible on Kaggle, comprises metadata for 45,000 movies from the Full MovieLens Dataset, along with 26 million ratings by over 270,000 users (*The Movies Dataset | Kaggle*, n.d.). GroupLens Research at the University of Minnesota's Department of Computer Science and Engineering, established Movielens in 1997 as a web-based recommender system to gather data for research on personalized recommendations. The utilized MovieLens dataset consists of tuples in the format <user, item, rating, timestamp>, representing a user's rating (on a 0-5 star scale) for a movie at a specific time (Harper & Konstan, 2016). This dataset, essential for education, research, and industrial applications, has seen significant engagement, with 140,000 downloads in 2014 and numerous citations in scholarly literature (Harper & Konstan, 2016). A search conducted in spring 2015 yielded 2,750 results on Google Books and 7,580 on Google Scholar for "movielens." Its popularity underscores the rapid expansion of research into personalization and recommendation systems. Datasets such as these are crucial for investigating and validating concepts within this domain. They have been instrumental in driving the adoption of predictive business analytics across various business sectors, such as utilizing market basket analysis for sales enhancement through better insights into customer purchasing behaviors or applying recommendation systems to forecast a user's future item preferences and suggest top choices.

2.2 Unsupervised Learning

Unsupervised learning algorithms identify patterns within unlabelled data without the need for predefined target outcomes (Al Mamun et al., 2022; Arikatla et al., 2021; Bane & Khyati, 2020; Glielmo et al., 2021; James et al., 2021; Keikhosrokiani et al., 2022; Keikhosrokiani & Asl, 2022; Keikhosrokiani & Pourya Asl, 2022; Suhendra et al., 2022). These algorithms, unlike their supervised counterparts, operate without explicitly defined outputs, relying solely on input data for learning. Various studies have highlighted examples of unsupervised learning algorithms, including Apriori, FP-Growth, Recommender Systems, SVD, and K-Mean Clustering (Arikatla et al., 2021; Bane & Khyati, 2020; Shah et al., 2017). Figure 1 illustrates a machine learning framework that encompasses both unsupervised and supervised learning methods.

Unsupervised learning offers the advantage of requiring minimal human intervention, notably eliminating the need for manual data labeling (Arikatla et al., 2021), unlike supervised learning. This reduction in manual effort allows for the processing of significantly larger datasets. Unsupervised learning thrives on discovering underlying structures in data without predefined target labels, leading to the identification of hidden patterns. As a result, unsupervised learning algorithms exhibit a high degree of versatility and are not confined to specific outcomes due to the emergence of these concealed structures (Bane & Khyati, 2020).

Figure 1. Machine learning framework with supervised and unsupervised learning

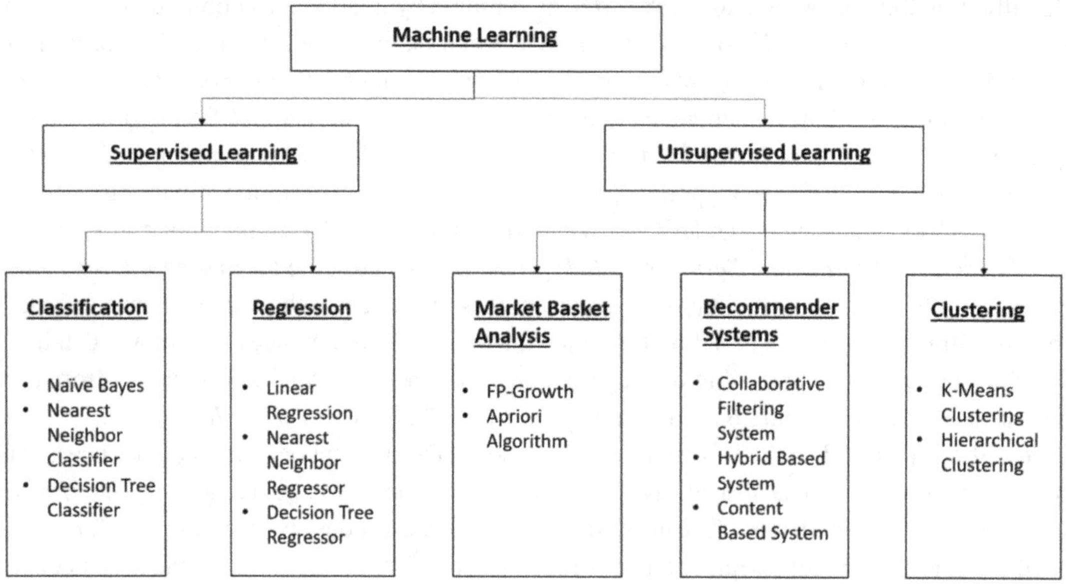

In comparison, unsupervised learning often presents greater challenges than its supervised counterpart. A primary difficulty lies in evaluating the effectiveness of unsupervised learning algorithms, as there lacks a universally agreed-upon method for validation against an independent dataset. While supervised learning allows for performance measurement through the accuracy of predictions against known labels, the absence of such ground truth in unsupervised learning complicates performance assessment. The challenge stems from the inherent nature of unsupervised learning, where evaluation metrics are less straightforward due to the lack of explicit targets.

2.3 Recommender Systems

Modern society grapples with the challenge of information overload. In response, recommender systems have become a vital information retrieval paradigm that addresses this issue (Deldjoo et al., 2020). These systems employ data-driven unsupervised learning techniques to propose items to users based on their likely preferences (Deldjoo et al., 2020; Shah et al., 2017; Stratigi et al., 2019). Generally, recommender systems fall into four categories: Collaborative Filtering, Content Filtering, Hybrid-based, and Context Aware (Deldjoo et al., 2020; Narke et al., 2020; Shraddha Gupta, 2020).

Goldberg et al., in 1992, introduced the concept of "Collaborative Filtering," envisioning an efficient information filtering process that incorporates human input (Goldberg et al., 1992). This method predicts a user's preferences by identifying similarities across users or items to estimate unknown ratings, thereby facilitating relevant recommendations (Deldjoo et al., 2020; Narke et al., 2020). Collaborative Filtering stands out because it does not require domain-specific knowledge to generate embeddings (Narke et al., 2020; Shraddha Gupta, 2020). This technique is subdivided into Memory-based and Model-based methods, making it adept at suggesting new items to users. Nevertheless, it faces a hurdle known as the cold start problem when introducing new items (Narke et al., 2020; Shraddha Gupta, 2020).

Additionally, the context-aware model represents a type of recommender system that incorporates contextual information to discern user preferences (Deldjoo et al., 2020). Contextual data may include factors such as location, time, or festive seasons. On the other hand, content-based filtering models utilize both the content information of items and the behavioral data of target users (Deldjoo et al., 2020; Hu et al., 2008). For instance, in the realm of movie recommendations, content properties might encompass actors, directors, production companies, and languages. Finally, hybrid recommender systems employ a combination of strategies from two or more types of recommender systems, offering a comprehensive approach to recommendations (Burke, 2002; Çano & Morisio, 2019a; Deldjoo et al., 2020).

2.4 Market Basket Analysis

Market basket analysis, a technique in data mining, enhances understanding of customer purchasing patterns. This method involves analyzing extensive datasets, such as purchase histories, to discover groups of products frequently bought together. For instance, "if a customer watch movies A and B, s/he is likely to also watch movie C (another item)"

The Apriori algorithm, developed by Agrawal and Srikant in 1994 (Agrawal & Srikant, 1994), stands as a prominent tool in market basket analysis (Sarker, 2021; Zhao et al., 2003), particularly for mining frequent itemsets (Chee et al., 2019). This process involves initially extracting frequent itemsets and subsequently generating association rules. The term "Apriori" denotes the use of prior knowledge about the properties of common itemsets. Utilizing a "bottom-up" approach, the Apriori algorithm aims to reduce search volume by adhering to two principles: "all subsets of a frequent itemset must be frequent; and if an itemset is infrequent, then all its supersets must also be infrequent"(Agrawal & Srikant, 1994; Chee et al., 2019). Despite its widespread use, the Apriori algorithm faces limitations, including the potential need to generate a large number of candidate itemsets as the count of frequent k-itemsets rises (Chee et al., 2019), which can extend the time required for candidate generation, especially when compared to the FP-Growth method (S.Mythili & R. Mohamed Shanavas, 2013).

In addition to the Apriori algorithm, the Frequent Pattern Growth (FP-Growth) method, introduced in 2000 (Han et al., 2000), stands out as another notable technique in association rule mining. The FP-Growth algorithm addresses the Apriori algorithm's shortcomings (Mustakim et al., 2018), by efficiently identifying frequent itemsets without needing to generate candidate itemsets (Chee et al., 2019; S.Mythili & R. Mohamed Shanavas, 2013). This method employs a divide and conquer strategy and requires only two scans of the database to determine the support count.

Researchers have conducted numerous experiments to compare the performance of the Apriori and FP-Growth algorithms (Hidayat et al., 2019; Mustakim et al., 2018; S.Mythili & R. Mohamed Shanavas, 2013). Findings from these studies indicate that FP-Growth outperforms Apriori in terms of speed and efficiency. A summary of the comparison between the Apriori and FP-Growth algorithms is presented in Table 1.

3. METHOD

The proposed research framework is illustrated in Figure 2. The description of each stage will be further explained.

Table 1. Comparison between apriori and FP-growth algorithms

Parameters	Apriori	FP-Growth
Storage structure	Array based	Tree based
Search strategy	Breadth First Search	Divide and conquer
Technique	Join and prune	Constructs conditional frequency pattern tree which satisfy minimum Support
Number of Database scans	K+1 scans	2 scans
Memory utilization	Large memory (candidate generation)	Less memory (No Candidate generation).
Database	Sparse/dense datasets	Large and medium data sets
Run time	More time	Less time

- *Data Preparation*

During the data preparation phase, we perform data cleaning and preprocessing to ensure the quality and integrity of the data. This involves formatting and validating data values to eliminate issues such as missing values, duplications, incorrect indexing, and incompatible formats..

- *Modelling*

In the modelling phase, we select and apply various techniques, calibrating some parameters to their optimal values. For instance, conducting Market Basket Analysis requires constructing models using the Apriori and FP Growth Algorithms. Developing a Recommender System involves creating models based on collaborative filtering (memory-based and model-based), content-based, context-based, and hybrid filtering approaches. The processes of data preparation and modelling are closely connected; during modelling, one might identify data issues or conceive new data ideas.

- *Evaluation*

Before the final model deployment, evaluating the models with suitable performance metrics is essential. This evaluation ensures the model aligns with the business's nature and objectives. It's crucial to ascertain whether the model overlooks any critical business issues. For example, a model that excels in precision but lacks recall may not be optimal if the business values recall more highly. Therefore, we must use various performance metrics to evaluate and select the most appropriate model for deployment.

3.1. Data Understanding

In this module, we will abstract a description of the data from the selected dataset, generate several visualization idioms to better understand the data, and show how to transform the data for Market Basket Analysis (MBA) and Recommender Systems.

Figure 2. Proposed research framework

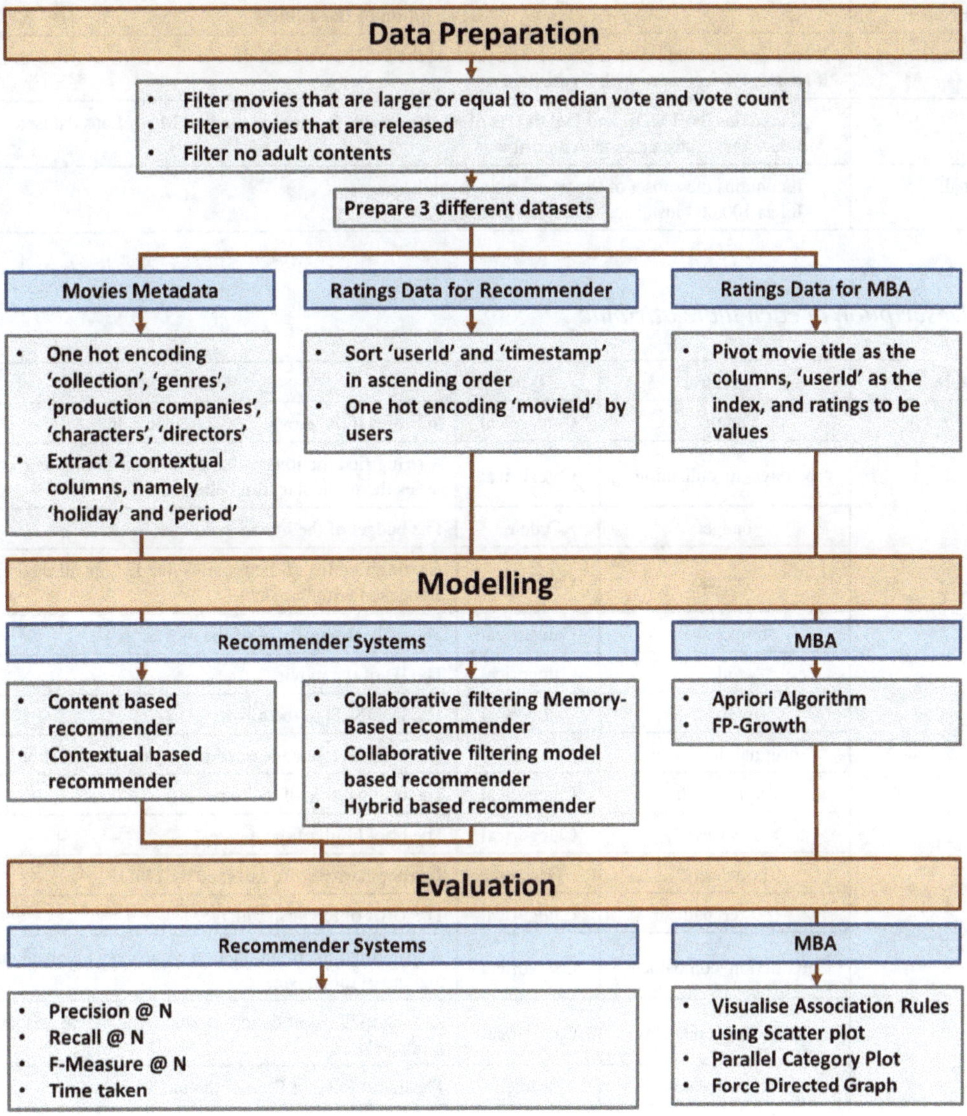

3.1.1 Data Description

The dataset that we used is titled "The Movies Dataset" (*The Movies Dataset | Kaggle*, n.d.). This dataset, derived from MovieLens, encompasses 26 million ratings from 270,000 users across 45,000 movies. It is organized into seven tables, with our study focusing primarily on three: movies_metadata.csv, links.csv, and ratings_small.csv. Table 2 provides a summary of the contents and dimensions of each table, while Table 3 offers details on the types of attributes and descriptions for each table's attributes.

Table 2. Description of the tables

Table Name	Description of the Table
'movies_metadata' (.csv)	· It contains information on all movies featured in the Full MovieLens dataset. · It has 45,466 instances with 24 attributes.
'links' (.csv)	· It contains the TMDB and IMDB IDs of all the movies featured in the Full MovieLens dataset. · It has 45,843 instances with 3 attributes.
'ratings_small' (.csv)	· It contains the subset of the users' ratings on the movies. · It has 100,004 instances with 4 attributes.

Table 3. Description of each table attribute

Table	Attribute	Type	Description
'movies_metadata' (.csv)	adult	Categorical	Indicates if the movie is X-Rated or Adult.
	belongs_to_collection	Categorical	A stringified dictionary that gives information on the movie series the particular film belongs to.
	budget	Ordered	The budget of the movie in dollars.
	genres	Categorical	A stringified list of dictionaries that list out all the genres associated with the movie.
	homepage	Categorical	The official homepage of the movie.
	id	Categorical	The ID of the movie.
	imdb_id	Categorical	The IMDB ID of the movie.
	original_language	Categorical	The original language in which the movie was shot.
	original_title	Categorical	The original title of the movie.
	overview	Categorical	The brief blurb of the movie.
	popularity	Ordered	The popularity score assigned by TMDB.
	poster_path	Categorical	The URL of the poster image.
	production_companies	Categorical	A stringified list of production companies involved with the making of the movie.
	production_countries	Categorical	A stringified list of countries where the movie was shot/ produced in.
	release_date	Ordered	Theatrical Release Date of the movie.
	revenue	Ordered	The total revenue of the movie in dollars.
	runtime	Ordered	The runtime of the movie in minutes.
	spoken_languages	Categorical	A stringified list of spoken languages in the film.
	status	Categorical	The status of the movie (Released, To Be Released, Announced, etc.)
	tagline	Categorical	The tagline of the movie.
	title	Categorical	The official title of the movie.
	video	Categorical	Indicates if the movie has a video available on TMDB.
	vote_average	Ordered	The average rating of the movie.
	vote_count	Ordered	The number of votes by users, as counted by TMDB.

Table 3 continued

Table	Attribute	Type	Description
'links' (.csv)	movieId	Categorical	The ID of the movie.
	imdbId	Categorical	The IMDB ID of the movie.
	tmdbId	Categorical	The TMDB ID of the movie.
'ratings_small' (.csv)	userId	Categorical	The ID of the user.
	movieId	Categorical	The ID of the movie.
	Rating	Ordered	The user's rating of the movie.
	timestamp	Ordered	The time when the movie is rated by the user.

3.1.2 Exploratory Data Analysis (EDA)

To the best of our knowledge, conducting exploratory data analysis is essential for obtaining a thorough and precise comprehension of the data before forming any hypotheses. When beginning to work with the MovieLens dataset, what initially comes to mind? Starting with the formulation of appropriate questions to pose to our dataset is advisable, followed by determining the methods for manipulating the data sources to obtain the required answers. Given the abundance of details in the MovieLens dataset awaiting exploration, we opted to concentrate on only five attributes pertinent to our study. For each attribute, we formulated one to three questions for the MovieLens dataset to answer.

3.1.2(a) Genre

TMDB categorizes our movie collection into 20 distinct genres. Among these, 'Drama' emerges as the predominant genre, representing 44.66% of the movies that identify as drama films. Conversely, the 'TV Movie' genre is the least common, comprising only 1.69% of all movies. Positioned in second place, 'Comedy' encompasses 29.11% of the films, noted for their significant humor. The genres occupying the top ten rankings include 'Thriller,' 'Romance,' 'Action,' 'Horror,' 'Crime,' 'Documentary,' 'Adventure,' and 'Science Fiction.' Figure 3 displays the total movie count for each genre.

3.1.2(b) Release Date

Although the dataset of 45,000 movies does not encompass the entire history of cinema, it presumably includes all major films produced by the world's leading film industries, such as Hollywood and Bollywood. Under this assumption, we categorize the movies according to their release dates to calculate the total number of movies released each decade. The resulting line graph, displayed in Figure 4, reveals a consistent increase in movie production from the 1870s through the 1980s. Subsequently, the volume of movies surged, doubling from 5,617 in the 1990s to 11,078 in the 2000s, indicating a 97% growth in production. The rise in movie numbers persisted into the 2010s, culminating in a peak of 12,615 movies by 2017.

Figure 3. The total number of movies of each genre

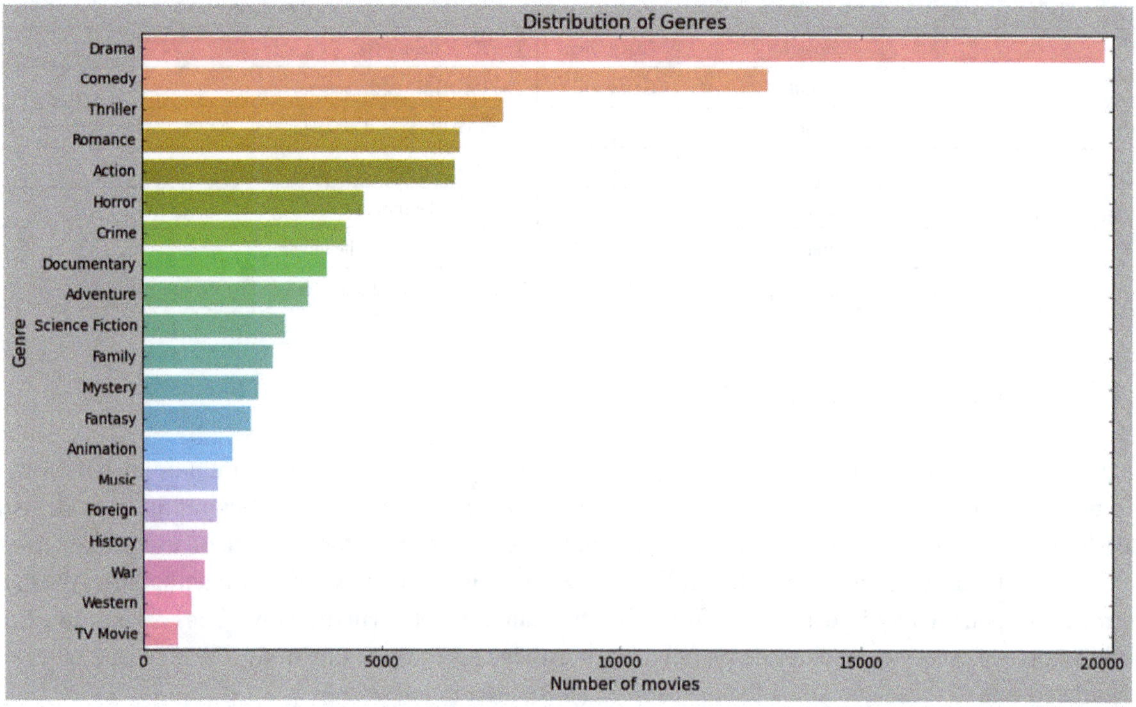

Figure 4. The total number of movies released by decade

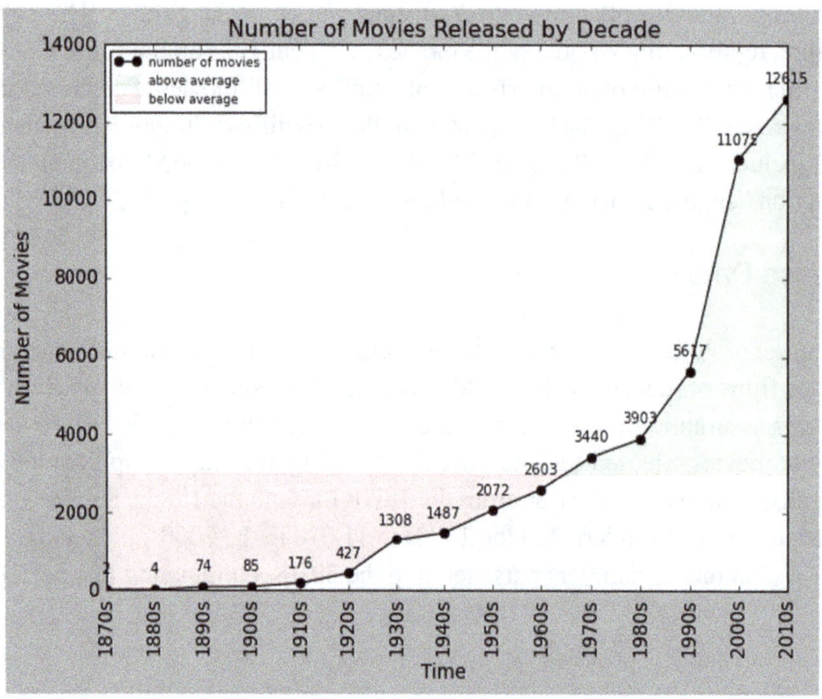

3.1.2(c) Vote Count

Figure 5 reveals that the distribution of 'vote count' is highly skewed to the right, exhibiting a median of merely 10 votes. Additionally, it shows that 2,788 movies did not receive any votes, whereas the highest number of votes received by a single movie was 14,075. This distribution suggests that TMDB votes might not be as indicative or persuasive as IMDB scores, considering that half of the movies garnered only 10 votes.

Figure 5. The distribution of 'vote_count'

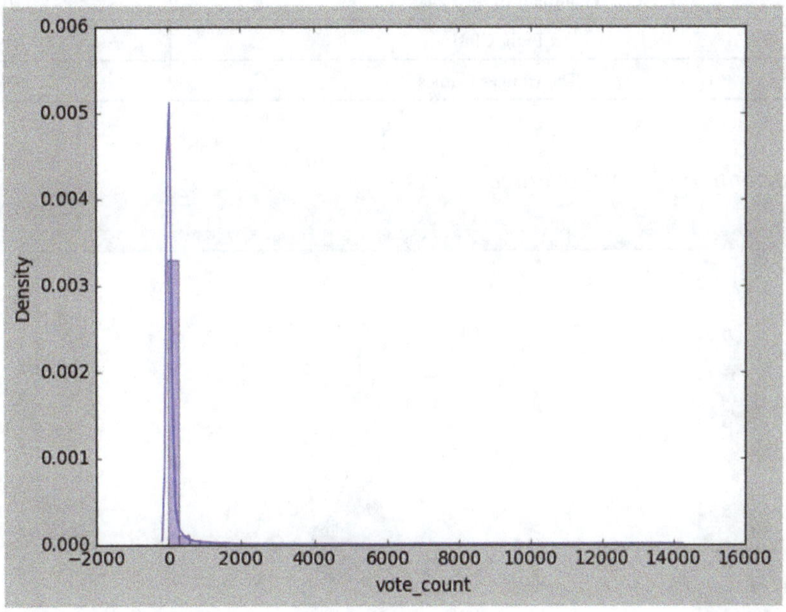

Table 4 reveals that two of Christopher Nolan's films, 'Inception' and 'The Dark Knight,' which received both critical acclaim and commercial success, occupy the top two spots on our list. They are followed by 'Avatar', 'The Avengers', 'Deadpool', 'Interstellar', 'Django Unchained', 'Guardians of the Galaxy', 'Fight Club', and 'The Hunger Games'.

3.1.2(d) Vote Average

Before visualizing the distribution of 'vote average', we observed that 2876 movies had zero average ratings. This observation does not necessarily indicate that these movies are of poor quality; it may simply mean they have not yet received any ratings. Consequently, we chose to address these zero values through median imputation, replacing them with the median value of the vote average. The summary statistics suggest that TMDB users are stringent in their ratings, with an average rating of only 6.01 out of 10, and half of the movies scoring 6.1 or lower (Figure 6).

Table 4. Top 10 most critically acclaimed movies in terms of vote counts

No.	Title	Vote Count
1	Inception	14075
2	The Dark Knight	12269
3	Avatar	12114
4	The Avengers	12000
5	Deadpool	11444
6	Interstellar	11187
7	Django Unchained	10297
8	Guardians of the Galaxy	10014
9	Fight Club	9678
10	The Hunger Games	9634

Figure 6. The distribution of 'vote_average'

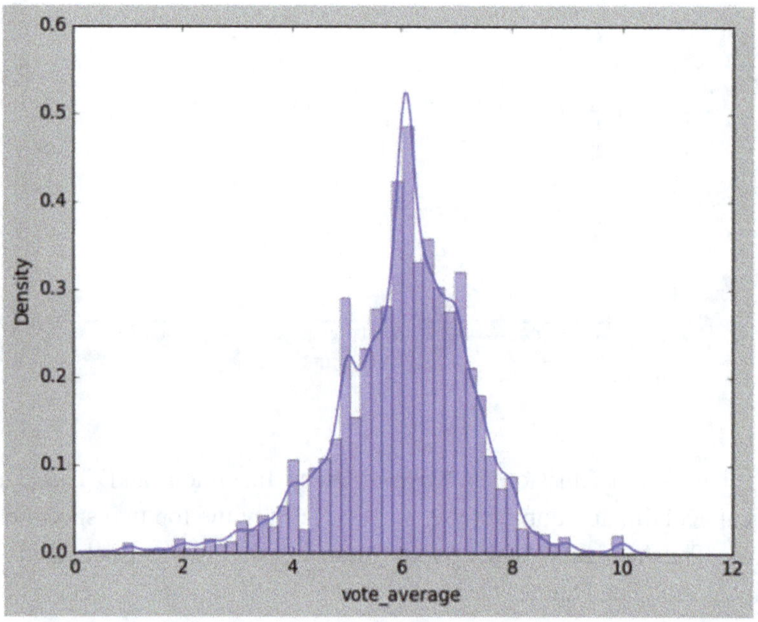

To ensure the credibility of the movie ratings, we focused on movies that received more than 163 votes, placing them above the ninth percentile for vote counts. According to Table 5, 'Dilwale Dulhania Le Jayenge' emerges as the most critically acclaimed film in the TMDB database, securing a 9.1 TMDB score from 661 users. 'Planet Earth' claims the second position with an average TMDB score of 8.8. It is also significant that all other top-rated movies appear in IMDB's Top 250 Movies list.

Table 5. Top 10 most critically acclaimed movies in terms of vote average

No.	Title	Vote Average	Vote Count
1	Dilwale Dulhania Le Jayenge	9.1	661
2	Planet Earth	8.8	176
3	The Shawshank Redemption	8.5	8358
4	The Godfather	8.5	6024
5	Your Name.	8.5	1030
6	The Dark Knight	8.3	12269
7	Fight Club	8.3	9678
8	Pulp Fiction	8.3	8670
9	Schindler's List	8.3	4436
10	Whiplash	8.3	4376

3.1.2(e) Rating

Figure 7 reveals that the most common rating is 4 on a scale of 5. Additionally, ratings between 1 and 3 are less frequent compared to those between 3 and 5. This suggests that users tend to rate movies more often when they enjoy them rather than when they dislike them.

Figure 7. The overall distribution of movie ratings

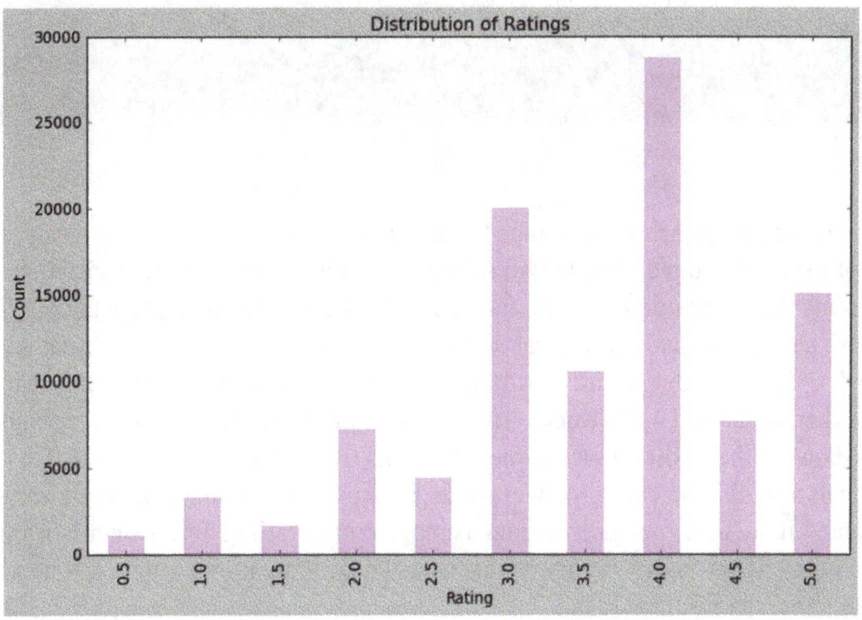

Upon analyzing the distribution of movie ratings by genre (Figure 8), it emerges that thirteen out of twenty genres display boxplots with a median rating of 4, and first and third quartiles of 3 and 4, respectively. Conversely, genres such as 'Animation', 'Foreign', and 'TV Movie' exhibit boxplots with higher ratings, evidenced by an upward shift and a broader interquartile range. The genres 'Documentary', 'Music', 'War', and 'Western', however, show a lower median score of 3.5, yet share the same interquartile range observed in the majority of genres.

Figure 8. The distribution of movie ratings per genre

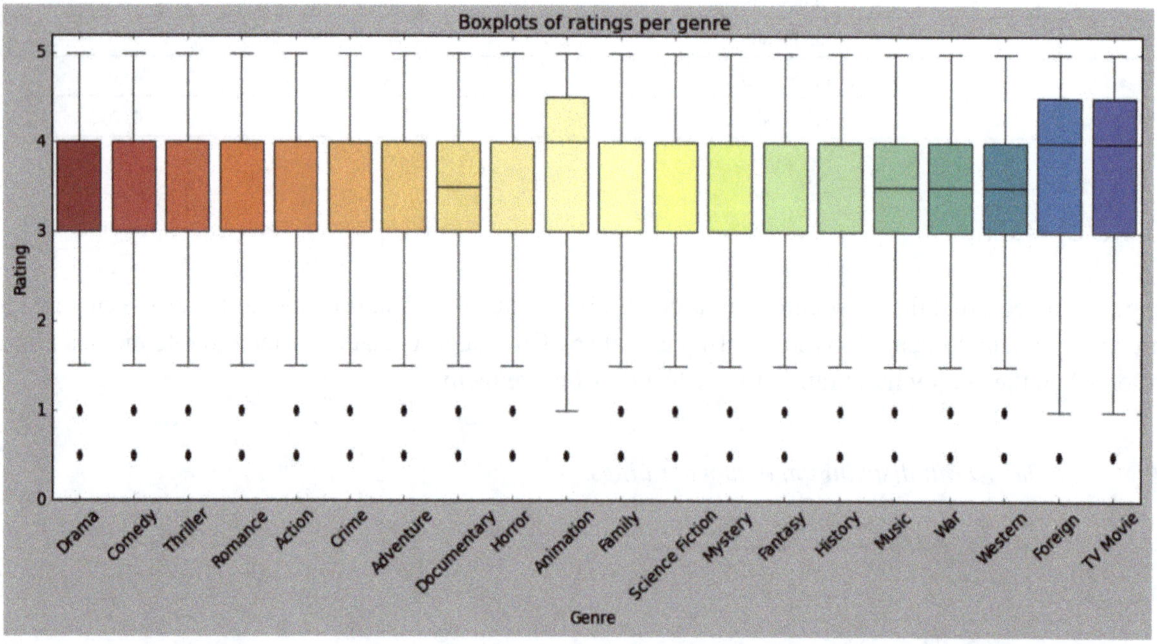

In this section, we group the movie ratings by 'movie id' to calculate both the mean ratings and the total number of users who rated each movie. Figure 9 features three different visualizations: the top histogram presents the distribution of mean ratings, the right histogram displays the distribution of the number of users per movie, and the central scatter plot illustrates the bivariate relationship between these two metrics. The distribution of mean ratings is negatively skewed, indicating that most movies received ratings between 3 and 4. Conversely, the distribution of the number of user ratings is extremely right-skewed, showing that most movies garnered ratings from only a small pool of TMDB users. The scatter plot reveals a significant cluster of data points, indicating that movies with a mean rating between 3 and 4.5 attracted more user ratings, while areas representing ratings lower than 3 or higher than 4.5 saw fewer data points. This analysis suggests that users tend to rate movies more frequently if they find them enjoyable rather than if they do not.

Figure 9. Number of users against mean rating (rating_small.csv)

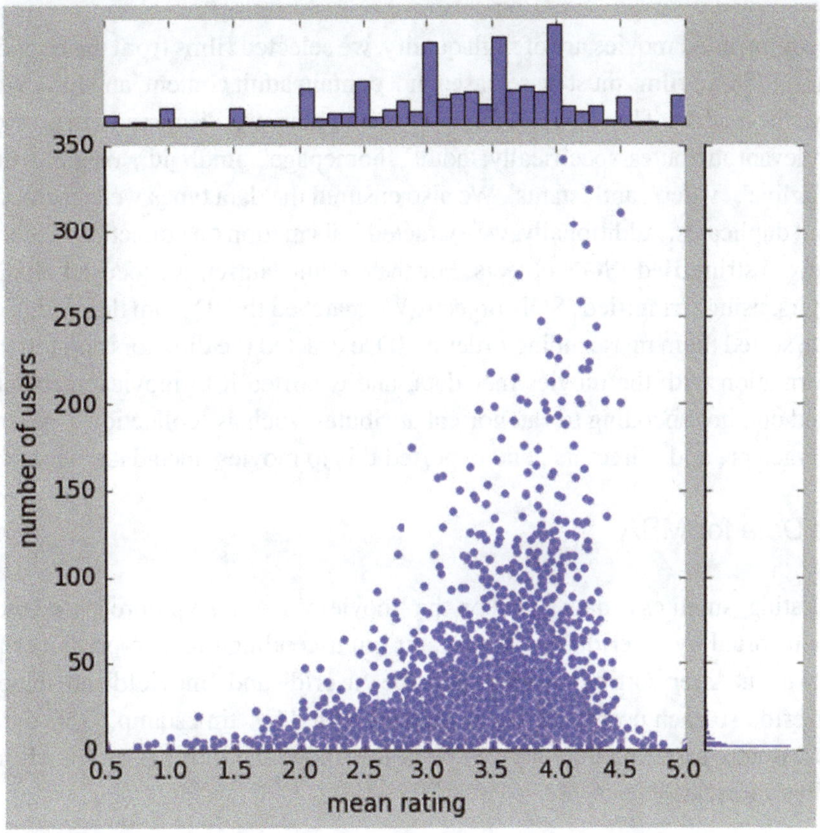

3.2 Data Preparation

To accomplish the task outlined before, integration of three distinct datasets is necessary. Table 6 below outlines the purpose of each dataset. Additionally, to fulfill the requirements for Market Basket Analysis (MBA) and recommender systems, a few assumptions are established as follows:

- Users who rate the movies are those who have either purchased or watched the movies.
- Users who have not rated the movies are considered uninterested in the movies.
- All users reside in the United States, and timestamps follow the country's standard, facilitating the implementation of a context-based recommender system

Table 6. Dataset purposes

Dataset	Purposes
Movies Metadata	To develop content and context-based recommender.
Ratings Data for Recommenders	To develop collaborative, hybrid and context-based recommender.
Ratings Data for MBA	To develop market basket analysis.

3.2.1 Movies Metadata

To ensure the recommended movies are of high quality, we selected films from the movies metadata that met specific criteria. These films must be released, not contain adult content, and have vote averages and counts at or above the median. The rationale for using the median was discussed in a previous section. We then removed irrelevant attributes, specifically: 'adult', 'homepage', 'imdb_id', 'original_title', 'overview', 'poster_path', 'tagline', 'video', and 'status'. We also ensured the data types were correct and eliminated all null values and duplicates. Additionally, we extracted information on collections, genres, and production companies from stringified JSON objects. For the credits dataset, we focused on directors and the top three characters, using stringified JSON objects. We matched the ID from the credits dataset with the movies metadata, sorted them in ascending order by ID, extracted the directors and top three characters, merged this information with the movies metadata, and exported it to movies_metadata_cleaned.csv. Lastly, we applied one-hot encoding to categorical attributes, such as 'collection', 'genres', 'production companies', 'characters', and 'directors', and exported this to movies_metadata_ohe.csv.

3.2.2 Ratings Data for MBA

We filtered the 'rating_small.csv' data based on the 'movieId' from the preprocessed movies metadata. The data was then sorted by 'userId' and 'timestamp' in ascending order to predict which movies users would watch next. After sorting, we dropped the 'userId' and 'movieId' attributes and grouped 'movieId' by 'userId', so each user had a list of movies sorted by 'timestamp'. This data was exported to ratings_all.csv. Before experimentation, we one-hot-encoded the rating data, transforming the list of movies into a binary format.

3.2.3 Ratings Data for Recommender

Similar to the MBA ratings data, we filtered the 'rating_small.csv' based on 'movieId' from the preprocessed movies metadata. We extracted two contextual columns from 'timestamp': 'holiday' and 'period' (e.g., 'early morning', 'morning', 'noon', 'evening', 'night', 'latenight') to support the contextual recommender system. We then performed a stratified split to divide the rating data into an 80% training subset and a 20% testing subset, maintaining proportional user representation. This stratification ensured users contributing to predictions in the training set also appeared in the testing set, allowing for effective evaluation of the recommender system's performance. Finally, we reshaped the data into a pivot table with 'title' as columns, 'userId' as the index, and 'rating' as values, ensuring no duplicates in movie titles.

3.2.4 Transformed Data Description

We have outlined the data transformation process for both recommender systems and market basket analysis tasks. Table 7 describes the transformed dataset, which is now prepared for analysis.

Table 7. Transformed dataset description

Dataset	Attributes	Attributes Type	Scale of Dataset	Description
Movies Metadata	movieid	Categorical	(15510, 1392)	The ID of the movie.
	budget	Ordered		The budget of the movie in dollars.
	popularity	Ordered		The popularity score assigned by TMDB.
	revenue	Ordered		The total revenue of the movie in dollars.
	runtime	Ordered		The runtime of the movie in minutes.
	vote_average	Ordered		The average rating of the movie.
	vote_count	Ordered		The number of votes by users, as counted by TMDB.
	title	Categorical		The original title of the movie.
	belongs_to_collection (OHE*)	Categorical		One-Hot-Encoded movie series that the particular film belongs to.
	genres (OHE*)	Categorical		One-Hot-Encoded genres associated with the movie.
	original_language (OHE*)	Categorical		One-Hot-Encoded original language in which the movie was shot.
	production_companies (OHE*)	Categorical		One-Hot-Encoded production companies involved with the making of the movie.
	production_countries (OHE*)	Categorical		One-Hot-Encoded countries where the movie was shot/produced in.
	directors (OHE*)	Categorical		One-Hot-Encoded directors involved in the movies.
	characters (OHE*)	Categorical		One-Hot-Encoded characters involved in the movies.
Ratings Data for Recommenders (Before split into train and test subsets)	userid	Categorical	(84157, 6)	The ID of the user.
	datetime	Categorical		The extracted datetime column from timestamp .
	holiday	Categorical		To identify if a rating is it made in a holiday.
	period	Categorical		The period of a day according to the rating timestamp (i.e., night, morning, noon & etc).
	title	Categorical		The official title of the movie.
	rating	Ordered		The user's rating of the movie.
Ratings Data for MBA	userid	Categorical	(671, 5682)	The ID of the user.
	movieId (OHE*)	Categorical		One-Hot-Encoded movieId.

* One-Hot-Encoding (OHE) transforms the categorical value into a new categorical column and assign a binary value of 1 or 0 to those column.

3.3 Modelling of Recommender System

This module presents the implementation and analysis of recommender systems, developed using Python within the Jupyter Notebook environment. As previously mentioned, we aim to develop four types of recommender systems: Collaborative Filtering (CF) System, Content-based System, Hybrid-based

System, and Context Aware System. Within the Collaborative Filtering System, we will explore two sub-categories: memory-based and model-based. Memory-based CF Systems, such as User-to-User CF and Item-to-Item CF, employ similarity measures like Pearson Correlation to determine the similarity among users and items. However, they suffer from scalability issues. We will conduct a detailed analysis of these scalability challenges following the implementation phase. Meanwhile, model-based CF systems will be implemented as well. In this section, we will implement and discuss six different recommender systems, as illustrated in Figure 10.

Figure 10. Recommender systems overview

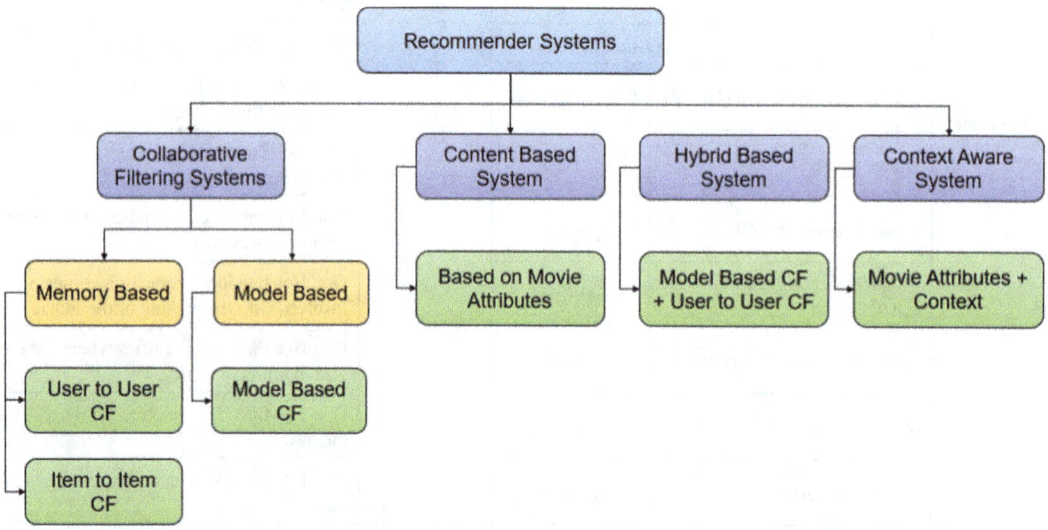

3.3.1 Collaborative Filtering

The foundational principle of collaborative filtering posits that individuals with similar preferences in the past will likely exhibit similar preferences in the future (Çano & Morisio, 2019b). This concept hinges on identifying items that a specific user might find relevant from a vast pool of options ("filtering") by leveraging the preferences of a multitude of users ("collaboration") (Peter et al., 2016). Therefore, collaborative filtering necessitates the comprehensive availability of information about every item-user interaction, along with metrics that gauge a user's preference for an item. In this context, we use 'rating,' on a scale from 1 to 5, as the metric for preference. Typically, not every user watches or rates every movie, leading to a scenario where the item-user matrix is replete with zeros due to its sparsity, and the rating matrix is filled with many missing values. In this study, we interpret such missing values to imply a lack of interest or the absence of a purchase to watch the movie, in contrast to non-missing values that indicate interest or the presence of a purchase to watch the movie.

3.3.1(a) User-to-User Collaborative Filtering System

Generating personalized recommendations for a user via collaborative filtering involves identifying users with similar tastes and recommending items they have appreciated but the targeted user has not yet explored. This process follows the preliminary data stratification and reshaping into a 'pivot' matrix (Gabriel, 2019; Grab N Go Info, 2022; Peter et al., 2016). The steps to implement this user-to-user recommendation approach are as follows.

1. Normalize the matrix (rows= users, columns = movies).
2. Find the most similar users based on rating behavior using Pearson Correlation toward a particular user.
3. Get the list of non-interacted top-5 weighted score movies from most similar users
4. To evaluate the performance:
   a. Identify whether top-5 weighted score movies are in the test-set movie.
   b. Repeat the steps above by implementing on the rest of the users.
   c. Compute performance metrics of AUC ROC, Precision, Mean Average Precision, Recall and F-measure.
   d. Repeat the steps above by implementing on top-10 and top-20 weighted score movies.

This approach is also referred to as "user-based top-N recommendation" (Peter et al., 2016). The initial step of normalizing the matrix addresses the treatment of null values. By normalizing the matrix and subsequently replacing null values with zeros, we indicate that these null values represent an average rating on a row-by-row basis. A critique work (Gabriel, 2019) highlights an issue with initially substituting null values with zeros, potentially misleadingly suggesting that an absence of rating is inferior to the lowest possible rating. Instead, it's more accurate to consider such an absence as a neutral position, where zero signifies an average rating and negative values indicate a dislike for the movie.

Following this, we calculated a proximity measure to determine the distance between our user and each of the other users. A commonly used method for measuring the proximity between two users is the Pearson correlation of their ratings (Peter et al., 2016).

We identify the most similar users for a specific user by arranging the Pearson Correlation measures in descending order. The crucial question arises: what constitutes the baseline for identifying the most similar users? To address this, we established a threshold for Pearson Correlation at 0.5659, derived from calculating the 90th percentile of all Pearson Correlation measures across the matrix. Consequently, the users falling within the 90th percentile of similarity measures are considered the most similar to a given user. Subsequently, we aim to identify movies rated by these most similar users that the target user has not yet rated, marking these as potential recommendations for the target user. Prior to finalizing these recommendations, we calculate a weighted score by combining the similarity measures with the ratings given by the most similar users. This ensures that potential recommendations from users with higher similarity scores and higher ratings receive a greater weighted score. To determine this weighted score, we multiply the similarity measures by the rating scores of the potential recommendations. After calculating these scores, we arrange them in descending order and select the top-N movies for recommendation. Implementing this user-based top-N recommendation strategy, Table 8 illustrates an example of selecting the top-10 movie recommendations for user ID 22.

Table 8. Compute weighted score based on the most similar users

Conditional Column	Weighted Score
The Wicker Man	1.34
Dead Man's Shoes	1.34
Dylan Moran: Monster	1.34
Mysterious Skin	1.34
The Darjeeling Limited	1.34
The Big Short	1.09
My Life in Pink	1.09
Sophie's Choice	1.09
The Great Dictator	1.05
Miracle Mile	1.00

We have illustrated the method for extracting the top-N movies for a user. However, to evaluate the effectiveness of our recommender system, we must replicate these calculations for every user to generate their recommended movie lists. Initially, we divided the data into training and testing subsets through stratified splitting. The testing subset contains the movies that users have actually watched. Thus, we compare the recommended movies to this testing subset to determine if the recommended movies match the movies in the testing subset. This evaluation method draws inspiration from the study by (Gabriel, 2019).

Subsequently, we calculated a variety of performance metrics to assess the effectiveness of the recommender system. These metrics include ROC AUC, Precision@N, Mean Average Precision@N, Recall@N, and F-Measure@N. Additionally, we conducted the evaluation using three different sizes of top-N recommendations: top-N = 5, top-N = 10, and top-N = 20.

3.3.1(b) Item-to-Item Collaborative Filtering System

In scenarios where the user base significantly exceeds the item pool, finding similar items can be more efficient and quicker than identifying similar users. However, in our case, the dataset contains a greater number of movies than users, with 3,375 movies compared to 671 users. Consequently, the computation for an item-based recommender system is slower than that for a user-based system under these conditions. The item-based collaborative filtering system estimates ratings for an item based on the ratings of similar items. A key distinction between item-based and user-based approaches is the orientation of the item-user matrix. Specifically, in the item-based system, the matrix is transposed: 'userId' represents the columns, and movie 'titles' are the rows. This contrasts with the user-based approach, where movie 'titles' are the columns and 'userId' the rows'.

The techniques of implementing item-based recommender are very similar to user-based, where the steps are described below.

1. Normalize the matrix (rows= movies, columns = users).
2. Find the most similar movies based on rating behavior using Pearson Correlation toward a particular user.

3. Get the list of non-interacted top-5 weighted score users from most similar movies
4. To evaluate the performance:
    a. Identify whether top-5 weighted score users are in the test-set.
    b. Repeat the steps above by implementing on the rest of the movies.
    c. Compute performance metrics of AUC ROC, Precision, Mean Average Precision, Recall and F-measure.
    d. Repeat the steps above by implementing on top-10 and top-20 weighted score movies.

After normalizing the matrix, we compute the similarity measure between items instead of users. With 3,656 movies in this study, we generate a Pearson Correlation matrix of dimension (3656, 3656), as depicted in Figure 11.

Figure 11. Compute Pearson correlation among items

	(500) Days of Summer	...And Justice for All	10 Cloverfield Lane	10 Things I Hate About You	11:14	12 Angry Men	12 Years a Slave	127 Hours	13 Assassins	13 Going on 30	13 Tzameti	1408	16 Blocks	17 Agai
(500) Days of Summer	1.000000	0.037672	0.009367	0.217008	-0.220182	0.019597	0.357962	0.945810	0.246391	0.139482	0.905945	0.931332	0.118548	0.00141
...And Justice for All	0.037672	1.000000	-0.009401	0.291604	-0.196565	0.226112	0.044947	-0.102910	-0.124663	0.001035	0.025213	0.032081	0.047912	0.0000E
10 Cloverfield Lane	0.009367	-0.009401	1.000000	-0.397384	0.092234	0.120598	0.260508	-0.003830	0.009093	0.790926	-0.011869	-0.007153	0.056935	0.0326C
10 Things I Hate About You	0.217008	0.291604	-0.397384	1.000000	-0.148291	0.089602	0.025306	0.137386	0.146811	0.064158	0.087942	0.076014	-0.196260	0.5606:
11:14	-0.220182	-0.196565	0.092234	-0.148291	1.000000	0.228101	0.550764	-0.206212	-0.127065	-0.087694	-0.166841	-0.185062	-0.147101	-0.3075‹

To illustrate, consider movie A as an example. We identify the most similar movies to movie A, selecting those in the 90th percentile of the similarity measures, a method detailed in the prior section. Subsequently, we aim to compile a list of potential users who have rated the movies most similar to movie A. For each of these potential users, we calculate a weighted score for movie A by multiplying the rating by the similarity measures. Following this calculation, we sort the weighted scores in descending order and select the top N users. Thus, these top N users are the recommended audience for movie A, and we implement the item-based top-N recommendation for this movie. To evaluate the effectiveness of the item-based recommender system, we extend the prediction process to include not just movie A but all 3,375 movies in the dataset, aiming to generate recommended 'userId' for each movie. We then assess the accuracy of these predictions by comparing them against the test subset. After that, we have computed a diversified of performance metric to evaluate the recommender. The evaluation is also repeated for three types of topN, which are topN =5; topN = 10 and topN = 20.

3.3.1(c) Model-Based Collaborative Filtering System

The model-based recommender system differs from memory-based systems, such as user-based and item-based, in that it does not necessitate the computation of similarity measures. Instead, it utilizes a model-based approach. This method generally offers a faster computation speed compared to memory-based systems, as it eliminates the need to calculate similarity measures for each observation. A prominent example of a model utilized in recommender systems is the latent factor model, such as Singular Value Decomposition (SVD). For this study, SVD has been selected to implement the model-based recommender system. The implementation steps are outlined as follows:

1. Normalize the matrix (rows= users, columns = movies).
2. Apply the SVD Algorithm on the matrix.
3. Get the list of non-interacted top-5 weighted score movies from the SVD Measures
4. To evaluate the performance:
    a. Identify whether top-5 weighted score movies are in the test-set movie.
    b. Repeat the steps above by implementing on the rest of the users.
    c. Compute performance metrics of AUC ROC, Precision, Mean Average Precision, Recall and F-measure.
    d. Repeat the steps above by implementing on top-10 and top-20 weighted score movies.

In this study, the model-based recommender employs a matrix structure with rows representing users and columns representing items, a configuration echoed in related works (Gabriel, 2019; Vaibhav, 2020). We initially normalize the matrix because the Singular Value Decomposition (SVD) algorithm cannot process null values. Consequently, we address null values by replacing them with zeros following normalization. Subsequently, we apply SVD, decomposing the matrix into three simpler matrices: "U," "sigma," and "VT." The dimensions of these matrices are illustrated in Figure 4.11. To compute the predicted movie scores, we first perform a dot product between "U" and "sigma" to obtain "U_sigma," and then a second dot product between "U_sigma" and "VT." This method of using the dot product to compute recommended movie scores also finds support in the works of (Gabriel, 2019). After executing the dot product, we reconstruct the matrix back into a Pandas dataframe, maintaining the same dimensions as prior to the dot product operation.

Subsequently, we transpose the matrix on which SVD was applied, configuring it so that columns represent 'userId' and rows represent movie 'title'. Transposing the matrix facilitates the sorting of recommended scores in descending order and enhances the efficiency of information retrieval. Table 9 displays the top-10 recommended movies for 'userId' 22.0.

Similar to the process used in previous recommender systems, we need to generate all recommended movies for each user and evaluate them based on the testing subset. We will then repeat the process for different numbers of top recommendations: topN = 5, topN = 10, and topN = 20.

Table 9. Get top-N movie score for a user

Title	22.0
The Lord of the Rings: The Fellowship of the Ring	0.65
The Lord of the Rings: The Two Towers	0.63
The Matrix	0.62
The Lord of the Rings: The Return of the King	0.62
The Empire Strikes Back	0.61
Fight Club	0.60
Star Wars	0.60
The Silence of the Lambs	0.60
Return of the Jedi	0.59
Se7en	0.59

3.3.2 Hybrid-Based Filtering

As noted in a study by Çano and Morisio (Çano & Morisio, 2019b), hybrid recommender systems blend two or more recommendation strategies to leverage their complementary strengths. Some studies propose hybrid models that fuse various collaborative recommenders to create a hybrid-based filtering mechanism (Aljunid & Huchaiah, 2021; Dong et al., 2017). Moreover, a prevalent approach to hybrid recommenders involves calculating a weighted score from different systems (Jeffery, 2021). This method combines outputs from each model using static weightings. In this chapter, we integrated user-based and model-based recommenders to calculate their combined weighted score. We assigned equal weights to both recommenders, calculating the hybrid score by multiplying the scores from both recommenders. Therefore, if a movie A recommended by the user-based system appears in the topN, but the same movie A recommended by the model-based system does not, the hybrid outcome will consider inputs from both systems, thus lowering the ranking of movie A from the user-based perspective. After computing the hybrid score, we sort the scores in descending order and select the recommended movies that rank within the topN. Figure 12 presents a Python syntax for generating topN movies with a hybrid score in descending order for 'userId' 22.

Figure 12. Compute hybrid score

	conditional_column	weighted_score	title	model_score	hybrid_score
4	Mysterious Skin	1.338882	Mysterious Skin	0.529360	0.708751
1	The Wicker Man	1.338882	The Wicker Man	0.528555	0.707672
2	Dylan Moran: Monster	1.338882	Dylan Moran: Monster	0.528555	0.707672
3	Dead Man's Shoes	1.338882	Dead Man's Shoes	0.528555	0.707672
0	The Darjeeling Limited	1.338882	The Darjeeling Limited	0.526621	0.705083

Once we obtain the hybrid score for a user, we must perform computations again to identify recommended movies for each user. Initially, we divided the data into training and testing subsets through stratified splitting, where the testing subset comprises movies actually watched by users. Thus, we compare the recommended movies with the testing subset to ascertain if the recommended movies are included there. This evaluation process has been carried out for three different numbers of top recommendations: topN = 5, topN = 10, and topN = 20.

3.3.3 Content-Based Filtering

Content-based filtering operates on the principle that individuals who appreciated items with specific characteristics in the past are likely to favor similar items in the future (Çano & Morisio, 2019b). This method utilizes item attributes to compare items with user profiles and generate recommendations. For this study, we encoded 1378 columns representing attributes of movies, such as collections they belong to, languages, actors, production countries, and more. We applied one-hot encoding to the movies' attributes. Therefore, by analyzing the attributes of previously watched movies, we aim to predict the features of movies a user is likely to prefer. This approach mirrors the technique used in the model-based recommender system, where we first normalize the data before applying the SVD algorithm to forecast prediction scores. We conduct this process for different numbers of top recommendations: topN = 5, topN = 10, and topN = 20.

3.3.4 Context-Aware Filtering

The MovieLens dataset does not directly provide contextual data. However, we succeeded in deriving two contextual attributes, 'holiday' and 'period,' from the existing dataset columns to complete the study's requirements. Additionally, due to the absence of location information about users, we assume they observe holidays as recognized in the United States. This assumption allows us to consider whether a user's rating was influenced by it being a holiday. Furthermore, we categorized the timing of each user's movie rating into six distinct periods. Figure 13 displays a pie chart illustrating the two contextual attributes we extracted.

Figure 13. One hot encode context data

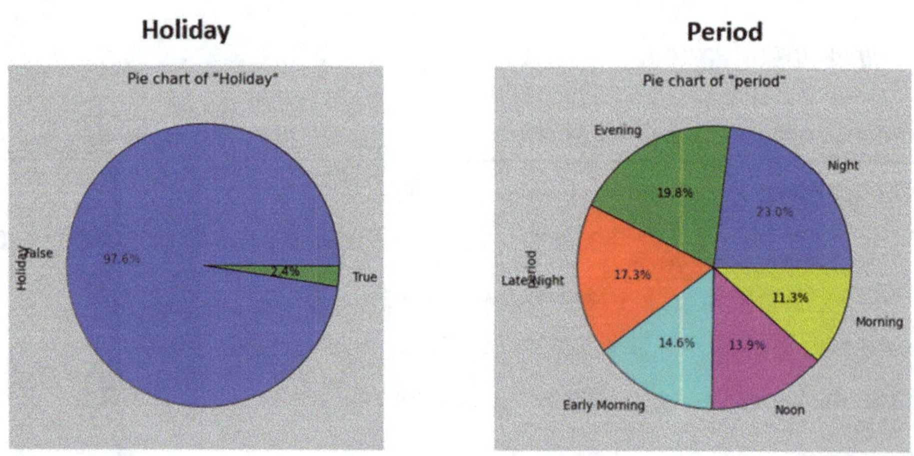

We then encoded the extracted contextual columns in binary format and combined them with the movies' metadata. Following this merge, the dimension of the resulting matrix was (671, 1384). In a manner akin to the model-based recommender system, we normalized this data and then applied the SVD algorithm to forecast the prediction score, as depicted in Figure 14.

Figure 14. Matrix subset for context-based recommender

	Early Morning	Evening	Late Night	Morning	Night	Noon	belongs_to_collection_Asterix and Obelix (Animation) Collection	belongs_to_collection_Babylon 5 Collection	belongs_to_collection_Charlie Chan (Warner Oland) Collection	bel
1.0	0.005434	0.005434	0.019782	0.005458	0.005419	0.005469	0.005519	0.005535	0.005519	
2.0	0.005951	0.005893	0.005945	0.055329	0.005836	0.005912	0.005519	0.005504	0.005519	
3.0	0.005549	0.013801	0.026194	0.005512	0.012726	0.005607	0.005520	0.005508	0.005519	
4.0	0.059779	0.032021	0.021656	0.049804	0.005390	0.005403	0.005517	0.005573	0.005519	
5.0	0.005187	0.005136	0.005455	0.005086	0.079178	0.005079	0.005519	0.005478	0.005519	

As with the earlier recommender systems, we must generate all the recommended contextual and content data for each user and evaluate these recommendations using the testing subset. This evaluation process is repeated to produce different outcomes for topN = 5, topN = 10, and topN = 20, with the results presented accordingly.

3.4 Modelling of Market Basket Analysis (MBA)

The primary aim of this section is to analyze the MovieLens dataset to identify patterns in customers' movie-watching habits. We accomplish this through Market Basket Analysis (MBA), a data mining method retailers use to enhance sales by understanding customer buying patterns more deeply. A typical rule found in MBA takes the form "A→B," where A represents the antecedent and B the consequent. This implies that if a customer enjoys movie A, they might also enjoy movie B, or it might allow us to predict the customer's next movie choice. The key outcome of this section is to uncover the associations between movies that users watch. We executed this analysis using two rule-generating algorithms: the Apriori Algorithm and the FP-Growth Algorithm.

3.4.1 Select the Attributes Based on Your Understanding

The MovieLens dataset does not inherently serve as a transactional dataset; rather, it compiles ratings that 671 users have assigned to specific movies. In our analysis, we regarded each user ID as a market basket, treating the movie IDs as the items purchased within that basket. We opted for movie IDs over titles to avoid confusion arising from multiple movies sharing the same title. Given that movie information and user ratings reside in separate dataframes, we executed two merge operations to amalgamate these datasets. Initially, we merged the 'movies' dataframe with the 'links' dataframe through an inner join. Subsequently, we employed another inner join to merge the 'links' dataframe with the 'ratings' dataframe, using the 'movield' column as the basis for this operation.

Subsequently, we organized the data so that each row represented an individual user and each column corresponded to a distinct movie ID. Within this arrangement, a value of 1 indicates that a user has rated a movie, while a value of 0 denotes the absence of a rating. Figure 3.2 displays the dataframe that emerged after applying one-hot encoding to the 'MovieId' column. This transformed dataframe, consisting of 671 rows and 5682 columns, is prepared for application in the rule-generating algorithms.

3.4.2 Create the Association Rules (AR)

To conduct Market Basket Analysis (MBA), various rule generation algorithms are available. However, for this study, we chose to implement the Apriori Algorithm and the FP-Growth Algorithm. Since Scikit-learn does not offer support for these algorithms in the context of MBA, we utilized the mlxtend machine learning package, which provides implementations for both the Apriori Algorithm and FP-Growth to identify frequent itemsets. Our focus was on itemsets that do not exceed a length of 3 and have a minimum support threshold of 20%. Consequently, we generated frequent item sets using the apriori() and fpgrowth() functions and introduced a new column to denote the length of each itemset. Following this, we filtered the item sets to meet our predefined criteria, as detailed in Table 10.

Table 10. Fixed criteria for apriori and FP-growth parameters

Parameters	Criteria	Values
Min_support	Equal to	0.2
Frequent_itemsets length	Less than or equal to	3.0
Frequent_itemsets support	Large than or equal to	0.2

3.4.3 Calculate Support, Confidence, and Lift for Each AR

Subsequently, we generated association rules from the identified frequent itemsets, taking into account their respective support, confidence, and lift values. Within the association_rule() function, it is possible to define the metric of interest and apply a minimum threshold. For our analysis, we established a minimum lift threshold of at least 1. This approach resulted in the generation of 534 rules using both the Apriori Algorithm and FP-Growth, all of which surpassed the minimum support level of 20% and the minimum lift level of 1. Nonetheless, it became evident that multiple rules featured the same set of products but in a different sequence of antecedent and consequent. Therefore, it is feasible to further condense the results derived from these rules illustrated in Figure 15 and 16 respectively.

Figure 15. The first five association rules generated via the apriori algorithm

antecedents	consequents	antecedent support	consequent support	support	confidence	lift	leverage	conviction
(1)	(260)	0.368107	0.433681	0.244411	0.663968	1.531004	0.084770	1.685311
(260)	(1)	0.433681	0.368107	0.244411	0.563574	1.531004	0.084770	1.447880
(296)	(1)	0.482861	0.368107	0.228018	0.472222	1.282839	0.050273	1.197270
(1)	(296)	0.368107	0.482861	0.228018	0.619433	1.282839	0.050273	1.358864
(1)	(318)	0.368107	0.463487	0.217586	0.591093	1.275317	0.046973	1.312066

Figure 16. The first five association rules generated via the FP-growth algorithm

antecedents	consequents	antecedent support	consequent support	support	confidence	lift	leverage	conviction
(296)	(356)	0.482861	0.508197	0.344262	0.712963	1.402927	0.098874	1.713379
(356)	(296)	0.508197	0.482861	0.344262	0.677419	1.402927	0.098874	1.603130
(593)	(356)	0.453055	0.508197	0.338301	0.746711	1.469334	0.108060	1.941665
(356)	(593)	0.508197	0.453055	0.338301	0.665689	1.469334	0.108060	1.636037
(296)	(593)	0.482861	0.453055	0.333830	0.691358	1.525991	0.115067	1.772101

3.4.4 Determine the Minimum Support

Our experiments involved testing various minimum support values, specifically 0.1, 0.15, 0.2, and 0.25. We ultimately chose to generate frequent item sets with a minimum support of 20% (min_support = 0.2). This decision was informed by two primary considerations. First, limitations in available memory led to 'out of memory' errors when setting the minimum support below 0.1. Second, as demonstrated in Table 11, there was a noticeable decrease in the number of frequent item sets as the minimum support value increased. Therefore, we selected this minimum support value to balance the need for a sufficient number of examples without an overwhelming abundance.

Table 11. The number of frequent itemsets generated for different minimum support values

Minimum Support	Number of Frequent Itemsets
0.10	36722
0.15	1863
0.20	268
0.25	76

3.4.5 Select The Number of AR to Give the Meaning of Your Associations

To make the association rules more meaningful and to simplify visualization, we decided to refine the dataframe that contained these rules. Our strategy involved focusing on rules where only one item formed the consequent, leading to the division of the dataframe into two smaller ones based on the quantity of items in the antecedent. Specifically, one dataframe retained all rules involving two items as antecedents, and the other included rules with three-item antecedents. Within each dataframe, we arranged the rules by descending "Lift" values and then selected the top 50 rules demonstrating the highest lift.

4. ANALYSIS AND RESULTS

This section will cover the outcomes from both the Recommender Systems and Market Basket Analysis (MBA). The performance of Recommender Systems will be evaluated using various metrics such as ROC AUC, Precision@N, Mean Average Precision@N, Recall@N, Mean Average Recall@N, and F1@N. For the MBA, three visualization techniques were employed to elucidate the association rules.

4.1 Recommender Systems

We explored six different recommender system approaches, aiming to identify the most effective model. Experiments were conducted with three variations of the topN parameter: 5, 10, and 20. The performance of each recommender, under different topN settings, was assessed using metrics such as ROC AUC, Precision@N, Mean Average Precision@N, Recall@N, Mean Average Recall@N, and F1@N. The outcomes of these evaluations are presented in Table 12.

Table 12. Performance of recommender systems

Recommender	TopN	ROC AUC	Precision @N	Mean Average Precision @N	Recall @N	Mean Average Recall @N	F1 @N
Collaborative User Based	5	0.518	0.010	0.283	0.002	0.042	0.003
	10	0.535	0.010	0.140	0.004	0.051	0.006
	20	0.058	0.011	0.091	0.008	0.073	0.009
Collaborative Item Based	5	0.512	0.004	0.216	0.004	0.190	0.004
	10	0.523	0.004	0.110	0.009	0.200	0.005
	20	0.557	0.005	0.058	0.022	0.219	0.008
Collaborative Model Based	5	0.648	0.067	0.227	0.013	0.093	0.022
	10	0.725	0.063	0.141	0.026	0.101	0.036
	20	0.801	0.057	0.095	0.046	0.128	0.051
Hybrid Based	5	0.526	0.012	0.241	0.002	0.046	0.004
	10	0.036	0.011	0.149	0.004	0.057	0.006
	20	0.566	0.012	0.092	0.010	0.084	0.011
Content Based	5	0.671	0.080	0.233	0.080	0.233	0.080
	10	0.379	0.152	0.201	0.152	0.201	0.152
	20	0.483	0.244	0.253	0.245	0.255	0.245
Context Based	5	0.661	0.078	0.243	0.078	0.243	0.078
	10	0.364	0.150	0.206	0.150	0.206	0.150
	20	0.481	0.246	0.255	0.247	0.257	0.246

In the field of information retrieval, the formulas for precision and recall differ from those traditionally learned in machine learning classification tasks. The distinctions between the well-known formulas and those used for information retrieval are summarized in Table 13.

Table 13. Description of precision and recall in different context

Metrics	Context	Formula	Description
Precision	Classification	$\frac{True\ Positive}{True\ Positive + False\ Positive}$	Positive predictive value
	Information Retrieval	$\frac{Number\ of\ correctly\ predicted\ labels}{Total\ number\ of\ predictions}$	Fraction of retrieved objects that are relevant to the query
Recall	Classification	$\frac{True\ Positive}{True\ Positive + False\ Negative}$	True positive rate
	Information Retrieval	$\frac{Number\ of\ correctly\ predicted\ labels}{Total\ number\ of\ actual\ labels}$	Fraction of the relevant objects that are successfully retrieved

We employed metrics suited for information retrieval to assess the recommender systems, given that they do not constitute supervised learning tasks, meaning they lack classification labels. In this framework, precision helps determine the proportion of correctly predicted movies out of all the predicted ones. It's possible to evaluate precision and recall at a specific cutoff rank, denoted as @N. Precision becomes particularly valuable when the cost of a false positive is high. For instance, if a company finds that suggesting random, uninteresting movies to a user leads to customer attrition, prioritizing precision can help mitigate this issue. Upon determining precision, the next step involves calculating the mean average precision. This metric offers a more comprehensive representation of precision, as advocated by (Tan, 2019). Table 14 details the formulas for mean average precision and recall (Tan, 2019).

Table 14. Description of mean average precision and recall

Metrics	Formula	Description
Mean Average Precision	$mAP = \frac{1}{N}\sum_{i=1}^{N} AP_i$	· AP = Average Precison · N = Sample Size
Mean Average Recall	$mAR = \frac{1}{N}\sum_{i=1}^{N} AR_i$	· AR = Average Recall · N = Sample Size

Subsequently, we visualized the mean average precision using a bar chart, as depicted in Figure 17. Our findings revealed that the Collaborative User-Based Recommender System, with a topN setting of 5, outperformed all others in this metric. In other words, this system achieved the highest average of correctly predicted movies out of all predictions when compared with the other recommender systems. These results support the assumption underlying user-based recommendations: individuals with similar preferences in the past are likely to exhibit similar tastes in the future, a principle that proves effective for this dataset.

Figure 17. Mean average Precision@N

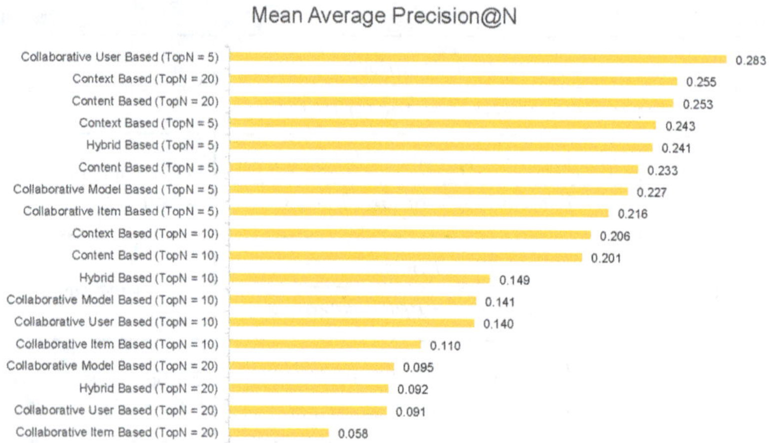

Meanwhile, recall provides an answer to questions like, "Out of all the actual movies (i.e., movies that users have watched), what fraction have been correctly predicted?" We prioritize recall when the cost of a false negative is significant. For instance, if a company finds that offering relevant movies is crucial for retaining users rather than suggesting movies of no interest, then in such scenarios, the recall metric becomes more valuable for evaluating the recommender system. Figure 18 illustrates the bar chart comparing each recommender system based on mean average recall. We found that the context-based recommender system achieved the highest performance according to this metric. In other words, this system had the highest average of correctly predicted movies out of all movies watched by the users. Moreover, the performance pattern of the context-based recommender system consistently surpassed that of the content-based recommender system whenever the topN values were equal. This pattern suggests that incorporating contextual information improves the outcomes of recommendations.

Figure 18. Mean average Recall@N

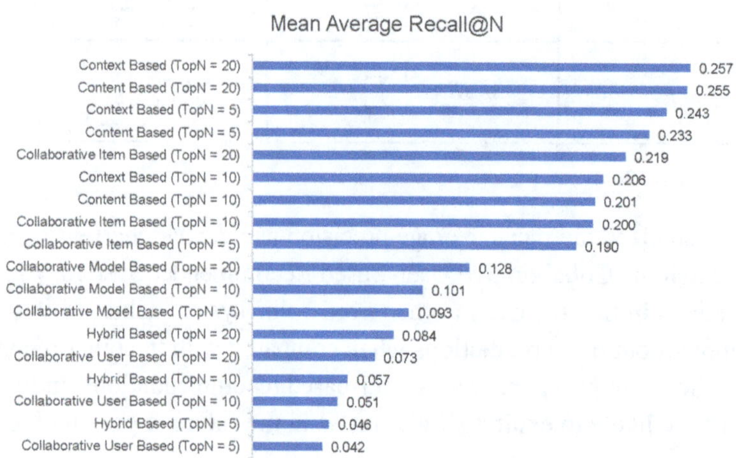

Since the user-based recommender system demonstrated the highest performance in mean-average precision, we chose this model for further visualization of the results. We can also visualize the performance results using a confusion matrix, as shown in Figure 19. The visual representation revealed a pattern: as topN increases, the ratio of true positives also increases. This outcome is expected because an increase in topN means more candidates are considered for matching with the true labels. The use of a confusion matrix for evaluating the recommender system is discussed in this paper (Del et al., 2008).

Figure 19. Confusion matrix of user-based recommender

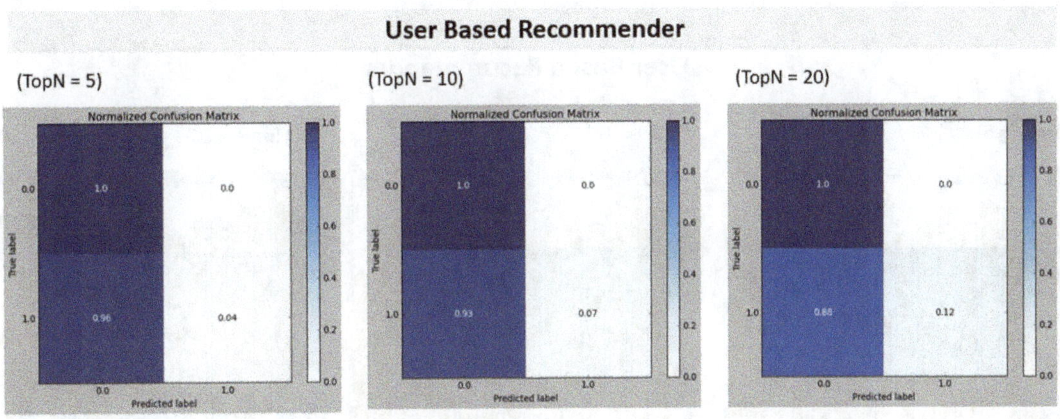

In addition to using a confusion matrix, we visualized the results through a bar chart that compares the number of true label movies with the number of predicted movies, as illustrated in Figure 20. Our goal was to identify the top 15 most frequently occurring movies in the testing set, such as 'The Silence of the Lambs', 'Pulp Fiction', 'Forrest Gump', etc. (these movies appear as x-axis labels). We selected these movies because they also frequently occur among the ground truth labels. We then examined how many of these movies the recommender system predicted across various topN values, as depicted by the blue bars in the chart. Similar to the pattern observed in the confusion matrix, the number of predictions matching these movies increases with higher topN values. However, does this mean that a higher topN necessarily improves the recommender system? The answer is no. As we observed in the mean average precision@N, higher topN values do not always enhance performance because they also contribute to an increase in false predictions. So, why visualize this data? By recognizing the patterns illustrated below, movie streaming companies can refine their recommender systems by assigning greater weight to these movies, thereby making the final recommendations more relevant to users.

Finally, this study clarifys and demonstrates why memory-based recommender systems do not scale as efficiently as model-based systems. The primary reason is that memory-based systems must identify the nearest neighbor of the target user or item (depending on whether it is user-based or item-based) for each prediction. Consequently, each prediction depends on different neighbors, unlike the one-size-fits-all approach of model-based systems. Model-based systems, on the other hand, rely on a predefined model, such as Singular Value Decomposition (SVD), eliminating the need to recalculate the similarity score after applying the SVD algorithm. As a result, model-based systems are significantly faster than memory-based systems, especially when dealing with a large number of users or items. For instance, in a scenario with a million users in the database, a user-based recommender system would need to compute a million similarity scores to obtain the overall performance metric. The model-based system requires 129.2 seconds to compute the results for three different topN values (i.e., 5, 10, and 20), whereas the memory-based system takes only 10.75 seconds. Therefore, if prediction speed is a critical factor for a streaming company, it would be advisable not to rely solely on memory-based recommenders, as they consume significantly more time than model-based systems.

Figure 20. Comparison of actual labelled movies with predictions

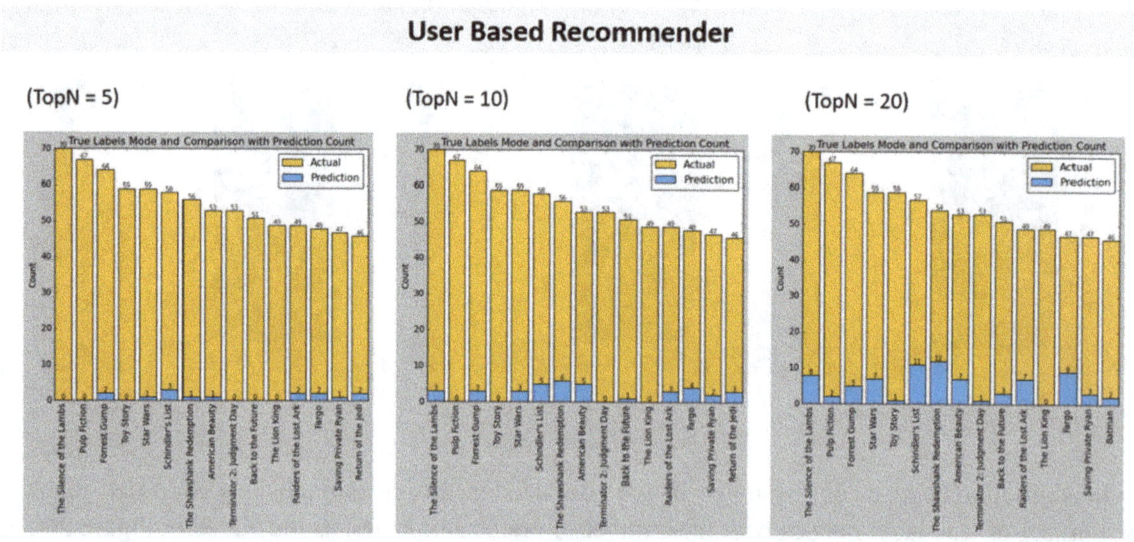

4.2 MBA

In this section, we introduce three visualization methods to analyze the association rules identified earlier: scatter plots, parallel category plots, and force-directed graphs. Subsequently, we will delve into three specific rules for a detailed discussion.

4.2.1 Scatter Plot

Figures 21 and 22 display the 2-item and 3-item association rules via scatter plots. This method plots each rule as a point, with the x and y axes representing support and confidence, respectively, and color indicating the lift value. Hovering over a point reveals a text label with the rule's support, confidence, and lift details. According to Munzner (Munzner, 2014), catter plots excel in providing overviews, characterizing distributions, identifying outliers and extreme values, and assessing the correlation between two attributes. Thus, they are apt for visualizing association rules.

In the scatter plots shown in Figures 21 and 22, the significant 2-item association rules (highlighted in dark purple) all feature movies from "The Lord of the Rings Collection". For instance, the 2-item rule with the highest lift, at 31.84%, suggests that viewers of "The Lord of the Rings: The Return of the King" are also likely to watch "The Lord of the Rings: The Two Towers", with a high confidence level of 89.20%. Likewise, the 3-item rule with the highest lift involves movies from the same collection, where "The Fellowship of the Ring" and "The Two Towers" predict viewing "The Return of the King".

Figure 21. Scatter plot for 2-item association rules

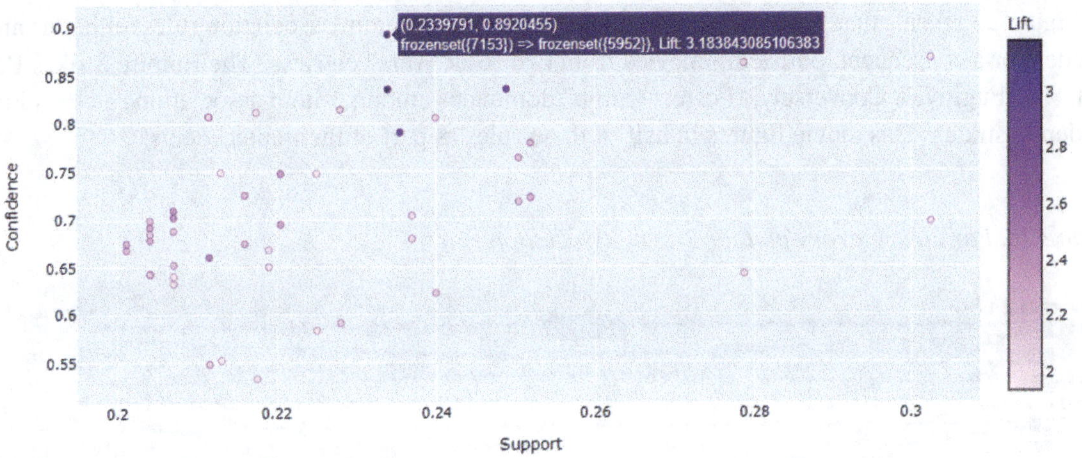

Figure 22. Scatter plot for 3-item association rules

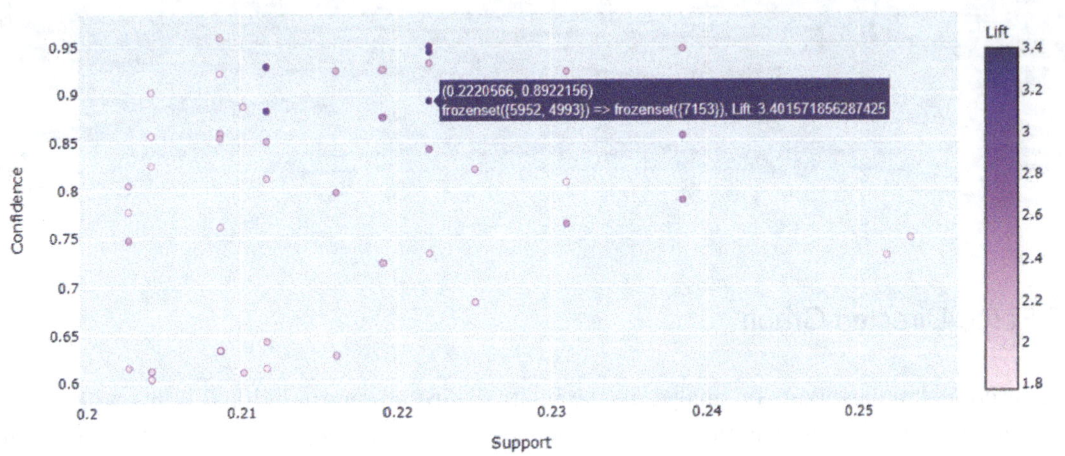

4.2.2 Parallel Category Plot

Figures 23 and 24 display the 2-item and 3-item association rules using parallel categories plots, respectively. References such as (Yang, 2005) and (Parallel Categories Diagram in Python, n.d.), highlight the suitability of parallel category plots for visualizing multi-dimensional categorical datasets. Yang et al. introduced an innovative approach to employing parallel plots for depicting frequent itemsets and complex many-to-many association rules (Parallel Categories Diagram in Python, n.d.).

In these plots, the plot represents each antecedent and consequent of the association rules by a series of vertical rectangles. Each rectangle corresponds to a movie ID that appears as either an antecedent or a consequent. The height of each rectangle indicates the frequency of the movie ID's occurrence. Ribbons connect these rectangles to illustrate the relationships between antecedents and consequents. Hovering over a rectangle with the mouse pointer reveals a tooltip that indicates the number of rules featuring that movie as either an antecedent or a consequent.

Figure 23 reveals that "The Matrix" frequently appears in 2-item association rules, either as an antecedent or a consequent, outpacing movies from two "Star Wars" entries, "The Empire Strikes Back" and "The Fugitive". Conversely, "Forrest Gump" dominates among 3-item association rules, as Figure 24 demonstrates. This movie figures in half of these rules as part of their antecedents.

Figure 23. Parallel category plot for 2-item association rules

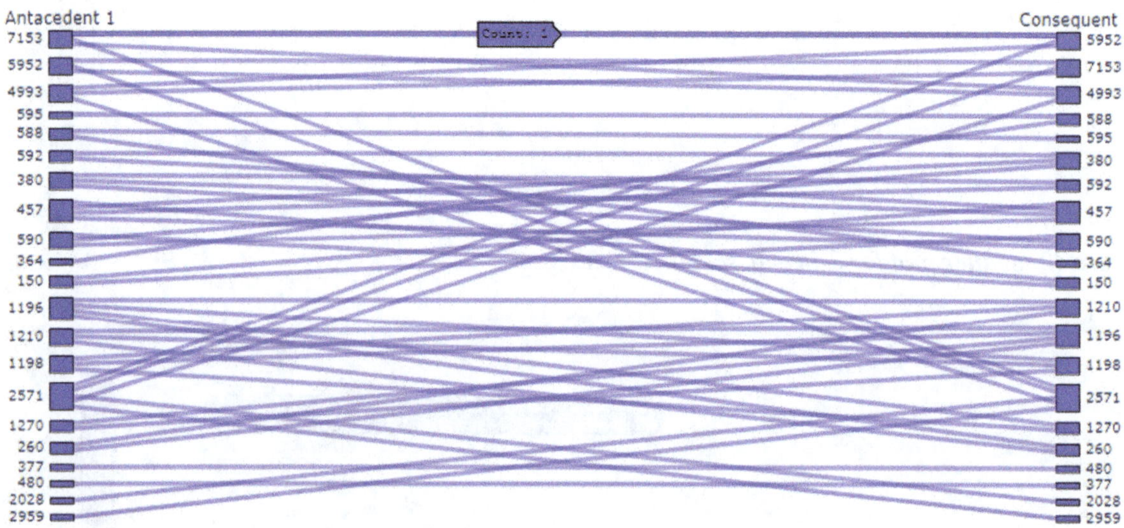

4.2.3 Force-Directed Graph

Graph-based techniques focus on analyzing the relationships among individual items within a set of rules, finding extensive application in association rule mining. Yen et al. have introduced a uniform graph-based methodology for identifying three distinct types of association rules: primitive, generalized, and multiple-level association rules. Another study by Appice and Buono presented a graph-based visualization tool aimed at aiding data miners in analyzing multi-level spatial association rules generated by AREA, a spatial data mining system. Despite the widespread use of graph-based visualizations, they can become overcrowded, making them practical only for smaller sets of rules. To mitigate visual clutter, we have limited our demonstration to fifty rules.

Figure 24. Parallel category plot for 3-item association rules

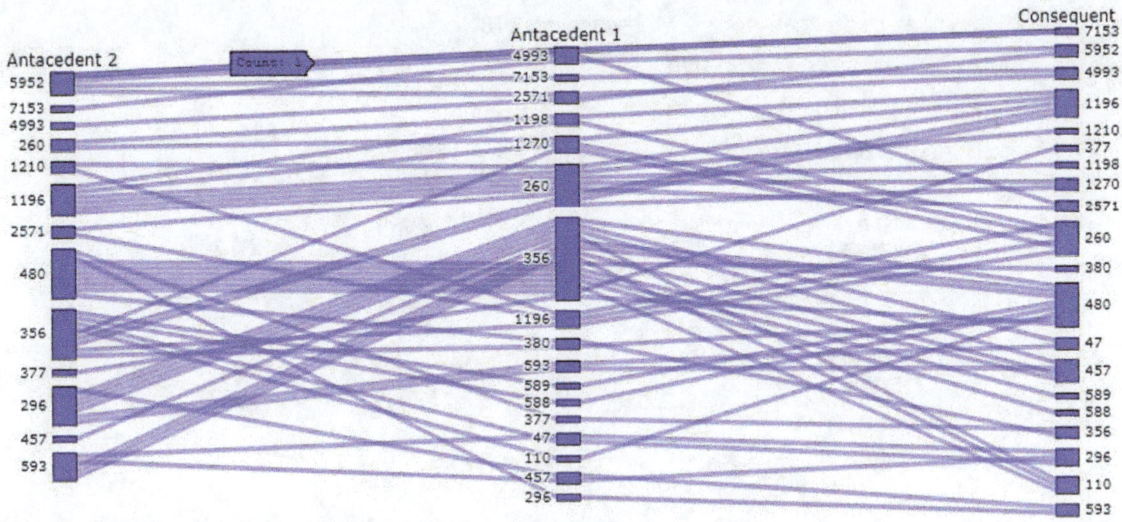

Figures 25 and 26 illustrate the association rules using force-directed graphs, generated with the "NetworkX" package in Python. This layout algorithm draws movies involved in numerous rules, and rules common to many movies, towards the center, while those featured in fewer rules are displaced to the edges. Nodes representing rules are colored pink, whereas movie nodes are purple. Additionally, the size of each node correlates with its degree in the graph, reflecting the count of connections it has. Consequently, nodes with a larger size are connected to a higher number of rule nodes.

Figure 25 identifies "The Matrix," bearing the ID 2571, as the largest node, indicating its frequent inclusion in the majority of rules. Similarly, within the realm of 3-item association rules, "Forrest Gump," carrying the ID 356, emerges as the largest node due to its prevalence in these rules. This observation aligns with findings from the parallel category plot discussed in the preceding section.

4.2.4 Analysis of Meaningful Association Rules

Upon visualizing a select sample of association rules through three different visualization methods, we extend our analysis to a broader dataset of association rules, evaluating them based on three key metrics: support, confidence, and lift. Consequently, we select three significant association rules for detailed examination as shown in Table 15.

Table 15. Three selected association rules for analysis

No.	Association Rule	Support	Confidence	Lift
1	{Pulp Fiction} → {Forrest Gump}	0.344	0.713	1.403
2	{Jurassic Park, Speed} → {Forrest Gump}	0.209	0.959	1.889
3	{The Lord of the Rings: The Two Towers, The Lord of the Rings: The Fellowship of the Ring} → {The Lord of the Rings: The Return of the King}	0.222	0.892	3.402

Figure 25. Force-directed graph for 2-item association rules

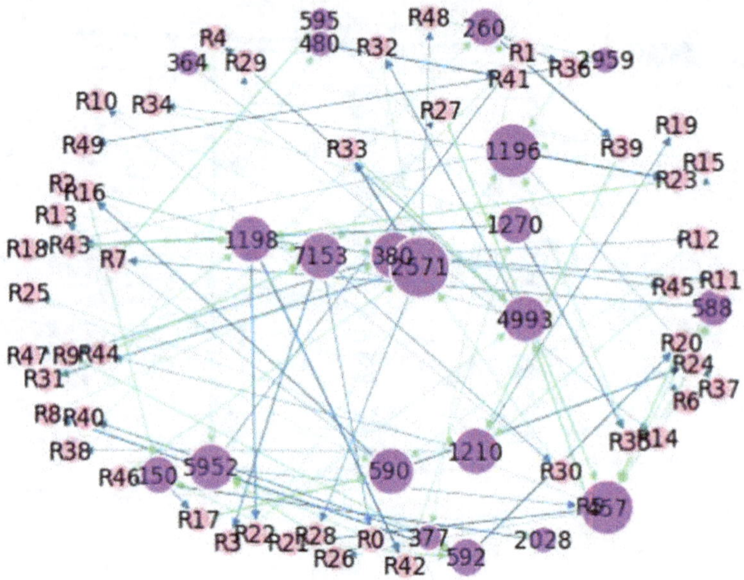

Figure 26. Association graph for 3-item association rules

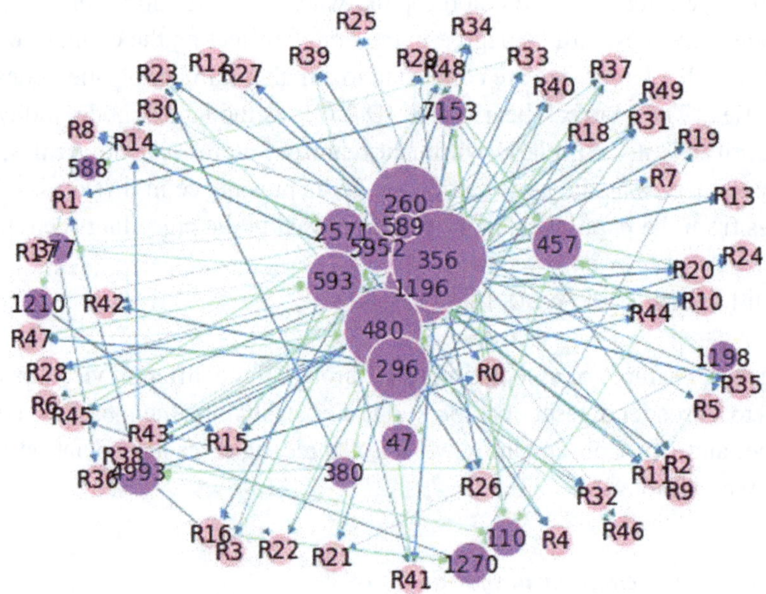

The first rule, {Pulp Fiction} → {Forrest Gump}, boasts the highest support at 34.4%, suggesting that approximately one-third of the 671 users have watched both "Pulp Fiction" and "Forrest Gump." This high support level stems from the frequent occurrence of both movies in users' viewing histories, not only because of their genre differences but also due to their high average ratings of over 8 and their presence in the top 250 movies on IMDb, as well as being among the top-rated on TMDB. This popularity likely drives their high co-occurrence among users.

Conversely, the rule {Jurassic Park, Speed} → {Forrest Gump} demonstrates the highest confidence of all analyzed rules. Confidence measures the likelihood that users who watched one set of movies also watched another, indicating a 95.9% probability that viewers of "Jurassic Park" and "Speed" will watch "Forrest Gump." However, the inherent popularity of "Forrest Gump" inflates this confidence, as it is a movie many users are likely to watch regardless of prior viewing history. Therefore, evaluating an association rule's merit requires considering additional metrics beyond confidence alone. With a support of 20.9% and a lift value over 1, this rule suggests a positive correlation between watching "Jurassic Park" and "Speed" and the likelihood of watching "Forrest Gump," recommending it to viewers of the former movies.

Furthermore, we established a minimum lift threshold of 1 to ensure all generated rules indicate a positive correlation between the antecedent and consequent. The third rule, {The Lord of the Rings: The Two Towers, The Lord of the Rings: The Fellowship of the Ring} → {The Lord of the Rings: The Return of the King}, exhibits the highest lift, reinforcing the intuitive notion that viewers of the first two movies in "The Lord of the Rings" series are highly likely to watch the concluding film, "The Return of the King." This rule, supported by more than 20% and with a confidence level of 89.2%, underscores why recommender systems often suggest sequels or series continuations.

This analysis underscores the importance of not relying solely on a single metric, such as confidence, when evaluating association rules. High confidence levels can be misleading, reflecting the frequent occurrence of the consequent rather than a meaningful association. Thus, a comprehensive evaluation involving all three discussed metrics—support, confidence, and lift—is crucial for identifying optimal association rules. Additionally, visualization tools offer significant value by enabling the extraction of actionable insights from a vast array of association rules.

5. DISCUSSION AND CONCLUSION

In this last module, discussion, conclusion, limitation and future work are discussed.

5.1 Recommender Systems

Nearly all data-rich companies stand to gain from implementing recommender systems (Cem, 2022). Beyond the movie streaming sector, as demonstrated in this study, e-commerce represents another field ripe for the benefits of recommender systems, thanks to its vast array of data, including numerous customers and their diverse online behaviors. These systems can efficiently replace rule-based systems by leveraging this extensive data. Without a recommender system, an e-commerce business that relies solely on promoting high-rated items might fail to offer the personalized experience consumers seek, potentially driving them toward competitors who provide more relevant item recommendations (Zander et al., 2015). urthermore, the proliferation of e-commerce has not only expanded the range of choices available to consumers but also introduced the challenge of information overload (Jiang et al., 2019). Without recommender systems, users might find it exceedingly time-consuming to navigate and extract relevant information from an e-commerce platform.

To address this challenge, numerous studies have adopted the collaborative filtering system in this domain (Jiang et al., 2019; Linden et al., 2003; Singh & Rishi, 2020). Collaborative filtering operates on the premise that individuals with similar preferences in the past will likely maintain similar preferences in the future. This system utilizes a user-item matrix, as illustrated in Table 16 below. The dimensions of this matrix represent the ratings users have provided. Typically, this matrix is sparse, filled with numerous null values, because a user only rates items they have purchased or shown interest in, making it unfeasible for them to rate every item in the entire e-commerce platform.

Table 16. Item-user matrix for e-commerce

User_ID	Item_ID_A	Item_ID_B	Item_ID_C	...	Item_ID_D	Item_ID_E
1	5	Null	Null	...	3	Null
2	Null	3	Null	...	5	Null
⋮	⋮	⋮	⋮	⋱	⋮	⋮
99999	Null	4	Null	...	Null	Null
100000	2	Null	Null	...	Null	5

Following the division of data into training and testing subsets through stratified user splitting, we can proceed to implement both the collaborative user-based recommender system and the model-based recommender system through the steps outlined as follows:

Collaborative User-Based Recommender System

1. Normalize the pivoted matrix (rows= users, columns = movies, values= ratings).
2. Find the most similar users based on rating behavior using Pearson Correlation toward a particular user.
3. Get the list of non-interacted top-5 weighted score movies from most similar users
4. To evaluate the performance:
   a. Identify whether top-5 weighted score movies are in the test-set movie.
   b. Repeat the steps above by implementing on the rest of the users.
   c. Compute performance metrics of AUC ROC, Precision, Mean Average Precision, Recall and F-measure.
   d. Repeat the steps above by implementing on top-10 and top-20 weighted score movies.

Collaborative Model-Based Recommender System

1. Normalize the pivoted matrix (rows= users, columns = movies, values= ratings).
2. Apply the SVD Algorithm on the matrix.
3. Get the list of non-interacted top-5 weighted score movies from the SVD Measures
4. To evaluate the performance:
   a. Identify whether top-5 weighted score movies are in the test-set movie.
   b. Repeat the steps above by implementing on the rest of the users.

c. Compute performance metrics of AUC ROC, Precision, Mean Average Precision, Recall and F-measure.
d. Repeat the steps above by implementing on top-10 and top-20 weighted score movies.

The purpose of normalizing the matrix initially is to manage null values by converting them to 0, where a 0 value post-normalization represents an average score on a row-wise basis. Following the completion of all steps, we will compile the results to determine which recommender system exhibits superior performance. Should the prediction speed be a concern for the e-commerce platform, it becomes necessary to assess the prediction speed of each recommender system and incorporate this metric into our evaluation. Typically, a memory-based recommender system consumes more time than a model-based one because it requires calculating the similarity score for each observation. E-commerce companies often depend on the speed of their platform to operate without significant delays. Therefore, it is advisable for the e-commerce platform to carefully consider the trade-offs between performance metrics and prediction speed.

5.2 MBA

Market Basket Analysis (MBA) finds wide application across numerous fields beyond marketing research and e-commerce, thanks to its ability to uncover relationships between entities and objects that often appear together. In the realm of road traffic safety studies, MBA can identify factors contributing to severe traffic crashes and their interdependencies by examining sets of factors that frequently co-occur in car accidents.

In the context of MBA for analyzing road traffic accidents, we treat each car accident as a "market basket," with the attributes' categories acting as the "purchased products" within this basket. To illustrate, consider ten severe casualty reports, each containing three descriptive aspects: weather conditions, vehicle type, and road alignment at the time of the accident. As demonstrated in Figure 27, each attribute falls into one of three categories: weather conditions (sunny, raining, snow), vehicle type (bus, private car, truck), and road alignment (uphill, downhill, curvey). The initial step involves translating the textual data from the severe casualty reports into a numerical format suitable for association rule mining. The transformed data is presented in Table 16, where each row corresponds to a car accident and each column to a category with its associated factor.

Table 16. The numerical representation of ten severe casualty crashes

ID	Weather_Sunny	Weather_Raining	Weather_Snow	...	Road_Uphill	Road_Curvy
1	1	0	0	...	1	0
2	0	1	0	...	1	0
3	0	0	1	...	0	1
⋮	⋮	⋮	⋮	⋱	⋮	⋮
9	0	1	0	...	0	0
10	1	0	0	...	0	1

Figure 27. Contributing factors to severe casualty crashes

Different algorithms for generating association rules will produce various results. The Apriori algorithm, for example, operates in two main stages during the rule generation process. Initially, it conducts an iterative search within the dataset of ten car accidents to identify frequent factor sets. Following this, it generates strong association rules from these frequent sets. It is crucial to set minimum threshold values for support, confidence, and lift to explore factor combinations commonly found in severe casualty crashes effectively. This approach ensures that the generated association rules offer significant value. For example, factor sets meeting or exceeding the minimum support are considered high-frequency item sets. Additionally, a lift value above one indicates a positive interdependence between the antecedent and consequent, making rules with a lift greater than one particularly interesting due to their higher level of significance.

Table 17. List of 2-item association rules

Rule ID	Antecedent	Consequent	Support	Confidence	Lift
1	Weather_Raining	Road_Curvey	0.18	0.53	2.85
2	Road_Downhill	Vehicle_Bus	0.23	0.80	2.10
3	Vehicle_Truck	Road_Downhill	0.23	0.76	2.03

Table 17 presents hypothetical values for support, confidence, and lift for the top three 2-item association rules. Rule ID 1, with the highest lift of 2.85 but the lowest support (0.18) and confidence (0.53), suggests that severe crashes on rainy days are likely to occur on curvy road surfaces. Consequently, government authorities are advised to take preventive measures such as installing warning signs, improving pavement conditions, and imposing speed limits to reduce the number of casualties and injuries from crashes. While this example highlights only three factors associated with severe car accidents, numerous other potential factors warrant consideration in real-life scenarios. Policymakers can leverage these insights to comprehend the causes of severe casualty crashes better and devise effective policies and safety countermeasures to mitigate the risk of car accidents.

Lastly, the Figure 28 shows the application of recommender system to an E-commerce website interface.

Figure 28. Sample e-commerce website platform interface

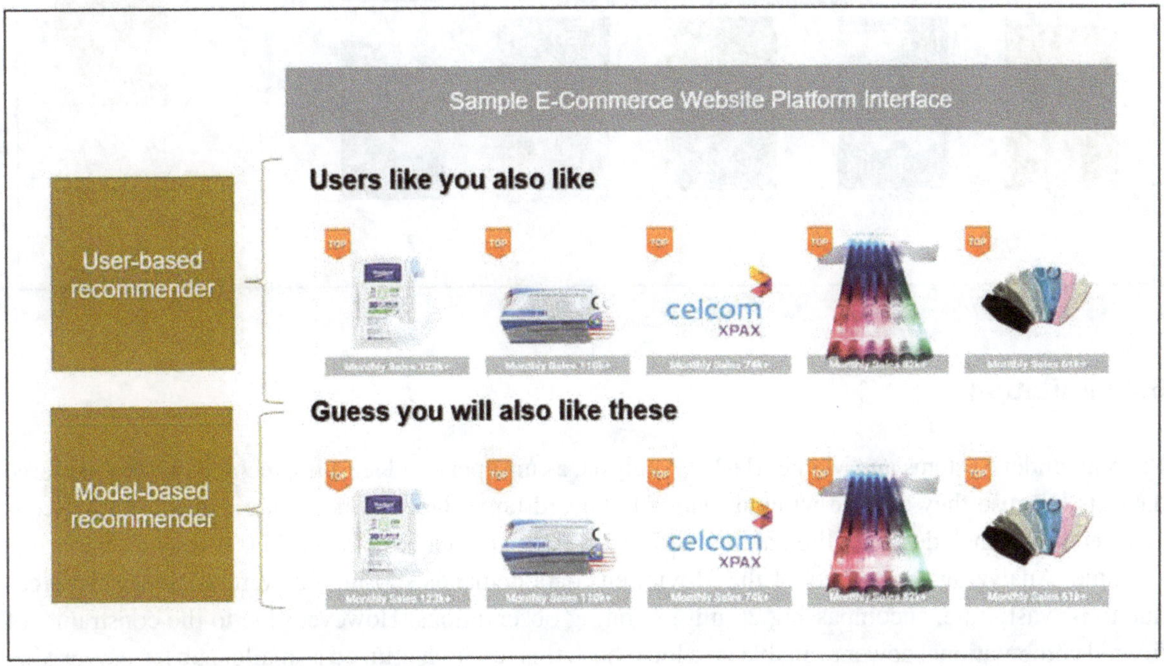

5.3 Conclusion

In today's era of information overload, many businesses move swiftly to harness emerging technologies and seamlessly integrate them into their operations. This is especially critical for subscription streaming services, where uncovering hidden associations between movies is key to delivering personalized recommendations to customers. Market basket analysis and recommender systems stand out as the most prevalent predictive analytics techniques in the business realm, boosting both customer satisfaction and sales revenue. In this chapter, we applied these techniques to the MovieLens dataset. Initially, we utilized recommender systems to propose movies that align with users' preferences. These systems not only assist service providers in content management but also empower users to effortlessly discover movies they are likely to enjoy. Additionally, through market basket analysis, we identified numerous rules with high lift values, enabling accurate movie recommendations. Consequently, such applications significantly enhance the overall user experience. Figure 29 illustrates a movie system interface that incorporates both recommender systems and market basket analysis for its audience.

Figure 29. Application of recommender systems and association rules to a movie system interface

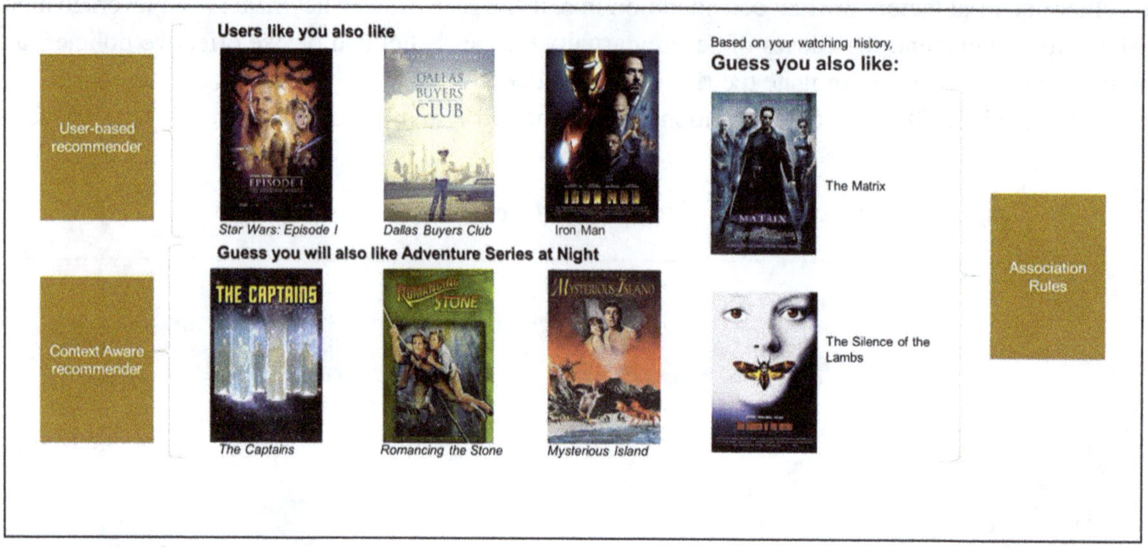

5.4 Limitation

Recommender Systems and Market Basket Analysis, as unsupervised learning techniques, require large datasets because they operate without manually tagged target labels. The comprehensive MovieLens Dataset, which includes 26 million ratings and 750,000 tag applications across 45,000 movies, is a prime example. Analyzing the entirety of the MovieLens data demands substantial computational resources due to its vast scale, encompassing 26 million rating observations. However, due to the constraints of limited computational power available on a local host, this research utilized a smaller subset, comprising 100,000 ratings from 700 users across 9,000 movies.

5.5 Future Work

The evaluation of Top-N for market basket analysis can serve as an objective method to assess the performance of both the Apriori and FP-Growth algorithms. Additionally, researchers have the option to utilize the ABC-RuleMiner, an association rule mining technique introduced in 2020 by (Sarker & Kayes, 2020). This method, by prioritizing the significance of linked contextual characteristics, effectively identifies redundant connections and extracts a set of non-redundant association rules. For future research, employing cloud computing to apply the unsupervised learning technique presents a viable solution, as it offers easy scalability for handling larger datasets.

REFERENCES

Agrawal, R., & Srikant, R. (1994). Fast algorithms for mining association rules. *20th International Conference on Very Large Data Bases.*

Al Mamun, M. H., Keikhosrokiani, P., Asl, M. P., Anuar, N. A. N., Hadi, N. H. A., & Humida, T. (2022). Sentiment Analysis of the Harry Potter Series Using a Lexicon-Based Approach. In P. Keikhosrokiani & M. Pourya Asl (Eds.), *Handbook of Research on Opinion Mining and Text Analytics on Literary Works and Social Media* (pp. 263–291). IGI Global. doi:10.4018/978-1-7998-9594-7.ch011

Aljunid, M. F., & Huchaiah, M. D. (2021). An efficient hybrid recommendation model based on collaborative filtering recommender systems. *CAAI Transactions on Intelligence Technology*, *6*(4), 480–492. doi:10.1049/cit2.12048

Arikatla, G., & Bhargav, C. (2021). *Movie prediction based on movie scriptsusing Natural Language Processing and Machine Learning Algorithms.* Blekinge Institute of Technology.

Bane & Khyati. (2020). Success of Bollywood Movie Using Machine Techniques: A Literature Review. *Mukt Shabd Journal.*

Burke, R. (2002). Hybrid Recommender Systems: Survey and Experiments. *User Modeling and User-Adapted Interaction*, *12*(4), 331–370. doi:10.1023/A:1021240730564

Çano, E., & Morisio, M. (2019). *Hybrid Recommender Systems: A Systematic Literature Review.* doi:10.3233/IDA-163209

Cem, D. (2022, February 9). *Recommendation Systems: Applications and Examples in 2022.* AIMultiple. https://research.aimultiple.com/recommendation-system/

Chee, C.-H., Jaafar, J., Aziz, I. A., Hasan, M. H., & Yeoh, W. (2019). Algorithms for frequent itemset mining: A literature review. *Artificial Intelligence Review*, *52*(4), 2603–2621. doi:10.1007/s10462-018-9629-z

Del, O., Félix, H., & Elena, G. (2008). Evaluation of recommender systems: A new approach. *Expert Systems with Applications*, *35*(3), 790–804. doi:10.1016/j.eswa.2007.07.047

Deldjoo, Y., Schedl, M., Cremonesi, P., & Pasi, G. (2020). Recommender Systems Leveraging Multimedia Content. *ACM Computing Surveys*, *53*(5), 1–38. doi:10.1145/3407190

Dong, X., Lei, Y., Zhonghuo, W., Yuxia, S., Lingfeng, Y., & Fangxi, Z. (2017). A hybrid collaborative filtering model with deep structure for recommender systems. *AAAI Conference on Artificial Intelligence.* 10.1609/aaai.v31i1.10747

Gabriel, M. (2019). *Recommender Systems in Python 101 | Kaggle.* https://www.kaggle.com/code/gsp-moreira/recommender-systems-in-python-101#Collaborative-Filtering-model

Glielmo, A., Husic, B. E., Rodriguez, A., Clementi, C., Noé, F., & Laio, A. (2021). Unsupervised Learning Methods for Molecular Simulation Data. *Chemical Reviews*, *121*(16), 9722–9758. doi:10.1021/acs.chemrev.0c01195 PMID:33945269

Goldberg, D., Nichols, D., Oki, B. M., & Terry, D. (1992). Using collaborative filtering to weave an information tapestry. *Communications of the ACM*, *35*(12), 61–70. doi:10.1145/138859.138867

Grab N Go Info. (2022, January 23). *(1) User-Based Collaborative Filtering In Python | Machine Learning - YouTube.* YouTube. https://www.youtube.com/watch?v=cxcFi3RDrEw

Gupta. (2020). A literature review on recommendation systems. *International Research Journal of Engineering and Technology (IRJET)*, 3600–3605.

Han, J., Pei, J., & Yin, Y. (2000). Mining frequent patterns without candidate generation. *SIGMOD Record*, *29*(2), 1–12. doi:10.1145/335191.335372

Harper, F. M., & Konstan, J. A. (2016). The MovieLens Datasets: History and Context. *ACM Transactions on Interactive Intelligent Systems*, *5*(4), 1–19. doi:10.1145/2827872

Hidayat, A. A., Rahman, A., Wangi, R. M., Abidin, R. J., Fuadi, R. S., & Budiawan, W. (2019). Implementation and comparison analysis of apriori and fp-growth algorithm performance to determine market basket analysis in Breiliant shop. *Journal of Physics: Conference Series*, *1402*(7), 077031. doi:10.1088/1742-6596/1402/7/077031

Hu, Y., Koren, Y., & Volinsky, C. (2008). Collaborative Filtering for Implicit Feedback Datasets. *2008 Eighth IEEE International Conference on Data Mining*, 263–272. 10.1109/ICDM.2008.22

James, G., Daniela, W., Trevor, H., & Robert, T. (2021). *Unsupervised learning*. Academic Press.

Jeffery, C. (2021, June 26). *7 Types of Hybrid Recommendation System*. Analytics Vidhya. https://medium.com/analytics-vidhya/7-types-of-hybrid-recommendation-system-3e4f78266ad8

Jiang, L., Cheng, Y., Yang, L., Li, J., Yan, H., & Wang, X. (2019). A trust-based collaborative filtering algorithm for E-commerce recommendation system. *Journal of Ambient Intelligence and Humanized Computing*, *10*(8), 3023–3034. doi:10.1007/s12652-018-0928-7

Keikhosrokiani, P. (2022). Handbook of Research on Consumer Behavior Change and Data Analytics in the Socio-Digital Era. doi:10.4018/978-1-6684-4168-8

Keikhosrokiani, P., & Asl, M. P. (2022). Handbook of Research on Artificial Intelligence Applications in Literary Works and Social Media. doi:10.4018/978-1-6684-6242-3

Keikhosrokiani, P., Asl, M. P., Chu, K. E., & Anuar, N. A. N. (2022). Artificial intelligence framework for opinion mining of netizen readers' reviews of Arundhati Roy's The God of Small Things. In Handbook of Research on Artificial Intelligence Applications in Literary Works and Social Media. doi:10.4018/978-1-6684-6242-3.ch004

Keikhosrokiani, P., & Fye, G. M. (2023). A hybrid recommender system for health supplement e-commerce based on customer data implicit ratings. *Multimedia Tools and Applications*. Advance online publication. doi:10.1007/s11042-023-17321-6

Keikhosrokiani, P., & Pourya Asl, M. (2022). *Handbook of research on opinion mining and text analytics on literary works and social media*. IGI Global. doi:10.4018/978-1-7998-9594-7

Linden, G., Smith, B., & York, J. (2003). Amazon. com recommendations: Item-to-item collaborative filtering. *IEEE Internet Computing*, *7*(1), 76–80. doi:10.1109/MIC.2003.1167344

Low, H. Q., Keikhosrokiani, P., & Asl, M. P. (2024). Decoding violence against women: Analysing harassment in middle eastern literature with machine learning and sentiment analysis. *Humanities & Social Sciences Communications*.

Movies And Entertainment Market Size Report, 2030. (n.d.). Retrieved June 3, 2022, from https://www.grandviewresearch.com/industry-analysis/movies-entertainment-market

Movies And Entertainment Market Worth $169.6 Billion by 2030. (n.d.). Retrieved June 3, 2022, from https://www.grandviewresearch.com/press-release/global-movies-entertainment-market

Munzner, T. (2014). Visualization Analysis and Design. In Visualization Analysis and Design. doi:10.1201/b17511

Mustakim, H., Herianda, D. M., Ilham, A., Daeng GS, A., Laumal, F. E., Kurniasih, N., Iskandar, A., Manulangga, G., Indra Iswara, I. B. A., & Rahim, R. (2018). Market Basket Analysis Using Apriori and FP-Growth for Analysis Consumer Expenditure Patterns at Berkah Mart in Pekanbaru Riau. *Journal of Physics: Conference Series*, *1114*, 012131. doi:10.1088/1742-6596/1114/1/012131

Mythili, M., & Mohamed Shanavas, A. (2013). Performance Evaluation of Apriori and FP-Growth Algorithms. *International Journal of Computer Applications*, *79*(10), 34–37. doi:10.5120/13779-1650

Narke, Lakshmi, & Azra, N. (2020). A comprehensive review of approaches and challenges of a recommendation system. *International Journal of Research in Engineering. Science and Management*, *3*(4), 381–384.

Parallel categories diagram in Python. (n.d.). Retrieved June 9, 2022, from https://plotly.com/python/parallel-categories-diagram/

Peter, B., Shmueli, G., & Nitin, P. (2016). *Data Mining for Business Analytics: Concepts, Techniques, and Applications with XLMiner*. John Wiley & Sons.

Sarker, I. H. (2021). Machine Learning: Algorithms, Real-World Applications and Research Directions. *SN Computer Science*, *2*(3), 160. doi:10.1007/s42979-021-00592-x PMID:33778771

Sarker, I. H., & Kayes, A. S. M. (2020). ABC-RuleMiner: User behavioral rule-based machine learning method for context-aware intelligent services. *Journal of Network and Computer Applications*, *168*, 102762. doi:10.1016/j.jnca.2020.102762

Shah, K., Salunke, A., Dongare, S., & Antala, K. (2017). Recommender systems: An overview of different approaches to recommendations. *2017 International Conference on Innovations in Information, Embedded and Communication Systems (ICIIECS)*, 1–4. 10.1109/ICIIECS.2017.8276172

Singh, M. K., & Rishi, O. P. (2020). Event driven Recommendation System for E-commerce using Knowledge based Collaborative Filtering Technique. *Scalable Computing: Practice and Experience*, *21*(3), 369–378. doi:10.12694/scpe.v21i3.1709

Stratigi, M., Li, X., Stefanidis, K., & Zhang, Z. (2019). *Ratings vs. Reviews in Recommender Systems: A Case Study on the Amazon Movies Dataset*. doi:10.1007/978-3-030-30278-8_9

Suhendra, N. H. B., Keikhosrokiani, P., Asl, M. P., & Zhao, X. (2022). Opinion Mining and Text Analytics of Literary Reader Responses: A Case Study of Reader Responses to KL Noir Volumes in Goodreads Using Sentiment Analysis and Topic. In P. Keikhosrokiani & M. Pourya Asl (Eds.), *Handbook of Research on Opinion Mining and Text Analytics on Literary Works and Social Media* (pp. 191–239). IGI Global. doi:10.4018/978-1-7998-9594-7.ch009

Tan, R. J. (2019, May 24). *Breaking Down Mean Average Precision (mAP) | by Ren Jie Tan | Towards Data Science*. Towards Data Science. https://towardsdatascience.com/breaking-down-mean-average-precision-map-ae462f623a52

The Movies Dataset. (n.d.). Retrieved June 3, 2022, from https://www.kaggle.com/datasets/rounakbanik/the-movies-dataset?select=movies_metadata.csv

Timur, O. (2020, June 17). *Machine learning - Item-Item Collaborative Filtering vs Market Basket Analysis - Cross Validated*. https://stats.stackexchange.com/questions/256012/item-item-collaborative-filtering-vs-market-basket-analysis

Top 10 Most Popular Subscription Streaming Services - All Top Everything. (n.d.). Retrieved June 3, 2022, from https://www.alltopeverything.com/most-popular-streaming-services/

Vaibhav, K. (2020, March 25). *Singular Value Decomposition (SVD) In Recommender System*. Analytics India Magazine. https://analyticsindiamag.com/singular-value-decomposition-svd-application-recommender-system/

Xian, Z., Keikhosrokiani, P., XinYing, C., & Li, Z. (2022). An RFM Model Using K-Means Clustering to Improve Customer Segmentation and Product Recommendation. In P. Keikhosrokiani (Ed.), Handbook of Research on Consumer Behavior Change and Data Analytics in the Socio-Digital Era (pp. 124–145). IGI Global. doi:10.4018/978-1-6684-4168-8.ch006

Yang, L. (2005). Pruning and visualizing generalized association rules in parallel coordinates. *IEEE Transactions on Knowledge and Data Engineering*, *17*(1), 60–70. doi:10.1109/TKDE.2005.14

Zander, S., Maria, R., Wetzel, S., & Sven, B. (2015). Does Personalisation Promote Learners' Attention? An Eye-Tracking Study. *Frontline Learning Research*, 1–13.

Zhao, Q., & Sourav, S. B. (2003). Association rule mining. *Survey (London, England)*.

Zhao, X., & Keikhosrokiani, P. (2022). Sales prediction and product recommendation model through user behavior analytics. *Computers, Materials & Continua*, *70*(2), 3855–3874. Advance online publication. doi:10.32604/cmc.2022.019750

Section 5
Social and Ethical Considerations in Technology

Chapter 14
Individual Privacy Should Be an Institutional Value:
Socio-Technical Design of University Data Collection Systems

Üzeyir Fidan
https://orcid.org/0000-0003-3451-4344
Usak University, Turkey

Nurettin Altay Boza
Usak University, Turkey

ABSTRACT

The objective of this chapter is to create a comprehensive socio-technical system that facilitates data collecting, processing, and reporting procedures within a university. Socio-technical system design is an interdisciplinary method that integrates social and technical elements. Consequently, the system was modeled concurrently, encompassing both the users and stakeholders as well as the software and hardware components. Throughout the development process, a thorough analysis was conducted to understand the requirements and expectations of university personnel regarding the system. This was achieved through the use of qualitative and quantitative data-gathering approaches. Based on the collected findings, prototypes were produced, and input was sought once again. A system that prioritizes user needs and has a high level of reliability was designed in the last phase. The purpose of the system is to enhance the university's ability to make decisions and plan strategically based on data. Additionally, it is anticipated that the system will boost employee motivation and productivity.

DOI: 10.4018/979-8-3693-1210-0.ch014

INTRODUCTION

Universities must adopt a more collaborative and stakeholder-focused strategy in order to effectively address the constant feedback from diverse stakeholders in the ever-evolving higher education landscape. For this purpose, several online feedback techniques, such as student satisfaction surveys, staff suggestion systems, and alumni relations management, are extensively employed. By integrating the data gathered in this manner into decision-making procedures, colleges embrace a more inclusive form of management. Nevertheless, according to scholarly sources, colleges often fail to give sufficient strategic consideration to online feedback systems and may have designs that are inefficient and lack clear objectives (Tadelis, 2016; Rabovsky, 2014; Shah & Nair, 2012). However, adopting an integrated socio-technical design approach that takes into account both technical and social aspects can greatly enhance the decision-making mechanisms of the institution and improve stakeholder satisfaction.

Universities employ a diverse range of online tools to methodically gather and examine input from their stakeholders (Hemsley-Brown & Oplatka, 2006). Student satisfaction surveys are the fundamental method of gathering data. The surveys, conducted at the conclusion of every semester, gather feedback on several aspects including courses, faculty, and infrastructure. Furthermore, employee suggestion and complaint systems are extensively employed, particularly for gathering data on administrative procedures. Through these tools, employees can conveniently submit their comments and concerns regarding any deficiencies or problems they observe. Alumni information systems are utilized for the purpose of establishing communication channels with former students and gathering their input regarding the university and educational programs. This information serves the dual purpose of enhancing alumni contacts and enhancing the educational experience. The data acquired from these various platforms are utilized as input in the decision-making procedures of universities, thereby contributing to stakeholder-centric management. Nevertheless, there can exist certain vulnerabilities in the design and operational procedures of these systems.

Given the stakeholders' worries and expectations regarding online feedback systems, certain challenges are particularly prominent. One of the primary obstacles to the utilization of such systems is the worry over the privacy and confidentiality of participants' data, as indicated by Howe et al. (2018). Employees prioritize maintaining the confidentiality of their identities and viewpoints to freely critique senior management, while students provide input to faculty members and university administration in a comfortable manner. Nevertheless, consumers also possess technological expectations, including the user-friendly nature of the data gathering instrument and its efficient and comprehensible structure. Hence, there is a distinct requirement for a comprehensive system architecture that can effectively tackle privacy and security issues at a societal level, while simultaneously offering a user-friendly data input framework at a technical one. Adopting such a design strategy is crucial in order to completely satisfy the expectations of stakeholders.

The online stakeholder feedback systems implemented in universities appear to be inadequate in facilitating a genuinely stakeholder-centered management approach by adequately resolving stakeholders' apprehensions over data protection and participation in the system (West et al., 2020). Universities' acquisition of student and employee data serves to facilitate administrative decision-making, although it also gives rise to concerns over individual privacy. Data use regulations in the majority of colleges are characterized by ambiguity and a lack of transparency (Hallak & Poisson, 2007), resulting in a sense of mistrust (Medina & Rufín, 2015).

This study focuses on the following research problems and plans to make a detailed evaluation of the data collection system developed at a state university in Turkey:

RQ1: To what degree do current online stakeholder feedback mechanisms employed by universities adequately tackle the privacy and security apprehensions of participants?
RQ2: Which socio-technical design concepts may be implemented to enhance stakeholder engagement and involvement in these systems?
RQ3: What design principles should be employed for the components of an online stakeholder feedback system (such as data entry infrastructure, data analytics, reporting, etc.) to enhance stakeholder engagement and contentment, and maximize the system's efficacy in decision-making procedures?

When designing systems to gather and assess stakeholder feedback in universities, a conflict arises regarding the balance between safeguarding individual privacy and enhancing organizational efficiency. According to the literature, socio-technical system design has a beneficial impact on the knowledge management and decision-making processes of companies (Malatji et al., 2019). Nevertheless, colleges lack an instance of a comprehensive application. Hence, this study investigates the online methods employed by universities to gather input from stakeholders, analyzing them from a socio-technical standpoint. The fundamental elements of such a system are recognized. The objective is to create application models that can effectively reconcile the university's efficiency objectives with the safeguarding of individuals' privacy, employing a socio-technical approach.

BACKGROUND

The significance of involving stakeholders in universities and incorporating their opinion into management choices has increased in recent years. This section provides a comprehensive analysis of the theoretical background and existing practices.

The literature highlights that involving stakeholders in decision-making processes enhances the legitimacy and application of outcomes, fosters the creation of innovative ideas, and effectively mitigates opposition to change (Edelenbos & Klijn, 2006; Mena & Palazzo, 2012). Stakeholder feedback serves as a crucial source of information for university management. Based on this data, it is possible to make essential enhancements and formulate new regulations (Mourad, 2017). These techniques are essential for a management model that is centered around ensuring the satisfaction of stakeholders. Universities encompass a diverse array of stakeholder groups, including students, professors, administrative staff, alumni, and others. Regularly monitoring the expectations and needs of these stakeholders is crucial for the university to accomplish its mission and vision objectives (Rupcic, 2019). Stakeholder feedback has become essential at this juncture.

Universities commonly implement surveys and feedback mechanisms such as student and employee satisfaction surveys, customer complaint systems, and alumni information forms (Aldridge & Rowley, 1998; Shah et al., 2017). The data collected from surveys and feedback is mostly analyzed using basic statistical techniques and then communicated to the appropriate departments. Nevertheless, the utilization of sophisticated analytical techniques such as data mining and artificial intelligence is not prevalent. Stakeholder feedback is widely recognized as a crucial input for decision-making systems, according to Goethel et al., (2019). Nevertheless, in reality, there can be discrepancies in converting this data into tangible policies and practices. There is currently no established systematic approach.

The socio-technical systems approach seeks to create cohesive systems that incorporate both social and technical aspects (Iwanaga et al., 2021). It is founded upon the three fundamental elements of individuals, procedures, and technology. Companies have started implementing socio-technical design principles in their information management and decision support systems in recent years (Govers & Van Amelsvoort, 2019; Münch et al., 2022). Organizations are adopting strategies that give priority to enhancing employee motivation, satisfaction, and performance. Aside from the advantages of offering a comprehensive viewpoint and enhancing stakeholder involvement, there are also drawbacks include difficulties in implementing and coordinating efforts, as well as incurring extra expenses (Khalid et al, 2023).

Online survey and evaluation tools are increasingly prevalent in stakeholder feedback studies undertaken in universities (Caeiro et al., 2020). One advantage is the ease of application. The protection and privacy of personal data in online systems is a significant issue (Nissenbaum, 2020). Specifically, individuals who wish to openly voice their critical perspectives are particularly concerned about the matter of maintaining anonymity. Alongside technological safeguards like data anonymization, access and authorization controls, and secure data transfer protocols, it is advisable to adhere to the principles of secrecy and voluntariness while designing processes (Pedreschi et al., 2008).

Upon reviewing existing studies, it becomes evident that colleges do not possess a comprehensive approach to managing stakeholder feedback (Manatos, Rosa & Sarrico, 2018). The majority of apps are comprised of separate and disconnected solutions that have been created independently. The objective of this project is to develop stakeholder feedback mechanisms within a socio-technical framework. Therefore, the objective is to offer higher quality information for decision-making procedures and enhance stakeholder satisfaction and sense of belonging (Dzimińska et al., 2018).

MATERIALS AND METHOD

Data and Ethics

Consulting the perspectives of all key stakeholders is crucial in the process of designing socio-technical systems to achieve the optimal balance between social and technological aspects (Iwanaga et al., 2021; Bryl, Giorgini & Mylopoulos, 2009). The study involves consulting with managers, practitioners, and other stakeholders who are users of the socio-technical system, to gather their experiences and perspectives during the data collection process.

The qualitative aspect of the research involved conducting focus group interviews and questionnaires. These activities were carried out with the authorization of the Social and Human Sciences Scientific Research and Publication Ethics Board, dated 09.11.2023, and identified as 2023-207. The interview and survey questions were developed by drawing upon pertinent literature and expert insights. Additionally, the participants were provided with a comprehensive explanation of the research's goal and scope.

During the data collection procedure, we prioritized research and publishing ethics, ensuring the confidentiality of participants and fostering a secure setting for them to openly discuss their experiences. The collected data underwent analysis while ensuring the protection of personal information through anonymization and strict adherence to the concept of confidentiality.

Model for System Design

The notion of "joint optimization of social and technical systems" introduced by Trist and Emery (1960) was embraced in the design of socio-technical systems. According to this idea, an almost perfect design should be achieved by considering the requirements of both the technical system and the social system (people) who use it (Trist, 1978).

Figure 1 showcases a system design model that highlights the interplay between social and technological system components, drawing inspiration from socio-technical theory (Walker et al., 2008). As per this concept, the elements of the technical system (hardware, software, network, etc.) would be impacted by the social system comprising of users and administrators. Conversely, the configuration and operation of the technical system will likewise exert influence on the social system.

Figure 1. Socio-technical system design model

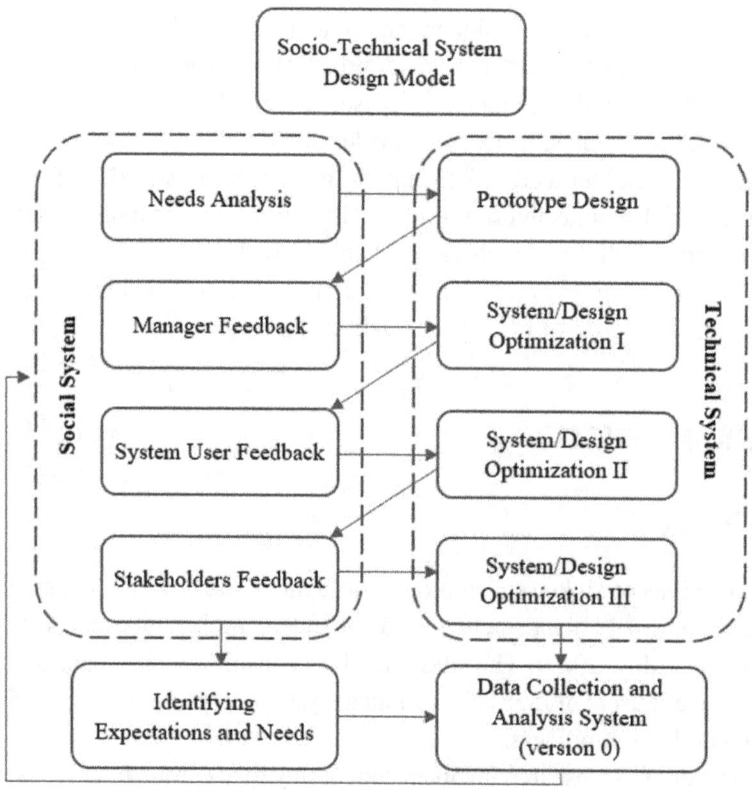

The suggested model takes into account the technical and social components of the system in a mutually interactive and jointly optimized manner. Therefore, this model, created as a modern implementation of socio-technical theory, is anticipated to enhance the overall performance and efficiency of the specific system.

Model for Technical System

The study utilizes a socio-technical system approach, which considers both social and technological system components. This approach is illustrated in Figure 1. The individuals who serve as administrators, implementers, designers, and users constitute the social system, whereas the technical system encompasses the hardware, software, network, and other technical infrastructure (Figure 2).

Figure 2. Technical system design model

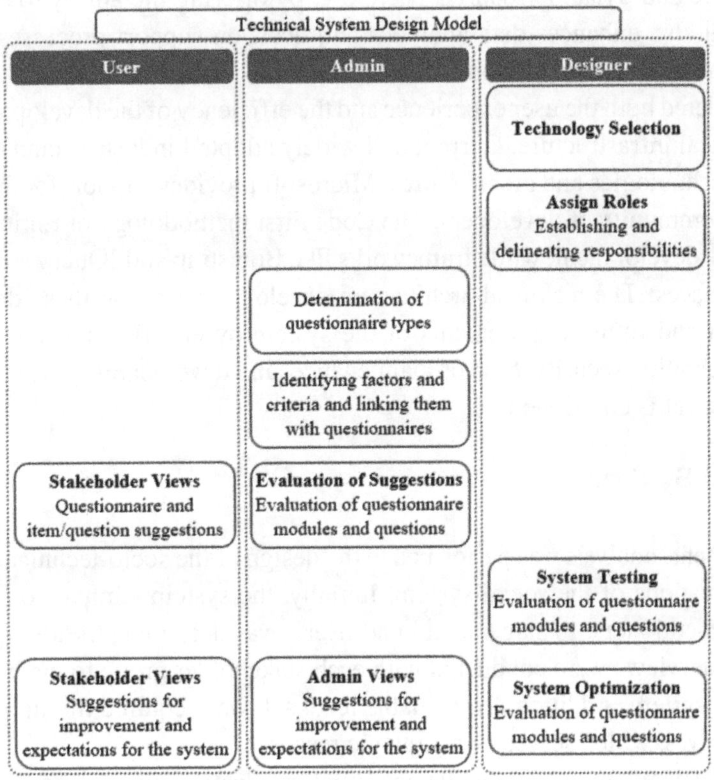

The study also noted the idea of co-optimization, which is a significant aspect of socio-technical design as proposed by Trist (1978). To gather information on the social aspect of the system, data was collected through focus group talks and questionnaires. Based on the findings, the technical infrastructure of the system was created to align with the requirements of the social system and assure the overall optimization of the system. Instead of treating the technical system components separately, a development approach was implemented that considered the connection between the social and technological systems, while also addressing the demands of all stakeholders. This method is anticipated to have a beneficial impact on the overall performance of the system.

The created socio-technical system's technological infrastructure is designed using a layered architecture. The presentation layer was implemented using the C# programming language within the asp.net MVC (Model-View-Controller) architectural pattern, which is built upon the .NET Framework. The

MVC pattern enhances flexibility and simplifies maintenance by separating the presentation, business logic, and data access elements of the program.

The data is structured using MS SQL Server 2019, which is Microsoft's widely accepted relational database management system. It is designed with a robust architecture that ensures both high availability and scalability. A data access layer was constructed by utilizing Entity Framework 6, an object relational mapping (ORM) framework, to establish a mapping between the database objects and the application. Access to the database is encapsulated within the object-oriented programming paradigm.

The design of the interface incorporates open source tools like Bootstrap, JQuery, and ApexCharts to create a visually appealing user experience that is compatible with mobile devices and enables the creation of interactive and dynamic reports. Therefore, by offering the ability to customize access for various user roles, it also enhances data analytics and decision support processes through the use of detailed graphics and visualization options.

This study considered both the user experience and the efficiency of the development processes when designing the technical infrastructure. Current and widely adopted industry standards were prioritized in the selection of technologies and architectures. Microsoft provides support for .NET technology and it has a substantial community of developers. The Code First methodology of Entity Framework allows for efficient database development, while frameworks like Bootstrap and JQuery aid in creating visually appealing user interfaces. The technical architecture developed based on these decisions is designed to fulfill the present and future requirements of the system by ensuring features such as scalability, adaptability, manageability, security, ease of maintenance, and developability. Therefore, a life cycle of sustainable development is envisioned.

Model for Social System

A thorough requirements analysis was performed in the design of the socio-technical system to ascertain the needs and expectations of the social system. Initially, the system's impact on several stakeholder groups, including practitioners, managers, and end-users, was determined. Subsequently, focus group investigations and interviews were conducted with each stakeholder group to methodically gather their requirements for the system. Additionally, valuable feedback was acquired through a survey conducted among senior executives, which served as a strategic resource.

A prototype was created and evaluated using a pilot application, in accordance with the input collected. The evaluation of test findings and user experiences was once again conducted using focus groups. The prototype was enhanced in accordance with the received requests. The findings section provides a comprehensive account of the input gathered from the focus groups, as well as an in-depth analysis of the key needs expressed.

The final system design had a seamless interplay between the technological infrastructure and user requirements, taking into account the aforementioned discoveries. The inputs from the social system analysis were effectively employed in the technological design, following the principle of joint optimization. Consequently, the optimization of customer happiness was achieved alongside the enhancement of technical performance.

RESULTS

Within the framework of the socio-technical system approach, this study involved doing stakeholder analysis and defining user roles. The primary stakeholder group identified for system utilization consists of individuals employed in the academic and administrative units of the university who are accountable for data collecting and analysis procedures.

The purpose of focus group research was to thoroughly examine the expectations and experiences of this particular group of stakeholders. A total of 47 user representatives participated in face-to-face focus group interviews. Four distinct sessions were arranged to facilitate the participants in articulating their viewpoints regarding the system, and qualitative data were gathered from 10-15 users in each session. Based on the discoveries, the system's interactions with user roles were simulated and technological needs were established. Table 1 displays the descriptive data for the groupings.

Table 1. Focus group participant characteristics

Age	Gender	Term of Office	Implementer Profile	Age	Gender	Term of Office	Implementer Profile
		Group I				Group II	
34	F	8	administrative	28	F	2	academic
31	M	5	academic	28	M	2	academic
30	F	5	academic	39	F	14	administrative
30	M	4	administrative	36	M	10	academic
31	F	6	administrative	33	M	8	academic
39	M	17	administrative	37	F	15	academic
41	M	16	administrative	27	M	2	academic
43	F	21	academic	42	M	20	academic
43	M	20	academic	41	M	18	academic
34	F	8	administrative	35	F	9	academic
34	F	8	academic	26	F	3	administrative
27	M	5	administrative	36	F	14	administrative
		Group III				Group IV	
27	F	1	academic	35	M	9	academic
39	F	13	academic	39	M	13	administrative
31	F	6	administrative	36	M	11	administrative
27	M	1	academic	41	M	15	academic
38	M	13	administrative	32	M	7	academic
37	M	15	academic	37	F	15	administrative
37	F	12	administrative	42	F	17	administrative
43	M	21	administrative	42	M	20	administrative
29	M	6	administrative	36	F	13	academic
40	F	14	administrative	41	M	15	administrative
33	M	7	administrative	40	M	14	administrative
40	F	18	administrative				

The participants' experiences and expectations were documented during the focus group talks using a comprehensive data collection method. Every session was meticulously documented using a tape recorder and preserved for subsequent transcription. Furthermore, both the moderator and the assistant moderator independently recorded their own observations and highlighted the most important aspects. The findings from all these data sources were summarized and the main themes were identified using qualitative analysis techniques.

Figure 3 presents the visual representation of the data analysis results acquired from the Group 1 interview. The keywords in question are derived exclusively from the data obtained from the focus group. Thus, adhering to the qualitative research tradition, the produced results were guaranteed to accurately represent the perspectives of the participants.

Figure 3. Highlights from the Group I meeting

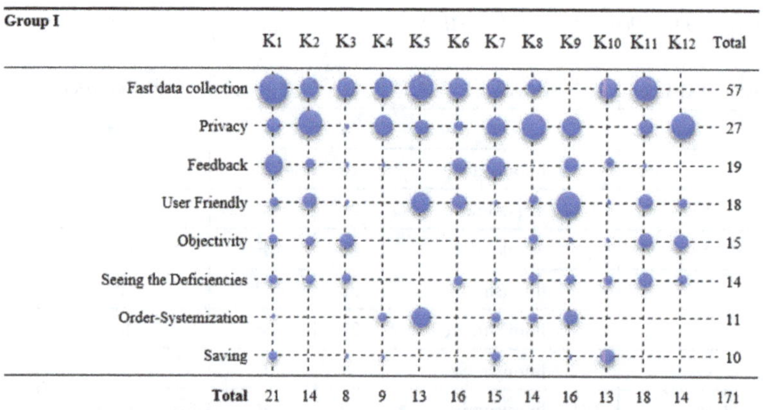

The analysis results based on the data obtained from Group 2's discussion are visualized in Figure 4.

Figure 4. Highlights from the Group II meeting

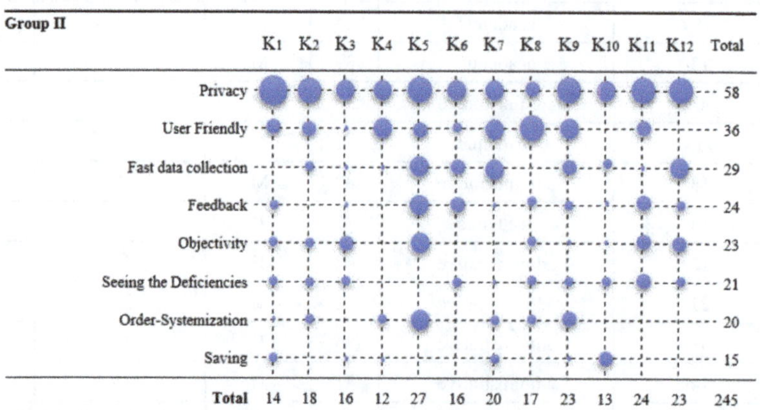

Figure 5 presents the visual representation of the data analysis results derived from the Group 3 interview.

Figure 5. Highlights from the Group III meeting

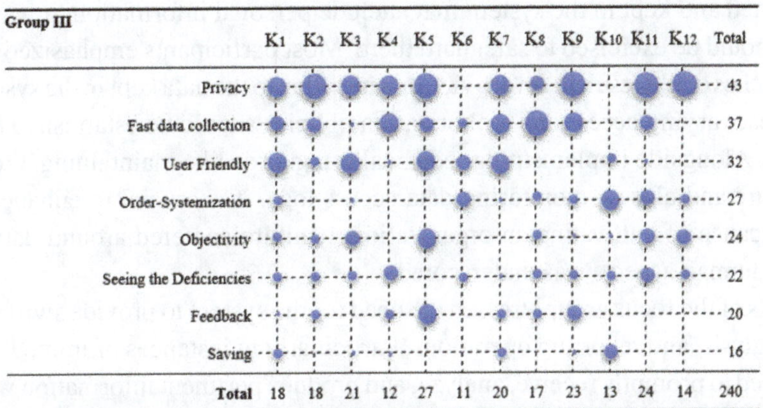

The analysis results based on the data obtained from Group 4 meeting are visualized in Figure 6.

Figure 6. Highlights from the Group IV meeting

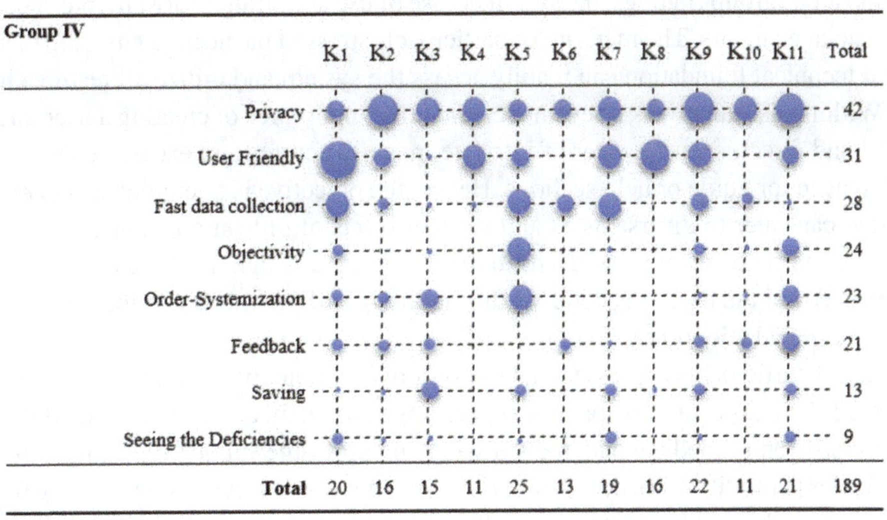

The qualitative data collected from the focus group meetings underwent a thorough analysis, which uncovered significant conclusions. Upon comparison analysis of the viewpoints offered in the four distinct focus group sessions, some recurring themes were identified:

- Strong emphasis on data privacy and security
- Efficient and seamless data acquisition and dissemination
- User-friendly and streamlined interface

Data privacy and security emerged as a significant concern among focus group participants. Given that the data inputted and kept in the system may include personal information, it was emphasized that extreme caution should be exercised to safeguard them. Most participants emphasized that unauthorized access or data breaches could result in severe victimization due to the data kept in the system. Furthermore, it was proposed that varying access and authorization policies should be established based on the level of data sensitivity. Alongside implementing technical safeguards like maintaining a robust information security architecture and closely monitoring data access logs, it is crucial to enhance user awareness. Hence, the significance of cultivating an organizational culture centered around data security in both technological and human aspects was underscored.

The participants of the focus group stressed the need for the system to provide swift and uninterrupted data gathering, analysis, and reporting operations. Particularly in instances of immediate data input, the system is anticipated to promptly receive, analyze, and produce pertinent information without delay. This anticipation is founded on the necessity for expeditious decision-making. Managers express apprehension about having to make judgments based on delayed and obsolete data when real-time data flow cannot be guaranteed. Conversely, it was also mentioned that any disturbances in the systems would have an adverse impact on business operations. Consequently, the participants expressed a need for the system to prioritize accessibility and agility, and possess the ability to promptly address immediate demands through a scalable infrastructure. This will facilitate the creation of seamless dynamic reports and infographics.

Based on the focus group findings, the system's ease of use and straightforward interface design were identified as crucial elements. The majority of participants stressed the need of ensuring that individuals lacking a solid technical foundation can readily access the system and utilize all features in an instinctive manner. Within this framework, they underscored the importance of creating a user interface that is uncomplicated and direct, steering clear of intricate menu structures and excessive choices, as well as minimizing the need for guide or help sections. Hence, the objective is to employ a versatile and adaptable system that can cater to diverse users and varying levels of utilization. Consequently, a considerable proportion of participants expressed a need for an interface design that is easy to use, intuitive, and focused on the needs of the user. It is believed that adopting and actively using the system will boost its potential for widespread adoption.

The majority of participants expressed that the system may potentially store personal or institutional data and stressed their expectations for its safeguarding. Simultaneously, it was noted that they place significant emphasis on immediate data transmission and up-to-the-minute reporting. Ultimately, they insisted on effortless usability and a design that is intuitive for users at every step, starting from inputting data to conducting analysis. The system design was significantly influenced by these three key results. The technological infrastructure and interface design were organized to fulfill these prioritized requirements. The social system analysis yielded tangible outcomes.

An examination of the keywords utilized in the focus group research offers important insights into the underlying motivations for word selection. Fielding and Lee (1997) argue that words have multiple meanings depending on the context. Contextual keyword analysis aims to study the relationship between words and the words that surround them.

Consistent with the objective of including all relevant parties in the development of the socio-technical system, input was also gathered from the university senior management, who are members of the senate. In order to achieve this objective, a preliminary version of the system was presented to high-level administrators via a pilot application during the developmental stage. After the initial meeting, a digital questionnaire was created to assess the overall viewpoints and anticipations of the administrators regarding the system. The survey was conducted with senior executives utilizing the system's internal framework. Thus, the system's functionality was tested and valuable input was obtained from the management level. Based on the gathered results, enhancements were implemented for the final iteration of the system. Early involvement of high management positively impacted the system design process.

A web-based questionnaire was created to gather the perspectives of top-level executives regarding the system. The survey has 12 closed-ended questions that assess the demographic attributes of the participants and their overall viewpoints on the system. Additionally, there are 2 open-ended questions to delve into their expectations of the system in detail. Table 2 presents the demographic characteristics, including age, gender, and position, of the top managers who took part in the survey.

Table 2. Senior management participant characteristics

	Gender	Title	Age
Senator 1	Female	Associate Professor	37
Senator 2	Female	Officer/Administrative	39
Senator 3	Male	Officer/Administrative	46
Senator 4	Female	Researcher	39
Senator 5	Female	Officer/Administrative	33
Senator 6	Male	Associate Professor	40
Senator 7	Male	Professor	65
Senator 8	Male	Professor	54
Senator 9	Male	Officer/Administrative	44
Senator 10	Male	Associate Professor	44
Senator 11	Male	Associate Professor	50
Senator 12	Male	Associate Professor	40
Senator 13	Female	Associate Professor	38
Senator 14	Male	Officer/Administrative	54

The distribution and statistics of the responses given to the 5-point Likert scale questionnaire consisting of 12 items are shown in Table 3.

Ultimately, the subjective viewpoints gathered from the open-ended questions of the survey underwent thorough examination of the content, were assigned codes, organized into categories based on common themes, and the results were presented visually in Figure 7-8.

Q1: What is the first term that comes to mind when thinking of a Data Collection and Analysis System?

Table 3. Online questionnaire and first impressions

Items	Strongly Disagree	Disagree	Undecided	Agree	Strongly Agree
The interface design of the module has a simple and understandable structure.	0 0,00%	0 0,00%	1 7,14%	7 50,00%	6 42,86%
Access to the module is simple.	0 0,00%	0 0,00%	0 0,00%	5 35,71%	9 64,29%
Ready-made questionnaire templates in the module make it easy to implement.	0 0,00%	0 0,00%	0 0,00%	5 35,71%	9 64,29%
The module facilitates the data collection process for the units.	0 0,00%	0 0,00%	0 0,00%	6 42,86%	8 57,14%
The module is useful for storing/retaining data.	0 0,00%	0 0,00%	1 7,14%	5 35,71%	8 57,14%
The module provides benefits to the relevant units by reporting the results.	0 0,00%	0 0,00%	0 0,00%	6 42,86%	8 57,14%
The module benefits management in the process of informed decision-making.	0 0,00%	0 0,00%	1 7,14%	6 42,86%	7 50,00%
The reports generated by the module benefit the quality management process.	0 0,00%	0 0,00%	0 0,00%	5 35,71%	9 64,29%
The module reduces the time cost for the data collection process of the units.	0 0,00%	0 0,00%	2 14,29%	4 28,57%	8 57,14%
The report types produced by the module are sufficient.	0 0,00%	0 0,00%	2 14,29%	8 57,14%	4 28,57%
Information about the module is sufficient.	0 0,00%	0 0,00%	1 7,14%	7 50,00%	6 42,86%
User manuals are easy to access within the module.	0 0,00%	0 0,00%	2 14,29%	3 21,43%	9 64,29%

Figure 7. Expectations from the system

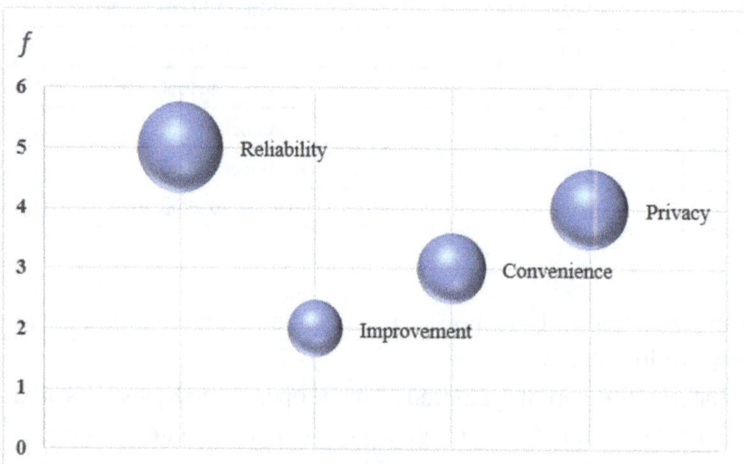

The emphasis placed on the idea of "Reliability" suggests that there are high standards and demands for the effectiveness and uninterrupted operation of the system. The precision and ease of access to data that will serve as the foundation for decision-making processes are crucial. The term "improvement" signifies that the system is perceived as a catalyst for enhancing institutional capability over a period of time. The term "convenience" implies that the system is anticipated to possess a user-friendly and instinctive interface that may be easily utilized by employees of all ranks. The focus on "Privacy" underscores the importance of safeguarding and preserving data with care and caution.

By evaluating these keywords comprehensively, the primary dimensions of senior management's expectations from the system become apparent.

Q2: In your opinion, what is the most powerful aspect of the Data Collection and Analysis System?

Figure 8. Strengths of the system

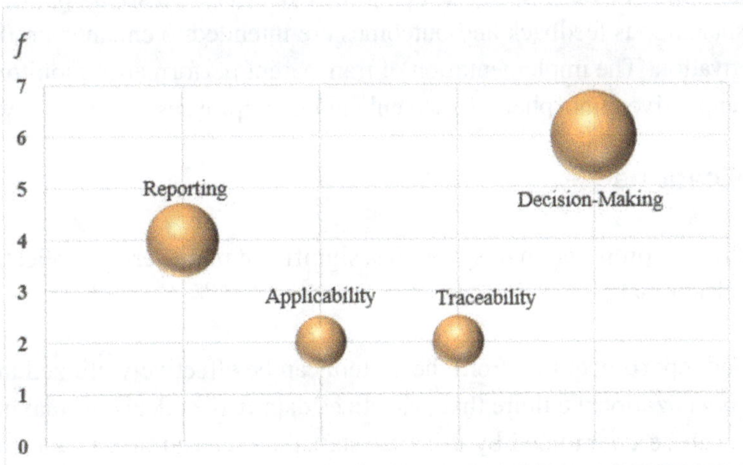

"Reporting" denotes the capacity of the system to convert and display data into significant reports and visual representations. "Applicability" underscores the capacity of the gathered data to inform tangible decisions and practical uses. "Traceability" pertains to the significance of being able to precisely investigate the origin of the data and the process of its modification. Ultimately, "Decision-Making" pertains to the system's capacity to facilitate well-informed decision-making, which is its primary desired outcome.

Collectively, these terms indicate the strategic advantages of the Data Collection and Analysis System. Senior management acknowledges the system's high value. The extensive dataset and multidimensional analysis allowed for a complete evaluation of senior managers' expectations and ideas for the system from a holistic standpoint. The collected results have furnished useful insights for determining the ultimate configuration of the system.

CONCLUSION

This study adopts a comprehensive socio-technical system approach that takes into account the simultaneous optimization of social and technical system components. An in-depth analysis was conducted on the experiences and expectations of both senior management and practitioners on the system, using qualitative and quantitative data collection methodologies. The findings have identified the technical infrastructure needs on one side, and the interface design and usability characteristics on the other side. The social and technical system components were created in continuous interaction and harmony, in accordance with the philosophy of joint optimization.

The established socio-technical system seeks to enhance the organization's ability to convert its data into valuable information, hence bolstering decision-making processes. The technology provides managers with immediate reports and trend analysis, enabling them to make precise and data-informed decisions. Simultaneously, the capacity to formulate forecasts and estimations regarding the future would effectively enhance company strategic planning procedures. The firm can quickly evaluate its overall performance and trends in specific areas thanks to holistic data visualization opportunities.

The system's instantaneous feedback and outcomes are intended to enhance productivity by stimulating employee motivation. The implementation of transparent performance monitoring is expected to foster a favorable competitive atmosphere, hence enhancing employees' productivity.

Managerial Implications

The socio-technical system proposed in this work has significant managerial implications for university management and decision makers.

- The data sets and reports acquired from the system can be effectively utilized in decision-making processes. An organizational culture that prioritizes data-driven decision-making can be formed.
- Strategic goals can be determined by utilizing statistical measurements and trend analysis conducted on various units.
- The user did not provide any text. By consistently monitoring performance indicators, it becomes possible to conduct studies on corporate performance management and process improvement.
- The user did not provide any text. The data warehouse infrastructure enables the generation of retrospective reports and time series studies, which will aid in future forecasting.
- Integrating and visualizing data across many departments would enhance institutional synergy.

Based on these findings, it is evident that the system has the capacity to make substantial contributions to university management.

Practical Implications

The advanced socio-technical system also provides substantial practical advantages for practitioners and end-users:

- The system will be made more accessible and easier to use through the implementation of a user-friendly interface design.

- The web-based architecture will enable convenient access to the system from many places and devices.
- The provision of online data entry and immediate reporting assistance will result in time savings.
- Performance monitoring can be facilitated by analyzing statistics and trends derived from various units.
- A comprehensive and coherent data structure would enhance the dependability of studies and reports.

These tangible contributions will promote the acceptance and efficient utilization of the system. Additionally, it will result in increased production.

Directions for Future Research

The study involved designing and modeling a socio-technical system. However, its execution and assessment of its impact will provide valuable insights for future investigations. Within this particular framework, several recommendations might be put forth:

- The implemented system should be deployed university-wide, and user feedback should be gathered.
- The measurement of productivity increase rates in various units should be done objectively, and the impacts of the system should be quantified.
- The investigation can focus on how it affects performance criteria such as student happiness, employee motivation, and the quantity of scientific publications.
- The extent to which system outputs and reports are used in decision-making processes can be analyzed.
- Comparable systems can be established at several universities, enabling the execution of comparative analysis.

Conducting these monitoring and comparison studies will enhance the existing body of knowledge on the design of socio-technical systems.

Funding Information

This research did not get any dedicated support from any public, private, or not-for-profit organizations.

REFERENCES

Aldridge, S., & Rowley, J. (1998). Measuring customer satisfaction in higher education. *Quality Assurance in Education*, *6*(4), 197–204. doi:10.1108/09684889810242182

Bryl, V., Giorgini, P., & Mylopoulos, J. (2009). Designing socio-technical systems: From stakeholder goals to social networks. *Requirements Engineering*, *14*(1), 47–70. doi:10.1007/s00766-008-0073-5

Caeiro, S., Sandoval Hamón, L. A., Martins, R., & Bayas Aldaz, C. E. (2020). Sustainability assessment and benchmarking in higher education institutions—A critical reflection. *Sustainability (Basel), 12*(2), 543. doi:10.3390/su12020543

Dzimińska, M., Fijałkowska, J., & Sułkowski, Ł. (2018). Trust-based quality culture conceptual model for higher education institutions. *Sustainability (Basel), 10*(8), 2599. doi:10.3390/su10082599

Edelenbos, J., & Klijn, E. H. (2006). Managing stakeholder involvement in decision making: A comparative analysis of six interactive processes in the Netherlands. *Journal of Public Administration: Research and Theory, 16*(3), 417–446. doi:10.1093/jopart/mui049

Emery, F. E., & Trist, E. L. (1960). Socio-technical systems. *Management Science. Models and Techniques, 2*, 83–97.

Fielding, N. G., & Lee, R. M. (1997). Applications of computer software in the sociological analysis of qualitative data. *Bulletin de Methodologie Sociologique, 57*(1), 3–24. doi:10.1177/075910639705700101

Goethel, D. R., Lucey, S. M., Berger, A. M., Gaichas, S. K., Karp, M. A., Lynch, P. D., Walter, J. F. III, Deroba, J. J., Miller, S., & Wilberg, M. J. (2019). Closing the feedback loop: On stakeholder participation in management strategy evaluation. *Canadian Journal of Fisheries and Aquatic Sciences, 76*(10), 1895–1913. doi:10.1139/cjfas-2018-0162

Govers, M., & Van Amelsvoort, P. (2019). A socio-technical perspective on the digital era: The Lowlands view. *European Journal of Workplace Innovation, 4*(2). Advance online publication. doi:10.46364/ejwi.v4i2.589

Hallak, J., & Poisson, M. (2007). *Corrupt Schools, Corrupt Universities: What can be done?* International Institute for Education Planning.

Hemsley-Brown, J., & Oplatka, I. (2006). Universities in a competitive global marketplace: A systematic review of the literature on higher education marketing. *International Journal of Public Sector Management, 19*(4), 316–338. doi:10.1108/09513550610669176

Howe, N., Giles, E., Newbury-Birch, D., & McColl, E. (2018). Systematic review of participants' attitudes towards data sharing: A thematic synthesis. *Journal of Health Services Research & Policy, 23*(2), 123–133. doi:10.1177/1355819617751555 PMID:29653503

Iwanaga, T., Wang, H. H., Hamilton, S. H., Grimm, V., Koralewski, T. E., Salado, A., Elsawah, S., Razavi, S., Yang, J., Glynn, P., Badham, J., Voinov, A., Chen, M., Grant, W. E., Peterson, T. R., Frank, K., Shenk, G., Barton, C. M., Jakeman, A. J., & Little, J. C. (2021). Socio-technical scales in socio-environmental modeling: Managing a system-of-systems modeling approach. *Environmental Modelling & Software, 135*, 104885. doi:10.1016/j.envsoft.2020.104885 PMID:33041631

Khalid, R., Landini, S., Valasai, G. D., Khalid, F., & Sandwell, P. (2023). Towards equitable and inclusive energy systems for remote off-grid communities: A socio-technical assessment of solar power for village Helario in Tharparkar, Pakistan. *Renewable and Sustainable Energy Transition, 4*, 100067. doi:10.1016/j.rset.2023.100067

Manatos, M. J., Rosa, M. J., & Sarrico, C. S. (2018). Quality management in universities: Towards an integrated approach? *International Journal of Quality & Reliability Management*, *35*(1), 126–144. doi:10.1108/IJQRM-04-2016-0046

Medina, C., & Rufín, R. (2015). Transparency policy and students' satisfaction and trust. *Transforming Government: People. Transforming Government*, *9*(3), 309–323. doi:10.1108/TG-07-2014-0027

Mena, S., & Palazzo, G. (2012). Input and output legitimacy of multi-stakeholder initiatives. *Business Ethics Quarterly*, *22*(3), 527–556. doi:10.5840/beq201222333

Mourad, M. (2017). Quality assurance as a driver of information management strategy: Stakeholders' perspectives in higher education. *Journal of Enterprise Information Management*, *30*(5), 779–794. doi:10.1108/JEIM-06-2016-0104

Münch, C., Marx, E., Benz, L., Hartmann, E., & Matzner, M. (2022). Capabilities of digital servitization: Evidence from the socio-technical systems theory. *Technological Forecasting and Social Change*, *176*, 121361. doi:10.1016/j.techfore.2021.121361

Nissenbaum, H. (2020). Protecting privacy in an information age: The problem of privacy in public. In *The Ethics of Information Technologies* (pp. 141–178). Routledge. doi:10.4324/9781003075011-12

Pedreschi, D., Bonchi, F., Turini, F., Verykios, V. S., Atzori, M., Malin, B., ... Saygin, Y. (2008). Privacy protection: regulations and technologies, opportunities and threats. *Mobility, Data Mining and Privacy: Geographic Knowledge Discovery*, 101-119. doi:10.1007/978-3-540-75177-9_5

Rabovsky, T. M. (2014). Using data to manage for performance at public universities. *Public Administration Review*, *74*(2), 260–272. doi:10.1111/puar.12185

Rupcic, N. (2019). Organizational learning in stakeholder relations. *The Learning Organization*, *26*(2), 219–231. doi:10.1108/TLO-02-2019-221

Shah, M., Cheng, M., & Fitzgerald, R. (2017). Closing the loop on student feedback: The case of Australian and Scottish universities. *Higher Education*, *74*(1), 115–129. doi:10.1007/s10734-016-0032-x

Shah, M., & Nair, C. S. (2012). Student surveys and feedback: Strategic solution for all tertiary education institutions. *Studies in Learning, Evaluation. Innovation and Development*, *9*(1).

Tadelis, S. (2016). Reputation and feedback systems in online platform markets. *Annual Review of Economics*, *8*(1), 321–340. doi:10.1146/annurev-economics-080315-015325

Trist, E. L. (1978). On socio-technical systems. *Sociotechnical systems: A sourcebook*, 43-57.

Walker, G. H., Stanton, N. A., Salmon, P. M., & Jenkins, D. P. (2008). A review of sociotechnical systems theory: A classic concept for new command and control paradigms. *Theoretical Issues in Ergonomics Science*, *9*(6), 479–499. doi:10.1080/14639220701635470

West, D., Luzeckyj, A., Searle, B., Toohey, D., Vanderlelie, J., & Bell, K. R. (2020). Perspectives from the stakeholder: Students' views regarding learning analytics and data collection. *Australasian Journal of Educational Technology*, *36*(6), 72–88. doi:10.14742/ajet.5957

KEY TERMS AND DEFINITIONS

Data Analytics: It involves analyzing data obtained from surveys and feedback with various statistical or artificial intelligence techniques.

Decision Support System: These are platforms that aim to provide information to the management's decision-making processes.

Privacy: Data privacy pertains to safeguarding personal information against illegal or improper utilization. Online survey anonymity exemplifies this phenomenon.

Questionnaire: This is a research methodology that seeks to gather data from certain groups of people by using well-organized and standardized questions. This study employed surveys targeting various stakeholder groups.

Socio-Technical System: It is a holistic system design method that takes into account both social and technical factors simultaneously. It highlights the synergy between humans and technology.

Stakeholder Feedback: The groups affected by the activities and decisions of the University (students, employees, graduates, etc.) express their assessments, suggestions, and expectations for these processes.

Chapter 15
Sentiment Analysis of User Reactions to Meta's Threads Launch and Twitter's X Renaming:
A Comparative Study Using DistilBERT and Machine Learning

Anukansha Sharma
Amity University, Noida, India

Piyush Kumar
https://orcid.org/0000-0003-1669-5903
Amity University, Noida, India

Ronit Bali
Amity University, Noida, India

G. M. Nandana
Amity University, Noida, India

Shuchi Mala
Amity University, Noida, India

ABSTRACT

The massive dataset generated by social media platforms has attracted researchers interested in sentiment analysis. Natural language processing (NLP) has become popular for retrieving useful knowledge from user-generated content. In this chapter, the authors conducted a sentiment analysis of comments from Meta's new product, Threads, in competition to Twitter. Authors have tested the system with real-time comments. A dataset of 12,000 comments was extracted from YouTube using the YouTube API containing keywords such as "Threads," "Twitter," and "X." The authors used DistilBERT to weigh the comments and segregate them into positive and negative. Machine learning algorithms were used to analyze the weighted data, and logistic regression was found to outperform random forest and KNN in providing an accuracy of 85.95%. The study highlights the importance of sentiment analysis in understanding user-generated content and its potential applications in the digital era.

DOI: 10.4018/979-8-3693-1210-0.ch015

INTRODUCTION

Sentiment analysis has been trending for the past years and it is considered as a practice of applying NLP or the natural language processing and text analysis procedures to detect and obtain subjective data from the written material (Al Mamun et al., 2022; Chu et al., 2022; Fasha et al., 2022; Hussein, 2018; Keikhosrokiani, 2022; Keikhosrokiani & Asl, 2022a; Keikhosrokiani & Pourya Asl, 2022; Low et al., 2024; Suhendra et al., 2022). It is mentioned that sentiment analysis is the method of collecting and analyzing people's sentiments, thoughts, and reactions regarding various topics, products, texts, and facilities (Wankhade et al., 2022). Taboada, (2016) refers to sentiment analysis as an attempt made to automatically determine the sentiment contained in the text. Further, (Medhat et al., 2014) mentions that it is the computational treatment of thoughts, feelings, and bias of the text. It provides an automated method for mining the target audience's thoughts and attitudes (Rahman et al., 2023). It will convert raw data into meaningful data and help researchers in figuring out what sort of sentiment can be formulated from the dataset based on public opinion. The output for these analyses can be grouped under positive or negative feedback (Diekson et al., 2023). From this, it can be said that sentiment analysis is a way by which one is able to understand what people's feelings or emotions are regarding a product or a service.

Due to advancement in technology, sentiment analysis has its uses in multi-disciplinary fields. Earlier, there used to be articles, newspapers, and people used to gather in the evening to discuss about the trending topics, but this has changed after social media platforms are discovered. People are keener on posting and expressing about their sentiment with the outside world in real time. Thus, in recent times, many microblogging platforms like Twitter(X), Instagram, and Threads are becoming popular with the general audience to express their opinion of various trending topics. These topics may include reaction to elections, wars, commercials, news, reviewing a place (Roy, 2023), stock market and many more. It can be attributed to the success factor in ease of communication and usage of technology in real time. These platforms have evolved to become bigger tools to reach the masses.

But these platforms have their own downfalls and shortcomings. With the advent of sharing news articles online easily, we are seeing plenty of fake news which is spreading.

Social media platforms are a huge source of data. It produces a huge chunk of data every minute. Text data, image, audio, videos are available for almost everything on the social media irrespective of the sentiment of people (John & Keikhosrokiani, 2022; Keikhosrokiani et al., 2022; Keikhosrokiani & Asl, 2022b; P. Kumar et al., 2022a; Ravichandran & Keikhosrokiani, 2023). As a plethora of information, news, comments, etc. are available, it becomes nearly impossible to decide what is correct or incorrect and a clear differentiation among the opinions is not formed.

One of the ways to trace and check the validity of such news is through sentiment analysis (SA). To assess the reliability of the information and its sources, analysis may be integrated with additional techniques like image analysis and source verification. Detecting trends in the sentiment of information connected to certain ideas can assist in determining whether certain narratives or fake news articles acquire popularity.

Customer satisfaction is a measurement of how happy or unhappy the customer is after they have utilized the product or services. These include conducting surveys and ratings, which support in improving and making required changes in the product and services.[1] Sentiment analysis is one of the ways by which a company or an organization can understand customer satisfaction about their product or services.

This can be achieved by identifying popular hashtags, doing real time marketing, collaborating with influencers, and encouraging them to create content. In this way it will help in creating timely and relevant content to audiences. SA may assist businesses in understanding how their rivals are interacting with social media trends and whether there is a potential to differentiate themselves in capitalization on a trend. It can be used to measure the campaign's impact by analyzing sentiment and engagement indicators. Additionally, it aids in the collection of feedback from social media users, allowing businesses to change and optimize their advertising campaigns in real time. It will allow brands to create their promotional efforts which are aligned with trends that will have a long-term influence rather than go away.

Because of numerous industrial applications, SA has piqued the interest of many researchers. SA techniques can be broadly classified into five types like Machine Learning-based, lexicon-based, linguistic rule-based, contextual embedding and ensemble based. Sentiment analysis based on machine learning automatically categorizes text qualities and trains an algorithm to find patterns and correlations in labeled text data while using a system that counts the quantity of positive, neutral, and negative words in a text, a sentiment score is determined by analyzing the frequency and intensity of these words.is done using Lexicon based sentiment analysis. The linguistic rule based is well-liked method offers a collection of manually created predetermined rules and patterns to help choose phrases that convey emotion. This approach may not be appropriate for more complex analyses and texts because it mainly relies on rules and word lexicons. The contextual method uses neural networks to extract word nuance and complexity from a given document by iterating through unsupervised machine learning training models. To build vector representations of words and phrases in relation to surrounding text, deep learning algorithms are used in this process. The term "bank" may then be distinguished between a riverbank and a financial organization. Finally, the ensemble utilizes the model that has been trained on social listening to assess financial reporting data, ensemble sentiment analysis can extend models across diverse domains and yield more accurate and dependable overall findings. Ensemble analysis may be performed using a variety of methods, such as voting, weighting, and meta. [2] In this chapter our focus is limited to only two major social media, i.e., Twitter "X" and Threads.

TWITTER

Twitter is one of the most used social media applications. People from across the globe use the application, ranging from average people, to influencers, models, politicians, and kids. The United States has the highest number of twitter users consisting of 95.4 million. In the year 2023, the value of the company is $41.09 billion generating a profit of $4.4 billion in 2022. It has around 528.3 million monthly active users which are monetized. Overall twitter has 56.4% male users and 43.6% female users. 30% of the customers want to see brands' presence and advertisements on twitter. India ranks 3rd after the US and Japan for the total number of users by having 27.25 million active users. Further, 82% percent of the people use twitter for entertainment purposes, and more than half of the twitters' users use the application for news purposes, and it is number 1 in terms of fetching news.[3]

THREADS

Threads is a new application launched by Meta on 5th July 2023. It is like twitter used for multi-purpose activities. Currently it has 130 million users and within 1 hour, after its launch the application surpassed one million users and Neymar is the most followed user in the Threads. It took just 4 days to reach one hundred million while apps like ChatGPT took around 2 months to reach the same. Users now only use the app for three minutes a day on average. On the other hand, two hundred million people use Twitter every day, logging on for 31 minutes on average.[4]

The goal of the chapter is to evaluate the hype when Threads app was launched in July 2023 and Twitter rebranded itself to "X" based on the sentiment of the public. Secondly, the goal was to compare the accuracies of machine learning models and compare the accuracy of positive and negative sentiments.

The remaining paper can be arranged as follows. Part 2 addresses related work, Part 3 explains methodology, Part 4 examines the results and discussion, and Part 5 discusses the final views on the planned work and future work.

LITERATURE REVIEW

A study was conducted to estimate the ability of Tweets in assessing the sentiment influence of COVID-19 cases in Greece. The authors collected around 150000 tweets from around 19000 users having a sum of around 2,800,000 words for almost one year and were examined towards sentiment dictionaries which included English to Greek and other one was in Greek. The authors then estimated the positive, negative, and neutral sentiments of people and further segregated the emotions into six main categories including – surprise, disgust, happiness, anger, sadness, and fear. Finally, the authors calculated the correlation between the COVID-19 cases and people's sentiments and sentiments and volume of data. It was found that most predominant sentiments were Surprise with 25.32% and Disgust with 19.88% of these COVID-19 cases. At a significance level of $p < 0.01$, the correlation coefficient (R2) for the Vader lexicon is – 0.07454 for cases and – 0.,70668 for tweets, while for the other lexicon it was – 0.93095 and 0.167387-9 (Samaras et al., 2023).

An study discussed customer satisfaction with the services offered with Traveloka. The authors downloaded tweets related to Traveloka and collected 1200 tweets related to the website. The authors applied three machine learning algorithms including Support Vector machine, Logistic regression, and Naïve Bayes. The outcomes represent that SVM outperforms other algorithms and by providing better accuracy and concluding the response of tweets about Traveloka (Diekson et al., (2023).

Xu et al., (2023) studied the sentiments of people during the Russia – Ukraine War. They gathered a dataset consisting of 2537 tweets regarding the war. The objective of the study was to establish the dependability of the LSTM model with Sastrawi in sentiment analysis in Indonesian and to weigh the working of the model with the collected Twitter dataset regarding the war. The outcome of this study was positive, negative, and neutral sentiments which were 54.7%, 35% and 10.2% respectively. The outcomes found from this research implies that the LSTM model with Literature can provide better consequences in sentiment analysis with a forecast accuracy of 82%.

Li et al., (2023) examined the concerns, sentiments, and their disparity with time regarding online classes by students and teachers on Reddit. Sentiment analysis was applied to find their feelings and changes. For concerns, the authors conducted Topic modeling in the posts. As an outcome, it was found that the various concerns about online classes, such as severe false actions, showed suspicions about former approaches to solve difficulties in online lessons. The researchers collected data around 19818 posts posted from 01/01/2020 to 30/04/2022. It was found that the overall sentiments were neutral. The sentiment of students inclines to be negative, airing a sense of depression and uncertainty, which exhibits approval-seeking actions. On the contrary, the teachers' sentiment is much more rational and positive. Further, findings have revealed that cheating in online classes is worrying as a regular and shared concern.

Halawani et al., (2023) proposed an automated sentiment analysis on social media using Harris hawk optimization with deep learning model (ASASM-HHODL). This model processes original social media comments in a useful format further, it uses fastText-based word inserting and skip-gram to investigate the reduction of language processing dependency on data-pre-processing. Further, the ABiLSTM – attention-based bidirectional long-short-term model is developed for class of sentiments. The results showed promising working over recent state-of-the-art approaches.

Alaei et al., (2023) discussed the uncertainty challenge by suggesting a context-aware dictionary-based target-oriented sentiment analysis technique that integrates contributions from both humans and machines to present an alternative method to measuring sentiment in partial tourism-related data. The research makes a working contribution by building a target dictionary exactly for tourism sentiment analysis. Thus, the authors further propose a case of targeted-oriented emotion and sentiment analysis of posts from Twitter for the gold coast of Australia as a tourist destination. The researchers collected 102,170 tweets around the topic and out of which a subset of 6000 comments were filtered for analysis purposes after removing all the incorrect data. Out of these 6000, around 279 posts were positive while 168 were neutral and only 28 were negative posts. For the remaining data, an annotation agreement was applied. The agreement relating to annotators at the post level was 74.9%, increasing to 79.4% at the sentence level and 92.3% for sensitive words, presenting a sound basis for successive studies.

Jain et al., (2023) proposed two different methods to understand the decision made by sentiment analysis by visualizing the results. In this paper, interpretability has been applied on NLP-based sentiment analysis utilizing data from various social media sites such as Facebook, Reddit, and Twitter. With VADER – Valance Aware Dictionary for sentiment Reasoning, heatmaps are produced, which account for visual validation of the findings, thus increasing clarity. Further, LIME – Local Interpre-Table Model-Agnostic Explanations have been used to provide in-depth insight into the predictions. It has been learnt through an experiment that the anticipated system can exceed several ongoing systems devised to challenge interpretability. Using VADER to analyze sentiments resulted in 69.52% accuracy with precision of 64.88%.

Ermakova et al., (2023) compared and evaluated solutions using two experimental studies. Firstly, based on tweets about airline service quality, the authors test solutions of six vendors with different market power like Amazon, IBM, Google, Microsoft, MeaningCloud and Lexalytics and make their classification reports. Secondly, the authors compare two services with various data over time. For this purpose, 14640 records were taken from the Kaggle platform. After cleaning the data, there were 13,519 tweets ready for experiment purposes. The comparison was made between Google cloud natural language API and Meaning Cloud Sentiment Analysis API. Clearly, Google Cloud Natural Language API outperformed Meaning Cloud Sentiment Analysis API.

Rahman et al., (2023) studied the pre-processing, methods, and machine learning models for the multi-class categorization of sentiment. Further, the authors enhanced the performance so that they can propose a multi-layer class model. The researchers have applied decision tree, support vector machine and Naïve Bayes and compared it with the single-layered architecture with multi-tier models. In this paper, the authors took the movie reviews for the purpose of analysis. A total of 156,060 reviews were downloaded out of which data was biased towards neutrality. It was found that overall accuracy of multi-layered architecture of naïve bayes was greater than SVM and Decision tree both in multi-tier architecture and single-tier model.

Mohamed et al., (2023) explored the social trends analytics using LexDeep approach to find the risk of domestic income shortfall during the COVID-19. The authors collected twitter reviews using Twint App for the period of 09/03/2019 to 17/03/2020 and during the period 18/03/2020 to 21/08/2021. Further, the tweets were annotated using VADER and deep learning models were applied to it. Various research was done using several embeddings, such as simple embedding, Global Vectors, and Word2Vec, to categorize the opinions expressed in the tweets. The performance of each LexDeep model was calculated and compared with a support vector machine (SVM). Lastly, the authors evaluated the unemployment rates before and after the pandemic to get a gist of percentage through the social media input analysis. The Lexdeep model with simple embedding performed better than SVM.

Costola et al., (2023) investigated the impact of the flow of coronavirus news and its formation in the stock market. The researchers examined 203,086 online posts and articles with respect to COVID-19 and published in three different platforms during the period January to June 2020.The authors applied machine learning algorithms such as BERT model which is widely adapted by the financial market. It was found that the outcomes have significant relation between opinion scores and S&P500.

Roy, (2023) explored customer online review emotions and accommodation experience that differ among luxury, mid-tier, and low-tier hotels. The sentiment analysis and natural language processing techniques were applied to determine aspects of hotel staying services. The authors have extracted data from TripAdvisor for hotels in Darjeeling. It was found that luxury accommodations have a subjective approach whereas the low-tier rooms hotels have an objective approach.

Gangrade et al., (2019) applied Thayer's Model to conduct sentiment analysis. The authors have extracted sentiment from keywords of sentiment using the hashtags from Instagram. Sentiment categories are applied to user postings, and the similarity between the sentiment adjective candidates and sentiment keywords is measured to ascertain sentiments. The outcomes show that the average accuracy rate for all sentiments is 90.7%.

Alatabi & Abbas, (2020) proposed a new opinion analysis technique in which a process of extracting polarity from social media platforms has been designed. The authors have applied the Bayesian Rough Decision Tree algorithm. The authors extracted 6000 posts out of which 4000 were Facebook comments and 2000 were movie reviews. Out of 4000 movie reviews 2000 were positive and 2000 were negative. Similarly, out of 2000 movie reviews, 1000 were positive while 1000 were negative. The accuracy of the proposed algorithm is more than 95% of the data. The normal decision tree algorithm gave an accuracy of 98.95% while that of BRDT algorithm gave an accuracy of 99.625%.

Gallagher et al., (2019) investigated the usage of text mining techniques in conjunction with sentiment analysis to better comprehend what consumers are saying about goods, services, and interactions with a business. If customers are given the chance to provide free text feedback instead of rating a product on a scale of one to five, do they really say what they think? The authors examine the relationship between structured data, such as user review ratings or satisfaction ratings, and unstructured customer sentiment, which takes the form of verbatim feedback. The writers rate a verbatim piece of feedback using different Sentiment Analysis techniques, and then classify it as good, negative, or neutral. They examine the possible business insights by comparing this normalized sentiment score to the matching rating score. The findings show that a company cannot get its whole customer experience information from a single, stand-alone statistic.

Ramanathan et al., (2022) examined the direct impacts of "social-media-induced purchase intention" on customer satisfaction using a structural equation model and data gathered from the online services sector. They also examine the mediating function of e-commerce and online sales (e-safety, e-information, and e-advertisement) on consumer happiness and discover that a novel factor—"e-safety"—mediates the association between consumer purchase intention and customer happiness in addition to social media advertising and information sharing. According to our findings, when a consumer makes an online purchase, an online e-trust relationship can be formed between them and the service provider.

Hasson et al., (2019) investigated the possibility of using social media data in place of traditional customer satisfaction surveys. The following actions were taken to assess this strategy, utilizing Twitter consumer feedback data: 1) Applying sentiment analysis to every Tweet to compare the general sentiment regarding various goods and/or services. 2) Building a network of hashtags to improve the Twitter customer feedback inquiry process. 3) Considering content and added value, comparing consumer opinion from survey replies with comments from social media. The authors discovered that social media offers benefits over conventional surveys.

Bozkurt et al., (2021) worked on this study to examine how consumer engagement habits are influenced by how consumers perceive businesses' social media interaction, taking into consideration the moderating effects of brand type and social media platform. The authors carried out two different surveys that were conducted to measure the construct of interests. The Model 1 was managed to review the regulating roles of product type and platform. According to the findings, consumers are more likely to purchase brand offerings, recommend the brand in exchange for financial incentives, tell their friends and family about the brand on social media, and offer comments and ideas for brand improvement when they believe a brand is active on social media as opposed to inactive.

Anto et al., (2016) worked on customer reviews serving as benchmarks for a company's functioning and success. The feedback from customers will provide the manufacturer with the accurate outcome of his goods. Considering the input, one can adjust his product as needed. However, most consumers never do provide comments. This work focuses on the method of automatically delivering feedback using information gathered from Twitter to circumvent the challenge of providing input. Through opinion mining, these data streams are filtered, examined, and feedback is gathered. Here, we mostly examine the cell phone data. According to the trials, the sentimental analysis is 80% accurate. The authors' approach can give businesses quick, insightful feedback.

Kim, (2021) examined text mining techniques and suggests a few substitute measures for gauging consumer sentiment. The results indicate that, in contrast to online review ratings, sentiment scores may be less susceptible to extreme bias. Online reviews had a skewed distribution towards extreme values, although sentiment scores tended to follow a normal distribution. Combining sentiment ratings and review durations might offer a fresh perspective on gauging excitement.

Al-Otaibi et al., (2018) used the leveraged Twitter data to extract insights from data that concealed popular sentiment. Positive or negative sentiment in tweets is classified using the support vector machine algorithm, and unigram is employed as a feature extraction technique. Large training datasets were used in the studies, and the algorithm produced results with a high accuracy of about 87%.

Kang & Park, (2014) applied the combination of sentiment analysis and VIKOR and created a new paradigm for measuring customer satisfaction for mobile services. Customer happiness for mobile services may be precisely quantified using a sentiment-analysis strategy that concurrently analyzes maximum group utility and individual regret with VIKOR, a compromise ranking method of the multicriteria decision making (MCDM) approach. The proposed methodology is primarily divided into two phases: customer satisfaction measurement and data gathering and preparation. As per the author's point of view the suggested customer-review-based method not only saves time and effort when gauging customer happiness, but it also accurately represents the opinions of actual consumers.

Wisnu et al., (2020) used the opinion mining and sentiment analysis to gauge public satisfaction with Indonesia's digital payment services (OVO, GO-PAY, and LinkAja). This study uses data from Twitter and goes through many steps, including data cleaning, feature selection, and classification using two machine learning approaches that includes the Naïve Bayes classifier and the K-Nearest Neighbor. After the raw data is cleaned up and the proper features for the classification procedure are extracted, the model is validated, and classification is carried out. Regarding the classification algorithm, this study reveals that KNN outperforms Naive Bayes in terms of accuracy.

S. Kumar et al., (2019) aimed a unique multimodal architecture that combines several data sources—namely, physiological signals and worldwide evaluations that are acquired independently for the product and its brand—to anticipate consumer product ratings. Natural Language Processing (NLP) technology is used to extract and evaluate the reviews given by viewers worldwide to calculate the compound score, which is used as a global rating. The electroencephalogram (EEG) signals of the participants were recorded simultaneously while watching different products on computer's screen. Using self-report for each product seen, valence scores for product ratings are derived from EEG to establish a local rating. An increased valence score is indicative of a participant's inherent attraction to a product. EEG data is modeled using random forest-based regression approaches to provide a local rating framework for rating prediction. Additionally, by combining local and global ratings, an optimization approach based on Artificial Bee Colonies (ABC) is employed to improve the framework's overall performance. 40 individuals, 25 of whom were male and 15 of whom were female, had their EEG information recorded while they browsed 42 distinct goods on an e-commerce website.

Miranda & Sassi, (2014) provided a Sentiment Analysis-based method to support the assessment of client satisfaction in an online job search company in Brazil. We examined a database maintained by an online job search firm that included customer reviews gathered via a form for canceling services. In addition to other parameters, this database includes a client-assigned score and a remark on the services. Using software developed in Python, we classified the sentiment indicated in the user comments and computed the correlation between the sentiment score and the client-assigned score.

Kozłowski & Korzeniewski, (2024) aimed to evaluate Polish hotel service investments made between 2018 and 2020. The evaluation was conducted by looking at the relationship between the amount of money spent on hotels in Poland's powiats and voivodeships and the feedback that guests left in online reviews on the websites of specific travel agencies. The approach used to assess the sentiment of text texts involves the use of an unsupervised classification algorithm to Polish.

METHODOLOGY

In this chapter the authors have applied an already pre-trained sentiment analysis model, that is, DistilBERT and compared the accuracies with different machine learning algorithms that has been discussed in detail in this section. The process flow of the methodology is shown in Figure 1.

The steps of the methodology process flow are as follows:

1. Data Extraction - The dataset has been extracted from YouTube comments. A total of 54691 comments were extracted containing keywords *"Twitter", "X", "Threads"*.

Figure 1. The process flow of the methodology

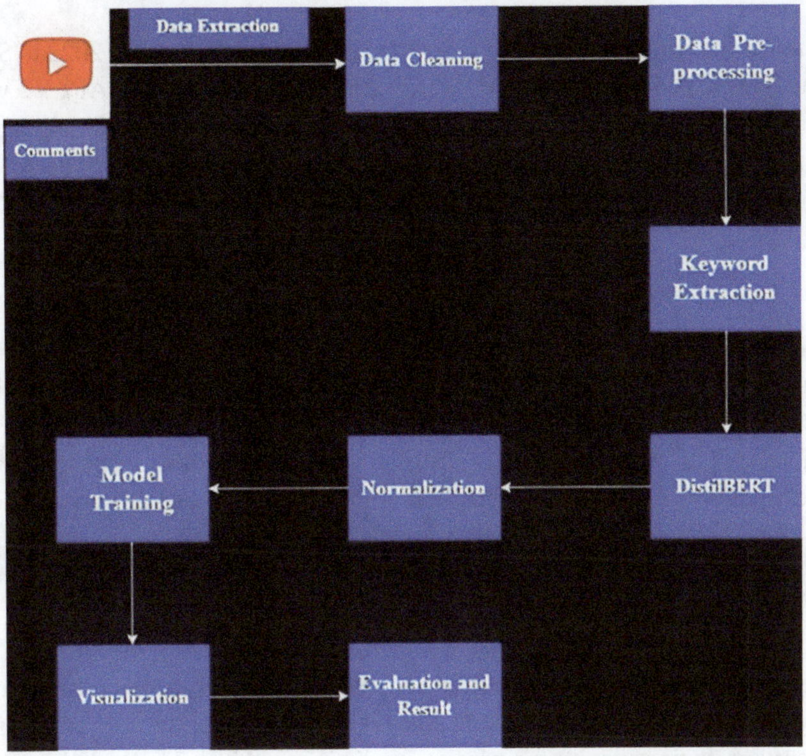

2. Data cleaning - Data was cleaned and the comments were removed which did not have *"X," "Threads", "twitter"* keywords. Further, the dataset contained dates of comments in textual format, which was converted into data format and after all the cleanup, the total of 12069 comments were available for further processes.
3. Data preprocessing - In the pre-processing stage, the data comments were tokenized, and punctuation were removed, and capital letters were converted to lower case wherever necessary followed by lemmatization and finally the preposition words like "as," "of," "in," etc. were removed.
4. Keyword Extraction - After the preprocessing was completed, the authors extracted the keywords for further usage. The main keywords were *"X," "threads," and "twitter"* along with positive and negative keywords.
5. DistilBERT - the pre-trained DistilBERT was applied on the preprocessed dataset to calculate sentiment score and to segregate the comments in positive and negative.
6. Normalization - The weights were applied based on "likes" for each comment received and then normalization values were multiplied by the score of DistilBERT to validate their intensity.
7. A. Model Training - 3 different algorithms were used on the weighted dataset. These algorithms included Random Forest, KNN, Logistic regression.

   B. Data Visualization - Based on the normalization, graphs were plotted, and necessary interpretations were noted down.
8. Evaluation and Result - Based on the model training, the accuracy, precision, F1-score, and Recall were calculated and compared.

DATASET

The dataset was extracted from the YouTube videos for the time of September 2022 to September 2023. A total of around 54691 YouTube comments were extracted. The YouTube API V3 was used for the purpose of collection of data. The API is free, and it has a variety of purposes ranging from blogging, managing subscriptions, uploading videos, extracting queries and many more. The API can be applied in all sorts of programming languages, such as python, Java, .NET, PHP, etc.[5]

DistilBERT

It is a pre-trained model for tiny general-purpose NLP that, like its predecessors, may be fine-tuned to perform well on a variety of tasks. By using knowledge distillation during the pre-training phase, we can reduce the size of a BERT model by 40% and yet keep 97% of its language comprehension skills, making it 60% quicker. This approach utilizes distillation to generate task-specific models.(Sanh et al., 2019) It accurately predicts the masked tokens (but not the next sentence objective) and finds a cosine resemblance between the student and instructor models' hidden states.[6]

KNN

It is a machine learning algorithm that supervises and makes comparable assumptions in close quarters. Selecting the appropriate value for K is crucial since it minimizes the number of mistakes the writers make while preserving their capacity for precise prediction-making. The technique becomes slower as the number of variables rises, despite its versatility in being able to be used for both regression and classification.[7]

RANDOM FOREST

A well-liked supervised machine learning approach for classification and regression issues in machine learning is the Random Forest approach. A Random Forest classifier uses many decision trees on different dataset subsets and averages them to increase the dataset's predicted accuracy. Its foundation is the idea of ensemble learning, which is the act of merging several classifiers to solve a challenging issue and enhance the model's functionality. Every tree is unique and possesses unique qualities, varieties, and attributes. Furthermore, since the decision tree only ever views 30% of the data, the dataset does not need to be divided into train and test sets.[8]

LOGISTIC REGRESSION

A sigmoid function is used in a basic logistic regression. whether the collection has values that fall into positive or negative categories. Logistic regression is the better option in the scenario. The value is in the interval of 0 to 1. There are three types of logistic regressions: ordinal, multinomial, and binary. Since there were only two outcomes for the dataset—positive and negative—binary logistic regression is utilized in this chapter. (P. Kumar et al., 2022b). The equation of the logistic regression is given as mentioned as in eq.1.

$$sig(x) = \frac{1}{1+e^{-x}} \tag{1}$$

RESULTS

From the above dataset, 55000 comments were extracted using the YouTube API with the keywords like *"X", "Twitter" and "Threads'*. After the data was cleaned by removing punctuations, changing the words from uppercase to lower case and many more, the data then preprocessed in which the lemmatization, removal of prepositional words were done and finally positive and negative words along with major keywords *"X," thread" and "twitter"* were extracted. These constituted about 12000 comments which were then trained on DistilBERT. This model calculated the sentiment score and segregated the comments into positive and negative comments. Based on these scores the following values were found.

TWITTER (X)

As illustrated in Figure 2, there were around 61% of comments which had negative viewpoints for twitter and only 39% of the comments were positive.

Further, it was found that the 61% of negative comments constituted more than 1000 comments while around 1750 and above of the comments were positive as shown in Figure 3 and it can be said that over a period of a year (Sept 2022 - Sept 2023) the ratio of positive to negative comments is around 40:60 and people usually don't like using the application. Another fact is that people have negative sentiment about twitter or X is that Twitter announced $8 for the cost of blue tick which verifies their account. Most people do not want to pay $8/month and want to express their point of view without any charge.

THREADS

Threads was launched by Meta on 5th July 2023 in competition to Twitter. People can express short videos, posts, comments within a limit of 500 characters just like twitter. As shown in Figure 4, about 56% of YouTube comments consist of negative sentiments about Threads application and only 44% of the public were having positive sentiments.

As illustrated in Figure 5, approximately 92% negative sentiments consisted of more than 6000 comments whereas ten thousand comments were positive.

Further, the weighted data was vectorized using TF-IDF. Maximum features used in it was 2500 and minimum and maximum "df" used was 1.0. Then the data was trained through different machine learning algorithms and based on their accuracies it can be evaluated that logistic regression is better in comparison of Random Forest and KNN. Accuracy of logistic regression was found to be 85.956% while that of random forest was 85.874% and for KNN was 83.140% as shown in Table 1.

Figure 2. Sentiment classification of comments about Twitter (X)

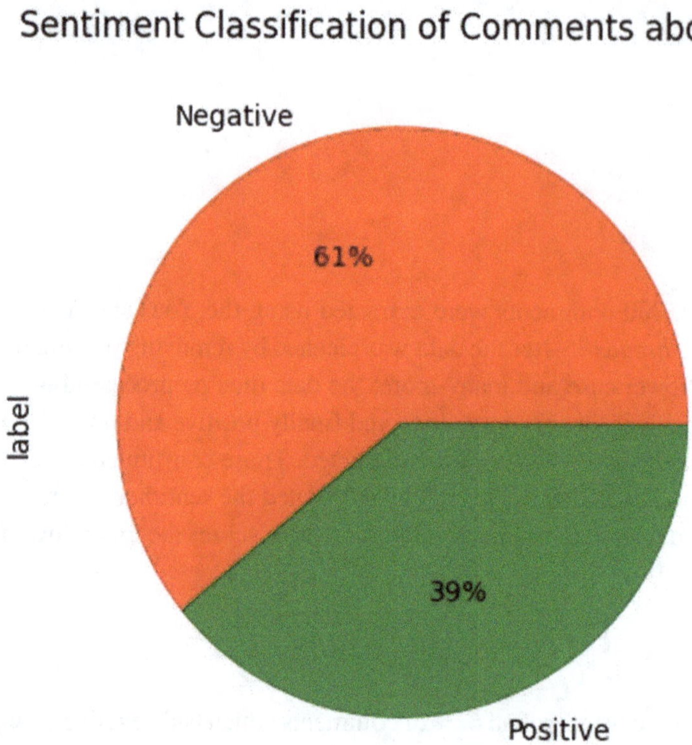

Figure 3. Bar graph representing the number of comments each sentiment has on X

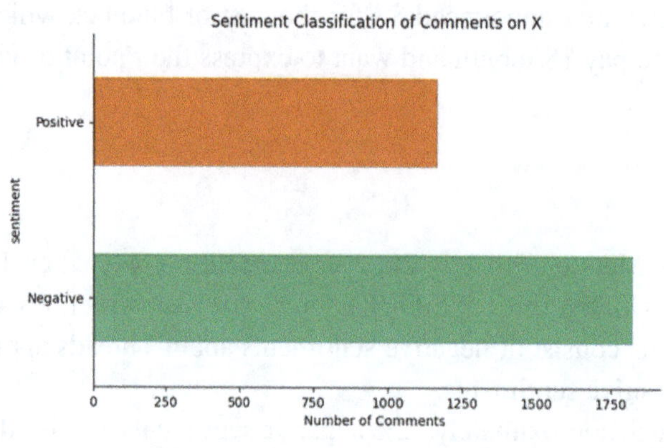

Based on the positive and negative comments, the precision for positive comments in logistic regression was estimated to be 86% while that for negative comments was found to be 84% as shown in Table 2.

Based on the positive and negative comments, the precision for positive comments in Random Forest was estimated to be 87% while that for negative comments was found to be only 75% as shown in Table 3.

Figure 4. Sentiment classification of comments about Threads

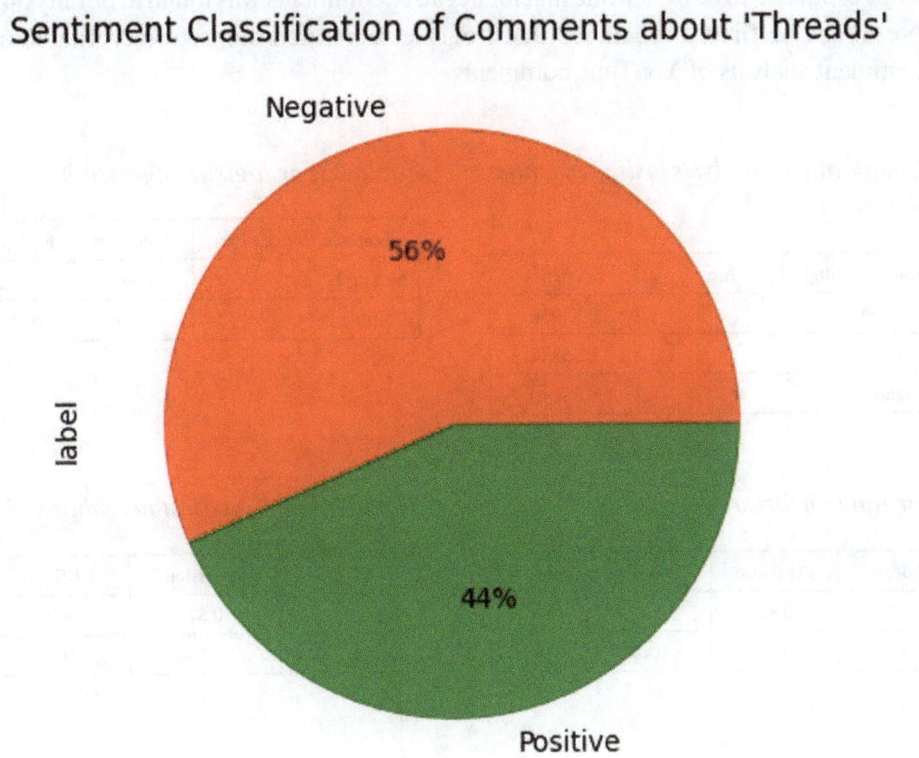

Figure 5. Bar graph representing the number of comments each sentiment has on Threads

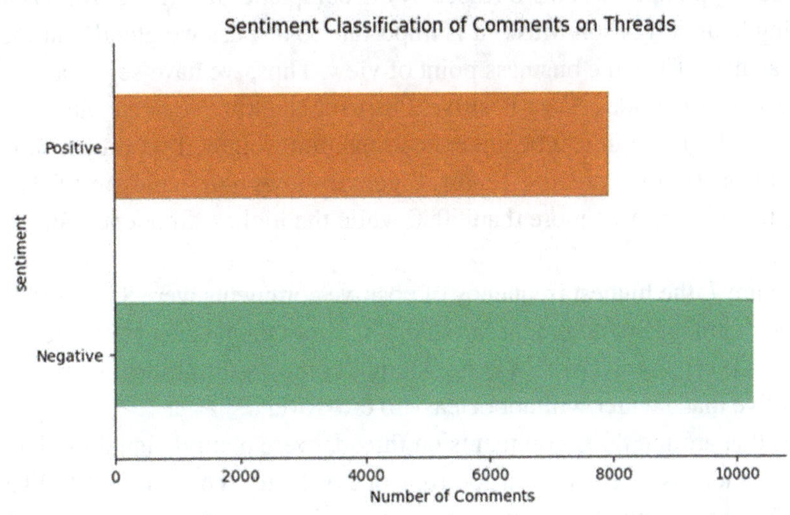

Based on the positive and negative comments, the precision for positive comments in KNN with K-value of 14 was estimated to be 87% while that for negative comments was found to be only 54% (Table 4).

Therefore, it can be finally concluded that Logistic regression outperformed Random Forest and KNN for sentiment analysis of YouTube comments.

Table 1. Comparative analysis using machine learning algorithm

Machine Learning Algorithm	Accuracy
Logistic Regression	0.85956
Random Forest	0.85874
K-Nearest Neighbor	0.83140

Table 2. For logistic regression

Logistic Regression	Precision	F1-Score	Recall
Negative	0.86	0.92	0.99
Positive	0.84	0.40	0.26

Table 3. For random forest

Random Forest	Precision	F1-Score	Recall
Negative	0.87	0.92	0.98
Positive	0.75	0.44	0.31

Table 4. For K-nearest neighbor

KNN	Precision	F1-Score	Recall
Negative	0.87	0.90	0.94
Positive	0.54	0.41	0.33

DISCUSSION

From the above results, the key concepts of sentiment analysis are discussed in this section. The sentiment analysis focuses on the polarity of the comments that include Positive, Negative, and Neutral.[9] When it comes to new applications being released by big companies like that of META and Twitter being renamed after being bought by Elon Musk, it is important to discuss weighted sentiment score and the graded sentiment analysis from the business point of view. Thus, we have segregated all the comments in 5 different aspects that includes -Very Positive, Positive, Neutral, Negative, and Very Negative.[9]

From Figure 6 and Figure 7, it can be understood that the weighted sentiment score from -1 to 0 is negative while that from 0 to 1 is positive scores. Figure 6 shows that the highest frequency of negative comments for the threads app was more than 5000 while the highest frequency for positive comments were near to 1000.

Similarly, in Figure 7, the highest frequency of positive comments were 800 for the X app while that of highest frequency for negative comments around 200. From the business perspective view of Twitter (X) it is a good sign as even though META is launching its competitor product named Threads, the users of Twitter are positive that Twitter will not be easy to crossover.

Figure 8 shows that around 8000 comments on threads were neutral signaling that people were not sure about the application, as whether it is a good app or a bad one. While around 4000 people were positive with the fact that a new application countering twitter is going to be launched and more than 2000 were happy and very positive about the application as it is going to give tough competition to Twitter. On the contrary, 3000 comments were negative and more than 2000 were very negative signaling that people didn't like the Threads application.

Figure 6. Histogram representing the weighted sentiment score on Threads app comments

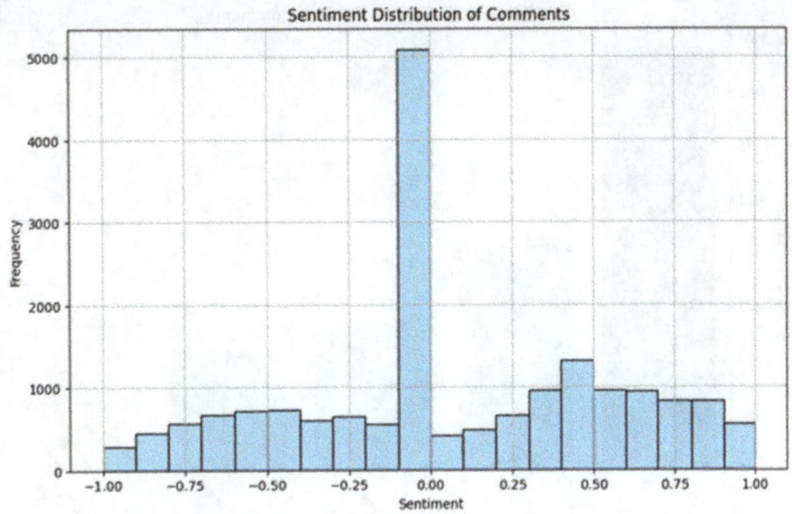

Figure 7. Histogram representing the weighted sentiment score on Twitter (X) app comments

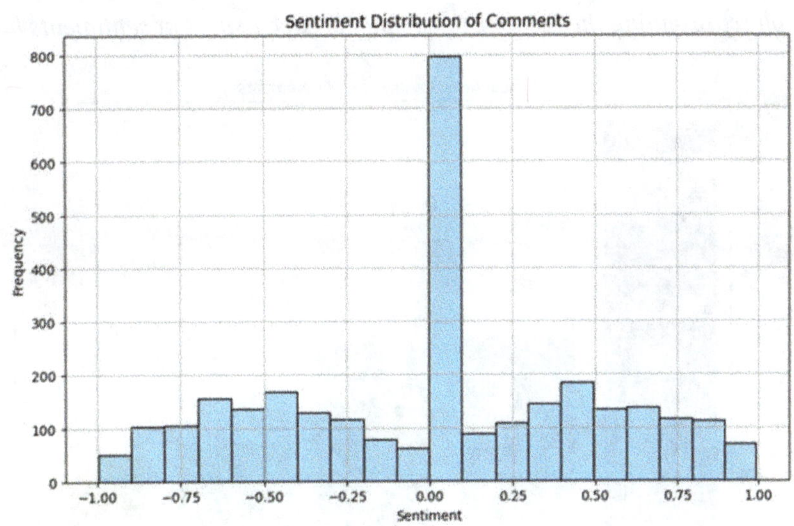

Figure 9 shows that around 1200 comments on threads were neutral signaling that people were not sure about the X application and renaming of the application done by the Elon Musk. While around 4000 people were positive with the fact that a new application countering twitter is going to be launched and more than 2000 were happy and very positive about the application as it is going to give tough competition to Twitter. On the contrary, 3000 comments were negative and more than 2000 were very negative signaling that people didn't like the Threads application.

Figure 8. Bar graph representing the number of comments each aspect of sentiments has on Threads

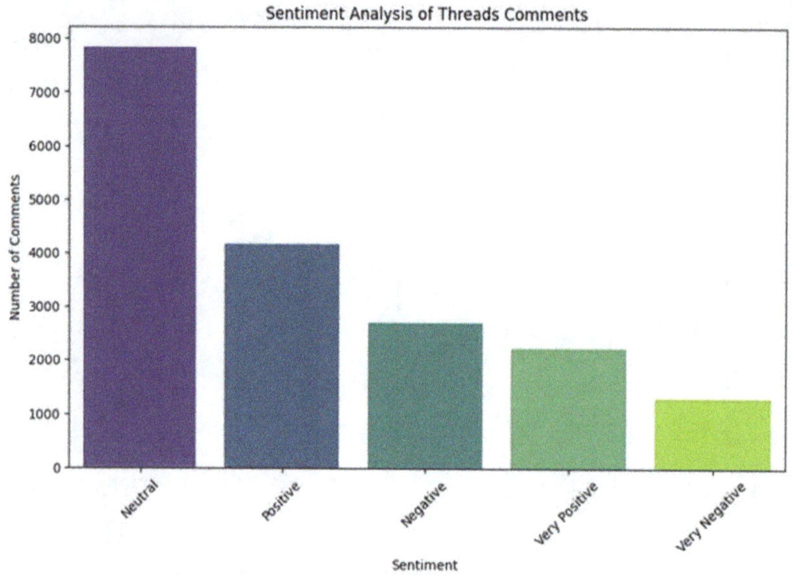

Figure 9. Bar graph representing the number of comments each aspect of sentiments has on Twitter (X)

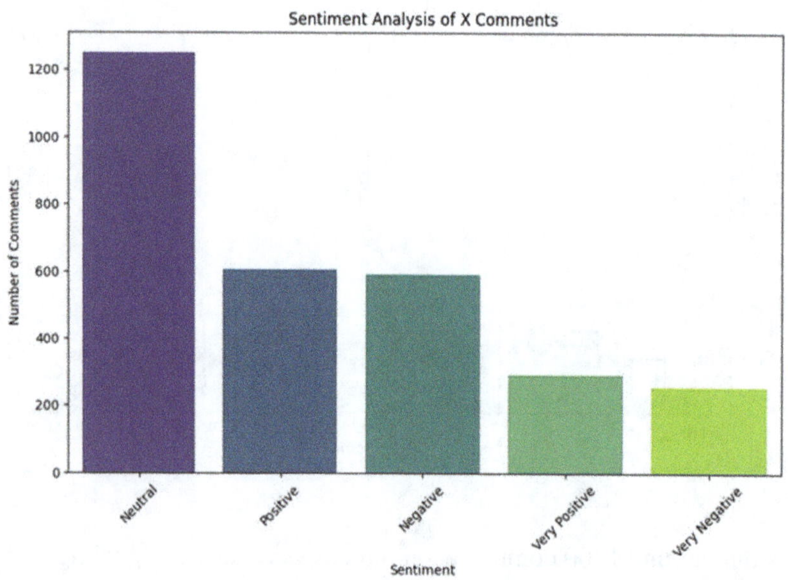

CONCLUSION AND FUTURE SCOPE

From the above results obtained following conclusions can be drawn:

1. **Rebranding from Twitter to X**: After the following move and spending a lot of money, the public has an overall negative view. Because the original app aesthetic was associated with the brand vision.

Users for a long time had a connection with the icon and its visual. This step has led to confusion and disappointment from the audience as it has lost its unique selling point and is not able to stay competitive in the market.

2. **Launch of Threads**: With the launch of Threads by Meta, the company wanted to stay up to date with the market. Developing and marketing a completely new product has led to their sales increase dynamically but the sentiment of the audience can be attributed to a negative view. This can be accounted for by the hype of the new app with better features and customer engagement. But as the number from the above dataset is received the hype has died down and only a stable number of users are continuing to use the app on daily bases.

In future research the authors can use the larger dataset with multiple different deep learning techniques and machine learning (supervised and unsupervised) which can be implemented and compared with this paper results. Also, in the above dataset any new parameter or variable can be added which will add more depth and better results can be predicated. A new hybrid model can be created and implemented using the above results and dataset.

REFERENCES

Al Mamun, M. H., Keikhosrokiani, P., Asl, M. P., Anuar, N. A. N., Hadi, N. H. A., & Humida, T. (2022). Sentiment Analysis of the Harry Potter Series Using a Lexicon-Based Approach. In P. Keikhosrokiani & M. Pourya Asl (Eds.), *Handbook of Research on Opinion Mining and Text Analytics on Literary Works and Social Media* (pp. 263–291). IGI Global. doi:10.4018/978-1-7998-9594-7.ch011

Al-Otaibi, S., Alnassar, A., Alshahrani, A., Al-Mubarak, A., Albugami, S., Almutiri, N., & Albugami, A. (2018). Customer Satisfaction Measurement using Sentiment Analysis. *International Journal of Advanced Computer Science and Applications*, *9*(2). Advance online publication. doi:10.14569/IJACSA.2018.090216

Alaei, A., Wang, Y., Bui, V., & Stantic, B. (2023). Target-Oriented Data Annotation for Emotion and Sentiment Analysis in Tourism Related Social Media Data. *Future Internet*, *15*(4), 150. doi:10.3390/fi15040150

Alatabi, H. A., & Abbas, A. R. (2020). Sentiment Analysis in Social Media using Machine Learning Techniques. *Iraqi Journal of Science*, 193–201. doi:10.24996/ijs.2020.61.1.22

Anto, M. P., Antony, M., Muhsina, K. M., Johny, N., James, V., & Wilson, A. (2016). Product rating using sentiment analysis. *2016 International Conference on Electrical, Electronics, and Optimization Techniques (ICEEOT)*, 3458–3462. 10.1109/ICEEOT.2016.7755346

Bozkurt, S., Gligor, D. M., & Babin, B. J. (2021). The role of perceived firm social media interactivity in facilitating customer engagement behaviors. *European Journal of Marketing*, *55*(4), 995–1022. doi:10.1108/EJM-07-2019-0613

Chu, K. E., Keikhosrokiani, P., & Asl, M. P. (2022). A Topic Modeling and Sentiment Analysis Model for Detection and Visualization of Themes in Literary Texts. *Pertanika Journal of Science & Technology*, *30*(4), 2535–2561. Advance online publication. doi:10.47836/pjst.30.4.14

Costola, M., Hinz, O., Nofer, M., & Pelizzon, L. (2023). Machine learning sentiment analysis, COVID-19 news and stock market reactions. *Research in International Business and Finance, 64*, 101881. doi:10.1016/j.ribaf.2023.101881 PMID:36687319

Diekson, Z. A., Prakoso, M. R. B., Putra, M. S. Q., Syaputra, M. S. A. F., Achmad, S., & Sutoyo, R. (2023). Sentiment analysis for customer review: Case study of Traveloka. *Procedia Computer Science, 216*, 682–690. doi:10.1016/j.procs.2022.12.184

Ermakova, T., Fabian, B., Golimblevskaia, E., & Henke, M. (2023). A Comparison of Commercial Sentiment Analysis Services. *SN Computer Science, 4*(5), 477. doi:10.1007/s42979-023-01886-y

Fasha, E. F. B. K., Keikhosrokiani, P., & Asl, M. P. (2022). Opinion Mining Using Sentiment Analysis: A Case Study of Readers' Response on Long Litt Woon's The Way Through the Woods in Goodreads. In Lecture Notes on Data Engineering and Communications Technologies (Vol. 127). doi:10.1007/978-3-030-98741-1_20

Gallagher, C., Furey, E., & Curran, K. (2019). The Application of Sentiment Analysis and Text Analytics to Customer Experience Reviews to Understand What Customers Are Really Saying. *International Journal of Data Warehousing and Mining, 15*(4), 21–47. doi:10.4018/IJDWM.2019100102

Gangrade, S., Shrivastava, N., & Gangrade, J. (2019). Instagram Sentiment Analysis: Opinion Mining. SSRN *Electronic Journal*. doi:10.2139/ssrn.3372757

Halawani, H. T., Mashraqi, A. M., Badr, S. K., & Alkhalaf, S. (2023). Automated sentiment analysis in social media using Harris Hawks optimisation and deep learning techniques. *Alexandria Engineering Journal, 80*, 433–443. doi:10.1016/j.aej.2023.08.062

Hasson, S. G., Piorkowski, J., & McCulloh, I. (2019). Social media as a main source of customer feedback. *Proceedings of the 2019 IEEE/ACM International Conference on Advances in Social Networks Analysis and Mining*, 829–832. 10.1145/3341161.3345642

Hussein, D. M. E.-D. M. (2018). A survey on sentiment analysis challenges. *Journal of King Saud University. Engineering Sciences, 30*(4), 330–338. doi:10.1016/j.jksues.2016.04.002

Jain, R., Kumar, A., Nayyar, A., Dewan, K., Garg, R., Raman, S., & Ganguly, S. (2023). Explaining sentiment analysis results on social media texts through visualization. *Multimedia Tools and Applications, 82*(15), 22613–22629. doi:10.1007/s11042-023-14432-y PMID:36747895

John, S. A., & Keikhosrokiani, P. (2022). COVID-19 fake news analytics from social media using topic modeling and clustering. In Big Data Analytics for Healthcare: Datasets, Techniques, Life Cycles, Management, and Applications. doi:10.1016/B978-0-323-91907-4.00003-0

Kang, D., & Park, Y. (2014). Review-based measurement of customer satisfaction in mobile service: Sentiment analysis and VIKOR approach. *Expert Systems with Applications, 41*(4), 1041–1050. doi:10.1016/j.eswa.2013.07.101

Keikhosrokiani, P. (2022). Handbook of Research on Consumer Behavior Change and Data Analytics in the Socio-Digital Era. doi:10.4018/978-1-6684-4168-8

Keikhosrokiani, P., & Asl, M. P. (2022a). Handbook of Research on Artificial Intelligence Applications in Literary Works and Social Media. doi:10.4018/978-1-6684-6242-3

Keikhosrokiani, P., & Asl, M. P. (2022b). Introduction to artificial intelligence for the analytics of literary works and social media: A review. In Handbook of Research on Artificial Intelligence Applications in Literary Works and Social Media. doi:10.4018/978-1-6684-6242-3.ch001

Keikhosrokiani, P., Asl, M. P., Chu, K. E., & Anuar, N. A. N. (2022). Artificial intelligence framework for opinion mining of netizen readers' reviews of Arundhati Roy's The God of Small Things. In Handbook of Research on Artificial Intelligence Applications in Literary Works and Social Media. doi:10.4018/978-1-6684-6242-3.ch004

Keikhosrokiani, P., & Pourya Asl, M. (2022). *Handbook of research on opinion mining and text analytics on literary works and social media*. IGI Global. doi:10.4018/978-1-7998-9594-7

Kim, R. Y. (2021). Using Online Reviews for Customer Sentiment Analysis. *IEEE Engineering Management Review*, *49*(4), 162–168. doi:10.1109/EMR.2021.3103835

Kozłowski, M., & Korzeniewski, J. (2024). Studying the effectiveness of investments in hotel services using customer sentiment analysis. *Quality & Quantity*. Advance online publication. doi:10.1007/s11135-023-01808-3

Kumar, P., Chauhan, R., Goyal, R., Bhati, N., Garg, S., & Mala, S. (2022). Skin cancer prediction using big data analytics and AI techniques. In *Big Data Analytics for Healthcare* (pp. 201–218). Elsevier. doi:10.1016/B978-0-323-91907-4.00011-X

Kumar, S., Yadava, M., & Roy, P. P. (2019). Fusion of EEG response and sentiment analysis of products review to predict customer satisfaction. *Information Fusion*, *52*, 41–52. doi:10.1016/j.inffus.2018.11.001

Li, S., Xie, Z., Chiu, D. K. W., & Ho, K. K. W. (2023). Sentiment Analysis and Topic Modeling Regarding Online Classes on the Reddit Platform: Educators versus Learners. *Applied Sciences (Basel, Switzerland)*, *13*(4), 2250. doi:10.3390/app13042250

Low, H. Q., Keikhosrokiani, P., & Asl, M. P. (2024). Decoding violence against women: Analysing harassment in middle eastern literature with machine learning and sentiment analysis. *Humanities & Social Sciences Communications*.

Medhat, W., Hassan, A., & Korashy, H. (2014). Sentiment analysis algorithms and applications: A survey. *Ain Shams Engineering Journal*, *5*(4), 1093–1113. doi:10.1016/j.asej.2014.04.011

Miranda, M. D., & Sassi, R. J. (2014). *Using Sentiment Analysis to Assess Customer Satisfaction in an Online Job Search Company*. doi:10.1007/978-3-319-11460-6_2

Mohamed, A., Muhammad Zain, Z., Shaiba, H., Alturki, N., Aldehim, G., Sakri, S., Farik Mat Yatin, S., & Mohamad Zain, J. (2023). LexDeep: Hybrid Lexicon and Deep Learning Sentiment Analysis Using Twitter for Unemployment-Related Discussions During COVID-19. *Computers, Materials & Continua*, *75*(1), 1577–1601. doi:10.32604/cmc.2023.034746

Rahman, H., Tariq, J., Ali Masood, M., & Subahi, A., Ibrahim Khalaf, O., & Alotaibi, Y. (2023). Multi-Tier Sentiment Analysis of Social Media Text Using Supervised Machine Learning. *Computers, Materials & Continua*, *74*(3), 5527–5543. doi:10.32604/cmc.2023.033190

Ramanathan, U., Williams, N. L., Zhang, M., Sa-nguanjin, P., Garza-Reyes, J. A., & Borges, L. A. (2022). A New Perspective of E-Trust in the Era of Social Media: Insights From Customer Satisfaction Data. *IEEE Transactions on Engineering Management*, *69*(4), 1417–1431. doi:10.1109/TEM.2020.2985379

Ravichandran, B. D., & Keikhosrokiani, P. (2023). Classification of Covid-19 misinformation on social media based on neuro-fuzzy and neural network: A systematic review. *Neural Computing & Applications*, *35*(1), 699–717. Advance online publication. doi:10.1007/s00521-022-07797-y PMID:36159189

Roy, G. (2023). Travelers' online review on hotel performance – Analyzing facts with the Theory of Lodging and sentiment analysis. *International Journal of Hospitality Management*, *111*, 103459. doi:10.1016/j.ijhm.2023.103459

Samaras, L., García-Barriocanal, E., & Sicilia, M.-A. (2023). Sentiment analysis of COVID-19 cases in Greece using Twitter data. *Expert Systems with Applications*, *230*, 120577. doi:10.1016/j.eswa.2023.120577 PMID:37317687

Sanh, V., Debut, L., Chaumond, J., & Wolf, T. (2019). *DistilBERT, a distilled version of BERT: smaller, faster, cheaper and lighter*. Academic Press.

Suhendra, N. H. B., Keikhosrokiani, P., Asl, M. P., & Zhao, X. (2022). Opinion Mining and Text Analytics of Literary Reader Responses: A Case Study of Reader Responses to KL Noir Volumes in Goodreads Using Sentiment Analysis and Topic. In P. Keikhosrokiani & M. Pourya Asl (Eds.), *Handbook of Research on Opinion Mining and Text Analytics on Literary Works and Social Media* (pp. 191–239). IGI Global. doi:10.4018/978-1-7998-9594-7.ch009

Taboada, M. (2016). Sentiment Analysis: An Overview from Linguistics. *Annual Review of Linguistics*, *2*(1), 325–347. doi:10.1146/annurev-linguistics-011415-040518

Wankhade, M., Rao, A. C. S., & Kulkarni, C. (2022). A survey on sentiment analysis methods, applications, and challenges. *Artificial Intelligence Review*, *55*(7), 5731–5780. doi:10.1007/s10462-022-10144-1

Wisnu, H., Afif, M., & Ruldevyani, Y. (2020). Sentiment analysis on customer satisfaction of digital payment in Indonesia: A comparative study using KNN and Naïve Bayes. *Journal of Physics: Conference Series*, *1444*(1), 012034. doi:10.1088/1742-6596/1444/1/012034

Xu, A., Tiffany, T., Phanie, M. E., & Simarmata, A. (2023). Sentiment Analysis On Twitter Posts About The Russia and Ukraine War With Long Short-Term Memory. *SinkrOn*, *8*(2), 789–797.

ENDNOTES

1 https://asq.org/quality-resources/customer-satisfaction

2 https://www.sfmagazine.com/articles/2023/june/five-approaches-to-sentiment-analysis

3 https://www.demandsage.com/twitter-statistics/#:~:text=Twitter%20has%20around%20528.3%20million,daily%20active%20users%20(mDAU)
4 https://explodingtopics.com/blog/threads-users
5 https://developers.google.com/youtube/v3
6 https://huggingface.co/docs/transformers/model_doc/distilbert
7 https://towardsdatascience.com/machine-learning-basics-with-the-k-nearest-neighbors-algorithm-6a6e71d01761
8 https://www.simplilearn.com/tutorials/machine-learning-tutorial/random-forest-algorithm
9 https://monkeylearn.com/sentiment-analysis/#:~:text=Sentiment%20analysis%20focuses%20on%20the,not%20interested).

Section 6
Sustainability Initiatives

Chapter 16
Green Theatre Index:
Measuring the Effectiveness of Climate-Smart Approaches and Benchmarking

Ronald Ma
University of Melbourne, Australia

Lily Clements
https://orcid.org/0000-0001-8864-0552
IDEMS International, UK

ABSTRACT

The effectiveness of climate-smart approaches is of significant concern because theatres contribute up to 33% of the hospital carbon footprint and 42% of revenue. Despite overwhelming advancements in climate-smart green theatre research, benchmarking remains a challenge. A single index representing their improvements has significant potential to increase control over and to promote their approaches. That is, this study does not stop at an inquiry about climate-smart approaches but also moves a step further and explores a possible outcome measure for the evolution of magnitudes, particularly in favour of the green theatre index (GTI). A function (clinical_theatre_emissions) was created in the R package Carbonr to calculate carbon emission. A time series emission data by theatre were consolidated as GTI using Fisher ideal index. The GTI proves a feasible and accurate consolidated outcome measure for carbon emissions to track and benchmark climate-smart strategies and could be applied in the real-world settings.

INTRODUCTION

One-hundred and ninety-two countries are currently implementing the Kyoto Protocol to reduce carbon emissions in accordance with agreed targets for our planetary wellbeing. Australia is no exception. The Protocol holds parties to account for rigorous monitoring and transparent reporting. Healthcare itself contributes to a significant source of pollution, which has a high cost on the environment, and subsequently the detriment of patient wellbeing due to its carbon footprint. Australian hospitals have been

DOI: 10.4018/979-8-3693-1210-0.ch016

placed second to the food industry in terms of waste by seven percent of the country's overall carbon footprint (Shum et al., 2020).

Climate-smart strategies for operating theatres (green theatre approaches) are of significant concern around the world, because theatres contribute twenty to seventy percent of the hospital carbon footprint and 42% of hospital revenue (Babu et al., 2019; Shum et al., 2020; Wu & Cerceo, 2021).

Carbon emissions have broader environmental and health implications, because they could potentially reverse decades of our health progress by changing climate patterns, temperature, precipitations, drought, floods and rising sea levels. Climate-related mortality is increasing due to cardiovascular diseases and asthma from coal power, and pandemics from altered habitats. All social determinants of health will be affected by climate change, from clean air, water and soil to food systems, sanitation and healthcare workforce.

Incineration alone could produce three kilograms of carbon dioxide for every kilogram of clinical waste (T. Southorn, A. Norrish, K. Gardner, & R. Baxandall, 2013; K. H. Wyssusek, Keys, & van Zundert, 2019). Although representing only a relatively limited physical portion of a hospital, theatres usually consume three to six times the energy of other rooms to incinerate high volumes of waste (Novosel et al., 2022). The majority of ozone-depleting anaesthetic gases, which have a global warming potential of over 2000 times that of carbon dioxide, are released into the atmosphere and significantly affect climate change. Therefore, climate-smart strategies targeting the operating theatre have the highest impact on the health of the patient within the healthcare industry.

Until now, benchmarking of green theatre approaches has not received sufficient attention. Previous research done on this subject overlooked a measure to track the progress and comparison analyses. The literature has been much more reticent in investigating ways of benchmarking and reporting frameworks. Therefore, the benchmarking of green approaches and a consensus on clear protocols remain a challenge despite overwhelming enthusiasm and advancements in green theatre research.

A single statistical index to benchmark their improvements has a significant potential to increase control over and to promote planetary wellbeing. That is, this study does not stop at an inquiry about green theatre approaches but also moves a step further and explores a possible standardised outcome measure for the evolution of magnitudes, particularly in favour of the "Green Theatre Index (GTI)" to track and benchmark the effectiveness of climate-smart strategies in operating theatres.

GTI is a weighted index inspired by Consumer Price Index (CPI) comprising two criteria: quantities of the different theatre wastes (clinical waste in kilograms and electricity in Kilowatts Hours) and corresponding tCO2e (tonnes of carbon dioxide equivalent) to find the percent change over a period of time. The GTI will serve as an indicator of the rate of the green theatre progress for tracking and benchmarking purposes.

STRUCTURE OF THE CHAPTER

This chapter proceeds with the introduction followed by a brief literature review on the green theatre approaches with a summary of the current knowledge gap of lacking a benchmarking measure. The methodology section will explain the study design, the source of data and the structure of the dataset. The data analysis section is the heart of the paper where the development of the carbonr R package to calculate CO2 emissions for the different types of theatre waste such as clinical waste and anaesthetic gases. The visualisation of the results in terms of plots and graphs is also included at the end of the data analysis section.

The findings section will describe the correct way of interpretations from the results. The limitation of the study will be briefly described before the discussion section, which provides a summary of where future efforts could be focused on.

The conclusion section will follow the discussion section and summarise the significance of this paper to the audience.

GREEN THEATRE APPROACHES IN THE LITERATURE

A literature search was conducted in June, 2023 of Web of Science, MEDLINE and EMBASE with search terms including all time periods and languages: "operating room", "operating theater", "operating theatre", "surgery", or "surgical procedure" (Topic) and "green or sustainab*", "carbon footprint", or "carbon emission" (Topic) and "measure or outcome*", "measurement, or benchmark*" (Topic). A total of 1,654 results were obtained and their abstracts were screened for relevance to the topic. Duplicates were removed and full-text articles were evaluated from the final result of eighty-two papers. These final papers were full-text accessible written in English demonstrating the PICO framework on climate-smart actions (I = intervention) in the operating theatres (P = population) with any outcome on ecological impact (O = outcome) in comparison to control groups (C = comparison). There were no control groups in these papers. This lack of benchmarking to track and compare the effectiveness of green theatre approaches drove the authors to carry out this study.

The overarching concept in these papers appears as '5Rs' (Recount, Reduce, Reuse, Recycle, and Reflect) to green the theatres. The purpose of the 5Rs is focused on providing insights into the objective quantification of the waste. Four themes appeared as waste audit, green strategies in individual operation, surveying staff attitudes and systematic reviews in order of frequency (de Ridder, Friedericy, van der Eijk, Dankelman, & Jansen, 2022; Dung, Toan, Huong, Mai, & Ha, 2023; Friedericy, van Egmond, Vogtlander, van der Eijk, & Jansen, 2022; Gatenby, 2011; Lattanzio et al., 2022; Lever, Smetana, Bechrakis, & Foerster, 2023; McGain, Story, Lim, & McAlister, 2017; Novosel et al., 2022; B. Pradere et al., 2023; Rizan, Lillywhite, Reed, & Bhutta, 2023; Siu, Hill, & MacCormick, 2017; T. Southorn et al., 2013; Wu & Cerceo, 2021; K. H. Wyssusek et al., 2019).

In the next section, these 5Rs in the current knowledge will be explained in detail.

The Concept of Recount

The concept of "recount" provides insight into the size of the problem by quantifying the waste in the theatres. It also highlights the issue on improperly segregated and discarded theatre wastes. Most waste audit papers are cross-sectional studies. This concept is represented in many waste audit studies and the quantity of waste is ranked by the type of operations. The total knee arthroplasty is one of the most wasteful procedures at 218.5kg, second to cataract procedures (233.6kg), in two 5-day audits at the Minneapolis Veterans Affairs Health Service (Rammelkamp, Dirnberger, Johnson, & Waisbren, 2021). This audit agrees with the finding from one of the earlier studies focusing on the breakdown of orthopaedic waste where arthroplasty cases are recognised as the most waste-producing surgeries (Kooner et al.,

2020). Despite being a short duration procedure, cataract surgeries contribute a significant volume of waste at 250g per phacoemulsification (Thiel et al., 2017).

Some papers compare the proportion of recyclable to non-recyclable waste and quantify the percentage of incorrectly segregated theatre waste. A Malaysian (Khor, Cho, Lee, & Chieng, 2020) and an Italian study (Amariglio & Depaoli, 2021) estimated that a half of waste was inappropriately segregated as general theatre waste, which could be recycled with a saving of 54kg with proper segregation (McKendrick, Snedden, Bunch, & McGregor, 2017).

Waste audit studies represent the largest body of knowledge and provide targeted strategies by ranking the most wasteful operations. These operations could be prioritised for benchmarking their GTI among participating theatres since they have the most greening potential.

One of the limitations of these studies would be that creating the most waste may not necessarily be proportional to the potential to reduce and reuse. The researchers in these studies seem to overlook the actual sources of waste within cataract and arthroplasty cases. Only cataract and orthopaedic procedures were considered by ranking the amount of waste, which may be measured with an inaccurate tool.

Furthermore, these waste audit studies have a tendency to stop at auditing and fail to follow up their audit data applications with targeted strategies to improve wastage. There is no strategy in these papers and implementation of changes to assess the improvement of these targeted strategies.

Green theatre approaches could expand their operations to understand the extent and source of waste and provide targets for future greening. Applications of the waste audit data together with benchmarking targeted greening strategies for cataract and arthroplasty procedures would prevent further deterioration in carbon footprints.

The Concept of Reduce

The concept of "reduce" is to reduce harmful and wasteful use in the operating theatres. One of the common themes in the literature was the amount of unnecessary waste related to opened yet unused equipment and surgical packs. The strongest approach in waste reduction strategies would be that the theatre waste is not generated in the first place and effort is not expended in formulating methods on how to reduce waste only after the waste being created. The concept is simply not bringing the waste into existence.

Many papers addressed reduction in surgical materials and energy resources. One of the significant approaches is focused on redesigning surgical kits into a customised minimalistic green kit based on the type of operation and surgeon preference. The greatest positive impact on carbon footprint was achieved in these 'bare essential' kits (Engler, Curley, Fu, & Bilec, 2022; Rouvière et al., 2022; Sanabria et al., 2020; Thiel et al., 2019; Thiel, Woods, & Bilec, 2018; Van Demark Jr, Smith, & Fiegen, 2018). These minimalist packs made waste savings of 0.3kg and 2.29kg per case in 128 wide-awake hand surgeries and 1099 skin cancer hand surgeries respectively (Thiel et al., 2019; Van Demark Jr et al., 2018).

Some papers are focused on surgical subspecialty and technique. The Cold technique in 60 adult tonsillectomies demonstrated the reduction of disposable equipment usage and saved 42kg to 51kg of waste compared to other techniques (Meiklejohn & Chavarri, 2021).

Desflurane and N2O were found to be the highest contribution to global warming. Reduction and intentional omission of the use of these gases had an estimated twenty-five percent reduction in Greenhouse Gases (GHG) per laparoscopies (Thiel et al., 2018), but there was no change in patient safety (Shoham, Baker, Peterson, & Fox, 2022).

Current literature also looked at the energy consumption of the operating theatres since operating theatres used more energy for ventilation and air conditioning than other areas of the hospital. Switching to occupancy-sensor lights and low-carbon sources clearly contributed a reduction of 33% in energy consumption (Thiel et al., 2018).

These waste reduction strategies appeared more effective than a simple waste audit by providing the measurement of the actual reduction in waste as outcomes. However, limitations can be seen in the proposal of the minimalist surgical packs for failing to measure the actual ecological impact and subsequent benchmarking of different '5Rs' strategies at multiple sites. They also focused on specific procedures like hand surgeries (Thiel et al., 2019). While these green packs were shown to have ecological benefits, these studies failed to mention what instruments were included in the pack and hence, providing guidelines, standards and protocols to implement this practice would be a challenge.

The support of hospital executives and equipment manufacturers beyond theatre staff seems to be as important as the strategy itself to have long-term success. It reveals the gap on current green theatre approaches that only focuses on the operating theatre itself and fails to include sufficient strategies on communication to involve hospital executives and sustainability officers for a long-term cultural change in the hospital. All staff level participation in green theatre approaches is the key to success for rethinking what should be used and produced in the first place.

The simple and effective practices should be incentivised and encouraged such as changing greener surgical techniques and reducing high GHG-producing anaesthetic gases. More research on the patient safety of these practices needs urgent attention in the hospital theatre budget allocations.

Although the use of occupancy-sensor lights and energy sources has no direct impact on the operations of the theatres and the patient safety, these administrative decisions could contribute to further greening of the theatres. The participation of the administrative staff in green theatre approaches is necessary and they would need a regular report on the benchmarking and tracking of waste reduction initiatives in the organisation.

The Concept of Reuse

This concept is based on the diligent reuse of any materials without compromising patient safety. Many papers mentioned 'Reuse' as a significant concept to consider when reducing carbon footprint (Guetter et al., 2018; Perry et al., 2023; Benjamin Pradere et al., 2023) although this is usually seen as going against regulations (Chang & Thiel, 2020).

Up to ninety-six percent reduction in waste were found when multi-use surgical stapling systems in sleeve gastrectomy and gastric bypass procedures (Meissner, Lichtnegger, Gibson, & Saunders, 2021). Similar findings were mentioned in laryngoscope blades (Rouvière et al., 2022) and haemostatic devices (Sanabria et al., 2020).

This concept of Reuse has limited literature since the emphasis of asepsis and patient safety are the priorities of any operating theatre. This also means that there is a huge gap in research that can be explored further. The literature identifies 'Reuse' as an important strategy but there is no clear protocol, standard, and guidelines on which materials can be reused safely and steps on sterilisation for reuse. Clear identifications of these protocols need more data on its effect on patient safety. There is also no literature on clinical outcomes. Only one study examined the risk to the patient, with the conclusion that there was lack of evidence to support the use of single-use instruments when considering instrument function, ease of use, patient safety, transmission of infection, and long-term patient outcomes.

However, safe intentional reuse of equipment has been shown to have no increase in infection or change to long-term patient outcomes (Siu et al., 2017).

The use of reusable gowns was found to be associated with lower waste and water use. These reusables provide 96% less waste by mass and 85% less water (Vozzola, Overcash, & Griffing, 2020). The transition from disposable to reusable surgical packs in two American hospitals resulted in 70% and 59% waste reduction (Conrardy, Hillanbrand, Myers, & Nussbaum, 2010). Only one literature found reusable surgical gowns to have no benefit over disposables in terms of their environmental impact and concluded that clear superiority of either reusable or single-use gowns and drapes cannot be demonstrated (Rutala & Weber, 2001). The McDowell study, commissioned by gown manufacturer Johnson & Johnson, found the nature of impacts to be too different to determine superiority, but it did find that manufacturing of the reusable gowns produced higher volatile organic chemical (VOC) emissions from dyeing and finishing compared with disposable counterparts (Overcash, 2012). Although these studies are limited and further study is required, the transition to reusables could be seriously investigated and considered as a long-term strategy.

Reusing can actually be more wasteful due to energy resources. Australia uses coal-based electricity, which can cause more environmental pollution and depletion of natural resources in the sterilisation process compared to producing single-use kits. However, it may not apply to other countries where electricity is powered by renewable energy. This suggests another gap in the literature on the sterilisation process and energy source.

The successful implementation of the 'Reuse' strategy needs further research on renewable energy, sterilisation processes and patient safety. The current literature suggests that green theatre approaches based on the 'Reuse' strategy is not the strongest intervention focus.

The Concept of Recycle

This concept is based on recycling everything that cannot be refused to use. This strategy appeared to be practical with targets for recycling paper and cardboard (K. H. Wyssusek et al., 2019) or aluminium blisters that were recognised to have the greatest impact on landfill, mineral, and fossil resources (Rouvière et al., 2022). Installing new recycling bins resulted in 67% of waste being recycled in comparison to the baseline 0% (McKendrick et al., 2017) and a 19% increase in recycled waste by increasing the size of recycling boxes (Treggiari, 2017).

Recycling approaches were effective and practical, which made a significant impact on reducing carbon footprint. The incremental changes such as increasing the size of recycling bags need long-term support from the hospital executives. Proper waste segregation methods could be a focus for implementation in all participating green theatres. As Thiel et al. (2018) suggest, recycling alone does little with a decrease less than 5% in GHG, but recycling-focused strategies implemented alongside other initiatives proposed in this paper can have positive compound effects.

Therefore, a recycling-focused strategy can be simple but practical effective methods by starting from education on the type of recyclable materials, improved waste segregation, installing more recycling boxes, and increasing their size. However, literature on this concept lacks benchmarking guidelines and measures to track improvements.

The Concept of Reflect

The concept of 'Reflect' is similar to the participatory action research principles, which include critical reflection of current practice, planning for the next step, acting on the initiative, and observing the outcomes (Green, O'Neill, Westphal, & Morisky, 1996). In the context of green theatre approaches, it encompasses the critical reflection and appraisal of staff attitudes to address barriers. Some of these obstacles were the lack of education and leadership in sustainability training. Rouvière et al. (2022) point out that ingrained habits and lack of communication should be addressed. Another study involving 524 surgical staff reported that 56.7% was unclear which items were recyclable and addressing barriers to recycling can significantly reduce waste and save healthcare resources (Azouz et al., 2019). Regulatory agencies limiting surgeon discretion for reusing supplies and manufacturers mandating single-use to limit liability are considered as perceived impact on excessive trash generation in ophthalmic theatres (Chang & Thiel, 2020).

A significant portion of the literature agreed that there was a willingness to improve environmental sustainability in the operating theatres and also accepted that there was excessive theatre waste (Chang & Thiel, 2020; Frewen, Grossman, & Basson, 2022a; Petre et al., 2019). However, one South Korean study suggested that many surgeons felt waste segregation was unnecessary and impeded surgical flow and patient care (Shinn et al., 2017).

While there was willingness to improve sustainability there were significant barriers that prevent successful implementation. For example, anaesthetists lack the knowledge and education to guide sustainable practice (Frewen et al., 2022a; Petre et al., 2019). Therefore, green theatre approaches need a national curricula reform that addresses education on sustainability and health consequences. Critical reflection exercises should be part of green theatre approaches.

Climate-smart strategies should start with surveys by asking open-ended questions to assess staff attitudes and barriers first. Then, it would be beneficial to form a green theatre team as the second step to involve administrative staff and theatre personnels for having leadership and executive support. Thirdly, the program could be designed on training, education and reporting of the progress.

Summary of the Gaps in the Current Body of Knowledge

There were diverse keywords to access sustainability papers and most papers originated in the United States of America. Significant gaps were found in research on green theatre standards, protocols, guidelines, databases, and measurements for a long-term implementation, especially benchmarking and reporting. The results from the literature were found to be difficult for any comparison since each study examined a different measure, different subspecialty and focus of waste (e.g., blue wrap or surgical instrument). We urgently need a standard statistical tool for benchmarking across green theatres across the board.

In summary, there is a need for statistical benchmarking tools and software for a long-term implementation to empower green theatre teams. This paper proposes a GTI, which will serve as a tool for the much-needed benchmarking to the current body of knowledge by using the powers of 'reproducible' R statistical open-source package, namely, carbonr. A dummy dataset will be used to demonstrate how green theatre teams could gather comprehensive data for their projects.

METHODOLOGY

Rationale for Choosing Carbonr R Package

R, a computer language and environment, has become a cornerstone in the realms of statistics and graphics. Its remarkable adaptability, manifested in over 20,000 packages within the Comprehensive R Archive Network (CRAN) and countless more across various platforms like GitHub, positions it as an indispensable asset for researchers and data scientists globally. R was created by Ross Ihaka and Robert Gentleman in the Department of Statistics at the University of Auckland in 1991 (Ihaka & Gentleman, 1996). Martin Machler contributed to R by using the GNU General Public License to make R free software, and hence, R version 1.0.0 was released to the public in 2000.

One package in R, carbonr, aims to conveniently calculate carbon-equivalent emissions. It facilitates a transparent, collaborative approach, making it an exemplary model for modern scientific research. The carbonr package and GTI serves the purpose of this research for the following advantages over other approaches.

1. **Open-Source Collaboration:** The global research community actively contributes to carbonr, ensuring its evolution and adaptability. Hosted on GitHub, it invites researchers to seamlessly integrate new functions and expand its capabilities.
2. **Transparency and Comprehensive Documentation:** Carbonr's methodology for calculating tCO2e is meticulously documented, grounded in robust government and academic research. Hosted under "IDEMSInternational/carbonr," it offers an open window into its inner workings, reinforcing trust and reliability.
3. **Maintenance and Repeatability:** carbonr's code and documentation, diligently maintained on GitHub, not only adhere to the principles of scientific repeatability but also ensure ease of replication in R, a testament to its robustness.

Our collaboration with the carbonr developers has extended its utility to encompass a broader spectrum of waste types found in operating theatres. This integration exemplifies the package's adaptability and readiness to embrace new challenges. By incorporating theatre waste, carbonr now provides a more comprehensive analysis, continually evolving to include additional waste types as needed, ensuring the tool remains adaptable and up-to-date.

Essentially, it would be hard to find a package which calculated these waste-types. However, the discovery of the open-source carbonr package, actively seeking collaboration, meant it was the right fit. By being open-source researchers could work alongside the package developers to ensure the inclusion of accurate calculations.

In summary, carbonr seems to be robust and meet the purpose of this research. It now has comprehensive coverage on theatre wastes and anaesthetic gases.

Rationale for Choosing GTI

The GTI is a way to express a change in a heterogenous group of theatre wastes. For example, the Consumer Price Index (CPI) encompasses about seven hundred items including health, transport and education services. Prices are measured in dollars per kilogram, yard, box, and many other different units. Only by transforming the prices of these many diverse goods and services to one index can the government keep informed of the overall fluctuation of inflation. Similarly, the GTI is conceptualised as an indicator to benchmark the improvements of green theatres over time.

In summary, the combination of the carbonr and GTI would be a perfect fit for benchmarking the progress of green theatre initiatives.

Study Design

A dummy dataset is used to demonstrate the technical aspects of tCO2e calculations powered by carbonr R package, which utilises the reproducible power of R programming language (Clements, 2023; R Core Team, 2023).

The calculated tCO2e is entered into a data frame for further calculations of GTI and plotting them in a time series to track and benchmark the progress among participating green theatres.

Source of Data

The dataset is constructed in ways that mimic a 'real-world' scenario. The data comprise a hypothetical hospital and a group of green theatres with associated theatre waste.

The Composition of the Dummy Dataset

The main dataset contains 4,386 observations of the following 6 variables in a spreadsheet format with six columns organised in rows for each record:

1. time: 21 entries, such as 1/02/2019 (4.90%); 1/12/2019 (4.90%); 1/05/2020 (4.88%) and 18 others (0 missing)
2. prices: Carbon credit unit price derived from dividing the total credits by the total tCO2e quantity. n = 4386, Mean = 35.03, SD = 1.00, Median = 35.03, MAD = 1.01, range: [31.56, 38.42], Skewness = 6.22e-03, Kurtosis = 0.01, 0% missing
3. quantities: tCO2e quantities. n = 4386, Mean = 153.97, SD = 327.18, Median = 22.40, MAD = 31.18, range: [2.12e-03, 3437.96], Skewness = 4.12, Kurtosis = 22.85, 0% missing
4. prodID: Product ID that represents the operation ID. n = 4386, Mean = 2.99e+05, SD = 1.59e+05, Median = 4.01e+05, MAD = 7226.19, range: [14215, 407860], Skewness = -0.89, Kurtosis = -1.13, 0% missing
5. retID: Retail ID that represents hospital ID. n = 4386, Mean = 1461.59, SD = 869.77, Median = 1032.00, MAD = 1.48, range: [1030, 3220], Skewness = 1.53, Kurtosis = 0.33, 0% missing
6. description: Product or the description of the operations. 6 entries, such as hepato-biliary-transplant (28.00%); general surgery (21.57%); colorectal (18.29%) and 3 others (0 missing)

Data Analysis

Developing R Function in Carbonr Package to Calculate CO2 Emission

Our objective was to enhance the functionality of the "carbonr" package by incorporating emissions resulting from operating theatres. While some functions, such as those for electricity and gas, general waste, disposables, and plastic waste, were already implemented based on the United Kingdom (UK) government report, we needed to develop additional functions to address specific requirements (UK Government, 2022).

Since the UK government report did not cover the new additions related to clinical data, we conducted a thorough review of reliable sources to gather the necessary information. Our research enabled us to identify CO2e estimates for the specific clinical waste components that must be included, such as syringes, needles, wet waste (e.g., specimens), and anaesthetics.

It is crucial to consider anaesthetics, particularly desflurane, as they make a substantial contribution to greenhouse gas (GHG) emissions (Varughese & Ahmed, 2021). Anaesthetics have a significant negative impact on the environment, underscoring the importance of including them in the package. However, we encountered a scarcity of research on CO2e emissions specifically related to anaesthetics. The limited availability of data and a range of estimated values contribute to this gap in knowledge. However, despite the scarcity of research on CO2e emissions related to anaesthetics, we recognised the importance of providing an estimate within the function. While the lack of comprehensive data presents challenges, we believe that including an estimation allows users of the package to have some insight into the potential environmental impact of anaesthetics. As more research becomes available, we plan to update the function with more accurate data to enhance the precision of the estimates. In addition, as part of our future updates to the package, we plan to incorporate Life Cycle Analysis (LCA) to provide a more comprehensive analysis of the emissions associated with anaesthetics.

Currently, inhalation anaesthetics are calculated by multiplying the weight used in tonnes (T) by the GWP100 value resulting in tCO2e (McGain, Muret, Lawson, & Sherman, 2020; K. Wyssusek, Chan, Eames, & Whately, 2022). The estimated propofol tCO2e estimate is calculated from the same approach, with the GWP100 value (Parvatker et al., 2019; Sherman, Le, Lamers, & Eckelman, 2012).

Wet clinical waste refers to clinical waste with high moisture content, such as biological specimens or fluids. To determine the CO2-e emissions from wet clinical waste, we utilised the values from the Australian Greenhouse 2023 document (Australian Government, 2023). In this calculation, emissions are derived using the equation: Clinical waste t CO2-e = Q x EF, where Q represents the tonnes of wet weight and EF denotes the emission factor (0.879).

By following these steps and Figures 1 to 3, we successfully incorporated emissions from operating theatres into the carbonr package, ensuring estimated tCO2e emissions for anaesthetics and wet clinical waste.

```
library(carbonr)
# create dummy data
df <- data.frame(time = c("10/04/2000", "10/04/2000", "11/04/2000",
"11/04/2000", "12/04/2000", "12/04/2000"),
theatre = rep(c("A", "B"), times = 3),
clinical_waste = c(80, 90, 80, 100, 120, 110),
```

```
electricity_kwh = c(100, 110, 90, 100, 100, 110),
general_waste = c(65, 55, 70, 50, 60, 30))
df
```

#> time theatre clinical_waste electricity_kwh general_waste

```
#> 1 10/04/2000 A 80 100 65
#> 2 10/04/2000 B 90 110 55
#> 3 11/04/2000 A 80 90 70
#> 4 11/04/2000 B 100 100 50
#> 5 12/04/2000 A 120 100 60
#> 6 12/04/2000 B 110 110 30
# get emissions and CPI (carbon price index)
clinical_theatre_data(df, time = time, name = theatre,
wet_clinical_waste = clinical_waste,
wet_clinical_waste_unit = "kg",
average = general_waste,
plastic_units = "kg",
electricity_kWh = electricity_kwh,
include_cpi = TRUE,
jurisdiction = "Australia",
year = 2023,
single_sheet = TRUE)
#> [[1]]
#> time theatre emissions carbon_price_credit
#> 1 10/04/2000 A 0.2990340 3.181279
#> 2 10/04/2000 B 0.2792765 2.971089
#> 3 11/04/2000 A 0.3119999 3.319217
#> 4 11/04/2000 B 0.2698696 2.871013
#> 5 12/04/2000 A 0.3186125 3.389565
#> 6 12/04/2000 B 0.2189492 2.329296
#>
#> [[2]]
# OR: Manually state a CPI value, and set single_sheet as FALSEd
clinical_theatre_data(df, time = time, name = theatre,
wet_clinical_waste = clinical_waste,
wet_clinical_waste_unit = "kg",
average = general_waste,
plastic_units = "kg",
electricity_kWh = electricity_kwh,
include_cpi = TRUE,
manual_price = 33.80,
single_sheet = FALSE)
#> [[1]]]
```

```
#> time theatre emissions carbon_price_credit
#> 1 10/04/2000 A 0.2990340 10.107348
#> 2 10/04/2000 B 0.2792765 9.439547
#> 3 11/04/2000 A 0.3119999 10.545597
#> 4 11/04/2000 B 0.2698696 9.121592
#> 5 12/04/2000 A 0.3186125 10.769102
#> 6 12/04/2000 B 0.2189492 7.400485
#>
#> [[2]]
#> [[2]][[1]]
#> [[2]]
#> [[2]][[2]]
```

Figure 1. Carbon price index (CPI) by theatre showing total emissions and total carbon price from theatre emissions by time of observation for benchmarking to track improvements

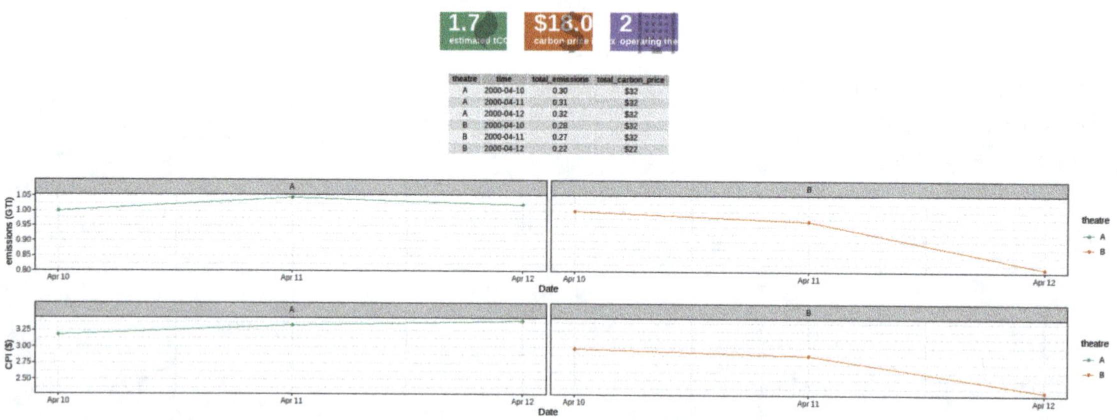

Calculating GTI

Index numbers like GTI is not a recent innovation and its history can be traced back to 1764 when an Italian G. R. Carli implemented the first index numbers (Chance, 1966). Carli used the simple average of relatives index number to report price fluctuations in Europe from 1500 to 1750. An index represents a change in a heterogenous group of items. The Consumer Price Index (CPI), for example, encompasses more than 200 categories, arranged into eight major expenditure groups. The CPI is the most noted measure of inflation for economists and used in many other contexts, such as deflation of time series data and conversion of nominal to real dollars (Bryan & Cecchetti, 1993). Therefore, the index number methodology suits the purpose of benchmarking to track green theatre improvements longitudinally.

Figure 2. CO2 emission by theatre

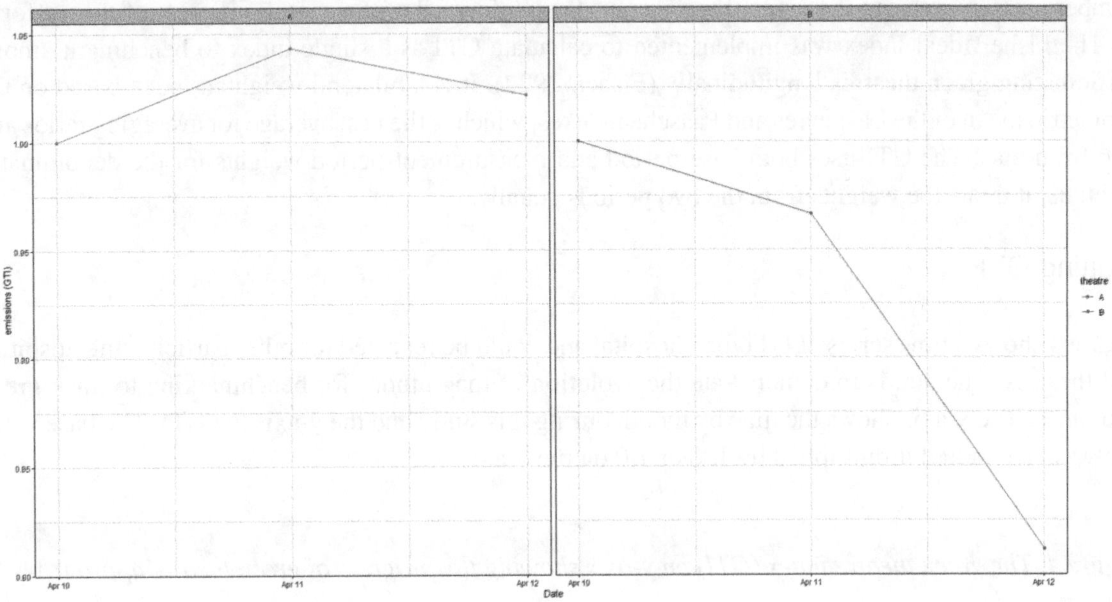

Figure 3. Carbon price index (CPI) by theatre

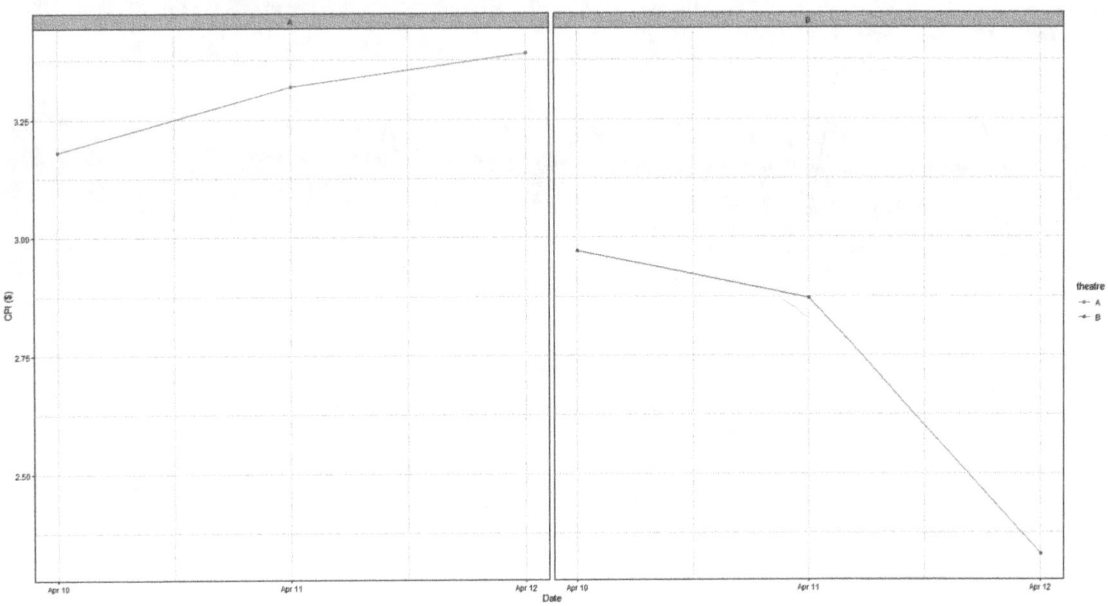

The GTI is an index number that expresses the relative change in the unit carbon credit and the tCO2e among participating green theatres from one period to another. In other words, GTI allows us to express an improvement change in carbon credit and tCO2e as a percent. It measures the evolution of magnitudes with a single number. The GTI utilises the powers of the index number being able to neutralise different units of measure on theatre waste as a carbon credit unit price and easier to assess the trend in a series of exceptionally large tCO2e numbers. Only by converting the carbon credits and tCO2e to one index number every month can the green theatre teams keep informed of the overall progress of their efforts.

The Fisher Ideal Index was implemented to calculate GTI as a single index to benchmark among participating green theatres longitudinally (Fisher, 1922). It is a bilateral weighted index based on the geometric mean of the Laspeyres and Paasche indexes, which is the best average for averaging ratios and free from bias. The GTI uses both base-period and measurement-period weights for the denominator and thus, it treats the weights from the two periods equally.

Plotting GTI

Figure 4 shows a time series of GTI for a hospital and could be repeated for other participating hospitals and theatres. The aim is to demonstrate the evolution of magnitudes for benchmarking to track green outcomes. The x-axis shows the time by month during this study and the y-axis the GTI. The base value is always a hundred if multiplied by 100 or 1.0 on the y-axis.

Figure 4. The green theatre index (GTI) on y-axis showing the progress of green theatre approaches by time on x-axis

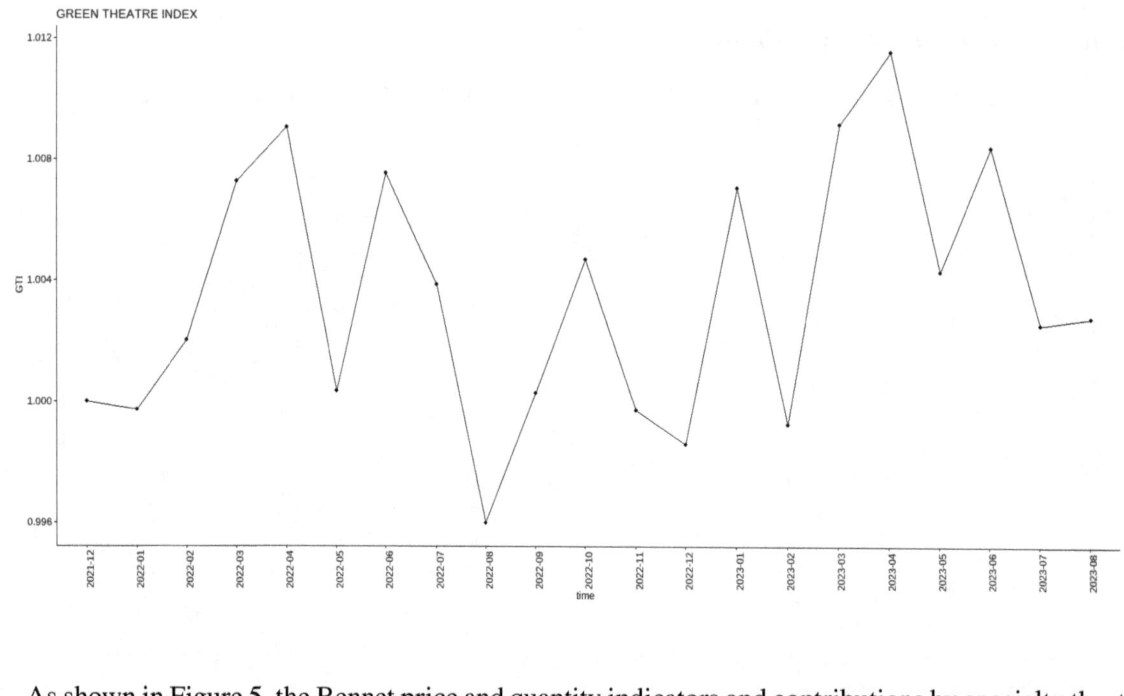

As shown in Figure 5, the Bennet price and quantity indicators and contributions by specialty theatre were calculated by using the bennet function from PriceIndices R package (Bialek, 2023; Białek, 2021, 2022). The price represents the unit price of carbon credit output from clinical_theatre_emissions function (Clements, 2023). The quantity represents the total tCO2e.

Figure 5. Bennet price and quantity contributions to the GTI where x-axis contains specialties and y-axis contributions (colorectal = colorectal surgery; ent = ear, nose, throat; gensurg = general surgery; hbt = hepatobiliary transplant; ortho = orthopaedics; paedsurg = paediatric surgery)

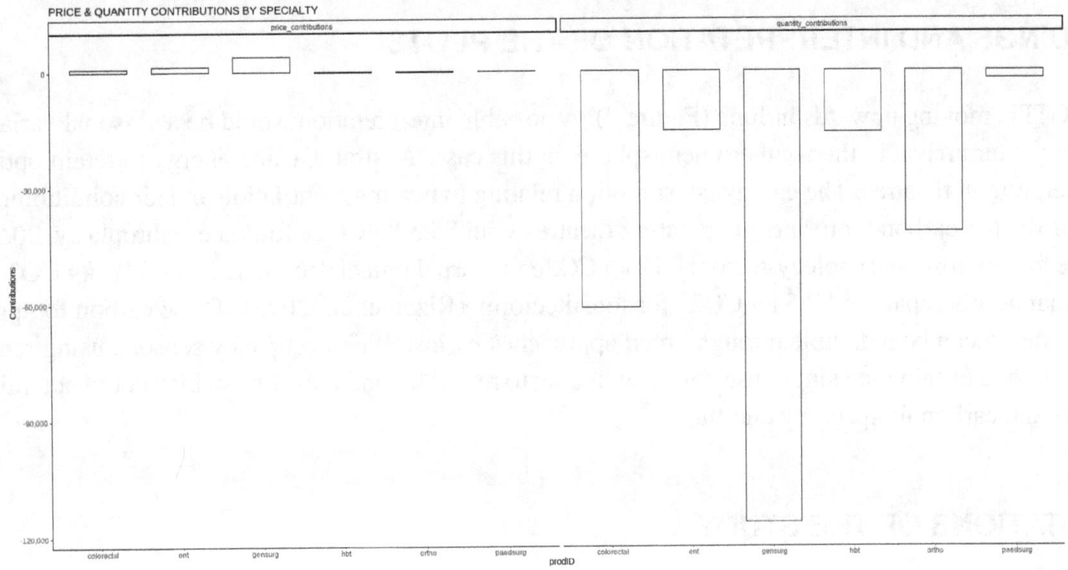

The contribution plot in Figure 6 demonstrates where to put our efforts to improve greenhouse emissions in our theatres. The plot highlights that Paediatric Surgery (paedsurg) is the least contributor in both the price (carbon credit unit price) and quantity (emissions) parameters and definitely has room to improve in subsequent green theatre implementations.

Figure 6. Mean carbon credit price by specialty where time on the x-axis and mean carbon credit dollars on the y-axis

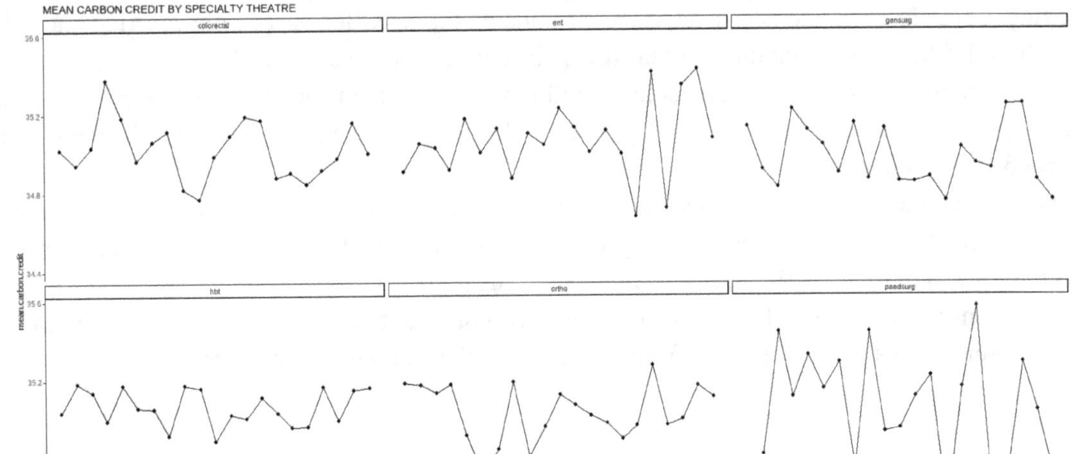

Figure 6 demonstrates the trends of the mean carbon credit price by specialty to show which specialty is making significant improvements, and in this case, General Surgery (gensurg).

FINDINGS AND INTERPRETATION OF THE PLOTS

The GTI is moving upwards in June (Figure 4). A possible interpretation would be a seasonal variation of the winter arrival in the southern hemisphere, in this case, Australia, using energy to retain optimal temperature in theatres. The energy consumption relating to heating, ventilation and air conditioning is one of the top carbon footprints in operating theatres with 85.5 kg CO2e for knee arthroplasty, 20.3 kg CO2e for laparoscopic cholecystectomy, 12 kg CO2e for carpal tunnel decompression, 11.7 kg CO2e for inguinal hernia repair and 7.5 kg CO2e for tonsillectomy (Rizan et al., 2023). These carbon footprints from energy can be reducible through green approaches by installing occupancy sensors, using renewable sources, eliminating single-use items, switching to reusables and recycling, which could potentially reduce the carbon footprint by one-third.

LIMITATIONS OF THE STUDY

The dummy dataset was specifically used in this research for a timely communication of this concept to the scientific community without any delay in a lengthy ethic approval. This limitation from the dummy dataset could also be an advantage for future research by substituting them with 'real-world' data to construct similar GTI for long-term implementation and benchmarking. A steep learning curve is usually expected in operating R statistical software for some green theatre teams without any programming experience, but the dividends for learning such a powerful statistical software outweigh its costs. This steep learning curve could also be viewed as a good trade-off for capacity building of current green theatre teams across the world. However, this drawback could be avoided by having a R programmer in the green theatre team. Moreover, carbonr now boasts a user-friendly function that generates an interactive dashboard, designed for effortless calculation of household and office emissions. This intuitive feature, employing a simple click-and-select interface, eliminates the need for users to have prior knowledge of R coding. Further collaboration could ensure a similar dashboard specifically for theatre emissions within the carbonr package. This advancement will not only democratise access to complex emissions data but also streamline the process, making it accessible and manageable for users regardless of their technical background.

Randomised controlled trials are needed to prove the effectiveness and efficiency of GTI itself and strive for a better measure for benchmarking since this paper's adoption of the Open-Source software methodology will definitely stimulate innovations on this topic.

The prevention of greenwashing, which is misrepresented as being 'green' when it is not environmentally sound, needs urgent attention from future researchers and policy makers.

DISCUSSION

We have seen green theatre initiatives worldwide recently and this trend is encouraging in terms of their enthusiasm and the volume of research published in various journals. However, all studies seem to be struggling to obtain necessary information on the requirements of the Kyoto Protocol on monitoring and reporting on a long-term basis. The current focus is still on surveying staff attitudes, individual operations and waste audit. Staff education and awareness need attention urgently since education proves significant reduction in theatre waste (Frewen, Grossman, & Basson, 2022b; Petre et al., 2019; Treggiari, 2017). As Mosquera et al pointed out, staff training in advanced waste management improved segregation of clinical waste and reduced costs (Mosquera, Andrés-Prado, Rodríguez-Caravaca, Latasa, & Mosquera, 2014). A green theatre team in the East of England was able to reduce theatre waste by 50% via education (T Southorn, AR Norrish, K Gardner, & R Baxandall, 2013).

The education program could include awareness of information collection, data entry, data warehousing, analyses and reporting to enhance the capability of green theatre teams. Comprehensive information management systems and processes in place will surely pave the way for informed decisions and continuous improvements. These systems, in turn, will transform themselves into a powerhouse of climate-smart actions with set goals and strategies.

One of the strategies would be benchmarking to track the effectiveness of green theatre teams as key performance indicators. This study stepped up its effort on this area of research into benchmarking with the GTI to track green outcomes. The GTI construction was based on the 'reproducible' powers of R programming language for green theatre team members to effectively and efficiently monitoring and reporting. The data structure and format were consistent with transparency and repeatability of science. The GTI R codes and documentations were based on the Open-Source software architecture for the benefits of the scientific community collaboration and further enhancements.

CONCLUSION

Climate-related mortality is approximately 150,000 per annum (0.3% of all deaths) and increasing in magnitudes due to cardiovascular diseases and asthma from coal power, and pandemics from altered habitats. Operating theatres contribute up to 33% of hospital greenhouse gas emissions and represent 42% hospital revenue. Therefore, the green theatre approaches seem to be the most relevant to planetary health and wellbeing. However, the green theatre approaches need a single and consolidated outcome measure to reduce theatre waste and greenhouse gases. This paper demonstrates the applicability of the GTI using the carbonr R package for benchmarking to track green theatre approaches as a measure of the evolution of magnitudes. Every step does count towards reducing the carbon footprint of the operating theatres. This study is just a single step in a long journey to achieve our ultimate goal of planetary wellbeing. It remains true that the first step must be in the right direction. The authors believe that our small step travels in the right path in a significant way to empower green theatre teams with this Green Theatre Index for the future of this planet. And start, for once, to think about Green Theatre Index.

REFERENCES

Amariglio, A., & Depaoli, D. (2021). Waste management in an Italian Hospital's operating theatres: An observational study. *American Journal of Infection Control, 49*(2), 184–187. doi:10.1016/j.ajic.2020.07.013 PMID:32663495

Australian Government. (2023). *Australian national greenhouse accounts faactors for individuals and organisations estimating greenhouse gas emissions February 2023.* Commonwealth of Australia

Azouz, S., Boyll, P., Swanson, M., Castel, N., Maffi, T., & Rebecca, A. M. (2019). Managing barriers to recycling in the operating room. *American Journal of Surgery, 217*(4), 634–638. doi:10.1016/j.amjsurg.2018.06.020 PMID:29958657

Babu, M. A., Dalenberg, A. K., Goodsell, G., Holloway, A. B., Belau, M. M., & Link, M. J. (2019). Greening the Operating Room: Results of a Scalable Initiative to Reduce Waste and Recover Supply Costs. *Neurosurgery, 85*(3), 432–437. doi:10.1093/neuros/nyy275 PMID:30060055

Białek, J. (2021). PriceIndices-a New R Package for Bilateral and Multilateral Price Index Calculations. *Statistika: Statistics & Economy Journal, 101*(2).

Białek, J. (2022). Scanner data processing in a newest version of the PriceIndices package. *Statistical Journal of the IAOS*, 1–29.

Bialek, J. (2023). *PriceIndices: Calculating Bilateral and Multilateral Price Indexes* (Version 0.1.7). Academic Press.

Bryan, M. F., & Cecchetti, S. G. (1993). *The consumer price index as a measure of inflation.* National Bureau of Economic Research Cambridge. doi:10.3386/w4505

Chance, W. A. (1966). A Note on the Origins of Index Numbers. *The Review of Economics and Statistics, 48*(1), 108–110. doi:10.2307/1924869

Chang, D. F., & Thiel, C. L. (2020). Survey of cataract surgeons' and nurses' attitudes toward operating room waste. *Journal of Cataract and Refractive Surgery, 46*(7), 933–940. doi:10.1097/j.jcrs.0000000000000267 PMID:32773547

Clements, L. (2023). *Carbonr: Calculating co2e emissions in R* (Version 0.0.0.9000). Academic Press.

Conrardy, J., Hillanbrand, M., Myers, S., & Nussbaum, G. F. (2010). Reducing medical waste. *AORN Journal, 91*(6), 711–721. doi:10.1016/j.aorn.2009.12.029 PMID:20510944

de Ridder, E. F., Friedericy, H. J., van der Eijk, A. C., Dankelman, J., & Jansen, F. W. (2022). A New Method to Improve the Environmental Sustainability of the Operating Room: Healthcare Sustainability Mode and Effect Analysis (HSMEA). *Sustainability (Basel), 14*(21), 13957. Advance online publication. doi:10.3390/su142113957

Dung, N. T., Toan, V. D., Huong, N. T. L., Mai, N. T., & Ha, N. N. M. (2023). Level of BTEX in the Areas of Domestic Waste Incinerators in Northern Vietnam: A Comprehensive Assessment of Contamination, Composition and Human Health Risk. *Bulletin of Environmental Contamination and Toxicology, 110*(5), 84. Advance online publication. doi:10.1007/s00128-023-03724-6 PMID:37093282

Engler, I. D., Curley, A. J., Fu, F. H., & Bilec, M. M. (2022). Environmental sustainability in orthopaedic surgery. *The Journal of the American Academy of Orthopaedic Surgeons, 30*(11), 504–511. doi:10.5435/JAAOS-D-21-01254 PMID:35412500

Fisher, I. (1922). The making of index numbers: a study of their varieties, tests, and reliability. Houghton Mifflin Company.

Frewen, L., Grossman, E., & Basson, C. (2022). Mostly harmless? A survey of South African anaesthetists' knowledge and attitudes regarding environmental sustainability in the operating theatre. *Southern African Journal of Anaesthesia and Analgesia, 28*(1), 35–39. doi:10.36303/SAJAA.2022.28.1.2658

Friedericy, H. J., van Egmond, C. W., Vogtlander, J. G., van der Eijk, A. C., & Jansen, F. W. (2022). Reducing the Environmental Impact of Sterilization Packaging for Surgical Instruments in the Operating Room: A Comparative Life Cycle Assessment of Disposable versus Reusable Systems. *Sustainability (Basel), 14*(1), 430. Advance online publication. doi:10.3390/su14010430

Gatenby, P. A. C. (2011). Modelling the carbon footprint of reflux control. *International Journal of Surgery, 9*(1), 72–74. doi:10.1016/j.ijsu.2010.09.008 PMID:20932944

Green, L., O'Neill, M., Westphal, M., & Morisky, D. (1996). The challenges of Participatory Action Research for health promotion. *The Journal of International Union of Health Promotion and Education.*

Guetter, C. R., Williams, B. J., Slama, E., Arrington, A., Henry, M. C., Möller, M. G., Tuttle-Newhall, J. E., Stein, S., & Crandall, M. (2018). Greening the operating room. *American Journal of Surgery, 216*(4), 683–688. doi:10.1016/j.amjsurg.2018.07.021 PMID:30055807

Ihaka, R., & Gentleman, R. (1996). R: a language for data analysis and graphics. *Journal of Computational and Graphical Statistics, 5*(3), 299–314.

Khor, H. G., Cho, I., Lee, K. R. C. K., & Chieng, L. L. (2020). Waste production from phacoemulsification surgery. *Journal of Cataract and Refractive Surgery, 46*(2), 215–221. doi:10.1097/j.jcrs.0000000000000009 PMID:32126034

Kooner, S., Hewison, C., Sridharan, S., Lui, J., Matthewson, G., Johal, H., & Clark, M. (2020). Waste and recycling among orthopedic subspecialties. *Canadian Journal of Surgery, 63*(3), E278–E283. doi:10.1503/cjs.018018 PMID:32437094

Lattanzio, S., Stefanizzi, P., D'ambrosio, M., Cuscianna, E., Riformato, G., Migliore, G., Tafuri, S., & Bianchi, F. P. (2022). Waste Management and the Perspective of a Green Hospital: A Systematic Narrative Review. *International Journal of Environmental Research and Public Health, 19*(23), 15812. doi:10.3390/ijerph192315812 PMID:36497884

Lever, M., Smetana, N., Bechrakis, N. E., & Foerster, A. (2023). Survey and reduction of waste production from eye surgery. *Die Ophthalmologie, 120*(9), 932–939. Advance online publication. doi:10.1007/s00347-023-01840-6 PMID:37052707

McGain, F., Muret, J., Lawson, C., & Sherman, J. D. (2020). Environmental sustainability in anaesthesia and critical care. *British Journal of Anaesthesia, 125*(5), 680–692. doi:10.1016/j.bja.2020.06.055 PMID:32798068

McGain, F., Story, D., Lim, T., & McAlister, S. (2017). Financial and environmental costs of reusable and single-use anaesthetic equipment. *British Journal of Anaesthesia, 118*(6), 862–869. doi:10.1093/bja/aex098 PMID:28505289

McKendrick, D., Snedden, L. J., Bunch, R., & McGregor, H. (2017). Pragmatic recycling of paper and cardboard in the operating theatre: An audit. *Journal of Perioperative Practice, 27*(3), 43–49. doi:10.1177/175045891702700302 PMID:29328742

Meiklejohn, D. A., & Chavarri, V. M. (2021). Cold technique in adult tonsillectomy reduces waste and cost. *Ear, Nose, and Throat Journal, 100*(5, suppl), 427S–430S. doi:10.1177/0145561319882779 PMID:31631678

Meissner, M., Lichtnegger, S., Gibson, S., & Saunders, R. (2021). Evaluating the Waste Prevention Potential of a Multi-versus Single-Use Surgical Stapler. *Risk Management and Healthcare Policy, 14*, 3911–3921. doi:10.2147/RMHP.S325017 PMID:34566440

Mosquera, M., Andrés-Prado, M. J., Rodríguez-Caravaca, G., Latasa, P., & Mosquera, M. E. (2014). Evaluation of an education and training intervention to reduce health care waste in a tertiary hospital in Spain. *American Journal of Infection Control, 42*(8), 894–897. doi:10.1016/j.ajic.2014.04.013 PMID:24913763

Novosel, S., Prangenberg, C., Wirtz, D. C., Burger, C., Welle, K., & Kabir, K. (2022). Climate change: How surgery contributes to global warming. *Die Chirurgie, 93*(6), 579–585. doi:10.1007/s00104-021-01551-1 PMID:35138418

Overcash, M. (2012). A Comparison of Reusable and Disposable Perioperative Textiles: Sustainability State-of-the-Art 2012. *Anesthesia and Analgesia, 114*(5), 1055–1066. doi:10.1213/ANE.0b013e31824d9cc3 PMID:22492184

Parvatker, A., Tunceroglu, H., Sherman, J., Coish, P., Anastas, P., Zimmerman, J., & Eckelman, M. (2019). Cradle-to-Gate Greenhouse Gas Emissions for Twenty Anesthetic Active Pharmaceutical Ingredients Based on Process Scale-Up and Process Design Calculations. *ACS Sustainable Chemistry & Engineering, 7*(7), 6580–6591. Advance online publication. doi:10.1021/acssuschemeng.8b05473

Perry, H., Reeves, N., Ansell, J., Cornish, J., Torkington, J., Morris, D. S., Brennan, F., & Horwood, J. (2023). Innovations towards achieving environmentally sustainable operating theatres: A systematic review. *The Surgeon, 21*(3), 141–151. doi:10.1016/j.surge.2022.04.012 PMID:35715311

Petre, M.-A., Bahrey, L., Levine, M., van Rensburg, A., Crawford, M., & Matava, C. (2019). A national survey on attitudes and barriers on recycling and environmental sustainability efforts among Canadian anesthesiologists: An opportunity for knowledge translation. *Canadian Journal of Anaesthesia, 66*(3), 272–286. doi:10.1007/s12630-018-01273-9 PMID:30547422

Pradere, B., Mallet, R., de La Taille, A., Bladou, F., Prunet, D., Beurrier, S., Bardet, F., Game, X., Fournier, G., Lechevallier, E., Meria, P., Matillon, X., Polguer, T., Abid, N., De Graeve, B., Kassab, D., Mejean, A., Misrai, V., & Pinar, U. (2023). Climate-smart Actions in the Operating Theatre for Improving Sustainability Practices: A Systematic Review. *European Urology, 83*(4), 331–342. doi:10.1016/j.eururo.2022.01.027 PMID:35151515

Pradere, B., Mallet, R., de La Taille, A., Bladou, F., Prunet, D., Beurrier, S., ... Lechevallier, E. (2023). Climate-smart actions in the operating theatre for improving sustainability practices: A systematic review. *European Urology, 83*(4), 331–342. doi:10.1016/j.eururo.2022.01.027 PMID:35151515

R Core Team. (2023). *R: A Language and Environment for Statistical Computing (Version 4.3.0)*. R Foundation for Statistical Computing.

Rammelkamp, Z., Dirnberger, J., Johnson, G., & Waisbren, S. (2021). An audit of all waste leaving the operating room: Can the surgical suite be more environmentally sustainable? *World Medical & Health Policy, 13*(1), 126–136. doi:10.1002/wmh3.397

Rizan, C., Lillywhite, R., Reed, M., & Bhutta, M. F. (2023). The carbon footprint of products used in five common surgical operations: Identifying contributing products and processes. *Journal of the Royal Society of Medicine, 116*(6), 199–213. Advance online publication. doi:10.1177/01410768231166135 PMID:37054734

Rouvière, N., Chkair, S., Auger, F., Alovisetti, C., Bernard, M., Cuvillon, P., Kinowski, J.-M., Leguelinel-Blache, G., & Chasseigne, V. (2022). Ecoresponsible actions in operating rooms: A health ecological and economic evaluation. *International Journal of Surgery, 101*, 106637. doi:10.1016/j.ijsu.2022.106637 PMID:35487421

Rutala, W. A., & Weber, D. J. (2001). A review of single-use and reusable gowns and drapes in health care. *Infection Control and Hospital Epidemiology, 22*(4), 248–257. doi:10.1086/501895 PMID:11379716

Sanabria, A., Kowalski, L. P., Nixon, I. J., Shaha, A., De Bree, R., Mäkitie, A. A., Rinaldo, A., & Ferlito, A. (2020). Considerations for environmentally sustainable head and neck surgical oncology practice. *American Journal of Otolaryngology, 41*(6), 102719. doi:10.1016/j.amjoto.2020.102719 PMID:32947153

Sherman, J., Le, C., Lamers, V., & Eckelman, M. (2012). Life Cycle Greenhouse Gas Emissions of Anesthetic Drugs. *Anesthesia and Analgesia, 114*(5), 1086–1090. doi:10.1213/ANE.0b013e31824f6940 PMID:22492186

Shinn, H. K., Hwang, Y., Kim, B.-G., Yang, C., Na, W., Song, J.-H., & Lim, H. K. (2017). Segregation for reduction of regulated medical waste in the operating room: A case report. *Korean Journal of Anesthesiology, 70*(1), 100–104. doi:10.4097/kjae.2017.70.1.100 PMID:28184276

Shoham, M. A., Baker, N. M., Peterson, M. E., & Fox, P. (2022). The environmental impact of surgery: A systematic review. *Surgery, 172*(3), 897–905. doi:10.1016/j.surg.2022.04.010 PMID:35788282

Shum, P. L., Kok, H. K., Maingard, J., Schembri, M., Bañez, R. M. F., Van Damme, V., ... Chandra, R. V. (2020). Environmental sustainability in neurointerventional procedures: A waste audit. *Journal of Neurointerventional Surgery, 12*(11), 1053–1057. doi:10.1136/neurintsurg-2020-016380 PMID:32680876

Siu, J., Hill, A. G., & MacCormick, A. D. (2017). Systematic review of reusable versus disposable laparoscopic instruments: Costs and safety. *ANZ Journal of Surgery, 87*(1-2), 28–33. doi:10.1111/ans.13856 PMID:27878921

Southorn, T., Norrish, A., Gardner, K., & Baxandall, R. (2013). Reducing the Carbon Footprint of the Operating Theatre: A Multicentre Quality Improvement Report. *Journal of Perioperative Practice*, *23*(6), 144–146. doi:10.1177/175045891302300605 PMID:23909168

Southorn, T., Norrish, A., Gardner, K., & Baxandall, R. (2013). Reducing the carbon footprint of the operating theatre: A multicentre quality improvement report. *Journal of Perioperative Practice*, *23*(6), 144–146. doi:10.1177/175045891302300605 PMID:23909168

Thiel, C. L., Fiorin Carvalho, R., Hess, L., Tighe, J., Laurence, V., Bilec, M. M., & Baratz, M. (2019). Minimal custom pack design and wide-awake hand surgery: Reducing waste and spending in the orthopedic operating room. *Hand (New York, N.Y.)*, *14*(2), 271–276. doi:10.1177/1558944717743595 PMID:29183168

Thiel, C. L., Schehlein, E., Ravilla, T., Ravindran, R., Robin, A. L., Saeedi, O. J., Schuman, J. S., & Venkatesh, R. (2017). Cataract surgery and environmental sustainability: Waste and lifecycle assessment of phacoemulsification at a private healthcare facility. *Journal of Cataract and Refractive Surgery*, *43*(11), 1391–1398. doi:10.1016/j.jcrs.2017.08.017 PMID:29223227

Thiel, C. L., Woods, N. C., & Bilec, M. M. (2018). Strategies to reduce greenhouse gas emissions from laparoscopic surgery. *American Journal of Public Health*, *108*(S2), S158–S164. doi:10.2105/AJPH.2018.304397 PMID:29698098

Treggiari, M. M. (2017). An initiative to optimize waste streams in the operating room: RECycling in the Operating Room (RECOR) Project. *AANA Journal*, *85*(2), 108. PMID:30501159

UK Government. (2022). *Greenhouse gas reporting: Conversion factors 2022*. UK Government.

Van Demark, R. E. Jr, Smith, V. J., & Fiegen, A. (2018). Lean and green hand surgery. *The Journal of Hand Surgery*, *43*(2), 179–181. doi:10.1016/j.jhsa.2017.11.007 PMID:29421068

Varughese, S., & Ahmed, R. (2021). Environmental and Occupational Considerations of Anesthesia: A Narrative Review and Update. *Anesthesia and Analgesia*, *133*(4), 826–835. doi:10.1213/ANE.0000000000005504 PMID:33857027

Vozzola, E., Overcash, M., & Griffing, E. (2020). An environmental analysis of reusable and disposable surgical gowns. *AORN Journal*, *111*(3), 315–325. doi:10.1002/aorn.12885 PMID:32128776

Wu, S., & Cerceo, E. (2021). Sustainability initiatives in the operating room. *Joint Commission Journal on Quality and Patient Safety*, *47*(10), 663–672. doi:10.1016/j.jcjq.2021.06.010 PMID:34344594

Wyssusek, K., Chan, K. L., Eames, G., & Whately, Y. (2022). Greenhouse gas reduction in anaesthesia practice: A departmental environmental strategy. *BMJ Open Quality*, *11*(3), e001867. Advance online publication. doi:10.1136/bmjoq-2022-001867 PMID:36002191

Wyssusek, K. H., Keys, M. T., & van Zundert, A. A. (2019). Operating room greening initiatives–the old, the new, and the way forward: A narrative review. *Waste Management & Research*, *37*(1), 3–19. doi:10.1177/0734242X18793937 PMID:30132405

Compilation of References

Abdelrahman, O., & Keikhosrokiani, P. (2020). Assembly line anomaly detection and root cause analysis using machine learning. *IEEE Access : Practical Innovations, Open Solutions*, *8*, 189661–189672. Advance online publication. doi:10.1109/ACCESS.2020.3029826

Abrardi, L., Cambini, C., & Rondi, L. (2022). Artificial intelligence, firms and consumer behavior: A survey. *Journal of Economic Surveys*, *36*(4), 969–991. doi:10.1111/joes.12455

Abrokwah-Larbi, K. (2023). The impact of customer focus on the performance of business organisations: Evidence from SMEs in an emerging West African economy. *African Journal of Economic and Management Studies.*

Abusweilem, M., & Abualoush, S. (2019). The impact of knowledge management process and business intelligence on organizational performance. *Management Science Letters*, *9*(12), 2143–2156. doi:10.5267/j.msl.2019.6.020

Acemoglu, D., & Restrepo, P. (2018). The race between man and machine: Implications of technology for growth, factor shares, and employment. *The American Economic Review*, *108*(6), 1488–1542. doi:10.1257/aer.20160696

Afolabi, I.T., Worlu, R. E. & Uwadia, C. O. (2016). Data Mining Approach for Target Marketing SMEs in Nigeria. *Covenant Journal of Informatics & Communication Technology, 4*(2).

Afolabi, I. T., Worlu, R. E., Adebayo, O. P., & Jonathan, O. (2019). Predicting Customer Behavior with Combination of Structured and Unstructured Data. 3rd International Conference on Science and Sustainable Development (ICSSD 2019). IOP Conf. Series. *Journal of Physics: Conference Series*, *1299*, 012041. doi:10.1088/1742-6596/1299/1/012041

Agrawal, R., & Srikant, R. (1994). Fast algorithms for mining association rules. *20th International Conference on Very Large Data Bases.*

Ahani, A., Nilashi, M., Zogaan, W. A., Samad, S., Aljehane, N. O., Alhargan, A., Mohd, S., Ahmadi, H., & Sanzogni, L. (2021). Evaluating medical travelers' satisfaction through online review analysis. *Journal of Hospitality and Tourism Management*, *48*, 519–537. doi:10.1016/j.jhtm.2021.08.005

Ahmad, H., & Mustafa, H. (2022). The impact of artificial intelligence, big data analytics and business intelligence on transforming capability and digital transformation in Jordanian telecommunication firms. *International Journal of Data and Network Science*, *6*(3), 727–732. doi:10.5267/j.ijdns.2022.3.009

Ajah, I. A., & Nweke, H. F. (2019). Big data and business analytics: Trends, platforms, success factors and applications. *Big Data and Cognitive Computing, 3*(2 C7 - 32), 1-30. doi:10.3390/bdcc3020032

Ajesh, A., Nair, J., & Jijin, P. S. (2016). A random forest approach for rating-based recommender system. *2016 International Conference on Advances in Computing, Communications and Informatics (ICACCI)*, 1293–1297. 10.1109/ICACCI.2016.7732225

Ajzen, I. (1991). The theory of planned behavior. *Organizational Behavior and Human Decision Processes, 50*(2), 179–211. doi:10.1016/0749-5978(91)90020-T

Akin-Adetoro, A & Salah Kabanda,S. (2020). Factors affecting the adoption of BYOD in South African small and medium enterprises. *Electron J Inf Syst Dev Ctries.*

Akter, S., Wamba, S. F., Gunasekaran, A., Dubey, R., & Childe, S. J. (2016). How to improve firm performance using big data analytics capability and business strategy alignment? *International Journal of Production Economics, 182,* 113–131. doi:10.1016/j.ijpe.2016.08.018

Al Haraisa, Y. E. (2017). Just-In-Time System and Its Impact on Operational Excellence: An Empirical Study on Jordanian Industrial Companies. *International Journal of Biometrics, 12,* 158. https://api.semanticscholar.org/CorpusID:55492018

Al Khuwaiter, M., AlKaabi, N., AlOlama, R., El Khatib, M., & AlAmiri, S. (2023). Managing Outsourcing in IT Software Services-A study of 3 Perspectives and 3 Industries in UAE. *International Journal of Business Analytics and Security, 3*(1), 103–124. doi:10.54489/ijbas.v3i1.206

Al Mamun, M. H., Keikhosrokiani, P., Asl, M. P., Anuar, N. A. N., Hadi, N. H. A., & Humida, T. (2022). Sentiment Analysis of the Harry Potter Series Using a Lexicon-Based Approach. In P. Keikhosrokiani & M. Pourya Asl (Eds.), *Handbook of Research on Opinion Mining and Text Analytics on Literary Works and Social Media* (pp. 263–291). IGI Global. doi:10.4018/978-1-7998-9594-7.ch011

Alaei, A., Wang, Y., Bui, V., & Stantic, B. (2023). Target-Oriented Data Annotation for Emotion and Sentiment Analysis in Tourism Related Social Media Data. *Future Internet, 15*(4), 150. doi:10.3390/fi15040150

Al-Aqrabi, H., Liu, L., Hill, R., Ding, Z., & Antonopoulos, N. (2013). Business Intelligence Security on the Clouds: Challenges, Solutions and Future Directions. *2013 IEEE Seventh International Symposium on Service-Oriented System Engineering,* 137-144. 10.1109/SOSE.2013.36

Alatabi, H. A., & Abbas, A. R. (2020). Sentiment Analysis in Social Media using Machine Learning Techniques. *Iraqi Journal of Science*, 193–201. doi:10.24996/ijs.2020.61.1.22

Alawida, M., Mejri, S., Mehmood, A., Chikhaoui, B., & Isaac Abiodun, O. (2023). A Comprehensive Study of ChatGPT: Advancements, Limitations, and Ethical Considerations in Natural Language Processing and Cybersecurity. *Information (Basel), 14*(8), 462. doi:10.3390/info14080462

Alazmi, A. R. R., & Alazmi, A. A. R. (2012). Data mining and visualization of large databases. *International Journal of Computer Science and Security, 6*(5), 295–314.

Al-Dhaen, F., Hou, J., Rana, N. P., & Weerakkody, V. (2021). Advancing the Understanding of the Role of Responsible AI in the Continued Use of IoMT in Healthcare. *Information Systems Frontiers*. Advance online publication. doi:10.1007/s10796-021-10193-x PMID:34493926

Aldridge, S., & Rowley, J. (1998). Measuring customer satisfaction in higher education. *Quality Assurance in Education, 6*(4), 197–204. doi:10.1108/09684889810242182

Aleisa, M. A., Beloff, N., & White, M. (2023). Implementing AIRM: A new AI recruiting model for the Saudi Arabia labour market. *Journal of Innovation and Entrepreneurship, 12*(1), 59. doi:10.1186/s13731-023-00324-w

Alenazi, S. A. & Alanazi, T.M. (2023).The Mediating Role of Sustainable Dynamic Capabilities in the Effect of Social Customer Relationship Management on Sustainable Competitive Advantage: A Study on SMEs in Saudi Arabia. *Sustainability. 15*(1952). doi:10.3390/su15031952

Alghamdi, N. A., & Al-Baity, H. H. (2022). Augmented Analytics Driven by AI: A Digital Transformation beyond Business Intelligence. *Sensors (Basel)*, *22*(20), 8071. doi:10.3390/s22208071 PMID:36298421

Alifah, S. K., Widyantara, P. B., & Puspasari, M. A. (2019). The Effect of Mental Workload towards Mental Fatigue on Customer Care Agent Using Electroencephalogram. *Proceedings of the 5th International Conference on Industrial and Business Engineering*, 173–177. 10.1145/3364335.3364367

Ali, O. T., Nassif, A. B., & Capretz, L. F. (2013, June). Business intelligence solutions in healthcare a case study: Transforming OLTP system to BI solution. In *2013 Third International Conference on Communications and Information Technology (ICCIT)* (pp. 209-214). IEEE. 10.1109/ICCITechnology.2013.6579551

Al-Jumaili, A. A., Ahmed, K. K., Al-Jalehawi, A. K., Al-Fatlawi, B. G., Al-Rekabi, M. D., Al-Sawad, O. S., Shari, F. H., & Sorofman, B. (2021). Evaluating the use of informational technologies by students of healthcare colleges for academic purposes over a five-year period. *Education and Information Technologies*, *26*(5), 5269–5289. doi:10.1007/s10639-021-10533-z PMID:33867808

Aljunid, M. F., & Huchaiah, M. D. (2021). An efficient hybrid recommendation model based on collaborative filtering recommender systems. *CAAI Transactions on Intelligence Technology*, *6*(4), 480–492. doi:10.1049/cit2.12048

Alkhatib, G., Bataineh, E., Fraihat, H., & Maamar, Z. (2007). An intelligent integrated e-Government framework: The case of Jordan. *Proceedings of the European Conference on e-Government, ECEG.*

Allen, R. (2020). *Digital Marketing Models: The Technology Acceptance Model.* Retrieved from https://www.smartinsights.com/manage-digital-transformation/digital-transformation-strategy/digital-marketing-models-technology-acceptance-model/

Alliant Energy. (2023). *Welcome to Alliant Energy.* Retrieved December 19, 2023 from https://www.alliantenergy.com/accountandbilling/customersupport/welcomepage

Alnidawi, A. B., & Omran, M. F. (2016). Human resource management activities adopted in the value chain model and their impact on the organizational sustainability - An empirical study of Jordanian pharmaceutical companies. *International Business Research*, *9*(9), 106–117. doi:10.5539/ibr.v9n8p106

Al-Okaily, A., Al-Okaily, M., Teoh, A. P., & Al-Debei, M. M. (2023). An empirical study on data warehouse systems effectiveness: The case of Jordanian banks in the business intelligence era. *EuroMed Journal of Business*, *18*(4), 489–510. doi:10.1108/EMJB-01-2022-0011

Al-Okaily, A., Teoh, A. P., & Al-Okaily, M. (2023). Evaluation of data analytics-oriented business intelligence technology effectiveness: An enterprise-level analysis. *Business Process Management Journal*, *29*(3), 777–800. doi:10.1108/BPMJ-10-2022-0546

Al-Otaibi, S., Alnassar, A., Alshahrani, A., Al-Mubarak, A., Albugami, S., Almutiri, N., & Albugami, A. (2018). Customer Satisfaction Measurement using Sentiment Analysis. *International Journal of Advanced Computer Science and Applications*, *9*(2). Advance online publication. doi:10.14569/IJACSA.2018.090216

Alter, S. (2015). Sociotechnical systems through a work system lens: A possible path for reconciling system conceptualizations, business realities, and humanist values in IS development. *1st International Workshop on Socio-Technical Perspective in IS Development*, 1–15.

Amande, N., Painho, M., & Oliveira, T. (2018). Geographic information technology usage in developing countries. A case study in Mozambique. *Geo-Spatial Information Science*, *21*(4), 331–345. doi:10.1080/10095020.2018.1523995

Amariglio, A., & Depaoli, D. (2021). Waste management in an Italian Hospital's operating theatres: An observational study. *American Journal of Infection Control*, *49*(2), 184–187. doi:10.1016/j.ajic.2020.07.013 PMID:32663495

Amira, V. Y. (2023). *Medium.com. How Tesla is using AI and Big Data Analytics in their Self Driving Cars?* Retrieved January 8, 2024, from https://medium.com/dare-to-be-better/how-tesla-is-using-ai-and-big-data-analytics-in-their-self-driving-cars-7072e410c1b8

Analytics, I. (2023). *India's own Cloud Service Providers*. Academic Press.

Anand, K. (2024). *How Intelligent Businesses Use Business Intelligence*. Retrieved January 7, 2024 from https://www.entrepreneur.com/growing-a-business/how-intelligent-businesses-use-business-intelligence/398669

Anderson, N., & Ozakinci, G. (2019). "It all needs to be a full jigsaw, not just bits": Exploration of healthcare professionals' beliefs towards supported self-management for long-term conditions. *BMC Psychology*, *7*(1), 38. doi:10.1186/s40359-019-0319-7 PMID:31234924

Angela, J., Suryono, I., & Wijaya, S. (2020). Profiling Indonesian Medical Tourists: A Motivation-Based Segmentation Study. *Journal of Economics, Business, &. Accountancy Ventura*, *23*(2), 205–217. Advance online publication. doi:10.14414/jebav.v23i2.2290

Anggadwita, G. & Mustafid, Q.Y. (2014). Identification of factors influencing the performance of small medium enterprises (SMEs). *Procedia-Social and Behavioral Sciences, 115,* 415-523.

Anh Hoang, D. T., Tran, H., Nguyen, B. T., & Tjoa, A. M. (2012). Towards the development of large-scale data warehouse application frameworks. *Lecture Notes in Business Information Processing*, *105*, 92–104. doi:10.1007/978-3-642-28827-2_7

Anto, M. P., Antony, M., Muhsina, K. M., Johny, N., James, V., & Wilson, A. (2016). Product rating using sentiment analysis. *2016 International Conference on Electrical, Electronics, and Optimization Techniques (ICEEOT)*, 3458–3462. 10.1109/ICEEOT.2016.7755346

Aoki, K. (2017). Mental Fatigue Measurement Using Visual Synchronization Tasks. *Proceedings of the 6th International Conference on Bioinformatics and Biomedical Science*, 37–43. 10.1145/3121138.3121164

Appel, T., Sevcenko, N., Wortha, F., Tsarava, K., Moeller, K., Ninaus, M., Kasneci, E., & Gerjets, P. (2019). Predicting Cognitive Load in an Emergency Simulation Based on Behavioral and Physiological Measures. *2019 International Conference on Multimodal Interaction*, 154–163. 10.1145/3340555.3353735

Ardagna, C. A., & Damiani, E. (2014, September). Business intelligence meets big data: an overview on security and privacy. *NSF Workshop on Big Data Security and Privacy*, 16-17.

Arefin, M. S., Hoque, M. R., & Rasul, T. (2021). Organizational learning culture and business intelligence systems of health-care organizations in an emerging economy. *Journal of Knowledge Management*, *25*(3), 573–594. doi:10.1108/JKM-09-2019-0517

Arikatla, G., & Bhargav, C. (2021). *Movie prediction based on movie scriptsusing Natural Language Processing and Machine Learning Algorithms*. Blekinge Institute of Technology.

Arnold, S. E. (1992). Information manufacturing: The road to database quality. *Database*, *15*(5), 32–39. https://dl.acm.org/doi/abs/10.5555/135054.135057

Arnott, Gao, Lizama, Meredith, & Song. (2019). Are business intelligence systems different to decision support systems and other business information systems? *ACIS 2019 Proceedings*. 66. https://aisel.aisnet.org/acis2019/66

Arnott, D., Lizama, F., & Song, Y. (2017). Patterns of business intelligence systems use in organizations. *Decision Support Systems, 97*, 58–68. doi:10.1016/j.dss.2017.03.005

Arnott, D., & Pervan, G. (2014). A critical analysis of decision support systems research revisited: The rise of design science. *Journal of Information Technology, 29*(4), 269–293. doi:10.1057/jit.2014.16

Arora, B. (2018). Big data analytics: The underlying technologies used by organizations for value generation. In Understanding the Role of Business Analytics: Some Applications (pp. 9-30). Springer Singapore. doi:10.1007/978-981-13-1334-9_2

Aruldoss, M., Lakshmi Travis, M., & Prasanna Venkatesan, V. (2014). A survey on recent research in business intelligence. *Journal of Enterprise Information Management, 27*(6), 831–866. doi:10.1108/JEIM-06-2013-0029

Arunachalam, D., Kumar, N., & Kawalek, J. P. (2018). Understanding big data analytics capabilities in supply chain management: Unravelling the issues, challenges and implications for practice. *Transportation Research Part E, Logistics and Transportation Review, 114*, 416–436. doi:10.1016/j.tre.2017.04.001

Arun, J., Hazaruthin, M. M., & Karthik, M. (2015). Analytics as a service delivery model for the cloud. *Technological Forecasting and Social Change, 168*, C7–C120766. doi:10.1016/j.techfore.2021.120766

Asgher, U., Khalil, K., Ayaz, Y., Ahmad, R., & Khan, M. J. (2020). Classification of Mental Workload (MWL) using Support Vector Machines (SVM) and Convolutional Neural Networks (CNN). *2020 3rd International Conference on Computing, Mathematics and Engineering Technologies (ICoMET)*, 1–6. 10.1109/iCoMET48670.2020.9073799

Ashrafuzzaman, Md., ASM, H, R, Adib., Sharif, H, M., & Tareq, A, M. (2022). The Impact of Social Media and Digital Marketing on Consumer Behavior. Handbook of Research on Consumer Behavior Change and Data Analytics in the Socio-Digital Era, 275-294. doi:10.4018/978-1-6684-4168-8.ch012

Ashrafuzzaman, Md., H, R., Rayesa, T., Nawrin, T., & Tasnuba, M. (2023). Application of Metaverse in the Healthcare Sector to Improve Quality of Life. Handbook of Research on Consumer Behavioral Analytics in Metaverse and the Adoption of a Virtual World, 292-320. doi:10.4018/978-1-6684-7029-9.ch014

Ashrafuzzaman, Md., Milu, M., A, Anika., K, Farzana., A, & Rahman, M. (2022). Big Data Analytics Techniques for Healthcare. Big Data Analytics for Healthcare Datasets, Techniques, Life Cycles, Management and Applications, 49-62. doi:10.1016/B978-0-323-91907-4.00015-7

Ataei, P., Gholamrezai, S., Movahedi, R., & Aliabadi, V. (2021). An analysis of farmers' intention to use green pesticides: The application of the extended theory of planned behavior and health belief model. *Journal of Rural Studies, 81*, 374–384. doi:10.1016/j.jrurstud.2020.11.003

Atnafu, D., & Balda, A. (2018). The impact of inventory management practice on firms' competitiveness and organizational performance: Empirical evidence from micro and small enterprises in Ethiopia. *Cogent Business & Management, 5*(1), 1503219. doi:10.1080/23311975.2018.1503219

Augustine, C. A., & Keikhosrokiani, P. (2021). *A Habit-Change Support Web-Based System with Big Data Analytical Features for Hospitals*. Doctive. doi:10.1007/978-3-030-70713-2_10

Australian Government. (2023). *Australian national greenhouse accounts faactors for individuals and organisations estimating greenhouse gas emissions February 2023*. Commonwealth of Australia

Ayoubi, E., & Aljawarneh, S. (2018). Challenges and Opportunities of Adopting Business Intelligence in SMEs: Collaborative Model. *DATA '18, October 1–2, 2018, Madrid, Spain*. Association for Computing Machinery.

Ayuningtyas, D., & Ariwibowo, D. A. (2020). The strategic role of information communication technology in succeeding medical tourism. *Enfermeria Clinica, 30*, 170–173. doi:10.1016/j.enfcli.2020.06.039

Azam, M., Khilji, A. B., & Khan, W. (2020). Knowledge management as a strategy & competitive advantage: A strong influence on success (A survey of knowledge management case studies of different organizations). *Public Policy and Administration Research*, *6*(10).

Aziz, N. A., Ismail, R., Omar, R., & Rahmana, I. (2021). Customer orientation and marketing innovation: A study of SMEs performance in East Coast Malaysia. *International Journal of Academic Research in Business & Social Sciences*, *11*(18), 202–219. doi:10.6007/IJARBSS/v11-i18/11628

Azmat, F., Lim, W. M., Moyeen, A., Voola, R., & Gupta, G. (2023). Convergence of business, innovation, and sustainability at the tipping point of the sustainable development goals. *Journal of Business Research*, *167*, 114170. doi:10.1016/j.jbusres.2023.114170

Azouz, S., Boyll, P., Swanson, M., Castel, N., Maffi, T., & Rebecca, A. M. (2019). Managing barriers to recycling in the operating room. *American Journal of Surgery*, *217*(4), 634–638. doi:10.1016/j.amjsurg.2018.06.020 PMID:29958657

Azvine, B., Cui, Z., Nauck, D. D., & Majeed, B. (2006, June). Real-time business intelligence for the adaptive enterprise. In *The 8th IEEE International Conference on E-Commerce Technology and The 3rd IEEE International Conference on Enterprise Computing, E-Commerce, and E-Services (CEC/EEE'06)* (pp. 29-29). IEEE. 10.1109/CEC-EEE.2006.73

Baars, H., & Kemper, H. G. (2008). Management support with structured and unstructured data—An integrated business intelligence framework. *Information Systems Management*, *25*(2), 132–148. doi:10.1080/10580530801941058

Babu, M. A., Dalenberg, A. K., Goodsell, G., Holloway, A. B., Belau, M. M., & Link, M. J. (2019). Greening the Operating Room: Results of a Scalable Initiative to Reduce Waste and Recover Supply Costs. *Neurosurgery*, *85*(3), 432–437. doi:10.1093/neuros/nyy275 PMID:30060055

Badakhshan, P., Wurm, B., Grisold, T., Geyer-Klingeberg, J., Mendling, J., & Vom Brocke, J. (2022). Creating business value with process mining. *The Journal of Strategic Information Systems*, *31*(4), 101745. doi:10.1016/j.jsis.2022.101745

Baesens, A. (2014). *Analytics in a big data world: The essential guide to data science and its applications.* John Wiley & Sons. doi:10.1002/9781119204183

Bahari, N. I. S., Ahmad, A., & Aboobaider, B. M. (2014). Application of support vector machine for classification of multispectral data. *IOP Conference Series. Earth and Environmental Science*, *20*(1), 012038. doi:10.1088/1755-1315/20/1/012038

Ballou, D. P., & Pazer, H. L. (1985). Modeling data and process quality in multi-input, multi-output information systems. *Management Science*, *31*(2), 150–162. doi:10.1287/mnsc.31.2.150

Ballou, D. P., Wang, R., & Pacer, H. (1998). Modeling information manufacturing systems to determine information product quality. *Management Science*, *44*(4), 462–484. doi:10.1287/mnsc.44.4.462

Bane & Khyati. (2020). Success of Bollywood Movie Using Machine Techniques: A Literature Review. *Mukt Shabd Journal.*

Banerjee, S., Nath, S. S., Dey, N., & Eto, H. (2015). Global Medical Tourism: A Review. In New Business Opportunities in the Growing E-Tourism Industry (pp. 114–131). IGI Global. doi:10.4018/978-1-4666-8577-2.ch007

Banerjee, A., Bandyopadhyay, T., & Acharya, P. (2013). Data Analytics: Hyped Up Aspirations or True Potential? *Vikalpa*, *38*(4), 1–12. doi:10.1177/0256090920130401

Baramichai, M., Zimmers, E. W. Jr, & Marangos, C. A. (2007). Agile supply chain transformation matrix: An integrated tool for creating an agile enterprise. *Supply Chain Management*, *12*(5), 334–348. doi:10.1108/13598540710776917

Barchielli, C., Marullo, C., Bonciani, M., & Vainieri, M. (2021). Nurses and the acceptance of innovations in technology-intensive contexts: The need for tailored management strategies. *BMC Health Services Research, 21*(1), 639. doi:10.1186/s12913-021-06628-5 PMID:34215228

Basile, L. J., Carbonara, N., Pellegrino, R., & Panniello, U. (2023). Business intelligence in the healthcare industry: The utilization of a data-driven approach to support clinical decision making. *Technovation, 120*, 102482. doi:10.1016/j.technovation.2022.102482

Battani, C., Cappelli, C., Francians, C., & Maurino, A. (2009). Methodologies for data quality assessment and improvement. *Association for Computing Machinery Computing Surveys, 41*(3), 1-52. https://doi.acm.org/10.1145/1541880.1541883

Bédard, Y., Gosselin, P., Rivest, S., Proulx, M. J., Nadeau, M., Lebel, G., & Gagnon, M. F. (2003). Integrating GIS components with knowledge discovery technology for environmental health decision support. *International Journal of Medical Informatics, 70*(1), 79–94. doi:10.1016/S1386-5056(02)00126-0 PMID:12706184

Bellamy, S. (2021). *Can mental workload in EEG tasks be classified using machine learning algorithms?* Northeastern University. doi:10.17760/D20399921

Berumen, A., & Cavanaugh, C. (2021). Developing a KPI-driven data strategy business strategy, data, and management practices. *Graziadio Business Review, 24*(2).

Bharadiya, J. P. (2022). Driving business growth with artificial intelligence and business intelligence. *International Journal of Computer Science and Technology, 6*(4), 28–44.

Bharadiya, J. P. (2022). Driving Business Growth with Artificial Intelligence and Business Intelligence. *International Journal of Computer Science And Technology, 6*(4), 28–44.

Bharadiya, J. P. (2023). A Comparative Study of Business Intelligence and Artificial Intelligence with Big Data Analytics. *American Journal of Artificial Intelligence*, 7(1), 24. doi:10.11648/j.ajai.20230701.14

Bharadiya, J. P. (2023). A comparative study of business intelligence and artificial intelligence with big data analytics. *American Journal of Artificial Intelligence*, 7(1), 24–30.

Bialas, C., Revanoglou, A., & Manthou, V. (2020). Improving hospital pharmacy inventory management using data segmentation. *American Journal of Health-System Pharmacy, 77*(5), 371–377. doi:10.1093/ajhp/zxz264 PMID:31754716

Białek, J. (2021). PriceIndices-a New R Package for Bilateral and Multilateral Price Index Calculations. *Statistika: Statistics & Economy Journal, 101*(2).

Bialek, J. (2023). *PriceIndices: Calculating Bilateral and Multilateral Price Indexes* (Version 0.1.7). Academic Press.

Białek, J. (2022). Scanner data processing in a newest version of the PriceIndices package. *Statistical Journal of the IAOS*, 1–29.

Bisgaard, S. (2008). Quality Management and Juran's Legacy. *Statistical Quality Control in Healthcare,* 390-401. doi:10.1080/08982110802317398

Bishop & Litch. (2000). Medical tourism can do harm. *BMJ (Clinical Research Ed.), 320*(7240), 1017. doi:10.1136/bmj.320.7240.1017 PMID:10753174

Bishop, S. (2018). *Using data-driven decision-making to enhance performance: A practical guide for organizations.* University of Maryland University College.

Black, D. W., & Grant, J. E. (2014). *DSM-5® guidebook: The essential companion to the diagnostic and statistical manual of mental disorders.* American Psychiatric Pub.

Blake, R., & Mangiameli, P. (2011). The effects and interactions of data quality and problem complexity on classification. *ACM Journal of Data and Information Quality*, *2*(2), 1–28. doi:10.1145/1891879.1891881

Blasco-Arcas, L., Hernandez-Ortega, B. I., & Jimenez-Martinez, J. (2016). Engagement platforms: The role of emotions in fostering customer engagement and brand image in interactive media. *Journal of Service Theory and Practice*, *26*(5), 559–589. doi:10.1108/JSTP-12-2014-0286

Blattberg, R. C., Kim, B., & Neslin S. A. (2008). Customer tier programs. In Database Marketing: International Series in Qualitive Marketing, 18, 579–605. Springer. https://doi.org/10.1007/978-0-387-72579-6_23

Boateng, R. (2022). *Data-driven enterprises in Africa- An evaluation of winners and losers*. Centre for the Study for the Economics of Africa.

Bohanec, M., Robnik-Šikonja, M., & Kljajić Borštnar, M. (2017). Decision-making framework with double-loop learning through interpretable black-box machine learning models. Industrial Management \&. *Data Systems*, *117*(7), 1389–1406.

Bonczek, R. H., Holsapple, C. W., & Whinston, A. B. (2014). *Foundations of decision support systems*. Academic Press.

Bozkurt, S., Gligor, D. M., & Babin, B. J. (2021). The role of perceived firm social media interactivity in facilitating customer engagement behaviors. *European Journal of Marketing*, *55*(4), 995–1022. doi:10.1108/EJM-07-2019-0613

Bratasanu, V. (2018). Leadership Decision-Making Processes in the Context of Data Driven Tools. *Quality - Access to Success*, 19.

Breaux, R., Dvorsky, M. R., & Becker, S. P. (2021). ADHD in COVID-19: Risk, resilience, and the rapid transition to telehealth. *The ADHD Report*, *29*(2), 1–9. doi:10.1521/adhd.2021.29.2.1

Breaux, R., Shroff, D. M., Cash, A. R., Swanson, C. S., Carlton, C., Bertollo, J. R., & Dahiya, A. V. (2023). Telehealth delivery of the RELAX intervention for families of adolescents diagnosed with ADHD: Preliminary treatment outcomes and evidence of acceptability and feasibility. *Evidence-Based Practice in Child and Adolescent Mental Health*, *8*(1), 24–38. doi:10.1080/23794925.2021.1970053

Brinkhues, R., Maçada, A. C., & Casalinho, G. (2014). Information Management Capabilities: Antecedents and Consequences. *Twentieth Americas Conference on Information Systems, Savannah, AISel.*

Bruckner, R. M., List, B., & Schiefer, J. (2002). Striving towards near real-time data integration for data warehouses. In *Data Warehousing and Knowledge Discovery: 4th International Conference, DaWaK 2002 Aix-en-Provence, France, September 4–6, 2002 Proceedings 4* (pp. 317-326). Springer. 10.1007/3-540-46145-0_31

Bryan, M. F., & Cecchetti, S. G. (1993). *The consumer price index as a measure of inflation*. National Bureau of Economic Research Cambridge. doi:10.3386/w4505

Bryl, V., Giorgini, P., & Mylopoulos, J. (2009). Designing socio-technical systems: From stakeholder goals to social networks. *Requirements Engineering*, *14*(1), 47–70. doi:10.1007/s00766-008-0073-5

Bughin, J., Chui, M., & Manyika, J. (2010). Clouds, big data, and smart assets: Ten tech-enabled business trends to watch. *The McKinsey Quarterly*, *56*(1), 75–86.

Bunyasi, G. N. W., Bwisa, H., & Namusonge, G. (2014). Effect of Access to Business Information on the Growth of Small and Medium Enterprises in Kenya. *International Journal of Business and Social Science*, *5*(10), 121–128.

Burke, R. (2002). Hybrid Recommender Systems: Survey and Experiments. *User Modeling and User-Adapted Interaction*, *12*(4), 331–370. doi:10.1023/A:1021240730564

Bustamante, A., Sebastia, L., & Onaindia, E. (2020). Bitour: A business intelligence platform for tourism analysis. *ISPRS International Journal of Geo-Information, 9*(11), 671. doi:10.3390/ijgi9110671

Caeiro, S., Sandoval Hamón, L. A., Martins, R., & Bayas Aldaz, C. E. (2020). Sustainability assessment and benchmarking in higher education institutions—A critical reflection. *Sustainability (Basel), 12*(2), 543. doi:10.3390/su12020543

California, U. S. (2022). *Research Guide on Theoritical Framework*. Retrieved from https://libguides.usc.edu/writingguide

Çano, E., & Morisio, M. (2019). *Hybrid Recommender Systems: A Systematic Literature Review*. doi:10.3233/IDA-163209

Cao, L., Zhang, C., & Liu, J. (2020). Ontology-based integration of business intelligence. *Web Intelligence and Agent Systems: An International Journal, 4*(3), 313–325.

Carey, S. (2018). *Heathrow turns to Power BI to predict passenger volumes ahead of time*. Retrieved from November 22, 2023, from https://www.computerworld.com/article/3427880/heathrow-turns-to-power-bi-to-predict-passenger-volumes-ahead-of-time.html

Caroline, L. (2024). *Top Ten Business Intelligence Failures*. Retrieved January 5, 2024 from https://www.intellectyx.com/blog/top-ten-business-intelligence-failures/

Carrera, P. M., & Bridges, J. F. (2006). Globalization and healthcare: Understanding health and medical tourism. *Expert Review of Pharmacoeconomics & Outcomes Research, 6*(4), 447–454. doi:10.1586/14737167.6.4.447 PMID:20528514

Cataldo, A., Pino, G., & McQueen, R. J. (2020). Size matters: The impact of combinations of ICT assets on the performance of Chilean micro, small, and medium enterprises. *Information Technology for Development, 26*(2), 292–315. doi:10.1080/02681102.2019.1684870

Catterall, R. (2012). Hey, what are you calling a "legacy system"? *IBM Data Management Magazine*, (2).

CavmakD.CavmakS. (2020). Using AHP to Prioritize Barriers in Developing Medical Tourism: Case of Turkey. https://papers.ssrn.com/abstract=3766688

Cem, D. (2022, February 9). *Recommendation Systems: Applications and Examples in 2022*. AIMultiple. https://research.aimultiple.com/recommendation-system/

Chance, W. A. (1966). A Note on the Origins of Index Numbers. *The Review of Economics and Statistics, 48*(1), 108–110. doi:10.2307/1924869

Chang, D. F., & Thiel, C. L. (2020). Survey of cataract surgeons' and nurses' attitudes toward operating room waste. *Journal of Cataract and Refractive Surgery, 46*(7), 933–940. doi:10.1097/j.jcrs.0000000000000267 PMID:32773547

Chauhan, C., Parida, V., & Dhir, A. (2022). Linking circular economy and digitalisation technologies: A systematic literature review of past achievements and future promises. *Technological Forecasting and Social Change, 177*, 121508. doi:10.1016/j.techfore.2022.121508

Chee, C.-H., Jaafar, J., Aziz, I. A., Hasan, M. H., & Yeoh, W. (2019). Algorithms for frequent itemset mining: A literature review. *Artificial Intelligence Review, 52*(4), 2603–2621. doi:10.1007/s10462-018-9629-z

Chege, S. M., & Wang, D. (2020). Information technology innovation and its impact on job creation by SMEs in developing countries: An analysis of the literature review. *Technology Analysis and Strategic Management, 32*(3), 256–271. doi:10.1080/09537325.2019.1651263

Chen, B., Wang, L., Li, B., & Liu, W. (2022). Work stress, mental health, and employee performance. *Frontiers in Psychology, 13*, 1006580. doi:10.3389/fpsyg.2022.1006580 PMID:36425815

Chen, H., Chiang, R. H. L., & Storey, V. C. (2012). Business intelligence and analytics: From big data to big impact. MIS Quarterly: Management. *Management Information Systems Quarterly*, *36*(4), 1165–1188. doi:10.2307/41703503

Chen, H., Chiang, R. H., & Storey, V. C. (2022). Business intelligence and analytics: From big data to big impact. *Management Information Systems Quarterly*, 1165–1188.

Chen, Y., Li, K. W., & Liu, S. (2008). A comparative study on multicriteria ABC analysis in inventory management. *2008 IEEE International Conference on Systems, Man and Cybernetics*, 3280–3285. 10.1109/ICSMC.2008.4811802

Chen, Y., & Lin, Z. (2021). Business intelligence capabilities and firm performance: A study in China. *International Journal of Information Management*, *57*, 102232. doi:10.1016/j.ijinfomgt.2020.102232

Chen, Z. S., Galatzer-Levy, I. R., Bigio, B., Nasca, C., & Zhang, Y. (2022). Modern views of machine learning for precision psychiatry. *Patterns (New York, N.Y.)*, *3*(11), 100602. doi:10.1016/j.patter.2022.100602 PMID:36419447

Cheuvront, D. (2020). *Heather Gardner shines a light on analytics and the energy industry*. IBM. Retrieved November, 14, 2023, from https://www.ibm.com/blog/heather-gardner-shines-a-light-on-analytics-and-the-energy-industry/

Choi, J. J., & Ngo-Ye, T. L. (2019). Selecting enterprise applications for curriculum: Insights from a teaching initiative. *Issues in Information Systems*, *20*(1), 195–203. doi:10.48009/1_iis_2019_195-203

Cho, Y. (2021). Rethinking Eye-Blink: Assessing Task Difficulty through Physiological Representation of Spontaneous Blinking. *Proceedings of the 2021 CHI Conference on Human Factors in Computing Systems*. 10.1145/3411764.3445577

Chuah, M. H., & Wong, K. L. (2012). Construct an enterprise business intelligence maturity model (EBI2M) using an integration approach: A conceptual framework. *Business Intelligence-Solution for Business Development*, 1-12.

Chu, K. E., Keikhosrokiani, P., & Asl, M. P. (2022). A Topic Modeling and Sentiment Analysis Model for Detection and Visualization of Themes in Literary Texts. *Pertanika Journal of Science & Technology*, *30*(4), 2535–2561. Advance online publication. doi:10.47836/pjst.30.4.14

Chung, Y., & Wang, W. (2004). The Levels of Information Technology Adoption, Business Network and a Strategic Position Model for Evaluating the Supply Chain. *Journal of Electronic Commerce Research*, *2*(5), 55–98.

Clarke, T. (2019). Creative destruction, technology disruption, and growth. In Oxford Research Encyclopedia of Economics and Finance. doi:10.1093/acrefore/9780190625979.013.393

Clements, L. (2023). *Carbonr: Calculating co2e emissions in R* (Version 0.0.0.9000). Academic Press.

Conley, E. C., Owens, D. R., Luzio, S. L., Subramanian, M., Ali, A. S., Hardisty, A., & Rana, O. (2008). Simultaneous trend analysis for evaluating outcomes in patient-centred health monitoring services. *Health Care Management Science*, *11*(2), 152–166. doi:10.1007/s10729-008-9061-z PMID:18581822

Connell, J. (2013a). Contemporary medical tourism: Conceptualisation, culture and commodification. *Tourism Management*, *34*, 1–13. doi:10.1016/j.tourman.2012.05.009

Conrardy, J., Hillanbrand, M., Myers, S., & Nussbaum, G. F. (2010). Reducing medical waste. *AORN Journal*, *91*(6), 711–721. doi:10.1016/j.aorn.2009.12.029 PMID:20510944

Cooke, J. A. (2013). Three trends to watch in 2013, Perspective. *Supply Chain Quarterly*, *1*, 11. doi:10.1111/jscm.12034

Costola, M., Hinz, O., Nofer, M., & Pelizzon, L. (2023). Machine learning sentiment analysis, COVID-19 news and stock market reactions. *Research in International Business and Finance*, *64*, 101881. doi:10.1016/j.ribaf.2023.101881 PMID:36687319

Couceiro, R., Duarte, G., Durães, J., Castelhano, J., Duarte, C., Teixeira, C., Branco, M. C., de Carvalho, P., & Madeira, H. (2019). Biofeedback Augmented Software Engineering: Monitoring of Programmers' Mental Effort. *Proceedings of the 41st International Conference on Software Engineering: New Ideas and Emerging Results*, 37–40. 10.1109/ICSE-NIER.2019.00018

Crosby, P. (1995). Philip Crosby's Reflections on Quality. McGraw-Hill. , ISBN 13. doi:10.4324/9780203027790-14

Cunningham, E. (2021). Artificial intelligence-based decision-making algorithms, sustainable organizational performance, and automated production systems in big data-driven smart urban economy. *Journal of Self-Governance and Management Economics*, *9*(1), 31–41.

Dabab, M., & Weber, C. (2018). Business intelligence and data analytics as a driver of dynamic capability strategic approach. *PICMET 2018 - Portland International Conference on Management of Engineering and Technology: Managing Technological Entrepreneurship: The Engine for Economic Growth, Proceedings*. 10.23919/PICMET.2018.8481750

Dang, H.-S., Nguyen, T.-M.-T., Wang, C.-N., Day, J.-D., & Dang, T. M. H. (2020). Grey System Theory in the Study of Medical Tourism Industry and Its Economic Impact. *International Journal of Environmental Research and Public Health*, *17*(3), 961. doi:10.3390/ijerph17030961 PMID:32033177

Darwazeh, D., Clarke, A., & Wilson, J. (2021). Framework for Establishing a Sustainable Medical Facility: A Case Study of Medical Tourism in Jordan. *WORLD (Oakland, Calif.)*, *2*(3), 351–375. doi:10.3390/world2030022

Das Chakladar, D., Dey, S., Roy, P. P., & Dogra, D. P. (2020). EEG-based mental workload estimation using deep BLSTM-LSTM network and evolutionary algorithm. *Biomedical Signal Processing and Control*, *60*, 101989. doi:10.1016/j.bspc.2020.101989

Davenport, T. H. (2006). *Competing on analytics, Harvard Business Review*. Harvard Business Press. doi:10.5860/CHOICE.44-6322

Davenport, T. H., Barth, P., & Bean, R. (2012). How Big Data is different. *MIT Sloan Management Review*, (Fall), 22–24. doi:10.7551/mitpress/12588.001.0001

Davenport, T. H., & Harris, J. G. (2007). *Competing on analytics – the new science of wining*. Harvard Business School Publishing Corporation. doi:10.1177/09722629211023024

Davenport, T. H., & Harris, J. G. (2007). *Competing on analytics – the new science of winning*. Harvard Business School Publishing Corporation. doi:10.5465/amr.2005.17293788

Davenport, T. H., Harris, J. G., & Morison, R. (2010). *Analytics at work – smart decisions, better results*. Harvard Business Press. doi:10.1108/14754391011050388

Davenport, T. H., & Prusiks, L. (2000). *Working knowledge: how organizations manage what they know*. Harvard Business Press. doi:10.1145/348772.348775

David, L. O., Nwulu, N. I., Aigbavboa, C. O., & Adepoju, O. O. (2022). Integrating fourth industrial revolution (4IR) technologies into the water, energy & food nexus for sustainable security: A bibliometric analysis. *Journal of Cleaner Production*, *363*, 132522. doi:10.1016/j.jclepro.2022.132522

Davis, F. D. (1989). Perceived Usefulness, Perceived Ease of Use, and User Acceptance of Information Technology. *Management Information Systems Quarterly*, *13*(3), 319–340. doi:10.2307/249008

Davis, F. D. (1993). User acceptance of information technology: System characteristics, user perceptions and behavioral impacts. *International Journal of Man-Machine Studies*, *38*(3), 475–487. doi:10.1006/imms.1993.1022 de la Hoz-Correa, A., Muñoz-Leiva, F., & Bakucz, M. (2018). Past themes and future trends in medical tourism research: A co-word analysis. *Tourism Management*, *65*, 200–211. doi:10.1016/j.tourman.2017.10.001

de Ridder, E. F., Friedericy, H. J., van der Eijk, A. C., Dankelman, J., & Jansen, F. W. (2022). A New Method to Improve the Environmental Sustainability of the Operating Room: Healthcare Sustainability Mode and Effect Analysis (HSMEA). *Sustainability (Basel)*, *14*(21), 13957. Advance online publication. doi:10.3390/su142113957

Debata, B. R., Patnaik, B., Mahapatra, S. S., & Sree, K. (2015). Interrelations of service quality and service loyalty dimensions in medical tourism: A structural equation modelling approach. *Benchmarking*, *22*(1), 18–55. doi:10.1108/BIJ-04-2013-0036

Deldjoo, Y., Schedl, M., Cremonesi, P., & Pasi, G. (2020). Recommender Systems Leveraging Multimedia Content. *ACM Computing Surveys*, *53*(5), 1–38. doi:10.1145/3407190

Del, O., Félix, H., & Elena, G. (2008). Evaluation of recommender systems: A new approach. *Expert Systems with Applications*, *35*(3), 790–804. doi:10.1016/j.eswa.2007.07.047

Deloitte & MHI. (2014). *The 2014 MHI Annual Industry Report – Innovation the driven supply chain.* https://www2.deloitte.com/content/dam/Deloitte/dk/Documents/process-and-operations/2015%20MHI%20Industry%20Report.pdf

Deloitte & MHI. (2016). *The 2016 MHI Annual Industry Report – Accelerating change: How innovation is driving digital, always-on Supply Chains.* http://cpbucket.fiu.edu/1168-geb6368x81168_emba-97075%2F2016-industry-report-2016-(1).pdf

Deming, W. E. (2000). *The New Economics for Industry, Government, Education* (2nd ed.). MIT Press. doi:10.7551/mitpress/11458.001.0001

Dhagarra, D., Goswami, M., & Kumar, G. (2020). Impact of Trust and Privacy Concerns on Technology Acceptance in Healthcare: An Indian Perspective. *International Journal of Medical Informatics*, *141*, 104164. doi:10.1016/j.ijmedinf.2020.104164 PMID:32593847

Dhakate, N., & Joshi, R. (2023). Classification of reviews of e-healthcare services to improve patient satisfaction: Insights from an emerging economy. *Journal of Business Research*, *164*, 114015. doi:10.1016/j.jbusres.2023.114015 PMID:37192884

Di Vaio, A., Hassan, R., & Alavoine, C. (2022). Data intelligence and analytics: A bibliometric analysis of human–Artificial intelligence in public sector decision-making effectiveness. *Technological Forecasting and Social Change*, *174*, C7–C121201. doi:10.1016/j.techfore.2021.121201

Diab, Z., & Awny, M. M. (2020). Data analytics maturity models: A systematic literature review. Towards the Digital World and Industry X.0. *Proceedings of the 29th International Conference of the International Association for Management of Technology, IAMOT 2020.*

Diekson, Z. A., Prakoso, M. R. B., Putra, M. S. Q., Syaputra, M. S. A. F., Achmad, S., & Sutoyo, R. (2023). Sentiment analysis for customer review: Case study of Traveloka. *Procedia Computer Science*, *216*, 682–690. doi:10.1016/j.procs.2022.12.184

Dietrich, B., Plachy, E. C., & Norton, M. F. (2014). *Analytics across the enterprise: How IBM realize business value from big data and analytics*. IBM Press Books. doi:10.1002/9781118936672

Dinter, B., & Lorenz, A. (2012). Social business intelligence: a literature review and research agenda. *Thirty Third International Conference on Information Systems*. https://aisel.aisnet.org/icis2012/proceedings/ResearchInProgress/104/

Diorio, S., Hummel, C., & Rogers, B. (2022). Revenue operations: A systems approach for turning analytics into growth. *Applied Marketing Analytics*, *7*(4), 306–317.

Dixon, S. (2023, Aug 31). *Social media: Statistics & Facts*. Statista. https://www.statista.com/topics/1164/social-networks/#topicOverview

Djerdjouri, M. (2020). Data and Business Intelligence Systems for Competitive Advantage: prospects, challenges, and real-world applications. *Mercados y Negocios*, (41), 5-18. https://www.redalyc.org/articulo.oa?id=571861494009

Dong, X., Lei, Y., Zhonghuo, W., Yuxia, S., Lingfeng, Y., & Fangxi, Z. (2017). A hybrid collaborative filtering model with deep structure for recommender systems. *AAAI Conference on Artificial Intelligence*. 10.1609/aaai.v31i1.10747

Dora, M., Kumar, M., & Gellynck, X. (2016). Determinants and barriers to lean implementation in food-processing SMEs—A multiple case analysis. *Production Planning and Control*, *27*(1), 1–23. doi:10.1080/09537287.2015.1050477

Doshi, R., Hiran, K. K., Mijwil, M. M., & Anand, D. (2023). To That of Artificial Intelligence, Passing Through Business Intelligence. In *Handbook of Research on AI and Knowledge Engineering for Real-Time Business Intelligence* (pp. 1–16). IGI Global. doi:10.4018/978-1-6684-6519-6.ch001

Dryglas, D., & Salamaga, M. (2018). Segmentation by push motives in health tourism destinations: A case study of Polish spa resorts. *Journal of Destination Marketing & Management*, *9*, 234–246. doi:10.1016/j.jdmm.2018.01.008

Duan, Y., Edwards, J. S., & Dwivedi, Y. K. (2019). Artificial intelligence for decision making in the era of Big Data—Evolution, challenges and research agenda. *International Journal of Information Management*, *48*, 63–71. doi:10.1016/j.ijinfomgt.2019.01.021

Dubey, R., Gunasekaran, A., & Childe, S. J. (2018a). Big data analytics capability in supply chain agility: The moderating effect of organizational flexibility. *Management Decision*. Advance online publication. doi:10.1108/MD-01-2018-0119

Dubey, R., Gunasekaran, A., Childe, S. J., Fosso Wamba, S., Roubaud, D., & Foropon, C. (2021). Empirical investigation of data analytics capability and organizational flexibility as complements to supply chain resilience. *International Journal of Production Research*, *59*(1), 1–19. doi:10.1080/00207543.2019.1582820

Dubey, R., Gunasekaran, A., Childe, S. J., Luo, Z., Wamba, S. F., Roubaud, D., & Foropon, C. (2018b). Examining the role of big data and predictive analytics on collaborative performance in context to sustainable consumption and production behaviour. *Journal of Cleaner Production*, *196*, 1508–1521. doi:10.1016/j.jclepro.2018.06.097

Dubey, R., Gunasekaran, A., Childe, S. J., Roubaud, D., Wamba, S. F., Giannakis, M., & Foropon, C. (2019b). Big data analytics and organizational culture as complements to swift trust and collaborative performance in the humanitarian supply chain. *International Journal of Production Economics*, *210*, 120–136. doi:10.1016/j.ijpe.2019.01.023

Dubey, R., Gunasekaran, A., Childe, S. J., Wamba, S. F., & Papadopoulos, T. (2016). The impact of big data on world-class sustainable manufacturing. *International Journal of Advanced Manufacturing Technology*, *84*(1–4), 631–645. doi:10.1007/s00170-015-7674-1

Dung, N. T., Toan, V. D., Huong, N. T. L., Mai, N. T., & Ha, N. N. M. (2023). Level of BTEX in the Areas of Domestic Waste Incinerators in Northern Vietnam: A Comprehensive Assessment of Contamination, Composition and Human Health Risk. *Bulletin of Environmental Contamination and Toxicology*, *110*(5), 84. Advance online publication. doi:10.1007/s00128-023-03724-6 PMID:37093282

Dzimińska, M., Fijałkowska, J., & Sułkowski, Ł. (2018). Trust-based quality culture conceptual model for higher education institutions. *Sustainability (Basel)*, *10*(8), 2599. doi:10.3390/su10082599

Ebrahim, A. H., & Ganguli, S. (2019). A comparative analysis of medical tourism competitiveness of India, Thailand and Singapore. *Tourism: An International Interdisciplinary Journal, 67*(2), 102–115.

Edelenbos, J., & Klijn, E. H. (2006). Managing stakeholder involvement in decision making: A comparative analysis of six interactive processes in the Netherlands. *Journal of Public Administration: Research and Theory, 16*(3), 417–446. doi:10.1093/jopart/mui049

Edge, D., Larson, J., & White, C. (2018, April). Bringing AI to BI: enabling visual analytics of unstructured data in a modern Business Intelligence platform. In Extended abstracts of the 2018 CHI conference on human factors in computing systems (pp. 1-9). doi:10.1145/3170427.3174367

Ediansyah, A., Arief, M., Hamsal, M., & Abdinagoro, S. B. (2022). A decade of medical tourism research: Looking back to moving forward. *Journal of Hospitality and Tourism Insights, 6*(5), 2158–2172. doi:10.1108/JHTI-06-2022-0250

Egberi, A. K., & Okpako-Uyeh, B. (2011). Competitive intelligence and marketing effectiveness of corporate business organizations in Nigeria. *International Journal of Economic Development Research and Investment*, (2), 3.

Eggert, M., & Alberts, J. (2020). Frontiers of business intelligence and analytics 3.0: A taxonomy-based literature review and research agenda. *Business Research, 13*(2), 685–739. doi:10.1007/s40685-020-00108-y

Ehsan, U., Liao, Q. V., Muller, M., Riedl, M. O., & Weisz, J. D. (2021). Expanding explainability: Towards social transparency in ai systems. *Proceedings of the 2021 CHI Conference on Human Factors in Computing Systems*, 1–19. 10.1145/3411764.3445188

El-Gohary, H. (2012). Factors affecting E-Marketing adoption and implementation in tourism firms: An empirical investigation of Egyptian small tourism organisations. *Tourism Management, 33*(5), 1256–1269. doi:10.1016/j.tourman.2011.10.013

Emery, J.C. (1969). *Organizational planning and control systems: Theory and management.* Macmillan. doi:10.1177/000271627039200187

Emery, F. E., & Trist, E. L. (1960). Socio-technical systems. *Management Science. Models and Techniques, 2*, 83–97.

Engler, I. D., Curley, A. J., Fu, F. H., & Bilec, M. M. (2022). Environmental sustainability in orthopaedic surgery. *The Journal of the American Academy of Orthopaedic Surgeons, 30*(11), 504–511. doi:10.5435/JAAOS-D-21-01254 PMID:35412500

Eom, S. (2020). DSS, BI, and data analytics research: current state and emerging trends (2015–2019). *Lecture Notes in Business Information Processing.*

Eraslan, E., Can, G., & Atalay, K. (2016). Mental workload assessment using a fuzzy multi-criteria method [Procjena mentalnog opterećenja primjenom neizrazite metode s više kriterija]. *Tehnicki Vjesnik (Strojarski Fakultet), 23*(3).

Erdin, C., & Ozkaya, G. (2020). Contribution of small and medium enterprises to economic development and quality of life in Turkey. *Heliyon, 6*(2), 2. doi:10.1016/j.heliyon.2020.e03215 PMID:32055722

Ermakova, T., Fabian, B., Golimblevskaia, E., & Henke, M. (2023). A Comparison of Commercial Sentiment Analysis Services. *SN Computer Science, 4*(5), 477. doi:10.1007/s42979-023-01886-y

E-Soft. (2022). *Hospital Information System (HIS).* Retrieved from https://www.e-soft.com.my/hospital.html

Evelson, B., & Nicolson, N. (2008). *Topic Overview: Business Intelligence-An Information Workplace Report.* Forrester.

Falcetta, F. S., de Almeida, F. K., Lemos, J. C. S., Goldim, J. R., & da Costa, C. A. (2023). Automatic documentation of professional health interactions: A systematic review. *Artificial Intelligence in Medicine, 137*, 102487. doi:10.1016/j.artmed.2023.102487 PMID:36868684

Fan, S., Lau, R. Y. K., & Zhao, J. L. (2015). Demystifying big data analytics for business intelligence through the lens of marketing mix. *Big Data Research, 2*(1), 28–32. doi:10.1016/j.bdr.2015.02.006

Fasha, E. F. B. K., Keikhosrokiani, P., & Asl, M. P. (2022). Opinion Mining Using Sentiment Analysis: A Case Study of Readers' Response on Long Litt Woon's The Way Through the Woods in Goodreads. In Lecture Notes on Data Engineering and Communications Technologies (Vol. 127). doi:10.1007/978-3-030-98741-1_20

Fattah, A. (2014). Cloud analytics: Derive insight without on-premises infrastructure. *IBM Data Management Magazine*, (8).

Fawcett, S. E., & Waller, M. A. (2014). Supply chain game changers—mega, nano, and virtual trends—and forces that impede supply chain design (ie, building a winning team). *Journal of Business Logistics, 35*(3), 157–164. doi:10.1111/jbl.12058

Fehrer, J. A., Woratschek, H., Germelmann, C. C., & Brodie, R. J. (2018). Dynamics and drivers of customer engagement: Within the dyad and beyond. *Journal of Service Management, 29*(3), 443–467. doi:10.1108/JOSM-08-2016-0236

Fernandez, J. L., Guiterrez, J. E., Castro, L. A., & Rodriguez, L. (2016). Integrating business analytics into SMEs in Mexico: Challenges and applications. *Avances en Interacción Humano-Computadora, 1*(1), 41–45. doi:10.47756/aihc.y1i1.13

Fielding, N. G., & Lee, R. M. (1997). Applications of computer software in the sociological analysis of qualitative data. *Bulletin de Methodologie Sociologique, 57*(1), 3–24. doi:10.1177/075910639705700101

Figalist, I., Elsner, C., Bosch, J., & Olsson, H. H. (2020, August). Breaking the Vicious Circle: Why AI for software analytics and business intelligence does not take off in practice. In *2020 46th Euromicro Conference on Software Engineering and Advanced Applications (SEAA)* (pp. 5-12). IEEE. 10.1109/SEAA51224.2020.00013

Figalist, I., Elsner, C., Bosch, J., & Olsson, H. H. (2022). Breaking the vicious circle: A case study on why AI for software analytics and business intelligence does not take off in practice. *Journal of Systems and Software, 184*, 111135. doi:10.1016/j.jss.2021.111135

Fishbein, M., & Ajzen, I. (1975). *Belief, attitude, intention and behaviour: An introduction to theory and research* (Vol. 27). Academic Press.

Fisher, I. (1922). The making of index numbers: a study of their varieties, tests, and reliability. Houghton Mifflin Company.

Fitriana, R., Eriyatno, T. D., & Djatna, T. (2021). Progress in Business Intelligence System research: A literature review. *International Journal of Basic & Applied Sciences IJBAS-IJENS, 11*(03), 118503–6464.

Fitzgerald, C., Letier, E., & Finkelstein, A. (2011). Early Failure Prediction in Feature Request Management Systems. *IEEE 19th International Requirement Engineering Conference,* 229-238. 10.1109/RE.2011.6051658

Fitzgerald, M., Kruschwitz, N., Bonnet, D., & Welch, M. (2014). Embracing digital technology: A new strategic imperative. *MIT Sloan Management Review, 55*(2), 1.

Fosso Wamba, S., Gunasekaran, A., Papadopoulos, T., & Ngai, E. (2018). Big data analytics in logistics and supply chain management. *International Journal of Logistics Management, 29*(2), 478–484. doi:10.1108/IJLM-02-2018-0026

Fountain, J. E. (2004). *Building the virtual state: Information technology and institutional change.* Rowman & Littlefield.

Fourie, L .E. (2015). Categorizing South African SMEs according to Customer Relationship Building practices. *Corporate Ownership & Control, 13*(1).

Francis, O. O. (2020). Evaluation of the implementation of business intelligence systems on SME results in Lagos State, Nigeria. *International Journal of Novel Research in Computer Science and Software Engineering*, *7*(3), 1–12.

Frewen, L., Grossman, E., & Basson, C. (2022). Mostly harmless? A survey of South African anaesthetists' knowledge and attitudes regarding environmental sustainability in the operating theatre. *Southern African Journal of Anaesthesia and Analgesia*, *28*(1), 35–39. doi:10.36303/SAJAA.2022.28.1.2658

Friedericy, H. J., van Egmond, C. W., Vogtlander, J. G., van der Eijk, A. C., & Jansen, F. W. (2022). Reducing the Environmental Impact of Sterilization Packaging for Surgical Instruments in the Operating Room: A Comparative Life Cycle Assessment of Disposable versus Reusable Systems. *Sustainability (Basel)*, *14*(1), 430. Advance online publication. doi:10.3390/su14010430

Gabriel, M. (2019). *Recommender Systems in Python 101 | Kaggle*. https://www.kaggle.com/code/gspmoreira/recommender-systems-in-python-101#Collaborative-Filtering-model

Gad-Elrab, A. A. (2021). Modern business intelligence: Big data analytics and artificial intelligence for creating the data-driven value. *E-Business-Higher Education and Intelligence Applications, 135.*

Gallagher, C., Furey, E., & Curran, K. (2019). The Application of Sentiment Analysis and Text Analytics to Customer Experience Reviews to Understand What Customers Are Really Saying. *International Journal of Data Warehousing and Mining*, *15*(4), 21–47. doi:10.4018/IJDWM.2019100102

Gallagher, M. W. (2012). Self-Efficacy. In V. S. Ramachandran (Ed.), *Encyclopedia of Human Behavior* (2nd ed., pp. 314–320). Academic Press. doi:10.1016/B978-0-12-375000-6.00312-8

Ganesan, S., & Gopalsamy, S. (2019). Business intelligence and advanced analytics: Impact and behavior of business decision making process. *International Journal of Recent Technology and Engineering, 8*(3 Special Issue), 375-379. doi:10.35940/ijrte.C1080.1083S19

Gangadharan, G., & Swami, S. N. (2004). Business intelligence systems: design and implementation strategies. Information Technology Interfaces. *26th International Conference on, 2004*, 139-144.

Gangrade, S., Shrivastava, N., & Gangrade, J. (2019). Instagram Sentiment Analysis: Opinion Mining. SSRN *Electronic Journal*. doi:10.2139/ssrn.3372757

García-Contreras, R., Muñoz-Chávez, J. P., & Muñoz-Chávez, R. L. (2023). Is the Idea of Human Replacement too Far-Fetched?: Artificial Intelligence as a Partner for the Public Sector. In *Handbook of Research on Applied Artificial Intelligence and Robotics for Government Processes* (pp. 93–113). IGI Global.

García-Contreras, R., Valle-Cruz, D., & Canales-García, R. A. (2021). Organizational selection: SMEs resilience and performance in COVID-19 age. *Estudios Gerenciales*, *37*(158), 73–84.

Gatenby, P. A. C. (2011). Modelling the carbon footprint of reflux control. *International Journal of Surgery*, *9*(1), 72–74. doi:10.1016/j.ijsu.2010.09.008 PMID:20932944

Gavurova, B., Cepel, M., Belas, J., & Dvorsky, J. (2020). Strategic management in SMEs and its significance for enhancing the competitiveness in the V4 countries: A comparative analysis. *Management & Marketing. Challenges for the Knowledge Society*, *15*(4), 557–569. doi:10.2478/mmcks-2020-0032

George, J., & Jeyakumar, M. K. (2020). A dimensional data model for healthcare revenue cycle analytics and business intelligence. *International Journal on Emerging Technologies*, *11*(3), 648–653.

Ghanem, S. K. R., & Hamid, N. A. A. (2021). Factors Influencing SME Performance: The Mediating and Moderating Role of Social Media Adoption and Organizational Culture. *Proceedings of the Second Asia Pacific International Conference on Industrial Engineering and Operations Management Surakarta.*

Giannakis, M., & Louis, M. (2016). A multi-agent based system with big data processing for enhanced supply chain agility. *Journal of Enterprise Information Management, 29*(5), 706–727. doi:10.1108/JEIM-06-2015-0050

Glielmo, A., Husic, B. E., Rodriguez, A., Clementi, C., Noé, F., & Laio, A. (2021). Unsupervised Learning Methods for Molecular Simulation Data. *Chemical Reviews, 121*(16), 9722–9758. doi:10.1021/acs.chemrev.0c01195 PMID:33945269

Goethel, D. R., Lucey, S. M., Berger, A. M., Gaichas, S. K., Karp, M. A., Lynch, P. D., Walter, J. F. III, Deroba, J. J., Miller, S., & Wilberg, M. J. (2019). Closing the feedback loop: On stakeholder participation in management strategy evaluation. *Canadian Journal of Fisheries and Aquatic Sciences, 76*(10), 1895–1913. doi:10.1139/cjfas-2018-0162

Goldberg, D., Nichols, D., Oki, B. M., & Terry, D. (1992). Using collaborative filtering to weave an information tapestry. *Communications of the ACM, 35*(12), 61–70. doi:10.1145/138859.138867

Gomwe, G., Potgiete, M., & Litheko, A. (2020). Business intelligence as a competitive advantage for SMMEs in the North West Province of South Africa. *Journal of Contemporary Management, 20*(1).

Gono, S., Harindranath, G., & Özcan, G. B. (2016). The adoption and impact of ICT in South African SMEs. *Strategic Change, 25*(6), 717–734. doi:10.1002/jsc.2103

Goodhue, D. L., & Thompson, R. L. (1995). Task-Technology Fit and Individual Performance. *Management Information Systems Quarterly, 19*(2), 213–236. doi:10.2307/249689

Govers, M., & Van Amelsvoort, P. (2019). A socio-technical perspective on the digital era: The Lowlands view. *European Journal of Workplace Innovation, 4*(2). Advance online publication. doi:10.46364/ejwi.v4i2.589

Govindan, K., Cheng, T. C. E., Mishra, N., & Shukla, N. (2018). Big data analytics and application for logistics and supply chain management. *Transportation Research Part E, Logistics and Transportation Review, 114*, 343–349. doi:10.1016/j.tre.2018.03.011

Grab N Go Info. (2022, January 23). *(1) User-Based Collaborative Filtering In Python | Machine Learning - YouTube.* YouTube. https://www.youtube.com/watch?v=cxcFi3RDrEw

Grabova, O., Darmont, J., Chauchat, J. H., & Zolotaryova, I. (2010). Business intelligence for small and middle-sized enterprises. *SIGMOD Record, 39*(2), 39–50. doi:10.1145/1893173.1893180

Graupner, E., Berner, M., Maedche, A., & Jegadeesan, H. (2014). Business intelligence & analytics for processes: A visibility requirements evaluation. *Tagungsband Multikonferenz Wirtschaftsinformatik 2014, MKWI 2014.*

Green, L., O'Neill, M., Westphal, M., & Morisky, D. (1996). The challenges of Participatory Action Research for health promotion. *The Journal of International Union of Health Promotion and Education.*

Gröger, C., Schwarz, H., & Mitschang, B. (2014). Prescriptive analytics for recommendation-based business process optimization. *Lecture Notes in Business Information Processing, 176*, 25–37. doi:10.1007/978-3-319-06695-0_3

Gualtieri, C. T., & Johnson, L. G. (2005). ADHD: Is objective diagnosis possible? *Psychiatry (Edgmont, Pa.), 2*(11), 44. PMID:21120096

Guarda, T., Santos, M., Pinto, F., Augusto, M. & Silva, C. (2013). Business intelligence as a competitive advantage for SMEs. *International Journal of Trade, Economics & Finance, 4*(187).

Guetter, C. R., Williams, B. J., Slama, E., Arrington, A., Henry, M. C., Möller, M. G., Tuttle-Newhall, J. E., Stein, S., & Crandall, M. (2018). Greening the operating room. *American Journal of Surgery, 216*(4), 683–688. doi:10.1016/j.amjsurg.2018.07.021 PMID:30055807

Gunasekaran, A., Papadopoulos, T., Dubey, R., Wamba, S. F., Childe, S. J., Hazen, B., & Akter, S. (2017). Big data and predictive analytics for supply chain and organizational performance. *Journal of Business Research, 70*, 308–317. doi:10.1016/j.jbusres.2016.08.004

Gupta, P., Pandey, B., Hussain, S., Kumar, A., Sharma, R., Yadav, M. K., Bhati, S., Khandelwal, A., Shyamal, S., Khan, A., Mohata, V., Khan, F., Sharma, K., Arora, K., Gandhi, T., Kumar, P., & Kundu, P. (n.d.). *Challenges and Strengths of Medical Tourism in Delhi NCR*. Academic Press.

Gupta. (2020). A literature review on recommendation systems. *International Research Journal of Engineering and Technology (IRJET)*, 3600–3605.

Gürdür Broo, D., Bravo-Haro, M., & Schooling, J. (2022). Design and implementation of a smart infrastructure digital twin. *Automation in Construction, 136*, 104171. doi:10.1016/j.autcon.2022.104171

Gürdür, D., Raizer, K., & El-Khoury, J. (2018). Data visualization support for complex logistics operations and cyber-physical systems. *14th International Joint Conference on Computer Vision, Imaging and Computer Graphics Theory and Applications*. 10.5220/0006569402000211

Gürdür, D., Vulgarakis Feljan, A., El-khoury, J., Kumar Mohalik, S., Badrinath, R., Pradeep Mujumdar, A., & Fersman, E. (2018). Knowledge Representation of Cyber-physical Systems for Monitoring Purpose. *Procedia CIRP, 72*, 468–473. doi:10.1016/j.procir.2018.03.018

Guru, S. K. (2023). Influence of big data analytics on business intelligence. In *Analytics Enabled Decision Making* (pp. 45–58). Springer Nature. doi:10.1007/978-981-19-9658-0_3

Habibi, A., Mousavi, M., Jamali, S. M., & Ale Ebrahim, N. (2022). A bibliometric study of medical tourism. *Anatolia, 33*(3), 415–425. doi:10.1080/13032917.2021.1954042

Hadoop. (2017). http://hadoop.apache.org

Hadoop. (n.d.). *Tutorials*. Retrieved November 11, 2023, from https://hadoop.apache.org/docs/r1.2.1/mapred_tutorial.html?source=post_page-----a4bb27bc930--------------------------------#MapReduce+-+User+Interfaces

Halawani, H. T., Mashraqi, A. M., Badr, S. K., & Alkhalaf, S. (2023). Automated sentiment analysis in social media using Harris Hawks optimisation and deep learning techniques. *Alexandria Engineering Journal, 80*, 433–443. doi:10.1016/j.aej.2023.08.062

Halkiopoulos, C., Dimou, E., Kompothrekas, A., Telonis, G., & Boutsinas, B. (2021). The E-Tour Facilitator Platform Supporting an Innovative Health Tourism Marketing Strategy. In V. Katsoni & C. van Zyl (Eds.), *Culture and Tourism in a Smart, Globalized, and Sustainable World* (pp. 609–623). Springer International Publishing. doi:10.1007/978-3-030-72469-6_39

Hallak, J., & Poisson, M. (2007). *Corrupt Schools, Corrupt Universities: What can be done?* International Institute for Education Planning.

Han, J., Pei, J., & Yin, Y. (2000). Mining frequent patterns without candidate generation. *SIGMOD Record, 29*(2), 1–12. doi:10.1145/335191.335372

Hansen, A. S., Telléus, G. K., Mohr-Jensen, C., & Lauritsen, M. B. (2021). Parent-perceived barriers to accessing services for their child's mental health problems. *Child and Adolescent Psychiatry and Mental Health, 15*(1), 1–11. doi:10.1186/s13034-021-00357-7 PMID:33514400

Harper, F. M., & Konstan, J. A. (2016). The MovieLens Datasets: History and Context. *ACM Transactions on Interactive Intelligent Systems, 5*(4), 1–19. doi:10.1145/2827872

Harsh, S. (1987). Decision Support Systems Definition and Overview. In *Proceedings of the American Agricultural Economics Association Extension Workshop*. Oklahoma State University.

Hart, M. L., & Porter, G. (2004). The impact of cognitive and other factors on the perceived usefulness of OLAP. *Journal of Computer Information Systems, 45*(2), 47–56.

Hasanzadeh, M., Delafrooz, N., Gholipoor Soleimani, A., & Shahroodi, K. (2021). Explaining the Model of Customer Value Co-Creation Behavior in the Development of Medical Tourism Industry of Guilan Province. *Urban Tourism, 8*(2), 141–159. doi:10.22059/jut.2021.327185.927

Hassan, N. R. (2019). The origins of business analytics and implications for the information systems field. *Journal of Business Analytics, 2*(2), 1–17. doi:10.1080/2573234X.2019.1693912

Hasson, S. G., Piorkowski, J., & McCulloh, I. (2019). Social media as a main source of customer feedback. *Proceedings of the 2019 IEEE/ACM International Conference on Advances in Social Networks Analysis and Mining*, 829–832. 10.1145/3341161.3345642

Haug, A., & Arlbjorn, J. S. (2011). Barriers to master data quality. *Journal of Enterprise Information Management, 24*(3), 288-303. doi:10.1108/17410391111122862

Haugh, A., Arlbjorn, J. S., & Pedersen, A. (2009). A classification model of ERP system data quality. *Industrial Management & Data Systems, 109*(8), 1053–1068. doi:10.1108/02635570910991292

Hazen, B. T., Boone, C. A., Ezell, J. D., & Jones-Farmer, L. A. (2014). Data quality for data science, predictive analytics, and big data in supply chain management: An introduction to the problem and suggestions for research and applications. *International Journal of Production Economics, 154*, 72–80. doi:10.1016/j.ijpe.2014.04.018

Hazen, B. T., Skipper, J. B., Ezell, J. D., & Boone, C. A. (2016). Big Data and predictive analytics for supply chain sustainability: A theory-driven research agenda. *Computers & Industrial Engineering, 101*, 592–598. doi:10.1016/j.cie.2016.06.030

HBR. (2012, October). Getting Control of Big Data. *Harvard Business Review*. Advance online publication. doi:10.1002/wcs.1379

Heathrow Airport. (2023). *Facts and figures*. Retrieved November 23, 2023, from https://www.heathrow.com/company/about-heathrow/facts-and-figures

Helical Insight. (n.d.). *Significance Of Business Intelligence In Social Media*. Retrieved January 8, 2024, from https://www.helicalinsight.com/significance-bi-social-media-2/

Hemsley-Brown, J., & Oplatka, I. (2006). Universities in a competitive global marketplace: A systematic review of the literature on higher education marketing. *International Journal of Public Sector Management, 19*(4), 316–338. doi:10.1108/09513550610669176

Hermawan, A., Kurnia, Y., Destiandi, N., & Kurnaedi, D. (2018). Modeling data mart using ETL (extract, transform, load) web service concept on the feeder with a dashboard. *IACSIT International Journal of Engineering and Technology, 6057-6059*. Advance online publication. doi:10.14419/ijet.v7i4.23127

Hidayat, A. A., Rahman, A., Wangi, R. M., Abidin, R. J., Fuadi, R. S., & Budiawan, W. (2019). Implementation and comparison analysis of apriori and fp-growth algorithm performance to determine market basket analysis in Breiliant shop. *Journal of Physics: Conference Series*, *1402*(7), 077031. doi:10.1088/1742-6596/1402/7/077031

Hmoud, H., Al-Adwan, A. S., Horani, O., Yaseen, H., & Al Zoubi, J. Z. A. (2023). Factors influencing business intelligence adoption by higher education institutions. *Journal of Open Innovation*, *9*(3), 9. doi:10.1016/j.joitmc.2023.100111

Holcombe, M. (2008). *Running an Agile Software Development Project*. Wiley. doi:10.1002/9780470385883

Hong, W. C. H. (2023). The impact of ChatGPT on foreign language teaching and learning: Opportunities in education and research. *Journal of Educational Technology and Innovation*, *5*(1).

Höpken, W., Fuchs, M., Keil, D., & Lexhagen, M. (2015). Business intelligence for cross-process knowledge extraction at tourism destinations. *Information Technology & Tourism*, *15*(2), 101–130. doi:10.1007/s40558-015-0023-2

Hoseini, B. L., Ajilian, M., Taghizade, M. H., Khademi, G., & Saeidi, M. (2014). *Attention deficit hyperactivity disorder (ADHD) in children: A short review and literature*. Academic Press.

Hossain, A., Quaresma, R., & Rahman, H. (2019). Investigating factors influencing the physicians' adoption of electronic health record (EHR) in healthcare system of Bangladesh: An empirical study. *International Journal of Information Management*, *44*, 76–87. doi:10.1016/j.ijinfomgt.2018.09.016

Hossain, M. I., Yusof, A. F., Hussin, A. R. C., lahad, N. A., & Sadiq, A. S. (2021). Factors influencing adoption model of continuous glucose monitoring devices for internet of things healthcare. *Internet of Things : Engineering Cyber Physical Human Systems*, *15*, 100353. doi:10.1016/j.iot.2020.100353

Hossain, M. S. (2017). Cloud-Supported Cyber–Physical Localization Framework for Patients Monitoring. *IEEE Systems Journal*, *11*(1), 118–127. doi:10.1109/JSYST.2015.2470644

Howe, N., Giles, E., Newbury-Birch, D., & McColl, E. (2018). Systematic review of participants' attitudes towards data sharing: A thematic synthesis. *Journal of Health Services Research & Policy*, *23*(2), 123–133. doi:10.1177/1355819617751555 PMID:29653503

Howson, C. (2013). *Successful Business Intelligence, Unlock the Value of BI & Big Data*. McGraw-Hill Education.

Huang, H., Zheng, O., Wang, D., Yin, J., Wang, Z., Ding, S., Yin, H., Xu, C., Yang, R., Zheng, Q., & Shi, B. (2023). ChatGPT for shaping the future of dentistry: The potential of multi-modal large language model. *International Journal of Oral Science*, *15*(1), 29. doi:10.1038/s41368-023-00239-y PMID:37507396

Huang, M.-H., & Rust, R. T. (2021). A strategic framework for artificial intelligence in marketing. *Journal of the Academy of Marketing Science*, *49*(1), 30–50. doi:10.1007/s11747-020-00749-9

Huh, Y. U., Keller, F. R., Redman, T. C., & Watkins, A. R. (1990). Data quality. *Information and Software Technology*, *32*(8), 559–565. doi:10.1016/0950-5849(90)90146-I

Hurbean, L., Militaru, F., Muntean, M., & Danaiata, D. (2023). The Impact of business intelligence and analytics adoption on decision making effectiveness and managerial work performance. *Scientific Annals of Economics and Business*, *70*(SI), 43-54. doi:10.47743/saeb-2023-0012

Husain, F. (2020). Investigating current state-of-the-art applications of supportive technologies for individuals with ADHD. *arXiv preprint arXiv:2005.09993*.

Hussein, D. M. E.-D. M. (2018). A survey on sentiment analysis challenges. *Journal of King Saud University. Engineering Sciences*, *30*(4), 330–338. doi:10.1016/j.jksues.2016.04.002

Hu, Y., Koren, Y., & Volinsky, C. (2008). Collaborative Filtering for Implicit Feedback Datasets. *2008 Eighth IEEE International Conference on Data Mining*, 263–272. 10.1109/ICDM.2008.22

Iansiti, M., & Lakhani, K. R. (2020). *Competing in the age of AI: Strategy and leadership when algorithms and networks run the world.* Harvard Business Press.

IBM. (2023). *IBM Cognos Analytics. Get answers faster with AI. IBM.* Retrieved November 10, 2023, from https://www.ibm.com/products/cognos-analytics

Ibrahim, A. E. A., Elamer, A. A., & Ezat, A. N. (2021). The convergence of big data and accounting: Innovative research opportunities. *Technological Forecasting and Social Change*, *173*, C7–C121171. doi:10.1016/j.techfore.2021.121171

Idoga, P. E., Toycan, M., Nadiri, H., & Çelebi, E. (2019). Assessing factors militating against the acceptance and successful implementation of a cloud based health center from the healthcare professionals' perspective: A survey of hospitals in Benue state, northcentral Nigeria. *BMC Medical Informatics and Decision Making*, *19*(1), 34. doi:10.1186/s12911-019-0751-x PMID:30782166

Ihaka, R., & Gentleman, R. (1996). R: a language for data analysis and graphics. *Journal of Computational and Graphical Statistics*, *5*(3), 299–314.

Imminent, A., Pacemen, P., & Alaska, E. (2015, October 16). Evaluating the quality of social media data in big data architecture. *IEEE Access : Practical Innovations, Open Solutions*, *3*, 2028–2043. doi:10.1109/ACCESS.2015.2490723

Ipinnaiye, O., Dineen, D., & Lenihan, H. (2017). Drivers of SME performance: A holistic and multivariate approach. *Small Business Economics*, *48*(4), 883–911. doi:10.1007/s11187-016-9819-5

Isık, Ö., Jones, M. C., & Sidorova, A. (2013). Business intelligence success: The roles of BI capabilities and decision environments. *Information & Management*, *50*(1), 13–23. doi:10.1016/j.im.2012.12.001

Iwanaga, T., Wang, H. H., Hamilton, S. H., Grimm, V., Koralewski, T. E., Salado, A., Elsawah, S., Razavi, S., Yang, J., Glynn, P., Badham, J., Voinov, A., Chen, M., Grant, W. E., Peterson, T. R., Frank, K., Shenk, G., Barton, C. M., Jakeman, A. J., & Little, J. C. (2021). Socio-technical scales in socio-environmental modeling: Managing a system-of-systems modeling approach. *Environmental Modelling & Software*, *135*, 104885. doi:10.1016/j.envsoft.2020.104885 PMID:33041631

Jacob, C., Bourke, S., & Heuss, S. (2022). From Testers to Cocreators—the Value of and Approaches to Successful Patient Engagement in the Development of eHealth Solutions: Qualitative Expert Interview Study. *JMIR Human Factors*, *9*(4), e41481. doi:10.2196/41481 PMID:36102548

Jagadeeswari, V., Subramaniyaswamy, V., Logesh, R., & Vijayakumar, V. (2018). A study on medical Internet of Things and Big Data in personalized healthcare system. *Health Information Science and Systems*, *6*(1), 14. doi:10.1007/s13755-018-0049-x PMID:30279984

Jain, A., Shah, D., & Churi, P. (2020). A Review on Business Intelligence Systems Using Artificial Intelligence. In S. Smys, J. Tavares, V. Balas, & A. Iliyasu (Eds.), *Computational Vision and Bio-Inspired Computing. ICCVBIC 2019. Advances in Intelligent Systems and Computing* (Vol. 1108). Springer. doi:10.1007/978-3-030-37218-7_107

Jain, D. S. (2018). Human resource management and artificial intelligence. *International Journal of Management and Social Sciences Research*, *7*(3), 56–59.

Jain, R., Jain, S., & Montano, C. B. (2017). Addressing diagnosis and treatment gaps in adults with attention-deficit/hyperactivity disorder. *The Primary Care Companion for CNS Disorders*, *19*(5), 24623. doi:10.4088/PCC.17nr02153 PMID:28906602

Jain, R., Kumar, A., Nayyar, A., Dewan, K., Garg, R., Raman, S., & Ganguly, S. (2023). Explaining sentiment analysis results on social media texts through visualization. *Multimedia Tools and Applications*, *82*(15), 22613–22629. doi:10.1007/s11042-023-14432-y PMID:36747895

Jaiswal, D., Chatterjee, D., Sarkar, A. S. M., Ramakrishnan, R. K., Pal, A., & Ghosh, R. (2023). Assessment of Mental Workloads Using Differential Dermal Potentials Recorded from in and around Ear. *Proceedings of the 8th Workshop on Body-Centric Computing Systems*, 1–6. 10.1145/3597061.3597257

Jalil, S., Rafi, S., LaToza, T. D., Moran, K., & Lam, W. (2023, April). Chatgpt and software testing education: Promises & perils. In *2023 IEEE International Conference on Software Testing, Verification and Validation Workshops (ICSTW)* (pp. 4130-4137). IEEE. 10.1109/ICSTW58534.2023.00078

Jallouli, R., Tobji, M. A. B., Piho, G., & McHeick, H. (2022). Guest Editorial. *Journal of Telecommunications and the Digital Economy*, *10*(2), 1–5. doi:10.18080/jtde.v10n2.590

James, G., Daniela, W., Trevor, H., & Robert, T. (2021). *Unsupervised learning*. Academic Press.

Janssen, M., Brous, P., Estevez, E., Barbosa, L. S., & Janowski, T. (2020). Data governance: Organizing data for trustworthy Artificial Intelligence. *Government Information Quarterly*, *37*(3), 101493. doi:10.1016/j.giq.2020.101493

Jarek, K., & Mazurek, G. (2019). Marketing and Artificial Intelligence. *Central European Business Review, 8*(2).

Jayender, P., & Kundu, G. K. (2021). *Intelligent ERP for SCM agility and graph theory technique for adaptation in automotive industry in India*. International Journal of Systems Assurance Engineering and Management. doi:10.1007/s13198-021-01361-y

Jeffery, C. (2021, June 26). *7 Types of Hybrid Recommendation System*. Analytics Vidhya. https://medium.com/analytics-vidhya/7-types-of-hybrid-recommendation-system-3e4f78266ad8

Jemima Jebaseeli, T., Anand Deva Durai, C., & Dinesh Peter, J. (2020). IOT based sustainable diabetic retinopathy diagnosis system. *Sustainable Computing : Informatics and Systems*, *28*, 100272. doi:10.1016/j.suscom.2018.08.004

Jha, M., Jha, S., & O'Brien, L. (2016). Big data and its impact on enterprise architecture. In The Human Element of Big Data: Issues, Analytics, and Performance (pp. 107-124). CRC Press. doi:10.1201/9781315368061

Ji, S., Li, Q., Cao, W., Zhang, P. & Muccini, H. (2020). Quality Assurance Technologies of Big Data Applications: A Systematic Literature Review. *Applied Sciences, 10*(8052), 1-31. doi:10.3390/app10228052

Jiang, L., Cheng, Y., Yang, L., Li, J., Yan, H., & Wang, X. (2019). A trust-based collaborative filtering algorithm for E-commerce recommendation system. *Journal of Ambient Intelligence and Humanized Computing*, *10*(8), 3023–3034. doi:10.1007/s12652-018-0928-7

John, S. A., & Keikhosrokiani, P. (2022). COVID-19 fake news analytics from social media using topic modeling and clustering. In Big Data Analytics for Healthcare: Datasets, Techniques, Life Cycles, Management, and Applications. doi:10.1016/B978-0-323-91907-4.00003-0

Jones-Farmer, L. A., Ezell, J. D., & Hazen, B. T. (2013). Applying control chart methods to enhance data quality. *Technometrics*. Advance online publication. doi:10.1080/00401706.2013.804437

Josiah, J. U., & Ekpo, N. S. (2019). Effect of Customer Relationship Management (CRM) on the Performance of SMEs on Hospitality Industry in Cross River State. *International Journal of Marketing and Communication Studies*, *4*(2).

Jun, T., Kai, C., Yu, F., & Gang, T. (2009, May). The research & application of ETL tool in business intelligence project. In *2009 International Forum on Information Technology and Applications* (Vol. 2, pp. 620-623). IEEE. 10.1109/IFITA.2009.48

Kahan, B. K., Strong, D. M., & Wang, R. Y. (2002). Information quality benchmarks: Product and service performance. *Communications of the ACM, 45*(4), 184–192. doi:10.1145/505248.506007

Kamel, S. (2020). The impact of business schools in transforming the society case: AUC School of Business. *Journal of Economic and Administrative Sciences, 36*(1), 38–63. doi:10.1108/JEAS-10-2018-0110

Kamunge, M. S., Njeru, A., & Tirimba, O. I. (2014). Factors Affecting the Performance of Small and Micro Enterprises in Limuru Town Market of Kiambu County. Kenya. International Journal of Scientific and Research Publications, 4(12).

Kang, D., & Park, Y. (2014). Review-based measurement of customer satisfaction in mobile service: Sentiment analysis and VIKOR approach. *Expert Systems with Applications, 41*(4), 1041–1050. doi:10.1016/j.eswa.2013.07.101

Kaplan, R. S., & Norton, D. P. (1993). Putting the Balanced Scorecard to Work. *Harvard Business Review*, (September-October), 4–17. doi:10.1016/B978-0-7506-7009-8.50023-9

Kasim, T., Zijad, D., Mahir, H., & Merima, H. (2018). The use of business intelligence (BI) in small and medium-sized enterprises (SMEs) in Bosnia and Herzegovina, Economic Review. *Journal of Economics and Business, University of Tuzla. Faculty of Economics, 16*(2), 23–37.

Kasneci, E., Seßler, K., Küchemann, S., Bannert, M., Dementieva, D., Fischer, F., Gasser, U., Groh, G., Günnemann, S., Hüllermeier, E., Krusche, S., Kutyniok, G., Michaeli, T., Nerdel, C., Pfeffer, J., Poquet, O., Sailer, M., Schmidt, A., Seidel, T., ... Kasneci, G. (2023). ChatGPT for good? On opportunities and challenges of large language models for education. *Learning and Individual Differences, 103*, 102274. doi:10.1016/j.lindif.2023.102274

Kauffman, R. JSrivastava, JVayghan, J. (2012). Business and data analytics: new innovations for the management of E-commerce. Electronic Commerce Research and Applications, 11(2), 85–88. https://doi.org/10.1016/j.elerap.2012.01.001

Kaufmann, J., & Chamoni, P. (2014, January). Structuring collaborative business intelligence: A literature review. In *2014 47th Hawaii International Conference on System Sciences* (pp. 3738-3747). IEEE. 10.1109/HICSS.2014.465

Kaushik, P. (2022). Role and Application of Artificial Intelligence in Business Analytics: A Critical Evaluation. *International Journal for Global Academic & Scientific Research, 1*(3), 1-11. doi:10.55938/ijgasr.v1i3.15

Kavu, T. D., Mastara, P., Phiri, L., & Jari, B. (2014). A Cloud Mining Model for SMEs in E-commerce in Zimbabwe. *International Journal of Scientific and Engineering Research, 5*(4).

Kazeli, H. (2014). Cloud Business Intelligence. *Lecture Notes in Business Information Processing, 183*, 307–317. doi:10.1007/978-3-319-11460-6_26

Kazemi, A., Kazemi, Z., Heshmat, H., Nazarian-Jashnabadi, J., & Tomášková, H. (2024). Ranking factors affecting sustainable competitive advantage from the business intelligence perspective: Using content analysis and F-TOPSIS. *Journal of Soft Computing and Decision Analytics, 2*(1), 39–53. doi:10.31181/jscda21202430

Keikhosrokiani, P. (2022). Handbook of Research on Consumer Behavior Change and Data Analytics in the Socio-Digital Era. doi:10.4018/978-1-6684-4168-8

Keikhosrokiani, P. (2022a). Big Data Analytics for Healthcare: Datasets, Techniques, Life Cycles, Management, and Applications. doi:10.1016/C2021-0-00369-2

Keikhosrokiani, P., & Asl, M. P. (2022a). Handbook of Research on Artificial Intelligence Applications in Literary Works and Social Media. doi:10.4018/978-1-6684-6242-3

Keikhosrokiani, P., & Asl, M. P. (2022b). Introduction to artificial intelligence for the analytics of literary works and social media: A review. In Handbook of Research on Artificial Intelligence Applications in Literary Works and Social Media. doi:10.4018/978-1-6684-6242-3.ch001

Keikhosrokiani, P., & Asl, M. P. (2022b). Preface. In Handbook of Research on Artificial Intelligence Applications in Literary Works and Social Media. Academic Press.

Keikhosrokiani, P., & Kamaruddin, N. S. A. B. (2022). IoT-Based In-Hospital-In-Home Heart Disease Remote Monitoring System with Machine Learning Features for Decision Making. In Studies in Computational Intelligence (Vol. 1021). doi:10.1007/978-3-030-97929-4_16

Keikhosrokiani, P., Asl, M. P., Chu, K. E., & Anuar, N. A. N. (2022). Artificial intelligence framework for opinion mining of netizen readers' reviews of Arundhati Roy's The God of Small Things. In Handbook of Research on Artificial Intelligence Applications in Literary Works and Social Media. doi:10.4018/978-1-6684-6242-3.ch004

Keikhosrokiani, P. (2019). Perspectives in the development of mobile medical information systems: Life cycle, management, methodological approach and application. In *Perspectives in the Development of Mobile Medical Information Systems*. Life Cycle, Management, Methodological Approach and Application. doi:10.1016/C2018-0-02485-8

Keikhosrokiani, P. (2020). The Role of m-Commerce Literacy on the Attitude towards Using e-Torch in Penang, Malaysia. In *E-Business in the 21st Century* (Vol. 7, pp. 309–333). World Scientific. doi:10.1142/9789811231841_0013

Keikhosrokiani, P. (2020a). Behavioral intention to use of Mobile Medical Information System (mMIS). In P. Keikhosrokiani (Ed.), *Perspectives in the Development of Mobile Medical Information Systems* (pp. 57–73). Academic Press. doi:10.1016/B978-0-12-817657-3.00004-3

Keikhosrokiani, P. (2020b). Emotional-persuasive and habit-change assessment of mobile medical information Systems (mMIS). In P. Keikhosrokiani (Ed.), *Perspectives in the Development of Mobile Medical Information Systems* (pp. 101–109). Academic Press. doi:10.1016/B978-0-12-817657-3.00006-7

Keikhosrokiani, P. (2021a). IoT for Enhanced Decision-Making in Medical Information Systems: A Systematic Review. In G. Marques, A. Kumar Bhoi, I. de la Torre Díez, & B. Garcia-Zapirain (Eds.), *Enhanced Telemedicine and e-Health: Advanced IoT Enabled Soft Computing Framework* (pp. 119–140). Springer International Publishing. doi:10.1007/978-3-030-70111-6_6

Keikhosrokiani, P. (2021b). Predicating Smartphone Users' Behaviour Towards a Location-Aware IoMT-Based Information System: An Empirical Study. *International Journal of E-Adoption, 13*(2), 52–77. doi:10.4018/IJEA.2021070104

Keikhosrokiani, P. (2023). *Handbook of Research on Consumer Behavioral Analytics in Metaverse and the Adoption of a Virtual World.* IGI Global., doi:10.4018/978-1-6684-7029-9

Keikhosrokiani, P., & Asl, M. P. (2022c). *Handbook of research on opinion mining and text analytics on literary works and social media.* IGI Global. doi:10.4018/978-1-7998-9594-7

Keikhosrokiani, P., & Fye, G. M. (2023). A hybrid recommender system for health supplement e-commerce based on customer data implicit ratings. *Multimedia Tools and Applications.* Advance online publication. doi:10.1007/s11042-023-17321-6

Keikhosrokiani, P., Mustaffa, N., & Zakaria, N. (2018). Success factors in developing iHeart as a patient-centric healthcare system: A multi-group analysis. *Telematics and Informatics*, *35*(4), 753–775. Advance online publication. doi:10.1016/j.tele.2017.11.006

Keikhosrokiani, P., Mustaffa, N., Zakaria, N., & Abdullah, R. (2020). Assessment of a medical information system: The mediating role of use and user satisfaction on the success of human interaction with the mobile healthcare system (iHeart). *Cognition Technology and Work*, *22*(2), 281–305. Advance online publication. doi:10.1007/s10111-019-00565-4

Keikhosrokiani, P., Mustaffa, N., Zakaria, N., & Sarwar, M. I. (2012). A proposal to design a location-based mobile cardiac emergency system (lmces). In *Global Telehealth 2012* (pp. 83–92). IOS Press. doi:10.3233/978-1-61499-152-6-83

Keikhosrokiani, P., Mustaffa, N., Zakaria, N., & Sarwar, M. I. (2012). A proposal to design a Location-based Mobile Cardiac Emergency System (LMCES). *Studies in Health Technology and Informatics*, *182*, 83–92. PMID:23138083

Keikhosrokiani, P., Zakaria, N., Mustaffa, N., Wan, T.-C., Sarwar, M. I., & Azimi, K. (2015). *Wireless Networks in Mobile Healthcare*. doi:10.1007/978-3-319-12817-7_30

Keller, A., Rimestad, M. L., Friis Rohde, J., Holm Petersen, B., Bruun Korfitsen, C., Tarp, S., Briciet Lauritsen, M., & Händel, M. N. (2021). The effect of a combined gluten-and casein-free diet on children and adolescents with autism spectrum disorders: A systematic review and meta-analysis. *Nutrients*, *13*(2), 470. doi:10.3390/nu13020470 PMID:33573238

Khalid, R., Landini, S., Valasai, G. D., Khalid, F., & Sandwell, P. (2023). Towards equitable and inclusive energy systems for remote off-grid communities: A socio-technical assessment of solar power for village Helario in Tharparkar, Pakistan. *Renewable and Sustainable Energy Transition*, *4*, 100067. doi:10.1016/j.rset.2023.100067

Khan, W. A., Chung, S. H., Awan, M. U., & Wen, X. (2020a). Machine learning facilitated business intelligence (Part I): Neural networks learning algorithms and applications. *Industrial Management & Data Systems*, *120*(1), 164–195. doi:10.1108/IMDS-07-2019-0361

Khan, W. A., Chung, S. H., Awan, M. U., & Wen, X. (2020b). Machine learning facilitated business intelligence (Part II): Neural networks optimization techniques and applications. *Industrial Management & Data Systems*, *120*(1), 128–163. doi:10.1108/IMDS-06-2019-0351

Khor, H. G., Cho, I., Lee, K. R. C. K., & Chieng, L. L. (2020). Waste production from phacoemulsification surgery. *Journal of Cataract and Refractive Surgery*, *46*(2), 215–221. doi:10.1097/j.jcrs.0000000000000009 PMID:32126034

Kikawa, C. R., Kalema, B. M., & Carol, M. N. (2019). A statistical analysis of business intelligence acceptance by SMEs in the city of Tshwane, Republic of South Africa. *Academy of Entrepreneurship Journal*, *25*(2).

Kim, R. Y. (2021). Using Online Reviews for Customer Sentiment Analysis. *IEEE Engineering Management Review*, *49*(4), 162–168. doi:10.1109/EMR.2021.3103835

Kirange, S. (2016). Role of business intelligence in decision-making for SMEs. KHOJ. *Journal of Indian Management Research and Practices*, (Special Issue), 41–47.

Kitchenham, B., & Charters, S. (2007). *Guidelines for performing Systematic Literature Reviews in Software Engineering*. Academic Press.

Kitsios, F., & Kamariotou, M. (2018). Decision support systems and strategic planning: Information technology and SMEs' performance. *Int. J. Decision Support Systems*, *3*(1/2), 53. doi:10.1504/IJDSS.2018.094260

Kng, C. K., Keikhosrokiani, P., & Asl, M. P. (2022). Artificial intelligence and human rights activism: A case study of Boochani's No Friend But the Mountains and his tweets on justice and equality. Handbook of Research on Artificial Intelligence Applications in Literary Works and Social Media. doi:10.4018/978-1-6684-6242-3.ch006

Kooner, S., Hewison, C., Sridharan, S., Lui, J., Matthewson, G., Johal, H., & Clark, M. (2020). Waste and recycling among orthopedic subspecialties. *Canadian Journal of Surgery*, *63*(3), E278–E283. doi:10.1503/cjs.018018 PMID:32437094

Korte, D., Ariyachandra, T., & Frolick, M. (2013). Business intelligence in the hospitality industry. *International Journal of Innovation, Management and Technology*, *4*(4), 429–434.

Kozłowski, M., & Korzeniewski, J. (2024). Studying the effectiveness of investments in hotel services using customer sentiment analysis. *Quality & Quantity*. Advance online publication. doi:10.1007/s11135-023-01808-3

Kronberga, K., Kirikova, M., & Kiopa, D. (2017). Navigating in the land of data analytics. *Lecture Notes in Business Information Processing*, *295*, 125–132. doi:10.1007/978-3-319-64930-6_9

Kučera, T., & Suk, A. (2019). The application of ABC analysis in the logistic warehousing processes. *Transport Means: Proceedings of the International Scientific Conference*.

Kumar, P., Chauhan, R., Goyal, R., Bhati, N., Garg, S., & Mala, S. (2022). Skin cancer prediction using big data analytics and AI techniques. In *Big Data Analytics for Healthcare* (pp. 201–218). Elsevier. doi:10.1016/B978-0-323-91907-4.00011-X

Kumar, S., Yadava, M., & Roy, P. P. (2019). Fusion of EEG response and sentiment analysis of products review to predict customer satisfaction. *Information Fusion*, *52*, 41–52. doi:10.1016/j.inffus.2018.11.001

Kumar, U. D. (2020). Analytics education. *IIMB Management Review*, *32*(1), 108–117. doi:10.1016/j.iimb.2019.10.014

Kune, R., Konugurthi, P. K., Agarwal, A., Chillarige, R. R., & Buyya, R. (2016). The anatomy of big data computing. *Software, Practice & Experience*, *46*(1), 79–105. doi:10.1002/spe.2374

Labde, S., Bhanushali, N., Thaker, R., & Singh, R. (2022). A Project on Statistical Analysis, ETL Automation, and Intelligence Reporting. *2022 2nd International Conference on Intelligent Technologies, CONIT 2022*.

Lada, S., Chekima, B., Karim, M. R. A., Fabeil, N. F., Ayub, M. S., Amirul, S. M., Ansar, R., Bouteraa, M., Fook, L. M., & Zaki, H. O. (2023). Determining Factors Related to Artificial Intelligence (AI) Adoption Among Malaysia's Small and Medium-Sized Businesses. *Journal of Open Innovation*, *9*(4), 100144. doi:10.1016/j.joitmc.2023.100144

Lafferty, C., & ... (2019). Sustainable Industry 4.0: Product decision-making information systems, data-driven innovation, and smart industrial value creation. *Journal of Self-Governance and Management Economics*, *7*(2), 19–24.

Lamarque, M., Moro Gutiérrez, L., Lamarque, M., & Moro Gutiérrez, L. (2020). Therapeutic Itineraries and Processes of Illness Care in Latin American Migrants: Conflicts, Negotiations, and Adaptations. *Migraciones Internacionales*, *11*. Advance online publication. doi:10.33679/rmi.v1i1.1796

LaMorte, W. W. (2019a). *Diffusion of Innovation*. Retrieved from https://sphweb.bumc.bu.edu/otlt/mph-modules/sb/behavioralchangetheories/behavioralchangetheories4.html

LaMorte, W. W. (2019b). *The Health Belief Model*. Retrieved from https://sphweb.bumc.bu.edu/otlt/mph-modules/sb/behavioralchangetheories/behavioralchangetheories2.html

Lateef, M., & Keikhosrokiani, P. (2022). Predicting Critical Success Factors of Business Intelligence Implementation for Improving SMEs' Performances: A Case Study of Lagos State, Nigeria. *Journal of the Knowledge Economy*. Advance online publication. doi:10.1007/s13132-022-00961-8

Latif, S. T. M. (2020). *Study of the effect of choice of organizational culture on artificial intelligence (AI) resources adoption*. NTNU.

Lattanzio, S., Stefanizzi, P., D'ambrosio, M., Cuscianna, E., Riformato, G., Migliore, G., Tafuri, S., & Bianchi, F. P. (2022). Waste Management and the Perspective of a Green Hospital: A Systematic Narrative Review. *International Journal of Environmental Research and Public Health, 19*(23), 15812. doi:10.3390/ijerph192315812 PMID:36497884

Laudon, K. C., & Laudon, J. P. (2014). *Management Information Systems, Managing the Digital Firm* (13th ed.). Pearson Education Limited.

Lavrač, N., Bohanec, M., Pur, A., Cestnik, B., Debeljak, M., & Kobler, A. (2007). Data mining and visualization for decision support and modeling of public healthcare resources. *Journal of Biomedical Informatics, 40*(4), 438–447. doi:10.1016/j.jbi.2006.10.003 PMID:17157076

Lee, C. K. H., Tse, Y. K., Ho, G. T. S., & Chung, S. H. (2021). Uncovering insights from healthcare archives to improve operations: An association analysis for cervical cancer screening. *Technological Forecasting and Social Change, 162*, 120375. doi:10.1016/j.techfore.2020.120375

Lee, H. (2023). The rise of ChatGPT: Exploring its potential in medical education. *Anatomical Sciences Education*, ase.2270. doi:10.1002/ase.2270 PMID:36916887

Lee, S. M., & Lee, D. (2020). Healthcare wearable devices: An analysis of key factors for continuous use intention. *Service Business, 14*(4), 503–531. doi:10.1007/s11628-020-00428-3

Lee, S. M., & Lee, D. (2020). Untact: A new customer service strategy in the digital age. *Service Business, 14*(1), 1–22. doi:10.1007/s11628-019-00408-2

Lee, Y. W., Pipino, L., Strong, D. M., & Wang, R. Y. (2004). Process-embedded data integrity. *Journal of Database Management, 15*(1), 87–103. doi:10.4018/jdm.2004010104

Leffa, D. T., Grevet, E. H., Bau, C. H. D., Schneider, M., Ferrazza, C. P., da Silva, R. F., Miranda, M. S., Picon, F., Teche, S. P., Sanches, P., Pereira, D., Rubia, K., Brunoni, A. R., Camprodon, J. A., Caumo, W., & Rohde, L. A. (2022). Transcranial direct current stimulation vs sham for the treatment of inattention in adults with attention-deficit/hyperactivity disorder: The TUNED randomized clinical trial. *JAMA Psychiatry, 79*(9), 847–856. doi:10.1001/jamapsychiatry.2022.2055 PMID:35921102

Lever, M., Smetana, N., Bechrakis, N. E., & Foerster, A. (2023). Survey and reduction of waste production from eye surgery. *Die Ophthalmologie, 120*(9), 932–939. Advance online publication. doi:10.1007/s00347-023-01840-6 PMID:37052707

Liebowitz, J. (2020). *Strategic intelligence: business intelligence, competitive intelligence, and knowledge management.* CRC Press.

Lim, S. L., Quercia, D., & Finkelstein, A. (2010). StakeNet: Using Social Networks to Analyse the Stakeholders of Large-Scale Software Projects. In *Proceedings of the IEEE 32nd International Conference on Software Engineering.* 10.1145/1806799.1806844

Lim, W. L., Sourina, O., & Wang, L. P. (2018). STEW: Simultaneous Task EEG Workload Data Set. *IEEE Transactions on Neural Systems and Rehabilitation Engineering, 26*(11), 2106–2114. doi:10.1109/TNSRE.2018.2872924 PMID:30281467

Linden, G., Smith, B., & York, J. (2003). Amazon. com recommendations: Item-to-item collaborative filtering. *IEEE Internet Computing, 7*(1), 76–80. doi:10.1109/MIC.2003.1167344

Li, S., Xie, Z., Chiu, D. K. W., & Ho, K. K. W. (2023). Sentiment Analysis and Topic Modeling Regarding Online Classes on the Reddit Platform: Educators versus Learners. *Applied Sciences (Basel, Switzerland), 13*(4), 2250. doi:10.3390/app13042250

Liu, Y., Han, T., Ma, S., Zhang, J., Yang, Y., Tian, J., ... Ge, B. (2023). Summary of ChatGPT-related research and perspective towards the future of large language models. *Meta-Radiology*, 100017.

Liu, J. C., & Wu, Y. (2014). Application of ABC Analysis in Inventory Management. *Advanced Materials Research, 1030–1032*, 2515–2518. . doi:10.4028/www.scientific.net/AMR.1030-1032.2515 PMID:31267820

Lopez-Garrido, G. (2020). *Self-Efficacy Theory*. Academic Press.

Low, H. Q., Keikhosrokiani, P., & Asl, M. P. (2024). Decoding violence against women: Analysing harassment in middle eastern literature with machine learning and sentiment analysis. *Humanities & Social Sciences Communications.*

Luen, W. K., & Hooi, C. M. (2016). In search of Malaysian companies with successful implementation of business intelligence initiatives. *Proceedings of the International Conference on Industrial Engineering and Operations Management.*

Lu, J. (2020). Data analytics research-informed teaching in a digital technologies' curriculum. *Transactions on Education, 20*(2), 57–72. doi:10.1287/ited.2019.0215

Lunt, N., Smith, R. D., Mannion, R., Green, S. T., Exworthy, M., Hanefeld, J., Horsfall, D., Machin, L., & King, H. (2014). *Implications for the NHS of inward and outward medical tourism: A policy and economic analysis using literature review and mixed-methods approaches*. NIHR Journals Library. https://www.ncbi.nlm.nih.gov/books/NBK263160/

Lu, X., Wijayaratna, K., Huang, Y., & Qiu, A. (2022). AI-enabled opportunities and transformation challenges for SMEs in the post-pandemic era: A review and research agenda. *Frontiers in Public Health, 10*, 885067. doi:10.3389/fpubh.2022.885067 PMID:35570947

Lyu, Q., Tan, J., Zapadka, M. E., Ponnatapura, J., Niu, C., Myers, K. J., Wang, G., & Whitlow, C. T. (2023). Translating radiology reports into plain language using ChatGPT and GPT-4 with prompt learning: Results, limitations, and potential. *Visual Computing for Industry, Biomedicine, and Art, 6*(1), 9. doi:10.1186/s42492-023-00136-5 PMID:37198498

Macdonald, E. M., Perrin, B. M., Hyett, N., & Kingsley, M. I. C. (2019). Factors influencing behavioural intention to use a smart shoe insole in regionally based adults with diabetes: A mixed methods study. *Journal of Foot and Ankle Research, 12*(1), 29. doi:10.1186/s13047-019-0340-3 PMID:31139261

Mach, M. A., & Abdel-Badeeh, M. S. (2010, November). Intelligent techniques for business intelligence in healthcare. In *2010 10th International Conference on Intelligent Systems Design and Applications* (pp. 545-550). IEEE. 10.1109/ISDA.2010.5687209

Machado, G. V., Cunha, Í., Pereira, A. C., & Oliveira, L. B. (2019). DOD-ETL: Distributed on-demand ETL for near real-time business intelligence. *Journal of Internet Services and Applications, 10*(1), 1–15. doi:10.1186/s13174-019-0121-z

Machkour, B., & Abriane, A. (2020). Industry 4.0 and its Implications for the Financial Sector. *Procedia Computer Science, 177*, 496–502. doi:10.1016/j.procs.2020.10.068

Madhani, P. M. (2020). Building a customer-focused strategy: Conceptual frameworks and research Propositions. *SSRN, 17*(3), 5–25. doi:10.2139/ssrn.3717410

Madugula, S., Pratapagiri, S., Phridviraj, M. S. B., Rao, V. C. S., Polala, N., & Kumaraswamy, P. (2023). Big data for the comprehensive data analysis of IT organizations. *Journal of High Technology Management Research, 34*(2 C7 - 100465). doi:10.1016/j.hitech.2023.100465

Magona,T ., Khumalo, S & du Plessis, T. (2021). Affordability of business intelligence tools suitable for SMEs decision making. *South African Journal of Information Management.*

Mamun, M., & Andaleeb, S. (2013). Prospects and Problems of Medical Tourism in Bangladesh. *International Journal of Health Services : Planning, Administration, Evaluation, 43*(1), 123–141. doi:10.2190/HS.43.1.i PMID:23527458

Manatos, M. J., Rosa, M. J., & Sarrico, C. S. (2018). Quality management in universities: Towards an integrated approach? *International Journal of Quality & Reliability Management, 35*(1), 126–144. doi:10.1108/IJQRM-04-2016-0046

Manis, K. (2023*). Empower Power BI users with Microsoft Fabric and Copilot. Microsoft Power BI Platform.* Retrieved November 22, 2023, from https://powerbi.microsoft.com/en-us/blog/empower-power-bi-users-with-microsoft-fabric-and-copilot/

Mansalis, B. (2023*). Real-world stories with Power BI: INTEGRIS Health, Embeds Power BI reports in Healthcare EMR to Provide Life Saving Data. Microsoft* [Video]. Retrieved October 20, 2023, from https://community.fabric.microsoft.com/t5/2021-MSBizAppsSummit-Gallery/Real-world-stories-with-Power-BI-INTEGRIS-Health-Embeds-Power-BI/td-p/1835298

Mao, K., Capra, L., Harman, M., & Jia, Y. (2011). A survey of the use of crowdsourcing in software engineering. *Journal of Systems and Software, 126*, 57–84. doi:10.1016/j.jss.2016.09.015

March, S. T., & Hevner, A. R. (2007). Integrated decision support systems: A data warehousing perspective. *Decision Support Systems, 43*(3), 1031–1043. doi:10.1016/j.dss.2005.05.029

Marín-Ortega, P. M., Dmitriyev, V., Abilov, M., & Gómez, J. M. (2014). ELTA: New approach in designing business intelligence solutions in era of big data. *Procedia Technology, 16*, 667–674. doi:10.1016/j.protcy.2014.10.015

Marjanovic, O. (2007, January). The next stage of operational business intelligence: Creating new challenges for business process management. In *2007 40th Annual Hawaii International Conference on System Sciences (HICSS'07)* (pp. 215c-215c). IEEE.

Martin, J. C., Bustamante-Sánchez, N. S., & Indelicato, A. (2022). Analyzing the Main Determinants for Being an Immigrant in Cuenca (Ecuador) Based on a Fuzzy Clustering Approach. *Axioms, 11*(2), 2. Advance online publication. doi:10.3390/axioms11020074

Masih, E. A. (2022). Feasibility of using QR code for registration & evaluation of training and its ability to increase response rate–The learners' perception. *Nurse Education Today, 111*, 105305. doi:10.1016/j.nedt.2022.105305 PMID:35220149

Mathrani, S. (2022). Enhancing production agility using enterprise systems. *Knowledge Management Research & Practice, 20*(1), 91–103.

McAfee, A., & Brynjolfsson, E. (2013). Big data: The management revolution. *Harvard Business Review, 90*(10), 61–68. doi:10.1111/npqu.11362 PMID:23074865

McGain, F., Muret, J., Lawson, C., & Sherman, J. D. (2020). Environmental sustainability in anaesthesia and critical care. *British Journal of Anaesthesia, 125*(5), 680–692. doi:10.1016/j.bja.2020.06.055 PMID:32798068

McGain, F., Story, D., Lim, T., & McAlister, S. (2017). Financial and environmental costs of reusable and single-use anaesthetic equipment. *British Journal of Anaesthesia, 118*(6), 862–869. doi:10.1093/bja/aex098 PMID:28505289

McKendrick, D., Snedden, L. J., Bunch, R., & McGregor, H. (2017). Pragmatic recycling of paper and cardboard in the operating theatre: An audit. *Journal of Perioperative Practice, 27*(3), 43–49. doi:10.1177/175045891702700302 PMID:29328742

Medhat, W., Hassan, A., & Korashy, H. (2014). Sentiment analysis algorithms and applications: A survey. *Ain Shams Engineering Journal, 5*(4), 1093–1113. doi:10.1016/j.asej.2014.04.011

Medina, C., & Rufín, R. (2015). Transparency policy and students' satisfaction and trust. *Transforming Government: People. Transforming Government, 9*(3), 309–323. doi:10.1108/TG-07-2014-0027

Megahed, F. M., Chen, Y. J., Ferris, J. A., Knoth, S., & Jones-Farmer, L. A. (2023). How generative ai models such as chatgpt can be (mis) used in spc practice, education, and research? an exploratory study. *Quality Engineering*, 1–29.

Mehrotra, P. (2021). Applications of Artificial Intelligence in the Realm of Business Intelligence. In *Research Anthology on Artificial Intelligence Applications in Security* (pp. 358–386). IGI Global. doi:10.4018/978-1-7998-7705-9.ch018

Mei, A. W. S., Hong, P. L., Keikhosrokiani, P., Xin, C. H., Ying, T. X., & Samat, N. (2021). A GIS-based Mobile Application to Improve Tourism Experience: A Case Study of Terengganu, Malaysia. *2021 International Congress of Advanced Technology and Engineering*, 1–10. 10.1109/ICOTEN52080.2021.9493443

Meiklejohn, D. A., & Chavarri, V. M. (2021). Cold technique in adult tonsillectomy reduces waste and cost. *Ear, Nose, and Throat Journal, 100*(5, suppl), 427S–430S. doi:10.1177/0145561319882779 PMID:31631678

Meissner, M., Lichtnegger, S., Gibson, S., & Saunders, R. (2021). Evaluating the Waste Prevention Potential of a Multi-versus Single-Use Surgical Stapler. *Risk Management and Healthcare Policy, 14*, 3911–3921. doi:10.2147/RMHP.S325017 PMID:34566440

Melbourne, U. o. (2022). *Writing an Abstract.* Retrieved from https://services.unimelb.edu.au/__data/assets/pdf_file/0007/471274/Writing_an_Abstract_Update_051112.pdf

Melchert, F., Winter, R., & Klesse, M. (2004). Aligning process automation and business intelligence to support corporate performance management. *Americas Conference on Information Systems. AMCIS*, 507.

Mena, S., & Palazzo, G. (2012). Input and output legitimacy of multi-stakeholder initiatives. *Business Ethics Quarterly, 22*(3), 527–556. doi:10.5840/beq201222333

Methaila, A., Kansal, P., Arya, H., & Kumar, P. (2014). Early heart disease prediction using data mining techniques. *Computer Science & Information Technology Journal, 24*, 53–59. doi:10.5121/csit.2014.4807

Microsoft Customer Stories. (2021). *Hospital network engages caregivers with Power BI analytics through visual storytelling that saves lives.* Retrieved November 22, 2023 from. https://customers.microsoft.com/en-us/story/1431800255709306489-integris-health-power-bi

Microsoft. (2023). *Create a narrative with Copilot for Power BI.* Retrieved November, 22, 2023 from https://learn.microsoft.com/en-us/power-bi/create-reports/copilot-create-narrative?tabs=powerbi-service

Mikalef P, Pappas IO, Krogstie J, & Giannakos M (2017). Big data analytics capabilities: A systematic literature review and research agenda. In Information Systems e-Business Management. https://doi.org/10.1007/s1025 7-017-0362-y

Miller, G. J. (2018, September). Quantitative comparison of big data analytics and business intelligence project success factors. In *Conference on Advanced Information Technologies for Management* (pp. 53-72). Cham: Springer International Publishing.

Miller, M., & Nyauncho, E. (2015). *Effective data mining and analysis for SME banking. Project technical note.* FSD Kenya.

Minh, Q. T., Thai, D. T., Duc, B. T., & Phat, N. H. (2022). Designing a data warehouse framework for business intelligence. *2022 International Conference on Data Analytics for Business and Industry, ICDABI 2022.* 10.1109/ICDABI56818.2022.10041706

Miocevic, D., & Crnjak-Karanovic, B. (2011). Cognitive and Information-Based Capabilities in the Internationalization of Small and Medium-Sized Enterprises: The Case of Croatian Exporters. *Journal of Small Business Management*, *49*(4), 537–557. doi:10.1111/j.1540-627X.2011.00335.x

Miranda, M. D., & Sassi, R. J. (2014). *Using Sentiment Analysis to Assess Customer Satisfaction in an Online Job Search Company*. doi:10.1007/978-3-319-11460-6_2

Mishra, S., & Tripathi, A. R. (2021). AI business model: An integrative business approach. *Journal of Innovation and Entrepreneurship*, *10*(1), 18. doi:10.1186/s13731-021-00157-5

Mishra, V., & Sharma, M. G. (2021). Framework for Promotion of Medical Tourism: A Case of India. *International Journal of Global Business and Competitiveness*, *16*(S1, Suppl 1), 103–111. doi:10.1007/s42943-021-00027-7

Mitchell, R. B., Woolridge, R. W., & Johnson, V. (2021). The role of nontechnical skills in providing value in analytics-based decision culture. *Journal of Education for Business*, *96*(1), 1–9. doi:10.1080/08832323.2020.1719961

Mixson, E. (2021). *Data Science at Netflix: How Advanced Data & Analytics Helps Netflix Generate Billions*. Retrieved January 4, 2024, from https://www.aidataanalytics.network/data-science-ai/articles/data-science-at-netflix-how-advanced-data-analytics-helped-netflix-generate-billions

Mognon, A., Jovicich, J., Bruzzone, L., & Buiatti, M. (2011). ADJUST: An automatic EEG artifact detector based on the joint use of spatial and temporal features. *Psychophysiology*, *48*(2), 229–240. doi:10.1111/j.1469-8986.2010.01061.x PMID:20636297

Mohamed, A., Muhammad Zain, Z., Shaiba, H., Alturki, N., Aldehim, G., Sakri, S., Farik Mat Yatin, S., & Mohamad Zain, J. (2023). LexDeep: Hybrid Lexicon and Deep Learning Sentiment Analysis Using Twitter for Unemployment-Related Discussions During COVID-19. *Computers, Materials & Continua*, *75*(1), 1577–1601. doi:10.32604/cmc.2023.034746

Mohammad, A. B., Al-Okaily, M., & Al-Majali, M. (2022). Business intelligence and analytics (BIA) usage in the banking industry sector: An application of the TOE framework. *Journal of Open Innovation*, *8*(4), 189. doi:10.3390/joitmc8040189

Moody, D. L., & Kortink, M. A. (2000, June). From enterprise models to dimensional models: a methodology for data warehouse and data mart design. In *International Workshop on Design and Management of Data Warehouses (DMDW'2000) DMDW* (p. 5). Academic Press.

Mosavi, N. S., & Santos, M. F. (2022). Implementation considerations for the applied business intelligence in health care. In *Advances in Decision Science and Management: Proceedings of Third International Conference on Decision Science and Management (ICDSM 2021)* (pp. 183-189). Springer Singapore. 10.1007/978-981-16-2502-2_19

Mosquera, M., Andrés-Prado, M. J., Rodríguez-Caravaca, G., Latasa, P., & Mosquera, M. E. (2014). Evaluation of an education and training intervention to reduce health care waste in a tertiary hospital in Spain. *American Journal of Infection Control*, *42*(8), 894–897. doi:10.1016/j.ajic.2014.04.013 PMID:24913763

Mourad, M. (2017). Quality assurance as a driver of information management strategy: Stakeholders' perspectives in higher education. *Journal of Enterprise Information Management*, *30*(5), 779–794. doi:10.1108/JEIM-06-2016-0104

Movies And Entertainment Market Size Report, 2030. (n.d.). Retrieved June 3, 2022, from https://www.grandviewresearch.com/industry-analysis/movies-entertainment-market

Movies And Entertainment Market Worth $169.6 Billion by 2030. (n.d.). Retrieved June 3, 2022, from https://www.grandviewresearch.com/press-release/global-movies-entertainment-market

Mudau, T. N., Cohen, J., & Papageorgiou, E. (2024). Determinants and consequences of routine and advanced use of business intelligence (BI) systems by management accountants. *Information & Management, 61*(1), 103888. doi:10.1016/j.im.2023.103888

Mudzana, T. (2016). *Business intelligence information systems success: A South African study* [Doctor of Philosophy Thesis]. University of Kwazulu-Natal, South Africa.

Mudzana, T., & Maharaj, M. (2015). Measuring the success of business-intelligence systems in South Africa: An empirical investigation applying the DeLone and McLean Model. *South African Journal of Information Management, 17*(1), 1–7. doi:10.4102/sajim.v17i1.646

Mugo, P. (2020). Porter's five forces influence competitive advantage in the telecommunication industry in Kenya. *European Journal of Business and Strategic Management, 5*(2), 30–49. doi:10.47604/ejbsm.1140

Münch, C., Marx, E., Benz, L., Hartmann, E., & Matzner, M. (2022). Capabilities of digital servitization: Evidence from the socio-technical systems theory. *Technological Forecasting and Social Change, 176*, 121361. doi:10.1016/j.techfore.2021.121361

Munzner, T. (2014). Visualization Analysis and Design. In Visualization Analysis and Design. doi:10.1201/b17511

Mustakim, H., Herianda, D. M., Ilham, A., Daeng GS, A., Laumal, F. E., Kurniasih, N., Iskandar, A., Manulangga, G., Indra Iswara, I. B. A., & Rahim, R. (2018). Market Basket Analysis Using Apriori and FP-Growth for Analysis Consumer Expenditure Patterns at Berkah Mart in Pekanbaru Riau. *Journal of Physics: Conference Series, 1114*, 012131. doi:10.1088/1742-6596/1114/1/012131

Mustapa, M. A. C., Amin, L., & Frewer, L. J. (2020). Predictors of stakeholders' intention to adopt nutrigenomics. *Genes & Nutrition, 15*(1), 16. doi:10.1186/s12263-020-00676-y PMID:32962632

Mutula, S., & Van Brakel, P. (2007). ICT skills readiness for the emerging global digital economy among small businesses in developing countries: A case study of Botswana. *Library Hi Tech, 25*(2), 231–245. doi:10.1108/07378830710754992

Mveku, B., Muzvidziwa, E., Mutero, T., & Matapo, S. (2022). The impact of ICT adoption decision-making: Case of Zimbabwean SME owner-managers. *International Journal of Research and Innovation in Applied Science, VII*(VI).

Mwaliko, E., Van Hal, G., Bastiaens, H., Van Dongen, S., Gichangi, P., Otsyula, B., Naanyu, V., & Temmerman, M. (2021). Early detection of cervical cancer in western Kenya: Determinants of healthcare providers performing a gynaecological examination for abnormal vaginal discharge or bleeding. *BMC Family Practice, 22*(1), 52. doi:10.1186/s12875-021-01395-y PMID:33706721

Myla, S., Marella, S. T., Karthikeya, K., Preetham, B., & Hasane Ahammad, S. K. (2019). The rise of "big data" in the field of cloud analytics. *International Journal on Emerging Technologies, 10*(4), 125–130.

Mythili, M., & Mohamed Shanavas, A. (2013). Performance Evaluation of Apriori and FP-Growth Algorithms. *International Journal of Computer Applications, 79*(10), 34–37. doi:10.5120/13779-1650

MyWam. (2022). *DoctorAssist: Hospital Management System*. Retrieved from https://wammap.com/hospital-information-system

Nader, J. (2022). Lean six sigma and design of experiments: an empirical case study from the dairy industry. *2022 International Conference on Interdisciplinary Research in Technology and Management, IRTM 2022 – Proceedings.*

Nahan-Suomela, R., & Lautamäki, S. (2013). The role of market orientation in the internationalization of SMEs. In *Cultural and Technological Influences on Global Business* (pp. 242–257). IGI Global. doi:10.4018/978-1-4666-3966-9.ch013

Najdawi, A., & Karan Patkuri, S. (2021). Modeling business intelligence process: toward smart data-driven strategies. *Proceedings of 2nd IEEE International Conference on Computational Intelligence and Knowledge Economy, ICCIKE 2021 C7 – 9410804*. 10.1109/ICCIKE51210.2021.9410804

Nalchigar, S., & Yu, E. (2013). From business intelligence insights to actions: A methodology for closing the sense-and-respond loop in the adaptive enterprise. *Lecture Notes in Business Information Processing, 165*, 114–128. doi:10.1007/978-3-642-41641-5_9

Nambiar, A., & Mundra, D. (2022). An overview of data warehouse and data lake in modern enterprise data management. *Big Data and Cognitive Computing, 6*(4 C7 - 132). doi:10.3390/bdcc6040132

Narke, Lakshmi, & Azra, N. (2020). A comprehensive review of approaches and challenges of a recommendation system. *International Journal of Research in Engineering. Science and Management, 3*(4), 381–384.

Nascimento, J., Frazão, N., Teixeira, S., & Ribeiro, A. C. (2022). Dashboard for the management and acceptance of customer orders. *Business Systems Research, 13*(3), 116–129. doi:10.2478/bsrj-2022-0028

Neaga, I., Liu, S., Xu, L., Chen, H., & Hao, Y. (2015). Cloud enabled big data business platform for logistics services: A research and development agenda. *Lecture Notes in Business Information Processing, 216*, 22–33. doi:10.1007/978-3-319-18533-0_3

Negash, S. (2004). Business Intelligence. *Communications of the Association for Information Systems, 13*, 177–195. doi:10.17705/1CAIS.01315

Nenzhelele, T. E., & Pellissier, R. (2013). Towards a universal definition of competitive intelligence. *South African Journal of Information Management, 15*(2), 1–7.

Ng, A. (2024, January 5). *How AI Could Empower Any Business* [Video]. https://www.youtube.com/watch?v=reUZRyXxUs4

Ng, I., & Nagalingham, S. (2023). Implementation of Business Intelligence Solution for United Airlines. *International Journal of Advanced Computer Science and Applications, 14*(1). Advance online publication. doi:10.14569/IJACSA.2023.0140192

Nguyen, D. K., Sermpinis, G., & Stasinakis, C. (2023). Big data, artificial intelligence and machine learning: A transformative symbiosis in favour of financial technology. *European Financial Management, 29*(2), 517–548. doi:10.1111/eufm.12365

Nguza-Mduba, B. (2020). *Intuitive competitive intelligence: the entrepreneurial path to success for small and medium-sized enterprises (SMEs) in the tourism sector in the Eastern Cape Province* [Doctor of Business Administration thesis]. University of Kwazulu-Natal.

Niccolai, J. (2011). *Residents Cut Energy Bills 11% in Smart Meter Test*. Retrieved November 11, 2023, from https://www.pcworld.com/article/482245/residents_cut_energy_bills_11_in_smart_meter_test.htm

Nikolic, S., Daniel, S., Haque, R., Belkina, M., Hassan, G. M., Grundy, S., ... Sandison, C. (2023). ChatGPT versus engineering education assessment: A multidisciplinary and multi-institutional benchmarking and analysis of this generative artificial intelligence tool to investigate assessment integrity. *European Journal of Engineering Education*, 1–56. doi:10.1080/03043797.2023.2248042

Nissenbaum, H. (2020). Protecting privacy in an information age: The problem of privacy in public. In *The Ethics of Information Technologies* (pp. 141–178). Routledge. doi:10.4324/9781003075011-12

Nofal, M. I., & Yusof, Z. M. (2013). Integration of business intelligence and enterprise resource planning within organizations. *Procedia Technology, 11*, 658–665. doi:10.1016/j.protcy.2013.12.242

Nourani, C. F. (2017). Virtual mobile interfaces, business intelligence, and analytics content processing. In Ecosystems and Technology: Idea Generation and Content Model Processing (pp. 189-222). Apple Academic Press. doi:10.1201/9781315365664

Novosel, S., Prangenberg, C., Wirtz, D. C., Burger, C., Welle, K., & Kabir, K. (2022). Climate change: How surgery contributes to global warming. *Die Chirurgie*, *93*(6), 579–585. doi:10.1007/s00104-021-01551-1 PMID:35138418

Nuryanti, H., & Andreas, S. P. (2017). The influence of knowledge management on business performance and competitive advantage in Riau food products on small and medium enterprises in Pekan Baru. *International Journal of Scientific & Technology Research*, *6*(10).

Nwanakwaugwu, A. C., Matthew, U. O., Kazaure, A. A., & Haruna, K. (2023). Data Mining Business Intelligence Applications in Retail Services Using Artificial Neural Networks. In *Handbook of Research on Cybersecurity Risk in Contemporary Business Systems* (pp. 186–210). IGI Global. doi:10.4018/978-1-6684-7207-1.ch010

Nwankwo, C. A., & Kanyangale, M. I. (2023). Customer Relationship Management and Survival of Manufacturing Small and Medium Enterprises in Nigeria. Journal of Economic and Social Development (JESD) – Resilient Society, 10(2).

Nylund, P. A., Ferras-Hernandez, X., & Brem, A. (2020). Automating profitably together: Is there an impact of open innovation and automation on firm turnover? *Review of Managerial Science*, *14*(1), 269–285. doi:10.1007/s11846-018-0294-z

Oesterreich, T. D., Anton, E., & Teuteberg, F. (2022). What translates big data into business value? A meta-analysis of the impacts of business analytics on firm performance. *Information and Management, 59*(6 C7 - 103685). doi:10.1016/j.im.2022.103685

Office, U. S. C. (2020). *Copyright in Derivative Works and Compilations.* Retrieved from https://www.copyright.gov/circs/circ14.pdf

Oliveira, A., & Bernardino, J. (2020). *Osspal assessment of self-service BI and analytics software.* Atas da Conferencia da Associacao Portuguesa de Sistemas de Informacao.

Olsen, D. H., & Dupin-Bryant, P. A. (2013). Combining business intelligence and stock market data: A primer for data analytics and business intelligence. *Journal of Applied Business Research*, *29*(1), 139–156. doi:10.19030/jabr.v29i1.7562

Olszak, C. M., & Ziemba, E. (2003), Business intelligence as a key to management of an enterprise. *Proceedings of Informing Science and IT Education Conference.* 10.28945/2672

Olszak, C. M., & Ziemba, E. (2007). Approach to building and implementing business intelligence systems. *Interdisciplinary Journal of Information, Knowledge, and Management*, *2*(1), 135–148. doi:10.28945/105

Omanin Siddiqua, P., Omanin, A., Faiza, S., Jafrin, & Ashrafuzzaman, M. (2022). Big medical data analytics for diagnosis. Big Data Analytics for Healthcare Datasets, techniques, Life Cycles, management and Applications, 111-124. doi:10.1016/B978-0-323-91907-4.00013-3

Omsa, S., Abdullah, I. H., & Jamali, H. (2017). Five Competitive Forces Model and the Implementation of Porter's Generic Strategies to Gain Firm Performances. *Science Journal of Business and Management*, *5*(1), 9–16. doi:10.11648/j.sjbm.20170501.12

Ong, I. L., Siew, P. H., & Wong, S. F. (2011). A five-layered business intelligence architecture. *Communications of the IBIMA*, *2011*, 1–11. doi:10.5171/2011.695619

Oracle. (2022). *What is IoT?* Retrieved from https://www.oracle.com/internet-of-things/what-is-iot/

Organization, W. H. (2020). *The top 10 causes of death.* Retrieved from https://www.who.int/news-room/fact-sheets/detail/the-top-10-causes-of-death

Orlikowski, W. J. (1992). The Duality of Technology: Rethinking the Concept of Technology in Organizations. *Organization Science, 3*(3), 398–427. doi:10.1287/orsc.3.3.398

Orlikowski, W. J., & Scott, S. V. (2008). Sociomateriality: Challenging the separation of technology, work and organization. *The Academy of Management Annals*, 2(1), 433–474. doi:10.5465/19416520802211644

Ou, L., & Peng, H. (2006, June). Knowledge and process based decision support in business intelligence system. In *First International Multi-Symposiums on Computer and Computational Sciences (IMSCCS'06)* (Vol. 2, pp. 780-786). IEEE.

Ouédraogo, D., Compaoré, I., & Nassè, T. B. (2022). Practice of business intelligence by SMEs in Burkina Faso. *International Journal of Management & Entrepreneurship Research*, *4*(1), 48–58. doi:10.51594/ijmer.v4i1.262

Overcash, M. (2012). A Comparison of Reusable and Disposable Perioperative Textiles: Sustainability State-of-the-Art 2012. *Anesthesia and Analgesia, 114*(5), 1055–1066. doi:10.1213/ANE.0b013e31824d9cc3 PMID:22492184

Padmanabhan, B., Hevner, A., Cuenco, M., & Shi, C. (2011). From information to operations: Service quality and customer retention. *ACM Transactions on Management Information Systems,* 2(4 C7 - 21). doi:10.1145/2070710.2070712

Pal, K. & Karakostas, B. (2020). Software Testing Under Agile, Scrum, and DevOps. In *Agile Scrum Implementation and Its Long-Term Impact on Organizations.* doi:10.4018/978-1-7998-4885-1.ch008

Pal, K. & Williams, I. (2021). Software Development Knowledge Management Using Web Portal. In *Digital Technology Advancements in Knowledge Management.* doi:10.4018/978-1-7998-6792-0.ch005

Pal, K. (2017). Supply chain coordination based on web services. In H. K. Chan, N. Subramanian, M. D.-A. Abdulrahman (eds) Supply Chain Management in the Big Data Era, (pp. 137-170). IGI Global. doi:10.4018/978-1-5225-0956-1.ch009

Pal, K. (2019). Markov Decision Theory Based Crowdsourcing Software Process Model. In Crowdsourcing and Probabilistic Decision-Making in Software Engineering: Emerging Research and Opportunities. Doi:10.4018/978-1-5225-9659-2-ch001

Pal, K. (2020). Framework for Reusable Test Case Generation in Software System Testing. In Software Engineering for Agile Application Development. Doi:10.4018/978-1-7998-2531-9-ch009

Pal, K. (2020). Information sharing for manufacturing supply chain management based on blockchain technology. In I. Williams (ed) Cross-Industry Use of Blockchain Technology and Opportunities for the Future, (pp. 1-17). IGI Global doi:10.4018/978-1-7998-3632-2.ch001

Pal, K. (2021). Applications of secured blockchain technology in manufacturing industry. In S. K. Pani, B. Patnaik, S. Lun, and X. Liu (ed) Blockchain and AI Technology in the Industrial Internet of Things. IGI Global. doi:10.4018/978-1-7998-6694-7.ch010

Pal, K. (2023). A Review of Big Data Analytics for the Internet of Things Applications in Supply Chain Management. *Applied AI and Multimedia Technologies for Smart Manufacturing and CPS Applications*, 221-245. doi:10.4018/978-1-7998-7852-0.ch005

Pal, K. (2023). Drivers of sustainable supply chain management using internet of things-based blockchain technology. In A. Taghipour (ed) Government Impact on Sustainable and Responsible Supply Chan. (pp. 171-201). IGI Global. doi:10.4018/978-1-6684-9062-4.ch010

Pal, K. (2017). A Semantic Web Service Architecture for Supply Chain Management, The 8th International Conference on Ambient Systems, Networks and Technologies (ANT 2017). *Procedia Computer Science*, *109C*, 999–1004. doi:10.1016/j.procs.2017.05.442

Pal, K., & Yasar, A. (2020). Internet of Things and blockchain technology in textile manufacturing supply chain data management. *Procedia Computer Science*, *170*, 450–457. doi:10.1016/j.procs.2020.03.088

Pan, B., Zhang, G., & Qin, X. (2018, April). Design and realization of an ETL method in business intelligence project. In *2018 IEEE 3rd International Conference on Cloud Computing and Big Data Analysis (ICCCBDA)* (pp. 275-279). IEEE. 10.1109/ICCCBDA.2018.8386526

Pantea, K., Norlia, M., Nasriah, Z., & Ahmad Suhaimi, B. (2019). User Behavioral Intention Toward Using Mobile Healthcare System. In A. Information Resources Management (Ed.), Consumer-Driven Technologies in Healthcare: Breakthroughs in Research and Practice (pp. 429-444). IGI Global.

Panteli, A., Kompothrekas, A., Halkiopoulos, C., & Boutsinas, B. (2021). An Innovative Recommender System for Health Tourism. In V. Katsoni & C. van Zyl (Eds.), *Culture and Tourism in a Smart, Globalized, and Sustainable World* (pp. 649–658). Springer International Publishing., doi:10.1007/978-3-030-72469-6_42

Papa, A., Mital, M., Pisano, P., & Del Giudice, M. (2020). E-health and wellbeing monitoring using smart healthcare devices: An empirical investigation. *Technological Forecasting and Social Change*, *153*, 119226. doi:10.1016/j.techfore.2018.02.018

Parallel categories diagram in Python. (n.d.). Retrieved June 9, 2022, from https://plotly.com/python/parallel-categories-diagram/

Pardo, T. A., & Gil-Garcia, J. R. (2005). *Understanding the Complexity of E-Government: Multi-method Approaches to Social Phenomena*. American Society for Public Administration.

Parker, S., & Wall, T. D. (1998). *Job and work design: Organizing work to promote well-being and effectiveness* (Vol. 4). Sage. doi:10.4135/9781452231518

Parssian, A. (2006). Managerial decision support with knowledge of accuracy and completeness of the relational aggregate functions. *Decision Support Systems*, *42*(3), 1494–1502. doi:10.1016/j.dss.2005.12.005

Parvatker, A., Tunceroglu, H., Sherman, J., Coish, P., Anastas, P., Zimmerman, J., & Eckelman, M. (2019). Cradle-to-Gate Greenhouse Gas Emissions for Twenty Anesthetic Active Pharmaceutical Ingredients Based on Process Scale-Up and Process Design Calculations. *ACS Sustainable Chemistry & Engineering*, *7*(7), 6580–6591. Advance online publication. doi:10.1021/acssuschemeng.8b05473

Parveen, F., & Bhavsar, A. (2023). Attention Based 1D-CNN for Mental Workload Classification Using EEG. *Proceedings of the 16th International Conference on PErvasive Technologies Related to Assistive Environments*, 739–745. 10.1145/3594806.3596582

Passlick, J., Grützner, L., Schulz, M., & Breitner, M. H. (2023). Self-service business intelligence and analytics application scenarios: A taxonomy for differentiation. *Information Systems and e-Business Management*, *21*(1), 159–191. doi:10.1007/s10257-022-00574-3

Pedreschi, D., Bonchi, F., Turini, F., Verykios, V. S., Atzori, M., Malin, B., ... Saygin, Y. (2008). Privacy protection: regulations and technologies, opportunities and threats. *Mobility, Data Mining and Privacy: Geographic Knowledge Discovery*, 101-119. doi:10.1007/978-3-540-75177-9_5

Pernici, B. & Scannapieco, M. (2002). *Data quality in Web Information Systems*. doi:10.1007/3-540-45816-6_37

Perry, H., Reeves, N., Ansell, J., Cornish, J., Torkington, J., Morris, D. S., Brennan, F., & Horwood, J. (2023). Innovations towards achieving environmentally sustainable operating theatres: A systematic review. *The Surgeon, 21*(3), 141–151. doi:10.1016/j.surge.2022.04.012 PMID:35715311

Peter, B., Shmueli, G., & Nitin, P. (2016). *Data Mining for Business Analytics: Concepts, Techniques, and Applications with XLMiner*. John Wiley & Sons.

Peters, M. A., Jackson, L., Papastephanou, M., Jandrić, P., Lazaroiu, G., Evers, C. W., Cope, B., Kalantzis, M., Araya, D., Tesar, M., Mika, C., Chen, L., Wang, C., Sturm, S., Rider, S., & Fuller, S. (2023). AI and the future of humanity: ChatGPT-4, philosophy and education–Critical responses. *Educational Philosophy and Theory*, 1–35. doi:10.1080/00131857.2023.2213437

Petre, M.-A., Bahrey, L., Levine, M., van Rensburg, A., Crawford, M., & Matava, C. (2019). A national survey on attitudes and barriers on recycling and environmental sustainability efforts among Canadian anesthesiologists: An opportunity for knowledge translation. *Canadian Journal of Anaesthesia, 66*(3), 272–286. doi:10.1007/s12630-018-01273-9 PMID:30547422

Phillips-Wren, G., Daly, M., & Burstein, F. (2021). Reconciling business intelligence, analytics and decision support systems: More data, deeper insight. *Decision Support Systems, 146*, 113560. doi:10.1016/j.dss.2021.113560

Piccinini, E., Hanelt, A., Gregory, R. W., & Kolbe, L. M. (2015). *Transforming industrial business: the impact of digital transformation on automotive organizations.* Paper Presented at the 2015 International Conference on Information Systems: Exploring the Information Frontier.

Pipino, L. L., Lee, Y. W., & Wang, R. Y. (2002). Data quality assessment. *Communications of the ACM, 45*(4), 211–218. doi:10.1145/505248.506010

Pisner, D. A., & Schnyer, D. M. (2020). Support vector machine. In A. Mechelli & S. Vieira (Eds.), *Machine Learning* (pp. 101–121). Academic Press. doi:10.1016/B978-0-12-815739-8.00006-7

Ponelis, S. & Britz, J. (2011). The role of business intelligence in information-intensive small businesses: initial results from an interpretive study. *MWAIS 2011 Proceedings, 9*(23), 345-361.

Ponis, S. T., & Christou, I. T. (2013). Competitive intelligence for SMEs: A web-based decision support system. *International Journal of Business Information Systems, 12*(3), 243–258. doi:10.1504/IJBIS.2013.052449

Popescu, G. H., Valaskova, K., & Horak, J. (2022). Augmented reality shopping experiences, retail business analytics, and machine vision algorithms in the virtual economy of the metaverse. *Journal of Self-Governance and Management Economics, 10*(2), 67–81.

Popovič, A., Hackney, R., Coelho, P. S., & Jaklič, J. (2012). Towards business intelligence systems success: Effects of maturity and culture on analytical decision making. *Decision Support Systems, 54*(1), 729–739. doi:10.1016/j.dss.2012.08.017

Porter, M. (2001). The value chain and competitive advantage. In *Understanding Business: Processes; Barnes, D. (Edited)* (pp. 50–66). Routledge. doi:10.1201/9781420025569.ch8

Porter, M. E. (1980). *Competitive Strategy: Techniques for Analyzing Industries and Competitors*. Free Press.

Power, D. J. (2015). 'Big data' decision making use cases. *Decision Support Systems V—Big Data Analytics for Decision Making: First International Conference, ICDSST 2015, Belgrade, Serbia, May 27-29, 2015 Proceedings, 1*, 1–9.

Pradere, B., Mallet, R., de La Taille, A., Bladou, F., Prunet, D., Beurrier, S., Bardet, F., Game, X., Fournier, G., Lechevallier, E., Meria, P., Matillon, X., Polguer, T., Abid, N., De Graeve, B., Kassab, D., Mejean, A., Misrai, V., & Pinar, U. (2023). Climate-smart Actions in the Operating Theatre for Improving Sustainability Practices: A Systematic Review. *European Urology*, *83*(4), 331–342. doi:10.1016/j.eururo.2022.01.027 PMID:35151515

Prevedello, L. M., Andriole, K. P., Hanson, R., Kelly, P., & Khorasani, R. (2010). Business intelligence tools for radiology: Creating a prototype model using open-source tools. *Journal of Digital Imaging*, *23*(2), 133–141. doi:10.1007/s10278-008-9167-3 PMID:19011943

Publishing, H. H. (2020). *Mind & Mood.* Retrieved from https://www.health.harvard.edu/topics/mind-and-mood

Quboa, Q., & Mehandjiev, N. (2017). Creating intelligent business systems by utilizing big data and semantics. *Proceedings - 2017 IEEE 19th Conference on Business Informatics, CBI 2017.*

Qu, H., Shan, Y., Liu, Y., Pang, L., Fan, Z., Zhang, J., & Wanyan, X. (2020). Mental Workload Classification Method Based on EEG Independent Component Features. *Applied Sciences (Basel, Switzerland)*, *10*(9), 3036. Advance online publication. doi:10.3390/app10093036

R Core Team. (2023). *R: A Language and Environment for Statistical Computing (Version 4.3.0).* R Foundation for Statistical Computing.

Rabovsky, T. M. (2014). Using data to manage for performance at public universities. *Public Administration Review*, *74*(2), 260–272. doi:10.1111/puar.12185

Ragazou, K., Passas, I., Garefalakis, A., & Zopounidis,C. (2023). Business intelligence model empowering SMEs to make better decisions and enhance their competitive advantage. *Discover Analytics.*

Rahman, H., Tariq, J., Ali Masood, M., & Subahi, A., Ibrahim Khalaf, O., & Alotaibi, Y. (2023). Multi-Tier Sentiment Analysis of Social Media Text Using Supervised Machine Learning. *Computers, Materials & Continua*, *74*(3), 5527–5543. doi:10.32604/cmc.2023.033190

Rahman, M. A., Hossain, M. S., Islam, M. S., Alrajeh, N. A., & Muhammad, G. (2020). Secure and Provenance Enhanced Internet of Health Things Framework: A Blockchain Managed Federated Learning Approach. *IEEE Access : Practical Innovations, Open Solutions*, *8*, 205071–205087. doi:10.1109/ACCESS.2020.3037474 PMID:34192116

Rahman, M. M. (2023). AI for ADHD: Opportunities and Challenges. *Journal of Attention Disorders*, *27*(8), 797–799. doi:10.1177/10870547231167608 PMID:37039127

Rahman, T., Ghosh, A. K., Shuvo, M. H., & Rahman, M. (2015). Mental stress recognition using K-nearest neighbor (KNN) classifier on EEG signals. *Int. Conf. Materials, Electronics & Information Engineering (ICMEIE)*, 1–4.

Raichle, M. E. (2015). The brain's default mode network. *Annual Review of Neuroscience*, *38*(1), 433–447. doi:10.1146/annurev-neuro-071013-014030 PMID:25938726

Rajagopal, S. (2011). Customer Data Clustering Using Data Mining Technique. International Journal of Database Management Systems, 3(4).

Raj, R., Wong, H. S., & Beaumont, A. J. (2016). Business Intelligence Solution for an SME. *CASE (Philadelphia, Pa.).*

Ramakrishnan, T., Kathuria, A., & Saldanha, T. J. (2020). Business intelligence and analytics (BI&A) capabilities in healthcare. In Theory and Practice of Business Intelligence in Healthcare (pp. 1-17). IGI Global. Doi:10.4018/978-1-7998-2310-0.ch00

Ramanathan, U., Williams, N. L., Zhang, M., Sa-nguanjin, P., Garza-Reyes, J. A., & Borges, L. A. (2022). A New Perspective of E-Trust in the Era of Social Media: Insights From Customer Satisfaction Data. *IEEE Transactions on Engineering Management*, *69*(4), 1417–1431. doi:10.1109/TEM.2020.2985379

Ram, J., Zhang, C., & Koronios, A. (2016). The implications of big data analytics on business intelligence: A qualitative study in China. *Procedia Computer Science*, *87*, 221–226. doi:10.1016/j.procs.2016.05.152

Rammelkamp, Z., Dirnberger, J., Johnson, G., & Waisbren, S. (2021). An audit of all waste leaving the operating room: Can the surgical suite be more environmentally sustainable? *World Medical & Health Policy*, *13*(1), 126–136. doi:10.1002/wmh3.397

Rana, N. P., Chatterjee, S., Dwivedi, Y. K., & Akter, S. (2022). Understanding dark side of artificial intelligence (AI) integrated business analytics: Assessing firm's operational inefficiency and competitiveness. *European Journal of Information Systems*, *31*(3), 364–387. doi:10.1080/0960085X.2021.1955628

Rana, T., Svanberg, J., Öhman, P., & Lowe, A. (2023). *Handbook of Big Data and Analytics in Accounting and Auditing*. Springer Nature. doi:10.1007/978-981-19-4460-4

Ranger, S. (2020). *What is the IoT? Everything you need to know about the Internet of Things right now.* Retrieved from https://www.zdnet.com/article/what-is-the-internet-of-things-everything-you-need-to-know-about-the-iot-right-now/

Rao, G. (2013). *Medical Tourism: Global Perspective* [dataset].

Rathore, P. S., & Sharma, B. K. (2022). Improving healthcare delivery system using business intelligence. *Journal of IoT in Social, Mobile, Analytics, and Cloud*, *4*(1), 11–23. doi:10.36548/jismac.2022.1.002

Ravichandran, B. D., & Keikhosrokiani, P. (2021). *An Emotional-Persuasive Habit-Change Support Mobile Application for Heart Disease Patients*. BeHabit. doi:10.1007/978-3-030-70713-2_25

Ravichandran, B. D., & Keikhosrokiani, P. (2023). Classification of Covid-19 misinformation on social media based on neuro-fuzzy and neural network: A systematic review. *Neural Computing & Applications*, *35*(1), 699–717. Advance online publication. doi:10.1007/s00521-022-07797-y PMID:36159189

Redjeki, S., Guntara, M., & Anggoro, P. (2015). Naive bayes classifier algorithm approach for mapping poor families potential. *Int. J. Adv. Res. Artif. Intell*, *4*(12), 29–33. doi:10.14569/IJARAI.2015.041205

Redman, T. C. (2014). *Statistics in Data and Information Quality*. Wiley. doi:10.1002/9781118445112.stat04018

Reid, G. B., & Nygren, T. E. (1988). The Subjective Workload Assessment Technique: A Scaling Procedure for Measuring Mental Workload. In P. A. Hancock & N. Meshkati (Eds.), *Advances in Psychology* (Vol. 52, pp. 185–218). North-Holland. https://doi.org/https://doi.org/10.1016/S0166-4115(08)62387-0

Reimer, B., Mehler, B., Coughlin, J. F., Godfrey, K. M., & Tan, C. (2009). An On-Road Assessment of the Impact of Cognitive Workload on Physiological Arousal in Young Adult Drivers. *Proceedings of the 1st International Conference on Automotive User Interfaces and Interactive Vehicular Applications*, 115–118. 10.1145/1620509.1620531

Reuille-Dupont, J. (2023). *The Power of Algorithms and Big Data: A Marketing Perspective on Consumer Manipulation in Business*. Academic Press.

Rizan, C., Lillywhite, R., Reed, M., & Bhutta, M. F. (2023). The carbon footprint of products used in five common surgical operations: Identifying contributing products and processes. *Journal of the Royal Society of Medicine*, *116*(6), 199–213. Advance online publication. doi:10.1177/01410768231166135 PMID:37054734

Rizzi, S. (2012). Collaborative business intelligence. *Business Intelligence, 1*, 186-205. 10.1007/978-3-642-27358-2_9

Romano, M., Contu, G., Mola, F., & Conversano, C. (2023). Threshold-based Naïve Bayes classifier. *Advances in Data Analysis and Classification*. Advance online publication. doi:10.1007/s11634-023-00536-8

Ronen, B., & Spiegler, I. (1991). Information as inventory: A new conceptual view. *Information & Management, 21*(4), 239–247. doi:10.1016/0378-7206(91)90069-E

Rosário, A. T., & Dias, J. C. (2023a). How Industry 4.0 and Sensors Can Leverage Product Design: Opportunities and Challenges. *Sensors (Basel), 23*(3), 1165. doi:10.3390/s23031165 PMID:36772206

Rosário, A. T., & Dias, J. C. (2023b). Marketing Strategies on Social Media Platforms. *International Journal of E-Business Research, 19*(1), 1–25. doi:10.4018/IJEBR.316969

Rosário, A. T., Lopes, P. R., & Rosário, F. S. (2023). Metaverse in Marketing: Challenges and Opportunities. In A. Khang, V. Shah, & S. Rani (Eds.), *Handbook of Research on AI-BasedTechnologies and Applications in the Era of the Metaverse* (pp. 204–227). IGI Global. doi:10.4018/978-1-6684-8851-5.ch010

Rosenbusch, N., Brinckmann, J., & Bausch, A. (2011). Is innovation always beneficial? A meta-analysis of the relationship between innovation and performance in SMEs. *Journal of Business Venturing, 26*(4), 26. doi:10.1016/j.jbusvent.2009.12.002

Rospigliosi, P. A. (2023). Artificial intelligence in teaching and learning: What questions should we ask of ChatGPT? *Interactive Learning Environments, 31*(1), 1–3. doi:10.1080/10494820.2023.2180191

Roßmann, B., Canzaniello, A., von der Gracht, H., & Hartmann, E. (2018). The future and social impact of big data analytics in supply chain management: Results from a Delphi study. *Technological Forecasting and Social Change, 130*, 135–149. doi:10.1016/j.techfore.2017.10.005

Rouhani, S., Ashrafi, A., Zare Ravasan, A., & Afshari, S. (2016). The impact model of business intelligence on decision support and organizational benefits. *Journal of Enterprise Information Management, 29*(1), 19–50. doi:10.1108/JEIM-12-2014-0126

Rouvière, N., Chkair, S., Auger, F., Alovisetti, C., Bernard, M., Cuvillon, P., Kinowski, J.-M., Leguelinel-Blache, G., & Chasseigne, V. (2022). Ecoresponsible actions in operating rooms: A health ecological and economic evaluation. *International Journal of Surgery, 101*, 106637. doi:10.1016/j.ijsu.2022.106637 PMID:35487421

Roy, G. (2023). Travelers' online review on hotel performance – Analyzing facts with the Theory of Lodging and sentiment analysis. *International Journal of Hospitality Management, 111*, 103459. doi:10.1016/j.ijhm.2023.103459

Rubio Valdehita, S., López Núñez, M. I., López-Higes Sánchez, R., & Díaz Ramiro, E. M. (2017). Development of the CarMen-Q Questionnaire for mental workload assessment. *Psicothema*. Advance online publication. doi:10.7334/psicothema2017.151 PMID:29048320

Ruhanen, L. (2019). The prominence of eco in ecotourism experiences: An analysis of post-purchase online reviews. *Journal of Hospitality and Tourism Management, 39*, 110–116. doi:10.1016/j.jhtm.2019.03.006

Rupcic, N. (2019). Organizational learning in stakeholder relations. *The Learning Organization, 26*(2), 219–231. doi:10.1108/TLO-02-2019-221

Rutala, W. A., & Weber, D. J. (2001). A review of single-use and reusable gowns and drapes in health care. *Infection Control and Hospital Epidemiology, 22*(4), 248–257. doi:10.1086/501895 PMID:11379716

Ružarovsk'y, R., Holubek, R., Janìček, M., Velìšek, K., & Tirian, G. O. (2021). Analysis of the Industry 4.0 key elements and technologies implementation in the Festo Didactic educational systems MPS 203 I4. 0. *Journal of Physics: Conference Series, 1781*(1), 12030. doi:10.1088/1742-6596/1781/1/012030

S4. (2017). http://incubator.apache.org/s4.

Saeed, A. M. M., Widyaningsih, A., & Khaled, A. S. D. (2023). Activity-based costing (ABC) in the manufacturing industry: A literature review. *Journal of Development Economics*, *8*(2).

Sagiroglu, S., & Sinanc, D. (2013, May). Big data: A review. In *2013 international conference on collaboration technologies and systems (CTS)* (pp. 42-47). IEEE.

Sahay, B. S., & Ranjan, J. (2008). Real time business intelligence in supply chain analytics. *Information Management & Computer Security*, *16*(1), 28–48. doi:10.1108/09685220810862733

Saheb, T., & Izadi, L. (2019). Paradigm of IoT big data analytics in the healthcare industry: A review of scientific literature and mapping of research trends. *Telematics and Informatics*, *41*, 70–85. doi:10.1016/j.tele.2019.03.005

Salisu, I., Sappri, M. B. M. & Omar, M. F. B. (2021) The adoption of business intelligence systems in small and medium enterprises in the healthcare sector: A systematic literature review. *Cogent Business & Management, 8*(1).

Salisu, I., Bin Mohd Sappri, M., & Bin Omar, M. F. (2021). The adoption of business intelligence systems in small and medium enterprises in the healthcare sector: A systematic literature review. *Cogent Business & Management*, *8*(1), 1935663. doi:10.1080/23311975.2021.1935663

Samarasinghe, K. R., & Medis, A. (2020). Artificial intelligence based strategic human resource management (AISHRM) for industry 4.0. *Global Journal of Management and Business Research*, *20*(2), 7–13. doi:10.34257/GJMBRGVOl20IS2PG7

Samaras, L., García-Barriocanal, E., & Sicilia, M.-A. (2023). Sentiment analysis of COVID-19 cases in Greece using Twitter data. *Expert Systems with Applications*, *230*, 120577. doi:10.1016/j.eswa.2023.120577 PMID:37317687

Sanabria, A., Kowalski, L. P., Nixon, I. J., Shaha, A., De Bree, R., Mäkitie, A. A., Rinaldo, A., & Ferlito, A. (2020). Considerations for environmentally sustainable head and neck surgical oncology practice. *American Journal of Otolaryngology*, *41*(6), 102719. doi:10.1016/j.amjoto.2020.102719 PMID:32947153

Sandu, D. I. (2008). Operational and real-time Business Intelligence. *Revista Informatica Economică, 3*(47), 33-36. https://revistaie.ase.ro/content/47/06Sandu.pdf

Sanh, V., Debut, L., Chaumond, J., & Wolf, T. (2019). *DistilBERT, a distilled version of BERT: smaller, faster, cheaper and lighter*. Academic Press.

Santi, R. P., & Putra, H. (2018). A systematic literature review of business intelligence technology, contribution and application for higher education. *2018 International Conference on Information Technology Systems and Innovation, ICITSI 2018 - Proceedings C7 – 8696019.*

SAP. (n.d.). *What is SAP HANA?* Retrieved November 14, 2023, from https://www.sap.com/uk/products/technology-platform/hana/what-is-sap-hana.html

Sapateiro, C. M., & Bernardo, R. M. (2020). Crossing human factors research and business intelligence. *International Journal of Enterprise Information Systems*, *16*(3), 78–92. doi:10.4018/IJEIS.2020070106

Sarker, I. H. (2021). Machine Learning: Algorithms, Real-World Applications and Research Directions. *SN Computer Science*, *2*(3), 160. doi:10.1007/s42979-021-00592-x PMID:33778771

Sarker, I. H., & Kayes, A. S. M. (2020). ABC-RuleMiner: User behavioral rule-based machine learning method for context-aware intelligent services. *Journal of Network and Computer Applications*, *168*, 102762. doi:10.1016/j.jnca.2020.102762

SAS Institute. (2023). *Foxwoods Resort Casino relies on SAS® Viya® to determine optimal staffing, enhance the guest experience and maximize profits*. Retrieved November 20, 2023, from https://www.sas.com/tr_tr/customers/foxwoods.html

SAS. (2023). *Sas Viya For Learners.* Retrieved November 14, 2023, from https://www.sas.com/tr_tr/software/viya-for-learners.html

Sathi, A. (2012). *Big data analytics: Disruptive technologies for changing the game.* doi:10.1002/9781119205005.ch9

Scheps, S. (2008). *Business Intelligence For Dummies.* Wiley Publishing.

Schink, H. (2009). Current state and future challenges of real-time ETL. *Proceedings 2nd student conference on software engineering and database systems.*

Schoeman, F., & Seymour, L. F. (2020). Understanding the Low Adoption of AI in South African Medium Sized Organisations. *Proceedings of 43rd Conference of the South African Institute of Computer Scientists and Information Technologists.*

Sechi, G. M., Migliori, M., Dassi, G., Pagliosa, A., Bonora, R., Oradini-Alacreu, A., ... Team, R. (2020). Business Intelligence applied to Emergency Medical Services in the Lombardy region during SARS-CoV-2 epidemic. *Acta Biomedica, 91*(2), 39. doi:10.2196/preprints.19062 PMID:32420923

Serumaga-Zake, P. A. (2017). The role of user satisfaction in implementing a Business Intelligence System. *South African Journal of Information Management, 19*(1), 1–8. doi:10.4102/sajim.v19i1.736

Sexton, C. C., Gelhorn, H. L., Bell, J. A., & Classi, P. M. (2012). The co-occurrence of reading disorder and ADHD: Epidemiology, treatment, psychosocial impact, and economic burden. *Journal of Learning Disabilities, 45*(6), 538–564. doi:10.1177/0022219411407772 PMID:21757683

Sezgin, E., & Yıldırım, S. Ö. (2014). A Literature Review on Attitudes of Health Professionals towards Health Information Systems: From e-Health to m-Health. *Procedia Technology, 16*, 1317–1326. doi:10.1016/j.protcy.2014.10.148

Shahbaz, M., Gao, C., Zhai, L., Shahzad, F., & Hu, Y. (2019). Investigating the adoption of big data analytics in healthcare: The moderating role of resistance to change. *Journal of Big Data, 6*(1), 6. doi:10.1186/s40537-019-0170-y

Shahbaz, M., Nasir, M. A., Hille, E., & Mahalik, M. K. (2020). UK's net-zero carbon emissions target: Investigating the potential role of economic growth, financial development, and R\&D expenditures based on historical data (1870–2017). *Technological Forecasting and Social Change, 161*, 120255. doi:10.1016/j.techfore.2020.120255 PMID:32904903

Shah, K., Salunke, A., Dongare, S., & Antala, K. (2017). Recommender systems: An overview of different approaches to recommendations. *2017 International Conference on Innovations in Information, Embedded and Communication Systems (ICIIECS)*, 1–4. 10.1109/ICIIECS.2017.8276172

Shah, M., Cheng, M., & Fitzgerald, R. (2017). Closing the loop on student feedback: The case of Australian and Scottish universities. *Higher Education, 74*(1), 115–129. doi:10.1007/s10734-016-0032-x

Shah, M., & Nair, C. S. (2012). Student surveys and feedback: Strategic solution for all tertiary education institutions. *Studies in Learning, Evaluation. Innovation and Development, 9*(1).

Sheppard, C. E., Lester, E. L. W., Chuck, A. W., Kim, D. H., Karmali, S., de Gara, C. J., & Birch, D. W. (2014). Medical tourism and bariatric surgery: Who pays? *Surgical Endoscopy, 28*(12), 3329–3336. doi:10.1007/s00464-014-3613-8 PMID:24969849

Sherman, J., Le, C., Lamers, V., & Eckelman, M. (2012). Life Cycle Greenhouse Gas Emissions of Anesthetic Drugs. *Anesthesia and Analgesia, 114*(5), 1086–1090. doi:10.1213/ANE.0b013e31824f6940 PMID:22492186

Shinn, H. K., Hwang, Y., Kim, B.-G., Yang, C., Na, W., Song, J.-H., & Lim, H. K. (2017). Segregation for reduction of regulated medical waste in the operating room: A case report. *Korean Journal of Anesthesiology, 70*(1), 100–104. doi:10.4097/kjae.2017.70.1.100 PMID:28184276

Shoham, M. A., Baker, N. M., Peterson, M. E., & Fox, P. (2022). The environmental impact of surgery: A systematic review. *Surgery*, *172*(3), 897–905. doi:10.1016/j.surg.2022.04.010 PMID:35788282

Shollo, A., & Galliers, R. D. (2016). Towards an understanding of the role of business intelligence systems in organizational knowing. *Information Systems Journal*, *26*(4), 339–367. doi:10.1111/isj.12071

Shongwe, T., Malatji, M., & Pretorius, J. H. C. (2022). Telecommunications customer service improvement through big data analytics. *2022 IEEE 28th International Conference on Engineering, Technology and Innovation, ICE/ITMC 2022 and 31st International Association for Management of Technology, IAMOT 2022 Joint Conference – Proceedings.*

Short, C. E., & Short, J. C. (2023). The artificially intelligent entrepreneur: ChatGPT, prompt engineering, and entrepreneurial rhetoric creation. *Journal of Business Venturing Insights*, *19*, e00388. doi:10.1016/j.jbvi.2023.e00388

Shum, P. L., Kok, H. K., Maingard, J., Schembri, M., Bañez, R. M. F., Van Damme, V., ... Chandra, R. V. (2020). Environmental sustainability in neurointerventional procedures: A waste audit. *Journal of Neurointerventional Surgery*, *12*(11), 1053–1057. doi:10.1136/neurintsurg-2020-016380 PMID:32680876

Siegel, E. (2015). *Predictive analytics: The power to predict who will click, buy, lie or die.* doi:10.1002/9781119172536

Sigman, B. P., Garr, W., Pongsajapan, R., Selvanadin, M., McWilliams, M., & Bolling, K. (2016). Visualization of Twitter data in the classroom. *Decision Sciences Journal of Innovative Education*, *14*(4), 362–381. doi:10.1111/dsji.12108

Sinclair, R. (2011). *Textile and Fashion: Materials, Design and Technology.* doi:10.1016/B978-1-84569-646-7.50019-6

Singh, P., Ghosh, S., Saraf, M., & Nayak, R. (2020). A Survey Paper on Identifying Key Performance Indicators for Optimizing Inventory Management System and Exploring Different Visualization Tools. *2020 4th International Conference on Intelligent Computing and Control Systems (ICICCS)*, 627–632. 10.1109/ICICCS48265.2020.9121036

Singh, M. K., & Rishi, O. P. (2020). Event driven Recommendation System for E-commerce using Knowledge based Collaborative Filtering Technique. *Scalable Computing: Practice and Experience*, *21*(3), 369–378. doi:10.12694/scpe.v21i3.1709

Sinha, N., Singh, P., Gupta, M., & Singh, P. (2020). Robotics at workplace: An integrated Twitter analytics – SEM based approach for behavioral intention to accept. *International Journal of Information Management*, *55*, 102210. doi:10.1016/j.ijinfomgt.2020.102210

Siu, J., Hill, A. G., & MacCormick, A. D. (2017). Systematic review of reusable versus disposable laparoscopic instruments: Costs and safety. *ANZ Journal of Surgery*, *87*(1-2), 28–33. doi:10.1111/ans.13856 PMID:27878921

Skountridaki, L. (2017). Barriers to business relations between medical tourism facilitators and medical professionals. *Tourism Management*, *59*, 254–266. doi:10.1016/j.tourman.2016.07.008

Skyrius, R., Kazakevičienė, G., & Bujauskas, V. (2013). The relationship between management decision support and business intelligence: developing awareness. In Advances in information systems and technologies (pp. 587-598). Springer. doi:10.1007/978-3-642-36981-0_54

Smith, W. B. Jr. (1993). Total Customer Satisfaction as a Business Strategy. *Quality and Reliability Engineering International*, *9*(1), 49–53. doi:10.1002/qre.4680090109

Snyder, J., Crooks, V. A., Johnston, R., & Dharamsi, S. (2013). "Do your homework…and then hope for the best": The challenges that medical tourism poses to Canadian family physicians' support of patients' informed decision-making. *BMC Medical Ethics*, *14*(1), 37. doi:10.1186/1472-6939-14-37 PMID:24053385

Sohail, N., & Sheikh, T. H. (2018). A study of inventory management system case study. *Journal of Dynamical and Control Systems*, *10*(10), 1176–1190.

Sony, M., & Naik, S. (2020). Industry 4.0 integration with socio-technical systems theory: A systematic review and proposed theoretical model. *Technology in Society*, *61*, 101248. doi:10.1016/j.techsoc.2020.101248

Southorn, T., Norrish, A., Gardner, K., & Baxandall, R. (2013). Reducing the Carbon Footprint of the Operating Theatre: A Multicentre Quality Improvement Report. *Journal of Perioperative Practice*, *23*(6), 144–146. doi:10.1177/175045891302300605 PMID:23909168

Spark. (2017). https://spark.incubator.apache.org

Spiel, K., Hornecker, E., Williams, R. M., & Good, J. (2022). ADHD and technology research–investigated by neurodivergent readers. In *Proceedings of the 2022 CHI Conference on Human Factors in Computing Systems* (pp. 1-21). 10.1145/3491102.3517592

Srivastava, S. K. (2007). Green Supply-Chain Management: A State-of-the-Art Literature Review. *International Journal of Management Reviews*, *9*(1), 53–80. doi:10.1111/j.1468-2370.2007.00202.x

Staniar, B., & Ngo, T. (2023). *How to build a sales effectiveness program for LinkedIn Sales Navigator with Tableau.* Retrieved November 11, 2023, from https://www.tableau.com/blog/how-build-sales-effectiveness-program-linkedin-sales-navigator-tableau

Stock, J. R. (2013). Supply chain management: A look back, a look ahead. *Supply Chain Quarterly*, *2*, 22–26. doi:10.4324/9780203124451-17

Stodder, D. (2013). *Achieving greater agility with business intelligence: Improving speed and flexibility for BI, analytics, and data warehousing*. TDWI Research.

Stoll, J. (2024). *Revenue generated by Netflix from 1st quarter 2013 to 3rd quarter 2023.* Retrieved January 5, 2024, from https://www.statista.com/statistics/273883/netflixs-quarterly-revenue/

Stone, M. D., & Woodcock, N. D. (2014). Interactive, direct and digital marketing: A future that depends on better use of business intelligence. *Journal of Research in Interactive Marketing*, *8*(1), 4–17. doi:10.1108/JRIM-07-2013-0046

Storm. (2017). https://storm.incubator.apache.org

Stratigi, M., Li, X., Stefanidis, K., & Zhang, Z. (2019). *Ratings vs. Reviews in Recommender Systems: A Case Study on the Amazon Movies Dataset.* doi:10.1007/978-3-030-30278-8_9

Subramanian, P., Palaniappan, S., Vedamanikam, M., Bharat, N. U., & Sinnasamy, S. (2016). Exploring the effectiveness of data mining techniques for lung cancer prediction. Tableau. *Business intelligence: A complete overview.* Retrieved October 22, 2023, from https://www.tableau.com/learn/articles/business-intelligence#bi-analysis

Suhendra, N. H. B., Keikhosrokiani, P., Asl, M. P., & Zhao, X. (2022). Opinion Mining and Text Analytics of Literary Reader Responses: A Case Study of Reader Responses to KL Noir Volumes in Goodreads Using Sentiment Analysis and Topic. In P. Keikhosrokiani & M. Pourya Asl (Eds.), *Handbook of Research on Opinion Mining and Text Analytics on Literary Works and Social Media* (pp. 191–239). IGI Global. doi:10.4018/978-1-7998-9594-7.ch009

Supply Chain Council. (2010). http://supply-chain.org/f/down-load/726710733/SCOR10.pdf

Tableau. (2023). *LinkedIn empowers thousands of salespeople with Tableau, reducing customer churn.* Retrieved November 11, 2023, from https://www.tableau.com/solutions/customer/linkedin-dives-deep-into-petabytes-data-tableau

Taboada, M. (2016). Sentiment Analysis: An Overview from Linguistics. *Annual Review of Linguistics*, *2*(1), 325–347. doi:10.1146/annurev-linguistics-011415-040518

Tadelis, S. (2016). Reputation and feedback systems in online platform markets. *Annual Review of Economics*, *8*(1), 321–340. doi:10.1146/annurev-economics-080315-015325

Tai, A. M., Albuquerque, A., Carmona, N. E., Subramanieapillai, M., Cha, D. S., Sheko, M., Lee, Y., Mansur, R., & McIntyre, R. S. (2019). Machine learning and big data: Implications for disease modeling and therapeutic discovery in psychiatry. *Artificial Intelligence in Medicine*, *99*, 101704. doi:10.1016/j.artmed.2019.101704 PMID:31606109

Tallarigo, R. (1999). Job and Work Design: Organizing Work to Promote Well-Being and Effectiveness. *Personnel Psychology*, *52*(2), 510.

Talukder, M. S., Sorwar, G., Bao, Y., Ahmed, J. U., & Palash, M. A. S. (2020). Predicting antecedents of wearable healthcare technology acceptance by elderly: A combined SEM-Neural Network approach. *Technological Forecasting and Social Change*, *150*, 119793. doi:10.1016/j.techfore.2019.119793

Tamang, M. D., Shukla, V. K., Anwar, S., & Punhani, R. (2021, April). Improving business intelligence through machine learning algorithms. In *2021 2nd International Conference on Intelligent Engineering and Management (ICIEM)* (pp. 63-68). IEEE. 10.1109/ICIEM51511.2021.9445344

Tam, L., Tyquin, E., Mehta, A., & Larkin, I. (2021). Determinants of attitude and intention towards private health insurance: A comparison of insured and uninsured young adults in Australia. *BMC Health Services Research*, *21*(1), 246. doi:10.1186/s12913-021-06249-y PMID:33740968

Tan, R. J. (2019, May 24). *Breaking Down Mean Average Precision (mAP) | by Ren Jie Tan | Towards Data Science*. Towards Data Science. https://towardsdatascience.com/breaking-down-mean-average-precision-map-ae462f623a52

Tarek, B. H., & Adel, G. (2016). Business intelligence versus entrepreneurial competitive intelligence and international competitiveness of North African SMEs. *Journal of International Entrepreneurship*, *14*(4), 539–561. doi:10.1007/s10843-016-0194-8

Tavera Romero, C. A., Ortiz, J. H., Khalaf, O. I., & Ríos Prado, A. (2021). Business intelligence: Business evolution after industry 4.0. *Sustainability (Basel)*, *13*(18), 10026. doi:10.3390/su131810026

Tcukanova, O. A., Yarskaya, A. A., & Torosyan, A. A. (2022). Artificial intelligence as a new stage in the development of business intelligence systems. *Proceedings of the 2022 International Conference "Quality Management, Transport and Information Security, Information Technologies", IT and QM and IS 2022*. 10.1109/ITQMIS56172.2022.9976832

TechInside. (2019). *Uber'in yapay zekası iş ve eğlence gezilerini ayırt edecek*. Retrieved January 6, 2024 from https://www.techinside.com/uberin-yapay-zekasi-is-ve-eglence-gezilerini-ayirt-edecek/

Telukdarie, A., & Sishi, M. N. (2018). Enterprise definition for industry 4.0. *IEEE International Conference on Industrial Engineering and Engineering Management*.

Teoh Yi Zhe, I., & Keikhosrokiani, P. (2021). Knowledge workers mental workload prediction using optimised ELANFIS. *Applied Intelligence*, *51*(4), 2406–2430. Advance online publication. doi:10.1007/s10489-020-01928-5

Teubner, T., Flath, C. M., Weinhardt, C., van der Aalst, W., & Hinz, O. (2023). Welcome to the Era of ChatGPT et al. *Business & Information Systems Engineering*, *65*(2), 95–101. doi:10.1007/s12599-023-00795-x

The Movies Dataset. (n.d.). Retrieved June 3, 2022, from https://www.kaggle.com/datasets/rounakbanik/the-movies-dataset?select=movies_metadata.csv

Thiel, C. L., Fiorin Carvalho, R., Hess, L., Tighe, J., Laurence, V., Bilec, M. M., & Baratz, M. (2019). Minimal custom pack design and wide-awake hand surgery: Reducing waste and spending in the orthopedic operating room. *Hand (New York, N.Y.), 14*(2), 271–276. doi:10.1177/1558944717743595 PMID:29183168

Thiel, C. L., Schehlein, E., Ravilla, T., Ravindran, R., Robin, A. L., Saeedi, O. J., Schuman, J. S., & Venkatesh, R. (2017). Cataract surgery and environmental sustainability: Waste and lifecycle assessment of phacoemulsification at a private healthcare facility. *Journal of Cataract and Refractive Surgery, 43*(11), 1391–1398. doi:10.1016/j.jcrs.2017.08.017 PMID:29223227

Thiel, C. L., Woods, N. C., & Bilec, M. M. (2018). Strategies to reduce greenhouse gas emissions from laparoscopic surgery. *American Journal of Public Health, 108*(S2), S158–S164. doi:10.2105/AJPH.2018.304397 PMID:29698098

Timur, O. (2020, June 17). *Machine learning - Item-Item Collaborative Filtering vs Market Basket Analysis - Cross Validated.* https://stats.stackexchange.com/questions/256012/item-item-collaborative-filtering-vs-market-basket-analysis

Titareva, T. (2021). *Leadership in an Artificial Intelligence Era.* Academic Press.

Tong-On, P., Siripipatthanakul, S., & Phayaphrom, B. (2021). The implementation of business intelligence using data analytics and its effects towards on performance in the hotel industry in Thailand. *International Journal of Behavioral Analytics, 1*(2).

Top 10 Most Popular Subscription Streaming Services - All Top Everything. (n.d.). Retrieved June 3, 2022, from https://www.alltopeverything.com/most-popular-streaming-services/

Torkzadeh, L., Jalilian, H., Zolfagharian, M., Torkzadeh, H., Bakhshi, M., & Khodayari-Zarnaq, R. (2021). Market segmentation in the health tourism industry: A systematic review of approach and criteria. *Journal of Policy Research in Tourism, Leisure & Events, 0*(0), 1–20. doi:10.1080/19407963.2021.1988622

Trabucchi, D., & Buganza, T. (2019). Data-driven innovation: Switching the perspective on Big Data. *European Journal of Innovation Management, 22*(1), 23–40. doi:10.1108/EJIM-01-2018-0017

Trappey, A. J. C., Trappey, C. V., Govindarajan, U. H., & Sun, J. J. H. (2021). Patent value analysis using deep learning models-the case of IoT technology mining for the manufacturing industry. *IEEE Transactions on Engineering Management, 68*(5 C7 - 08941278), 1334-1346. doi:10.1109/TEM.2019.2957842

Treggiari, M. M. (2017). An initiative to optimize waste streams in the operating room: RECycling in the Operating Room (RECOR) Project. *AANA Journal, 85*(2), 108. PMID:30501159

Trist, E. L. (1978). On socio-technical systems. *Sociotechnical systems: A sourcebook*, 43-57.

Trkman, P., McCormack, K., de Oliveira, M. P. V., & Ladeira, M. B. (2010). The Impact of Business Analytics on Supply Chain Performance. *Decision Support Systems, 49*(3), 318–327. doi:10.1016/j.dss.2010.03.007

Troidl, A. (2023). *Boost Social Selling Success With Sales Navigator Analytics.* Tribalimpact.com. Retrieved November 19, 2023, from https://www.tribalimpact.com/blog/boost-social-selling-success-with-sales-navigator-analytics#:~:text=%2B59%25%20total%20revenue%20influenced%20by,Sales%20Navigator%20to%20find%20customers

Tsai, M. L., Ong, C. W., & Chen, C. L. (2023). Exploring the use of large language models (LLMs) in chemical engineering education: Building core course problem models with Chat-GPT. *Education for Chemical Engineers, 44*, 71–95. doi:10.1016/j.ece.2023.05.001

Tsumoto, S., Hirano, S., & Hanada, E. (2003, November). Internet-based decision support: towards E-hospital. In *Proceedings 27th Annual International Computer Software and Applications Conference. COMPAC 2003* (pp. 595-600). IEEE. 10.1109/CMPSAC.2003.1245401

Tumpa, Z. N., Saifuzzaman, M., Rabby, S. F., Crearie, L., & Stansfield, M. (2020, December). *Understanding business intelligence in the context of mental healthcare sector of Bangladesh for improving health services. In 2020 IEEE 8th R10 Humanitarian Technology Conference (R10-HTC)*. IEEE.

Turban, E. & Aronson. (2001). *Decision Support Systems and Intelligent systems* (6th ed.). Prentice Hall.

Turban, E., & Watkins, P. R. (1986). Integrating expert systems and decision support systems. *Management Information Systems Quarterly, 10*(2), 121–136. doi:10.2307/249031

Tutunea, M. & Rus, V. (2015). Business intelligence solutions for SMEs. *Procedia Economics and Finance, 3*, 865-870.

UK Government. (2022). *Greenhouse gas reporting: Conversion factors 2022*. UK Government.

Uwagaba, J., Omotosho, T. D., & George, G. O. (2023). *Exploring the Barriers to Artificial Intelligence Adoption in Sub-Saharan Africa's Small and Medium Enterprises and the Potential for Increased Productivity*. World Wide Journal of Multidisciplinary Research and Development.

Vaibhav, K. (2020, March 25). *Singular Value Decomposition (SVD) In Recommender System*. Analytics India Magazine. https://analyticsindiamag.com/singular-value-decomposition-svd-application-recommender-system/

Vaisman, A., & Zimányi, E. (2012). Data Warehouses: Next Challenges. In Business Intelligence. eBISS 2011. Lecture Notes in Business Information Processing, vol 96 (pp. 1-26). Springer. doi:10.1007/978-3-642-27358-2_1

Vajawat, B., Varshney, P., & Banerjee, D. (2021). Digital gaming interventions in psychiatry: Evidence, applications and challenges. *Psychiatry Research, 295*, 113585. doi:10.1016/j.psychres.2020.113585 PMID:33303223

Vajirakachorn, T., & Chongwatpol, J. (2017). Application of business intelligence in the tourism industry: A case study of a local food festival in Thailand. *Tourism Management Perspectives, 23*, 75–86. doi:10.1016/j.tmp.2017.05.003

Valle-Cruz, D., García-Contreras, R., & Muñoz-Chávez, J. P. (2022). Mind the Gap: Towards an Understanding of Government Decision-Making based on Artificial Intelligence. *DG.O 2022: The 23rd Annual International Conference on Digital Government Research*, 1–9.

Valle-Cruz, D., Muñoz-Chávez, J. P., & García-Contreras, R. (2023). Towards the Understanding of Consumer Behavior in the Metaverse: A Systematic Literature Review Using the PRISMA Methodology. Handbook of Research on Consumer Behavioral Analytics in Metaverse and the Adoption of a Virtual World, 1–21. doi:10.4018/978-1-6684-7029-9.ch001

Valle-Cruz, D., Fernandez-Cortez, V., & Gil-Garcia, J. R. (2022). From E-budgeting to smart budgeting: Exploring the potential of artificial intelligence in government decision-making for resource allocation. *Government Information Quarterly, 39*(2), 101644. doi:10.1016/j.giq.2021.101644

Valle-Cruz, D., Fernandez-Cortez, V., López-Chau, A., & Sandoval-Almazán, R. (2021). Does Twitter Affect Stock Market Decisions? Financial Sentiment Analysis During Pandemics: A Comparative Study of the H1N1 and the COVID-19 Periods. *Cognitive Computation*, 1–16. PMID:33520006

Valle-Cruz, D., & García-Contreras, R. (2023). Towards AI-driven transformation and smart data management: Emerging technological change in the public sector value chain. *Public Policy and Administration*. doi:10.1177/09520767231188401

Valle-Cruz, D., García-Contreras, R., & Gil-Garcia, J. R. (2023). Exploring the negative impacts of artificial intelligence in government: The dark side of intelligent algorithms and cognitive machines. *International Review of Administrative Sciences*. doi:10.1177/00208523231187051

Van Demark, R. E. Jr, Smith, V. J., & Fiegen, A. (2018). Lean and green hand surgery. *The Journal of Hand Surgery, 43*(2), 179–181. doi:10.1016/j.jhsa.2017.11.007 PMID:29421068 van Heck, G., van den Berg, J., Davarynejad, M., van Duin, R., & Roskott, B. (2010). Improving Inventory Management Performance Using a Process-Oriented Measurement Framework. In J. E. Quintela Varajão, M. M. Cruz-Cunha, G. D. Putnik, & A. Trigo (Eds.), *ENTERprise Information Systems* (pp. 279–288). Springer Berlin Heidelberg. doi:10.1007/978-3-642-16402-6_30

Varughese, S., & Ahmed, R. (2021). Environmental and Occupational Considerations of Anesthesia: A Narrative Review and Update. *Anesthesia and Analgesia, 133*(4), 826–835. doi:10.1213/ANE.0000000000005504 PMID:33857027

Vashisht, V., Kamya, S., & Vashisht, M. (2020). Defect prediction framework using neural networks for business intelligence technology-based projects. *2020 International Conference on Computer Science, Engineering and Applications, ICCSEA 2020 C7 – 9132944.*

Venkatesh, V., Morris, M. G., Davis, G. B., & Davis, F. D. (2003). User Acceptance of Information Technology: Toward a Unified View. *Management Information Systems Quarterly, 27*(3), 425–478. doi:10.2307/30036540

Verma, A., Yurov, K. M., Lane, P. L., & Yurova, Y. V. (2019). An investigation of skill requirements for business and data analytics positions: A content analysis of job advertisements. *Journal of Education for Business, 94*(4), 243–250. doi:10.1080/08832323.2018.1520685

Viégas, F. B., & Wattenberg, M. (2007). Artistic data visualization: Beyond visual analytics. *Proceedings of the 2nd International Conference on Online Communities and Social Computing*. 10.1007/978-3-540-73257-0_21

Viken, A., Höckert, E., & Grimwood, B. S. R. (2021). Cultural sensitivity: Engaging difference in tourism. *Annals of Tourism Research, 89*, 103223. doi:10.1016/j.annals.2021.103223

Villar, A., Zarrabeitia, M. T., Fdez-Arroyabe, P., & Santurtún, A. (2018). Integrating and analyzing medical and environmental data using ETL and Business Intelligence tools. *International Journal of Biometeorology, 62*(6), 1085–1095. doi:10.1007/s00484-018-1511-9 PMID:29516156

Vishwakarma, M., & Kesswani, N. (2023). A new two-phase intrusion detection system with Naïve Bayes machine learning for data classification and elliptic envelop method for anomaly detection. *Decision Analytics Journal, 7*, 100233. https://doi.org/https://doi.org/10.1016/j.dajour.2023.100233

Vodithala, S., & Bhukya, R. (2023). A Novel Political Optimizer-Based Feature Selection with an Optimal Machine Learning Model for Financial Crisis Prediction. *International Journal of Cooperative Information Systems, 2350020*. Advance online publication. doi:10.1142/S021884302350020X

Vozzola, E., Overcash, M., & Griffing, E. (2020). An environmental analysis of reusable and disposable surgical gowns. *AORN Journal, 111*(3), 315–325. doi:10.1002/aorn.12885 PMID:32128776

Wada, M., Noda, Y., Iwata, Y., Tsugawa, S., Yoshida, K., Tani, H., Hirano, Y., Koike, S., Sasabayashi, D., Katayama, H., Plitman, E., Ohi, K., Ueno, F., Caravaggio, F., Koizumi, T., Gerretsen, P., Suzuki, T., Uchida, H., Müller, D. J., ... Nakajima, S. (2022). Dopaminergic dysfunction and excitatory/inhibitory imbalance in treatment-resistant schizophrenia and novel neuromodulatory treatment. *Molecular Psychiatry, 27*(7), 2950–2967. doi:10.1038/s41380-022-01572-0 PMID:35444257

Wade, R. (2020). *Advanced Analytics in Power BI with R and Python: Ingesting, Transforming, Visualizing*. Springer International Publishing. doi:10.1007/978-1-4842-5829-3

Waliszewski, K., & Warchlewska, A. (2020). Attitudes towards artificial intelligence in the area of personal financial planning: A case study of selected countries. *Entrepreneurship and Sustainability Issues, 8*(2), 399–420. doi:10.9770/jesi.2020.8.2(24)

Walker, G. H., Stanton, N. A., Salmon, P. M., & Jenkins, D. P. (2008). A review of sociotechnical systems theory: A classic concept for new command and control paradigms. *Theoretical Issues in Ergonomics Science*, *9*(6), 479–499. doi:10.1080/14639220701635470

Waller, M. A., & Fawcett, S. E. (2013). Data science, predictive analytics, and big data: A revolution that will transform supply chain design and management. *Journal of Business Logistics*, *4*(3), 77–84. doi:10.1111/jbl.12010

Walter, C., Cierniak, G., Gerjets, P., Rosenstiel, W., & Bogdan, M. (2011). *Classifying mental states with machine learning algorithms using alpha activity decline*. ESANN.

Walumweya, M., & Phiri, J. (2022). Adopt effective competitive strategies in response to environmental challenges for the national public broadcasting corporation in developing countries: A participatory approach. *Open Journal of Business and Management*, *10*(1), 175–191. doi:10.4236/ojbm.2022.101011

Wand, Y., & Wang, R. Y. (1996). Anchoring data quality dimensions in ontological foundations. *Communications of the ACM*, *39*(11), 86–95. doi:10.1145/240455.240479

Wang, D., Churchill, E., Maes, P., Fan, X., Shneiderman, B., Shi, Y., & Wang, Q. (2020). From human-human collaboration to Human-AI collaboration: Designing AI systems that can work together with people. *Extended Abstracts of the 2020 CHI Conference on Human Factors in Computing Systems*, 1–6.

Wang, Y. (2016). What are the biggest obstacles to the growth of SMEs in developing countries? An empirical evidence from an enterprise survey. *Borsa Istanbul Review*, *16*(3).

Wang, H., Tao, D., Yu, N., & Qu, X. (2020). Understanding consumer acceptance of healthcare wearable devices: An integrated model of UTAUT and TTF. *International Journal of Medical Informatics*, *139*, 104156. doi:10.1016/j.ijmedinf.2020.104156 PMID:32387819

Wang, L. (2019). Research and Implementation of Machine Learning Classifier Based on KNN. *IOP Conference Series. Materials Science and Engineering*, *677*(5), 052038. doi:10.1088/1757-899X/677/5/052038

Wang, R. Y. (1998). A product perspective on total data quality management. *Communications of the ACM*, *41*(2), 58–65. doi:10.1145/269012.269022

Wang, R. Y., Storey, V. C., & Firth, C. P. (1995). A framework for analysis of data quality research. *IEEE Transactions on Knowledge and Data Engineering*, *7*(4), 623–640. doi:10.1109/69.404034

Wang, R. Y., & Strong, D. M. (1996). Beyond Accuracy: What data quality means to data consumers. *Journal of Management Information Systems*, *12*(4), 5–33. doi:10.1080/07421222.1996.11518099

Wang, W., Chen, L., Xiong, M., & Wang, Y. (2021). Accelerating AI Adoption with Responsible AI Signals and Employee Engagement Mechanisms in Health Care. *Information Systems Frontiers*. Advance online publication. doi:10.1007/s10796-021-10154-4

Wang, X., Tian, Q., Zhu, M., Wang, Y., Wang, B., Jing, X., Yokoi, H., Li, L., Liu, Z., Huang, W., Chen, S., Liu, Z., & Li, G. (2023). Towards Optimizing the Quality of Long-Term Physiological Signals Monitoring by Using Anhydrous Carbon Paste Electrode. *IEEE Transactions on Biomedical Engineering*, *70*(2), 423–435. doi:10.1109/TBME.2022.3193115 PMID:35867372

Wankhade, M., Rao, A. C. S., & Kulkarni, C. (2022). A survey on sentiment analysis methods, applications, and challenges. *Artificial Intelligence Review*, *55*(7), 5731–5780. doi:10.1007/s10462-022-10144-1

Ward, M. J., Marsolo, K. A., & Froehle, C. M. (2014). Applications of business analytics in healthcare. *Business Horizons*, *57*(5), 571–582. doi:10.1016/j.bushor.2014.06.003 PMID:25429161

Washington, P., Park, N., Srivastava, P., Voss, C., Kline, A., Varma, M., Tariq, Q., Kalantarian, H., Schwartz, J., Patnaik, R., Chrisman, B., Stockham, N., Paskov, K., Haber, N., & Wall, D. P. (2020). Data-driven diagnostics and the potential of mobile artificial intelligence for digital therapeutic phenotyping in computational psychiatry. *Biological Psychiatry: Cognitive Neuroscience and Neuroimaging*, *5*(8), 759–769. doi:10.1016/j.bpsc.2019.11.015 PMID:32085921

Watson, H. J., Wixom, B. H., Hoffer, J. A., Anderson-Lehman, R., & Reynolds, A. M. (2009). Real-time business intelligence: Best practices at Continental Airlines. *EDPACS The EDP Audit, Control, and Security Newsletter*, *40*(6), 1–16. doi:10.1080/07366980903484935

Watts, D. J. (1999). *Small Worlds. The Dynamics of Networks between Order and Randomness*. Princeton University Press. doi:10.1515/9780691188331

Watts, S., Shankaranarayanan, G., & Even, A. (2009). Data quality assessment in context: A cognitive perspective. *Decision Support Systems*, *48*(1), 202–211. doi:10.1016/j.dss.2009.07.012

Weber-Lewerenz, B., & Vasiliu-Feltes, I. (2022). Empowering Digital Innovation by Diverse Leadership in ICT—A Roadmap to a Better Value System in Computer Algorithms. *Humanistic Management Journal*, *7*(1), 117–134. doi:10.1007/s41463-022-00123-7

Weichbroth, P., Zurada, J., & Olszak, C. (2024). Exploring the Benefits, Challenges, and Opportunities of Collaborative Business Intelligence. *Proceedings of the 57th Hawaii International Conference on System Sciences*. https://hdl.handle.net/10125/106408

Werner, M., Wiese, M., & Maas, A. (2021). Embedding process mining into financial statement audits. *International Journal of Accounting Information Systems*, *41*, C7–C100514. doi:10.1016/j.accinf.2021.100514

West, D., Luzeckyj, A., Searle, B., Toohey, D., Vanderlelie, J., & Bell, K. R. (2020). Perspectives from the stakeholder: Students' views regarding learning analytics and data collection. *Australasian Journal of Educational Technology*, *36*(6), 72–88. doi:10.14742/ajet.5957

Williams, A., Suler, P., & Vrbka, J. (2020). Business Process Optimization, Cognitive Decision-Making Algorithms, and Artificial Intelligence Data-driven Internet of Things Systems in Sustainable Smart Manufacturing. *Journal of Self-Governance and Management Economics*, *8*(4), 39–48.

Williams, M. D., Rana, N. P., & Dwivedi, Y. K. (2015). The unified theory of acceptance and use of technology (UTAUT): A literature review. *Journal of Enterprise Information Management*, *28*(3), 443–488. doi:10.1108/JEIM-09-2014-0088

Williamson, O. (1996). The Mechanisms of Governance. doi:10.2307/3117318

Wisnu, H., Afif, M., & Ruldevyani, Y. (2020). Sentiment analysis on customer satisfaction of digital payment in Indonesia: A comparative study using KNN and Naïve Bayes. *Journal of Physics: Conference Series*, *1444*(1), 012034. doi:10.1088/1742-6596/1444/1/012034

Wixom, B. H., & Ross, J. W. (2018). How to Monetize Your Data, MIT Sloan Management Review. *Spring Issue*, *58*(3), 10–13. doi:10.7551/mitpress/11633.003.0009

Wolniak, R., & Grebski, W. (2023). Functioning of predictive analytics in business. Silesian University of Technology Scientific Papers. Organization and Management Series, 175, 631-649. doi:10.29119/1641-3466.2023.175.40

Wong, A. (2024). *5 Reasons your business intelligence solution is failing you*. Retrieved January 5, 2024, from https://www.tellius.com/5-reasons-your-business-intelligence-solution-is-failing-you/

Wu, C. (2003). Lean manufacturing: A perspective of lean suppliers. *International Journal of Operations & Production Management*, *23*(11), 1349–1376. doi:10.1108/01443570310501880

Wu, S., & Cerceo, E. (2021). Sustainability initiatives in the operating room. *Joint Commission Journal on Quality and Patient Safety*, *47*(10), 663–672. doi:10.1016/j.jcjq.2021.06.010 PMID:34344594

Wyssusek, K. H., Keys, M. T., & van Zundert, A. A. (2019). Operating room greening initiatives–the old, the new, and the way forward: A narrative review. *Waste Management & Research*, *37*(1), 3–19. doi:10.1177/0734242X18793937 PMID:30132405

Wyssusek, K., Chan, K. L., Eames, G., & Whately, Y. (2022). Greenhouse gas reduction in anaesthesia practice: A departmental environmental strategy. *BMJ Open Quality*, *11*(3), e001867. Advance online publication. doi:10.1136/bmjoq-2022-001867 PMID:36002191

Xian, Z., Keikhosrokiani, P. XinYing, C., & Li, Z. (2022). An RFM Model Using K-Means Clustering to Improve Customer Segmentation and Product Recommendation. In P. Keikhosrokiani (Ed.), Handbook of Research on Consumer Behavior Change and Data Analytics in the Socio-Digital Era (pp. 124–145). IGI Global. doi:10.4018/978-1-6684-4168-8.ch006

Xu, A., Tiffany, T., Phanie, M. E., & Simarmata, A. (2023). Sentiment Analysis On Twitter Posts About The Russia and Ukraine War With Long Short-Term Memory. *SinkrOn*, *8*(2), 789–797.

Yaman, T. T., & Bilgic, E. (2019). Is business analytics education sufficient in business schools? The case in Turkish business schools. *Proceedings - 2019 3rd International Conference on Data Science and Business Analytics, ICDSBA 2019 C7 – 9270212*. 10.1109/ICDSBA48748.2019.00040

Yang, J., Li, H. B., & Wei, D. (2023). The Impact of ChatGPT and LLMs on Medical Imaging Stakeholders: Perspectives and Use Cases. *Meta-Radiology*, 100007.

Yang, L. (2005). Pruning and visualizing generalized association rules in parallel coordinates. *IEEE Transactions on Knowledge and Data Engineering*, *17*(1), 60–70. doi:10.1109/TKDE.2005.14

Yang, X., Chen, A., PourNejatian, N., Shin, H. C., Smith, K. E., Parisien, C., Compas, C., Martin, C., Costa, A. B., Flores, M. G., Zhang, Y., Magoc, T., Harle, C. A., Lipori, G., Mitchell, D. A., Hogan, W. R., Shenkman, E. A., Bian, J., & Wu, Y. (2022). A large language model for electronic health records. *NPJ Digital Medicine*, *5*(1), 1–9. doi:10.1038/s41746-022-00742-2 PMID:36572766

Yang, Y., Hu, J., Liu, Y., & Chen, X. (2020). Doctor Recommendation Based on an Intuitionistic Normal Cloud Model Considering Patient Preferences. *Cognitive Computation*, *12*(2), 460–478. doi:10.1007/s12559-018-9616-3

Yazici, M. E., & Nastjuk, I. (2022). Security issues in data analytical environments. *17th International Conference on Wirtschaftsinformatik, WI 2022*.

Yee, L. S., & Keikhosrokiani, P. (2022). Hospital data analytics system for tracking and predicting obese patients' lifestyle habits. In *Big Data Analytics for Healthcare*. Datasets, Techniques, Life Cycles, Management, and Applications. doi:10.1016/B978-0-323-91907-4.00004-2

Yi, Q., Hoskins, R. E., Hillringhouse, E. A., Sorensen, S. S., Oberle, M. W., Fuller, S. S., & Wallace, J. C. (2008). Integrating open-source technologies to build low-cost information systems for improved access to public health data. *International Journal of Health Geographics*, *7*(1), 29. doi:10.1186/1476-072X-7-29 PMID:18541035

Yunna, W., & Yisheng, Y. (2014). The competition situation analysis of the Shale gas industry in China: Applying Porter's five forces and scenario model. *Renewable & Sustainable Energy Reviews*, *40*, 798–805. doi:10.1016/j.rser.2014.08.015

Yu, X., Xu, S., & Ashton, M. (2023). Antecedents and outcomes of artificial intelligence adoption and application in the workplace: The socio-technical system theory perspective. *Information Technology & People*, *36*(1), 454–474. doi:10.1108/ITP-04-2021-0254

Zahay, D., Sihi, D., Muzellec, L., & Johnson, D. S. (2019). The marketing organization's journey to become data driven. *Journal of Research in Interactive Marketing, 13*(2), 162–178. doi:10.1108/JRIM-12-2018-0157

Zahedi, F. (1993). *Intelligent systems for business: expert systems with neural networks.* Wadsworth Pub. Co.

Zahor, N., Khan, Z., Meyer, M., & Laker, B. (2023). Internal entrepreneurial behaviour of internationalising African SMEs-Towards a new research agenda. *Journal of Business Research*, 154.

Zaiane, Xin, & Han. (1998). Discovering Web access patterns and trends by applying OLAP and data mining technology on Web logs. *Proceedings IEEE International Forum on Research and Technology Advances in Digital Libraries*, 19-29. . doi:10.1109/ADL.1998.670376

Zainol, A. F., Keikhosrokiani, P., Asl, M. P., & Anuar, N. A. N. (2022). Artificial intelligence applications in literary works: Emotion extraction and classification of Mohsin Hamid's Moth Smoke. Handbook of Research on Artificial Intelligence Applications in Literary Works and Social Media. doi:10.4018/978-1-6684-6242-3.ch005

Zander, S., Maria, R., Wetzel, S., & Sven, B. (2015). Does Personalisation Promote Learners' Attention? An Eye-Tracking Study. *Frontline Learning Research*, 1–13.

Zeithaml, V. A., Berry, L. L., & Parasuraman, A. (1990). *Delivering quality service: Balancing customer perceptions and expectations*. Free Press. doi:10.5860/CHOICE.28-0390

Zeng, L., Xu, L., Shi, Z., Wang, M., & Wu, W. (2006). *Techniques, processes, and enterprise solutions of business intelligence.* Paper presented at the 2006 IEEE International Conference on Systems, Man, and Cybernetics, Taipei. 10.1109/ICSMC.2006.385050

Zeng, D., Chen, H., Lusch, R., & Li, S. H. (2010). Social media analytics and intelligence. *IEEE Intelligent Systems, 25*(6), 13–16. doi:10.1109/MIS.2010.151

Zhang, Z., & Zhang, P. (2015). Seeing around the corner: An analytic approach for predictive maintenance using sensor data. *Journal of Management Analytics*, *2*(4), 333–350. doi:10.1080/23270012.2015.1086704

Zhao, J. L., Fan, S., & Hu, D. (2014). Business challenges and research directions of management analytics in the big data era. *Journal of Management Analytics*, *1*(3), 169–174. doi:10.1080/23270012.2014.968643

Zhao, Q., & Sourav, S. B. (2003). Association rule mining. *Survey (London, England).*

Zhao, R., Liu, Y., Zhang, N., & Huang, T. (2017). An optimization model for green supply chain management by using a big data analytic approach. *Journal of Cleaner Production, 142*, 1085–1097. doi:10.1016/j.jclepro.2016.03.006

Zhao, X., & Keikhosrokiani, P. (2022). Sales prediction and product recommendation model through user behavior analytics. *Computers, Materials & Continua*, *70*(2), 3855–3874. Advance online publication. doi:10.32604/cmc.2022.019750

Zhao, Y., Zhang, L., Zeng, C., Lu, W., Chen, Y., & Fan, T. (2023). Construction of an aspect-level sentiment analysis model for online medical reviews. *Information Processing & Management*, *60*(6), 103513. doi:10.1016/j.ipm.2023.103513

Zhi, Z., & Guixian, Z. (2010). Notice of retraction: developing a framework for business intelligence systems in Southwest, China. *2010 3rd International Conference on Computer Science and Information Technology,* (7), 182-184.

Zhong, R. Y., Huang, G. Q., Lan, S., Dai, Q. Y., Chen, X., & Zhang, T. (2015). A big data approach for logistics trajectory discovery from RFID-enabled production data. *International Journal of Production Economics, 165*, 260–272. doi:10.1016/j.ijpe.2015.02.014

Zhong, R. Y., Lan, S., Xu, C., Dai, Q., & Huang, G. Q. (2016). Visualization of RFID-enabled shopfloor logistics Big Data in Cloud Manufacturing. *International Journal of Advanced Manufacturing Technology*, *84*(1–4), 5–16. doi:10.1007/s00170-015-7702-1

Zhou, C., Stephen, A., Cao, X., & Wang, S. (2021). A data-driven business intelligence system for large-scale semi-automated logistics facilities. *International Journal of Production Research*, *59*(8), 2250–2268. doi:10.1080/00207543.2020.1727048

Zhou, X., Chen, S., Liu, B., Zhang, R., Wang, Y., Li, P., Guo, Y., Zhang, H., Gao, Z., & Yan, X. (2010). Development of traditional Chinese medicine clinical data warehouse for medical knowledge discovery and decision support. *Artificial Intelligence in Medicine*, *48*(2-3), 139–152. doi:10.1016/j.artmed.2009.07.012 PMID:20122820

Zhu, W., Zhang, C., Liu, C., Yuan, J., Li, X., Wang, Y., & Jiang, C. (2023). Recognition of Pilot Mental Workload in the Simulation Operation of Carrier-Based Aircraft Using the Portable EEG. *Proceedings of the 2023 3rd International Conference on Human Machine Interaction*, 43–49. 10.1145/3604383.3604391

Ziaee, M., Shee, H. K., & Sohal, A. (2023). Big data analytics in Australian pharmaceutical supply chain. *Industrial Management & Data Systems*, *123*(5), 1310–1335. doi:10.1108/IMDS-05-2022-0309

About the Contributors

Pantea Keikhosrokiani is currently a postdoctoral researcher at the Faculty of Information Technology & Electrical Engineering as well as Faculty of Medicine as part of 6GESS program. She received the Bachelor of Science degree in electrical and electronics engineering. She further perused the master's degree in information technology and PhD in service system engineering, information system from the School of Computer Sciences, Universiti Sains Malaysia (USM), Malaysia. She was a Teaching Fellow with the National Advanced IPv6 Centre of Excellence (Nav6), USM, where she is currently a Senior Lecturer with the School of Computer Sciences since 2018. Her recent books and articles were published by distinguished publishers (Elsevier, Springer, Taylors and Francis, and IGI Global). Her research interests include AI-augmented information systems, database systems, health and medical informatics, business intelligence, behavioral analytics, opinion mining, big data, and technopreneurship.

* * *

Nasuha Lee Abdullah holds a Doctorate degree in Engineering Business Management and is currently a senior lecturer at School of Computer Sciences, Universiti Sains Malaysia. Prior joining USM, Nasuha has been in the Electrical and Electronics (E & E) manufacturing industry for over 15 years specializing in Quality Management. Her current research interest is in Information System and Information Technology (IS/IT).

Cheryll Anne Augustine has finished her undergraduate degree in Computer Sciences, Information System Engineering from School of Computer Sciences, Universiti Sains Malaysia. She is pursuing her Master's degree from the same school now.

Ioana Bolog has a Medical Doctor (MD) degree in Medicine and has 29 years of experience in multinational Pharma in areas ranging from Commercial, Research & Development, Business Development, Learning and Training, both at local/regional and global levels. She is a certified professional in talent development and training management, learning design and managing learning technologies. Her main interests are around creating learning strategies that bring organisational impact, internal consulting, agile learning methodologies, innovation in the learning space and leadership development. She is involved in various cross-functional working groups across various industries with a main focus in life sciences. She has done volunteer work for Healthcare Business Women Association, mentors young professionals and supported social entrepreneurship causes.

Nurettin Boza, after completing his undergraduate education in Management Information Systems, continues his master's degree in the same field. Continuing his academic development, Boza currently works as a senior software developer in the IT Department at Uşak University.

Lily Clements is a data scientist with a PhD in statistics. She is committed to working with data to support positive social impact, and is involved in a number of exciting projects at her workplace, IDEMS International.

Rigoberto García-Contreras is an Associate Professor at the National School of Higher Education, Leon Unit, National Autonomous University of Mexico (UNAM). Visiting Professor at the School of Accounting and Administration of the Autonomous University of State of Mexico. His research interests are related to Intangibles Management, Artificial Intelligence in Organizations, and Knowledge Economics in Organizations. Ph.D. in Economic and Administrative Sciences, Master in Administration with a specialization in Organizational Management and Bachelor in Administration from the Autonomous University of State of Mexico. He did a research stay at the Laboratory of Personality Psychology, National University of Córdoba, Argentina. Associate Researcher at the Public Innovation and Artificial Intelligence Laboratory (I-Lab Mexico). Member of the National System of Researchers Level 1 (SNI-CONACyT).

Üzeyir Fidan received his master's degree in Statistics from Afyon Kocatepe University in 2013. He received his doctorate degree in Management Information Systems from Gazi University in 2022. Continuing his academic development, Fidan currently serves as a senior lecturer at Uşak University. He has many publications at national and international levels on Decision Support Systems, Artificial Intelligence Applications, Data Analytics and Digitalization.

Nandana G. M. is currently working for Accenture, Bangalore as Application Development Senior Analyst. She has completed Master of Computer Science and Engineering from Amity School and Engineering, Amity University, Noida. With a rich background in machine learning & data science, Nandana has contributed significantly to the field through research papers. She has a keen interest in data science and is excited to share insights and contribute to the discourse through future publications.

Minna Isomursu is a professor, 6G enabling sustainable society, Digital Health, University of Oulu. She is an experienced Research Professional - knows how to navigate in European research ecosystem. Dreams about using digital technologies and data for making us healthier and happier. She is currently working in Business Finland funded More Stamina project to examine digital therapeutics for fatigue management, and Digital Europe funded Reboot Skills to upskill professionals in manufacturing industry.

Piyush Kumar is currently working in Tata Consultancy Services Limited, Gandhinagar, Gujrat as a PMO lead for the past 1.5 years. He has completed his master's in business administration in Finance and Information Technology from Amity Business School, Amity University, Noida, Uttar Pradesh, India. He has worked closely with national and international authors, editors, and healthcare practitioners. He has publication experience for several research publications, conferences, and book chapters in the domains of healthcare, telemedicine, Artificial Intelligence, machine learning, and deep learning. He is also an active reviewer for international journals that include "Informatics in Medicine Unlocked" and

"Bulletin of Electrical Engineering and Informatics". Piyush Kumar has experience in analysing the data by designing charts, and graphs and creating dashboards out of it which provide key information. He has been working on various analytics tools such as IBM SPSS, Tableau and MS Excel to extract meaningful knowledge from data.

Kah Win Lee, a corporate data scientist with a Master's degree in Data Science and Analytics graduated from Universiti Sains Malaysia (2022), has earned the title of Kaggle Notebook Master, achieving a ranking of #230. Contributions include publications such as Brain Tumor Identification, Child or Adult Classification, and Plant Crops Multi-Class Classification.

Ronald Ma graduated with Bachelor of Medicine and Bachelor of Surgery, and specialised in surgery. He graduated with Post-graduate Diploma and Master of Public Health with First Class Honours from The University of Auckland in 2004 following which he was awarded the Doctor of Philosophy at the School of Population Health. He is currently employed in the Department of Medicine, University of Melbourne, Austin Health. He writes and presents on the issues of Public Health, Epidemiology, the Participatory Action Research approaches to promote the well-being of ethnic minorities, and Health Economics including Clinical Costing.

Andréia de Bem Machado has a PhD in Engineering and Knowledge Management. Postdoctoral fellow at the Federal University of Santa Catarina. Evaluator of the National Institute of Educational Studies and Research Anísio Teixeira (Ministry of Education Brazil). She is an Ad Hoc evaluator of National and International Journals. Evaluator in the PNLD Infantile Education program. Consultant in the production of low vision UNESCO teaching material. She has been working in the educational field for over 25 years. She is part of the scientific committee of national and international journals. Currently the areas of study are: innovation, innovation in the public sector, entrepreneurship, smart cities, education, special education and digital pedagogical model. She likes to innovate in the art of researching and disseminating knowledge.

Shuchi Mala currently works at the Department of Computer Science and Engineering, Amity University. Shuchi does research in spatial data modelling, Geoinformatics (GIS) and optimization.

Mune Moğol Sever started working in the service sector after working in the manufacturing industry for a short time. She is Assistant Professor in Anadolu University. She has a double major in industrial engineering and economics, a master's degree in tourism management, and a doctoral degree in the same field. She has written a book titled "Industry 5.0 = Industry 4.0 + Society 5.0 Technology for People" and various research articles on service operation management and digitalization. She conducts undergraduate courses on production management and quality management in service enterprises and master's courses on operations management and marketing research in service processing.

J. Patricia Muñoz-Chávez is a Ph.D. Associate Professor at the Technological University of the Metropolitan Area of the Valley of Mexico. Her research interests are related to Organizations, Higher Education, and Organizational Behavior. She holds a Ph.D. in Strategic Planning and Technology Management (Popular Autonomous University of the State of Puebla.), a Master's Degree in Management, and a Bachelor's Degree in Accountant (Autonomous University of the State of Hidalgo). She did a research stay at the University of Malaga, Spain. She has publications in several national and international journals and publishers. She is a member of the National System of Researchers of Mexico.

Kamalendu Pal is currently associated with the Department of Computer Science, School of Science and Technology at City, University of London. He has a diverse academic background, having received a BSc (Hons) degree in Physics from Calcutta University, India, followed by a Postgraduate Diploma in Computer Science from Pune, India. He has also worked as a research assistant for the government of India's two research and development organizations, under the Council of Scientific and Industrial Research (CSIR). Later, Kamalendu graduated with his MSc in Software Systems Technology from the University of Sheffield, a Postgraduate Diploma in Artificial Intelligence from Kingston University, an MPhil in Computer Science from University College London, an MBA from the University of Hull, and a diploma in Higher Education teaching practice from City, University of London, United Kingdom. Kamalendu is an accomplished researcher, having published over a hundred international research articles (including book chapters) in the scientific community. His research papers have been published in prestigious journals such as the ACM SIGMIS Database, Expert Systems with Applications, Decision Support Systems, and international conferences. His research interests include various fields of computer science - such as knowledge-based systems, decision support systems, teaching and learning practices, blockchain technology, software engineering, service-oriented computing, sensor network simulation, and supply chain management. Kamalendu is also on the editorial board of an international computer science journal. He is a member of the British Computer Society, the Institution of Engineering and Technology, and the IEEE Computer Society.

Antonio Pesqueira is a healthcare and pharmaceutical commercial and supply chain management leader, with an emphasis on technological advancements and process improvement. Concurrently, he holds esteemed academic positions as a professor and research fellow at ISCTE/IUL. Within the Technology and Architecture Research Department, he contributes to the Ph.D. program, focusing his research on digital technologies, healthcare data management, blockchain, and the nexus of innovation and business management. He has notably chaired the Pharmaceutical Supply Chain & Security World Forum and is often invited as a keynote speaker at events such as the Pharma Track & Trace, and Serialization & Labeling Summit. Co-authored more than 20 scholarly articles and book chapters that have been featured in prestigious scientific journals. These include the Journal of Business Research, Future Generations Computer Systems, Journal of Medical Systems, Knowledge Management, WSEAS Transactions on Business and Economics, and Information Systems Frontiers, to name a few. Moreover, his outstanding contributions have been acknowledged at various peer-reviewed international conferences. Furthermore, serves as a reviewer for journals including Pharmaceutical Medicine (PHMA) and BMC Medical Informatics and Decision Making. He possesses certifications in data science and agile coaching and plays an instrumental role in the scientific review committee for the AICONF'23 program at Oxford University.

Moussa Pourya Asl is currently affiliated with the Faculty of Humanities, University of Oulu. He received his PhD in English Literature from Universiti Sains Malaysia, where he worked as a Senior Lecturer of literary studies from 2018 to 2023. His primary research area is in diasporic literature and gender and cultural studies. He has published several articles in the above-mentioned areas.

Albérico Travassos Rosário is a Ph.D. Marketing and Strategy of the Universities of Aveiro (UA), Minho (UM) and Beira Interior (UBI). With affiliation to the GOVCOPP research center of the University of Aveiro. Master in Marketing and Degree in Marketing, Advertising and Public Relations, degree from ISLA Campus Lisbon-European University | Laureate International Universities. Has the title of Marketing Specialist and teaches with the category of Assistant Professor at IADE-Faculty of Design, Technology and Communication of the European University and as a visiting Associate Professor at the Santarém Higher School of Management and Technology (ESGTS) of the Polytechnic Institute of Santarém. He taught at IPAM-School of Marketing | Laureate International Universities, ISLA- Higher Institute of Management and Administration of Santarém (ISLA-Santarém), was Director of the Commercial Management Course, Director of the Professional Technical Course (TeSP) of Sales and Commercial Management, Chairman of the Pedagogical Council and Member of the Technical Council and ISLA-Santarém Scientific Researcher. He is also a marketing and strategy consultant for SMEs.

Anukansha Sharma is a computer science undergraduate highly involved in the fields of Artificial Intelligence, Geospatial Analysis and Data Science. She pursues her interests by actively engaging in researches and aims at providing a positive societal impact.

Anukansha Sharma is a final-year BTech CSE student passionate about Artificial Intelligence, Machine Learning, and Data Science. She explores these fields through research papers and actively engages in hackathons, aspiring to use technology to create a positive societal impact.

Maria José Sousa (Ph.D. in Management) is a University Professor and a research fellow at ISCTE/IUL and of CIEO (Algarve University). Her research interests currently are public policies and political science, innovation and business management issues. She is a best seller author in ICT and People Management and has co-authored over 70 articles and book chapters and published in several scientific journals (e.g. Journal of Business Research, UAIS, Future Generations Computer Systems, Journal of Medical Systems, I. J. of Knowledge, Culture and Change Management, Knowledge Management, Wseas Transactions on Business and Economics, Information Systems Frontiers and others), she has organized and peer-reviewed international conferences. She is also External Expert of COST Association - European Cooperation in Science and Technology.

David Valle-Cruz, Ph.D., MInf, BEng, is an Assistant Professor in the Science Department at the Universidad Autónoma del Estado de México and is a member of the Mexican National System of Researchers. David is a Computer Engineer, he holds a Master of Informatics, and a Ph.D. in Economics and Management. He has been a visiting researcher at the Center for Technology in Government (CTG), SUNY Albany, NY, and at the Computer Science and Multi-Agent Systems Laboratory of CINVESTAV, Guadalajara, Mexico. His articles have been published in leading journals, including Government Information Quarterly, Cognitive Computation, First Monday, Information Polity, and International Journal of Public Sector Management (among others). His research interests are related to Applied Artificial Intelligence, Social Media, and Emerging Technologies in the Public Sector.

Index

A

B

C

D

E

F

G

H

I

K

L

M

N

O

P

Q

R

S

T

U

W

www.ingramcontent.com/pod-product-compliance
Lightning Source LLC
LaVergne TN
LVHW060255011026
849161LV00011B/2718